Media Studies

Texts, Production, Context

2nd Edition

Paul Long and Tim Wall

PEARSON

Harlow, England • London • New York • Boston • San Francisco • Toronto • Sydney • Auckland • Singapore • Hong Kong
Tokyo • Seoul • Taipei • New Delhi • Cape Town • São Paulo • Mexico City • Madrid • Amsterdam • Munich • Paris • Milan

Pearson Education Limited
Edinburgh Gate
Harlow
Essex CM20 2JE
England

and Associated Companies throughout the world

Visit us on the World Wide Web at:
www.pearson.com/uk

First published 2009
Second edition published 2012

© Pearson Education Limited 2012

ISBN 978-1-4082-6951-0

British Library Cataloguing-in-Publication Data
A catalogue record for this book is available from the British Library

Library of Congress Cataloguing-in-Publication Data
A catalog record for this book is available from the Library of Congress

10 9 8 7 6 5 4 3 2 1
16 15 14 13 12

Typeset in 9.5/12 pt ITC Giovanni Std by 73
Printed and bound by Rotolito Lombarda, Italy

Media Studies

Visit the *Media Studies* Companion Website second edition at **www.doingmediastudies.com** to find valuable **student** learning material including:

- Extra case studies
- Annotated weblinks
- Suggestions for answers to questions in the book
- Blog offering you opportunities to comment and showcase your work

At our website you will find updates on topics from this book, more case studies, and activities which will extend your skill at doing media studies.

You will be able to follow links to other websites which feature the latest information on the state of the media, and add ones that you have found useful yourself. There will be examples of different people's attempts to answer the questions we set in this book, and ways they incorporated them into their own assignments. You will also be able to comment on your own approaches so that other students – who also use the book – can see, respond and discuss.

You can receive alerts each time something new happens, and we encourage everyone who uses the book to offer interesting material in whatever media form is best suited. We welcome your written comments and ideas, photographs, videos and audio. This is your learning community, built around a book that helps you become a successful media scholar.

Contents

List of contributors   xi

Guided tour   xii

Acknowledgements   xiv

Introduction: Getting started: 'doing' media studies   **1**

What is media studies?   **1**
The context of media and media studies   **6**
How to use this book   **14**
What then will this book enable you to do?   **18**
Getting started – just do it   **18**
Suggested reading sources   **19**

Part One: Media texts and meanings   **26**

Chapter 1 How do media make meaning?   **28**

Thinking about media meanings   **28**
Thinking about media as texts   **30**
Analytical tools: rhetoric   **33**
Analytical tools: semiology   **50**

Summary   **66**
Further reading   **67**

Chapter 2 Organising meaning in media texts: genre and narrative   **70**

Asking questions about genre and narrative   **70**
Studying genre   **72**
Narrative, narratology and genre study   **82**
Bringing genre and narrative together   **95**

Summary   **96**
Further reading   **98**

Chapter 3   Media representations   **100**

Asking questions about representations   **100**
Conceptualising and defining representation   **102**
Media professionals and the 'politics' of representation   **116**
Method: content analysis   **122**
Representations of individuality: stars, personalities, celebrities   **124**

Summary   **127**
Further reading   **129**

Chapter 4   Reality media   **130**

Thinking about 'reality media'   **130**
Conceptualising reality and realism   **132**
Dominant practices and forms of reality media   **139**
Reality, truth, freedom, ethics and responsibility   **149**

Summary   **155**
Further reading   **157**
Appendix: Analysing texts   **158**

Part Two: Producing media   **166**

Chapter 5   The business of media   **168**

Thinking about media businesses   **168**
Investigating media businesses   **171**
Political economy of media   **172**
Organisational studies   **185**
The culture of production – media professionals,
  creative workers   **192**
Media business in the digital age   **197**

Summary   **201**
Further reading   **202**

Chapter 6   Media regulation and policy   **204**

Thinking about media regulation and policy   **204**
Regulation and public policy   **207**
Policy and regulation analysis   **210**
Issues in policy and regulation   **218**

Summary   **230**
Further reading   **231**

Chapter 7   Media production in a global age   **234**

Thinking about global media production   234
What's global about global media?   237
Studying the impact of global media – further themes
    and ideas   264

Summary   267
Further reading   268

Part Three: Media audiences   272

Chapter 8   Producing audiences: what do media
do to people?   **274**

Thinking about audiences   274
What is an audience?   276
Propaganda and manipulating audiences   286
Media effects and moral panics   290
From effects to influence   295

Summary   296
Further reading   299

Chapter 9   Investigating audiences: what do
people do with media?   **300**

Thinking about what audiences do with media texts   300
Identifying audience activity   303
From 'effects' to uses and gratifications   304
Discovering the audience: media, context and meaning   310
Researching media audiences   330
Ethics and audience research   337

Summary   339
Further reading   341

Part Four: Media and social contexts   342

Chapter 10   Media power   344

Thinking about media power   344
Conceptualising power   346
Media and power   349
Ideology   351
Discourse, power and media   363

Summary   367
Further reading   368

Chapter 11   Conceptualising mass society   370

Asking questions about 'mass society' and media   370
Contexts: mass society, mass media and social change   373
Theories of mass society   373
Who are 'the masses'?   387

Summary   393
Further reading   394

Chapter 12   Modernism, postmodernism and after   396

WTF?   396
Conceptualising the modern   398
Modernists, modernism and media   399
Postmodernism and postmodernity   407
Critiquing postmodernism?   418

Summary   422

Chapter 13   The consumer society and advertising   424

Configuring consumer society   424
Historical context of consumerism and advertising   426
Cultures of consumption   427
Theorising the consumer society   428
Branding, identity and consumption   433
The organisation and practice of advertising in the digital age   434
Rejecting consumption as a modus operandi: adbusting
    and 'culture jamming'   441
The future of advertising and marketing   442

Summary   444
Further reading   446

Part Five: Historiography   **448**

Chapter 14 Media histories   **450**

Exploring media and history   450
Thinking about media history   453
Doing historiography   461
Sources and archives   465
Writing media history   472

Summary   481

Conclusion: Doing your media studies   **482**

What you will need to do   483
What you will need to cover   484
What to do next   486

Glossary   488
References   491
Index   505

Supporting resources

Visit **www.doingmediastudies.com** to find valuable online resources

Companion Website

- Extra case studies
- Annotated weblinks
- Suggestions for answers to questions in the book
- Blog offering you opportunities to comment and showcase your work

For more information please contact your local Pearson Education sales representative or visit **www.doingmediastudies.com**

List of contributors

Vian Bakir is Senior Lecturer in Journalism in the School of Creative Studies And Media, Bangor University. She is the author of Sousveillance, Media and Strategic Political Communication: Iraq, USA, UK (Continuum, 2010) and Torture, Intelligence and Media in the War on Terror: Evaluating Sousveillance in Political Communication Struggles. (in preparation, Ashgate, 2012). She has published elsewhere on western media and Iraq in K.Randell & S.Redmond (eds.) The War Body on Screen (2009) and the Journal of Popular Communication. She has co-edited a book (with David Barlow) on Communication in the Age of Suspicion: Trust and the Media (Palgrave-Macmillan, 2007).

Andrew McStay is Lecturer in Media Culture in the School of Creative Studies And Media, Bangor University. the School of Creative Enterprise at the London College of Communication, University of the Arts. He is the author of The Mood of Information (Continuum, 2011) and Digital Advertising (Palgrave-Macmillan, 2009). Work in preparation includes: Deconstructing Privacy. For Peter Lang and The Mode of Seduction: A Critical Investigation into Creativity in Advertising. for Routledge. His blog can be found at: http://advertising-communications-culture.blogspot.com/

Oliver Carter is Lecturer in Media Studies in the Birmingham School of Media, Birmingham City University and an active researcher exploring the political economy of Euro-Cult film fandom.

Faye Davies is Senior Lecturer in Media and Cultural Studies in the Birmingham School of Media, Birmingham City University and is engaged in research into production practices in mainstream TV and Alternative film.

Andrew Dubber is Knowledge Transfer Fellow in Music Industry Innovation, Birmingham School of Media and the editor of 'New Music Strategies', a highly influential blog on the music business and new media. For insight into his various works and online presence start here: http://andrewdubber.com/

Guided tour

reality, stereotypes are sometimes seemingly inescapable and even necessary to media texts and the information and pleasure that we gain from them. There is a complication perhaps in that while some stereotypes seem so prevalent across media our perception of them is also conditioned by their currency in other sectors of society and other modes of communication. Racist and sexist stereotypes for instance pre-date mass media forms, occurring in religious tracts, paintings, drama, jokes, folk tales and so on. Most of us both recognise and may call on stereotypes (consciously or unconsciously) in a variety of situations. Jokes can depend upon stereotypes for their point and punchline ('There's these two rosbifs …'), they come to hand very easily in sporting competitions when passions and stakes run high ('The natural discipline of the Germans will be a force to contend with in this tournament') or when doing many everyday things such as driving ('Women drivers!'). The ubiquity of stereotypes does rather disguise their constructedness in media texts therefore, as we have a tendency to see them as natural, to an extent 'believing' in them.

We can identify a range of functions for stereotypes in media texts and relate them to broader social and historical contexts; however, that in part explains them and undermines their obviousness and our acceptance of them. On the one hand, they provide an ordering process in the face of the contingency and

Doing media studies

We don't need to be media students to recognise the concept of stereotype or instances of its manifestation and occurrence. It is one of those ideas that have become 'common sense' to a degree (although sometimes at the cost of clarity and precision, as we'll explore). Make a list of any *five* stereotypes from media that you can identify. Some are suggested in our 50 Cent example as pointers, but think about the cast of characters in a computer game such as the variations on *Grand Theft Auto*. Outline a list of characteristics for each one and an instance of their appearance in media.

Doing media studies encourages you to try out the ideas covered in the text.

---

being human, of being good and bad – without badness being an index of all members of that group – of figures whose pre-eminent characteristic is not defined through their skin colour or culture! In fact it is rare for whiteness to be referenced as related to race or ethnicity at all (see Dyer, 1997).

Method: content analysis

For a moment we should dwell upon the issue of representation as 'proportionality', i.e. how many people from a group are represented, how frequently and to what degree and extent representations exist in media forms. This issue is usefully dealt with via a specific mode of media research: content analysis. You might wonder about this title as all of the methods we've thus far employed are about studying and interpreting the content of media texts – broadly textual analysis. We use the term 'content analysis' in very specific ways, however.

Content analysis is a quantitative method of analysing the denotative content of media output based upon defined samples and recognisable categories.

Content analysis is a means of counting the amount or frequency with which elements occur in media texts. It is a method that aims at objectivity by counting those things that are 'unproblematically' denoted or manifested in media content, such as the use of particular words or the appearance of particular images. A case in point would be the use of 'terrorist' or 'fundamentalist' in conjunction with 'Islam' in radio news reports for instance. While such terms might be full of connotations this method relies upon harvesting data before any interpretation of the term in its contextual setting is made. In order to work effectively this method deals with significance at the level of quantity – not only

Definitions explain the important terms, so that you have a quick and usable starting point when you encounter a new idea.

---

movie about US backpackers chasing girls and fun, before descending into a horror tale in which the protagonists are lured to a Slovakian town in order to be graphically tortured to death. By any estimation, the scenes depicted are harrowing and extremely explicit (a woman has a blowtorch taken to her face, for instance). Is this entertainment? Is it commentary (we watch rich Europeans torturing young people for kicks, which is what we are doing in turn by watching the movie)? Is it the same old prejudice against a constructed 'other' (the brutal Slovak)? Is it just another example of spectacular excess? Is there any point in asking such epistemologically based, 'modernist' questions wherein one might expect to locate motive and meaning?

Films such as *Hostel*, as well as phenomena like first-person shooter video games, 'death metal' music and 'Gangsta' rap, also exemplify a related aspect of the characterisation of postmodern media. This suggests that such works assume 'amoral' positions, in which who is good or bad and what position we are meant to take on the world represented is indistinct. In fact, the amorality includes the consumer, too, as we are not invited to take a critical distance but simply wallow in the pleasures of shooting and torturing people, and so on. In such examples and conclusions, we see an example of postmodernism as a moment in which 'anything goes'.

Case Study

The Simpsons

The animated TV show *The Simpsons* is the quintessential postmodern text. Its gestation, its character and the responses it generates encapsulate the nature of postmodern society. Matt Groening, the creator of the show, was heavily influenced by the alternative, underground culture that developed in the 1960s and 1970s, and first came to prominence as a comic book writer/artist with his satirical strip *Life in Hell*. This misanthropic look at the world usually centred on the situation of a rabbit by the name of Binky or a gay couple called Akbar and Jeff. The strip came to the attention of some of the producers on a 1980s TV live-action comedy sketch show, *The Tracey Ullman Show*, and Groening was asked to develop some animations of his work for it. Instead, he came up with *The Simpsons*

as a series of skits that proved so popular they won a spin-off deal.

The Simpsons features the eponymous family that comprises dad Homer (whose name evokes the great Greek author of *The Iliad* and *The Odyssey*), mother Marge, and their children Bart (an anagram of Brat), Lisa and Maggie. These are all named after Groening's own parents and siblings. Stories take place in an American town called Springfield, the exact location of which is uncertain (it is Midwest but also by the sea!).

In the course of their adventures, the family have confronted their own foibles at home, work, school and in society at large. They have travelled in time and space and met God and the Devil, as well as an incredible array of historical and living celebrities who have provided voices for the show – including former British prime minister Tony Blair, who 'appeared' during his time in office.

Many episodes consciously play with the conventions of animation and the sitcom genre, endlessly quoting and pastiching both popular and high culture. In its time, the show – one

Case studies highlight examples from a wide variety of media around the world, which bring the subject alive.

---

420   Part 4   MEDIA AND SOCIAL CONTEXTS

Thinking aloud

What is an intellectual and what do they do?

Some of the debates about postmodern thought concern the degree to which thinkers seem to be complicit with some of the pessimistic conclusions they come to – about politics, meaning and social action, for instance. Such debates centre upon the function of ideas in society and the role of the intellectual therein.

Intellectuals include academics in universities, along with other educators, and also embrace technocrats who manage organisations, scientists and technologists who design the machines of the modern age, social and political leaders, and, of course, people who work in media, managing ideas and forms of communication. Modern 'mass' societies require people who can solve problems, organise production and state services, and communicate ideas. For this reason, over the twentieth century the role of intellectuals grew in scale and importance, and their power to influence and control ideas grew as well. The social group of intellectuals, then, is central to understanding modernity, postmodernity and postmodernism.

People who earn their living through research and thinking can be thought to inhabit a particularly privileged position when it comes to evaluating society – they have the time, space and authority, literally, to stop and think! Thus, as Noam Chomsky has argued, thinkers have certain obligations. Writing at the height of the Cold War and appalled at the manner in which some scientists, economists and other thinkers were actively supporting American action in Vietnam, he declared that:

> With respect to the responsibility of intellectuals … [they] are in a position to expose the lies of governments, to analyse actions according to their causes and motives and often hid-

Western democracy provides the leisure, the facilities, and the training to seek the truth lying hidden behind the veil of distortion and misrepresentation, ideology and class interest, through which the events of current history are presented to us.

(Chomsky, 1967).

Much of postmodern thought, while provocative, may also be indicative of an abnegation of the responsibility of the intellectual. To announce the end of history while people still struggle for life, or to celebrate the consumer society as dominant when so many do without, might seem a little premature.

Ultimately intellectuals are but another social group the identity and integrity of which is as recuperated and commodified as any other. 'Highbrow' journals such as *Prospect* or *Foreign Affairs* have produced lists of 'top' public intellectuals. This hit parade approach was recently added to by *The Observer* which sought to evaluate the role and place of the intellectual in British life, doing so with a list of 300 contenders:

> But if the list is anything to go by, then the dominant professions from which contemporary British public intellectuals are drawn are journalists (20%), writers (19%), historians (14%) and critics (13%).

A big surprise is the relatively poor showing of thinkers whom one would expect to be making a significant impact on public discourse – philosophers (4%), scientists (4%), economists (3%) and politicians (2%). But the main conclusion to be drawn from this survey is that the trope that intellectuals begin at Calais is simply wrong. The British aversion to the I-word seems to be at odds with the facts. This country has an impressive array of lively, creative and argumentative minds. And if you doubt that, just watch them take this thesis to pieces.

Thinking aloud pushes you to think further about the issues under discussion, inviting you to come to a more sophisticated analysis of the concepts.

ods of historical research, and the re-presentation of the past. We specifically use the term to refer to the writing of history based on analysis, evaluation and the selection of authentic, original source materials and the use of these in a narrative. Finally, historiography can be used to mean a selection of historical literature, usually relevant to a specific topic or subject. So, it can refer to the articles and books about the coming of sound in cinema in the USA, the development of sound broadcasting in Europe, or the nature of the press during the First World War.

and debates about the 'effects' of media forms on audiences on to the history of their pleasure in cinema. A cautionary take on such a tale suggests that it is far too easy to reproduce unthinking perspectives on media audiences of the past as somehow primitive and further back along a kind of developmental curve that leaves us in a privileged position. We might indeed be more socially and materially privileged than some of our forebears but we should not imagine that our perception, acuity or pleasure is in any way necessarily superior. The story here relies upon the counterpoint of a 'developmental' sense of history – that of historical development as rupture or fracture. The story relies upon a sense of cinema as 'invention', a new device complete with new practice (representing movement in real time), impacting upon the world as something revolutionary.

'Cinema' (or 'kinema' as it came to be known at that early time – from the Greek for motion) was in place already by the time of its supposed 'invention'. By this we do not mean at the technological level as a particularly original amalgamation of lenses, celluloid strips, process and development but as a series of professional practices centred upon public entertainment. Photography, itself the basis for cinema (16 frames a second on those first cameras and projectors), was being used by figures such as Eadweard Muybridge (1830–1904), Etienne Marey (1830–1906) and T.A. Edison (1847–1931) in devices such as the Kinetoscope in order to 'show' motion. Theories of the 'persistence of vision' were already well known and exploited in 'flickerbook' animations – a quick succession

Key thinker

E. H. Carr (1892–1982)

E. H. Carr's *What Is History?* (1961) is one of the most influential of all works dealing with the philosophy behind the historian's project. Some of the central arguments are provocative for anyone with a faith in the idea that history merely records the facts of the past. He argues that such 'objective' or 'empiricist' history is not possible. Carr suggested that the problem with such views is that the historian, as man or woman, cannot divorce themselves from the age in which they live, from the outlook and interests that characterise social perception and with that the perception of the past and what it means. He thus distinguished between 'facts of the past' (things that happened) and 'historical facts' (the things that happened that historians select for their stories of the past). So, he argued that when we read histories we need to recognise that what constituted facts were decisions made by historians, that 'facts speak only when the historian calls on them: it is he who decides to which facts to give the floor, and in what order of context' (Carr, 1961: 11). This is not to suggest that Carr thought history a redundant enterprise but instead that we should, in approaching any account, 'examine the historian' for who they are and where (or when) they come from as much as what they have to say to us! He saw historiography as 'an unending dialogue between the past and present' (Carr, 1961: 30).

Key thinkers give succinct biographies of the key people who have provided the intellectual backbone of media studies.

New media, new media studies

Online memory making

In 2000, couple Steve and Julie Pankhurst launched the website Friends Reunited (www.friendsreunited.com). Inspired by the US-based Classmates.com, the Pankhursts provide a place for people to find out about what their old schoolmates were up to and to re-establish contact with each other. The site organised exchanges between subscription-paying members based around listed schools and universities. By the end of its first year Friends Reunited could claim several thousand members, within another year over 2 million – an incredible take-up rate. At one point, the site claimed 18 million users, although not all were fully registered subscribers. Like most web-based ventures the success of the site can be measured in financial terms and its waxing and waning fortunes are indicative of the uncertainties of modern media. The site was acquired by the UK independent TV company ITV plc in 2005 for £120 million. In March 2009, ITV announced that it would sell Friends Reunited as part of wider restructuring, selling the site for £25 million to brightsolid Limited, a firm owned by DC Thomson, a publishing firm most famous for comics such as the *Beano*).

Friends Reunited is in many ways a paradox: its operation and speed of success were only possible because of that most modern of media, the internet, yet the site is effectively retrospective – based on memory and nostalgia. The site is organised around forums dedicated to sharing memories of school, teachers and growing up, as well as wider aspects of social life. The comments in its public forum generated some controversy and several libel cases, and it was cited in the break-up of numerous marriages as old flames reignited relationships. There have been spin-off CDs, books and TV programmes as well as imitators and spoof sites (*Convicts Reunited anyone?*). Subscribers to the site range from 'silver surfer' users in their later years, to individuals just out of school who are not only using the site as a contact base but seek to memorialise their recent experiences.

Friends Reunited can tell us a lot about the relationship between history and media. Although we may not always realise it, the site enables us to explore our own personal histories, and if we participate in it, to make that history. On the site our school lives are produced by what is recorded there, and we select what is there, for our own ends, both well meant and malicious. Ultimately, in its social media organisation and various forums, it has offered intensified, perhaps even new, ways of developing collective memory and can be compared with the Facebook group discussed at the head of this chapter and other projects like it. The challenge for new scholars is to get to grips with the continuities of such media but also the way in which they challenge our thinking about media forms and social activities such as memory making.

New media, new media studies focuses on ways of thinking about new media forms and highlights specific examples.

Summary

Investigating and producing media history

In this chapter we have explored what we mean by history, and discussed what features of media history make it distinctive. We have also discussed some of the limitations of media history as it has been practised. With a critical awareness of this work you will be able to produce thoughtful historiographies of your own. The ideas and approaches that we have sketched out here offer only a starting point for thinking about this enterprise and one that needs to be considered in conjunction with the insights and approaches set out in the rest of the book. In the same way, it is hard to conceive of any of those other approaches – to regulation, text, audiences and so on, that does not in some way, implicitly or explicitly, deal with aspects of the historical in what they have to say about the media.

What we need, as scholars and thinkers, are names, concepts, frameworks and ideas for locating the ways in which we navigate our way around our subject in an attentive manner. We cannot do everything; and we cannot actually capture the past other than in a partial sense, and sometimes our job as scholars is to acknowledge such limitations. In doing so, however, we can at least sketch out how we might offer further avenues for work and consideration – had we time enough!

If you have followed through the discussion and activities you should now be able to challenge yourself to produce your own histories. These might be set as an assignment, or you may choose to give a historical dimension to a dissertation. Whatever their form it is useful to have a checklist of approaches based upon the schema we laid out in this chapter.

At the beginning we set out the things you should aspire to do by the end. If you have followed through the chapter and our exercises, drawing upon skills already developed the things you should be able to

- Discuss the distinctive features of media histories, and explain the uses and limitations of media as history.
- Generate questions for studying media history.
- Produce a timeline to represent the chronology of media development.
- Research relevant primary and secondary sources and evaluate their reliability as historical evidence.
- Make research plans for histories based upon aesthetic, political-economic, technological and socio-cultural approaches.

It is certainly important that you can with some clarity explain what we mean by history and something of the considerations and skills of historiography. It is certainly helpful if you can write these out as simple definitions and a skill toolkit.

The skill toolkit includes the ability to generate research questions, often derived from contemporary issues, or from absences in current histories. It is certainly worth skimming through the chapter and making a list of the absences we have highlighted, as they will give you an extensive range of possible historiographies that you could apply to a range of media. Equally important is the ability to abstract chronologies in your area of study from secondary sources, or from initial research, and represent them on a timeline. This provides an overview for all your subsequent work.

At a more advanced level you will need to identify, analyse and interpret primary sources, often using archives. As you select and incorporate them into a written account you need to make judgements about their reliability as evidence for any claims you are going to make. It is one of the qualities of a good media historian that they are sensitive to what can be claimed, and what cannot. The greatest challenge, though, is writing up the history. Here you need to choose an appropriate approach – emphasising aesthetic, political-economic, technological, or socio-cultural factors – but contextualising it with an awareness of the

Chapter summaries pull together the main themes discussed and remind you of the principal arguments.

We began this part by listing some newspaper headlines that illustrate ways of thinking about media power. We have also provided illustrations for each of three models of media power – media forms are powerful, media *make* people powerful and the media as *agents* of power. You should now find three of your own examples. These can be drawn from any sources – media, academia or even from conversations you might hear about you every day. Never neglect the 'common-sense' ways in which audiences feel about media. In each of your examples, think about *how* the source relates to the power model – what evidence or assumptions are present? Is an argument about media presented? Are you convinced?

Develop a dossier on media power. Outline what kinds of concerns (if any) you, or social groups, might have about this power. What are we able to do about such concerns? In light of some of the evidence of how individuals and social movements are using new media, what arguments are there for thinking about democratic possibilities and potential for resistance to power? Is there evidence of 'new media' used as a tool for the powerful, for repressive purposes?

Further reading

Eagleton, T. (2007) *Ideology: an Introduction*, London and New York: Verso.
Eagleton is a literary theorist and his work is informed by Marxist approaches to analysis. This book explores some of the key thinkers and works on the subject of ideology and, despite claims that the concept has waned as an object of understanding in recent years, he brings this up to date. Eagleton is a witty and erudite writer who brings very complex ideas to life with ease, always aware of the historical and contemporary context, which is used to provide illumination.

Matheson, D. (2005) *Media Discourses: Analysing Media Texts*, Maidenhead: Open University Press.
This book offers a detailed insight into the use of discourse as concept and method in the analysis of a range of media texts, in order to explore who 'talks', what is represented and how power relations are challenged or reinforced. Matheson explores different media genres, such as news, advertising and weblogs.

Miller, D. and Philo, G. (eds) (2000) *Market Killing: What the Free Market Does and What Social Scientists Can Do About It*, Harlow: Longman.
The various authors in this book argue that the expansion of the free market in the last part of the twentieth century produced a rise in inequality and violence, and allowed a criminal economy and the degradation of social and cultural life. Its main objective is to question the position of academia on these developments, suggesting that many academics in the social sciences, media and cultural studies have avoided critical issues and

Further reading suggestions at the end of each chapter lead you towards books and articles that will help you explore the topics in greater detail.

Acknowledgements

Author acknowledgements

This book – in its original version and this second edition – took a long time to develop and to write and thus there are many individuals who have aided and abetted the principal authors who are Paul Long and Tim Wall.

Our thanks must be expressed firstly to Andrew Taylor of Pearson who suggested the project and who has proven to be such a supportive editor from the outset. Jane Lawes who took on the task of coaxing a second edition out of us in spite of Andrew's experience. Others at Pearson have been equally supportive: Janey Webb and Steven Jackson, our desk editor Elizabeth Wright as well as Debra Weatherley and Linda Dhondy. Stuart Hay played an invaluable part as development manager for the project in its original phase, reading the manuscript and posing questions that made for a much better book. With respect to the second edition, special thanks must go to Michael Fitch for his diligent copy-editing, useful challenges and suggestions and his appreciation as non-specialist reader. Again, in an age when publisher-author relations have been pared down to the barest of exchanges, the team at Pearson have been superb, and it is with the greatest pleasure and surprise that we have reached the point of publication of a second edition.

We must of course thank those authors who aided us in expanding the scope of the book. Substantial contributions from Vian Bakir and Andy McStay serve the tone of this book well and their chapters speak to their distinctive expertise and we hope that readers will seek out their other work in exploring their place in media studies. Colleagues from the Birmingham School of Media contributed material and ideas that made chapters materialise. Faye Davies contributed to the chapter on representation and audiences while Oliver Carter's broad input is notable in particular in the chapters on audiences as well as case studies of snuff movies and 'Ghostwatch'. The ever inimitable Andrew Dubber provided substantial material for the development of the chapter on media business and continuing suggestions for thinking about the nature of media studies. Jon Hickman and Inger-Lise Bore contributed work on new media and fandom while Andrew Richardson provided sketches of the contemporary reality of creative labour.

Those various individuals who read the final manuscript in advance of publication offered comments which made the project and lengthy gestation seem worth it at last. Many thanks indeed to you and we hope that our readers agree with the kind comments displayed on the cover of this book.

Individuals in the Interactive Cultures research team (http://interactivecultures.org/) in the Birmingham Centre for Media and Cultural Research, merit a special mention. The close reading, diligence and skills of Dr. Nick Webber, Jon Hickman and Jez Collins aided in ensuring that the first edition made it to publication. Thanks to colleagues in the Birmingham School of Media, Birmingham City University – notably Brett Taylor, Sue Heseltine, Vanessa Jackson and Ellie Gibbons whose delightful photography enhances the first chapter.

We would like to express our appreciation to all of those other colleagues – in academia and across various media companies, who have offered stimulating ideas, insights, suggestions and provocations in our development as scholars and pedagogues and in the development of this book. Special thanks to Karl

Rawstrone for the positive feedback and to BCU colleagues who have used the book as a teaching aid in the last few years. Likewise, and emphatically, this work is dedicated to the many students who have responded to our ideas and methods over the years. They have demonstrated the value of active engagement with media texts, production and contexts and their ideas and questioning approach continues to inform their professional lives whether as media professionals or in other walks of life. Since the first edition we have been very pleased to see the book 'in action' and to hear positive comments from those at whom it is aimed. Their feedback and ideas have helped us in particular with the development of the second edition.

Tim Wall would also like to thank those former colleagues whose example as highly skilled teachers, and whose ideas generously offered in stimulating discussions, have found their way into the approaches used in this book: Dave Swann, David Hesmondhalgh, Dave Hinton, Steve Spittle, and Ben Calvert. I'd also like say thank you to Nadine, Matty and Carys whose forbearance in the face of too many of my evenings and weekends spent working made it possible to finish in the end.

Paul Long would like to thank Tim Wall for his wisdom, guidance and indulgent aid over the years. While we each wrote, and rewrote, different parts of this book, the tone and approach is very much a synthesis of our joint philosophy. Very special thanks go to Debra, Martha and Eve for their indulgence and understanding during the writing of this book.

Publisher acknowledgements

The publishers would like to thank the anonymous panel of reviewers for their comments on the first edition and their suggestions for a second.

The publishers would further like to thank Paul Long for his lead in updating and adding to this second edition and both authors for the dedication, effort and skill they demonstrated in producing the book in the first place.

We are grateful to the following for permission to reproduce copyright material:

Text

Extract on page 2 from *Oxford English Dictionary*, Oxford University Press (Oxford University Press 1997), definition of 'Media Studies'. By permission of Oxford University Press; Extract on page 8 adapted from Life through a lens: how Britain's children eat, sleep and breathe TV, *The Guardian*, 16 January 2008 (Ward, L.), Copyright Guardian News & Media Ltd. 2008; Extract on pages 9–10 from What is the point of media studies?, *Independent*, 27 August 2006 (Luckhurst, T.), www.independent.co.uk/news/media/what-is-the-point-of-media-studies-413472.html; Extract on pages 39–40 from *The Style Guide*, The Economist Newspaper Ltd (The Economist 2012), © The Economist Newspaper Limited, London (2012); Extract on page 70 abridged from 'Ol' dusty tale' by Kenneth Turan, *Los Angeles Times*, 29 July 2011, with permission from the Los Angeles Times; Extract on page 116 adapted from Tuned Out, Stonewall (2005), www.stonewall.org.uk/media/tuned_out_gay_people_in_the_media/default.asp; Extract on pages 143–144 from Vanessa Jackson, Degree Leader Television (BCU), former BBC Series Producer, in response to author's query; Extract on pages 148–149 from http://www.takeabreak.co.uk © H Bauer Publishing; Extract on page 217 adapted from National Union of Journalists Code of Conduct, http://www.nujtraining.org.uk/page.phtml?category=policy&id=316, National Union of Journalists; Extract on page 240 from http://online-journalismblog.com/ and http://www.paulbradshaw.co.uk, Paul Bradshaw; Extract on pages 253–254 from *Managing the Challenge of WTO Participation: 45 Case Studies*, Cambridge University Press (Gallagher, P., Low, P., Stoler, A. L. 2005), Case Study 3 by Abul Kalam Azad, http://www.wto.org/english/res_e/booksp_e/casestudies_e/case3_e.htm; Extract on pages 280–281 from Children boost their parents' web use, Research Report, 01.05.08, http://advertising.microsoft.com/uk/internet-research-children-boost-parents-web-use, Microsoft; Extract on page 288 adapted from an interview with Noam Chomsky, www.chomsky.info/ © 1992, excerpt used with permission of Roam Agency; Extract on pages 338–339 from Oh goodness, I am watching reality TV, *European Journal of Cultural Studies*, 11(1), pp. 9–10, p.11 (Skeggs, B., Thumin, N. and Wood, H. 2008), copyright © 2008 by Sage Publications. Reprinted by permission of Sage; Extract on page 349 from Last of the moguls. Rupert Murdoch is the last member of a dying breed. Time for him to step back, *The Economist*, 21 July 2011 (Anon), © The Economist Newspaper Limited, London (2011); Extract on pages 362–363 from http://advocacy.globalvoicesonline.org/ by Noha Atef, editor of Totureineygpt.net blog, Global Voices Advocacy site is licensed as Creative Commons Attribution 3; Extract on page 379 from Radio Listeners in Panic, taking War Drama as Fact: Many Flee Homes to Escape 'Gas Raid from Mars' – Phone Calls Swamp Police at Broadcast of Wells' Fantasy, From The New York Times, 31 October 1938 © 1938 The New York Times. All rights reserved.

Picture Credits

The publisher would like to thank the following for their kind permission to reproduce their photographs:

(Key: b-bottom; c-centre; l-left; r-right; t-top)

© 2010 Amazon.com, Inc. or its affiliates: 439; Alamy Images: imagebroker 73, Kevin Walsh 316, PhotoEdit 383, The Art Gallery Collection 360r, vario images GmbH & Co.KG 181, 234; Bridgeman Art Library Ltd: Private Collection / Photo © Lefevre Fine Art Ltd., London 401; Corbis: Alessandra Benedetti 352, Bettmann 360cr, Henry Diltz 458t, Mike Stewart/ Sygma 412, Patrick Guis / Kipa 360l, Sean Adair / Reuters 458b, Sygma 455; Getty Images: 130, 320, 344, AFP 5, 106b, 199, 244, 300, Simone Joyner 106t, SSPL 94b, WireImage 56; H. Bauer Publishing: 148; Heeb Media LLC ("Heeb"): 121; Image courtesy of The Advertising Archives: 28, 50, 159, 278, 431t, 431b, 436; Lime Pictures: 314; Linden Research, Inc.: 327l, 327r; Mary Evans Picture Library: 286, 287; Mirrorpix: 35, 37; NASA: 459; nisyndication.com: 293, 427; PARIS MATCH/SCOOP: 158; Photography by Eleanor Gibbons, www.eleanorgibbons.com, Eleanor Gibbons: 42l, 42c, 42r, 43t, 43b, 44tl, 44tr, 44b, 53; Reuters: Yiorgos Karahalis 105; Rex Features: DeeDee DeGelia & Brent Winebrenner & DeGelia / Mood Board 374, Kevin Foy 208, ITV 147, Sipa Press 260, 360cl, Richard Young 414, Mohamad Zaid 145; The Kobal Collection: David James / New Line 194, Polygram / Spelling 90; TopFoto: 94t

All other images © Pearson Education

Every effort has been made to trace the copyright holders and we apologise in advance for any unintentional omissions. We would be pleased to insert the appropriate acknowledgement in any subsequent edition of this publication.

Getting started: 'doing' media studies

What is media studies?

The reader can be forgiven for thinking that this is an odd question with which to begin a book called *Media Studies* but it is symptomatic of the way that the authors do things, the way that we will proceed and the way that we want to work with you in order for you to become media scholars. We challenge you with questions throughout the text to encourage your critical thinking and approach to doing your own research.

As established media teachers and scholars, 'we' – the authors – pose rhetorical questions in order to engage and lead 'you' – the reader – through ways of thinking about what appear to be 'common-sense' ideas about media. We do this in order to pose further research questions and develop activities, to support a claim that herein is, in some manner, media studies. We suggest that media studies is something active that we will do together and that, as a result of building upon the bases set out in this book, you'll be able to continue studying effectively and rewardingly. In this introduction we will attempt an initial definition and map of the nature and scope of media studies and its object of study. We will introduce some arguments for why such an enterprise has value and what this entails in terms of scholarly application and theorisation. Indeed, we'll try to clarify exactly what scholarship and theory involve. Finally, we'll set out some of the philosophy informing the way in which you will be approaching media studies – its texts, production and contexts – and how to make the best use of this book and its special features.

First steps

Asking a basic question like 'What is media studies?' is a conventional way of beginning scholarly work. Books like this one often offer a core definition of the subject under examination. Such definitions attempt to get to the heart of the subject, to identify the elements that bind it together, making it coherent and recognisable. At first glance media studies appears to be simple to define. The name is a giveaway: obviously, media studies is the study of media! Furthermore, through using such a definition we can get directly to the heart of our enterprise.

Alas, if only it were that simple! To attempt to offer such a definition of this field and leave it there would fail to reveal the complexity of what media studies encompasses, let alone articulate what exactly is meant by the various media and how they are studied.

The variety and range of the subject and the various approaches are thus worth dwelling on as a means of outlining where media studies comes from, the various things it attempts to do and the particularities entailed that distinguish it from our everyday activities and encounters with media, such as walking past an advertising hoarding, watching television or opening a web page.

Since the 1970s at least, courses in media studies and related subjects within its domain have been a growth area in further and higher education around the world. The subject and this growth has also been the object of some controversy and debate – as we discuss below. Nonetheless, courses are well established in the English-speaking world in particular – not only in Australasia, North America and the UK but also across Europe from Spain to Scandinavia. Courses and independent traditions of studying media can be found elsewhere, of course, developing in response to demand and to the need to comprehend an increasingly 'mediatised' world. Across Asia, media studies is an established area of study with many courses combining theory and practice. Sites such as the Communication University of China, which has a student body of over 15,000 individuals, offer evidence of how training for media industries combines with a critical assessment of the role of media in contemporary society, in particular in a country like China itself which has undergone enormous cultural change in recent decades and where media forms play an important and sometimes controversial part (see p. 234)

Thus, courses have proven popular perhaps because they deal with media that have come to matter more and more in everyday life – economically and culturally. Perhaps, too, there is a patina of glamour about the subject. Admittedly, there is also a perception among some prospective students that media studies might provide an easier ride than some other subjects – after all, who doesn't already know something substantial about TV, magazines or social networking? You couldn't make the same claim for palaeontology.

Media studies has become a noun. Sometimes it gets capital letters as a proper noun, although not consistently, as you'll note when you look around at individual courses, books and articles. This excerpt from the *Oxford English Dictionary* is useful in providing us with a definition (*the* definition perhaps) and in outlining instances of the use of the term, as well as some perspectives on the field.

> *media studies n. (freq. with sing. concord; also occas. in the sing. form as media study) analysis of the mass media; study of the media as an academic discipline.*
>
> *[1951 Amer. Sociol. Rev. 16 174 Mass media studies have, on the whole, tended to conceive of the audience as a series of discrete individuals.] 1968 Audiovisual Instr. Jan. 12/2 Experience gained in the nascent film study and screen education programs can provide guidelines for *media study. 1975 Times Educ. Suppl. 4 Apr. 54 (heading) Stephen Thomas and Brian Thomas on introducing media studies into primary schools. 1977 Gay News 24 Mar. 23/2 Dennis . . . went to the University of Massachusetts, where he received a BA in media studies. 1994 Daily Tel. 27 Aug. 15/4 It has been an uphill struggle to persuade universities to accept entrants with A-level subjects such as media studies.*

In universities across the world, media studies is now an established academic field that offers salaried posts to tutors who determine curricula, publish articles and books within the subject area and appear as 'authorities' on media forms they purport to make sense of. Individuals are occasionally awarded not inconsiderable funds and credit for the work that they do which, in turn, informs the said curricula, attracting thousands of students who can gain higher-level qualifications. The current 'Media Courses and Multimedia Courses directory' that is run jointly by the British Film Council and Skillset lists details of some 9412 courses across the British Isles that includes film, TV, radio and web authoring (www.bfi.org.uk/education/talkscourses/mediacourses/ [accessed 1/7/11]). In 2008, in the UK, the body responsible for ensuring the quality of such programmes provided a statement that gave some sense of the scope of media-related educational fields in this country:

> *Degree programmes in communication, media, film and cultural studies are characterised by a diversity of emphases, drawing in different ways on [. . .] disciplinary and professional sources [. . .] and offering a range of approaches to theoretical, critical, practical and creative work within these fields. Often combining the search for thorough knowledge and*

understanding with the development of students' creative and reflexive capacities in innova-
tive ways, they offer programmes relevant to students' futures, both in work and as citizens.

(The Quality Assurance Agency for Education [2008], Directory of Media and
Multimedia Courses [Second Edition]; available at: www.qaa.ac.uk/Publications/
InformationAndGuidance/Documents/CMF08.pdf)

We can see on the basis of the definition above that media studies is *more* than simply the study of media; it is also a set of practices for defining the study of media and organising studies of existing academic studies of the media. It can also be thought of as a means of authorising and validating studies of media; after all – and as we discuss below and throughout this book – there are plenty of people who dismiss media forms and media studies as essentially ephemeral and lacking seriousness.

However, it is important to note that there were students of media long before the professionalisation and institutionalisation of this field known as media studies. If you examine the backgrounds of media studies academics and authors (such as the authors of this book and those others who contributed to it), you will discover that they were trained in and inhabit a range of different disciplines and subjects. To name the most obvious, these encompass the study of English language and literature, psychology, sociology, history, economics, political science and anthropology. Thus, media studies, the noun, refers to a meeting place for a lot of different people with differing approaches, questions and agendas.

When all of these individuals, with their differing approaches, first came together – with all of their dialogues, interaction and disagreements – media studies became much more than the sum of these parts. What linked them all was the central object of study and a sense that it merited attention.

Media studies can be thought of therefore as a field of study rather than a discipline with its own discrete concepts, traditions and methods for doing research and finding things out. While it is influenced by those disciplines listed above, it also interacts with cognate (intellectually similar) fields concerned with the study of communications, journalism, film and television, popular music, photography and new media forms such as computer games and the internet. In this way it can often appear a very dynamic field of enterprise but also one that can be very hard to pin down.

The extent and variety of the field can be gauged by the continued proliferation of articles, books and websites dedicated to the various topics and domain of study of media. Specialist academic journals, for instance, usually published monthly, quarterly or at other intervals, are where one would expect to find evidence of the latest research work, theoretical debates and reviews of the latest monographs (individual, extended research projects) and collections. Some typical journal titles dedicated to the study of media are listed in the annotated bibliography at the end of this chapter.

Not surprising, then, that many of us would wish to turn to a guide such as this one to help get started. Guides like this, of which there are many, help us to develop confidence enough to navigate a way through media studies in order to make sense of the field, and of why and how academics do what they do in order to make associated ideas and approaches work for us. In order to do this, we do need to spend some time examining our foundational terms a little further in order to support our approach. In doing so we could reflect upon the question: what are the various media of media studies?

Defining media: what are the media of media studies?

Linguistically, 'media' is the plural of medium. A medium refers at base to one thing between two others. Our usage reflects a conception of a medium of communication as being a conduit through which messages are channelled and pass between one person and another or from one to another. Thus, 'the media' has become a conventional term used to describe modern means of electronic communication. Like a number of plural words, 'media' is often used as if it were a singular form, because it has become a catch-all concept and shorthand term. We attempt to avoid this usage in this volume, where possible, for reasons set out below.

One pitfall of using 'media' as a singular, catch-all term is that it elides differences between industries and forms that are quite particular. Too often, this usage also allows misleading generalisations that, among other things, serve to give a sense of coherence to media industries, institutions and forms as if these things were conscious entities. This usage also tends to obscure the roles and responsibilities of individual agents (creative workers, owners, producers, etc.) across media institutions and forms.

Generally, then, 'the media' has been taken to refer to those various industries and forms first fully founded in the nineteenth century, such as newspapers, magazines, photography and film. While the landmark UK newspaper title *The Times* was founded in 1785 (as *The Universal Daily Register*), its status was properly cemented with the invention of the steam-powered printing press in 1814 and the appearance of a range of competitors in the Victorian age. Although the first photographic image was captured in 1826 by the Frenchman Nicéphore Niépce, the development of the medium by Louis Daguerre, Hercules Florence, William Fox Talbot and George Eastman industrialised and popularised 'taking' and consuming photographs. The age of film was inaugurated by a public display by the French Lumiére brothers in 1895, although the equipment and means to achieve this had been around for several years by that time.

'The media' of media studies encompasses, too, the broadcast media of the twentieth century – radio (né 'wireless' and effectively invented in the nineteenth century out of contributions by figures such as Thomas Edison and Nikola Tesla, among others) and television. It extends to the study of popular music (including recordings and live performances), the internet in all of its variety and, more recently, computer games. We should note, also, those practices that operate at the intersection of these various media, such as advertising, public relations and the aforementioned internet, which provides the site for much that is new but also offers platforms for and instances of what seems quite familiar.

The use of the qualified term for these various forms – '*mass* media' – reflects a concern with the manner in which various media forms send messages (broadly conceived), from a *single* source to many destinations simultaneously or in a similar form to an anonymous *mass* of people, who constitute the audience, consumers, listenership, readership, community and so on.

Thus, media studies as a field covers all of those forms listed above, while, traditionally, media such as telephones and faxes have not been included due to the fact that they deliver single messages to individuals. Of course, one could argue that, with the advent of text messaging systems and the exponential advance in mobile technologies, the place of the telephone needs to be reconsidered in our pantheon. The most recent generation of phones act as receivers for radio, TV and the internet, as well as offering owners the ability to play games and record still and moving images, and providing a means of interpersonal communication through microblogging social networks such as Twitter. A figure like the singer Lady Gaga for instance numbers 'followers' in the tens of millions, all of whom are privy to her promotional messages, statements on events of the day and her conversations with fans and other celebrities.

Some forms that are clearly aimed at a mass audience – like popular fiction publishing (the Mills and Boon series of romances, Jacqueline Wilson books for children, etc.) or popular pictorial art (prints by the popular Scottish artist Jack Vettriano for instance) – tend to be excluded from the domain of media studies because subjects such as English literature or art and design have considered these forms to be within their province. Mixed media forms such as comic books, on the other hand, seem to be open to claims from allcomers. Comics have considerable cultural importance in countries such as France and Japan but, in the UK and USA, their status as popular entertainment has dwindled in recent decades.

Source: Ben Radford/Corbis

From one to many: a graphic illustration of how electronic mass communication reaches out to audiences.

These distinctions do not suggest that there is not an occasional overlap across disciplines and the consideration of forms. This is particularly important when one takes on board the incredible and international 'synergies' of promotion in the launch of a book such as *Harry Potter and the Deathly Hallows*, which took place in tandem with gaming, film, TV and music spin-offs (see Chapter 5 for a discussion of such processes).

However, simply identifying the various media that are or are not the object of our study does not in itself define media studies as a mode of study and the way that it should proceed. If we were to consider media as mere conduits for communication our approach would be a straightforward descriptive activity. We would ask: what was the message, who sent it and to whom? Such a model, while useful, does not account for any effect that any medium itself has on the transmission of messages. After all, once we begin to consider the scale of mass communication we are no longer working with a model analogous to a two-way conversation. The very different natures of the range of media forms already listed should draw our attention to this issue. In what way are film and television similar and where do they diverge in how they communicate? How do they compare with radio, or the web, or even the press? If the comparisons seem odd, don't forget that these are all media constituting the subject of 'media studies'.

With this sense of commonality and difference in media forms in mind, we could, or should, therefore, examine the technical manner in which messages are transmitted, asking questions about the message itself, what happens to it in the process of communication and, indeed, consider who receives it and in what circumstances.

One of the most renowned communication theorists to draw attention to this aspect of the media was the Canadian Marshall McLuhan (1911–80). As a popularising academic, his aim was to avoid obscurity in order to communicate his ideas to a broader reading public. In doing so, a number of his observations were elevated to catchphrases, even clichés, for the modern age of mass communication, with the detail and nuance of his argument often neglected. Thus, his term 'the global village' (McLuhan, 1964) describes the manner in which communications have reduced traditional limits of space and time across the globe. This is a phrase that seemed pertinent to the age of satellite broadcast and seems prescient given the advent of the internet.

The key phrase from McLuhan's writings that will serve us here is 'the medium is the message' (McLuhan, 1964). This phrase encapsulates the essence of one of the key insights for those who wish to take the study of media *as* media seriously and see media studies as a field distinct from the domain of sociology, literary studies, politics, psychology or business studies for instance.

McLuhan's notion encapsulates a variety of grander ideas but there is one point worth focusing on here. He was trying to point out that if we concentrate upon the individual messages of contemporary media forms alone – the content, if you like – then a greater significance will be missed. What is important about any one medium is that it is more than a mere conduit for communication, and certainly not one which is 'pure' in leaving the message untouched in the form that it reaches us. McLuhan teaches us that it is the form and dimension of an individual medium that contributes to meaning. In his argument, it is the very nature of mass media which impacts upon the make-up of modern society. Because of media forms we live, think and communicate differently from those generations who came before these forms.

> In a culture like ours, long accustomed to splitting and dividing all things as a means of control, it is sometimes a bit of a shock to be reminded that, in operational and practical fact, the medium is the message. This is merely to say that the personal and social consequences of any medium – that is, of any extension of ourselves – result from the new scale that is introduced into our affairs by each extension of ourselves, or by any new technology. [. . .]
>
> The instance of the electric light may prove illuminating in this connection. The electric light is pure information. It is a medium without a message, as it were, unless it is used to spell out some verbal ad or name. This fact, characteristic of all media, means that the 'content' of any medium is always another medium. The content of writing is speech, just as the written word is the content of print, and print is the content of the telegraph. If it is asked, 'What is the content of speech?', it is necessary to say, 'It is an actual process of thought, which is in itself nonverbal.' An abstract painting represents direct manifestation of creative thought processes as they might appear in computer designs. What we are considering here, however, are the psychic and social consequences of the designs or patterns as they amplify or accelerate existing processes. For the 'message' of any medium or technology is the change of scale or pace or pattern that it introduces into human affairs.
>
> McLuhan (1964: 23–4)

The context of media and media studies

Media are of course the sum of much more than form and message. Media studies might also encompass examinations of the effect or influence that consuming media messages has on society in general or on individual audience members. We might look at the manner in which producers work and how their activities are organised and financed. The domain of media studies also considers the significance of media in society and in turn offers a challenge to consider wider social issues and meanings – after all, and as we suggest later, modern society is simply inconceivable without media! These approaches lead us to think of media in context.

A context, broadly speaking, refers to the setting for something. Here, we mean to locate media output, organisations, audiences, practices, policies and so on against those aspects of society that have a bearing upon the possible ways in which all of these aspects can be meaningful. To speak of context means that we are interested in the way in which societies are organised, how ideas are established, accepted and distributed within societies and how the languages we use are involved in and influence these ideas and the organisation of any society. We use the plural languages here to refer to both the different ways in which we speak as individuals in our society (dialects, accents, slang) and the manner in which media products 'speak'. To suggest that media forms 'speak' is to treat the images, sounds, designs and shapes that make them and they make as part of a repertoire of communication (see Chapter 1).

The wider issue of context, while introduced in brief at this juncture, is so complex that it forms the basis for many of the questions and approaches within media studies and is something that to varying degree informs every subsequent chapter of this book.

Validating the field: why study media?

So far, so good, then: media studies can be said to 'exist' as a field with its own object of study. We can track the lineaments of the field in terms of approaches and theoretical and analytical presumptions, identify 'star names' and dominant ideas, as well as map where the field is manifest in established locations in educational institutions.

However, just because something is established and authorised in this way does not mean that its value and meanings are self-evident to us and don't merit further exploration. We should ask what seems to be a very impertinent question here in order to satisfy ourselves in proceeding (and in order to reassure you of your purchase of this book perhaps): why should we study media? Is it simply that media exist and warrant attention *because* they exist? On one level this would be an acceptable rationale for study (the pursuit of knowledge is its own end), albeit a tautological one. By this measure, however, we could argue for a 'motor-car studies' or 'washing-machine studies' for instance, as both are ubiquitous pieces of hardware that are integral to modern life in the same manner as the iPad or television. Thus, why one phenomenon is studied in particular ways and not another is worthy of reflection as a means of making sense of what we do and the variety of ways in which we do it.

A starting point for an argument for the study of media is to consider economic evidence, in all of its variety. Consider, for instance, the relatively old-fashioned and often under-examined sector of magazines and children's comic books. In a report by the market research company Mintel from April 2010 on the UK sector, we learn that this sector underwent a significant downturn in 2009 with sales of children's comics and magazines totalling £125 million, a fall of 8 per cent between 2008 and 2009 in a market traditionally resilient to economic turbulence. The available sample for this survey was 76 titles, a decline from 86 in 2006 and 83 in 2008 ('Children's Comics and Magazines – UK – April 2010' Mintel International Group Limited; http://oxygen.mintel.com/sinatra/oxygen/display/id=517923).

Excluding books, the newspaper is the oldest of the non-electronic mass media, with industry and form repeatedly affected if not usurped by once 'new' media such as radio, television and latterly the internet. However, reports of the death of the press have, time and again, proven premature. The *World Press Trends* of 2006 reveals that, in the first five years of the new millennium, 2001–5, paid-for and free daily newspapers increased in number by more than 14 per cent over that period. In 2005 for instance, in a survey of 78 countries across all continents, 8267 daily paid-for titles were counted with a combined circulation of 448,503 million copies (World Association of Newspapers, 2006). Undoubtedly, the market in countries such as the USA has declined, hit hard by challenges for advertising revenue from free online sources. In growing economies such as India, while online access and use is still limited to around 7 per cent of the population, rising literacy rates have boosted readership for newspapers – part of a print industry worth an estimated £2.8bn (see: Roy Greenslade, 'Indian newspaper market 'is on fire'', Guardian Online 13 May 2011 (www. guardian.co.uk/media/greenslade/2011/may/13/newspapers-india; accessed 1/7/11).

We could go on but these facts, alongside charges for TV subscriptions, purchase of cinema and concert tickets, CDs or music downloads, and so on, represent significant economic activity in modern societies of all descriptions. Whether revenues are expanding or declining, the point is that this economic activity also gives some indication of related social and cultural activities and the consequential interleaving of media into our lives. As this extract from a newspaper report on a survey conducted by another market research company Childwise (www.childwise.co.uk) reveals, the consequences engender barely concealed concerns about what such interleaving means – particularly for the young.

> . . . based on interviews with 1,147 children in 60 schools around England, Scotland and Wales [the report] found television viewing now averages 2.6 hours a day across the age group, though one in 10 say they watch more than four hours daily.
>
> [. . .]
>
> It found that 58% watch during their evening meal, while 63% lie in bed watching the screen (rising to almost three-quarters of 13 to 16-year-olds). Two-thirds – particularly the youngest children – watch before school, and 83% turn on the television after returning home.
>
> [. . .]
>
> Computers are also now a key part of children's private worlds. 'The internet is now an essential part of most young people's lives', says the study, with 85% of five to 16-year-olds accessing the net, and over a third (including a quarter of five to six-year-olds) owning a computer or laptop of their own. On average, they go online just over four times a week, spending two hours each time.
>
> The survey shows a rise in internet use, particularly among younger children, driven primarily by a boom in the use of social networking sites, primarily Bebo. Communication, says the report, 'has overtaken fun (e.g. online games) as the main reason to use the internet and study is now far behind'.
>
> Almost three-quarters (72%) of children have visited a social networking site, and over half have set up their own profile – sometimes lying about their age to sidestep minimum age safeguards. Children as young as eight are now signing up.
>
> Source: Lucy Ward (2008) 'Life through a lens: how Britain's children eat, sleep and breathe TV', Guardian, 16 January. Copyright Guardian News & Media Ltd 2008.

Ultimately, recourse to quantitative figures doesn't actually tell us everything but they are a starting point for provoking thought and debate about the rationale for our field of study and the obvious significance of media as economic and social forces.

What matters is that media matter to us. Newspapers, web, tweets, television, radio present us with information – from political analysis to details of which celebrity is dating which celebrity. Films entertain us; popular music provides us with soundtracks to our lives and emotions ('they're playing our tune'). Playing computer games – in person or as a member of online interactions – allows us to be a part of communities. Media might contribute to our status as citizens ('I watched the election broadcast on TV and I'm never voting for that lot!') or as consumers ('I shop online – therefore I am') or potential miscreants ('I file-share'). What matters is that media have significance in our lives, providing meanings and pleasure, activity, stimulation and distraction and that this is achieved in very particular ways for great numbers of people.

In this way, we would argue that media are qualitatively different from many other modern phenomena, such as our earlier examples of motor cars and washing machines, which are both economically valuable and meaningful in their own way. However, is this variety, wealth, activity and particular meaningfulness of media forms then not worthy of dedicated and serious attention?

We'll make one point repeatedly throughout this book. While media studies is often concerned with the meaning of media forms, we all of us consume media products and know what they mean. If we did not then we would not get much from our media consumption in terms of meanings and pleasure, unless we were a particular kind of masochist, perhaps. But then media are not simply means for transmitting messages to us, 'loud and clear', nor is it simply that media production is another area of production like car-making (even if that metaphor underwrites one fount of serious critical theory, as we'll see later – see Chapter 11).

The nature of the variety of media is such that they are integral to our everyday lives, virtually from the moment that we're born. How media forms make meaning (and indeed how producers view that process of making meaning) is too often treated as if transparent, natural and obvious. A good example that we go into in much detail in a later analysis comes from the world of advertising (pp. 158–165). Advertisements for women's perfumes and men's aftershaves work hard to convey to us a whole set of values associated with the product presented in any one advert, not least of all that they are for women and men respectively although they don't always say so. Adverts convey 'reasons' for why we should favour that product in the absence of any knowledge, necessarily, of what it smells like ('smello-o-vision' is not quite widespread yet). However, these 'reasons' do not appear as such, if at all. Adverts rarely 'tell' us anything directly – for example, this product smells like roses, is sophisticated, and will attract the opposite sex and make you happy as a consequence. While drawing upon speech, body language, writing and so on, adverts, like many media forms, communicate through their own sets of conventions, drawing upon social ideas, working allusively as well as directly and unequivocally by turn. Try thinking about this when you next take a look at such an advert or, indeed, when watching a film or listening to music. Think about how your media product communicates, what your response to it is, whether you can explain this and how you understand it.

So, we'll spend some time arguing that meaning and practices are not transparent, natural and obvious and to treat them in this way – as many of us do – presents huge conceptual problems. Media studies offers some means of engaging with these problems.

For anyone willing to take the study of media seriously, it is worth taking on board these arguments for the simple fact that the existence of media studies continues to generate controversy in some quarters. Media professionals, politicians and other academics, among others, have on occasion heaped opprobrium on our field. It is worth thinking about why this is so and what media scholars have done in order to risk ridicule.

There are media practitioners who take exception to the way in which their work is scrutinised and interpreted by media scholars. Then there are those media studies courses that dare to incorporate practical elements into their curricula. Objections are brought to bear against both theory and vocational production courses because they implicitly and explicitly demystify media work and practices. Some of these practices include real myths – the 'nose for news', 'rat-like cunning' or 'objectivity' of the born reporter, or the 'intuition' of the great record label A&R man, for instance, as well as the creative individualism of the TV or film director. Such ideas are all problematised (and equally celebrated) by the theorist, especially when they serve to impede eager individuals from pursuing media careers.

Evidence – the argument against media studies?

Cambridge University called them a 'soft' option this week. John Humphrys thinks they're pointless. In the more macho parts of journalism, real journos don't study. They roll up their sleeves and report.

Yet thousands of young people sign up to media studies courses. They have helped produce former Channel 4 chief executive Michael Jackson (Westminster University); Sunday Times editor John Witherow (Cardiff School of Journalism); Royal Television Society Young Journalist of the Year 2004 Mark Daly (University of Stirling); and hundreds of others. So what's the problem?

Until the late 1990s, seasoned journalists relished opportunities to rubbish media studies. It was the modern equivalent of 1960s sociology, a fool's paradise jammed full of bearded Marxists with 'sweetie mice for brains'. When Chris Woodhead, the former chief inspector of schools, condemned it as 'vacuous' and 'quasi-academic', there were cheers in newsrooms from Brighton to Inverness.

Some still feel that way. John Humphrys, the presenter of Radio 4's Today *programme, says: 'Even more kids are doing it now and it is sillier than it ever was. Where are they going to find jobs? If you decide after a proper degree in English, history or economics to do a one-year post-graduate course in journalism at a good university, all well and good. But the idea of three years at university doing journalism is barmy.'*

Source: Tim Luckhurst (2006) 'What is the point of media studies? ', *Independent,* 27 August (www. independent.co.uk/news/media/what-iisi-the-point-of-media-studies-413472.html)

Some arguments against media studies are predicated on a conflation of the frivolity of much media content and the approach to making sense of it. The study of 'Mickey Mouse' for example implies that the field itself is a 'Mickey Mouse' one. Of course, the venerable Mickey, one of the world's most recognisable images (loved and reviled in equal measure), is also the historical fount of the success of an entertainment corporation which in 2010 posted an increase for the year of 20 per cent in its net income figure (attributable to Disney) to $3.96 billion on a 5 per cent rise in revenue to $38 billion. Of the company's outstanding achievement for that year, CEO Robert A. Iger commented in his letter to shareholders that:

Toy Story 3 *is at once a gorgeous work of art, a great example of how new technology can make entertainment even more compelling, and a story that speaks to all of us. It shares the DNA of Disney classics like* Snow White, Pinocchio *and* Beauty and the Beast; *deeply human stories that appeal to people across cultures and ages and are enjoyed every day the world over.*

(http://a.media.global.go.com/corporate/investors/annual_report/2010/media/global/pdf/ letter-to-shareholders.pdf; accessed 1/7/11).

No 'value' in a study of the economics or cultural claims made here then?

There is a suspicion among media scholars that objections to what we do sometimes evince elitist and anti-democratic positions. There is little comparative complaint about the study of traditional and established subjects such as classical languages or the literature of the distant past for instance, which is usually read by a relatively small and particularly educated section of society. However, when we turn to the popular and to mass media, then 'massness' itself, ubiquity, ephemeral qualities (perceived and literal – in that much media content is not made to last) and occasional silliness are used to claim that the popular is intrinsically unattractive and unworthy of attention. That these things might be the very basis of genuine pleasure (what could be more suspect than pleasure?) and meaning, let alone study, is dismissed.

One familiar argument goes that not only have mass media 'dumbed down' society at large over time, but the availability of qualifications allowing young people to study media is undermining the value of education itself. This argument is a selective and circuitous one and worth taking seriously for a moment – before it is dismissed.

We should not be too worried about such attacks on the field, however. In the past, similarly predicated objections have been raised against now well-established disciplines such as literary studies and sociology. Occasionally, these continue to be manifested in attacks on the worth of subspecies of fields and disciplines with unimpeachable credentials (women's history, black history? The very thought!).

The argument for the study of media is self-evident to those with eyes to see and ears to hear the world about them (and maybe dextrous thumbs with which to manoeuvre through various game worlds). That the existence of media studies generates such responses might actually be taken as evidence that its practitioners are doing something right. Yet the value of the field is ultimately supported by the nature of scholarly approaches, the way that evidence, insight and arguments are presented in comparison with the expectations and rigour of wider, shared standards. Its value is manifested, too, in the success and quality of the things that its students do and say as a result of study in this field.

Studying media: becoming a scholar and theorist

One argument about what constitutes media studies, as an academic field that one can pursue at university, would have it that, far from being the simple study of media, it is, in fact, the study of studies of media. In this it is not unlike many traditional disciplines that inform the field, such as history, literary studies and sociology.

Students often ask tutors why such courses are based around the study of other people's ideas about media, when we could turn on the television, open a newspaper or log on to the internet and begin studying media straight away. To understand the value of this approach, we need to consider what scholarship and theory entail.

Being a scholar and taking up a scholarly position towards research and its purpose involves taking on a different perspective from that which we normally inhabit in our everyday encounters with media. This is not to imply that scholars, theorists or researchers are in any way better than 'ordinary' people. For instance, in our everyday interactions we often evaluate and discuss media forms in very subjective, individualised and unsystematic ways. We might find ourselves 'rating' songs or TV shows, for instance, or bemoaning the lack of realism in a film ('it's a bit far-fetched'), or expressing amazement at an aspect of a news story in the papers. We have recourse to repertoires of terms and descriptions for media works – 'cool', 'crap', 'a classic', 'on another level' – that are meaningful to us and those with whom we speak, but are very difficult to consider as objectively meaningful. Of course, most scholars do enjoy media products and seek out the kinds of information that they present about the world, but they have different motives when consuming media forms in their guise as scholars. While conscious of their own involvement in the consumption of media meanings (and pleasures), they attempt to achieve a 'critical distance' from the world of media, to 'make strange' or distance the everyday assumptions involved in consuming television, reading a newspaper or talking about the latest record releases.

A critical distance is useful, as it is very easy to take a lot for granted, to accept unquestioningly those assumptions that we have held for a long time, rather than opening up our minds to new possibilities and ways of answering questions about media. Thus one of the real pleasures of the intellectual study of studies of media is the way in which striking new ideas present us with ways of assessing and rethinking our assumptions (although sometimes we may confirm them!).

A further reason for studying the work of others is that it allows us to 'stand on the shoulders of giants' and to consider how our own questions might have been anticipated and dealt with already. Academics have been investigating and writing about media for as long as it has existed as a concept. Indeed, some of the questions and issues we think of as modern and pertinent to the media were being posed by Ancient Greek philosophers such as Socrates and Plato over 2000 years ago. As this quote from Plato's *Republic* suggests, ancient attitudes resonate in relation to our modern pleasures:

> *Any musical innovation is full of danger to the whole state, and ought to be prohibited . . . when modes of music change, the fundamental laws of the state always change with them.*

(Plato, *The Republic*)

We would suggest that by grasping the existing academic work, comparing and contrasting it, relating it to our own experience of contemporary media, we can begin to develop a fuller picture of questions asked and maybe even develop some useful answers to those questions.

To theorise is to consider the wider contexts and significance of individual media products and our use of and pleasure in them. In our case this may be media output (TV shows, songs, photographs) as well as aspects of the production or experience of that output by audiences – or a perspective on all three. Knowledge and analysis lead to insights and propositions about the significance of an object of study, based on evidence often produced at a remove from our own subjective perspective of an object.

Thus, as scholars, what we could do with in order both to understand and explain how media make meaning – in ways that we can all agree upon – is a common technical language that defers subjective judgements. In this way, we should be like the most effective of media producers and, although even 'objective' academics rarely escape their subjectivity, by using a set of clearly defined terms we can support precisely argued and detailed arguments about media with our analyses. Analysis, when properly presented and illustrated, aims to convince others of an interpretation and argument in order to make grander points about value, effect and so on. Subjects that we go on to explore such as power, ideology, pleasure, realism, postmodernism and so on are all predicated upon analysis and argument about media texts and their meanings.

Many students, not to mention journalists and even media professionals, are suspicious of the project and terminologies of academic analysis. Certainly, some theorists can be very flowery, obscure and downright boring in their writing and seemingly deliberately difficult in their choice of vocabulary. Sometimes this is for very good reasons. Students too can misunderstand the utility of a specialist language, deploying terms willy-nilly in their writing. At base, understanding the value of accurate language and precision will aid in the development of scholarly procedure and its rewards – intellectually for its own sake, in developing your powers of argument and explanation and, indeed, in the responses and marks that you get from using the work of others.

Producers as theorists

It is often said of famous photographers, pop stars, film directors and so on that they have an 'instinctive' or 'intuitive' grasp of their form. We would argue that this is a rather romanticised notion that presents a dead end to understanding how media workers learn and practise their skills and trade. Rather than rely upon the romantic appeal to individual genius (but we wouldn't want to deny it either), we suggest that media producers are instead better understood to be effective at combining and exploring the possibilities of the technical languages and cultural ideas at their disposal. In fact, effective media producers share a lot of ground with academics, despite some obvious differences and occasional antipathy between the two.

It should be stated that while some theorists do tend to set themselves apart from producers – intellectually, politically, socially – what they do and the manner in which they think about media is not so particular to them. Across the various fields of media production, practitioners themselves have been particularly active in generating debates, principles and theories around the making of media 'products' and the means in which they are understood. This practice has been particularly fruitful and important in the field of film, for instance. Here we can cite film-makers such as the Russian Sergei Eisenstein (1899–1948), Paul Rotha (1907–84) and John Grierson (1898–1972) in the UK or the French *nouvelle vague* (new wave) group including Jean-Luc Godard (1930–), François Truffaut (1932–84) and Claude Chabrol (1930–). These directors and producers wrote film criticism, and commentaries on their guiding principles for film and views of the medium that set terms for the way that their work and the work of others could be made and viewed.

Film or cinema was one of the first mass-media forms to be accepted into the field of higher education as a dedicated and serious object of study (although rarely referred to in academic circles by so cursory and frivolous a term as 'the movies'). This was due, in part, to the seriousness of its treatment as 'the seventh art' by such theorists–practitioners. In the same 'aesthetic' mode, film theory has also sometimes intersected with that of photography in how practitioners have conceptualised the representative and realist qualities of their medium, for the way that it impacted upon political and philosophical ways of seeing the world.

Here, for instance, is an extract from an interview in the *Times of India*, in which director Rajkumar Gupta speaks about his film *Aamir*, which concerns the travails of a Muslim man against a backdrop of terrorism in Mumbai.

> I thought of Aamir *as the story of a common man and his dilemma and the troubled times that we live in, and how and where our socio-political structure has gone wrong. Regardless of community, people have responded to* Aamir *as the story of the common man. They feel this could happen to any one of us. . . . I don't want to segregate myself as a film-maker. In* Aamir, *I wanted to tell a story. I wasn't consciously making a statement. Also I did feel that people from the majority community where I belong perceive the minority in ways that aren't the truth. There are foot soldiers in terrorism and extremism who wouldn't know anything about the actual happenings. I wanted to make sure* Aamir *was accessible to as many people as possible. I didn't want to restrict it to a message-oriented statement . . . Fortunately or unfortunately, I don't watch too many films. Nevertheless I was accused of lifting* Aamir *from Filipino director Neill de la Llana's* Cavite. *I love the works of Frank Capra and Martin Scorsese. My favourite film is Vittorio de Sica's* Bicycle Thieves. *I love Mani Ratnam's work, who doesn't? The film-maker that I truly admire is Bimal Roy.*
>
> *Source:* Subhash K. Jha (2008) *'It's equally tough for all outsiders in Bollywood',*
> 20 June http://timesofindia.indiatimes.com accessed 01/01/12

Here, then, is a thinking media worker fully attuned to the way in which his medium deals with particular stories and reaches its audience without becoming reduced to a 'message'. He reflects upon his own intentions and responsibilities, as well as the relationship of the film with his own inspirations from other films.

Beyond film, we should also consider the manner in which journalists and broadcasters have defined the professional, philosophical and ethical aspects of their fields, offering a measure by which their practices, and the worth and social role of the press and broadcast media, might be judged. This self-consciousness and reflective quality can be tracked, too, in the domain of PR and advertising and, indeed, a founding figure in the former field, Edward Bernays, was directly influenced by theories of his uncle, Sigmund Freud (see p. 286). Currently, the rise of digitised technologies and the internet, and their infiltration into every part of life, have presented all of us with questions about communication, community, privacy, copyright and ownership, as well as identity and many, many more such issues. You will find plenty of examples of these questions and what academics and producers have to say about them throughout this book.

That some media creative workers do intellectualise and reflect upon their work, its meaning and their responsibilities is important for understanding the value of our own scholarly approach. As more of us become in some way 'producers' of media, however, we are, all of us, confronted by such issues and how we might play a part in thinking them through and contributing to debates about the meaning and role of media in contemporary life.

Using the tools of the trade

A useful metaphor for a great deal of what scholars do with their equipment, which consists of theories, methods, jargon and so on, is that of the car mechanic. Presented with a faulty car, any mechanic worth their salt will commence by diagnosing the problem by listening to the account of the driver and then by paying attention to either bodywork or the engine, or wherever the fault is supposed to lie. In order to address the problem and get to the root of it to effect repairs, the mechanic works through a series of methodological steps, using particular tools to do particular things. It would be very unusual indeed (and a little worrying for the driver) to see the mechanic systematically going through their toolbox and trying each tool against the source of the problem: 'Does the screwdriver work on this sparkplug? No? How about my wrench . . . ?' Mechanics employ tools in response to particular needs.

As scholars, therefore, we can think of ourselves to some extent as 'clean-fingered' mechanics. Equipped with a series of typical questions in order to address our subject, we have at our fingertips a series of tools (theories, analytical research techniques) developed to do different things in response to different purposes, questions and problems. What we do in this book is introduce a range of theories, techniques and conventional jargon used by media scholars in order to empower you to produce and develop your own responses to media.

How to use this book

It is worth stating what this book is *not*. It is not, for instance, an encyclopaedic repository of the entire range of ideas about media. Nor is it a narrative of media and media studies from the invention of the cave painting to Wikipedia. It is, in many ways, necessarily selective in what it does cover and that coverage is viewed from particular perspectives. Some ideas and approaches from the field are privileged and presented in detail, while others are sketched in briefly. This is due to the expediency of space and focus, but for the sake of transparency and self-reflexivity we should say that this is partly due to the authors' own preferences, schooling and perspective as scholars from the Anglophone community. To some degree, therefore, we have attempted to compensate for a parochial tendency in our own experience of media industries, content and names by taking a consciously international perspective.

As a comparison, you would find other books advertised as textbooks on media studies similar but different in focus and approach. For some venerable scholars who recommend or use such books in their own teaching, this work will be too forward; for others, too 'backward'. Nonetheless, the book is intended as a usable resource that will only make sense or have value for the reader if it is used to *do* media studies. Our belief is that learning takes place through activity, whether in response to theoretical premises through debate or reflection or through the exploration of subjects (ideas and objects of study) via research and analysis.

In this book, we have one overriding aim: to make the study of media 'come alive' for the reader and to get the reader engaged in media studies as an active process. We do this as experienced teachers and authors, drawing upon a wealth of work in the field, testimonies from practitioners, consumers and students and because, for all of us, media in all varieties are exciting, provocative and important enough to merit serious attention.

While we flatter ourselves (and assure our editors and publishers) that we can achieve this task for the reader, ultimately this won't fully work unless you take on the responsibility of doing this work too. Sometimes this involves stopping to reflect and think, sometimes conducting some research of your own – chancing your hand. We can tell you what media studies is and even set tasks for you to parrot these descriptions (sometimes examinations can appear to work in this way but there are no 'tests' herein). What purpose would this serve? When we claim that what we offer is in some way media studies we're presenting you with a basic set of equipment with which to go off and make more sense of what the giants have done and what active researchers are doing. Above all, we have organised this book as a basis for your activities as researchers. Media studies will come alive for you and mean something when you do it, not at the end of this book, but as you work through it from front to back, or dip into it as and when interest or need takes you.

Above all, it will work for you if you engage with these ideas, consider them and test them out in your everyday encounters with media, from the websites you surf to the music you listen to, from the films you watch through to the thousands of visual images and advertisements you glimpse or hear throughout the day.

Organisation of the book

Our approach to active learning is reflected in the organisation and supporting features of this book. There are five parts to this book: media texts; media production; media audiences; media and society; and finally media histories. Each part has its own chapter or chapters and a brief introduction outlining what the part is about and why it is organised in this manner. As you will discover, there is a lot of cross-referencing between chapters. This reflects the fact that on offer here are a variety of perspectives and organising principles designed to address key areas of concern in particular ways. However, each area is not discrete or self-enclosed and a well-equipped media scholar needs to be aware of these perspectives and what kinds of ideas and approaches can be drawn upon in studying media. For instance, a study of media as business – a chapter within the producing media part – cannot afford to ignore historical issues, which are covered in the last chapter. A study of media audiences would be redundant without some consideration of the nature of what meanings media products hold for them.

Chapters within each part are organised in order to lead you through a range of ways of investigating and engaging with the theories, techniques and various media forms. A number of supporting features serve to highlight the central thrust of each chapter as an environment for active learning.

Introductions and 'what we will do in this chapter'

Each chapter opens with a brief illustrative media example that highlights some of the issues that will be explored in that chapter. We then describe the things that 'we' will explore together in the chapter and provide a list of key terms and key thinkers referred to throughout the chapter. It is important to note these names and terms not only for accuracy's sake but also in order to give credit where credit is due. We also itemise what you *should* be able to do at the chapter's end. However, this list will only have value if you follow the chapter through thoroughly by engaging actively and in depth with the learning features outlined below.

Doing media studies

Each chapter presents a number of achievable activities and suggestions for research that the reader should complete if they wish to develop their skills of media analysis and theorisation. These activities may invite you to write a few hundred words, you might need to visit a music concert, buy a newspaper, go online or even talk to friends in order to generate material. These activities are placed at strategic points in each chapter. At the head of each chapter where appropriate you will find an activity entitled *Getting started*; others occur throughout the chapters and at the end you'll find a final activity of more substance designed to provoke thought, develop insights and get you to apply skills acquired thus far.

The authors sincerely believe in the evidence of their experience as tutors, and indeed as students of the media, that knowledge and insight come through exploration and application of ideas in relation to the things we find interesting. Tackling theses activities will be the most important way of using this book.

Case studies

Ideas and methods of investigation are no use if left abstract and inert. Each chapter is laden with passing illustrative instances of media practices and ideas that underline the theories and methods we explore. Each chapter presents detailed case studies produced by the authors, sometimes derived from 'the classics', and even from the work of students, that serve as examples of 'how to do' media studies in support of what you do. The variety of case studies serves also to illustrate the complex and pluralistic manner in which such research is conducted, presenting an array of openings for the reader's own research interests.

Definitions of key terms

You will have noticed from the outset that we set great store by examining the very terms upon which we proceed ('what is media studies?'). One of our first principles as scholars is to ask questions, exploring and evaluating the terms of our investigation and establish what we mean when we employ particular words and phrases.

As we have mentioned, media studies, like many other scholarly fields, utilises what sometimes seem like unusual or impenetrable jargon words, seemingly at odds with 'common-sense', everyday usage or meaning. An apparent oxymoron, such as postmodernism (see Chapter 12), is one such instance, or perhaps the more regular use of *sign* or even *rhetoric* (see Chapter 1). That we could also cite *simulacrum, two-step flow* or *pseudo-individualisation* would have you reaching for a dictionary, although even that resource may not be able to help here.

As mentioned, these words and the wider media studies phrasebook serve a particular and very important purpose in pinpointing the nature and assumptions behind scholarly work and the meaning and insight that the scholar produces and attempts to communicate. Most terms and phrases – political economy, historiography, ethnography and so on – are shared with other fields and disciplines, indicating the inter-disciplinary nature of our work and the outward-looking nature of scholarly work. As far as possible, therefore, throughout this book we outline and define some of the key terms that inform the field, their derivation and how they are employed in context.

Overall, key terms and definitions are collated in a final glossary, which serves as a 'one-stop' reference point when you need to remind yourself of an idea or cross-reference it.

Key thinkers

Knowing something about the ideas of important individuals who have defined the field, as well as the context in which their ideas were produced, can sometimes aid in the appreciation and recollection of their insights or maybe just their names. Thus we offer some brief intellectual biographies of both theorists and practitioners as a way of bringing the history, thought and practice of media studies to life.

Do note, however, that personal biographical material is rarely of more than passing interest, although some egregious individuals manage to work such stuff into their course-work essays for no reward ('Little did Professor Zeiss Ikon realise when he was born in 1899 that he would one day produce a masterwork of media studies . . . ').

Key texts

The aim of scholarly research is usually to conduct original investigations and analyses of the primary sources of the media: its products, professionals, organisations, audiences and so on. However, all scholarly work must acknowledge existing approaches and insights, even if we wish to reject them and move into new modes of thought and investigation. These are the books, chapters and journal articles, and occasionally lectures or conference contributions that constitute the secondary sources of the scholar's work: the giant's shoulders that we stand upon to gain a better view.

Throughout this book we draw attention to some of the field's foundational and most influential studies, theories and polemics, as well as more recent, innovative and, as yet, relatively unknown works. We do this through references, quotes, discussions, introductions and, occasionally, in lengthier extracts. We can't present these works in their entirety or offer much more than a very partial précis. It is the reader's task, therefore, to seek out material in order to explore ideas in their original and extended form. In serious scholarly work, there is no substitute for reading and, to this end, alongside key text boxes, etc. you will find, at the end of each chapter, annotated further reading lists with guidelines and questions designed to aid your comprehension of this material.

Thinking aloud

Many media theories, or the theories employed by media scholars in order to make sense of media forms, organisations, audiences and contexts, can provoke controversy and debate. The nature of theories and generalisations, derived from the observation and interpretation of phenomena, is built around evidence and argument and are sometimes based upon polemical agendas or simply present us with challenging insights. This might include the observations of semiology on the relationship of the world and how we seek to describe it through language (see Chapter 1), feminist protests about misogynistic media representations (see Chapter 3) or the Marxist precept that it is not enough to describe the world, 'the point is to change it' (see Chapter 10).

Media research and theories are also prompted in response to provocative ideas about media – the power forms have over people (influence, effects) or the power they give to people (stars, owners) – as well as provocative things that media say and do (newspaper witch-hunts for paedophiles, bringing salacious material into the household in the form of sexual material in magazines for teens, TV shows, internet sites and so on).

'Thinking aloud' boxes serve briefly to give you a moment to reflect, to stop and think about the ramifications of an issue or approach. They also seek to highlight in more detail ongoing controversies and engagements with theory, as well as instances of media practice that might grab our attention. In tandem with suggestions for further work and

New media, new media studies

The extent to which 'digital' media have changed traditional forms such as TV, radio or the press has probably been overstated. Claims such as 'the newspaper is dead', for instance, overemphasise the idea of endings rather than framing transformations and continuities. Nonetheless, new scholars, born into the digital world, are well placed to engage with new media practices in all their variety.

For this edition we have introduced this section in order to bring into focus some of the ways of thinking about new media forms and how they might challenge long-standing modes of thinking and analysis in media studies. Enhanced and extended aspects of interactivity, wide access to the means of production and the challenge to the boundaries between audiences and producers for instance, not to mention the advent of social media, present us with much material to analyse. Business models for industry, aesthetics, meanings, audience activity and so on are all areas for us to consider for how they challenge established practices in media and in media studies.

reading, the aim is to make media studies 'come alive' and prompt your own engagement with the field.

Summary

If you begin with and maintain an interest in and attention to the scholarly study of media, it will offer its own reward. On the other hand, we live in an 'audit culture', where a measurable customer service and quality assurance (i.e. a return for your money) is paramount, even in education. Thus, just as at the beginning of each chapter we outline what you should be able to do, we reiterate these points at the end of each chapter. If you have followed our advice, taken on the tasks we have set and followed up ideas for reading and so on, you should be raring to go further.

What then will this book enable you to do?

We expect that readers of this book will come to it in order to enhance their studies as fully enrolled college- or university-level students, whether in media or cultural studies, or some other discipline that has led them to consider media. Beyond the apparent satisfaction with the pursuit of knowledge for its own sake, then, we should also consider the range of ways in which knowledge of and engagement with media might have further value. We've already sketched out the centrality of media to modern life and how they have a part to play in underwriting our role as citizens. If we take on board the proposition that media messages are not simple transmissions of information but that their mode of transmission is important, as well as the context of the circulation of that message, we can appreciate how media literacy might aid our political acuity.

The very fact of contemporary media enterprise, economy and fiscal worth would surely merit some attention, along with awareness of how media forms and organisations are governed and upon what imperatives regulation proceeds. Again, this can be very different from other sectors of industry: the performance of a car is one thing, but why people might pay for a film or popular music performance to the extent that they do is another. We should not forget, either, that many of us who study media are already practitioners or seek careers in media organisations. It is only fair to point out that this book won't get you a job, nor will most degrees in media studies. But, then, degrees in English literature don't aim to produce authors. However, as our words on media practitioners indicate, the most successful and thoughtful individuals are highly conscious, reflective, thinking professionals. If you aim to be a worker in the media or wider cultural industries, you need to develop an understanding of the institutions you will find yourself in, how to navigate them and indeed how to make sense of media output and how to articulate your ideas. If this is your aim, then we hope to help you.

Ultimately, this book won't enable you to do anything – only you are able to achieve things for yourself, through action and engagement with the things we suggest and out of your own initiative.

Getting started – just do it

What we seek to develop, in tandem with the engaged reader, are skills of analysis that integrate and synthesise ideas, testing theories and indeed theorising about the significance of a range of media-related phenomena and practices. This means that the reader who finds this book successful will become more than a reader. They will be an active thinker and researcher, and what they do will indeed be media studies.

The serious and genuinely motivated scholar has already begun to ask valuable questions about media before acquiring this book. In order to develop reflective skills and a focus, however, the reader should ask her- or himself the following questions before turning over and proceeding to engage with this book:

- What is it about media that interests me?
- What is happening in various media at the moment?
- In what ways is what is happening across media (or in my media life) significant and how can I make sense of these events and developments beyond the level of self-interest?

If you are prepared to ask such questions and keep asking others like them, and are prepared to turn over the page and engage, then you will be well on your way to being a media scholar.

Suggested reading sources

Media studies journals

These titles (and there are many others – see the References at the end of this book) can be found in most large city libraries, as well as the libraries of universities and colleges, depending upon the needs and focus of any media and communications courses. While some journals offer a general coverage of the field, some are more specialist in their attention to specific media forms and practices.

Such journals are where you will find examples of the latest research, questions and debates in the media studies field, as well as reviews of the latest books and conferences. In this way the interested scholar can develop detailed insights into the field, learning from new and established scholars about how to 'do' media studies.

Journalism Studies

(www.tandf.co.uk/journals/titles/1461670X.asp)

This is published six times a year. It has contributors from around the world who discuss relevant topics surrounding news, politics, current affairs, public relations and advertising. Its intended audience is not just academic but also includes journalistic practitioners. The scope of *Journalism Studies* includes:

- the history of journalism,
- the sociology of journalism,
- journalism and new media,
- journalism and policy,
- women and journalism,
- journalism and regulation,
- journalism ethics,
- media ownership and journalism,
- minorities and journalism.

Doing media studies

'First steps'

This is where *you* can begin to explore the value of media for yourself in terms of their importance in your everyday life. You can do this by completing the very simple activity described here.

Using a simple diary format over the period of a week, keep a close record of all of your activities, including how much time you watch television, time spent online, whether or not you bought a paper or what music you listened to.

Of course, you could keep a very rough record of everything *else* you do, too, comparing and contrasting the hours spent on different activities. You might also consider the personal cost of this media consumption (subscriptions, hardware).

Once you have completed this activity you could generate some provocative and challenging questions to get you thinking about what you've discovered. For instance, what would you do with all of this time if mass media did not exist?

As an indicator of what can be achieved, here's a response from one of our own students who completed this task as part of their studies.

> I was asked to keep a diary of my media consumption over the period of one week. Here are the results. I have to say that I am a little embarrassed by the findings, I am sure that I have more of a life than what the findings suggest (the timings are approximate)

Monday

Listened to the radio in the morning while having breakfast (30 mins)

Listened to music on my iPod on the way to university (45 mins)

Viewed numerous advertising billboards while on the way to university

Read the free *Metro* newspaper while on the bus

Watched some extracts from films in my Film Rhetoric class

Checked my email while at university and surfed the net (45 mins)

Listened to music on my iPod on the way home (45 mins)

Viewed numerous advertising billboards while on the way home

Played on my Xbox 360 (90 mins)

Watched television with my flatmates (120 mins)

Read the *New Musical Express* magazine which I bought earlier (£2.10)

Chatted to friends on MSN and Facebook, surfed net (120 mins)

Sleep!

Tuesday

Watched TV news while having breakfast (30 mins)

Listened to music on my iPod on the way to university (45 mins)

Viewed numerous advertising billboards while on the way to university

Read the free *Metro* newspaper while on the bus

Checked my email while at university and surfed the net (45 mins)

Listened to music on my iPod on the way home (45 mins)

Viewed numerous advertising billboards while on the way home

Watched television with my flatmates (120 mins)

Went to the cinema to see a film (cost £5)

Chatted to friends on MSN and Facebook (60 mins)

Sleep!

Wednesday

Watched TV news while having breakfast (30 mins)

Listened to a podcast on my iPod on the way to university (45 mins)

Viewed numerous advertising billboards while on the way to university

➡️

Read the free *Metro* newspaper while on the bus

Listened to music on my iPod on the way home (45 mins)

Viewed numerous advertising billboards while on the way home

Bought some DVDs and CDs while out shopping (£15)

Played on Xbox 360 (90 mins)

Went to see a live band (£10)

Sleep!

Thursday

Watched television (90 mins)

Listened to music on my iPod on the way to university (45 mins)

Viewed numerous advertising billboards while on the way to university

Read the free *Metro* newspaper while on the bus

Listened to music on my iPod on the way home (45 mins)

Viewed numerous advertising billboards while on the way home

Watched television with flatmates (120 mins)

Went out to a club, danced to music (£5 entry, 300 mins)

Sleep!

Friday

Listened to the radio in the morning while having breakfast (30 mins)

Listened to music on my iPod on the way to university (45 mins)

Viewed numerous advertising billboards while on the way to university

Read the free *Metro* newspaper while on the bus

Checked my email while at university and surfed the net (45 mins)

Listened to music on my iPod on the way home (45 mins)

Played on my Xbox 360 (90 mins)

Watched two films with my flatmates (240 mins)

Saturday

Surfed net (60 mins)

Listened to music while surfing net (60 mins)

Played on Xbox 360 (120 mins)

Watched television (180 mins)

Read friend's copy of the *Sun* (10 mins)

Played on friend's Wii (120 mins)

Went out to a club, danced to music (£6 entry, 300 mins)

Sunday

Watched television (60 mins)

Surfed the net (120 mins)

Listened to music while surfing net (60 mins)

Played on Xbox (60 mins)

Watched a film (90 mins)

Surfed the net (120 mins)

Observations

When it comes to my media consumption I seem to have a routine. I regularly listen to music while on the way to and from university and also read the free newspaper. I spend a lot of time online and also watching television/movies. I had no idea I spent so much time online, it goes so quickly. I imagine that this routine might be viewed differently if I itemised every tune, site and programme that fitted into these hours. I didn't really spend that much money during the week on media. Obviously, things like my iPod, Xbox 360, DVD player did cost money and quite a lot too. It is interesting to see how some of my consumption is on my own but some is with friends. Overall, I am quite surprised by how much time I spend consuming the media.

Some questions that I thought would be worth researching include:

- How does my media routine compare with the other people I sometimes share my consumption with?

- What pleasures do I get from playing on my Xbox 360?

- Why are some media consumed on your own when other times it is a group activity?

(See www.tandf.co.uk/journals/titles/1461670X.asp)
Recent articles include:

- The 'objectivity' ideal and its limitations in twentieth-century British journalism
- Ethics and eloquence in journalism
- Nation, culture and identity in a French-language Corsican newspaper
- Emerging media in peril: Iraqi journalism in the post-Saddam Hussein era.

It also has a sister journal called *Journalism Practice*, which is devoted to the study and analysis of significant issues arising from journalism as a field of professional practice.

Mass Communication and Society

(www.informaworld.com/smpp/title~content=t775653676)

This is published four times a year. It publishes articles from a wide variety of perspectives and approaches that advance mass communication theory. It draws heavily from many other disciplines, including sociology, psychology, anthropology, philosophy, law and history. Recent articles include:

- Towards a model of interactivity in alternative media: a multilevel analysis of audiences and producers in a new social movement network
- Editing conservatism: how *National Review* magazine framed and mobilised a political movement
- Broadcast and cable network news coverage of the 2004 presidential election: an assessment of partisan and structural imbalance
- Towards a measure of community journalism.

Media, Culture and Society

(http://mcs.sagepub.com/)

This is possibly the most well-known media studies journal, and has been in existence for almost 30 years. It is published every two months and features articles on all media, drawing on different disciplines and approaches. A number of influential and important articles have been featured in *Media, Culture and Society* which have had enormous impact across the field. It is a must-use resource for all media scholars due to the large archive of material it has. Recent articles include:

- Contra flow from the Arab world? How Arab television coverage of the 2003 Iraq war was used and framed on Western international news channels
- Politics, religion and the media: the transformation of the public sphere in Senegal
- The realities of virtual play: video games and their industry in China
- Securing vision: photography and US foreign policy.

New Media and Society

(http://nms.sagepub.com/)

The field of new media studies is fast-moving with important developments happening constantly. Due to the slow process of publishing books, many tend to be out of date or slightly behind when discussing these developments. This is when a journal such as *New*

Media and Society is most useful, as it allows scholars to be aware of what research is currently being undertaken in this exciting field. Published every two months, *NMS* has been in existence for 10 years. Recent articles include:

- Taking risky opportunities in youthful content creation: teenagers' use of social networking sites for intimacy, privacy and self-expression
- Can filesharers be triggered by economic incentives? Results of an experiment
- Social networks and cellphone use in Russia: local consequences of global communication technology
- Forums for citizen journalists? Adoption of user-generated content initiatives by online news media.

Participations

(www.participations.org/)

This is a new journal and it differs from the other journals discussed here as it is published only online. It is devoted to audience and reception studies, areas that are not as well supported by stand-alone journals as are other fields of research. It has been in existence since late 2003. The aims of *Participations* are to:

- publish research from many approaches, without the limitations on length and presentation of evidence which can cramp and weaken such work;
- encourage open debate between different approaches and methodologies;
- encourage collaborations across academic disciplines, areas and countries;
- provide a place where people may with ease find materials and bibliographies for use in teaching and research training;
- provide a focal point for the development of the broad field, including holding conferences and other kinds of forum.

(See www.participations.org/introduction.htm)

Participations is a particularly useful resource for media scholars as it is available for free and does not require a subscription to access. The titles of recent articles give a sense of the range of subjects covered:

- 'Other' or 'one of us'?: the porn user in public and academic discourse
- 'You've Made Mistress Very, Very Angry': Displeasure and Pleasure in Media Representations of BDSM
- Everyday Talk: Investigating Media Consumption and Identity Amongst School Children
- Speculations on Spoilers: Lost Fandom, Narrative Consumption and Rethinking Textuality
- Television, Sexual Difference and Everyday Life in the 1970s: American Youth as Historical Audience
- Get a Real Job: Authenticity on the Performance, Reception and Study of Celebrity.

Screen

(www.gla.ac.uk/services/screen/)

This was first published in 1952, when it was known as *The Film Teacher*, changing its name to *Screen Education* in 1959, a name it kept until 1969, from when it was simply called *Screen*. Its aim has been to develop the field of film studies and assist in defining it. It provides a forum where controversial issues surrounding film can be debated and discussed among academics. *Screen* has also encompassed television as well as film. A number of important and influential articles have appeared in *Screen*, one of the most well known being Laura Mulvey's 1975 article 'Visual pleasure in narrative cinema', which appeared in volume 13, issue 3. Recent articles have included:

- 'The viewers have . . . taken over the airwaves?' Participation, reality TV and approaching the audience-in-the-text
- The television personality system: televisual stardom revisited after film theory
- 'Paranoia, paranoia, everybody's coming to get me': *Peep Show*, sitcom and the surveillance society.

Media studies online

There are many individual academic blogs, research websites, open-access online journals and so on that have appeared in recent years. These are places to encounter research in progress as well as contribute to debates about media studies. These sites are, for good or bad, more immediate and responsive to media events when compared to the processes of print publication although this does have a tendency to raise questions about 'peer review' and reliability among those suspicious of the online world.

Some of the most interesting sites are (their own words in italics):

A Manifesto for Media Education

(www.manifestoformediaeducation.co.uk/)

This is a key site for anyone interested in media education in the context of arguments about the value of the field and the role of media in contemporary society. Anyone seriously interested in understanding the field should examine this site and engage with it.

This project is an attempt to develop a shared understanding, some shared reasons, for media education. We hope it will stimulate discussion within course teams and with students. We imagine it will lead to conversations about how we teach and what specific things we teach, but those are secondary questions. We believe we may uncover many reasons but it seems better to have articulated many as opposed to none [. . .]

On this website you will find a variety of writers' summations of their reasoning for media education. These will be context specific and at times may feel at odds with one another. However we hope that by the end of the process we will have a better, more sustaining understanding of the purpose of what we do and that we will be able to draw on this understanding to keep us on track in the classroom and in defending and advocating our subject in the future.

Antenna

(http://blog.commarts.wisc.edu/)

Antenna is a collectively authored media and cultural studies blog committed to timely yet careful analysis of texts, news, and events from across the popular culture spectrum. The site regularly responds to new works and developments in television, film, music, gaming, digital video, the Internet, print, and the media industries.

Antenna is intended to address a broad public inside and outside the university walls. Within those walls, though, it further intends to bridge the gap between scholarly journals, which remain the paradigm for scholarly discourse but too often lack the ability to reply to issues and events in media with any immediacy, and single-author media scholar blogs, which support swift commentary but are limited in their reliance upon the effort and perspectives of individuals. Coordinated by a group of writers who draw on a variety of approaches and methodologies, Antenna, therefore, exists as a means to analyze media news and texts, both as they happen and from multiple perspectives.

[. . .]

Antenna's goal is to create a forum in which readers and contributors participate in active, open, and thoughtful debate about media and culture.

Culture Machine

(www.culturemachine.net/)

Culture Machine is a series of experiments in culture and theory.

The aim of Culture Machine is to seek out and promote the most provocative of new work, and analyses of that work, in culture and theory from a diverse range of international authors. Culture Machine is particularly concerned with promoting research which is engaged in the constitution of new areas of inquiry and the opening of new frontiers of cultural and theoretical activity. It is also committed to the generation of possibilities for new scholarship and research.

Flow

(http://flowtv.org/)

Flow is an online journal of television and media studies launched in October 2004. In our 6 year history we have published over 900 columns from over 300 authors from around the U.S. and the world. Flow's mission is to provide a space where researchers, teachers, students, and the public can read about and discuss the changing landscape of contemporary media at the speed that media moves.

PART ONE

MEDIA TEXTS AND MEANINGS

As a starting point for our studies we should consider how media industries are organised around a process of production, distribution and consumption.

Media companies such as Disney, News International, Canal+, Bertelsman and so on are organised as businesses with departments covering finance, production, recruitment and so on that allow them to function as effective economic entities. Individuals in such departments oversee the production of saleable materials through research, development, cultivation of the creative process and final realisation of product to its packaging ready for delivery. Consider a Nintendo video game as the end product of such a process. This product is developed and produced, then marketed and distributed: you can buy games in shops, by mail order or over the internet – maybe even borrow them from friends or obtain illegal 'pirated' copies. Finally, media products are consumed by viewers, listeners, web surfers, readers and so on. With Nintendo and its products, consumers spend hours mastering games, moving through each level relating to the pleasure, attraction and rewards they get from them.

In this first part of the book we are concerned with this final stage – media *output* – in very particular ways. For most of us our main experience of the media is as consumers of its output. What we 'consume' is the meaning of that output in newspaper stories, pop songs, billboard advertisements, radio and TV shows, films, photographs, computer games and websites. This meaning is the basis of the thrills, pleasures and informational aspects of media forms in all their variety – the very basis of their existence and success.

The four chapters in this part of the book are intended to lead you through a step-by-step process of thinking about media output and meanings and some of the key terms by which media studies describes and makes sense of this output through interpretation. Beginning with the acknowledgement of the fact that we already know what meanings media forms have, we aim to equip you with some procedures and tools that will aid you in making sense of *how* media make meaning and how we understand those meanings.

We'll look first at the nature of texts and methods of rhetorical and semiological analysis. In Chapter 2 (Organising media in media texts: genre and narrative) we look at the different categories of media texts in terms of genre as well as consider how stories are organised in terms of narrative. In the third chapter (Media representations) we pay attention to the way in which all media 'represent' the world (fictional or otherwise) and in particular to how we think about individuals and groups and what is at stake in such representations. Finally, Chapter 4 (Reality media) develops these themes further by thinking of the relationship of media meanings and the worlds media depict or construct in terms of the truth claims they make or are assumed to make. In addition we'll tie all of these threads together in an extended analysis of a media text in order to work through ways of making sense of how meaning is made.

Chapters in this section:

Chapter 1: How do media make meaning?
Introduces the concept of text and the tools of rhetorical and semiological analysis that aid the understanding of how media meanings are made

Chapter 2: Organising meaning in media texts: genre and narrative
Examines types of media text and the conventions governing meaning and the organisation and structuring of stories and representation

Chapter 3: Media representations
Develops the idea of media representation to consider the specific issues and ways in which social groups and individuals are represented in media forms

Chapter 4: Reality media
Evaluates the relationship of media forms and meanings with the real, truth, fact and authenticity as well as our expectations of these ideas

CHAPTER 1

How do media make meaning?

What is this image, what exactly is going on here and how do I know what it is and what it means?

Source: The Advertising Archives

Thinking about media meanings

Consider the image reproduced here and ask yourself some simple questions of the kind that we rarely ask (because we *know* the answers already): what is this image and what is it telling me? How do I *know* what it is saying to me and how is it saying it?

Some readers might leap to respond along the lines of 'it is obvious what it is: it is an advertisement for Sony Ericsson!' We would agree that it might well be an advertisement but there is nothing at all obvious here that tells us that this is such a media product, nor does it say anything about Sony Ericsson products — at least explicitly and unequivocally.

There is some written text here to guide our interpretation: 'I [. . .] coding the future'. The trademark for Sony Ericsson is placed after the I, in a place redolent of the slogan

famous from many tourist T-shirts ('I ♥ New York', for instance). There is 'rhyme' of the green and white Sony Ericsson trademark in the shaping of the many zeroes and ones that dominate the image mainly to the left of the frame. Such sequences are of course those of the binary language which forms the basis of computer coding behind our digital world. In tandem with this evocation of the basis of computing are the floating plus signs, musical notes, the .com suffix and @ symbol that we associate with e-communication addresses and identities. All of these items are part of a flux of cloud in neon pinks and purples.

What does all of this mean then and what are we meant to take from it? Is there a discernible message about Sony Ericsson on offer or simply a feeling that one might associate with the exciting idea of

'I [Sony Ericsson] coding the future'? Is this a glimpse at a vision of the virtual space inside of a Sony Ericsson processor, privy to what the future might actually look like at the digital level? Seen from one angle, the outline of the trademark zooms to the left like a binary comet, the clouds a rocket-like exhaust from a long tail of zeroes and ones as Sony Ericsson forges ahead at speed, scattering the symbols of our current digital world like ninepins.

While some of us might 'get' what this media text offers without a second thought, others might not be best placed to 'read' its meanings (on occasion, gaining no meaning at all) and may even misinterpret it completely. Your reading might be completely at odds with ours for instance and readers may even consider that we have 'over-read' this media product. How we react may in fact relate to the skill with which this media product has been put together and its level of success in communicating with audiences.

Whatever our reactions, we could agree that while this is a very simple-looking piece of media output, one that graces billboards, pages of magazines, websites and so on in order to reach millions, it is, in fact, a very sophisticated image

indeed. It is sophisticated in that it is full of meaning and it draws upon a range of conventions and associations, with little or no attempt made to notify us of the fact that it is 'doing' something. That something is that it is communicating ideas about Sony Ericsson as a company and producer of 'cutting-edge' products.

It is worth noting, too, that like many advertisements nowadays this one

does not exhort us to buy a product or, indeed, tell us anything significant about any one item from among the Sony Ericsson portfolio.

Beginning to ask questions about the selection and organisation of the constituent parts of media images such as this one — without recourse to its creators — and thinking about meaning and the terms of analysis are the objectives of this first chapter.

What we will we do in this chapter

This chapter introduces the concept of the text as a way of focusing on and analysing the meaning of media output. We will move on to explore the ways in which media make meaning, by defining and using tools of rhetorical analysis and then semiological analysis. The kinds of questions we ask of our apparently simple advert, and the way in which we might make sense of how it makes sense, can be extended to newspaper articles, web pages, popular music recordings, magazine covers, films, computer games and all media products.

By the end of this chapter you should be able to:

- ■ Distinguish between the artefactual, commodity and textual aspects of media outputs.

- ■ Systematically identify the rhetorical devices involved in producing and organising meaning in media texts.

- ■ Utilise tools of rhetorical and semiological analysis in support of detailed interpretations and arguments about the meaning of media texts.

- ■ Begin to conceptualise the relationship of media meanings to social contexts.

KEY TERMS: ▶ affect; analysis and interpretation; artefact; cognition; commodity; construction; diachronic; langue; meaning; multi-accentuality; paradigm; parole; polysemia; rhetoric; semiology; synchronic; syntagm; text.

Thinking about media as texts

Most people experience media as consumers – solely through various forms of output, the end result of media production. That is to say we read newspapers, magazines and comics, we watch films and TV shows, listen to the radio and music, as well as using the internet and playing computer games. And, of course, we experience a range of media products in a variety of places – a pop song can appear on the radio, as a soundtrack to a film or in the background of a TV show.

We can distinguish between ways of labelling media output and understanding function and meaning by considering the following three-part relationship:

- First, the output of the media has a physical form as an artefact. Media artefacts include DVD discs, tabloid-sized newspapers, reels of celluloid film, hard-copy photographs or even the digital signals that make up a downloadable song by any music band. These are all physical forms.

- Secondly, there is the economic value embodied in media output, in terms of commodity status. Here we refer to the cost and price that are put on media production and media products – the cost of a cinema ticket, which adds to the revenue of a film alongside DVD rentals and sales, for example. Even when we don't necessarily pay directly for media products (encounters with advertising hoardings being one example, or songs heard over supermarket PAs or on commercial radio) we are encountering an economic chain in which the value and cost of the media artefact is in some way related to some other expenditure that we might make. Either way, payment has been entered into by the consumer with some kind of return on investment – hopefully a profit – expected by the producer.

- Thirdly, we can consider media output as a site for the generation of meaning value: what media outputs say and how they speak, and what meanings output has for us as individuals and social beings. Meaning here refers to the ways in which we are affected psychologically, emotionally, culturally, physically and intellectually by media output: the way in which media forms entertain, stimulate, inform us – giving us pleasure, shock or food for thought.

When we study texts, we are interested in asking questions about meaning rather than the physical results of production, distribution and consumption, or the way that output is produced, marketed and sold as a commodity defined by its economic status. Of course, we should be aware of the way in which these three ways of labelling media output interact, but for now let us insist upon the distinction as a means of exploring the particularities of text and the construction and relay of meanings.

Here, the use of the term 'text', as distinct from 'artefact' and 'commodity', displays the debt owed by the field of media studies to English literature. In literary studies, texts are books, poems or plays, which are read and analysed in terms of the meanings derived from the selection and deployment of words alone. Typeface, cover images, quality of paper, publisher and price are rarely, if ever, invoked as having any pertinence to the thrust of a narrative, metre or structure in the act of interpretation.

This debt to English literature is echoed also in the way in which we sometimes refer to analysis as providing a 'reading' of texts that encompass photographs, movies, pop music and so on. Likewise, in interpreting the text as a 'creative' and meaningful product of the various media we aim to go beyond mere description in order to articulate fully what it has to say to us about the world.

Making sense of textual meaning

It appears to be a very simple matter to understand the meaning of media output as text – millions of us do it every day as a matter of course. We log on to websites, listen to the

Doing media studies

Making sense of media products

Identify *five* media products in your possession or that you have encountered in your consumption today. For each media product think of its status as artefact, commodity and text.

■ How useful and straightforward are these categories for understanding your media products?

■ Does any confusion between categories arise?

■ What are the advantages and disadvantages to distinguishing between media as artefact, commodity and text?

radio and watch TV. We encounter advertising across all media forms in a myriad of ways. So fast and so often do they appear that individual adverts barely register in our consciousness. But then we don't have to stop and pay attention in the face of each advert we come across – if it were necessary to do so the roads might be blocked when we drive down the street past billboards and posters on the sides of bus stops or in shop windows! The rapidity with which we encounter media output and make sense of it, at least superficially, is thus shared across all media and is a key characteristic of contemporary life. Making sense of media texts is habitual, a constant in our everyday existence.

When we watch TV or listen to the radio, presenters and actors usually speak our language and refer to things, places and people we recognise in familiar ways: if they did not, the media might not retain our attention. We also understand aspects of the output of media that are harder to explain in the same way as written or spoken language or recognisable images. Popular music doesn't use words alone, sometimes making its sounds out of musical instruments as well as from 'found' sounds such as electronic blips and beeps taken from computer games and mobile phones. Even visual media such as film, TV and photography use aspects of light, colour and so on in a creative, allusive manner.

With these observations in mind, we can think about the work of making meaning in three ways. We very rarely stop to consider how media make meaning or indeed the range of meanings any one of the many thousands of media products might contain for us as individuals or for the many millions they are aimed at. When we read newspapers, watch films, look at photographs or play games, their meanings appear to be simple because we have no need to recall the work that has gone into preparing us for the act of reading or interpretation.

First, this work is that of media producers themselves. The expectations and ideas of writers, film-makers, musicians, programmers and designers, as well as the conventions and institutions they work within and the contexts that they share with us as consumers, all contribute to the way in which meaning can occur.

Secondly, we media consumers do 'work' that results from our upbringing and those wider cultural, social and historical contexts we navigate in our lives. Of course, to pay attention to the general factors contributing to and affecting our understanding of any media output might prove counterproductive to its purposes (polemic, entertainment, educational, selling goods, etc.) and our reasons for consuming it (pleasure, information, 'vegetating', etc.).

Thirdly, the main work that has gone into preparing us for our ongoing consumption and pleasure in media is our regular acquaintance with their various forms: newspapers, TV and so on. This encounter with media and the acquisition of a sense of how various forms work is akin to our acquisition of our mother tongue – it starts pretty much from the day we're born, often unwittingly or without choice. We live in a media-saturated world, surrounded by media texts that even those who object to such a situation can hardly avoid.

Thus, media products come in a range of guises and make meaning through a variety of means, with many purposes, as part of a relationship between producer and consumer. Therefore, we can see that texts and textual meanings are always contextualised. In each case meaning is inflected first and foremost by the manner and mode of communication.

To illustrate what is at stake here, consider a very simple example – the typeface used in the presentation of the words in this book and available to you on any computer. In what ways is the meaning of a simple word like 'horror' affected here by the typographic *choices* made and deployed?

HORROR   Horror

Horror   HORROR

Imagine this word and any of the typefaces used here (or any available to you) on a film poster, in a comic book, on a pop-up page on an internet website, or on a T-shirt or DVD cover. Perhaps we can imagine such things without the usual accompanying image or even any use of colour, and even then such absences are important choices in each medium's textual meanings.

Why analyse media texts?

By developing critical skills for the analysis of media forms and meanings we want to draw attention to the fact that media and their products are *not* natural, or 'just there'. How they operate and convey the world to us is not necessarily an obvious matter or consensual, however much it appears to be that way.

While we should not dismiss casual ways of referring to the various media and what they provide – as a 'window on the world', 'the real thing', etc. – our first lesson is to appreciate that such phrases tend to reflect the habitual manner in which we consume any medium. Our acquaintance as consumers with the variety of media forms rarely involves establishing a critical distance from them. We know already what media are saying to us, so we rarely bother to ask questions about how they make meaning that might, in turn, lead to questions of why they make meaning in the ways that they do and prompting questions about what might be at stake.

We want to develop a mode of analysis in order to deal with the issue of how media make meaning in order to ponder the stakes involved in the ubiquity of forms in our lives and in society at large. Such an approach, when properly executed, presented and illustrated, aims systematically to convince others of one's interpretation in order to support any argument or to make grander points about the social value, cultural insights and even the effects of media texts.

Doing media studies

Getting to grips with textual meaning

■ For one week, keep a 'media studies' diary: make a note of the conversations you have or overhear about media and their meanings. What kinds of things do people say about media and their understanding of media (do they say anything at all)? How do people describe their experience of media and the meanings media have for them?

■ Identify a current item in the news. Watch as many TV news bulletins related to this story as you can, as well as listening to radio accounts or looking for web accounts of the story. Get hold of coverage of the same story in the newspapers. What similarities and differences are you able to identify across these versions of the story? Pay attention to the facts and detail of the story but also to the manner in which it is presented. How does each medium impact upon the story, do you think?

Tools for analysing media texts

Many of us often struggle to convey exactly what media texts mean to us with any precision and we often resort to very generalised evaluative expressions ('cool', 'OK', 'brilliant', 'rubbish', 'far-fetched', etc.). We do, however, tend to pinpoint some very precise things when we talk about how moving a film is, how funny a radio interview is, how exciting or involving a pop song or computer game has been, or how concerned we are by the issues presented by a newspaper story. But these examples suggest an often under-developed way of speaking, where conversation tends to the superficially descriptive, rather than any systematic approach to an understanding of why we might exhibit such reactions towards media texts.

As scholars, what we need in order both to understand and explain how media make meaning – in ways that we can all agree upon – is a common technical language that, as far as possible, avoids wholly subjective judgements. In this way, we should be like the most effective of media producers and, although even 'objective' academics rarely escape their subjectivity, by using a set of clearly defined terms we can support schematic and methodical analyses of media texts with precisely argued and detailed interpretations. We can employ particular and transferable terms that will allow us to make sense of similar operations but different characteristics across media forms. These terms compose a 'meta-', or greater, framing language to make sense of media. What matters most is that we use this to get to grips with some methodical means of making sense of how meaning is made.

Here, we explore and enlist two interrelated approaches to explain how the selection and organisation of media resources make meaning. These are two approaches that attend to different aspects of media meaning in different ways, asking different questions but ultimately working together as resources both in support of interpretations of the way in which meaning works and claims for the social significance of media meanings.

Analytical tools: rhetoric

Rhetoric
is the construction and manipulation of language by the creator of a text for affective purposes.

Cognition
refers to the way in which we, as individuals, acquire knowledge as well as apply it – the process through which we comprehend events and ideas in order to come to understand the world.

For many people, the experience of consuming media texts feels very personal and intimately connected with the way we think of ourselves and indeed interact with others, in a spontaneous, unconscious manner. We laugh, we cry, we get excited – scared, agitated, concerned – in our consumption. In those media that deal with 'actuality' – such as newspapers, broadcast news, website updates and documentaries, and photographic reportage – we experience a parade of people talking or writing to us as individuals, supported by images of things which are explained in familiar terms for us. In the story telling media – like film and TV drama or comedy, or comic books – we are placed in the position of spectators at the creation of events, whether 'realistic' or fantastic, which seem to be unfolding before our vicarious point of view.

We feel this personal involvement (most of the time) because the producers of media texts have mastery over a series of production techniques that we can label 'media rhetoric'. The first step in our approach to comprehending the manner in which texts are meaningful we therefore call rhetorical analysis.

Rhetorical analysis asks: how are media texts put together as media texts? How do they organise and present meaning? Rhetorical analysis approaches media texts and their meanings as constructed out of the use of available techniques, styles and conventions in any medium. The intention of this construction is to position audiences in particular ways in order to elicit emotional, psychological or physical responses from them.

Ultimately, the aim of media in organising meaning is to get audiences to pay attention, and so aid **cognition** or their interpretation of the media text as a mode of communication. In this way we can examine photography, typography, film frames, page layout and design, musical conventions and so on, as well as the particularities of the use of words in the press and magazine journalism, in broadcasting, in songs, on websites, in dramatic dialogue and across all media forms.

This approach to considering media forms and the way that they express ideas, to represent and inflect the real world or to construct fictional worlds, is one step towards overcoming a sense that the media simply reflect the world in some straightforward manner, operating as transmitters of information-based messages. In fact, rhetorical analysis suggests that meaning is not mainly about information, the tangible content of the media, but is tied to the way that we learn about that information: its presentation and the particularities of the medium. As we learnt from Marshall McLuhan (1964) in the introduction: 'the medium is the message'.

Modern media are involved in a complex and sophisticated activity of social communication. We may not always recognise this activity because media workers are so skilful that their communication often seems 'natural' and 'obvious', partly due to our familiarity with media forms.

Rhetoric, language and meaning

In order to clarify our use of the term media rhetoric, it is useful to distinguish it from those other related concepts that inform media studies: language and meaning.

- **Language** is the material out of which a single instance of communication is created. It provides the basic units – in words and phrases, images and sounds – as well as rules that determine how they can be organised in texts – grammar and syntax.
- **Rhetoric** is the way in which language is manipulated to a particular purpose, such as the creation of emotion in poetry. Applied to media, we can think of the evocation of fear when watching a horror film or feelings of excitement and urgency when playing video games. Likewise, when we watch the news, certain subjects will cause us to attend to the story with concern and proper seriousness.
- **Meaning** refers to the interpretation of messages by the reader of the text.

Like the grammatical directions and conventions underpinning written and spoken language, rhetoric is concerned with the organisation of vocabulary. However, while grammar refers to organisation according to rules, rhetoric is about organisation according to results. For example, we can illustrate this point by looking at a recent front page of a popular British daily newspaper depicting the widespread social disturbances of the summer of 2011 (see p. 35). During the period of unrest, the front pages of many popular daily newspapers presented graphic responses to what was perceived to be a challenge to law and order. As in all tabloid headlines, the aim was to grab the interest of the potential reader, presenting the front page not as an objective perspective on events but instead to evoke and ride on the emotions of the reader – evoking fear, concern and anger for instance. The silhouetted image of a woman jumping for her life from a blazing building illustrates the results of unthinking mob violence (mob rule becomes the even more judgemental 'yob rule'). Her anonymity makes her a symbol for a broader peril. The front page presents a conjunction of fear-inducing images and ideas – the imperilled woman, the injured policeman, a riotous 'hoodie' – and speaks to the reader on their terms: the idealised '*Daily Mirror* reader', for example, the common man or woman, engaging their attention and concern.

Such examples suggest that rhetoric involves more than simply aiming to be effective in communication – getting a message across in an economic fashion ('man bites dog', 'our aspirin clears headaches fast'). When we focus upon the rhetoric of acts of communication, we are interested in more than the conveyance of information; we connect the form that the communication takes with the possible response made to reading it. Such emotional responses are usually known as *affective responses*. Rhetoric is the art of manipulating these affective responses.

Source: Mirrorpix

> Captioning. This refers to the use of verbal text to accompany visual text. Where this is used (appearing within a picture or alongside it, whatever the context — a gallery, in a publication or on a webpage), it is of vital importance in the interpretation given to the picture. Captioning may 'anchor' the meaning of images and our response to them, reaffirming interpretation or undermining it by degree. For instance, a picture of a figure such as Osama bin Laden might, depending upon context and intent, be underlined by captions as disparate as 'evil terrorist' or 'defender of the faith'. In captioning, therefore, we can see an overlap with aspects of presentation as outlined above.

The classical origins of rhetoric: some lessons and abiding concerns

If we take another definition of rhetoric as 'the art of persuasive communication and eloquence', this indicates the way in which rhetorical analysis is concerned with style, composition and argument. Rhetoric, as an idea and a skill that could be learnt, practised and deployed, developed in the Ancient World. In fourth-century BC Athens, it was essential to be able to speak effectively for participation in the public life of this original democracy, as exemplified by Aristotle's famous *Art of Rhetoric*. Rhetoric in this context was used to appeal to an audience of one's peers, to convince them of the validity of your position in a topic by the use of both reasoned argument and emotion: content accentuated by presentation and delivery.

Many European cultures, from the Romans onwards, were influenced by ideas of rhetoric, making its teaching and study central to their educational system and modes of communication, from the arts to religious treatises and sermons. The study of rhetoric reached its height during the Renaissance, later becoming associated with the kinds of rote learning found in English schools in the nineteenth century. In this instance, its association acquired the negative implications of a series of limiting structures guiding the manner in which one was expected to speak and understand the value of verbal communication. For insights into this history see Barilli (1989). This book has a particularly interesting chapter on McLuhan and the rhetoric of technology. You could also look at Herrick (2008).

We retain this sense of language use in our phrases that dismiss the 'empty rhetoric' of an argument or excuse 'a figure of speech'. The idea of rhetoric has had a similar influence on the Continent and, most interestingly, despite its equivalent decline, has been important to the development of structuralism, deconstruction and concepts of discourse, manifesting itself in the development of the kind of theoretical vocabulary that has proven useful to media scholars and which is discussed throughout this book.

You may have encountered the term 'rhetoric' elsewhere and, like many terms used in both academic and non-academic ways, we must be careful not to confuse meanings. We've mentioned 'empty rhetoric' and you may have often asked or been asked a 'rhetorical question'. The first concept relates to the idea that arguments can be convincingly put, suggesting that one has heard something quite profound, yet be ultimately insubstantial. The second concept is sometimes mistakenly taken to refer to questions without answers. In fact, a rhetorical question is one designed to achieve particular ends. If someone asks of us, 'Do you think I've got all day?' the aim is to prompt us into action in the service of such an obviously busy and important person.

Dictionary definitions of 'rhetoric' suggest that it has come to imply insincerity or exaggeration. Such negative associations come from a common perspective that to respond to ideas and words emotionally is inferior to a considered intellectual response. Although we should recognise this sense – and it will come up in our investigations elsewhere – we want to underline a more neutral sense of rhetoric.

We hope that a closer examination of media texts enhances rather than reduces the pleasure that we derive from them as media consumers. We want to comprehend both emotional and intellectual responses to media texts, valuing them while being attuned to the motives and manipulations at work in their production.

Rhetorical convention and media

What is important to establish is the idea that rhetorical techniques consist of a series of conventions that can be learned, practised and understood. In the original sense, the emphasis of rhetoric was on verbal manipulation. It was about using well-chosen and well-organised words to achieve the desired affective response. However, the modern media text communicates through a number of channels, not just the spoken or written word, and so we use the term rhetoric to cover the choice and delivery of images, sounds and non-verbal interpersonal communication, as well as any other vehicle for conveying meaning.

Each medium has particular rhetorical devices that are used by its practitioners and, of course, recognised and comprehended by audiences in particular ways. It is possible to draw up lists of rhetorical devices for every medium: the particularities of print media, popular music, photography or film and television, and also to label them in groups for the sake of comparison. We should allow for crossover between media forms, of course, as no medium is discrete and self-contained, but here we offer a list of devices and ways of systematically identifying rhetoric that help to organise our approach to texts.

Please note that we've ordered our exploration of media rhetoric in particular ways in order to aid the development of your thinking about the construction of media texts. You may find this a limiting list, merely a starting point for categorising media rhetoric. If so, you should by all means develop further categories useful to you and your understanding of media texts.

Identifying rhetorical media tools and techniques

Verbal rhetoric

Verbal rhetoric refers to the word as written and spoken. It is a label that points to the choice of words, the vocabulary used in media communication. It is concerned with what is written and spoken, although for our purposes not immediately with how it is written or spoken, which is a matter of presentation and worthy of further inflection (see below).

Affect
The intellectual, emotional, psychological or physical responses to the rhetorical address of media texts.

Different styles of journalism use words in different ways to generate **affects** as we've seen in the tabloid examples above. Particular choices of words speak volumes about the product in which they appear. The distinction between the types of language used in a British tabloid newspaper such as the *Sun* is quite apparent when compared with the 'broadsheet' or 'quality' end of the market, manifest in publications such as its stablemate *The Times*.

Like poetry, popular music often uses words and phrases in interesting, idiosyncratic ways that are familiar but at a remove from our everyday use. A UK band like the Arctic Monkeys, whose members employ colloquial terms such as 'mardy' (meaning touchy or moody) in their songs, have accentuated their individuality. This is compounded by the singer's emphatic Northern accent – a matter of presentation that we discuss below. In the same way, the language and terminology conventionally used in gangsta rap songs when compared with that in country music songs would also illustrate this point. Again, the pronunciation and dialects associated with the delivery of both types of music is a matter of presentation.

The panel on p. 38 uses some UK newspaper headlines to outline the key rhetorical figures and labels for the ways that words are used every day in the print media. These choices – whether language is 'plain' or euphemistic for instance – relate to each media institution and say much about the values directing it and its relationship with its audience. Here, we signal the type of paper: populist 'tabloid', which places emphasis on pictures over words, deploying colloquialisms; and 'quality', which tends to offer more extensive and wordy coverage.

While we can compare newspapers and the markets they serve – the assumed audiences they speak to or with – we could similarly examine the language of broadcasters and the vocabulary available to them. Differences between talk and pop radio, between DJs of different cultural backgrounds, would all serve as points of attention.

Case Study

Reliable sources and unreliable words

One morning in 2003, UK radio broadcasters set in motion a series of events that called into question the honesty of the British government over the rationale for the war in Iraq and the reputation of the BBC, and which led directly to the death of civil servant Dr David Kelly. Part of a broadcast on Radio 4's *Today* programme, at 6.07 a.m. on 27 May 2003, involved an exchange between presenter John Humphrys and defence correspondent Andrew Gilligan. The topic of their conversation concerned the nature of government claims that Iraq had weapons of mass destruction (WMDs) that could be launched at British targets at 45 minutes' notice. Here is a crucial part of the exchange:

Humphrys: This in particular, Andy, is Tony Blair saying they'd be ready to go within 45 minutes?

Gilligan: That's right, that was the central claim in his dossier . . . we've been told by one of the senior officials in charge of drawing up that dossier . . . that actually the government probably, erm, knew that that 45-minute figure was wrong before, even before, it decided to put it in . . . Downing Street, our sources says . . . ordered it [the dossier] to be sexed up, to be made more exciting.

The choice of the phrase 'sexed up' immediately became the object of the story itself as it unfolded. Dispute over this term led to Gilligan's resignation on the basis of his choice of phrase, which was deemed to be misleading and unrepresentative of what the government had actually done with its information. This episode in turn contributed to the

Source: Mirrorpix

Hutton and Butler inquiries about the British government's use of intelligence (see www.the-hutton-inquiry.org.uk/content/report/chapter01.htm#a7).

Source: http://news.bbc.co.uk/1/hi/uk_politics/3892809.stm

Common verbal rhetorical devices – examples from newspapers practice

These examples paraphrase the kinds of rhetorical practices familiar from the headlines of tabloid and 'quality' newspapers that we encounter everyday.

ALLITERATION

Typical of tabloid style

'Naughty Nun's furtive fling'

Alliteration is the repetition of starting letters of words in a phrase or sentence, effectively creating a kind of affective rhythm. In this example there are two alliterative phrases in the headline.

RHYME and ALLUSION

Typical of tabloid style

'Sarky gets narky at Carla's malarky'

'Itsy bitsy, teeny weeny, Gaga's a dream in her bikini'

Rhyme is an obviously poetic rhetorical device. It is used relatively sparingly in such media forms, except for humorous intent as here. The second headline makes use of an enduring pop song and is also therefore allusive. Allusions make direct or indirect references to other ideas, places, people or texts, generating affect based around the pleasure of recognition.

Rhymes and alliteration are often used in advertising to make a product memorable. A classic example here would be advertisement catchphrases such as 'Beanz Meanz Heinz' or 'PPPPick up a Penguin'.

EUPHEMISM

Typical of tabloid style

'Wife takes knife to cheating hubbie's meat and two veg'

Euphemism is the substitution of more acceptable terms for those that might offend some people.

As controversies over profanity in popular music, on TV or in film suggest, words have a power to shock – threatening or alienating potential audiences as well as treading the boundary of legality.

Sometimes words might be 'bleeped' or edited out in songs or, as in dubbed versions of film, similar yet less offensive phrases voiced over the original.

METAPHOR

Typical of quality style

'Libya is a pressure-cooker set to explode'

Metaphor is the substitution of one idea for another. This headline gives a vivid portrait in one metaphorical phrase of the socio-political conditions in one particularly troubled country.

Metaphor is sometimes confused with **SIMILE** where one idea is compared to another, for example, 'English footballers are like bulldogs'.

METONYM

Typical of quality style

'Face to face'

Metonym refers to a part of something used to represent it as a whole (e.g. 'I've bought some wheels' for 'I've bought a car'). This headline substitutes 'face' for the two people concerned. You may also find the term **SYNECDOCHE** used in place of metonym, and for our purposes these terms can be used interchangeably.

ELLIPSES

Typical of tabloid style

'You murdering b@*!$@%s

An ellipsis is simply the omission of data, usually of what we take to be obvious. It is often written as a row of three dots. In conversation, missing information is supplied non-verbally through the way in which we inflect language and express ourselves: 'What on earth . . . ?' The use of ellipses in this headline fakes coyness about the use of bad language.

CLICHÉ

Typical of quality style

'High noon: Obama sends ultimatum'

Cliché is the use of well-worn phrases, ideas, metaphors, allusion and so on to generate recognition, quickly deploying meaning.

Thinking aloud

These kinds of labels relate to spoken and written words but they can also have application to the visual and aural aspects of the media covered below. You could compile your own indicative list but think of the hoot of an owl, or a creaky floorboard or door used to evoke atmosphere in a scary movie – a cliché if ever we heard one!

Presentational rhetoric

Our category of 'presentational rhetoric' opens up an enormous variety of factors to take into account in analysis of media meanings. We can begin the exploration of this category by asking: what happens to words once they are chosen and deployed in media texts?

The earlier example of the typeface used on the word HORROR is a good example of what we have in mind here for the written word when it is inflected by typographic and design choices (see p. 32). Similarly, when we encounter the spoken word, presentation is concerned with how people speak – accents, volume, emphasis, pace, pauses and so on. Such things contribute to how we respond to the nature of the words chosen.

For instance, a presenter on a station such as the BBC's World Service is expected to sound authoritative, clear and reliable. It may be something of a shock to some listeners around the world therefore when the voice is changed, as it occasionally is, by the inclusion of speakers with regional British accents, perhaps speaking of 'yow'/you or 'sarf'/south or 'oop North' for 'up North'. In more informal radio programmes in the UK, such as those on popular music stations such as Radio One or Capitol, to have a regional accent and casually colloquial delivery has not only become acceptable but has become expected, and perhaps even a necessity for gaining and retaining certain audiences. Across the world, the march of MTV in its local guise and the employment of younger presenters with a casual approach to delivery clearly illustrates the issues here, especially when compared with the manner in which traditional newsreaders deliver their material.

Case Study

Rhetoric and media producers

Media producers work to particular guidelines about how they use available media languages and express themselves in their particular fields that are often published in style guides and in-house manuals. Here is an example from the 'style guide' of the respected UK-based journal *The Economist*:

'Tone'
The reader is primarily interested in what you have to say. By the way in which you say it you may encourage him either to read on or to stop reading. If you want him to read on:
[. . .]

Use the language of everyday speech, not that of spokesmen, lawyers or bureaucrats (so prefer let to permit, people to persons, buy to purchase, colleague to peer, way out to exit, present to gift, rich to wealthy, break to violate) . . . It is sometimes useful to talk of human-rights abuses but often the sentence can be rephrased more pithily and more accurately. 'The army is accused of committing numerous human-rights abuses' probably means 'The army is accused of torture and murder'.

Avoid, where possible, euphemisms and circumlocutions promoted by interest-groups. In most contexts the hearing-impaired are simply deaf. Female teenagers are girls, not women. The underprivileged may be disadvantaged, but are more likely just poor. Decommissioning weapons means disarming.

And man sometimes includes women, just as he sometimes makes do for she as well. However, it is often possible and even preferable to phrase sentences so that they neither give offence to women nor become hideously complicated. Using the plural can be a helpful device. Thus 'instruct the reader without lecturing him' is better put as 'Instruct readers without lecturing them'. But some sentences resist this treatment . . . Avoid also chairpersons (chairwoman is permissible), humankind and the person in the street – ugly expressions all. And, so long as you are not insensitive in other ways, few women will be offended if you restrain yourself from putting or she after every he.

[. . .]

Do not be hectoring or arrogant. Those who disagree with you are not necessarily stupid or insane. Nobody needs to be described as silly: let your analysis show that he is. When you express opinions, do not simply make assertions. The aim is not just to tell readers what you think, but to persuade them; if you use arguments, reasoning and evidence, you may succeed. Go easy on the oughts and shoulds.

[. . .]

Do not be too didactic. If too many sentences begin Compare, Consider, Expect, Imagine, Look at, Note, Prepare for, Remember or Take, readers will think they are reading a textbook (or, indeed, a style book). This may not be the way to persuade them to renew their subscriptions.

Source: You can read this online at www. economist.com/research/styleGuide/ and it is also published in hardback form for the general reader/writer as 'an invaluable companion for everyone who wants to communicate with the clarity, style and precision for which *The Economist* is famous'. © The Economist Newspaper Limited, London (2008)

This guide is given to all journalists who write for this publication. It is unlikely, therefore, that anyone who consistently avoided these rules – writing in text speak or a version of the tabloid style seen above – would find their work in print. Such guides do particular jobs that relate to the image of the media consumer constructed by its producers – ensuring that they get what they paid for (here a high standard of journalism and reportage).

You should seek out other versions of such guides – for TV, radio, film and so on. Otherwise you should bear in mind their existence as we proceed through the next few pages. As we suggest, rhetoric when applied to media forms and communication is about much more than the types of words employed and how they are arranged.

By paying attention to issues of presentation, if we think about words we can see how the manipulation of delivery creates complexity and affects 'affect'. This applies to the way that something is said but is also accentuated through accompanying gestures. Television presenters in actuality programming, as well as the actors in fictional forms, are taught to be aware of the vital importance of the non-verbal aspects of their delivery – those aspects of interpersonal communication we call 'body language'.

There are non-verbal rhetorical devices that have been specifically devised for television. For example, the presenter of a news programme will frequently nod in the direction of a supposed colleague about to give a report, even though the colleague may not literally be sitting in the direction of the nod. The viewer is expected to interpret the nod as implying that the speaker is in the same studio and that there is no continuity lost between the two shots. In practice, however, the inserted speaker may well present in a pre-recorded sequence. There is no malicious deceit intended here (although the created illusion is deceitful); the intent is to avoid disruption in the comprehension and attention of the audience. Occasionally things can go wrong, although there is never any sense that the deceit is exposed – we as viewers enter into the deceit willingly.

Presentational rhetoric also allows for the way in which sound can be used to create 'space', distance and ambiance. In radio, for instance, sound effects – 'natural' background noises – are employed to signal that we are outside, and footsteps approaching or moving away fade in and fade out. Most films and TV programmes nowadays employ 'foley' operators in order to create sounds to support the images we see, in order to accentuate 'realism' and 'verisimilitude' (see Yewdall, 2007).

Doing media studies

Analysing *mise en scène*

Watch a TV detective drama, paying attention to presentational issues. How would you describe the *mise-en-scène*? What elements strike you as most important to the presentation of the drama? What kind of mood does the programme's staging aim for? How does this show compare with other kinds of drama such as soap opera or even comedy shows?

Of course, under this category of presentation we need to account for the choices of décor and location in audio-visual media, as well as the appearance of items in photographs and on the page (printed or web-based). One way is through the concept of *mise en scène*. This is a French term originating in theatre to label all the contents of the stage and their arrangement. It was taken up by film critics as a way of labelling everything within the film frame and, as such, overlaps with the theatrical in labelling those things 'staged' for the camera. This can refer equally to the way in which reality is captured for the benefit of documentary film or the way that it is arranged in support of fictional film. Furthermore, this term also labels all of the things we perceive on a screen which affect our perception, such as lighting arrangements and the relationship of on-screen and off-screen space. Aspects of *mise en scène* include, therefore: setting, costume and make-up, lighting and movement in the frame, as well as the acting and gestures of performers and presenters. It is a term that we can employ not only for the analysis of film but also for TV, photographic content, computer games and some aspects of websites (see Bordwell and Thompson, 1988: 196–228).

The lesson for us here in a consideration of rhetoric is that, while words are important, and they are sometimes the most important aspect of media forms, they constitute only one element in the text. The way that words are presented and inflected, amplified and obscured, and sometimes are completely absent, is an important reminder that media communication is about much more than words – even when words appear to be primary, on speech radio for instance or in pop songs. The word 'love' can produce a very different affect when voiced in the context of a speed metal song or of a slow R & B tune.

As a broad category, 'presentation' directs us to consider the very organisation of sound (its amplification), the choice of instrumentation in a piece of music (acoustic

Key text

Simon Frith: 'Why do songs have words?'

Sociologist and popular music scholar Simon Frith has posed the question 'Why do songs have words?' He offers a means of considering the rhetoric of pop songs and how they create meaning. The issue here is that there is no reason why music should be accompanied by words and, even though most songs comprise music and lyrics, the latter are often misheard. In spite of this, analysts have tended to concentrate on words as the index of what songs mean and how they have value for consumers. Frith usefully points out all of the other rhetorical aspects of performance – sound and so on – that condition lyrical meaning and may in fact relegate words to a minor role in a song for its listeners:

In songs, words are a sign of a voice. A song is always a performance and song words are always spoken out, heard in someone's accent. Songs are more like plays than poems: song words work as speech and speech acts, bearing meaning not just semantically, but also as structures of sound that are direct signs of emotion and marks of character. Singers use non-verbal as well as verbal devices to make their points – emphases, sighs, hesitations, changes of tone; lyrics involve pleas, sneers and commands as well as statements and messages and stories (which is why some singers, such as the Beatles and Bob Dylan in Europe in the sixties can have profound significance for listeners who do not understand a word they are singing). (Frith, 1988: 120).

instead of electric guitar, falsetto instead of bass vocals), the colours of magazine or web page backgrounds. It is not that presentation is a simple category that means everything and nothing – it serves as a lead-in point to considering the nature of media choices and organisation.

Photographic devices

Some media forms need specialised terms for the particular rhetorical choices and techniques available within that medium for dealing with content. The act of pointing a camera and taking on a point of view, of focusing or obscuring aspects of a scene seen though a lens, underlines the power of the photographer and the medium over which they have control.

The images on these pages demonstrate five of the most common devices used in photography and in other forms of rhetoric used in the capture and construction of media images: composition; retouching; cropping; juxtaposition and montage. Our list here might also apply to drawings, collages and so on, as used in advertisements and animations, as well as material deployed on websites, etc. These devices are common enough to be picked up in newspapers and magazines by you in order to identify and explore them in use. They should not be taken as exhaustive or unchangeable, though, any more than is our list of verbal devices.

Editorial rhetoric

This category refers in general to the organisation of the moving image, although it has relevance to audio media such as radio and music and, indeed, the use of sound within TV and film.

Source: Eleanor Gibbons

Composition. This refers to selecting angles, lighting, lens, framing and other elements of the construction of photographs. We can also include here the distance between lens and object. It matters whether the object is seen 'close up', in which only some of the object under scrutiny is in the frame, at some kind of medium distance, meaning all or most of the object can be seen clearly within the frame, or whether things are seen in 'long shot', where the object is contextualised against background and so on within the frame.

Source: Eleanor Gibbons

Retouching. This refers to ways of accentuating aspects of a picture (tonal distinctions, amplifying or dulling colour for instance), as well as processing out or substituting unwanted elements within a picture.

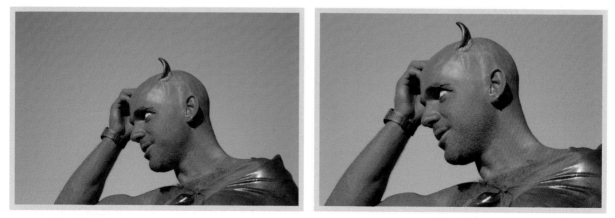

Source: Eleanor Gibbons

Cropping. A subtler and more immediate rhetorical device than retouching is to cut out unwanted material by adjusting the edges of the picture. This can be done 'in the camera' during a shoot or in processing afterwards.

Juxtaposition. This refers to the placing of one picture or part of a picture alongside another. We may read them as constituting a single text and thus come to a third meaning. Juxtaposition may also take place in the frame at the point of composition, of course, wherein objects are thrown together due to the choice and perspective taken by the photographer or image maker.

Source: Eleanor Gibbons

Montage: a step beyond juxtaposition is the merger of two or more images into a seamless whole to create a new text.

Source: Eleanor Gibbons

Primarily, our concern under this heading is with the rhetoric of the moving image (film, TV, computer games) and how technology and the grammar of the image are used, both of which have a great deal to do with the demands of narrative and realism (see Chapters 2 and 3). For the moment, though, let us begin to think about sequence and available rhetorical devices.

Whether on celluloid, on videotape or in digitised form we can think first of all of the ways in which our categories from photography and presentation – *mise en scène*

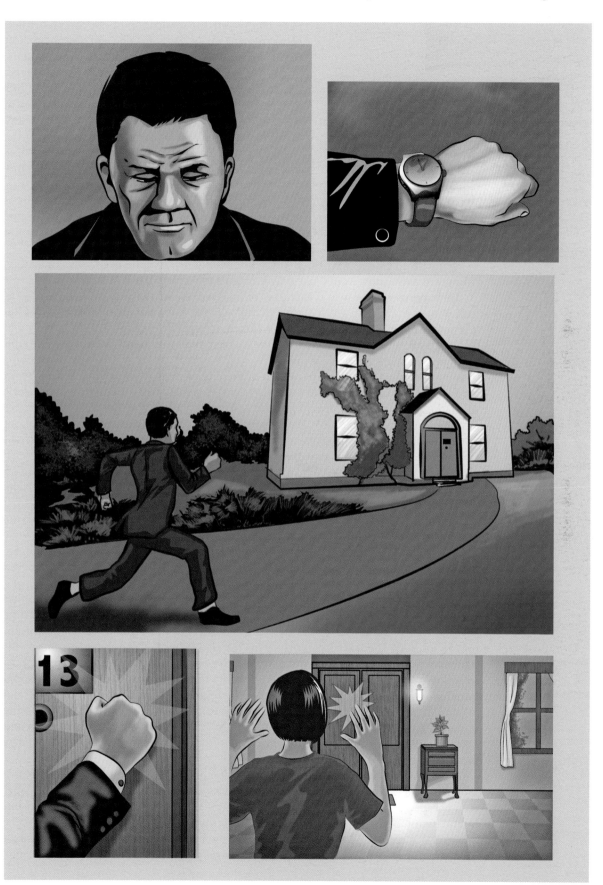

Thinking aloud

The list of rhetorical devices available to pho-tography was formulated by the practices and conventions of a pre-digital age. Is there any way in which this list is altered or added to by technologies of digitisation?

particularly – are the foundation of our comprehension of any moving image. Let's imagine and describe a short film sequence to illustrate this point and combination.

At first, we see a close-up of a person's face glancing downward in a worried manner. A close-up in this instance usually encompasses all of the key features of the face. The scene 'cuts' suddenly to another close-up, of someone's arm and wristwatch. A cut is simply the change from one view to another in film or TV, images that have been 'shot' by different cameras or by the same camera at different times. These shots are then sequenced or edited together.

The next shot is of a house, with a person running away from camera towards its front door (we don't see the person's face but clothing and hair suggest that they are the same person as in the previous sequence). The next scene is the interior of a room and the sound of pounding on a door.

Even with this brief description you will possibly perceive the beginnings of a story, although the five shots would take only moments to present in real time.

The important point here is that a set of images presented in such a way invites us to read them as a sequence, given our familiarity with the 'grammatical' organisation of film. It is possible that such shots could all be filmed on separate occasions – it is unlikely that they would be shot in the seconds it takes to 'read' them, although TV studios with multiple camera set-ups can achieve this.

We could take a still image from each of these brief shots and analyse it separately. In the first, for instance, we would recognise signs of anxiety from the non-verbal rhetoric which the actor uses. A juxtaposition of this image with a still from the second shot forces a connection between the two. The person is looking at their watch and worried about time. The producer of this sequence might have shot the same sequence in a different fashion. We could have had a medium-shot (usually referring to the full or partial framing of a person or object by the camera) showing a person looking at their watch without a cutaway (i.e. when another shot is inserted to show what the character is looking at). Here, the affective response demanded of the audience is more dependent upon the non-verbal rhetoric of the actions of the actor than the rhetorical organisation of shots. It is up to the film-maker to choose whether the story is better told through lengthier shots and a single scene or a rapid sequence. In this instance, the rapid cutting could be used to accentuate the anxiety of the individual and mood of the scene, although this is not solely achieved through rapid cutting.

Here we can identify three elements in the way in which these scenes work together in such a sequence to produce an effect (impression of a connection in space and time between shots) and affective response (urgency, anxiety – intrigue as to what is beginning to unfold). The first element concerns the significance of the image presented – its sign value – which we go on to discuss in more detail below, under our discussion of semiology. This aspect is shared across all media forms (the anxiety could be conveyed in other ways, too). The second element is the framing – shared with photography and other aspects of illustration. The final element of editing – sticking together or juxtaposing scenes of movement – is integral to film, although we should recognise how radio and popular music make use of sequential editing in the same manner to create wholly new meanings from disparate elements.

The repeated rhetorical device that we've described in our sequence is known as a motivated cut. An illusion has been created of a person looking down at a watch, anxious because of time. There is a motivated connection between the two, cued in our interpretation of the sequence by the editing. In much the same manner, the third scene of a house is connected by the fact that it is edited in sequence. The fact that the figure is running away, coupled with the quick cut, suggests a motivated link between anxiety, time and action – the 'illusion' of action continues. The third scene also acts, belatedly, as what is known as an establishing shot. The house identifies a space for the focus of action; we see it from within and without if we accept the motivated link with the fourth scene. The last scene (interior) might be shot elsewhere – in a studio, for instance – while the other four are shot 'on location'. An association is made between the actions seen in scenes 1 to 3 and the pounding on the door, confirming the link (we assume the person running 'against' time to the door to be the source of the knock that the person inside responds to).

All of this is, of course, a constructed illusion but one that, if done well, involves us – partly through intrigue (what is happening? why?), as well as the evocation of anxiety and concern (the affective response – again, effective if this has been done well). It is doubtful whether a skilled producer would worry very much about how to present this short element of a greater story. The rhetorical organisation would seem to come 'naturally', as an obvious way to present the tale. The tale might also be told by using a continuous shot, as well as a moving camera that might be equally effective and affecting. Less so, perhaps, would be a reliance on the actor or a voice-over 'explaining' what was happening.

Any effective use of rhetoric tends to go unnoticed, however, simply because we are so used to this technique: we take it for granted, usually only noticing when it is done badly or in a very unusual manner. For film and TV, as well as computer gaming, editing rhetoric contributes to and organises our sense of space and time. The length of shots, alongside the rapidity and perspective of 'cuts' between shots, are what give a text its particular rhetorical character and aid sense making, recognition, involvement and pleasure on the part of audiences. This is true for 'real-life' or 'actuality' media (current affairs, news, documentary) programming as well as fiction.

Sequence length and organisation also have relevance when considering radio. Dramas and 'actuality' make use of cutaways and the editing together of different material, recorded at different times and sometimes used to evoke difference in space and time, to produce similar effects to the moving image.

Analysis and the individual perspective

A question worth asking yourself is: how does any attempt to analyse 'affect' and meaning relate to the kinds of likely responses in the majority of an audience? We might, of course, make idiosyncratic readings but this might be perverse given the manner in which media texts seek to address audiences. Any answer here will relate to how informed our analysis is by our own position as media consumers. Thus, it is always useful to begin with our own intuitive responses to media texts – these really do matter, as does a response to the text as a cohesive whole – rather than beginning with an attempt to 'spot' rhetoric at work.

Of course, while our own position as a consumer is an important starting point, we should recognise its limits. If we find ourselves relatively unaffected by a media text, for instance, and if we were to rely on this subjective starting point alone, we might get stuck. To usefully move beyond our own response, we should think of an implied rhetorical position for the audience, just as we think of the rhetoric constructing the text. If confronted with a response along the lines of 'this does nothing for me' we should ask instead, 'how is this text asking me to respond?'.

This is not to suggest that we should be overly concerned about absolutely right and wrong analyses as such, but in certain circumstances it would be perverse to go against what seems a likely or 'intended' affect. However, do be cautious about claiming intent on behalf of producers – without direct access, one cannot be sure and, even then, 'affects' may be far more or far less significant than producers planned.

Thus, to pursue the point about affect and the position of the audience. Portentous tones from newsreaders on the occasion of natural disasters mean that we are expected

Doing media studies

Organising and interpreting the rhetoric of the moving image

Nowadays films, games and TV programmes make use of scripts and storyboard visualisations to map out camera work and the placing of actors and presenters, as well as giving cues for the use of sound and music. This is usually presented in the form of a storyboard – very much like a comic book (see for example our five 'film shots' on pp. 45–6).

In the early days of the film industry, producers would often work without a script at all, formulating shots and sequences based upon detailed scenarios – short stories in prose. The skill of the production team lay in how they interpreted this scenario within the developing rhetorical conventions of the medium.

For this activity, produce a short storyboard for the following scenario that conveys the information and sequence in a creative fashion.

Scenario

NIGHT: In an opulent but joyless grand mansion house, a sick, old man lies on his deathbed attended by several anxious aides and servants. He clutches a glass globe, which contains a winter's scene encased in water. He tries to mutter some words and drops the globe, dying with 'Rosebud' the only clearly heard utterance.

DAY: Newspaper headlines proclaim the death of this rich man while reporters crowd around the mansion eager to gain the story of his last hours.

Thinking aloud

Think of rhetoric as a means to an end – media language appealing to us as members of a potential audience in the first instance and then, once our attention has been won, working in support of the maintenance of our attention in the face of enormous distraction and competition for that attention (and, of course, our cash!). Consider, for instance, trawling through the dial on a radio or through TV stations on the occasions when we're not searching for anything in particular (we're not always habitual viewers, listeners or readers). How then do media producers seize our attention for their products in a saturated field of similar products? We go to a magazine rack and may be confronted with several publications all dealing with a subject we might be interested in. Many of these works may even feature the same kinds of content and, superficially at least, may seem indistinguishable. On what basis do we make choices in such an instance?

to respond to stories appropriately (concern, sympathy or outrage perhaps) and recognise the basis for shared interpretations. Occasionally, when watching a film, we may find that its technique or budget might militate against the aspirations of its creators. Then we might find ourselves sneering at its appearance and failure, responding to it in ways that were unintended simply because it is not effective in marshalling rhetoric.

One final word on the 'implied audience' is worth making. Students sometimes leap to the conclusion that a text featuring particular social groups is providing a cue and a clue to the audience that is being addressed. There is some value in this, of course. If we take hip-hop music as an example, it is a cultural form derived from African-American experiences and histories. Interestingly, however, it is consumed across a huge variety of cultures, notably white middle-class Americans, who became the key audience for this genre in the 1990s. To assume a direct correlation between appearance and audience, then, is a fallacy and requires some consideration (if this were the case then the main consumers of pornography would be women!).

Case Study

Rhetorical analysis

Source: The Advertising Archives
How does media rhetoric work in this media text?

This magazine uses a range of rhetorical techniques to address its potential readers and do its 'work' in appealing to them among all the others available. The cover layout is typical of many popular magazines and this one belongs to the more sophisticated end of a range of publications which are aimed at women readers. The title 'Elle' (untranslated from the title of the original French publication, meaning she or her) dominates in the largest type, at the head of the page/cover, although this is partly obscured by a medium-sized shot of musician Lily Allen (the 'cover star'). Straplines for features in the magazine are roughly arranged around her body and rather neatly the promise of 'How to get gorgeous hair now' is placed by Allen's raven-coloured locks.

Allen is posed in a rather exaggerated fashion, looking directly at the lens and thus out at the

reader. Her face is emphatically framed by the double LL of the title and, just in case we don't recognise her immediately and understand that she is the main attraction, her name is highlighted to the left along with what one assumes is the agenda for discussion on the pages within and which offers a menu based on potential reader interests: fashion, music, babies.

This banal list of items on Allen is interesting for how it underlines the rather unequivocal nature of the cover straplines. Interestingly, and while Allen is the dominant feature, her strapline is rather slighter than the importance of the announcement that the magazine contains 'The New Trends'. Like most of the cover items, this speaks directly to the reader: 'Key looks to suit *you*', 'How to handle *your* critics', while other items on gaining gorgeous hair (now!), friendship, success and cosmetic surgery are assessments and guides speaking to the assumed concerns of the reader (or what the reader *should* be concerned with!).

We can note the presentation of the cover in terms of the colours used – mainly a range from the blue end of the spectrum, anchored by the title logo, which dominates in colour too – and also the elegance of Allen's attire. We've noted how the cover speaks to the reader and while its verbal rhetoric lacks wit perhaps, its muted nature in tone and typographical design is one that flatters the potential reader a little. Note, for instance, how the cosmetic surgery strapline (bottom right) is rather subdued in among purple-pink colours. Such instances underline how this cover does not seek to 'scream' at the reader in vulgar fashion and desperation but works with confident elegance.

With such observations we're starting to move beyond the organisation of the text in terms of available rhetorical techniques and on to a differently nuanced way of thinking about meaning. Such issues can be illustrated by asking questions about what kinds of ideas about women, femininity and elegance are presented by this media text and this rhetorical arrangement. To understand further aspects of the text, the way that meaning is created and some of the complexity of the answers to such questions, we need another approach that will complement and build upon rhetoric. This is called semiology.

Analytical tools: semiology

Semiology

means, literally, 'the study of signs'.

Most academic disciplines seem to have an 'ology' somewhere in their scope. It indicates that they are a serious, systematic and logical endeavour. The Greek *logos* – from whence we get the suffix -ology – indicates a rational principle and order to explaining phenomena. The 'ology' of media studies (although not ours alone) is called **semiology**. The prefix *sem* comes from the Greek for sign (rather than the Latin for half) and is to be found in words such as *sem*aphore – signalling with flags or lights – and *sem*antics – the study of meaning in linguistics.

Developed long before and outside media studies, semiology is particularly useful for us in studying the process of media communication. As we have suggested previously, communication has sometimes been seen as a process by which information passes from one person to another, or from one to many in the case of mass media forms such as broadcasting. In emphasising the conveyance of information, this process approach to understanding communication assumes that meaning is, literally, a matter of encoding and decoding what needs to be communicated. The media operate as mediators in this process – the bit in between the communicator and receiver/s. Semiology takes another perspective to communication as mediation, rather in the manner of our rhetorical approach, by seeking to identify the factors that contribute to the way in which meaning is made in the act of mediation – *how* the content of media messages come to have significance and mean what they do.

Semiology is the attempt to explain how things mean what they mean and the various ways in which things mean what they do. It is therefore the study of meaning and the different systems that make meaning possible. These 'systems' include images, colour, bodily gestures and music, as well as the various fields of mass communication, i.e. media forms in all their variety. Where rhetoric draws our attention to the importance of what someone is saying (e.g. on a TV screen), along with the setting, the way that they speak and so on, in placing and 'affecting' us, semiology goes further to consider *why* specific things – a 'posh' accent, a black face, a suit and tie, a steel-grey backdrop, the street rather than the studio – mean what they do.

Our approach to investigating meaning is further complicated by the technical language used in semiology. Often, it seems that the technical language used is simply there in order to baffle outsiders, i.e. non-academics. However, one of the reasons why technical language is employed is to ensure that we all have a shared set of precise and agreed-upon terms. This allows us to proceed quickly to investigate meaning in a particular and precise manner, and to underline the interpretations we make and the way that we present them. With its set of technical concepts, we use semiology with the aim of explaining the way in which meaning is created. Ultimately, semiological approaches suggest that any explanation is not to be found in the text alone, nor in the mind of the person reading the text, but in interaction between text and reader.

Foundations of semiology

The basis of semiology is to be found in the conceptions of two visionary yet very different thinkers working at the start of the twentieth century. These are Ferdinand de Saussure and Charles Sanders Peirce. They provided a basic set of templates for the work done by later thinkers in semiology, such as Roland Barthes and Umberto Eco, who took de Saussure's and Peirce's ideas in directions they most likely could not have anticipated, offering a range of applications in the study of meaning in media and culture.

Both de Saussure and Peirce sought to move beyond the consideration of everyday communication acts (what is said between individuals in any socially located situation) to work at a more generalised, theoretical and abstract level, in order to identify the systems and systematic processes governing communication, meaning and sense-making in modern societies.

Key thinker

Ferdinand de Saussure (1857–1913)

De Saussure was a Swiss linguist whose innovation lay in a move from philology and etymology (studying where language and words originate historically, or diachronically) to examine the structure of language in use (its synchronic function – see below). He did not publish widely during his life and his most influential work, *Course in General Linguistics* (1993), was published posthumously in 1916, built from lecture notes made by his students at the University of Geneva.

His work was influenced by the sociologist Emile Durkheim, as well as the political philosopher Karl Marx (see Chapter 10). His ideas were appropriated by later thinkers and structuralists such as the anthropologist Claude Lévi-Strauss and Roland Barthes.

Key thinker

Charles Sanders Peirce (1839–1914)

Peirce was an influential American philosopher of 'pragmatism' who wrote widely on mathematics, logic and the sciences. His invention of 'semiotics' – at virtually the same time as de Saussure's semiology – resulted from his logical approach to philosophy as a doctrine of signs designed to make sense of the world. Below, we tend to favour de Saussure's approach to explaining signification, as Peirce's was somewhat different in emphasis.

For Peirce, the sign or 'representamen' describes how something meant something to someone, standing for something in his or her mind, communicating with those to whom the communication was addressed. In this argument, all communication is built therefore upon the relation of 'representamen', interpreter and idea. His works set out a complex variety of classes of sign that has not proven amenable to practical use. However, his idea of sign–object relationships – ICON, INDEX and SYMBOL – is resonant and is dealt with below.

Note: Semiotics or semiology?

Any survey of the field will reveal that different people use alternative names to refer to the study of signs. The term 'semiology' comes from a suggestion in the work of de Saussure. Peirce called his approach 'semiotics' and many writers prefer this name. It does not really matter which you use as the terms can be considered to be interchangeable to underline the approach to analysis. However, one should always be aware in contexts such as this one that our précis is there as a stepping stone for the serious scholar to probe further in order to fully assess the distinctions in such original thinking.

Core ideas in the semiological approach

The first stage in getting to grips with semiology is to understand the core assumptions made in this approach. We can see these as three contentions that consolidate some of the ideas we've been touching upon already.

Thinking aloud

Psychologically, setting aside its expression in words, our thought is simply a vague, shapeless mass. Philosophers and linguists have always agreed that were it not for signs, we should be incapable of differentiating any two ideas in a clear and constant way (Saussure, 1893).

One of the most provocative suggestions of de Saussure's approach to language is that our conceptualisation of the world, of reality, of meaning, can only occur because we have a language – as well as other modes of representation – to do so. Thus, language does not describe the world: it is possibly constitutive of it! In the pages that follow we outline some of de Saussure's terms in common use in semiology.

First, media texts are seen as constructions. In media studies, we often use the term 'construction' to refer to the production of texts. In this we are emphasising the idea that texts are not 'natural' occurrences but are manufactured, that the way in which meaning is produced has involved a set of choices. There is an obvious sense in which the newspaper we read or the TV programme we watch is manufactured – part of an industrialised, technical process pursued by media workers. When we think of things in this way, we are recognising that media products are constructed as artefacts and as texts that are sites of meaning. Simply put, this means that, as well as being manufactured as print on paper, sounds in a musical recording or as moving images, they are manufactured or constructed out of elements of language and existing meanings. Thus, one of the main aims of semiological analysis has always been to examine how media conventions compare with written or spoken language, in order to generate and deploy meaning.

Secondly, the semiological approach starts with the acceptance that meanings are the result of social convention rather than any 'essential' property inherent in things themselves, or in the relationship of words or other signs to the things or concepts depicted. If meaning was an essential property of things themselves then the meaning would be present 'in' things or, for us, the text for all time, fixed and unmovable, and any interpretation would be either right or wrong. However, we only read a text in a particular way because we are used to associating particular signs with particular words or images (or sounds) included in a text. In semiology, then, meaning is seen as socially determined. It is social convention that is the source of meaning. Following de Saussure, we view these conventions as the organisation and rules of language.

We can formulate a third contention based upon the ideas of construction and social values underpinning meaning. If texts are constructed from language (as written and spoken, or from media 'languages'), and the meaning of language is created by social conventions, then the meaning of the text is as much the result of these conventions as it is the intentions of the people who produced the texts.

In the study of fine art or English literature there is, traditionally, an emphasis placed upon individual artists or authors – the creative genius as the fount of the value of the artistic product (see p. 80). In media studies, we tend to emphasise the view that socially conventional meanings and the forces that determine them are as important as, if not more important than, the conscious intentions of the text's producer or producers. In this approach, a single text is seen not as indicative of the originality or singularity of a producer but as telling us something about social convention. So, the meaning of a news article, for instance, or a piece of popular music, is not fixed by journalist or musician, producer or designer, singer or songwriter, but by the conventions that are used both by the media workers who produce texts and the readers who consume them.

This is of vital importance because it allows us to understand that the language we use will be interpreted in ways that go well beyond our individual intentions. These sorts of meanings are often referred to as 'hidden meanings' or 'subtexts' because they seem to be things of which we are not primarily conscious and are subsumed to the obvious or 'main' message of a text. Debates about racist or sexist language would be good examples of some of the things we are thinking of here.

Semiology in textual analysis: sign, signifier and signified

Semiological thought proposes that the basic unit of communication systems is the sign. If we think of those things we usually recognise and label as signs around us – road signs, exit signs, shop signs – this will give us an idea of the central premise here. Think of traffic lights, for instance, and the use of red, amber and green in signalling stop, get ready and go. Semiology suggests that there is nothing intrinsic to the colour red that demands 'stop' (elsewhere red might mean 'danger', 'hot', 'sexy' or simply not amber, green or blue, for instance). On each set of traffic lights, the red light works to direct us to stop, just as green tells us to go.

De Saussure's foundational work concentrated on written and spoken language and, for the purposes of explaining how words work as signs, he suggested that signs could be thought of as consisting of two indivisible aspects: signifier and signified.

The signifier refers to the physical properties or aspects of a sign that lead them to be perceived in some way. In spoken language, this could be a word as it is spoken (it has a physical existence as audible sound waves) or written (these words, on this page, exist as lines, curves and circles recorded in ink). The signified is the conceptual aspect of the sign – the association or idea conjured up by our perception of the signifier.

We hear or read a word such as 'dog' and we think of what de Saussure would term 'dogness', i.e. the concept signified or triggered by the signifier. We could get somewhat distracted here by discussion about the apparent imprecision of the signified. You might automatically think of your dog, or any other specific dog, for instance, but how do you know that that was the dog I had in mind? Our image here pinpoints a specific individual dog that represents a particular type of dog that, in turn, conjures up a heap of associations, the operation of which we'll qualify below.

For our purposes, we can move on by noting that, when we communicate, we put words together to create meanings in specific ways. Our attempts at communication are sometimes precise and literal: 'I took my dog to the vet's on Smith Street', and sometimes more nuanced, metaphorical even: 'You look dog-rough!' or 'I'm going to kill that dog of a boyfriend of mine' (neither phrase would merit a trip to the vet or the police, we assume). Semiology provides us with tools with which to make sense of both the precision of meaning in use but also the way that meaning can sometimes escape 'intention' (I did not have your dog in mind at all!).

While some new scholars will struggle with these propositions and ideas, perhaps treating language and communication as a more transparent thing than it is, we should at least understand that, once we accept the centrality of the sign and the

Source: Eleanor Gibbons

This picture of a dog presents us with the sign 'dog'. The 'signifier' (the image itself, with two-dimensional physical properties made up of coloured ink dots in the photograph) presents the 'signified' of both 'dogness' and this particular dog captured in the image.

explanatory aspect of signifier and signified – which are always indivisible – we can begin to explore the wider ideas of semiology. De Saussure's intent was not to present a conceptual idea of the elements of the sign which would lead us to analyse each sign individually with regards to its components, but merely to suggest something fundamental about the operations of language. To focus on the analysis of signs at the level of signifier and signified, as if this was the basis of understanding, would be a mistake. The object of our attentions must remain at the level of the sign but the conceptualisation of the function of a sign will prove useful in getting to grips with the way that meaning works at different levels.

In de Saussure's study, the consequences of which we continue to deal with, he drew attention to the apparent arbitrariness of language within systems of signification. This means, for instance, that there is nothing about the collection of bound papers, ink, illustrations and so on that you hold in your hand which demands that it be termed a 'book'. It is merely convention that gives it this label, which is distinctive within the system of language simply by being a choice that is not hook, look, cook or any other word and that, when placed in an order of signification ('I hold in my hand a book' might be one order), operates as a noun. Likewise, nothing about a four-legged furry animal that wags its tail and chases cats demands that it should be called 'dog' – convention and culture confer this label. We need only look to the written and spoken variety of languages around the world to see the enormous variety of methods and conventions for describing the world (dog becomes, for example, *chien, hund, perro*). If things themselves had properties that demanded specific labels, language differentiation would not exist!

Media signs

As a linguist, de Saussure was interested in written and spoken language as a signifying system. Language consists of a lexicon of words (hundreds of thousands in the English language) made of phonemes and letters – the sounds of speech and the lines on a page which constitute writing – which, when combined into sentences, according to rules of grammar and conventions of usage, have significance and communicate meaning. De Saussure also suggested that the same approach could be brought to bear on any form of communication or signifying system. Just as words (as signs) are collected together to make a particular piece of communication in writing or conversation (these sentences for instance), de Saussure suggested that we could break down other pieces of non-word communication into basic units or individual signs.

In looking at modern mass media, that would mean we could extend the semiological approach in order to identify the signs in, and signifying practices of, computer games, TV programmes, podcasts, magazine articles, adverts, pieces of music or films. Of course, some signs would be words (written or spoken), but others would be images or parts of images (colours, typefaces, representations of people, places) or aspects of sound.

As we learnt in our approach to rhetoric, the manner in which a word is used or inflected – spoken or written – has the potential to condition its impact in particularly affective ways. We can see how one can delve much more deeply here, beyond affect, especially when we begin to think about the associated meanings that a certain typeface has on a page or a mode of delivery in acting or speech.

Identifying semiological tools and techniques

Signs – selection and combination

It is rare for us to encounter simple signs individually and, as such, we are confronted by them in the context of greater signifying systems. For sure, we might pass road signs, or

Langue

is a term which refers to a whole system of signification and its elements – the distinctions and oppositions which allow meaning to emerge, determined by the rules and principles of combination shared by the communities who recognise and use this system of signification. (Thus, alongside 'French' we could identify the langue of food and its presentation in menus, which order food from starter to dessert and coffee.)

Parole

refers to any particular 'utterance', 'expression' or 'statement' derived from the system of signification or langue.

Paradigm and syntagm

refer to the principles or rules of how language or any signifying system is put together. Paradigm is a term that refers to what we could call the 'vertical' relationship between any words in a sentence or sign in a system – an element which could be substituted for another similar sign. Signs in language are organised in linear fashion to make more complex structures such as sentences or 'syntagms' which demonstrate the possibilities of paradigmatic selection.

Thus, in a sentence (or syntagm) such as 'it was a lovely sunny day' the adjective 'lovely' – selected from a huge paradigmatic set – might be substituted for another such as 'beautiful'. This mode of description has relevance to the mass media, as we'll see in our discussion of genre in the next chapter.

rush around looking for the sign indicating 'Men' or 'Women' when we need to relieve ourselves urgently. However, in conversation or when apprehending mass media we encounter a proliferation of signs combined together in creating meaningful texts.

In newspapers, single written word signs are combined into sentences, paragraphs and then into full stories. These written elements are then combined with other words presented in larger typefaces to form headlines, often further combined with photographs, diagrams or other forms of illustration (courtroom drawings for instance). Such illustrations are themselves combinations of different elements, perhaps facial features, hairstyles, clothing and background elements such as the location of the image.

In television programmes, combinations appear even more complex. Single spoken words are combined into lines of dialogue, which are combined with visual elements in the frame (*mise en scène*) such as the facial features of the presenters or actors, their hairstyles, clothing, the furnishing of the studio or images of outdoors. All of these signs are part of an animated text, inflected by the rhetoric of lighting, camera perspective and framing, as well as the editing process.

In any instance, the media workers who produced the text chose each sign and then combined them together. Even when confronted by actuality out in the field while reporting or shooting on location, processes of selection and combination have taken place. By this means a text is constructed and signifies in tandem with and indivisible from its affective operation. In semiology, meaning is viewed as being determined by the selection of signs and their combination in texts. For this reason semiology is a method that makes sense of the process and signifying results of selection and combination.

English-speaking students and users of semiology will come across a number of semiological terms derived directly from the French of de Saussure. These technical terms are worth outlining here in order to indicate the systematic nature of this approach and also to aid your familiarity with terms that are sometimes deployed in academic work without qualification.

Whether we use such terms or not they have a function and use in supporting analysis of the way that meaning works. Such tools are not the object of the analysis of texts, and the best way to become familiar with them is to use them as appropriate in relation to the starting point of the meaning of a text.

Verbal and visual signs

It is easy to 'spot' verbal signs – each word is clearly a sign itself. In spoken and written language, words constitute a minimum element of meaning, easily distinguished from each other and usually organised in linear fashion (in the Western world we read from left to right and top to bottom of the page, spoken words come one after another). It is far harder to do this with other types of sound and images. The reason for this is that images, particularly photographs (or 'moving' photographs in the form of film or seamless video sequences) seem like reality and not like verbal signs at all. We can take in a photograph in its entirety immediately, just as we would when looking at 'the world'. Also, it is sometimes hard to accept that images do not have an essential meaning. If we look at a photograph of a tree, it seems obvious that it means 'a tree' (and indeed a specific tree at that) because it looks like a tree – a specific tree. You do not need to attend to social convention to work that one out! We've seen plenty of trees and, in encountering an image of a tree, we know that it is indeed a tree! There is no need to learn a special language or principles of meaning to understand this, in the same way that we learn to speak, read and write, under the tutelage of parents and teachers.

Furthermore, it is hard to be sure in any exact way what the signs are in a non-word-based text. It is difficult to identify a clear, distinct basic unit that is equivalent to a word when we examine film trailers or instrumental dance tracks, for instance. Can we think of images and musical (or other) sounds as signs in the same way as words, as comprising signifier and signified?

Diachronic and synchronic

De Saussure's originality lay in his attention to the study of language and the processes of meaning-making in use at a particular time – in other words taking a **synchronic** approach. A **diachronic** approach would attend to changes in language over time in terms of its organisation and principles. For our purposes, we could study media signifying systems in this way – noting the ways that websites, for instance, have altered the ways in which they signify or 'mean' over a relatively short period.

The problem with thinking about non-word-based texts as constructions made up of socially conventional language elements is that it seems to go totally against the widely held view that sounds or photographs are 'real'. Reality is the antithesis of the constructed. This sense is reinforced when we look at a TV report 'live' from the scene of some unfolding drama, or hear a live broadcast of an interview on radio. Images, particularly, seem more 'naturally' related to the objects that they represent. This sense of realism is a very strong feature of mass media and our consumption of it. It is an important object of semiological study and features in Chapter 4.

Ultimately, the point to bear in mind is that, once an object is 'captured' by a signifying system (a tree in digital photographic form or on filmic celluloid, for instance), it is no longer that original 'innocent' object. It now exists as a sign – something selected and embraced within a system of communication.

Complex signs – testing significance and getting to grips with analysing meaning

Signs – words in a sentence, sounds in a song, images and performances in films – work together to make a greater whole whose complexity is derived from their combination. We can think of such combinations as meaningful texts made out of complex signs. To change any element in the set-up of a complex sign or greater text would alter its meaning, although in each case we can see that some elements are more important than others.

The greatest test facing those new to semiology is making the leap from the recognition of the concept of the sign as an explanatory device to an examination of signs in use and, in particular, signs in use *together* as complex entities, as part of a textual system – be it a newspaper article, pop song, website or TV programme. We need to consider how to make sense of texts that are not only combinations of signs but are built upon very complex signs indeed. For instance, we have here a photograph from a newspaper (media artefact) reporting on a film premiere which works as a (media) text to present JLS (a pop band).

JLS

Source: Getty Images

Forgoing any detailed interpretation, just for the moment consider this text as a combination of visual signs – men, clothes, a public place and so on. We could get bogged down in the detail here – noting in rote fashion the significance of black hair, brown skin, etc., all of which are important individually. But to do so ignores their combination as greater units of meaning.

Each aspect of the image of each man constitutes, in itself, a complex sign: each man is dressed, posed and presented (all aspects explained as rhetorical organisation) in a particular way, constituting a site of various signs, creating a greater whole. And together they create a greater sign – the band JLS – as part of this photographic text. It is organised around particular rhetorical principles: medium-distance shot, clearly lit, the quartet organised and balanced along triangular principles with the tallest two inside, the shorter at either edge of the group. We might deduce that the rhetorical organisation comes from the choices and organisation of the photographer but also from the band itself – who are practised in the group pose and who are also supported by stylists and PR intermediaries who prepare them for just such an eventuality and who manage such moments.

This deconstruction seems straightforward enough, but it is intended to suggest that the basis to analysing such a text is not to ask 'where are the signs?'. We should understand immediately that every element is signifying – that's what signifying systems do. Nor should we look from top left to right and downwards, to 'scan' for signification – that is not how such texts work rhetorically or semiologically. Rather, we need to ask: what are the most significant elements of this text? Which signs are most meaningful and how are they meaningful within the organisational hierarchy of the text?

Looking for elements that are significant is the basis of a good approach to the evaluation of visual signs such as those that constitute this text – or indeed other types of complex media sign. We can ask ourselves if we were to change an element (or a variety of elements) would this alter meaning in any significant manner? We wouldn't do it literally but replacing one person, object or location (or sound, or accent) with another means we can judge the contribution that element makes to the meaning of the text. This is usually called a significance or 'commutation' test. It is unlikely that the significance of elements in a text will be absolute, that an element will be either entirely significant or not significant at all. All signs are significant but meaning and value are relative things. So some elements may be central to meaning as a whole – to substitute them would change the meanings of a text as a whole. Others, if substituted, may lead to no change at all or only slight inflections of meaning.

If we focus on words in a text then, clearly, the most basic parts of these significant elements will be the words selected. However, even words do not just contain verbal elements – in print or when spoken. Typography, size, colour, intonation, clarity, pitch, words on a page in a specific layout – all of these indicate how significance can be underwritten. Here, replacing the actual men in the image with others – those of another band like One Direction for instance, or anonymous models or even women – would be one way of identifying the most obvious aspect of signification here: that this is an image of the well-known band JLS. Setting aside this specificity for a second, we could think about how different the image might be if we replaced the kinds of clothes the men are wearing (substituting the casually co-ordinated primary colours with lamé, silver, white, gold, black leatherwear, branded sports jackets, hats, etc.), or placed them in a studio setting.

What the image means – and it means much more than simply conveying the two-dimensionally implicit label of 'This is JLS' – would change. While nowhere does it 'say so', just as it does not say 'JLS', we suggest that this text also signifies to some degree ideas of youth, masculinity, camaraderie, success and vibrancy that are not simply 'imported' to the text by a previous association with JLS's renown as a chart band (and success on the TV show *X Factor*) and what they stand for (i.e. from songs and gossip columns). This is a matter of the level of signification of signs combined in this text and the associations triggered beyond the level of simple recognition.

Denotation and connotation: levels of signification

De Saussure's idea of the sign did not concentrate on the signified or associated idea with any great detail but it is apparent from any understanding of his work that we cannot just think about the idea triggered by signs in simple terms. When we perceive signs, we do not usually think about one idea but potentially a whole range of ideas generated by the sign. This aspect of signification was most profitably explored by the French theorist Roland Barthes.

Barthes took up terms developed by de Saussure and Peirce and deployed them in productive ways to think about the social context and role of the media. The terms most interesting to us at this juncture are those of *denotation* and *connotation*. Barthes suggests that any sign will be associated with an initial aspect of signification but that this aspect will trigger further associations. The first aspect or level of signification is the most obvious, literal or generally agreeable. We see an image of a Union flag (the UK's official symbol): most of us would agree it is of a Union flag. This is the *denoted* level of meaning. In some circumstances of course it might serve to denote 'UK' – stamped on goods or the back of an Olympic runner, for instance.

Further associations, more abstract, debatable and contextual – depending upon who is deploying and interpreting the sign – would work at the level of *connotation*. Thus, a sign such as the Union flag might connote ideas such as Britishness, patriotism and unity. However, in some circumstances – on the cover of a pamphlet from the British National Party (a political party of the far right) for instance – connotations might be of exclusivity and hostility to non-British people (i.e. nationalism, possibly racism). Seen from the perspective of some people in countries such as Iraq or Afghanistan, the flag might connote 'liberator' or 'oppressor' in equal measure. Or, it might simply go unrecognised.

These terms are perhaps the most important to us in the area of interpretation. The denotative allows us to describe significant aspects of texts, using these as a basis for further levels of (connotative) interpretation.

Sign–object relations

Alongside the consideration of significant elements in a text and the triggering of associated ideas, we can also identify types of relationship between signs and the objects to which they

Key thinker

Roland Barthes (1915–80)

Barthes was a French literary critic and theorist, whose approach to semiology, applied to mass media and everyday culture, as well as his consideration of photography in particular, set in place some of the basic tools for media studies.

In his studies of literature, Barthes expressed a concern with the way in which literary language represented its particular worlds and conveyed social ideas – that representation is never 'innocent'. He attended to aspects of literary rhetoric that have great import to the kind of analysis we pursue in these chapters, noting how such systems of communication work in conventional ways to appear natural, disguising the values supporting them.

An early work of note was his collection of essays, *Mythologies* (Barthes 1972). These short analyses of aspects of popular culture (wrestling, films about Romans – see below – film stars' faces, new cars, steak and chips) were published in French magazines between 1954 and 1956, then collected and supported by a methodological essay 'Myth today'. Barthes's innovation was to draw upon de Saussure's semiology as a means of understanding contemporary cultural texts as signifying systems in a particular context (post-war France undergoing a consumer boom). He went on to refine his approach and apply it 'scientifically' to further aspects of signifying systems, such as fashion, offering radical critiques of the habitual manner in which we make sense of the world.

From: 'The Romans in films'

In Mankiewicz's *Julius Caesar*, all the characters are wearing fringes. Some have them curly, some straggly, some tufted, some oily, all have them well combed, and the bald are not admitted, although there are plenty to be found in Roman history. Those who have little hair have not been let off for all that, and the hairdresser – the kingpin of the film – has still managed to produce one last lock which duly reaches the top of the forehead, one of those Roman foreheads whose smallness has at all times indicated a mixture of self-righteousness, virtue and conquest.

What then is associated with these insistent fringes? Quite simply the label of Roman-ness. We therefore see here the mainspring of the Spectacle – the *sign* – operating in the open. The frontal lock overwhelms one with evidence, no one can doubt that he is in Ancient Rome. And this certainty is permanent: the actors speak, act, torment themselves, debate 'questions of universal import', without losing, thanks to this little flag displayed on their foreheads, any of their historical plausibility. Their general representativeness can even expand in complete safety, across the ocean and the centuries, and merge into the Yankee mugs of Hollywood extras: no matter, everyone is reassured, installed in the quiet certainty of a universe without duplicity, where Romans are Romans thanks to the most legible of signs: hair on the forehead (Barthes and Lavers, 1972: 55).

refer, which are particularly useful for those non-verbal languages that proliferate across the media. A sense of these relationships indicates the function of different signs within texts, aiding us also in comprehending and identifying the complex ways in which meaning works.

Peirce suggested three possible relationships between signs and the objects to which they refer. Do note that signs may overlap in terms of their function and the way that we enlist such terms to describe this function.

1. **Iconic relationship** This describes the physical similarities between a sign and its object. The smiley face icon is one of the most basic means of representing a human being and a human emotion, and one recognisable even to babies who have yet to develop language. Other simple signs of this nature might be stick men or women of

the kind one finds on toilet doors. Photographic depictions – still or moving – are the most obvious of signs that have an iconic relationship with the objects they depict.

2. **Indexical** The operation of this sign–object relationship is defined by cause (sign) and effect (object). 'Noises off' in film (owl or wolf calls in a scary movie for instance) are indicative of this relationship, as are footprints in the sand discovered by a castaway (other humans are here). You will note that these examples suggest that iconic signs can have a dual relationship with the object depicted or referred to – the image of a footprint is also iconic!

3. **Symbolic** Here the relationship of sign and object is a habitual or merely conventional one. This relationship is exemplified by words – spoken or written: there is no reason why a series of lines and circles such as CAT should describe a four-legged creature (nor is there any essential reason why the sound of the word should be seen as a reference to that creature!).

Alongside words we could add signifying objects, such as flags. Red, white and blue in various combinations represents ideas of the UK, the USA, France and various other nations, as well as the cultures and values that these countries are thought to represent. Some forms of brand identity are indicative of symbolic relations – the Nike swish, Adidas's three stripes or Orange's orange block would be good examples.

Organisation of signs in texts – media rhetoric and signification

Thus far we have concentrated on the singularity of signs without fully exploring the fact that texts are more than just a container for a series of signs. As the idea of media rhetoric teaches us, the way in which signs are organised and presented in texts is of vital importance to meaning.

When we learn to speak, read or write words, we do not just acquire vocabulary, we also learn a set of grammatical rules. These rules govern the way word signs are combined in a text so that they make sense. When we analyse texts, we don't just engage in a sign-spotting activity – this would result in banal lists and offer little insight into meaning. The contribution of signs to the meaning of a text is more than a matter of their individuality: how they are combined and relate to each other is important to the total meaning or meanings, ordering them, limiting them, sometimes opening the text up to multiple interpretations.

When signs are combined, their structural relationship is changed. Different signs combined in different ways are likely to create different readings. Combination has its greatest effect on the connotations of a text and can have a range of effects on the interpretation of signs. On the one hand, a certain combination may inflect the nature of the way that we read signs and the associations that are invited. On the other hand, signs may reinforce each other to support a particular reading, repeating associations through a variety of signifiers. Repetition (over space or time) encourages a reader's confidence in understanding something in a particular way. Sometimes the combination of signs can create a complete transformation in the associations we make. The reading of the signs combined might therefore be completely different from that of each sign presented separately. Because the meaning of signs is conventional, it is never fixed and absolutely certain. First, societies contain a range of people who have differing values and experiences in relation to those they might share. Likewise, societies are dynamic – some values are always subject to change, even as others endure. Thus, meanings are forever subject to challenge and we can understand this through concepts of polysemia and multi-accentuality.

Another theorist who was concerned with trying to construct a theory of semiology that understands the use of signs in the act of communication is helpful here: Valentin

Volosinov. This theorist was important in expanding upon the rather structure-centred approach of de Saussure, whose synchronic and structural approach to language function, as we've seen, tended to suggest that, despite the lived aspect of language, meaning resided in the relationship of words to each other. Thus a word such as dog signifies through virtue of not being hog, log or frog for instance.

Multi-accentuality refers to the concept that a sign has a central nucleus of meaning but that around this there is a range of other, close but distinct, possible meanings that can be identified. Volosinov's approach led him to argue that meaning was not simply a function of the system of signification and its operation. He saw that different aspects of the social relationship of the communicators was just as important as the system of available vocabulary and grammar. He proposed that we should not think of a sign as having a meaning determined by and fixed within the language system. He argued that, in use, signs have a slightly different meaning for different 'readers', or those at the receiving end of communication. He saw these differences as related to the differences in power between those involved in the act of communication. We could now see those differences in the connotation-level meaning of signs. Each sign has its own nucleus of meaning but slight differences or accents of meaning would be brought to bear depending upon the individual's position in the social relationship of power in society.

The concept of multi-accentuality is sometimes linked to a related concept – that of polysemia. A literal translation of the word would gives its meaning as many (poly) meanings (semia). However, it is important to distinguish between the multiplicity of readings possible because a text is ambiguous or abstruse (deliberately or otherwise), and those possible due to its polysemic nature. It is perhaps more productive to use the phrase 'many readings', to emphasise that the multiplicity of meanings come from different readings being made, rather than because the text lacks clarity as a construction or because its creator intended to be unclear about meaning.

Usually a text can be seen as polysemic because a range of different readers made different readings, rather than because one reader made a range of different readings. The latter case is only likely to happen if the text is ambiguous – or the reader is a poor media student. To understand the difference, we need to examine some of the ideas of yet another influential semiologist, the Italian Umberto Eco.

Codes: textual encoding and decoding

Eco enlists the idea of a code in order to explore the way that different readers are able to make different readings of a text. A code is a means for converting information into a special format to communicate it. We are all familiar with code as a device for spies and secret agents, as an aid for subterfuge or, more innocuously, in Morse code. Each code contains within it a limited number of elements to choose from in communicating. Morse code uses dots and dashes – the signs in its signifying system.

A code also has a set of rules which determine how each element may be used and combined with other elements. Morse code derives many of its rules from those of written grammar, which it attempts to stand in for. Of course, written language is a code too. There are a limited number of words that are available when we are writing and rules determine how they are combined (if we wish to make meaning). When you learn a language, you learn vocabulary and grammar. This is most apparent when you look at a language other than your own!

A signifying code is a specific language system. The code provides a range of possible signs and the rules that govern their combination. When we recognise the code a text is made from, we can then read it based upon a recognition and understanding of the relational nature of the signs and the way in which that combination inflects, reinforces or transforms the way that signs should be read in that code. In using the idea of a code and the concepts of encoding and decoding, Eco goes against the prevailing approach of most

Key thinker

Umberto Eco (1932–)

Eco is an Italian academic – Chair of Semiotics at the University of Bologna. He has written extensively on the semiotics of literature and of popular culture (see his analysis of James Bond in Chapter 2) for the benefit of his academic peers and for a popular audience through a range of newspaper columns.

He has achieved widespread fame for a series of complex yet bestselling books, such as *The Name of the Rose*. Later made into an equally celebrated film starring Sean Connery, this is a medieval detective story around signs and signification and the interpretation of texts. The title itself is a clue to the games that the author plays – derived as it is from Shakespeare's play in which Juliet says to Romeo 'What's in a name? That which we call a rose/By any other name would smell as sweet.' The name of the central character – William of Baskerville – is an allusion to Sherlock Holmes and the plot revolves around a missing text on the nature of laughter and its social role in undermining the pompous. All of this is set against the background of an inquisition – i.e. a fundamental and literalist interpretation of the Bible as the word of God used as a basis for the persecution of heretics or those whose interpretation of this text was aberrant (Eco, 2004).

semiologists by returning to the processual idea of communication. In essence his idea is a simple one. If the code which is utilised by the reader is a different one from that used to create the text, then a reading other than that intended by the creators will result. Eco uses the terms 'preferred' and 'aberrant' to refer to readings in this manner. Preferred reading is where the text is created and understood using the same code. An aberrant reading is where one code is used in production but the text is read using another.

It is important to emphasise that Eco does not see aberrant readings as 'wrong' and in this he differs greatly from those who model communication as a simple linear process. The notion of an aberrant reading then allows us to see that a range of different readings might be made of a particular text. It allows us to make connections to other concepts that we have introduced. Thus polysemia in a text is the result of various aberrant readings, made possible by the use of different codes. Media texts, being the complex things they are, offer many opportunities for polysemia, by drawing upon a wide range of signifying systems (think of an average website) and rhetorical strategies.

Polysemia and the media producer

Producers of media texts usually aim to ensure that polysemia is kept to a minimum. On one level polysemia could be viewed as a breakdown in communication, and in something as determined as an advert or news report, it could be something of a disaster. For this reason, media workers need to be skilled manipulators of media language and this is why media production is guided by so many professional rhetorical conventions, reinforced through institutional imperatives and resulting in relatively fixed codes when compared to contemporary art or literature. Of course, the relative rigidity of the codes and the control on the individual creativity of media workers is often seen as resulting in aesthetically inferior texts.

The main thing to think about here is how rhetorical techniques are deployed in order to direct and anchor meaning. An obvious example would include the captioning of photographs.

Uses and limits of semiology

So far, we have collated a set of analytical tools to allow us to undertake a comprehensive semiological analysis, 'deconstructing' texts in order to examine the way that they make meaning. We use these tools in total in a textual analysis in subsequent pages (p. 159–165). The one thing that we need to address, however, is whether or not we can be sure that our interpretations are convincing – shared by other readers or analysts – and not based simply upon a very personal and aberrant reading of the text.

Now, semiologists make no claim to objectivity, although there was once a 'dream of scientificity' to the enterprise. It is not possible, therefore, to present a reading as 'fact' or, for most of us, to draw upon our reputation as great thinkers or established academics in its support (and even then we should be prepared to express any disagreement with analyses). One approach is to draw on evidence that supports the general aspects of our interpretation rather than any personalised perspective. There are two ways in which we can do this – by demonstrating the inter-subjective nature of our reading (not relying upon what we think or feel alone), and by providing detailed structural support for our analysis.

The first approach could utilise some form of audience research in order to investigate the range of readings individuals make of a text, as well as the commonalities in their comprehension. We examine the different approaches to media audiences taken by media studies academics in Chapter 9. The second approach is achieved through the use of the Peircean, de Saussurian and Barthesian concepts we have introduced thus far. By using the conceptual ideas as analytical tools, we ensure that we are examining the functions of elements of the text and at the same time providing a range of evidence and explanation for our interpretation. If we make arguments for which are the most significant elements in a text, we can then consider how they work together to anchor and direct meanings.

There is no guarantee that an analysis is not partial, but the greater the accuracy with which we employ analytical tools, the more weight the reading has. In the end, the objective of an analysis is being persuasive – in academic study being persuasive depends upon the systematic and thorough nature of your approach.

Case Study

Mis-interpretations

Multi-accentuality, in tandem with opportunities for polysemia, can provide producers and readers with some interesting challenges and result in some curious texts with intended and unintended results. For instance, the US hip-hop clothing label Akademiks bought advertisement space on the sides of buses on the basis that it wanted to promote literacy. Supported by the city council, 200 buses in New York (as well as many in other US cities) were covered with adverts with the directive to 'Read books, get brain'.

Great embarrassment was caused when the phrase 'get brain' was revealed to be sexual slang used among the black community.

Source: www.guardian.co.uk/world/_2004/nov/06/usa.oliverburkeman

What issues arise in this instance of signification? What factors have impacted upon the generation and understanding of meanings?

Thinking aloud

Are producers semioticians?

We've already suggested that media producers are experts in the manipulation of media rhetoric – they have to be to be effective. On the other hand, we would suggest that they are also effective semioticians in their use and deployment of signification. This is, in part, a result of being familiar with social conventions and being situated in the culture that they share with us as readers. Things tend to 'mean' or signify in particular ways as if they were just naturally so. When the team – as well as the artists – involved in the JLS photo put it together, they did so with a degree of consciousness and apparent intuition, in order to get the image 'right'.

Furthermore, those who might wonder at the utility of semiological ideas should note how related ideas and methods have escaped way beyond the academic world. Principles, stated or implied, are often at the core of much contemporary cultural criticism in the media itself. The work of companies such as Semiotic Solutions has sought to apply the approach to the commercial world: 'to bring a radical new dimension of insight into traditional market research. Through semiotic analysis the critical element of cultural influence could be added to consumer psychology; suddenly we could see both halves of the consumption equation.' (www.semioticsolutions.com/home.php) As the company proposes in its offer of semiological masterclasses: 'Now you don't have to be an academic to understand and use the power of semiotics.'

Semiology (as bio-semiology) has even attended to such diverse things as the colours and markings of species of birds, and the markings on insects such as bees and wasps, as systems of signification with functions within nature.

New media, new media studies

New rhetoric, new signs?

To what extent does the form of new media present challenges to interpretation and to these tools we've introduced when compared to established media? Do our rhetorical tools extend unproblematically to video games, social media and webpages? Are new modes of signification presented by hyperlinks and the way in which digitisation offers spatial and temporal layers around any one word, image or logo?

On one hand, we can see the resonant ways in which new media forms utilise long-established conventions of photography and typography as well as enlisting and emphasising the social conventions of signs. Consider the Google homepage for instance. Here, we're thinking of the basic, unadulterated, unpersonalised version that is presented whenever you go to Google in order to perform an internet search. We are not yet thinking about the efficacy of the function of using Google, we just want to consider the presentation of the homepage and its signification.

That this is a 'page' is a starting point for the thinking about the fact that the web takes some of its cues from the idea of the book or more ambitiously, the

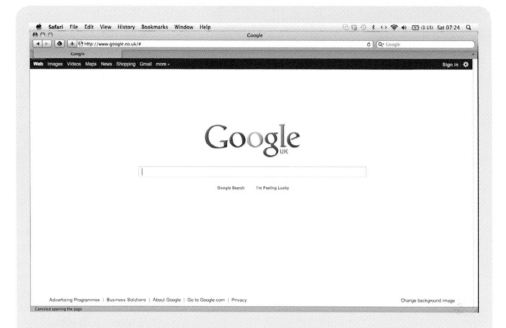

assembly of books and knowledge presented by a library. The Google search engine presented at this juncture is but a gateway that has no visible clues to the potentially overwhelming list of data that will result from typing in a search term and pressing the 'enter' button. This page is what is regularly called a design classic and aims at maximum efficiency and accessibility. It is tidily presented with the core function encapsulated in the wide box at the centre of the page. Additional inflections for any search (image, video etc.) are 'hyperlinked' or available in a dropdown menu. However simple they look then, webpages are sites in time and space which often reveal so much more that is co-present with a movement of the mouse.

Nonetheless, the sheer whiteness of the basic template of the Google homepage belies the way in which so much is at our fingertips. This has all the connotations of the clean page, of tidiness, organisation and reliability. Perhaps also a sense that this is a service for the user to employ for their needs: it is all about the user who will fill in this space with their requirements. In actual fact, this sense is belied by the way in which a hierarchy and preferential process comes into organising search results.

The whiteness of the page, with its culturally specific connotations of purity, at one with the unofficial Google motto 'Don't be evil', emphasises the company logo at the centre. The logo uses the Catull BQ typeface designed by Gustave Jaeger in 1982 for the Berthold company. The curves and soft qualities of this typeface deserve further reflection but are attractive and semi-informal in their affect, a quality accentuated by the rainbow range of colours employed to give body to the logo. While not childlike exactly, the use of mainly primary colours presents, alongside the dominant white of the page, the building block from which all further colours are made. Indeed, the rainbow quality is also one that accentuates an inclusive, fun and usable aspect of the homepage.

While such design aspects are an important part of the Google appeal we should remember that it is the efficacy of the search engine which has made the service so popular to the extent that the word has become a verb for internet users.

A useful task for you would be to take a look at other search engine pages in order to consider how they work in rhetorical and semiotic terms.

Summary

Conducting textual analyses

In this chapter we explored how media make meaning and how we might make sense of this process in scholarly and systematic ways. As a way of labelling the meaningful aspects of media products we introduced the idea of the media text, as distinct from the artefactual (physical) and commodity (economic) form of media products. We dwelt upon the idea of meaning as something obvious to us – we know what media texts mean already – but that we rarely stop to think about how they mean. We suggested that this is an important consideration for prompting us to step back from some of the habitual ways in which we often think of media forms and how they present the world to us.

We developed our discussion by introducing a range of analytical tools that allow us to precisely explore and outline how media texts are meaningful. We separated these for the benefit of understanding but insist that they must be combined in order to make analyses effective.

First, we introduced the concept of rhetoric or persuasive language here to explore the ways in which available media conventions (framing, design, acting styles and so on) are employed to organise and convey meaning. We drew upon some of the roots of this idea of persuasive language in order to think about how media rhetoric positions us as consumers of meaning and the kinds of affective responses media texts generate in us (attention, thrills, laughter, lust, etc.). In order to schematically detail media rhetoric we identified a series of rhetorical devices or labels to describe how media forms work. These were verbal rhetoric, presentational rhetoric, photographic devices and editorial rhetoric. Not all of these devices apply to all media forms, nor are they all present at all times when applicable – they are resources for us to draw upon. We sought to demonstrate these ideas and how they work in our support in a brief example of a rhetorical analysis of a magazine cover. This should give you a sense of how to perform this analysis and you will need to think about practising this approach against similar texts and other forms.

In the second part of this chapter we introduced the concept of semiology – the study of signs. We set out some of the foundational ideas and thinkers in semiology and the key concepts they provide us with. Core to the idea of semiology is the sign and signifying systems which gives us an approach to consider further how meaning works and where meaning is derived from. As semiology was formulated as an approach to linguistics, here we consider media conventions – visual, aural and so on – as akin to language (and of course media forms use written and spoken words too!). We suggested that media texts present us with combinations of complex signs and introduced a range of 'jargon' terms from semiology such as denotation and connotation in order to locate how meaning works and the different ways in which it works. Drawing upon some contemporary cultural and media theorists our discussion and examples of how to use, and why we use, semiology involved a consideration of the social contexts in which meaning is made. As meaning is formed out of the contextual and conventional understanding of signifying systems we therefore considered the ways in which meanings sometimes escape any intentions that media producers might have as well as the tactics they employ in order to anchor and direct the interpretations we make. Thus, ideas of polysemia and multi-accentuality serve to instruct us in some of the subjective aspects of our readings of media texts but that our tools, if employed properly and rigorously, serve to support any interpretations and arguments we wish to make about meaning.

You should now evaluate what you are able to do as a result of this chapter. If you have followed this chapter through, engaged with the activities and thought about the issues covered you should be able to:

- Distinguish between the artefactual, commodity and textual aspects of media outputs. If you are unsure about this distinction go back to the relevant discussion and examine a further range of media products in order to think through these ideas and how they help in making sense of media meanings.

- Define and identify the rhetorical devices involved in producing and organising meaning in media texts. Remember that different media forms employ different conventions. Our list of rhetorical devices gives us a resource to draw upon to make sense of different forms and how these devices might be combined. You can refine your understanding by paying attention to different types of media.

■ Utilise tools of rhetorical and semiological analysis in support of the interpretation of the meaning of media texts. Do remember that these devices were introduced in order to make sense of how media texts use available conventions to make meanings. We use these tools in order to underline our arguments about how meaning is made and where it derives from. Don't forget that our interpretations always begin with the text, not the tool.

■ Conceptualise the relationship of media meanings to social contexts. Media texts are not produced in a vacuum. What they say and what we make of them has something to do with the society we inhabit. Media texts are then about something, more than an assemblage of trite stories, thrills and so on – which are all important. You can get to grips with what we mean by the contexts for media meaning by examining some of the other chapters in this book but also by thinking critically about your own consumption.

Our aim in this chapter has not been to present a model approach to media textual analysis: there isn't one! We have some tools but no simple means of making a reading that is reproducible on every occasion we wish to make sense of what media 'mean'. This is something you will have do by being attuned and responsive to media products and confident in your use of these ideas.

It is worth reiterating that analysis always starts with our own reading as consumers and we try to make sense of that reading in relation to the signifying system, or combination of systems, before us. Concepts of rhetoric and rhetorical devices, as well as all of the terms from semiology, are tools to be employed as needed. They do not provide a list that needs to be consulted 'in order' every time we wish to understand the nature of texts. They will, however, fortify the arguments we wish to present to others about our interpretations of the value and social role of the media.

Doing media studies

Collating an analytical toolbox – reading texts

On a sheet of A4 paper, compile a list of all of the technical terms we've introduced so far and evaluate how far you understand them. Where you are unsure, return to the definition and discussion and explore the idea further through the recommended reading.

Whether fully secure in your understanding or not, you can explore these concepts best through application. Find a full-page advertisement from a magazine (or an alternative media text if you prefer) and briefly write up what it means to you. Then, using the terms introduced in this chapter, develop this into an analysis of meaning that pays close attention to rhetorical organisation and how the advertisement addresses its audience (what affect does it seek to produce?), along with its semiological meanings.

What ideas about its subject and context does it invoke in support of its product? How does it anchor meaning? What relationship is there between the rhetorical affects and the values associated with the product?

Further reading

Barthes, R. (1972) *Mythologies*, London: Vintage.
We used an extract from this highly influential work earlier in this chapter but the other articles are of great interest. The 'Myth today' article introduces Barthes's ideas and these are expanded further in his other essays as he looks at soap detergent advertisements and also wrestling, areas that are still pertinent today. Also of interest is Barthes's article 'The rhetoric

of the image', taken from his 1977 work *Image, Music, Text*. This essay looks at myths in modern advertising, problems with the semiotics of images and the way in which an Italian pasta advertisement connotes a sense of 'Italianicity'.

Berger, J. (1972) *Ways of Seeing*, Harmondsworth: Penguin.
Based on the BBC television series of the same name from the early 1970s, Berger's *Ways of Seeing* might seem a little outdated but it is still an important resource for the media scholar who wishes to understand the lineage behind some of the cultural ideas represented in visual images. Though it is generally concerned with fine art, the final essay on publicity and advertising is of particular interest.

Bignell, J. (2002) *Media Semiotics: an Introduction*, Manchester: Manchester University Press.
An indispensable book for those who wish to further their understanding of semiotics. Bignell carefully takes the reader through the process of semiological analysis, introducing different techniques and providing numerous examples drawn from all manner of media. He offers in-depth analyses of men's magazines, reality television shows and mobile phone text messaging.

Hill, C.A. and Helmers, M.H. (2003) *Defining Visual Rhetorics*, London: Lawrence Erlbaum.
Offering numerous contemporary and historical examples, *Defining Visual Rhetorics* looks at the persuasive techniques employed in media texts. The book opens with a study of Thomas E. Franklin's photograph from 11 September 2001, 'Firefighters at Ground Zero', and goes on to offer analyses of Hitchcock's *Vertigo*, magazines and political rhetoric. Though the examples are mainly American, this work is still of great value for those understanding media rheortic. Also, see Barry Brummett (2011) *Rhetoric in Popular Culture* (London: Sage) for a similar tome.

CHAPTER 2

Organising meaning in media texts: genre and narrative

Asking questions about genre and narrative

It's hard to say what is most depressing about *Cowboys and Aliens* — the film itself, or the fact that this was the best movie a posse of major Hollywood players could come up with.

A leaden mash-up of western and science-fiction elements that ends up noisy, grotesque and unappealing, this Jon Favreau-directed film features five producers (including Brian Grazer and Ron Howard), six executive producers (Steven Spielberg and Ryan Kavanaugh among them) and six credited writers, led by *Star Trek* rebooters Alex Kurtzman and Roberto Orci and *Lost*'s Damon Lindelof. No wonder the film plays like a business deal more than a motion picture.

Listed as a producer, not a writer, is Scott Mitchell Rosenberg, whose concept for the original graphic novel inspired the film. That's right, *Cowboys* doesn't even retell the story the graphic novel does; it sets out on its own. This is not a satisfying journey.

[...]

Both the cowboy and the alien halves of the venture play like tired retreads of once-vibrant material, and putting them together doesn't disguise the deficiencies — it doubles down on the losses.

[...]

With a script eager to embrace every witless western chestnut — talking is 'flapping your gums' to this crowd — and a passion for stock situations, *Cowboys and Aliens* displays one thumping cliché after another as if its bankrupt derivativeness was in some way reinventing the wheel.

Source: 'Ol' dusty tale by Kenneth Turan, *Los Angeles Times* Film Critic, 29 July 2011.

This review of a contemporary film is instructive. It reveals a number of common attitudes towards media texts and our consumption of them. The review is based upon a clearly expressed opinion, underlining the writer's own tastes and preferences for particular types of film achievement as well as his expectations and knowledge of the two types of film brought together in *Cowboys and Aliens*.

While we may not share the same tastes and prejudices expressed here, part of the pleasure that we find in popular media forms comes from our knowledge of them, their variety and the sense of how they work, or ought to work. There is pleasure, passion and meaning in the recognition of categories — of film, music, journalism, computer games, and so on — and judging what is done with them by producers. Sometimes we take pleasure in approving or rejecting unsuccessful experiments with the things we like and feel close to (tampering with the conventions and parameters of things we feel are almost 'natural' and unalterable).

What we will do in this chapter

This chapter develops our concern with texts, drawing upon skills of rhetorical and semiological analysis. Our aim is to consider the conventions and broader systems of meaning that order media texts in terms of genre analysis, and the way in which stories are ordered as narrative at rhetorical and semiological levels. We will add to the tools with which we make sense of media texts, what they mean in terms of their internal economy and in relation to wider institutional (media producers) and social contexts.

By the end of this chapter you should be able to:

- Outline the key terms used in the analyses of genre and narrative.

- Identify key theorists who have contributed to study in the area of genre and narrative.

- Apply the ideas of genre and narrative to the interpretation of a variety of media texts from different media sectors.

- Draw upon and synthesise a range of analytical skills to produce a detailed reading of the styles and meaning of media texts.

KEY TERMS: ▶ closure; convention; disruption, dynamism and hybridity; enigma; equilibrium; *fabula*; formalism; genre; narrative; narratology; plot and story; POV (point of view) and perspective; stable world, *syuzhet*.

Doing media studies

Getting started

In order to get thinking about the issues dealt with in this chapter, identify *one* specific text that you have recently consumed from *each* of the following media areas:

- journalism/the press/magazines
- radio
- photography
- advertising (print or audio-visual)
- video/computer gaming
- popular music
- film
- television
- webpage.

Think of a *general* term or label for each text that could be used to categorise it *within* each medium. (Is there a cue in the way that a listings magazine, catalogue, newspaper, TV channel or retailer locates your text or a webpage tags it?)

What features do your texts share with other similar texts from the same field (these could include use of rhetorical devices, storylines, types of words, recurring images, locations, etc.)?

Studying genre

Genre is a French word for 'kind', 'category' or 'type'. Its root resembles other words in English such as gene, genotype and gens – the Roman word for a group of families with common ancestors. We can also spot its echo in the word gender, the term we use to distinguish between masculine and feminine (see the discussion in the next chapter). Genre is enlisted here specifically as a term for the classification of particular types of media forms and content within each media group: for example, Grime, Hardhouse and Indie music; Bollywood, Giallo (a type of Italian thriller) and 'teen' movies; glamour, family and wildlife photography; travel, investigative and lifestyle journalism.

You will have a similar illustrative list from the opening activity that compares with this one. As you will appreciate from your own list, especially if it reflects your own preferences, categorisations are meaningful to both producers and consumers of texts. Genre is important to us as consumers in that it allows us to find texts that we like more easily. Or perhaps that should be genre allows producers to identify consumer preferences and organise their products so as to guide us to their products more easily.

Genre can be thought of as a signifying system, which relies on sets of codes and conventions shared by both producers and readers of texts. When we study the categorisation or types of texts we engage in genre study or genre criticism. Such approaches have a venerable history, stretching right back to the Ancient Greeks.

Genre critics in our field of study think about texts within any one medium – television for instance – in a variety of ways, and use a range of terminologies including those from rhetoric, aesthetics and semiology and from media professions themselves. Such scholars bring a range of agendas with them to their analyses. At a basic level, they are interested in highlighting the common features of different texts and how they can be grouped together, rather than analysing single texts in isolation. Nonetheless, some critics seek out generic texts that prove the rules of any group, but that also exhibit singularity and therefore difference.

Problems of definition

There is a paradox and obvious difficulty involved in defining genre. Any generic media text is both similar to and different from all others of its type. It has to be similar to other texts otherwise it would not be recognisably generic and it needs to be different to avoid being a simple copy. If generic texts were straight copies of each other, then after a while there would be little incentive for us to keep consuming them. The review that opens this chapter for instance bemoans the familiar clichés deployed in the film *Cowboys and Aliens* (dir. Favreau, 2011). Likewise, then, how do we know if a text fits a genre unless we've seen it and compared it with the many others like it? But on the basis of this similarity and difference we can't fully anticipate the character of any generic text or even, perhaps, any entire media genre. However, genre definitions are circuitous – we define genres based upon what we've seen or heard of media texts already, in anticipation of others that we might see or hear.

Consider the category of women's magazines. Any list of texts in this group could reasonably include such disparate publications as *The People's Friend, Take a Break, Woman's Own* in the UK, *Amica, Brigitte, Freundin* in Germany, as well as versions of *Elle, Vogue* and *Cosmopolitan* in both countries. These texts share common features but have as many differences not accounted for by language and culture, in tone, presentation, content and the address to their respective readerships. Commonalities, then, might include fashion spreads, features on women's health, lifestyle, articles on famous women, a majority of contributors who are women and so on, as well as a particular appearance to the cover, which usually (although not always) features a famous woman. Even where these publications might coincidentally or intentionally deal with the same content, their distinctiveness is apparent.

Of course, no one generic text tends to feature all of the elements of the wider category to which it might belong. A recognisable science-fiction film such as the aforementioned *Cowboys and Aliens* (dir. Favreau, 2011) features aliens and a threat to the planet Earth, but it is neither set in the future nor on other planets, it doesn't feature time travel, robots or many other generic elements such as we find in films such as *Star Wars* (dir. Lucas, 1977) *Total Recall* (dir. Verhoeven, 1990), *The Chronicles of Riddick* (dir. Twohy, 2004) or *I, Robot* (dir. Proyas, 2004). All of these films belong to the genre of science fiction: while being different they belong to the same genre.

In order to account for this similarity and difference, we can turn once more to the linguistic model introduced in our discussion of semiology, and to the concepts of syntagm and paradigm in particular. If any media genre is defined not only by any individual instance in use (a musical recording, a film, a magazine), but by all of the other texts within the group (nu metal music, films, magazines), then this is rather analogous to de Saussure's description of language systems that we explored in the previous chapter. Meaning comes from a relationship between the choice of elements, their organisation and expression in a particular manner distinct from all the other available choices and combinations within the lexicon of a language.

Any **genre** text could be described as a syntagmatic instance of the system, composed from a selection and ordering from an overall genre paradigm (science fiction, hard house music, women's magazines, first-person shooter computer games, etc.). Thus, each area of media can be classified into different sets or types of text according to textual form, often in conjunction with certain types of thematic content (Gangsta Rap and women's magazines rarely deal with similar issues or stories, overtly at least). Each generic grouping evinces particular codes and conventions, which makes us aware that they 'belong' to a particular genre. Based upon this discussion then we can offer this definition of genre in relation to the media field.

Genre

is a recognisable grouping, subset or type of media form comprising the paradigmatic elements (stories, rhetoric, signification) that are drawn upon in the creation of individual syntagmatic texts.

Genre: dynamism and exhaustion

The film theorists Robert Allen and Douglas Gomery suggest that genres provide audiences with a 'horizon of expectations' (Allen and Gomery, 1993: 84), a point that we can extend from film to other forms and genres. For instance, in a TV police series we expect a particular story arc involving detection and the ultimate dispensing of justice, a particular type of signification (paradigmatic, iconic features include police stations, police uniforms and procedures, etc.) under the thematic concern with crime. However, TV police series vary considerably, both at the present time (synchronically) and over time (diachronically). Thus, a key feature of genre is its abiding and changing nature and the degree of difference possible within each generic set. Despite the differences between *Law and Order (US or UK)*, *Morse*, *The Bill*, *Homicide*, *Starsky and Hutch*, *CSI (original, Miami, NY or Bradford)*, *Les Bleus*, *Spiral* and *La Squadra*, among many, many others, we still place them in the police series genre.

So, we should add to the above definition, that genres, although they consist of recognisable elements, are dynamic. We can best analyse a generic text by looking at its difference from the texts of other genres, or comparing it with other texts within its own generic paradigm diachronically (over time) and synchronically (at any one moment). As we have indicated in our definition, part of the dynamism of generic texts can be explained by the idea that they draw upon a considerable repertoire of elements, rather than each generic text drawing upon all of the codes and conventions available in a particular generic group.

We can understand the paradigm/syntagm further as media makers select items from a set menu and combine them in different, imaginative ways (although still ensuring that the 'meal' is recognisable and, in most cases, palatable). Generic texts, then, provide us with familiar pleasures in novel ways. Without differences between generic texts, they would soon lose their popularity, and without significant degrees of repetition, they would cease to be recognisably generic and popular for that reason. Nonetheless, we can point to the fact that certain genres have lost their popularity and effectively 'died out'. Such a list might include:

- western films,
- Hollywood musicals,
- rock concept albums,
- TV beauty contests,
- Nazi and Soviet propaganda films,
- British war comics,
- 'electro' music,
- cigarette advertising.

Depending upon your location, this list gives several random examples of forms and genres that have, by and large, fallen out of favour with producers and audiences alike. We can speculate that this has, perhaps, happened partly due to stylistic changes, or because such genres have seemingly exhausted themselves by the degree to which repetition has outweighed innovation or usefulness.

Some genres have been forced to change out of all recognition and even existence: by legislation in the case of cigarette advertising in the UK, military and political defeat in the case of Nazism and Soviet communism, and by social convention in the case of once popular but now potentially offensive sitcoms predicated on the 'inherent' humour of racial difference, such as the UK's *Love thy Neighbour* and *Mind Your Language*. Some genres, such as R&B in popular music, have been around for at least 60 years, but comparing what once constituted that genre with what it is now suggests some real problems when thinking of the continuity of genre.

A general point about generic exhaustion or redundancy is illustrated by the case of the western film (also a once popular domain for TV series) and its relation to aspects of the image and mythology of America. Theorists have argued that the West, in its earlier incarnation in books, comics and then films, starring once famous actors such as Tom Mix,

John Wayne and Audie Murphy, as well as TV series such as *Gunsmoke, Rawhide, Bonanza*, etc., reflected a sense of self-confidence and moral rectitude in its stories and a mythical dimension in its iconography.

A clichéd feature of such texts in the movies, presented in their most formulaic 'z-list' features (i.e. cheaply made), would be that the good guy always wears a white hat and the bad guys wear black ones (or, more often, war paint, as baddies were often Native Americans). Rugged, individualistic, skilful, moral and manly men, supported by equally rugged yet nevertheless feminine women, forged the values of civilisation out of the wilderness. However, on the occasion when America's image and status in the world came into question, particularly during the Cold War and against the backdrop of the Vietnam War, in which the boundaries of right and wrong – in relation to the actions of that nation – were harder to present as clearly demarcated, genre films began to problematise the image of the West and indeed the western itself. This began with films produced outside the US at first, such as the Italian 'spaghetti westerns' of Sergio Leone. Hollywood-produced works that took up the 'problem' with this genre include Arthur Penn's *Little Big Man* (dir. Penn, 1970) and later works, such as Clint Eastwood's *The Outlaw Josey Wales* (dir. Eastwood, 1976) and even his attempt at a revival in *Unforgiven* (dir. Eastwood, 1992) (see French, 2005; McVeigh, 2007).

Dynamic and hybrid genres

We have established that in media production there is a balance to be struck between difference and repetition in general, and in the difference between specific texts. There is a pull towards 'tried-and-tested' formats, which have in the past delivered large audiences or readerships for magazines and newspapers. However, the need for innovation encourages tampering with generic conventions to produce 'something different' in order to attract new audiences.

On television we get new programmes such as *Deadwood* (a new TV western!) and *CSI* (with all of its spin-offs), and also *Buffy the Vampire Slayer* and *Angel*, which offer a curious mix of traditional horror motifs, romance and teen drama (in a similar vein to *Dawson's Creek* or *Hollyoaks*). *Buffy*'s difference comes from mixing the supernatural with the banality of pubescent growing pains: 'My boyfriend's a vampire', 'We'll miss the prom because of the impending apocalypse', etc. *Dexter* features as its lead a 'good' serial killer (a figure popularised in thrillers such as *Hannibal, Saw*, etc.), who works as a forensic investigator (shades of *CSI*) in catching and punishing 'bad' serial killers. Alongside the western tradition discussed above we might number several instances where the genre has been 'mashed up' with other ideas, e.g. *Wild, Wild West* (dir. Sonnenfield, 1999), *The Burrowers* (dir. Petty, 2008), *Jonah Hex* (dir. Hayward, 2010) and the aforementioned *Cowboys and Aliens*.

Thinking aloud

The notion of disappearing genres might apply to the role of the Second World War in relation to that of the projection of the image of a country like the UK. This period was reproduced in endless films, TV series and in boys' comics in the decades after the Second World War (roughly 1945–79), but such depictions have now virtually disappeared.

How might we evidence and explain the decline of films, comics and dramatic TV series related to Britain's role in the Second World War? What kinds of methods would evaluate the nature of this decline in terms of the quantity of texts and their qualities?

Case Study

'Extinct' genres

Even a relatively recently invented form and technology such as video/computer gaming has its dead and dying genres (hereafter, we'll refer to computer gaming – 'video' seems an archaic prefix already!). The reasons for these changes may be due to technological innovations that have 'dated' earlier versions of games (limited speeds, graphics and sophistication), or perhaps other reasons, such as the way that a lack of innovation and repetition makes a genre redundant and unattractive to consumers after a while.

The top 10 'dead' genres from Gamespy.com are:

1. **Graphic Adventure.** Examples: The Space Quest and King's Quest games, Maniac Mansion, Monkey Island
2. **Beat 'Em Up.** Examples: Streets of Rage, Double Dragon, River City Ransom
3. **Full Motion Video.** Examples: Night Trap, Mad Dog McCree, Dragon's Lair
4. **Educational.** Examples: Oregon Trail, Where in the World is Carmen Sandiego?, Reader Rabbit

5. **Virtual Reality.** Examples: Virtual Boy, Power Glove, Various Horrible Stereoscopic Glasses
6. **Maze.** Examples: Pac-Man, Amidar, Crush Roller
7. **Text Adventure.** Examples: Zork, Trinity, Planetfall
8. **Light gun.** Examples: Duck Hunt, House of the Dead, Lethal Enforcers
9. **Puzzles.** Examples: Tetris, Bust-A-Move, Puyo Puyo
10. **Space Shooter or 'Shmups'.** Examples: Asteroids, Xevious, Space Invaders, R-Type, Radiant Silvergun

Source: Bowen, 2003

An update to the list is provided by 'Mappers United' and includes:

Alternative Sports Games

PC First Person Shooters

Survival Horror

Shoot 'Em Ups

Puzzle Games

Scrolling Beat 'Em Ups

Isometric RPGs

(www.mappersunited.com/forum/index.php?threads/top-ten-dying-game-genres.543/).

Doing media studies

Based upon a computer game of your choice, answer the following questions:

1. What are the generic features of any one group of games and how does your chosen game fit in with that group?
2. To what extent do computer games echo the features of other media forms and what features are unique to the medium?
3. Does your game tell a story in any way?

Alongside such innovations, we should also include generic parodies such as *Viz* comic, artists such as MC Frontalot within 'nerdcore rap', films such as *Scary Movie* (dir. Wayans, 2000), *Shaun of the Dead* (dir. Wright, 2004) or *Hot Fuzz* (dir. Wright, 2007), 'newspapers' such as the *Sunday Sport* or *National Enquirer* and TV shows such as *Brass Eye* and *The Office*, the latter poking fun at reality TV conventions. These texts are innovative because they stretch, play with and mix the codes and conventions of genres. But we find them interesting or funny precisely because they signify the codes and conventions of familiar genres while undermining them. Despite their lampooning style, they are still *recognisably* generic. All of these examples, while potentially parodic in intent or outcome, could also be labelled as *hybrid*: they mix different genres together to do something that is different and new (or which 'feels' new). They create new pleasures for existing audiences, perhaps amalgamating different groups or attracting new audiences, readers, etc.

Genre in context: production and consumption

Dynamic change and hybridity is not the only way that genres develop. Wholly new genres do come along in all areas of the media, to provide something different – new thrills for new audiences. However, new genres occasionally also fail to attract new audiences because they are simply unpopular, or when they do gain audiences, readers or consumers, they eventually lose their novelty value as they offer their own foundation of pleasurable repetition (see the discussion of cult media and fandom in Chapter 9).

This is certainly the case with still relatively recent televisual innovations in the form of UK docusoaps such as *Airport* or *Club Reps*, 'reality TV', with the acme being Endemol's internationally successful *Big Brother*, 'DIY/personal makeover' shows such as *Changing Rooms* or *Home Front*, and the 'idol'/'X factor' style knockout talent shows popular around the world. Of course, you might ask whether these are entirely new or merely hybrids or, as some suspect, possible parodies of existing genres! Lately, 'reality TV' shows have been joined by those that offer real people in 'modified' situations. Shows like *The Only Way Is Essex* and *Seven Days* in the UK and, in the US, *The Hills*, *Laguna Beach*, *The Real Housewives of Orange County* and *Jersey Shore* offer ordinary people saying unscripted lines but in scripted situations.

In television particularly (but also important in all other media areas), much generic innovation and repetition can be attributed to the increased competition in broadcasting, in particular the brutal economic fight for audience share and revenue in the digital age. As Nicholas Abercrombie points out:

Television's need for a constant stream of new programmes means a perpetual tension between using genre conventions to retain audiences and keep costs down, on the one hand, and, on the other, breaking and crossing genre boundaries to attract new audiences and stay ahead of the competition.

(Abercrombie, 1996: 45)

In the global age, where media companies are truly international organisations, generic innovation and repetition may be transported across cultural and linguistic boundaries. Recent developments in music participation programming (combining features of reality, talent and gaming formats) in American and British shows, such as *Singing Bee* and *Don't Forget the Lyrics*, for instance, have appeared anew on Italian TV as *Chi fermerà la musica* and *Canta e Vinci* respectively. The BBC's *Strictly Come Dancing* has been exported to over 32 countries, reappearing as *El Baile en TVN* (Chile), *Ples sa zvijezdama* (Croatia) and *Vild med dans* (Denmark), among others. On one level, this process is simply about the sale of a copyrighted format, its structure and name across boundaries, but there is nothing to prevent new versions of such programmes being inspired by their combination of pleasurable and successful features. What we end up with then is a range of media products which are different but the same.

We should note then that genre has an economic function equal to its aesthetic, rhetorical and semiologically meaningful function. Genre is of vital importance to media organisations such as those involved in TV and radio broadcasting because it allows them to gain regular and predictable audiences. Even in an age of apparent audience fragmentation, as 'niche' audiences become more and more important, competition is growing not only among the small fry but equally among large-scale, mainstream media organisations like

Ofcom's survey and generic 'pleasure'

In a report from 2006, the UK regulator Ofcom identified dissatisfaction among TV viewers with reliance among broadcasters on generic programming.

Another area of significant dissatisfaction in our survey and more generally across the qualitative research conducted relates to programme innovation . . . programme innovation and origination is an area of key importance to viewers. While the much-berated formats of reality TV and makeover shows continue to do well in terms of viewing figures, viewers feel strongly that this type of programming is derivative, and that more could be done to create original programming. 28% of the overall survey sample didn't feel that the main terrestrial channels were providing adequate amounts of first run programmes . . . Representatives of specialist interest groups highlighted some parts of the schedule where more innovation could usefully be introduced, singling out daytime television with its 'captive audience' as a largely wasted opportunity.

Source: Ofcom, 2006

ITV, Sky and the BBC. The reliance on genre programming, such as game shows, soap operas and, lately, docusoaps, reality TV and makeover shows, is a way of delivering audiences with the minimum of economic risk.

In the UK, both the BBC and the ITV network have been criticised for producing 'formulaic' programming (see Ofcom box). By this, critics often mean that the network has relied on particular types of popular programme genres and forsaken others, such as 'quality' drama and current affairs. We can see this argument echoed in critiques of contemporary Hollywood film and the way that it has eschewed 'serious', adult-oriented features. Instead, it relies upon big names (actors, directors) in generic blockbusters organised 'by numbers' in order to generate the biggest audiences, mainly immature audiences who are available for summer holiday release dates, and who will guarantee revenues of hundreds of millions of dollars (Biskind, 1999; Shone, 2005).

As we discuss below, it is common in critical discussion to equate the generic with dull predictability. For some theorists this, in turn, has predictable results on the cultural terrain and upon consumers themselves, i.e. they become dull and inured to stimulation and independent thought. When thinking about genre, we should be aware of such criticisms, but also of the cultural assumptions that lie behind them. Nonetheless, genres *are* important to audiences, just as much as they are to producers. You can't have one without the other. As we have already said, there is a pleasure to be found in repetition and the 'horizon of expectations' of generic texts. Perhaps this is down to conservatism on the part of consumers – why pay for something new whose rewards cannot be anticipated? Perhaps it is a question of taste. Either way we should be attentive to a question that is not always explicitly addressed in genre study: how *do* audiences find their way to *new* examples of genres they enjoy and to new genres?

One obvious way we can think of in which audiences might find their way is through the labelling of digital TV channels (documentary channels are divided into history, biography, travel, wildlife, etc.). Elsewhere, music and entertainment stores (online or in physical space) divide their content accordingly, as do newsagents with their racks of newspapers, magazines, comic books and so on. Online retailers, such as Amazon and Netflix, use software that interprets customer purchase choices and recommends material to them and browsers along these lines ('those who bought this DVD also liked . . .'). Alongside industry-generated marketing campaigns, reviewers in magazines, on the internet and on

TV keep us informed about new products, how they adhere to generic rules and how they compare with other texts. Consider the reference points of this review of a contemporary horror film for example:

> *Proving once again that horror is a genre that feasts upon its own entrails,* The Descent *duly devours and regurgitates an impressive smorgasbord of shockers. Marshall describes his movie as 'Deliverance goes underground', but this feisty thriller owes just as much to the town-and-country counterpoint of Wes Craven's* The Hills Have Eyes. *From the low-angled shots of an Evil Dead-style woodland cabin, to the iconic poses of Carrie (the blood-splattered Macdonald bears more than a passing resemblance to Sissy Spacek), Marshall leads us on a whistlestop tour of all his fan-boy favourites. Echoes of* Nosferatu, Aliens *and even Danny Boyle's* 28 Days Later *reverberate around these caves, with a feast of Fulci-style gore laid on for the hardcore horror fans. Breaking with the stalk-and-slash tradition of a single 'final girl' surviving to slay the beast, Marshall presents an ensemble chorus who turn upon one another as they descend into the mouth of madness.*

> Mark Kermode, 'What lies beneath: Neil Marshall's
> subterranean shocker is one of the best British horror films
> of recent years', *Observer*, 10 July 2005

We could problematise the relationship of such reviewers with the media texts and industries they appear to evaluate. While they offer publicity for such products (whether the review is positive or negative), what they also do is give us clues and cues with which to make sense of the range of media products on offer to us. Of course, what we do then, as consumers, is to perform our allotted role and buy our cinema ticket, tune in to the TV schedules or buy the latest hit record; we also spread the word!

We'll explore the nature of audiences more fully in Chapters 8 and 9, but it is worth dwelling on the relationship between certain forms of media, particular genres in fact, and the allegiances shown by audiences and readers as consumers of media texts. We could note in passing that certain genres and certain media forms attract particularly committed consumers – fans – who exhibit a remarkable discernment in what they consume and the way that they consume it. Here we could list the adherents of science fiction TV, those cultists who celebrate older shows, such as *Star Trek, Blake's Seven, X-Files* and *Dr Who*, as well as more recent ones, such as *Babylon 5* or *Falling Skies*. Then there are those music fans that devote themselves to collecting obscure records – usually vinyl – such as 'Northern Soul' aficionados. It is rarely the case that such devotion is shown to newspapers, advertisements or TV current affairs shows! This kind of activity attests perhaps to the extreme devotion and passions that certain genres can elicit from consumers.

Genre and limiting the horizon of expectations

Besides organising us as consumers of media texts, genres have an important determining role in meaning-making beyond the internal system and pleasurable dynamic of the text. More straightforwardly, genres offer us particular ways of seeing the world, while excluding others; in this they can be considered to be 'ideological' in nature. A full discussion of this concept can be found in Chapter 10 but in essence it refers to the way in which media objects present us with ways of seeing the world that are not necessarily in our individual and collective interest. Such ideas are not advertised as such but presented as if entirely self-evident, 'common-sense' even.

John Fiske and John Hartley (1989) talk of genres as 'agents of ideological closure' because they act to close down the meaning potential of a given text and the way that it is understood. The imaginative and symbolic spaces provided by media texts, instead of having a free rein, are ultimately conservative and predictable in structure and in the way they deal with their content, reinforcing a sense – however fantastic the scenario – that 'this is the natural order of things'. It is also the case that endless repetition across media forms is understood to limit the responses of consumers – as opposed to the uniquely challenging qualities of individualised 'art' (see also the discussion in Chapter 11).

This sort of closure can be seen in the western form that we touched upon above, with the triumph of particular values as embodied in the hero. Similarly with TV situation comedies, which traditionally have dealt in fairly narrow conceptions of the family, ethnicity, class and gender. In these cases, generic codes and conventions are mobilised – often using stereotypes (see Chapter 3) – to limit the range of meanings we can hope to make from our reading of the text. However, a cursory glance at some British TV sitcoms from the 1970s would indicate that this is a genre that has undergone significant changes, particularly in relation to issues such as race, gender and sexuality. That we nowadays might wince at the casual sexism of period pieces such as *George and Mildred* or *On the Buses*, or the racial insults of *Love Thy Neighbour* and *'Til Death Us Do Part* (they might be illegal under British law, in fact), suggests that these are not in any straightforward manner successful agents of ideological closure.

We should ask, too, whether audiences also winced in the same way as we might when these programmes were originally shown or whether they instead unproblematically accepted the ideological closure offered to them. How do those audiences respond who re-encounter such shows on rerun TV channels, or when they are viewed anew? What pleasures are involved as a result of seeking out such texts on video and DVD? We must be very careful about looking at older examples of media texts in whatever generic field as ideological and thinking of contemporary texts as somehow non-ideological. We are not easily able to identify the ideologies of our own time, precisely because they are the dominant values currently circulating in our society, treated casually and accepted as 'natural'. We can recognise the values of 1970s sitcoms just as we note the attitudes, sideburns, cars and clothes, because of the way that ideologies change over time. Like breakfast cereal, ideology appears to have a 'shelf life'.

Nonetheless, ideological or otherwise, genre is often referred to inside and outside contemporary academic media studies as indicating an inferior kind of text, often viewed as being typical of media output. What greater insult or dismissal can there be other than the claim that something is 'generic'? From this perspective the conventions of genre are viewed as formulaic devices, which exist because of the domination of a particular form of cultural organisation termed 'mass culture'. The term, in part, connotes the sense of the rather mechanical, production-line nature of media production (see Chapter 11 for a more detailed discussion). Such attacks on media genres and generic texts derive, in part, from a notion of 'high art' and the 'creative individual'. Certain groups of texts, usually great paintings, musical symphonies, Shakespearean tragedies, are presented as part of a 'canon' of all that is best in culture. The greatness of such texts is seen as dependent upon their uniqueness and creation by great individuals.

This latter approach was strongly influential on theories of media production that were influenced by such approaches from art and literary theory, which sought to find value among the products of the mass media rather than simply dismissing it all. Some media texts were identified as superior because they reflected the interests of singular creative geniuses. One instance of this approach is associated with film studies and the French term *auteur*, which means author. This clearly places the emphasis on creative individuals at the centre of production, rather than the social, cultural or even production conventions that give rise to many popular texts.

The opening up of the debate about cultural value was one of the central concerns of academic work in media and cultural studies from the 1950s. In part, this is because the group of people who are usually thought of as intellectuals and who conduct these debates have, in the past, been the group who defined cultural value (see Chapter 11).

Thinking aloud

Creativity in media?

The use of the term author (*auteur*) to ascribe creative status and worth to the director of film originated with a small group of critics, later film-makers, associated with the French critical journal *Cahiers du Cinéma* in the 1950s. Critics such as François Truffaut, Jean-Luc Godard and Eric Rohmer sought to celebrate directors who seemed to evince a personal style and vision, despite working under the constraints of the rather rigid Hollywood studio system of film-making (see Chapter 11). The aim was partly polemical (a *politique*), seeking to endorse those talents who made films that were truly filmic, using the language specific to the medium rather than producing static filmed plays or books – as they felt was the case with French cinema at that time (the boring 'Cinéma du papa' as the *Cahiers's* critics called it). Key studio-contracted directors, such as Howard Hawks, John Ford and Alfred Hitchcock, found themselves elevated to the status of true artists or *auteurs*, while their contemporaries were dismissed as mere journeymen or *metteurs en scène*. Later, this French approach was erroneously translated and taken up in the US and the UK as a *theory* of authorship (John Caughie, 1981).

The issue presented by this thread is whether or not media workers can be thought of as 'creative' in the same way as individual painters or writers, when so many forms are collaborative and so obviously determined by market demands and prescriptions.

Thinking aloud

Genre and hierarchies of value

> So poetry is something more philosophical and more worthy of serious attention than history (Aristotle).

It is worth mentioning Aristotle (382–322 BC) in a work on media studies in order to conceptualise the influence that generic criticism has had on our field's antecedents, namely drama and literary studies. Aristotle classified literature into the lyric, epic or narrative, and drama. These labels endure, alongside other core categories such as tragedy, comedy and satire. From the time of the Renaissance to the eighteenth century, these types of literature were treated as if they were ideal, fixed categories, rather like biological species, with their own subject matter, style and affect. In relation, critics and authors insisted upon the need to keep each category 'pure' and to avoid the mixing of forms, particularly as these were ranked in importance in relation to the kinds of social content with which they dealt. Epic and tragedy, with their grand themes and aristocratic subject matter and agents, reigned at the top, with comedy and the pastoral – both concerning coarser material – at the bottom.

It may be that, in our postmodern age (see Chapter 12), with our hybrid media genres, such rigidity and value judgements are redundant, especially in the field of popular culture – the mass media for us. Certainly, and as Charlotte Brunsdon (1997) has pointed out in her work on television, nowadays theorists rarely make explicit value judgements about media texts, yet we continue to celebrate and elevate certain genres above others. One way in which media theorists have implicitly expressed their preferences is through the media forms and genres that they have paid attention to – something you should note when searching for secondary materials in this area. Likewise, the next time that you see an awards ceremony on TV, for instance, consider the order in which the prizes are presented: usually ascending from 'frivolous' sitcoms and comedies to 'serious' drama, from series and soaps to stand-alone set-pieces and even to current affairs programmes.

The clarity of the division that was constructed between high and low culture starts to crack when applied to contemporary culture, which is so strongly based upon media texts. The problem for intellectuals has been complicated further when some groups of media texts – jazz and 'film noir' come to mind – came to be viewed as 'worthy', and started to collapse as the ideas of postmodernism (see Chapter 12) and celebrations of kitsch made liking Madonna's music or MTV almost compulsory among intellectuals (and particularly among media and cultural studies lecturers!).

Where have we got to?

At this point, it is worth pulling together a list of what constitutes genre, and the key points that we need to take forward. Thus, we can think of genre in three distinct ways:

1. as sets of codes and conventions concerning content, story, signification and thematic treatment (its aesthetic, stylistic dimension);

2. as a way for producers of media texts to organise audiences/consumers/readers (its economic dimension);

3. as a way for audiences to find types of media texts that appeal to them as a means of meeting and satisfying the 'horizon of expectations' (its consumer dimension).

Before we move on, however, it is worth sounding a note of caution about the classification of media texts. When we identify genres, we should be aware of the elasticity of the term, which is applied to very broad groups of texts (Hollywood films, pop music, tabloid newspapers), and to more specific groups of texts (the teen comedy, boy bands, redtops). We need to question the utility of such categorisations – for the producer, consumer *and* theorist. Exactly how meaningful and obvious is it to enlist classifying terms, and how are such terms themselves qualified and explained in use and in explanation of the media?

Narrative, narratology and genre study

Narrative
refers to the organisation of textual elements into a pattern in terms of space, time and perspective. It is the narrative that encourages us to read specific parts of the text as 'events' which are ordered through time (temporal succession) and which we conceive as the cause of other events (causation).

For certain genres we could list the kinds of specific stories that are repeatedly told. These might include: newspaper problem pages with tales of infidelities, the fatal attraction of one to another; computer games where players – through the figures they manipulate – progress on to greater dangers and rewards (at least in terms of points and kudos); and TV soaps that offer never-ending stories (any resolution is always the beginning of another thread or problem, unless characters die or leave the milieu of the regular action).

Some types of story cross over many different genres. One basic storyline, for instance, is repeated in adverts (film, radio, even still images), popular songs, films, TV shows, and even some news reports around the lives of celebrity individuals. The story? 'Boy meets girl' (or vice versa), with variations on that theme (boy loses girl, regains her and finds love, etc.). We see this structure repeated in newspaper gossip columns about celebrity love affairs, 'weepie' films and certainly many, if not most, pop songs. From Elvis and the Beatles to Coldplay and Dizzee Rascal, this is the basic template for pop's stories.

We now turn to consider the manner in which media texts tell such stories, how the worlds and events they tell of – fictional or otherwise – are organised and ordered and how this contributes to our understanding of them. Once more we will draw upon our repertoire of rhetorical and semiological terms and techniques in order to understand stories and storytelling as structures and signifying systems. The conventional terms we shall use here are **narrative** and narration.

Narrative as structure

We all seem to share a very strong sense of narrative structure, which probably comes from our social and individual perception of time itself (we get up when it gets light, go to bed when it gets dark), in conjunction with the vast number of stories we are told as children. If you take a look at the most basic of children's picture book readers or even at pre-school TV shows, such as *Teletubbies*, you can discern very simple and repetitive narratives: Po has ball, Po plays with ball, Po loses ball, Po finds ball once more. Theorists have suggested that it is through our acquisition of stories and a sense of our own place in them that we come to an understanding of our self and develop our individual subjectivity (Freeman, 1993). Certainly, children are always interested in making up stories of their own, and they have a keen awareness that a story, by convention, should have a start, a middle and an end. Such recognition is the basis of an understanding of narrative structure.

Work on narrative and narration has been developed in a number of academic disciplines and subjects – including literary studies, anthropology, psychology and film studies – and so there are a large number of concepts available for the study of narrative in the full range of media texts. There is even an attempt to see the study of narrative as a distinct intellectual and analytical activity, and so the term narratology has been coined to indicate its existence. The most developed work in examining narrative structure is to be found, unsurprisingly, in linguistics and in literary studies. The analysis of narrative structure was developed initially in the work of groups active at the beginning of the last century, such as those known as the Russian Formalists and the Prague School. Some of the theorists who are associated with this movement are Roman Jakobson and Vladimir Propp (see below), while more recent contributors to the field whose names you will encounter elsewhere include Gerard Genette and Tzvetan Todorov. Many of the ideas developed by these theorists were taken up and applied fruitfully to the study of film, which became theoretically rigorous (as opposed to the subject of casual, subjective critical observation) when it developed into a university subject in the 1960s and 70s. This development is associated with the work of analysts such as Christian Metz, journals such as *Screen* and a broader movement known as structuralism.

Propp's method

Propp's approach was to conceptualise stories as structures that were analogous to language systems. In the Formalist approach to language and literature, sentences were categorised and interpreted at the level of the morphemes. A morpheme is a meaningful linguistic unit consisting of a word, such as *play*, or a word element, such as *-ed* in *played*, that cannot be reduced to any smaller meaningful part.

Propp used this method and extended it to analyse folk tales, hundreds of them. Propp categorised these by their smallest narrative units – narratemes – leading to a series of conclusions about the shared structures of such stories. In *Morphology of the Folk tale* (Propp, 1928), he suggested that, although folk tales might have differences in plot, character and

Key thinker

Vladimir Propp (1895–1970)

Propp was a student of the Russian Formalists and a folklorist with an interest in the kinds of tales that were passed on from generation to generation among the Russian peasantry.

setting, they would share common structural features. These common features, Propp thought, had two principal elements:

1. Functions of characters: Propp suggested characters could be categorised by their function in the narrative, for example, villain, the donor, the dispatcher, the helper, the hero, the false hero, the princess and her father. Importantly, Propp suggested that a single character could fulfil more than one of these functions, or that a single function could be fulfilled by more than one character.

2. Narrative units descriptive of particular action: Propp suggested that there were 31 core narrative units, which could be found across all folk tales (at least those he examined). Below are some of Propp's narrative units.

   A member of a family leaves home (the hero is introduced);
   An interdiction is addressed to the hero ('don't go there', 'go to this place');
   The interdiction is violated (villain enters the tale);

   Hero leaves home;
   Hero is tested, interrogated, attacked, etc. preparing the way for his or her receiving magical agent or helper (donor);

   Hero and villain join in direct combat;
   Hero is branded (wounded/marked, receives ring or scarf);
   Villain is defeated (killed in combat, defeated in contest, killed while asleep, banished);
   Initial misfortune or lack is resolved (object of search distributed, spell broken, slain person revived, captive freed);
   Villain is punished;
   Hero marries and ascends the throne (is rewarded/promoted).

Importantly, Propp suggested that not all units will necessarily appear in all stories. However, when the units do appear, they do so in the order he suggests. While you may wonder whether this analysis and list provides us with any usable tools, we should note the statistical evidence of the work in uncovering the repeated structures of narratives. His work was therefore influential on many important theorists in various disciplines, such as Claude Lévi-Strauss, who sought to understand the myths and mores of pre-industrial societies.

In this spirit other scholars extended and applied the project to Western popular culture. The innovative work of Roland Barthes, for instance, is dealt with in Chapter 1 while film theorists took Propp's narrative functions and applied them to cinema with some success. For example, Will Wright in *Six Guns and Society* (1975) conducted a Proppean analysis of westerns.

In order to make the narrative units more useful as an analytical tool, Wright developed some narrative units more specifically applicable to the western. Below we reproduce some of Wright's list of narrative units, which he suggested would apply to all classic westerns (he divided westerns up into various types):

The hero enters a social group.

The hero is unknown to the society.

The hero is revealed to have an exceptional ability.

The villains are stronger than society; the society is weak.

The villains threaten society.

The hero fights the villains.

The hero defeats the villains.

The society is safe.

The society accepts the hero.

The hero loses or gives up his special status.

Peter Hutchings has suggested that Wright's use of 'Proppean' analysis is so particular as to be of little use outside the western (Hollows and Jancovich, 1995). However, what is interesting beyond this apparent bean counting is that Wright attempts to look at particular structural elements of the western and suggests that changes in narrative structure and function relate to wider changes in American society. As such, westerns have a mythic function in that they offer stories, which serve to bind us to a particular social order. Here, myth is profoundly ideological and serves to justify or explain society as it is, for instance winning consent for the dominant capitalist social order. On the other hand, and as we've seen above, the form may actually 'break down' or disappear when its central motif becomes untenable.

With a similar concern for popular literature, Italian semiologist Umberto Eco has focused on the work of a single author – deriving a basic narrative scheme in relation to the James Bond novels, although one could do much the same with the films. His schema was worked out in *The Bond Affair* (Eco, 1966). Here is an extract from the list:

M moves and gives a task to Bond.

The villain moves and appears to Bond.

Woman moves and shows herself to Bond.

Bond consumes woman: possesses her or begins her seduction.

The villain captures Bond.

Bond conquers the villain.

Ultimately, these kinds of studies are important in that they cause us to think of the consequences of these kinds of structural repetitions. They suggest that media forms are social practices, making a link between the stuff of symbolic stories and the values that we live by.

Stability – disruption – enigma – resolution

Our attention to narratology thus far has been largely based around film, as this is a relatively accessible medium and we expect that our references and illustrations will be recognisable to you. However, as a narrative medium we should note that not all films tell stories in the same way, nor in a conventional, recognisable manner. Not all films have the same narrative structure, but media theorists have suggested that we can see commonalities in the majority of commercial films produced in North America and Europe. This is based upon studies that suggest that film-makers in a variety of institutional settings established a set of conventions for the telling of fictional film stories that were largely in place by about 1915, and which continue still to dominate this form (see Bordwell, 1985). Mainstream entertainment films of the sort that are primarily organised around coherent storytelling for the purpose of entertainment are usually described as classic realist films. The narrative principles of such films are worth exploring as a basis for comparison and the analysis of other media.

Thinking aloud

Christopher Booker implicitly revisits the work of Propp and of Formalism. In his book *The Seven Basic Plots: Why We Tell Stories* (2005), Booker promises to unlock the secrets of stories, from the ancient Babylonian 'Epic of Gilgamesh' to more recent blockbuster films that have captured the popular imagination – *Star Wars* (dir. Lucas, 1977) and *Jaws* (dir. Spielberg, 1975), for instance.

The author compares plots from films, novels, operas and so on to reveal the reiteration of seven basic plots which are: rags to riches; quest; voyage and return; hero as monster; rebirth; comedy; and tragedy. This analysis is used to point out 'deeper structures' and the seeming universality of such templates in the tales we tell each other.

In a film, the formation of a coherent narrative is possible because of a hidden presumption about narratives we all share. In his work on narrative, Tzvetan Todorov (1977) has suggested that we infer the existence of a stable world, which pre-exists the story that is about to be recounted to us. The story starts at the point at which this stable world is disrupted, although the plot of the film often needs to establish the equilibrium of the filmic world first. While films may not open with the full establishment of the stable world (they may reorganise the temporality of the events we need to see in order to understand the narrative), it is usually the case that we are plunged into a milieu and the lives of protagonists as if they were ongoing, in the middle of their everyday business. A useful phrase for this situation from literary studies is that of *in media res* (into the middle of things).

The coherent internal story world portrayed in a film is usually referred to as the diegesis. Filmic or rhetorical elements that fall outside the coherent domain of the story – voice-overs and the soundtrack – are usually referred to as non- or extra-diegetic.

The disruption and state of dis-equilibrium comes – within the classic film text – usually in the form of an enigma. The enigma may be the central puzzle that a detective has to solve in a crime or mystery film, or perhaps the misunderstanding between a man and a woman that prevents their love blossoming, leaving us to wonder 'will they or won't they'. Good examples of such films, although there are thousands, would include the detective/noir *Se7en* (dir. Fincher, 1995) or 'romcoms' like *There's Something About Mary* (dir. Farelly and Farelly, 1998) or *What Happens in Vegas* (dir. Vaughan, 2008).

The enigma may also be the entry of a disruptive *force* into a particular milieu, such as a western town or an outer space location in a science fiction film (or the crossover of both in *Cowboys and Aliens*). Exactly what should be done about this disruption is what propels the film narrative along.

In *Star Wars* (dir. Lucas, 1977), the disruption and enigma centre upon the entry of two escaped robots, or 'droids', into the world of the bored young Luke Skywalker, who lives on the barren desert world of Tatooine. The thrust of the enigma he is presented with and needs to solve is: why does the little robot – R2D2 – need to contact the hermit Ben Kenobi and what information does he have to impart to him? If you know this film, you will be able to think through how this initial enigma evolves and unravels, and where it leads the protagonists.

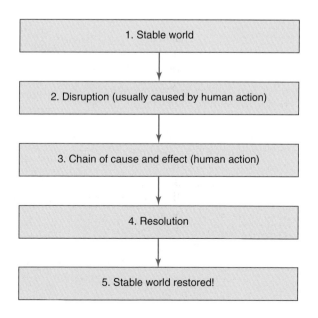

Any narrative film can close only when the enigma is solved, and the disruption challenged and dealt with or understood and set right. At this point, the film finishes and the status quo returns; equilibrium is re-established. The imagined world may have changed because of the events of the film – although not usually in any greater respect than through changes to the fictional characters – but it is again stable; well, at least until our next film. It is often easier to understand a set of concepts visually, so the figure shows the idea of cinematic narrative, summarised in a diagram.

Plot and story

One of the most useful tools for understanding structure and the relevance of narrative theory is the distinction that can be made between plot and story. Broadly, we construct the story in our heads from information narrated to us through the plot. This distinction has, according to film historian and theorist David Bordwell, a long history that may go back, once more, to the Greek Aristotle (Bordwell, 1985). Russian Formalists such as Viktor Shklovsky, writing in the first decades of the twentieth century, theorised this distinction between plot and story in some detail. As Formalists, Shklovsky and his collaborators were interested in the specific nature of artistic form (in literature, the 'literariness' of the language and structure that sets it apart from everyday speech and functional writing) and how it presented the world and could be used to generate responses.

The Formalists used two terms for narrative that are roughly analogous to our distinctions between plot and story. Thinking of these terms in relation to film, the first of these is:

fabula – sometimes translated as 'story'.

Fabula
The *fabula* is a pattern that film spectators create through assumptions and inferences: we do not see the *fabula* on the screen or hear it on the soundtrack.

Now, this might suggest that we can create any *fabula* we want from the story information narrated to us through the plot. Not so. Bordwell has highlighted some of the limits to the spectator's *fabula* construction:

> The fabula, *however imaginary, is not a whimsical or arbitrary construct. The viewer builds the* fabula *on the basis of prototype schemata (identifiable types of persons, actions, locales, etc.), template schemata (principally the 'canonic' story), and procedural schemata (a search for appropriate motivations and relations of causality, time, and space). To the extent that these processes are intersubjective, so is the* fabula *that is created.*

(Bordwell, 1985: 49)

So, although we create the *fabula* for ourselves, how we do so is constrained by the intersubjective nature of our schemata. Film relies on recognisable codes and conventions to narrate story information and we understand these conventions partly because they can draw upon specific, shared ways of understanding the world. We can think of our schemata as a framework for perceiving the world and these apply in all areas of the media. So, when faced by a newspaper story, a radio news bulletin or a feature film, we already have a set of preconceptions which we bring to the text. Importantly, this set of preconceptions has an important determining function on how we perceive the world. In short, meaning making is a social process, rather than a matter of individual whim.

Syuzhet
The *syuzhet* is the actual *arrangement and presentation* of the *fabula* in the film. The *syuzhet* is a *system* because it arranges elements – the story events – according to specific principles.

This leads us to ask a straightforward question. If the *fabula* is not a material part of the film, what do we call the material elements that allow us to construct the *fabula*? The plot is used to narrate the material for our *fabula* construction. Again the Russian Formalists developed a term for plot: *syuzhet* that we can understand in relation to film.

The concept of *syuzhet* is useful because it allows us to analyse the elements of a media form like film, which the consumer organises into a story. Of course, we should consider also the degree to which this idea aids our understanding of other forms, but there are three important principles that relate the *syuzhet* (plot) to the *fabula* (story).

1. Narrative 'logic'

When we construct the *fabula* in our heads, we perceive a set of events and construct relations between them. These relations are generally assumed to be *causal* (one element explains or leads to another). The *syuzhet* (plot) can assist this sense making by implying that events *are* causal and linear. But the *syuzhet* can also arrange events so as to block or complicate causal relations. Maybe an example would be useful here.

Aliens (dir. Cameron, 1986) is a film about, well, aliens. But it is the intention of the film-maker to build suspense, tension and anxiety among audience members. This is how the pleasures of such films are generated, and complicating the *syuzhet* is a good way to do this. For example, the *syuzhet* offers numerous 'false scares' to the spectator. We assume that the door opening or the tap on the shoulder will preface the arrival of the alien. Of course, they don't always, but this complication of the *syuzhet* is an essential feature of horror and thriller films. The actual *fabula* that we construct may be relatively straightforward (Phew! It was only one of the heroes after all behind the door!), but the journey to that construction is made deliberately more complex by the contradictory inference we make from the *syuzhet* cues. The ability of the *syuzhet* to deliberately mislead or complicate should alert us to the complexity of narrative and narration in film.

The *syuzhet* of a film is often far more complex than the *fabula* we construct as spectators. If this were not so, films would be dull, literal affairs. The development of ever more complicated *syuzhet* has allowed the pleasures of cinema to become far more complicated in turn. The *fabula* we construct around movies such as *Jaws* (dir. Speilberg, 1975), *Casablanca* (dir. Curtiz, 1942), *Se7en* (dir. Fincher, 1995), *The Sixth Sense* (dir. Shyamalan, 1999) and *Rear Window* (dir. Hitchcock, 1954) may still be fairly simple. But the twists and complications of the *syuzhet* serve to heighten our pleasure.

2. Time

The *syuzhet* can encourage us to construct events in any sequence; it can also suggest events are happening over any time span (a duration of hours, days, or even decades). Again, as with narrative logic, the organisation of time by the *syuzhet* can be used to assist or block our *fabula* construction. The representation of time has altered as film rhetoric has changed and developed. How time is represented by the *syuzhet* may also be influenced by genre codes and conventions and may even differ between individual films.

While films may often appear to be linear in organisation – i.e. they proceed to outline events chronologically – they do not always do so, sometimes adding to our pleasure and confusion. As the film-maker Jean-Luc Godard has said, in response to the argument that films should have a beginning, a middle and an end, 'Yes, but not in that order.' The disruption of the 'natural' order of time has proven useful to art cinema of the kind produced by Godard, challenging our habitual pleasures and sense of the world. But such disruption is also in evidence in more mainstream films, such as *Pulp Fiction* (dir. Tarantino, 1994) and *Memento* (dir. Nolan, 2000). The latter film is actually played out with the scenes arranged in reverse order. While it is not unusual in films to have flashbacks (also known as analepsis), flash*forwards* (prolepsis), although uncommon, are not unknown. The US TV series *Lost* has made use of flashforward devices in order to trick its audiences and add to its enigmatic development, so engendering audience loyalty.

Likewise, time can be slowed down – literally via slow-motion techniques and, more recently, 'bullet-time' technologies, as pioneered in *The Matrix* (dir. Wachowski and Wachowski, 1999). Slow motion involves the shooting of more frames per second than the usual 24 in celluloid film. 'Bullet time', used so effectively in the fight scenes in *The Matrix* and many films thereafter, uses upwards of 12,000 frames per second! Speeding things up involves shooting *fewer* frames per second but projecting them at normal speed. During the early period of film-making, film was shot at 16 frames per second and often, when such material is shown nowadays, it seems jerky and laughable to modern audiences, as it is projected at the modern 24 frames per second.

Other rhetorical devices that manipulate time include the use of montage editing or even hackneyed devices such as showing the falling leaves of a paper calendar. In *Groundhog Day* (dir. Ramis, 1993), reporter Bill Murray is condemned to repeat a single day of his life over and over. The motif used to signal this return to the start of each day is a brief instant of black screen and a close-up of an alarm clock as it clicks on to 6 o'clock in the morning.

In terms of our example from above of *Aliens* (dir. Cameron, 1986), we can note how some story information and a sense of time passing is conveyed very quickly via editing – the journey across the galaxy by spaceship, for instance. Some scenes are more protracted, especially as tension mounts. In the penultimate scene of the film, Ripley (Sigourney Weaver) has to rescue the child Newt from the clutches of the monsters' lair before the alien planet explodes. This is played out against the sound of an inexorable computer countdown to destruction and the wait for a rescue spaceship to arrive.

3. Space

In order for us to construct our *fabula* we need a sense of the space in which events occur, although this can sometimes be vaguely delineated or abstract (Bordwell, 1985). Sometimes this is intentional; sometimes it is down to creative teams who have a poor command of the language of cinema; or sometimes there is just a simple problem with continuity!

In Chapter 4 on realism, we will outline in more detail the way in which film and other media delineate space and produce a coherent sense of a reality.

Using the concepts

The concepts of *syuzhet* and *fabula* (you can use plot and story just as easily) help us to understand how films are constructed and how we make meaning from them. By manipulating narrative logic, time and space, the *syuzhet* can block or assist our *fabula* construction. It should add an interesting dimension to your rhetorical and semiological analysis of complex texts like films if you can suggest how the *syuzhet* presents story information, and, more importantly, why the *syuzhet* presents information in this way and with what effect. Our next section raises some issues around such questions.

Narration – point of view (POV), perspective and closure

The sum of our approaches to rhetoric, semiology and meaning systems such as genres and narrative should draw our attention to the unnatural yet naturalised way of doing things. In pursuit of storytelling, the formal qualities of media forms such as film are often 'effaced', that is they seem to appear or move seamlessly in conveying story information to us. We are not asked to pay attention to the rhetorical organisation of meaning systems. This is partly by design – in most mainstream commercial films the aim is to entertain through the effectiveness and economy of conveying gripping stories in an involving, effective and affective manner. It is also achieved for us as viewers via convention – we're so accustomed to the dominant film style that we rarely pay it much heed – it seems 'natural'. The questions we need to ask in our analyses of all media texts are some of the most suggestive ones that narratological study raises:

- What point of view (POV) are we presented with?
- Who is telling the story or looking, explicitly or implicitly?
- What kind of position are we, as consumers of the text, being asked to take or being placed in?

The whole truth? Bryan Singer's *The Usual Suspects* revolves around the testimony of one Verbal Kint concerning the devilish Keyser Söze, a tale which may not be wholly reliable.

Answers to such questions offer insights into the pleasures of media consumption but also into more troubling aspects of social power and ideology (see Chapter 10). To illustrate our point in an obvious manner: some films utilise the device of a voice-over, a spoken commentary that qualifies what we see and hear in the diegesis. This may be explicitly identified as the insights of one of the characters who plays a part in the story or, sometimes, someone completely unconnected to the action and even *un*introduced, acting out the role of an abstract narrator. A good example here would be old Hollywood movies that sought to adapt the Bible. Off screen, venerable actors would read out sections from the various books over the actions depicted: 'In the beginning God created the heaven and the Earth', etc.

More often than not, the question of who or what is telling the story in a film is not obviously suggested, as most films do not use the device of a spoken narration. Nonetheless, it is possible to analyse texts in terms of the narrative perspectives they offer on the action as it unfolds. Sometimes they present an omniscient, 'God's eye' view of events. This simply means that, in what we see and hear, we are privy to all important information and scenes wherever they take place.

As we saw in our discussion of the plot of the fictional form, sometimes we are not privy to all of the information we need in order to make sense of the story unfolding before us, as information is delayed. Generally, in such situations we are following the story as it is motivated by characters themselves, who unravel the enigma before them. To some degree a text that offers us a mixture of both of these approaches is the US TV show *CSI*. Story information is withheld from us in this series, as we follow the police pathologists as they seek to solve murder mysteries. And yet the camera also takes us to places and presents us with scenarios that are impossible for anyone to actually view (e.g. the pathway of a bullet boring into a human body!).

How should we express this attention to narrative perspective in our analyses? In film studies it is conventional to take a cue from the *auteur* approach and say that it is the director who is guiding us. Thus, one might write:

> *In Spielberg's bravura war film* Saving Private Ryan *(dir. Speilberg, 1998), he takes us right into the thick of the Normandy landings and the heat of battle, with its noise, blood, sweat and fear.*

It is also equally acceptable to refer to the film itself as if it were a conscious ordering entity, for example:

> *The film places us on the Omaha beach, landing with the American forces, right among the explosions and screams of fear and pain. Occasionally we cut to the Wehrmacht machine gunners, anonymous and crouching in their pillboxes.*

Derived from narratological studies of literature, we can also ask questions of the reliability of the narrator or narration. This issue is one that can be illustrated with reference to the example of our Spielberg film (see the case study below).

Theorists interested in the social role of the media have used analyses of narrative perspective as the precept for more seriously intended insights into the structure of films. One element of film that we should pay attention to in this respect is that of the resolution or closure of individual films. On the whole, narrative film tends to tie up the loose ends of its story in re-establishing the status quo. In doing this, however (especially in Hollywood film), films present a remarkably limited amount of possible endings that offer a particularly satisfying and rounded view of reality. These repetitions can be interpreted as ideological in character as they sanction the means by which resolution is achieved (violence, individual action by 'mavericks' and so on).

The repetitive nature of narrative structure and resolution is rather self-consciously alluded to in Paul Verhoeven's science fiction blockbuster *Total Recall* (dir. Verhoven, 1990). The film plays upon the conceit of identity and the manipulation of the mind. The central character, played by Arnold Schwarzenegger, decides to take an adventurous 'holiday', which is actually a series of imaginary experiences implanted in his mind. He is told that, by the end of his experience (which may or may not be the story as it subsequently unfolds before us, further complicating the narrative and narrational cues), he will have discovered aliens, killed the bad guys and will 'get the girl'. Such romantic endings are those that are most often asserted in film. This is where the male and female leads are reunited or finally united, whatever the preceding drama (e.g. the end of the world in *Independence Day* (dir. Emmerich, 1996) or *Terminator 3* (dir. Mostow, 2003)). The assertion of the heterosexual romance has been troubling for feminist scholars, who have problematised the representation and role of women in the media in general and in narrative film in particular.

What about other media forms?

As we've tried to indicate with our examples at the outset of this part of the chapter, we should not imagine that narrative is only to do with film or TV forms. In such media, the story appears to unfold in linear sequence, unravelling in front of us, often in 'real' time (although we could include comic books in that category of sequential images and events). Narrative is also a way of understanding the organisation of most media forms, from still images to written texts, and even websites and online pages – here, we're thinking of hyperlinks and how they manage progression through various stages of information in a linear or non-linear manner. Photographs may serve to capture events at a particular moment and invite our interpretation in inferring narrative events.

Likewise, narrative is not merely a matter of *fiction* ('telling stories' might be mistaken here for the spinning of fabricated yarns). A sense of what narrative and narration is will aid in the understanding of the news, of documentaries, photography and 'written' journalism. We will explore these ideas further in subsequent chapters.

Case Study

Unreliable narrators

The opening sequence of *Saving Private Ryan* is *not* the famous and harrowing recreation of the wartime landing on the beaches of Normandy but a scene set in contemporary France amidst the Allied cemeteries. We follow an old man (who we infer is a war veteran) and his family among the serried ranks of graves. As he pauses before one headstone, the camera closes in on his eyes. Heralded by portentous martial music, an immediate cut takes us back 60 years to Omaha beach at dawn on 6 June 1944.

This is an intriguing ploy on Spielberg's part. For the period of the film after this cut – heralding a flashback – we follow Captain Miller (Tom Hanks) and his platoon of marines. Based on this visual cue, what appears to be a motivated cut from the old man to the war, following Miller's search for the eponymous Private Ryan, it is 'natural' to infer that the veteran is Miller. This premise is also aided by Hanks's casting in the key role of the designated saviour of Ryan, the use of many minor actors and the anonymity and randomness of the slaughter in the opening scenes, among which only Hanks has any recognisable status for viewers.

However, by the penultimate scene it transpires that Miller does not survive the war and that the veteran we began the film with is Ryan. We cut back to him at the graveside reflecting upon these events. Spielberg may be making a point about the sacrifice of war, but this is a troubling narrative device (albeit

a minor one compared with the visceral realism of the recreation of war). Spielberg has played a trick on us but, narratively speaking, if the idea of the cue (Ryan's eyes, the cut, the reverie) is valid, then how can Ryan recall these events in a motivated flashback? In the film, he himself is a paratrooper who landed inland, away from the notorious and nearly disastrous beach landings. Perhaps we are guided by a reminiscence on the part of Ryan who is evoking the sacrifice made by so many others – not just for him but for all those saved from Nazi domination.

Another film that also offers an instance of an *unreliable* narration, and an identifiable narrator who directs and motivates the narration once he is introduced, is *The Usual Suspects* (dir. Singer, 1995). The convoluted story of a failed heist and a criminal mastermind known as 'Keyser Söze' is related by one Verbal Kint (Kevin Spacey) to a US customs officer played by Chazz Palminteri.

A series of flashbacks and details, mainly prompted by Kint's testimony under questioning, weave a convincing web of conspiracy, treachery and discussion of whether or not the almost superhuman, and mythical, Kaiser Söze actually exists. By the end of the film, however, the investigating officer is confronted by evidence suggesting that the story that he, and we, have been told is a *complete* fabrication. There may be no Keyser Söze and, logically, nothing of the events that we have been privy to can be considered to be viable in the construction of a convincingly reliable *fabula*. Like the detectives, we've been hoodwinked!

These examples highlight the way in which narrative perspective and organisation can add to the rhetorical 'affect' of the text (the visceral thrills of the Spielberg film, the 'con' of Singer's).

Still images, as they are used in advertising and in support of journalism, should interest us too, in terms of narrative. In adverts, there is often an implicit 'before and after' concerning the use of products. Headache tablets are enlisted to counter disruptions to the body, freeing up individuals to go back to their lives. Deodorants counter antisocial smells, making individuals better people, more attractive to the opposite sex and so on. In the field of journalism, in newspapers specifically, reporters search for and relate stories. The press (and TV and radio news) has particular narrative devices and phrases, shorthand and perspectives that are worthy of investigation. We've already mentioned pop music as a narrative form, and almost any song you hear throughout the day can be interpreted for its narrative organisation, although do note that this is not simply a matter of interpreting the words as if they were a script.

Key theory

'The gaze'

Inspired by 'structuralist' approaches to narrative and ideology (see Chapter 10), Laura Mulvey provided one of the key theoretical insights into film and its power to order and place us as spectators in particular viewing positions. In an article entitled 'Visual pleasure and narrative cinema' (1975), Mulvey argues that women in mainstream narrative film are subject to two modes of structural treatment and oppression.

First, they are presented for the pleasure of the spectator, which implies a privileging of the masculine 'gaze'. The narrative flow of films can be interrupted or 'frozen' to allow for the invitation to the viewer to look at female characters, whose bodies can be 'cut up' by the camera for our scrutiny and appreciation. Women exist, therefore, to 'be looked at' by the mechanism of cinema.

Secondly, women are often the objects of narrative investigation, sometimes the very enigma that propels the plot, for example *There's Something About Mary* (dir. Farrelly and Farrelly, 1998), *Pretty Woman* (dir. Marshall, 1990), or *She's All That* (dir. Iscove, 1999).

We can observe in relation, here, that narrative cinema is character-led. The motivations of the characters propel the story along. In this 'realist' cinema, a male hero figure is usually the prime motivator of the narrative, or what we call the subject. Female characters tend to be constructed as objects to be looked at and/or investigated.

Narration, then, is not a simple or innocent matter. Narratives and narration within texts echo and reinforce key questions we can ask about media production and social relations in general:

■ Who has the power to narrate, to present images and stories?

■ Who has access to resources, and to editorial control in terms of including, foregrounding, obscuring and excluding certain facts or information?

■ Who or what is foregrounded? Who or what is marginalised?

■ Who triumphs and who is punished in stories?

Case Study

Photography as narrative

From its inception, and even to the present day, photography has drawn upon a long pictorial tradition of narrative creativity and an understanding on the part of consumers that images tell stories. Images similar to this can be found in many family collections and archives such as the Ernest Dyche Collection held at the Birmingham City Central Library Archives in the UK. Dyche had a photographic practice in Birmingham in the 1950s and was patronised by the first wave of commonwealth immigrants from the West Indies and Asia. Individuals and their families had their portraits taken, dressed up in their finest clothes, not only to record themselves for themselves but to send images 'home' in order to signal their success and the prosperous life forged in the UK. Such images invite questions along the lines of: who are these people, where are they from and what are they up to? What did they do next? Incidentally, Dyche's images endure because he kept a copy of everything he made for his clients.

Source: TopFoto

While photographs capture a movement in 'media res' they invite interpretations in terms of the narrative they present – however posed the situation.

Source: Getty Images

When and where was this image taken? How are these people related? What brought them to this spot and what became of them?

Bringing genre and narrative together

We have now considered two major concepts in aiding our sense of how media make meaning. Genre and narrative are clearly recognisable – familiar but complex ideas. For us as media scholars these provide tools that, in conjunction with those of rhetoric and semiology, will allow us to produce sophisticated textual analyses. One thing to consider, again, here is that such analyses should always begin with the text as a whole. There is no point in bringing a list of tools to systematically dismantle our object of scrutiny: remember, we know what texts mean – we're interested in exploring *how* they mean. Building upon this presumption, we can of course read more deeply into texts to see that they do not just tell us about the stories and information they present ('boy meets girl', 'president to start war', 'maniac loose in girls' dormitory'). The very presentation, repetition, conventions and ordering of texts has something to tell us about the myths and ideas we live by. Thus, our tools are there to aid any argument we wish to bring to bear about such ideas concerning the social role of media. These will certainly be borne out as we turn to the issue of representation in the next chapter.

Overall, then, our task is not merely to describe but to interpret. The point of any analysis, therefore, is to have a point!

Case Study

Generic hybridity and narrative structure

The notorious and highly successful film *Blair Witch Project* (dir. Myrick and Sanchez, 1999) offers an interesting case study for bringing together genre and narratological study. Ostensibly, the film offers a story within a story. It tells of a group of student film-makers who set out to produce a documentary about the legend of the so-called 'Witch' associated with the Maryland town of Burkittsville, formerly Blair. The three members of the documentary crew go missing in the Maryland woods and later, so the film claims, the footage they shot is found and reassembled into the film we are watching.

Generically, the film is a horror film. It could be said to belong to a subgenre of suspenseful, supernatural, occult-type tales such as *The Exorcist* (dir. Friedkin, 1973) at one extreme and *The Haunting* (dir. de Bont, 1999) at the other. That said, it bears a remarkable similarity to a film called *The Last Broadcast* (dir. Avalos

and Weiler, 1998) and, in turn, you will find that *The Collingswood Story* (dir. Costanza, 2002) is 'inspired' by both. Subsequent films of this type include *Paranormal Activity* (dir. Peli, 2007), *Cloverfield* (dir. Reeves, 2008) and *Apollo 18* (dir. Lopez-Gallego, 2011) However, if *The Blair Witch Project* is a horror film, many of the key features we would associate with the genre are absent. There is no creepy music (no music at all in fact), no ghost, no realisation of 'fantastic/supernatural' incidents via special effects or make-up, there is no evident 'gore' and not really many rhetorical shocks in terms of sudden events in the progress of the story. There isn't even a 'witch' to speak of, that we see (although we may infer her presence in the story).

As a horror film, the feature relies upon many implied events and the creation of a sense of unease; it is often psychologically unsettling. Rhetorically, in terms of its stylistic features, the film appears to be a documentary, very much in keeping with a tradition of non-fictional film-making and, more recently, reality TV (the acting is largely improvised). It utilises direct-to-camera address on video and black-and-white film stock, mixing registers and references to 'realism', doing all that it can to connote that the events portrayed really did happen in this way. It relies very much on the 'less is more' premise in producing affect but also in conveying realism. TV camera crews that are present at news events, despite their efforts, do not always get perfect pictures or even a sense of what it is that is happening; often the authenticity of the pictures, however indistinct, is enough to underwrite the testimony of the reporter who is there to interpret and describe events for us. In using the motif or cue of a crew making a documentary, much of the film is structured as an investigation, the pursuit of the enigma of the Blair Witch. However, the orderly process of this investigation, apparently reassembled for our scrutiny, soon disintegrates into a panicked mess as the students get lost in the woods and suffer a series of threatening events.

Establishing a *meta*textual 'realism', the film benefited from its low-budget status and lack of significant achievement among its young cast and crew, who were all 'unknowns'. There was a creative approach to marketing in trailing the filmic story events via a TV documentary (or straight-faced 'mockumentary'), as well as a website devoted to the 'actual' legend of the 'Blair Witch' (an invented tradition that the cast themselves were encouraged to believe in – see www._blairwitch._com/). These supplementary texts made use of fabricated police reports about the disappearance of the student film-makers and the discovery of the footage. The website was created well in advance of the distribution deal that the film-makers won, which turned a 'no-budget' film into one of the most profitable of all time.

Even if we did not have this knowledge, and even if *The Blair Witch Project* was not discovered to be a fiction, it is susceptible to the kind of narrative and generic deconstruction that should make us suspicious at least. If we were to take a formalist approach, the tale, in its most basic structure, adheres to that of a classic cautionary fairy tale (which is what horror films are in essence), in terms of its progress, motifs and locations. Three students (the children) venture into the woods in search of knowledge of a witch (the quest), whereupon they become lost and persecuted, finally finding a house in the darkest part of the woods where they meet their end.

What we can conclude is that the film, as a genre piece, builds upon some of the generic conventions, and certainly uses particular types of narrative elements that are very old and very familiar, even if it narrates them in a very contemporary manner. What is interesting is that, as part of a genre – in film at least – that stretches back a century, we can note both that the genre has been remarkable persistent in its appeal and motifs *and* that it continues to change! Changes in the horror film have been closely linked to changes in society and something that you might usefully consider is the degree to which such films tell us about our social outlook and self-image (see Wells, 2000).

Summary

Exploring genre and narrative

In this chapter we have considered some of the ways in which meaning is organised in media texts and how media scholars have labelled these and understand their function. We began with an examination of the different types or genres of media texts. We saw how the idea of genre locates texts which are recognisable because of their similarities (characters, themes, settings and so on) but which are, of necessity, also different. This related to the dynamic nature of such forms but we also noted the way in which certain genres have become exhausted or died out just as genres mix, merge and, indeed, how new ones emerge. We saw how these characteristics related to the functions of genres for both producers and consumers. For us in the audience, genre is important in signalling pleasure and expectation but as we saw this is also, potentially, a limiting idea in terms of the social values presented and repeatedly asserted in texts.

In the second part of this chapter we explored narratology – the study of narrative or story organisation and how this relates to genre. Clearly, particular types of story recur in particular types of genres. Via the work of theorists such as Vladimir Propp, we examined the importance of narrative structures and how, at base, stories and motifs are organised in a surprisingly repetitive manner. Our exploration looked at narrative for how it organised and revealed story information through plotting. We saw how perspective, time, space and closure are all issues that we should pay attention to in media texts in order to understand the nuanced way in which meaning is made. We noted too that narratology, in looking at stories and questions of perspective, is not confined to fictional forms but that genres such as news and other types of current affairs forms are organised in similar ways. The consequences of such insights for understanding the social role of the media in presenting the world to us, offering perspectives and implicit interpretation, make these approaches vital.

You should now evaluate what you are able to do as a result of this chapter. If you have followed this chapter through, engaged with the activities and thought about the issues covered you should be able to:

■ Outline the key terms used in the analyses of genre and narrative. If you are not clear, go back and re-examine these terms and what they mean. If you need to, you might seek out the insights of others through the further reading.

■ Apply the ideas of genre and narrative to the interpretation of a variety of media texts from different media sectors. It is important that you test out these ideas and what they mean to you in use by exploring them across forms other than the examples we've used in this chapter.

■ Draw upon and synthesise a range of analytical skills to produce a detailed reading of the styles and meaning of media texts. The ideas in this chapter are meaningful when used in tandem with the rhetorical and semiological tools previously introduced. These are collective resources that if you are able to draw upon confidently will support the kinds of insights you are able to make into media texts.

When doing genre analysis it is important to bear in mind that genres are not static. They are marked by patterns of repetition and difference and they do change over time. Your own analysis will be able to offer comparisons between texts within a genre and also between genres but this will only be meaningful with some attention to the contexts in which this change and difference is located.

Ultimately, the sum of all of the contributions of the various theorists and approaches to genre and narrative should cement the ongoing argument in these chapters. There is nothing natural or given about media forms. They are susceptible to analysis, interpretation and understanding beyond mere acceptance of such a proposition, and we can move towards a greater degree of media literacy and reflexivity.

As you move on, the quality of your own analysis will be crucially determined by the extent to which you are able to critically engage with popular texts and the context in which they are produced. Not in the terms of whether they are good or bad – of course their effectiveness matters – but in how they work to organise our expectations, to provide us with pleasure and to mobilise particular ideologies and myths.

Doing media studies

Exploring genre and narrative

This final activity offers a way of exploring the application of genre and narrative theory to media forms in more depth. It will allow you to consolidate the insights and explorations of this chapter.

Choose a text from each of the following media areas:

■ website,

■ newspaper,

■ print advertisement,

■ pop song.

Identify the specific subgenre that each of your chosen texts belongs to (within newspapers there are lots of different types of article, while advertisement genres are often determined by the product). Itemise the generic features of each of your texts, as well as some features of the wider genre to which they belong that they might not exhibit. Explore the extent to which these features present a narrative, the way that it is plotted and the rhetorical devices used to narrate and convey the story told. Evaluate the extent to which the concept of narrative is useful to explaining the meaning of such non-filmic media forms.

Further reading

Altman, R. (1999) *Film/Genre*, London: British Film Institute.
A commonly referenced title when discussing film genre. Altman looks at how both audiences and producers make use of genre but is particularly interested in how different groups apply different meanings to genres. Previous works in this field had assumed film audiences to be passive yet Altman proposes that they are active in their consumption of film genres. Altman discusses how genres are born, how they develop, how they become mixed and also how to study them. Examples from numerous different genres are provided. This is the starting point for genre for the new media scholar.

Bordwell, D. and Thompson, K. (2003) *Film Art: An Introduction*, Boston: London, McGraw-Hill. Now in its eighth edition, *Film Art* is considered to be the most worthy starting point for film scholars as it provides an introduction to the key concepts required when studying and analysing film. Part three is entirely devoted to the study of genres and how they can be analysed. Detailed examples of the documentary, experimental and animated film genres are provided. No serious scholar of film should be without this important work.

Borthwick, S. and Moy, R. (2004) *Popular Music Genres: An Introduction*, Edinburgh: Edinburgh University Press.
Borthwick and Moy offer an introduction to popular music genre. The book takes a 'unidisciplinary' approach to studying music genre, providing textual analyses of the following 11 specific music genres: soul, funk, psychedelia, progressive, punk, reggae, synthpop, heavy metal, rap, indie and jungle. In addition, the context of these music genres is studied in order to gain an understanding of the historical importance of genre. Though some genres are neglected at the expense of others it still offers the reader detailed critical analysis of music genre.

Giltrow, Janet and Stein, Dieter (eds.) (2009) *Genres in the Internet: Issues in Genre*, John Benjamins Publishing, Philadelphia. This book offers a range of essays on the generic challenges of online sites such as blogs and other aspects of computer-mediated communication. It is useful in framing these analyses with concepts and frameworks drawn from rhetorical studies and in attempting a snapshot of the dynamic nature of the web and its changing forms, bringing well-established ideas to bear upon the core communicative aspects of online spaces.

Murray, J. (1998) *Hamlet on the Holodeck: The Future of Narrative in Cyberspace*, Cambridge, Mass.: MIT Press.
Murray explores the way in which digital technology challenges traditional narrative organisation. She focuses on the nature of interactive technologies and the new spaces afforded by hypertext links. This is a highly theoretical work in many respects but one that attempted to get to grips with the ramifications of the internet when it was still in its infancy. New researchers will find it useful to consider how their own media consumption might confirm and update some of the insights in this book.

Neale, S. (1999) *Genre and Hollywood*, London: Routledge.
Along with Altman (1999), Neale revived the study of film genre in this accessible work that serves as a comprehensive introduction to the field of film genre in Hollywood cinema. The first chapter offers definitions of genre, introducing relevant concepts. Most scholars will find Neale's detailed analyses of major Hollywood film genres to be of great interest, particularly focusing on the problematic categorising of the film noir genre. Like Altman, Neale is keen to stress the importance of genre when considering the economic purpose it serves for major Hollywood studios.

CHAPTER 3

(with contributions from Faye Davies)

Media representations

Asking questions about representations

The UK's travelling community has been the object of intense media an public interest as a result of the Channel 4 TV series *My Big Fat Gypsy Wedding*. It is a reality TV series (documentary seems a passé way of describing its entertainment objectives) which explore the nuptial rituals of Irish travellers in the UK. The series title references the Hollywood comedy of American-Greek mores *My Big Fat Greek Wedding* (dir. Joel Zwick, 2002).

A sense of responses to the series and its depiction of an often already vilified yet under-represented and unheard social group can be garnered in some newspaper column and blog headlines:

Big Fat Gypsy Weddings under fire for showing eight-year-olds 'pole dancing': Controversial show Big Fat Gypsy Weddings has come under fire for showing 'horrific' images of girls as young as six provocatively dancing in skimpy clothes and wearing full make-up. (*Metro*)

My Big Fat Gypsy Wedding claims to celebrate a unique traditional culture. Pull the other one, it makes Jordan look classy! (Jan Moir, *Daily Mail*)

Does My Big Fat Gypsy Wedding Spread Lies? (Jezebel.com)

Gypsy wedding show 'a big fat lie about us'. (*Cambridge News*)

Travellers' Times identified some of the problems with the series, notably its confusion over the distinctions between Romany peoples and travellers of Irish descent. Furthermore:

From Romany Gypsies outraged at Channel 4 describing the sexual assault of girls as a Gypsy tradition, to howls of protest from mums worried about kids as young as six getting spray tans, the series has opened a much needed nationwide debate on how the Gypsy and Traveller community is shown in the media.

Far from being a 'secretive community' Romany Gypsy people in particular are making their feelings plain on Facebook, Twitter, the Channel 4 website and by officially complaining to OFCOM the government's media regulator which has legal powers to punish Channel 4 if it decides it has broken its broadcasting code.

(Source: http://www.travellerstimes. org.uk/list.aspx?c=00619ef1-21e2- 40aa-8d5e-f7c38586d32f&n= ab717302-92fb-4487-82b1- 9f70934969b3)

Was the TV series manipulative and deceitful? Or is the issue one of interpretation, emphasis and perspective? How was this presentation related to the way in which newspapers responded and facilitated prodigious comments and a wider debate about this social group and its representation?

Perhaps any investigation of this subject would, in the first instance, need to survey the full range of reports about travellers (and how they are labelled as travellers, tinkers, Romani, gypsies etc.) and evaluate whether instances of such 'negative reporting' outweigh the positive or dispassionate ones. We could also turn to the readers of the press and the public at large to examine their perceptions of this social group. Perhaps we should ask the travellers themselves about how they feel about such reports. Either way, this case and the kinds of questions arising signal the issues surrounding representation in media which are dealt with in this chapter.

What we will do in this chapter

In this chapter we will develop our concern with media texts and their contexts by thinking about the issue of representation in general and focusing on it in particular through the representations of social groups and individual figures. This leads us to a discussion of stereotyping. We will explore the origins and function of stereotyping in media forms and some of the complex issues around such depictions: how they tell us about social relations as well as presenting questions about the 'politics' of representation as they pertain to the responsibilities of media producers and the role of media companies. We will further develop the issue of representations of specific social groups to examine the meanings of individuality as depicted in the guise of media stars, personalities and celebrities, and what these suggest to us about the social values embodied in our encounter with such depictions.

By the end of this chapter you should be able to:

- Identify and outline issues involved in thinking about representation and media.
- Define the concepts of representation, stereotyping and associated subcategories.
- Deploy rhetorical, semiological, genre and narrative skills to analysing media representations.
- Engage with debates around the depiction of individuals and social groups in media.

KEY TERMS: ▶ archetype; the burden of representation, celebrity; class; content analysis; gender; queer theory; race and ethnicity; representation; sexuality; star; stereotype.

Doing media studies

Getting started

Think about any media text that you have consumed today. What kinds of individuals and/or groups feature in your text ? These might include TV presenters from the news, participants in online forums, performers in music videos, as well as figures and groups in fictional and other factual forms. How would you categorise the individuals and/or groups depicted? What kinds of ideas and feelings about them do you have as a result of your media consumption?

Conceptualising and defining representation

In the modern world the majority of people gain the majority of their information and knowledge about the world through mass media texts. We find out about what is going on through a variety of media sources – Twitter, the TV news, documentaries, newspaper front pages, magazine gossip columns, web pages, phone text updates, RSS feeds and so on. We also find out about individual people (the ordinary and the extraordinary), about 'other' social and national groups (Norwegians, asylum seekers, paedophiles, 'Gangstas', Christians – supposing you don't fall into one, or all, of these groups already) and their environments through our media sources. If you don't already live there then you might access inner-city America – 'the ghetto' – in rap music, or Afghanistan's Helmand province in news reports, indicating this experiential aspect of the media.

In fact it is possible to feel very knowledgeable and educated about the world as a result of our media consumption. However, what is the nature of this knowledge? How reliable or accurate is it? How informed and enlightened are we exactly in this mediatised and information-saturated age? To what degree are we asked to engage with the processes and means by which information comes to us and to be critical about it and this process? Who is responsible for such information? These are extensions of the issues that we dealt with in preceding chapters via our examination of media rhetoric (choice of words, presentation, edit, perspective, etc.), narrative organisation (how story and plot are ordered), and how the media signifies, which we examined using the tools of semiology. The point here is that while media forms may have their own rhetoric and language that position us as audience members for entertainment purposes, they are not divorced from the social, cultural, political and historical contexts of their making. This is why representation is such an important area for consideration. It informs our outlook on various groups and cultures – our own and those of others – potentially in turn affecting how social relations are played out.

If we turn to dictionary definitions of the group of words around the verb 'to represent' we come across several distinct meanings. First, there is represent as meaning 'equivalence' or 'corresponding to'. This sense would most obviously fit one of the semiological terms we encountered previously: 'icon' (see p. 59). This relates to the types of relationship between any sign and its referent as outlined by Peirce (p. 51): iconic signs look like the thing that they represent. Thus, a stick man on a toilet door represents the men who are directed to use those facilities. A picture of Brad Pitt looks like, well, Brad Pitt. The point is of course that such a picture is not literally the thing it represents despite our tendency automatically to say of such an image, 'It's Brad Pitt.' The distinction serves to remind us all the time of the process of mediation.

This sense of representing as equivalence or correspondence would also have relevance to thinking semiologically about the symbolic relationship of any sign and its referent (p. 60). As we saw in our previous chapters this symbolic relationship refers to an arbitrary but conventionally agreed one. The amalgam of shapes or the letters CAT, in English at least, refer to a four-legged furry mammal or the idea of CAT, but there's nothing about such an animal that necessitates this label. Likewise, we generally accept that our own names (Paul Long and Tim Wall, the main authors of this book for instance) are labels that correspond to our status as actually existing individuals – they 'represent' us in signing photographs for our readers, in letters or maybe in leaving graffiti on a toilet door.

Another sense of the word concerns the idea of something or someone acting as a proxy or substitute for something or someone else. In relation to this sense, there is the idea of representative as agent or delegate – such as an MP, district councillor or congressman. The interesting aspect of this meaning is that in certain democracies we often find ourselves with representatives whom we did not vote for. The democratic system tends to favour the majority view, whether in one voting region or at a national level. It may happen therefore that your representative in this sense speaks on your behalf but evinces ideas and qualities you actively dislike and disagree with. Campaigns against the war in Afghanistan by US-led coalition forces in recent years for instance have engendered protests against governments that are expressed in the phrase 'not in my name!'.

Across media forms we find this sense of agency or proxy at work when a newspaper speaks of the interests of its readers, or when a radio newscaster asks of a reporter in the field or an interviewee 'what our listeners will want to know is… '. Here, as a self-proclaimed 'voice of the people' or a public servant, media professionals and organs such as newspapers operate in the role of representative of a community of interest even if it doesn't always accord with our individual perspective or range of preferences.

A further meaning of represent that we should remind ourselves of concerns the way in which things or individuals are deemed to typify or epitomise particular qualities, for example, 'Spanish tennis player Rafael Nadal embodies the virtues of sportsmanship' or 'The European Parliament tells us everything about what is wrong/right with the EU.' To extend this sense, we can talk of the way in which the songs of the Beatles 'represent' the 1960s for many of us who were and who were not there; Simon Cowell 'represents' all that is bad about the modern recording industry; movies such as *Transformers* 'represent' the modern Hollywood blockbuster ethos; the *National Enquirer* in the US most consistently 'represents' the style of the tabloid newspaper.

Representation

To represent something is to describe or depict it, to call it up in the mind by description, portrayal or imagination. To represent also means to symbolise, to stand for, to be a specimen of or to substitute for.

Let us pull together a general definition of **representation** then that will serve our purposes in thinking of media texts in this way.

We should also consider a related term that will become more important in our next chapter on reality media. This concerns the limited concept of *re*-presentation – to present again. 'Realist' actuality media such as documentary forms like the news and other forms of reportage in audio-visual media such as broadcasting and photography as well as print journalism are understood to tell us about the world directly. However, any form of representation can never provide a full picture or understanding of what is being *re*-presented. Media forms, however factual or however much invested in truth, 'realism' or authenticity, for instance, can never be fully faithful to subject matter if only due to the nature of the decisions made in their production.

Representation in particular – individuals and groups

In media studies the issue of representation is often dealt with quite specifically in a focus on the portraits of individuals and particular social groups. For instance, Liz Wells in a popular introductory work on photography defines representation in this fashion as 'ways in which individuals, groups or ideas are depicted' (Wells, 2004: 295). Wells's deployment of the term in this way indicates a consciousness of the lack of 'innocence' involved in such depictions. By innocence Wells is thinking along the same lines as us when we 'problematise' notions of 'transparency' in media depiction and the political, social grounding of representations. Our opening example of the depiction of travellers in the UK media indicates some of what is at stake if we think of the hostile affects such coverage might generate.

Let's imagine some typical representations and the issues raised around the depiction of individuals. Imagine a male newsreader from TV, shots of the missing child Madeleine McCann from the posters that have been sent around the world calling for her return, a CD cover featuring Elton John or George Michael. Here we're thinking of images but we

Thinking aloud

The idea of representation can be quite an abstract idea. More often than not, when confronted by imaginative content in forms such as film, TV or even popular music, we are confronted by representations of a world not taken to be necessarily or actually existing 'out there' – it is something fictional, fantastic and maybe idealised. In the case of popular songs it is often impressionistic, concerning aspects of romance, love and loss. In fact people sometimes feel disappointed that they cannot reach the standard set by such representations in the reality of their own experiences ('why can't real life be like it is in songs?'). Nonetheless, even in the most extreme fantasies there are still recognisable elements of our experience of the world as it actually is. Fantasies like horror stories and science fiction tales are anchored in familiar aspects of the world even when they break all the rules (serial killers are just so hard to kill!). *Star Wars* features human beings and aliens who act and speak rather like we do, remarkably so given that the films take place 'a long time ago, in a galaxy far, far away'.

We can refer back to our discussions in the preceding chapter of media language in order to ratify a general point about representation in terms of media as a form of language. Media forms represent the image of the world to us (iconically) and ideas about the world (symbols). However, all representations, in media or elsewhere, contain only a fraction of what could have been presented. Thus, we can claim that representations are selective in their portrayals (factual or otherwise in terms of a fictional milieu) and are thus 'abstractions' in the way in which they work at extricating, emphasising or inflecting limited elements or characteristics of what is on show or known. The evening news, for instance, makes selections of 'what matters in the world' and then gives us a very limited view of things through the reporter's viewpoint, other commentators, witnesses and so on. While editors seek to give us the 'big picture' this can never be more than partial.

We suggest then that it is best to think of the way in which media forms can be thought to actively construct their worlds. This applies to 'fact'-based media as well as to imaginative forms. To work with an idea of media construction, however, is not to suggest that media representations are as a whole 'false' or conspiratorially misleading or intentionally partial in what they say: far from it! We do rely upon the integrity of media to tell us about the world in the same way as we rely upon books, letters or word of mouth; we just need to attend to the manner in which all information never comes to us 'innocently' or innocent of interest or perspective. This is important for how we think about media forms in general but also for the very specific ways in which studies of representation have understood depictions of particular groups in society.

should not forget that representation takes place through all forms of media work: verbal rhetoric – words used in reports, scripts, jokes and so on, as well as via the modes in which those words are presented, inflected and delivered. The same goes for popular music in terms of lyrics, delivery and, of course, the music itself, which also works as a representational, rhetorical form.

The instances of representation that are suggested here are drawn from a variety of visual media sources. They are images of men and women in different roles and contexts: real people in the role of real people (inhabiting their own identities as presenters or as the objects of news, reality TV, etc.) as other images might be of real people in their roles as actors representing other, fictional individuals. We can agree on the straightforwardness of the claim that here is a picture of Mrs X, Ms Y or Mr Z, etc. Semiologically speaking, images are iconic (the representation looks like the thing it represents), working at the denotative, analogical, literal level. Yet, at a further level of signification we could claim (subject to detailed analysis and argument) that such figures as represented serve to 'connote' (p. 58) further levels of meaning and more complex and generalised ideas – aspects of contemporary society or culture. This then is the level of the symbolic level of representation.

We'll unpack these ideas in due course but we can gesture towards these complexities and connotations (which you can develop further) by offering some possible labels for the associational, connotative level of the images suggested: black middle-class professional man; gay man; imperilled child. While these representations are diverse they obviously do not reflect the full demographic of each basic group we might label in our society. Nor are they representative of media representations as a whole as we have made an arbitrary selection here to make a point.

In contemporary society such representations mediate and contribute to the construction of our knowledge and understanding of that wider society and all the individuals and groups that exist within it – including those that we ourselves think we belong to (Spanish people, football fans, music lovers, democrats, etc.). We even accept representations of cultures we have never been involved with and construct our understanding of them from media representations. These may be positive or they may be negative, inflecting in turn our disposition towards such groups, as our example of asylum seekers suggests. Media representations of groups are not independent of the rest of society and neither are they and what they represent unchanging (superficially at least), nor do they go unchallenged. This is not to suggest that they get 'better', more accurate or necessarily less offensive over time to those who are offended by them. Often such representations are lauded or vilified for the way in which they are considered to be positive or negative, 'realistic' or 'fabrications'. People and individuals who are being represented often have something to say about their depiction although the extent to which they are heard is another matter (imagine whether or not 'gypsies' complained to the newspapers about the series and stories referred to at the start of this chapter).

Why representations merit such responses, their implications and how we can make sense of them concerns us as we proceed. In drawing attention to how the media make use of and construct representatives we recognise how we ourselves categorise and identify social groups in particular and recognisable ways. To categorise individuals means generalising about them, identifying them as part of a wider class or group of things, people, etc. who possess some quality and qualities of experience in common – to themselves and to those who perceive them. To talk of the working class, for instance, identifies people by their economic status in the labour market; to talk of gay women identifies a

Trevor MacDonald: UK TV newsreader, middle-class, professional man. What else does this media figure 'represent'?

Source: Reuters

Source: Simone Joyner/Getty Images

Elton John, rock star in performance. What other ideas does this media figure 'represent'?

Source: Getty Images

The campaign to find Madeleine McCann. What do such images come to represent beyond the literal identification of this lost child?

group by both biological status and sexual orientation; to talk of the French identifies people by their geographical origin, nation and culture. To cite such categories, however objective we aim to be, begins to call up a range of ideas – connotations and myths – about these groups that are at the same time diffuse *and* limited.

To take the French, for instance, from the perspective of the UK invites positive connotations of a sophisticated culture (food, language, literature, romantic lovers) and of the rather ridiculous but repeated image of beret-wearing, Breton shirt-wearing bicycle riders with a string of onions around the neck. This is clearly an immediately limited idea but one that is recognisable from the circulation of signs in British society and their associations. The French have their own versions and labels for the British encapsulated in the label 'Les rosbifs' (roast beefs) which reduces a culture to a meat dish. (The Portuguese use 'bife' or 'steak' as a label for the same group.) This nickname does perhaps have something to do with the perennial image of 'John Bull' and his preferences while another label, 'Les fuck-offs', says something about the vulgar behaviour of Brits abroad as well as something about European perceptions of British attitudes to foreigners and Europe in particular. Such positive and negative labels and the ideas behind them are quite common in everyday usage and in the way in which media representations work as selective abstractions. These are manifest in the related concepts of archetype and stereotype.

Typing: archetype and stereotype

To refer to anyone as a 'type' is to define an individual by what they represent rather than for their unique qualities as individuals. Typification involves a form of shorthand, signified by appearance, behaviour, belief, etc. Anybody or anything can be dressed up or made to appear as a 'type' and we hear it particularly when reference is made to actors who are 'typecast' in particular roles. Such figures seem to evince a set of general conventions and expectations producers and consumers have about them as people as well as about society in general, i.e. that individuals can be recognised, categorised and limited in such a banal fashion.

In comparison, an archetype is a 'perfect' or idealised person or thing that exhibits certain core values and identities that offer a model or pattern for the way in which cultures are viewed. This ideal can be expressed as a positive or negative force. Pre-mass-media archetypal figures include the heroes, heroines and villains of mythology and ancient religions such as Hercules, Andromeda, Zeus and so on. Modern villains and heroes who epitomise the deep beliefs, values and preferences of society include figures such as Superman, Dracula or Sherlock Holmes. Time and again we see fictional figures as well as actual living individuals lauded as modern archetypes. Stereotypes by contrast seem more limiting in function and are often (although not always) negative.

Stereotype

Stereotyping is a process involving the expression of an exaggerated belief about a group that serves to qualify or justify the conduct towards that group of those who hold and express that belief.

We'll return to the **stereotype** but, for now, let us consider the archetype or 'ideal' as exemplified in the enduring figure of Superman whose cultural life encompasses his comic book origins, radio shows, TV programmes, films and records. The creation of Jerry Siegel and Joe Shuster, two young Jewish comic book creators in the 1930s, Superman evinces the idea of coming to America experienced by any other immigrant (he is an alien in the most literal sense in that he comes from outer space) and becoming the embodiment of America. His possible meanings are represented by his benign appearance and deeds, embodying 'truth, justice and the American way'. His very clothes, despite his origins in outer space, are indeed red, white and blue. Recent retellings of the story have Superman arriving on Earth, albeit landing in the Soviet Union and being raised as a good communist (Millar, 2004) or arriving in the UK and taking on the characteristics of the 'stiff-upper-lipped' English adopted culture (Johnson and Cleese, 2006)!

The distinction between archetype and the more familiar stereotype can sometimes seem blurred. This can be illustrated through a consideration of the popular and controversial music star 50 Cent (Curtis Jackson). Here is an extract from a newspaper feature on him which explicitly enlists the notion of the archetype:

> *The wealth of music Curtis Jackson released and his 2000 shooting conspired to turn 50 Cent the rapper into a local legend before his debut album had even been released. In some senses, he represents the latest incarnation of an archetype that crops up time and time again in popular music. Early blues singers often retold in song the story of the deadly confrontation between Billy Lyons and a pimp called Lee Shelton (known variously as Stagger Lee or Stagolee), two real-life characters from the Deep South whose 1895 shoot-out resulted in Lyons' death.*
>
> *In* Stagolee Shot Billy, *a book about the social history of the myth, writer Cecil Brown describes how Stagolee's persona as the 'bad black hero' feeds into our perception of characters as varied as Puff Daddy, OJ Simpson, Malcolm X and Huey Newton.*
>
> Chris Campion, 'Right on the money', *The Observer Music Monthly*, August 2005, p. 35.
> www.guardian.co.uk/music/2005/aug/21/popandrock2

This artist's genre of music – a stripped-down form of 'Gangsta Rap' – relating the travails of life for many African-Americans in urban America has been castigated for glorifying drug dealing and brutality. One theme of the criticism is that the cast of characters in the genre's recordings comprises a male group of 'niggas', 'pimps' and 'players' and a female group of 'bitches' and 'hos'. Taken as a partial and often offensive selection of African-Americans these representations then can be labelled with more pejorative intent as 'stereotypes'. For some people 50 Cent himself is a stereotype – at least in his media guise. (Representations are stereotypes, not people themselves – the distinction is an important one.) 'Fiddy's' image, like the cast of characters in his songs, is deeply objectionable to many not just because of a brutal 'realism' but because they repeat the limited range that has characterised representations of African-Americans in the mainly 'white' media.

A Frenchman by the name of Firmin Didot invented the term 'stereotype' in the nineteenth century. It derived from his printing practice and referred to an impression of an original piece of typography (where our word 'type' also comes from) used in the process of printing (a mode of reproduction) instead of the original. For our purposes the modern use of the term derives from the work of American theorist Walter Lippmann in his 1922 book *Public Opinion*. Sometimes, especially in reference to the media, we use the term in tandem with the damning label of cliché when making critical qualitative judgements – 'It was such a clichéd radio phone-in show, trawling out all of the usual stereotypical characters and opinions', etc. However, we more readily use the term to refer to impressions of individuals and groups. This is how we will anchor our definition.

Stereotypes: nature and function

Stereotypes are often, but not always, negative ascriptions and they tend to be limited in the range of meanings that they articulate. We could add that in this they are, like the more innocuous sense of 'typing', a form of shorthand, reducing the complexity of an individual, group or situation to a familiar and quickly understood and defining set of attributes. Ideas about the groups to which they refer are embodied and naturalised in media texts, in rhetorical manner and in narratives and generic conventions. They thus contribute to the way in which other groups understand and relate to those who are presented through such stereotypes.

If we suggest that stereotypes are usually more prevalent and readily associated with social groups who are in the minority in societies we can appreciate why those images and ideas about African-Americans from the gangsta rap of 50 Cent or asylum seekers from overseas mentioned above cause so much concern. We can add too that stereotypes are usually about those who are not just a minority but who have less power in society than the majority. In this way we can begin to think about how stereotypes work and where they come from as well as the various functions they serve.

According to Graeme Burton (Burton and Dimbleby, 1988: 70), it is the speed and intensity of the assumptions and predictions that are made about other persons on a slender basis that makes stereotyping so lethal and objectionable. However, given the limitations of media texts (or any representative form) in terms of the ability to be faithful to reality, stereotypes are sometimes seemingly inescapable and even necessary to media texts and the information and pleasure that we gain from them. There is a complication perhaps in that while some stereotypes seem so prevalent across media our perception of them is also conditioned by their currency in other sectors of society and other modes of communication. Racist and sexist stereotypes for instance pre-date mass media forms, occurring in religious tracts, paintings, drama, jokes, folk tales and so on. Most of us both recognise and may call on stereotypes (consciously or unconsciously) in a variety of situations. Jokes can depend upon stereotypes for their point and punchline ('There's these two rosbifs …'), they come to hand very easily in sporting competitions when passions and stakes run high ('The natural discipline of the Germans will be a force to contend with in this tournament') or when doing many everyday things such as driving ('Women drivers!'). The ubiquity of stereotypes does rather disguise their constructedness in media texts therefore, as we have a tendency to see them as natural, to an extent 'believing' in them.

We can identify a range of functions for stereotypes in media texts and relate them to broader social and historical contexts; however, that in part explains them and undermines their obviousness and our acceptance of them. On the one hand, they provide an ordering process in the face of the contingency and

Doing media studies

We don't need to be media students to recognise the concept of stereotype or instances of its manifestation and occurrence. It is one of those ideas that have become 'common sense' to a degree (although sometimes at the cost of clarity and precision, as we'll explore). Make a list of any *five* stereotypes from media that you can identify. Some are suggested in our 50 Cent example as pointers, but think about the cast of characters in a computer game such as the variations on *Grand Theft Auto*. Outline a list of characteristics for each one and an instance of their appearance in media.

Thinking aloud

It's just a joke?

The conjunction of stereotyping and driving motor cars is often an explicit feature of the BBC TV show *Top Gear*, indeed, it may be an aspect of the pleasure that many take in it. Presenters such as Jeremy Clarkson and James May appeal to many for their machismo and straight-talking manner, seemingly at odds with a contemporary landscape in which audiences, or those who claim to speak for them, are quick to take offence. In one 2011 edition, the presenters made disparaging remarks about Mexicans (repeating stereotypes that they were lazy and feckless), laughing that no one from the embassy in the UK was likely to complain as the ambassador would be asleep. However, the Mexican ambassador did complain, as did a number of others – 11 in total. While silence should not be taken as approval, there were plenty who complained in online forums of this situation and in favour of the presenters' use of 'humour'. These comments from the *Telegraph*'s website are typical:

11 viewers complained from an audience of millions . . . You know what, I am a london born man and I hate east enders for its stereo type cliche view of lundun tarn and I know it will offend me, so I am going to watch it, and then write in to complain of its content as offensive to londoners. The BBC should have apologised for this dark and violent soap being presented as 'drama' years ago . . .

At last some sanity coming back in a too PC world. welcome back Top Gear and lets have loads more controversial remarks. No one rapped virgin for having speedy gonzales, that advert was more racially stereoptyped than a joke said on top gear, albeit not a very good one. Get a sense of humour you miserable lot.

How far would you agree with such claims and instances in which the use of stereotypes is explained as a joke? Are there other instances where such stereotypes are regularly deployed in search of a laugh?

'messiness' of reality, offering a 'short cut' to meaning that nonetheless refers to 'the world', expressing something of the values and beliefs of those who hold the stereotype to be in some way indicative ('Yes, of course "they" are all like that, aren't they?'). Rhetorically and semiologically speaking, therefore, a stereotype functions metonymically as an index of a wider reality and set of values about the group the burden of which usually falls on a single figure. This is why they are subject to such fierce debate – on one hand vilified for their negative qualities and on the other hand dismissed as simple and expedient characters in dramas, comedies or reports where no 'offence' was intended.

We often think of stereotypes as in some way false, that they offer an inaccurate or misleading picture of individuals and social groups. However, the late media theorist Tessa Perkins (see below) argued that stereotypes are effective by virtue of the fact that they have some semblance to reality, that, however extreme or reductive, they contain a 'grain of truth'. This is not to excuse stereotypes where they are hurtful in any way but to find in them an explanation for their origin, existence and role. The limited intelligence of individuals in representations of Irish people in British culture and of African-Americans in American culture for instance echoes the fact that these groups were, historically, structurally and systematically oppressed and disadvantaged by those in power. Ireland was subject to oppressive British rule for centuries while the history of Americans of African origin is defined by the institution of slavery and its legacy. The language, demeanour and culture of the Irish and of black Americans – when judged on the terms of the dominant culture – can all be said to have been negatively affected by these histories and resultant power relations and have had a long-term impact upon positioning the group as inferior to those who have dominated them. In Germany, Turkish people filled gaps in the post-war workforce as *Gastarbeiter* and despite the necessity of their presence were treated as second-class citizens around whom stereotypes developed. David Horrocks and Eva Kolinsky have documented how even those at the bottom of the pile in German society were able to look down upon Turkish workers for being loud, garish in dress, dragging scores of children around with them – appearing as akin to an 'epidemic' (Horrocks and Kolinsky, 1996: 8). Comedy shows on German TV such as *Was guckst du?* have played on such stereotypes. As one online post by a viewer about this show comments (do note that this is a German-speaker posting in English so forgive any errors in expression):

> '*I don't get it – are all the German Turks so dumb?' That's the question you would ask yourself after watching the show! And it is very popular belong the Germans and most unfortunately belong some Turks as well. The protagonist of the most sketches is a Germanborn Turk – and he plays the stereotypic Turkish-descend bloke. Using all the time the slang and low grammatical knowledge – and often playing a violent orientated chauvinistic character. I'm aware that many Turkish people in Germany hate him – but the majority of them seems to have at least accepted the point of view the general public has of 'them'.*
>
> *The worst fact has to come: through the acceptance of this show in the German public more and more (especially young) Turks are more likely to become like the stereotypic character which is shown to them week by week – because this character is more and more accepted – even though as a clown. This leads towards a downward spiral in this minority-group – regarding financial income, prestige in higher level jobs, willing to acquire education.*

Posted at www.imdb.com/title/tt0279612/ (accessed 21 July 2008)

The point here is that these ideas about Turks are 'believable' (as this post attests), for the way in which they plug into recognisable and observable traits. First-generation Turkish workers in Germany are, of course, non-native speakers and this characteristic impacts upon the generation born to them when they settle in Germany; aspects of their culture and demeanour can seem alien to native Germans. These are easily spotted and latched on to as 'representative' traits just as they obscure so many others of infinite variety. Foregrounded in media stereotypes as in *Was guckst du?*, that while derived from humorous intent and played to excess in such shows, these representations appear to have a 'grain of truth' to them. That this is a partial and particularly inflected and reiterated truth should also be noted. Interestingly, Horrocks and Kolinsky also identify stereotypes of Germans held by Turkish workers. Among them they spoke of employers as cold, inhuman and

Key theory

Stereotyping stereotypes

Tessa Perkins in her article 'Rethinking stereotypes' (Perkins, 1997) suggests that there are a number of stereotypes about stereotypes themselves. These offer some interesting and important counterpoints to some of the themes presented elsewhere in this section. Perkins has written that these stereotypes of stereotypes include the idea that stereotypes are simple, and about minority or oppressed groups always erroneous in content and are necessarily negative and insulting. In addition stereotypes are held about groups with whom 'we' have little or no social contact; by implication, therefore, they are not held about the group to which 'we' belong.

Likewise she adds that stereotypes are thought to be 'rigid' and do not change over time, that because contradictory stereotypes exist then this is produced as evidence that they are erroneous, but of nothing else. She has more to say, but a final aspect of this list suggests that those who hold or believe a stereotype to be true means that behaviour towards a group is predictable.

That there are stereotypes of stereotypes does not mean that in the majority of instances in which we find them in use that they are not negative in some way. Or perhaps this 'stereotype' of negativity is noticeable because of the power of the negative and offensive representations. What Perkins does underline for us is the fact that, while stereotypes look so obvious and simple, their dimensions, use and function are revealed to be complex.

money-grabbing types. In this contrast we can see some of the complexities around stereo-types: any group can be subject to this process.

Let's explore these ideas about stereotypes and representations further by turning to some case studies concerning examples of social categories of **gender** and sexuality. These two examples are from a selection that includes race, class, ethnicity, religion, nation and so on, where some instructive work in this area has been done that will prove suggestive for anyone interested in other categories that we touch upon as we proceed. These two categories – gender and sexuality – will certainly aid us in understanding the cultural con-structedness of such categories and the role that representation plays in their definition from within and from without.

Gender
refers to the *cultural* nature of the differences between the *natural* biological sexes of male and female.

Gender and representation

At a biological level we can agree that men and women have important and obvious dif-ferences that are to do with their chromosomes and reproductive capacities. However, to what degree the state of being masculine or feminine follows from this physical nature is the subject of debate and controversy. We tend therefore to use the word 'gen-der' when referring to the sense that masculinity and femininity are social and cultural in nature.

To suggest that gender and sex are indistinguishable would, to some degree, rely upon a claim that our status as social beings is determined by our 'essential' or 'necessary' natures. Using the term 'essence' or 'necessity' in relation to gender or representation is to sug-gest that certain characteristics are 'innate' or natural, not a result of cultural convention. Here, it is useful to refer to Judith Butler, who theorised gender as 'performative' rather than innate or fixed. It certainly seems that both males and females have their gender asserted through a 'stylised repetition of acts' (Butler in Fuss, 1991: 140). These are all of those things we do that mark us out, to varying degrees, as 'masculine' or 'feminine'; for example, I might work out or put my make-up on (but I'm not saying which of these works in favour of which category). These acts are not necessarily consciously performed: I just know I need to be seen to be working out to assert my manhood, for example. These acts are not only prevalent and played out in the stories, sounds and images of popular televi-sion, film and music, but also in journalistic portrayals and depictions of the roles of men and women. Mass media texts around the world are dominated by images of ideologi-cally asserted 'femininity' and 'masculinity': how men and women are expected to look and behave. Although there do seem to be multiple versions of femininity and masculin-ity depicted in our media, these categories are still quite restrictive in terms of 'perform-ing' gender in terms of what is, and how it is, performed. We can see this in the research referred to in the key text.

'Performances' of gender we see in media (and around us in our culture) are perceived as 'natural' within society because they are so common; they are certainly not consciously viewed or necessarily consciously constructed. They are accepted by the majority of pro-ducers and viewers alike without question. This is, after all, the domain of 'nature', or so it seems (see the discussion of ideology in Chapter 10 for a detailed discussion of this idea). Producers of media texts may not be aware of their constructions but are unconsciously ingrained with notions of this constructed reality. This in turn has a bearing on how they are thought to inscribe social ideas – as opposed to 'nature' – into media texts.

Other arguments can be offered in support of the socially constructed, cultural aspect of gender. We could study media representations and how they record versions of what it means to be male or female and the way in which such representations record social values – aiding and abetting our identity formation. A study of *changes* in representations of men and women and the values and expectations of masculinity and femininity over the years, in any media form, might suggest that such categories are far from fixed.

Key text

Reel versus real world: older women and the Academy Awards

A useful example of the restrictiveness of the performance of femininity relates to the rather limited place for women of a certain age across the media and in film in particular. This has been explored by Elizabeth Markson and Carol Taylor who researched the relative invisibility of 'older' women in Hollywood movies. They studied over 1600 women nominated for Academy Awards between 1927 and 1990 and the nature of their role performances. They found that once past the age of 35 women rarely appeared in roles other than as stereotypical 'nag', 'hag', 'old bag', 'poor old thing' and so on. Their concluding statement is particularly affecting here when thinking about representations:

As women film goers, we keep hoping to see depictions of women's relationships with one another that have some ring of authenticity to our own experience and that of other women. We also hope to see our beloved female (and male) stars with whom we grew up as well as our age peers on the screen. As they age, the female (but not the male) stars virtually vanish from the screen into a black hole. The older we and they become the more time elapses between their performances. When an 'older' female star does appear in a film, she is either relegated to relatively little screen time or she portrays a character that neither we, nor we suspect, most women, would choose to emulate as a model for our own present or future lives. The 'women's pictures' we see, with rare exceptions, do not seem to ring true.

(Markson and Taylor in Davis *et al.*, 1993: 170–1)

Sexuality and representation

If we refer to sexuality, we are talking about the sexual preferences of individuals – whether they are attracted to men, women or both, or indeed anything else that causes an attraction and pleasure for those individuals. This sense should not reduce the issue of sexuality to that of physical sexual practice alone (if at all) but encompasses also the dress, attitude and expression of individuals and groups as well as the way in which they are categorised and understood by society in terms of legal definitions, rights and so on. So sexuality is not a thing of 'biology' here (although it may well be), but is understood as socially and culturally constituted – its historical and geographical variety and changes over time suggest as much.

In most societies, to be heterosexual is to be understood, variously, as part of the dominant group, to be 'normal', 'straight' and so forth. 'Heterosexual' is therefore a normative category, which is taken for granted, and about which all other categories circulate as outside of this norm. Indeed theorists such as Cathy J. Cohen have defined 'heteronormativity' as the practices (this would include representational practices), 'that legitimize and privilege heterosexuality and heterosexual relationships as fundamental and "natural" within society' (Cohen, 2005: 24). In the UK, for instance, heterosexuality (the attraction of men for women and vice versa) is serviced and governed by a range of traditions (e.g. the institution of marriage as distinct from the civil partnership), cultural conventions, laws (the age of consent) and financial incentives (tax relief for married couples and benefits for resulting children, etc.).

To be 'heterosexual' is to belong potentially to a diffuse group categorised by a range of practices and cultural conventions. One can be a 'ladies' man' or a 'loose woman', exhibiting one's status through excess or restraint in one's sexual activity – relative to conventional norms of course. One can be a 'male chauvinist pig' or a 'new man', 'new lad', 'new woman' and so on. The interesting thing about such 'new' formations is that they seem to reoccur with perplexing frequency over the decades. The Victorians, as much as we do, spoke about 'new women' challenging the mores of the age as well as the 'new man' defining the future!

Key theory

Queer theory

In their book *Gay Histories and Cultures*, Haggerty and Zimmerman (1999) relate the fluctuations in meaning of the term 'queer' and its parallels with the label 'gay' as well as the contentiousness in its usage. Originally queer was an English word designating something odd (as in the saying 'as queer as a clockwork orange' – from whence Anthony Burgess's book and Stanley Kubrick's film derive). It became applied to and used by gay men from early in the twentieth century where it had largely negative connotations. It was then appropriated as a badge of difference by an organisation called 'Queer Nation' from June 1990 in an attempt to assert difference and even to shock 'straights' as well as conservative 'assimilationist' homosexuals (Haggerty and Zimmerman, 1999: 723–4) aiming to 'fit in' with societal norms.

Our interest lies in the fact that the term was taken up by cultural theorists, prompted by thinkers like Tessa de Lauretis, in order to expand upon and identify those interested in the lives, experiences and culture of gay, lesbian and bisexual individuals in relation to problematising 'hetero-normativity'. The field is an innovative one, taking its cues particularly from the work of French theorist Michel Foucault and ideas of discourse (de Lauretis, 1991) (see also Chapter 10).

This use of this term has been described by Jenny Kangasvuo and Sanna Karkulehto (2006: 2) thus:

Despite and due to the word's many connotations, queer has become a very useful conceptual tool for research and theory that concentrates on sexuality, gender and a wide variety of non-normativities. Queer is a word that questions the meanings of stable and fixed categories of identity, hegemonic truths on relationships, families, reproduction and desire, and the relevance of universalized normativities. At the same time, queer promotes respect of individuality, diversity and plain fun. In academia queer reminds us that no paradigm, theory or axiom can perfectly explain the world – quite the contrary: when paradigms and theories become canonized they often lose their explanative, descriptive and critical power.

'Homosexuality' refers to same-sex preferences, male or female, although the term tends to be applied to men with 'lesbian' referring to women. There is an incredibly diverse list of labels and names, derogatory, positive, scientific, slang, etc. for these groups, many of them arising from the stereotypes associated with such sexual identities. These have largely been imposed from outside of the groups but are sometimes constructed from within. Sometimes the self-consciousness about stereotypes and intentional challenges are evidenced in the way in which labels have been appropriated – the 'reclaiming' of the term 'queer' for instance.

Students will often come across the acronym LGBT in relation to studies in this area. This stands for 'lesbian, gay, bisexual and transgendered' and refers to both the area of study into such identities and cultures and often a proclamation of the identities of academics themselves. ('Transgender' is a category referring to people whose gender identity does not directly relate to their biological, assigned or given sex.)

If we take homosexuality in the UK as an example (as we could for any other country), we could explore whether or not the range of representations today have expanded and, possibly, altered over time. Likewise we should be attuned to continuities: have they and the values that they evince stayed the same, in comparison with those of the recent past and the issues that have arisen around this category? A good reason for doing this is due to the way in which the status of homosexuals in the UK, legally and culturally, has been challenged and changed.

Until the Sexual Offences Act, passed in 1967, male homosexuality in the UK was illegal and punishable by a jail sentence or mental health treatment and this made it very difficult to represent this particular range of sexuality in the media in anything like a positive light. As Richard Dyer has related, the nature of this sexual identity could only be hinted at in media texts and in particular ways (Dyer, 1993, 2002). Homosexuality was seen from 'outside' – framed by the notion that it was a problem, was 'deviant' (when compared with heterosexuality), a disease or psychological condition which could be cured or was simply evidence of immorality, something to be ashamed of. Thus representations were often unsympathetic or when they were sympathetic they reproduced narratives and figures such as the troubled homosexual who was ill at ease with his or her condition, for example Dirk Bogarde in the film *Victim* (dir. Deardren, 1961) or *The Children's Hour* (dir. Wyler, 1961) or *The Killing of Sister George* (dir. Aldrich, 1968).

As homosexuality became decriminalised in the UK after 1967 (although widespread persecution endured and indeed continues) attempts were made to represent it in a more open manner. As a result there was a wider inclusion of media portraits and voices that evinced the 'lived reality' of homosexuals. These included the publication of newspapers such as *Gay Times* (www.gaytimes.co.uk/) from 1984, and TV shows such as *Out on Tuesday* which appeared with the launch of the terrestrial TV channel Channel 4 in 1982. However, these representations were certainly not always received by the 'mainstream' as non-threatening to the naturalised heterosexual state of normality. Laws may be changed but attitudes and culture take time to progress, if they do so at all. In the 1970s and 80s there was also a noticeable increase in available stereotypical images of homosexuals, implied at least through the 'campness' and effete manner of TV personalities such as Larry Grayson, John Inman and Kenneth Williams. They achieved recognition and status, albeit as parodic and relatively toothless and desexualised figures. More recently figures such as Graham Norton, Julian Clary and Alan Carr have achieved some success openly representing male homosexuality and sexual activity. That said, both have a *risqué* 'jester' role in TV and Clary has engendered moral outrages at some of his jokes that led to calls for sanctions and has resulted in a serious hiatus in his career.

On the one hand it could be argued that, in the main, contemporary representations of homosexuality are less automatically judgemental, more open and explicit, and representing an even wider range of homosexual-lived experience than what was once available. Again, this reflects the changing political, social and cultural contexts of our time that appear to some degree to be more accepting. Magazines aimed at the gay community such as *Attitude* (www.attitude.co.uk) appear on magazine racks in stores offering an accessible focal point for consumption alongside 'mainstream' magazines. These also testify to the visibility of this culture – its movement from a status of being hidden or perceived as shameful to being less so, in some quarters. Certainly, current representations are more explicit, open and diverse than ever before with such UK television series as *Queer as Folk* (1999), *Tipping the Velvet* (2002), and now even UK soaps such as *Coronation Street* and *EastEnders* have successfully introduced gay male characters with little controversy, at least that merited by this defining aspect of their representation.

Although it has been argued that this area of representation still requires positive development, as Western societies' understanding and accommodation of sexuality develops, the dominant representations that we see today are representative of our contemporary social ideas and values and an analysis of these texts can allow a scholarly insight into our naturalised and common-sense views about such groups. These ideas link closely to the ideas of power and – as our transcript and issue of debate below suggest – positive steps can easily be countered by the reappearance of typically negative stereotypes. Our explorations also evidence the suggestion that there is no 'ideal' representation, no absolute truth or reality that we are trying to assert or uncover in dealing with representation.

Stonewall is a lobbying and action group dedicated to equality and social justice for gay men and women. In 2005 its researchers examined the representations of gay people and related issues in 168 hours of peak-time programming on the BBC's two main channels. Alongside this analysis they conducted interviews and focus groups with viewers of varying sexualities.

Case Study

Just as things change . . . they stay the same

A key site relating to the growth of a plurality of representations in the UK media is that of Channel 4. Channel 4 was launched in 1982, in part to serve the needs of alternative and minority groups. The station was directed by a public service remit which has maintained this focus to varying degrees until the present day.

Soap operas and dramas such as *Brookside*, *Queer as Folk* and *Shameless* have represented class, race, sexuality and gender in ways which are different from the obscured or mildly palatable portrayals in the wider media and society. Channel 4 productions also explored issues of class, nationalism, drug use and a variety of subcultures through its film arm Channel 4 Films, later rebranded as Film 4 in 1998. Films such as *Trainspotting*, *The Crying Game*, *Beautiful Thing* and *Brassed Off* not only challenged dominant representations of British society but constructed wider versions of 'knowledge' about the groups portrayed.

The series *Queer as Folk* (1999) – see www. channel4.com/video/queer-as-folk/series-1/ – offered a controversial change in the representation of homosexuality on British (and later US) television. It offered a range of plotlines in which the sexuality of its characters was not the primary determinant; in fact the quality of being a gay man was normalised and presented as everyday. Unlike previous dramatisations of homosexuality as a 'problem' or defined in relation to mainstream or dominant versions of heterosexual conduct,

here were men who were part of a vibrant and sometimes independent culture. While it dealt with the familiar tropes of 'coming out' and the contemporary spectre of AIDS, these were part of a wider and multifarious range of stories in which characters were allowed to be multifaceted – detailed and complex and not reducible to their moral qualities (judging them as good or bad) or their positive or negative impact upon the world. They just were. More recently *Sugar Rush* has explored the growing pains of young gay women. This adaptation of a novel by Julie Burchill is described thus:

> *Sugar Rush* explores the world of Kim and her earth-shattering lust for the gorgeous and sassy Maria Sweet, otherwise known as Sugar. And if Sugar wasn't enough to blow Kim's mind, there's also her dysfunctional, embarrassing family – a mini-freak for a brother, an obsessively house-proud dad and a mum who's behaving as if she's the one who's 15 years old. Each episode is a different journey inside Kim's world as her wry observations take us into the mind of a screwed-up, loved-up, lustful adolescent experiencing the bright lights of Brighton and the rush of forbidden love for the first time. *Sugar Rush*, the riotous exploration of what it means to be young, horny and queer in 21st-century Britain.

Source: www.channel4.com/life/microsites/S/ sugar_rush/show.html 21/7/8

Both series took any sexual identities for granted in scenarios where characters were settled and unsettled, happy and discontented by turn. In this way, what has traditionally been structured as 'difference' becomes unremarkable. However, while these series are indicative of a 'progressive' quality in Channel 4 programming they are but individual series. Elsewhere and in some substantial research, the picture of how homosexuality is represented in UK TV is seen very differently.

The researchers sought to explore a number of questions. These included:

- How does the BBC portray gay people's lives?
- Does television have a positive or negative impact on gay people's lives?
- What impact does the portrayal of lesbians and gay men have on heterosexual people?

■ Does the BBC challenge homophobia, or does it reinforce it?

■ Do lesbian and gay licence-fee payers get value for money?

The resulting report *Tuned Out: The BBC's portrayal of lesbian and gay people* presented a number of findings which included:

> *Gay people and their lives are five times more likely to be described or portrayed in negative terms than in positive ones on the BBC. Gay lives were positively and realistically represented for just six minutes and depicted in negative terms or contexts for 32 minutes out of 168 hours of programming.*
>
> *During 168 hours of programmes there were 38 minutes of gay references, both positive and negative. This represented 0.4 per cent of broadcast time in 49 separate instances and included openly gay characters or personalities, direct and indirect references to gay people and gay sexuality, use of gay stereotypes and innuendo.*
>
> *Gay life is disproportionately over-represented in entertainment programmes, including game shows, chat shows and comedy. The majority, 72 per cent, of individual references to gay sexuality were made during entertainment programmes, despite entertainment comprising just 14 per cent of all programmes monitored.*
>
> *Lesbians hardly exist on the BBC. Where gender was specified during a reference to gay sexuality, 82 per cent of references were about gay men.*
>
> *Lesbian and gay issues are rarely tackled or even mentioned in factual programmes. These programmes, including consumer shows and documentaries, made up over half (54 per cent) of all programmes monitored, yet only 3 per cent of all individual gay references appeared within this genre.*
>
> *Gay people are often used as the subject of jokes on the BBC. Over half (51 per cent) of all gay references were designed for comic effect. Most of these revolved around stereotypes of sexually predatory or camp and effeminate gay men.*
>
> *The BBC relies heavily on clichéd stereotypes in its portrayal of gay people. It seems reluctant to present lesbian and gay people in everyday scenarios, such as stable relationships or family life.*
>
> *Source*: www.stonewall.org.uk/media/tuned_out_gay_people_in_the_media/default.asp. Stonewall, 'Tuned Out' (2005)

As researchers and theorists there may be reason to take issue with the premises of how some of this research was conducted but many of its findings are suggestive and insightful. As such they offer a very different perspective on the politics of representation than the more optimistic thrust set out above. These tensions serve ultimately then to reiterate the sense that this domain demands our attention. Our ongoing project should be to assess whether such reports are convincing and how, if at all, representations are changing.

Media professionals and the 'politics' of representation

Our studies thus far suggest that media representations are related to context and through investigation of stereotypes we can enhance our understanding of society and its power relations and hierarchies (see Chapter 11). However, it is all very well to ascribe the source to 'society' or 'culture' in the abstract but we should attend to questions of who *literally* is creating and producing representations and how they acquire the skills and power to do so. Who takes responsibility for stereotypes and how they appear? This is certainly a challenge presented by the research from Stonewall outlined previously and an explicit aspect of complaints about the humour of *Top Gear*. To take such issues seriously is to understand representation quite clearly as a political issue with real impact upon individual lives and social organisation. Thus, we need to track back in our study of texts to ask questions of the very creators of those texts, asking them to account for the material they put out to their audiences. Who is being spoken about or for, and in what manner? What of the issue of who speaks and who represents?

Here then we are focusing on media institutions and professionals and their responsibilities and involvement in the 'politics' of representation. There are various factors to be investigated in relation to these media workers. First, we could consider the demographics of those who are in the position to produce texts, or who have a huge impact in the production of the media in general, for example those who own media companies. By considering the demographics of such a group we can identify patterns of employment and access to the media, which may be based upon gender, ethnicity, sexuality, class, age and education. This is important as our background can impact on how we see the world and our perception of certain groups outside that which we define as our own. Think about your own background and upbringing, your sense of right and wrong, your cultural and religious ideas. All these factors impact on how you perceive certain events and in the same sense these factors impact on how media makers perceive and re-present events and issues.

One way of challenging representations is based then upon a perception of the limited access that the under- (or mis-) represented have to the means of expression by contributing to the production of media texts themselves. This approach connects the symbolic aspects of representation but also the literalness of the 'proxy' idea of representation we discussed earlier. One way of thinking about representation in terms of 'proxy' or 'substitute' is to question the way in which the 'make-up' of media adequately reflects or echoes that of society in general. The debate in this area takes on a number of issues. First, it concerns the nature of media institutions: do they recruit in an equal manner from the full range of the population? Secondly, it takes on the look, sound and expression of the media: are the various faces and voices of a plural society properly and proportionally represented? This issue was one taken up by Greg Dyke, the former Director General of the BBC. He once described that organisation as 'hideously white'. He was referring to the ethnic make-up of its workforce and how this impacted on its ability to serve and adequately reflect its audience. He claimed that:

> Ethnic minorities in the United Kingdom disproportionately don't use our services. Our research shows they don't think we're for them.

This mattered, he argued, for the following reasons:

■ how we are organised – for example, who we employ;
■ the services we choose to operate;
■ the content we run on those channels, networks and online sites.

Greg Dyke in 'Diversity in Broadcasting: a public service perspective' speech on 3 May 2002. www.bbc. co.uk/pressoffice/speeches/stories/dyke_cba.shtml

Concern with media workers' attitudes and values are often based upon the assumption that such attitudes influence stories, whether this is in terms of a transmission or their worldview, their political attitudes or their personal religious orientations for instance. We could investigate whether media workers can be thought to 'bias' media content in line with their own personal or group attitudes. This may also apply to various other media texts, be they fictional or factually based. Media professionals, like other social groups, don't necessarily set out to insult particular social groups or to portray them in a limited or negative light. Like the rest of us, they share in the recognition of existing images and ideas, drawing upon them as they communicate and make sense of the world. However, it is certainly the case that if we examine the history of representations we can find plenty of examples where stereotypes have been accentuated and deployed with a clearly malicious intent. One can think of propagandist portraits of fat, cigar-smoking capitalists, wearing

Case Study

Harry Roselmack and French TV

→ The appointment of reporter Harry Roselmack to an important and visible position on French TV gives a sense of the realities of issues and debates in the area of representation in media and the make-up of media organizations. In the summer of 2006, Roselmack took on the anchor role of France's most popular news programme on the TF1 channel for a period of six weeks. This appointment was one which made news itself in periodicals like *Le Parisien* which splashed Roselmack's face across the front page, the obviousness of his racial identity the implicit issue: he is a man of African origin by way of Martinique, in the French Caribbean. His role was to fill in for Patrick Poivre d'Arvor, a presenter who has anchored the broadcast since 1976 and who addresses over seven million viewers each evening.

Attention to Roselmack's presence and position continued throughout the summer, drawing comment from observers from outside France such as the *New York Times* which noted that France has a black population of around five million (around one million from the Caribbean). It was suggested by one contributor to the *Times*' coverage that this most visible of minorities is socially invisible. Thus, when it comes to equality and representational issues, the situation in France could be illustrated by the fact that more black people played on the national Football team at that point (13 of 23 players) than in the National Assembly (10 or 577 members, and none of the 10 from the French mainland). Minority figures in such prominent positions was, and is, still a rarity.

The *Times* reported how in 1999 a black writer by the name of Calixthe Beyala formally complained about this situation and demanded quotas for black people on television. Such actions contributed to an increasing diversity on French screens at least with TF1 hiring Madagascan-born Sébastien Folin in 2001 (as weather forecaster) and public broadcaster France 3 appointing Audrey Pulvar (from Martinique) to present its evening news bulletin (albeit one with half of TF1's audience).

The *New York Times* interviewed Roselmack who said of his appointment that: 'This is certainly no sign that we have arrived at a normalised situation [. . .] That will be the case the day people no longer make such a fuss when a black, North African or Asian colleague is hired'. For him, the appearance of a black face on television was not a signal of equality but had the potential to act as a trailblazer. The real object was to gain a significant presence for minorities in all areas of economic, political and cultural life: 'TV can play the role of pathfinder [. . .] But the other media and all industries in France, not to mention politics, have to go down the same path'.

Source: adapted from Katrin Bennhold, 'For French Blacks, a Face on TV News Is Only a Start', New York Times.Com, 14 August 2006.

pinstripe suits and top hats in posters used in the Soviet Union or the repetition of anti-Semitic images in the Nazi era (see p. 286 on propaganda). During the Rwandan genocide, national radio was tasked with generating hatred between the Tutsi and Hutu tribes (Thompson, 2007). Producers and audiences who share and deploy social stereotypes need to be on their guard, however. This may be for pragmatic reasons. Some of the ways of representing immigrants to the UK from Asia and the Caribbean that were common in the media in the 1950s and 60s and even 70s are now deemed to transgress production codes and guidelines (see below). Indeed, they may even be illegal according to legislation

Doing media studies

Read the article below from the *Press Gazette* which outlines some of the issues discussed in this section and how some individuals have sought to tackle them:

'National radio station to tackle ethnic issues' by Walé Azeez, 20 August 2004

Black Britain, the online news website, is advancing with plans to launch a nationwide commercial speech-based radio station, to address what it sees as a dearth of views from the country's ethnic minority communities on the airwaves.

Its founders said the 75 per cent talk station would provide the space for non-white Britons to discuss 'issues other than music and race', which they said were rarely catered for at present.

The as yet unnamed station will be in the mould of established speech radio channels such as BBC Radio 4 and LBC 97.3FM, according to its founders, who are in talks with venture capitalists in a bid to raise the £5m needed for the launch.

'It's going to be a station that ensures that individual's views on issues that affect us all are heard, rather than only speaking to them on issues of race,' said Kaye AdeniranOlule, the online news service's head of marketing.

He said communities that would also be represented included Chinese and South Asian. 'It's to do with talking about things that affect us as a people really. So, for example, when announcements are made in Downing Street or by the Chancellor of the Exchequer, we'd talk about how it affects us in any specific way besides how it affects everybody else.'

Kofi Kusitor, founder of Black Britain, added: 'If you look across the country we don't have a talk-based station. We can't always be doing music. I'm not mentioning names, but any time we're asked to appear on any mainstream programme worth its salt, it's almost always saying something about music, entertainment generally or fashion,' Kusitor said.

The Black Britain website was launched in July 1998 as a news and information services for black and ethnic minority communities.

What evidence are you able to find for the existence of other such projects? What do you think of such initiatives? Are they necessary? Any answers might depend upon your own cultural position and the extent to which your feel yourself to belong to a well- or under-represented group.

to outlaw racism. But unthinkingly offensive actions or malicious intentions and prejudices do not go unchecked by the media industries, or indeed by society at large in terms of audience responses, laws and regulations.

However, if we accept that media forms are perforce limited in their representation of the world and that texts offer constructions of the world then the notion of *mis*representation that often arises presents us with a problem. On what basis are our objections to the substance of individual representations based? Those who object to any depiction, or indeed who seek to construct 'positive' representations, may themselves fall into the trap of relying upon an idea of 'essential' meanings, insisting upon an innate idea of what something is or is not. To evaluate representations as accurate or misleading then may be an impossible task and, for any insistence upon the provision of positive images this may, in obscuring any negative images, compromise the sophistication of any view of a social group.

Overall, we can accept that representation is not 'innocent', that with such debates and contentiousness surrounding what is said, heard and viewed it is a political issue. A 'politics' of representation for those offended by the limited ways in which the social group they belong to is represented may not be about finding the perfect representation of that group because we could argue not only that there isn't one but why would we want one 'ultimate' representation to stand in for the whole of a group? The imbalances come into view here if we compare the representation of white people with other ethnic groups. We could argue that, in media around the world, white people are accorded the full range of

Advertising Standards Authority

From UK Radio Advertising Standards Code 13 Racial Discrimination

a. It is illegal (with a few exceptions) for an advertisement to discriminate on grounds of race.

b. Advertisements must not include any material which might reasonably be construed by ethnic minorities to be hurtful or tasteless.

The Race Relations Act 1976 (as amended) makes it unlawful to broadcast an advertisement which indicates or implies racial discrimination. There are a few exceptions, full details of which can be obtained from the Commission for Racial Equality on 020 7939 0000; website: www.cre.gov.uk.

Source: www.asa.org.uk/asa/

UK Press Editors' Code of Practice

Discrimination

(i) The press must avoid prejudicial or pejorative reference to an individual's race, colour, religion, gender, sexual orientation or to any physical or mental illness or disability.

(ii) Details of an individual's race, colour, religion, sexual orientation, physical or mental illness or disability must be avoided unless genuinely relevant to the story.

www.pcc.org.uk/cop/practice.html

Key theory

The burden of representation

Negative stereotypes are often objectionable because they are limited individually but are repeated incessantly within a limited range of representations. Groups who are subject to such repeated stereotypes are not afforded representation via the range of images that present them as equal to dominant groups who seem to 'naturally' represent the wealth of humanity. In addition, problems sometimes arise for media producers who belong to minority groups in that they become tasked by those groups and others (implicitly or explicitly) with taking on all of the politics involved in negative portrayals of that group, tasked with setting them right or having all of their work scrutinised for its politics as well as their attitudes, practices and so on. Theorist and practitioner Kobena Mercer has identified what this means for Black British artists in his essay 'Black art and the burden of representation' (1994). Here he draws together a number of the ways in which we have been thinking about media representation.

Whereas politicians and other public figures are elected into positions for which they speak as 'representatives', this role has fallen on the shoulders of black artists not so much out of individual choice but as a consequence of structures or racism that have historically marginalised their access to the means of cultural production. When black artists become publicly visible only one at a time their work is burdened with a whole range of extra-artistic concerns precisely because, in their relatively isolated position as one of the few black practitioners in any given field – film, photography, fine art – they are seen as 'representatives' who speak on behalf of, and who are thus accountable to, their communities. In such a political economy of racial representation where the part stands in for the whole, the visibility of a few token black public figures serves to legitimate, and reproduce, the invisibility, and lack of access to public discourse, of the community as a whole.

Source: Mercer, 1994: 240.

If we look at a field where there are many black artists – rap music for instance – we can see how this burden is still imposed. An artist such as 50 Cent, mentioned above, is perennially held to account for his work in relation to ideas of black America. A figure like Eminem who is spoken about because of his exceptionality as a 'white' rapper is rarely subject to the same questions in relation to white, working-class Americans.

Case Study
Heeb magazine and 'the burden of representation'

Source: Heeb Media LLC

Heeb magazine takes on and plays with Jewish stereotypes in a humorous and often controversial manner

One address to the 'burden of representation' that faces groups who challenge their negative representation in the media is to adopt a knowing, 'postmodern' approach (see Chapter 12). A good example here – often very controversial too – is suggested by *Heeb* magazine which ran from 2002–10. *Heeb* was a magazine by and about Jewish people and culture that presents Jewish stereotypes that are drawn upon by Jewish people themselves but also many of those constructed from 'without' as offensive stereotypes. Such depictions include those of the 'Jewish princess', the 'miserly' Jew, the 'worrier', the 'overbearing mother' and so on.

The manner in which these are used by this magazine seems to be playful and ironic, denying offence and hurtfulness by appropriating stereotypes, subverting and indulging them as if to say to the prejudiced: 'There's nothing you can say that we haven't said already ourselves.' The question is, however, whether this works effectively as many individuals have found some issues dealt with – the Holocaust for instance – to be beyond parody. Likewise, one wonders at the audiences for these jokes. Is it OK to poke fun at yourself if you belong to a minority among others in that minority? What if others from 'without' join in too? Are they being ironic?

Further to offending Jewish readers (and non-readers presumably), *Heeb* poked 'back' at other groups that historically had persecuted and caricatured Jews. The Winter 2004 edition pilloried Mel Gibson's movie *Passion of the Christ*, leading to the magazine being singled out in a report on 'anti-Catholicism' by the Catholic League. The report stated that:

> The editors who introduced the spread said that the death of Jesus was 'summarily blamed upon the Jews', until this 'fondly held belief seemed destined to fade forever' after Vatican II. A sexually suggestive Jesus wears a Jewish prayer shawl as a loin cloth, and the Blessed Mother was shown exposing her breasts and body piercing. The occupation of the model photographed as Mary Magdalene was described as 'Evangelist-cum-nymphomaniac country singer'. She was quoted as saying, 'Who killed Jesus? Ryan Adams.' The woman who was photographed as Pontius Pilate was quoted as saying, 'Christians believe the Jews killed Jesus; that is why there is so much anti-Semitism in the world. The church was created on that one simple anti-Semitic principle. Christians who say otherwise are making it up or misrepresenting their own religion.'

Given suspicions of Gibson's attitude to Jews in his films and in light of anti-Semitic remarks, something interesting is revealed in this instance about the cultural confidence expressed in *Heeb*'s attitudes and willingness to pick a fight.

(www.catholicleague.org/annualreport. php?year=2004&id=97#MAGS)

Source: www.heebmagazine.com/

being human, of being good and bad – without badness being an index of all members of that group – of figures whose pre-eminent characteristic is not defined through their skin colour or culture! In fact it is rare for whiteness to be referenced as related to race or ethnicity at all (see Dyer, 1997).

Method: content analysis

For a moment we should dwell upon the issue of representation as 'proportionality', i.e. how many people from a group are represented, how frequently and to what degree and extent representations exist in media forms. This issue is usefully dealt with via a specific mode of media research: content analysis. You might wonder about this title as all of the methods we've thus far employed are about studying and interpreting the content of media texts – broadly textual analysis. We use the term 'content analysis' in very specific ways, however.

Content analysis
is a quantitative method of analysing the denotative content of media output based upon defined samples and recognisable categories.

Content analysis is a means of counting the amount or frequency with which elements occur in media texts. It is a method that aims at objectivity by counting those things that are 'unproblematically' denoted or manifested in media content, such as the use of particular words or the appearance of particular images. A case in point would be the use of 'terrorist' or 'fundamentalist' in conjunction with 'Islam' in radio news reports for instance. While such terms might be full of connotations this method relies upon harvesting data before any interpretation of the term in its contextual setting is made. In order to work effectively this method deals with significance at the level of quantity – not only within a text but also across a range of texts. This might involve, for instance, surveying every edition of a specific newspaper within a set period, or all newspapers within the same period.

As such this method deals also with clearly demarcated parameters: identifying a manageable 'universe' that is to be the subject of analysis – television soap operas for instance or social networking sites. From this 'universe' it is necessary to specify the range of any sample of it – BBC soap operas, Facebook sites belonging to female members of the network 'Studying in Finland', for instance. Within these parameters and determined by the need to count things that can be counted in significant numbers clear coding categories are drawn up for the things that are to be counted – scenes in which someone smokes a cigarette in *EastEnders*, frequency of references to named celebrities, for example.

Content analysis may be used to identify the frequency with which certain individuals and/or groups appear in media although if we wish to determine such things at the level of race or ethnicity, not to mention class or sexuality, we can appreciate the problems that might arise: how exactly is race or ethnicity 'denoted' or 'manifested'? Our passing example above on soap opera for instance might set a category of 'Polish plumbers'. It would be hard to count such things in radio broadcasts or in popular music recordings without invoking a whole set of presumptions (gay people act in certain ways, 'foreigners' always talk differently!) about categories that are not made obvious or manifest. Even when we turn to images in photography, TV or film the manifest aspects of race or ethnicity can be problematic – physical markers such as skin tone, hair, facial dimensions are incredibly varied and not reducible to any average measure.

Nonetheless this approach is important for generated data and evaluating media content (references to 'media studies' in tandem with 'Mickey Mouse' in the press for instance at A-level results times). A range of software exists to aid such studies – intentionally or otherwise: online search engines, for instance, can be usefully employed in support of this method in limited ways. Such methods are integral too to those areas of media concerned with publicity and public relations: evaluating impact in terms of the frequency with which a client or product features in media or the column inches devoted to them.

Doing media studies

Studying content-based data

Tables 3.1 and 3.2 are derived from a study of American media – 'A Content Analysis: Reflections of Girls in the Media: A Study of Television Shows and Commercials, Movies, Music Videos, and Teen Magazine Articles and Ads'. This work was conducted by Nancy Signorelli, PhD of the University of Delaware, Department of Communication, for the Kaiser Family Foundation and Children Now in April 1997 (available at www.kff.org/content/archive/1260/gendr.html).

Take a look at the data and then answer the following questions:

1. According to the Census of the American population conducted in 2000, people of Hispanic origin account for 12.5 per cent of the population (USA Todays www._usatoday._com/_news/_census/_2001-04-03). Using the tables, what conclusions are you able to draw based upon the representation of this group in the US media?

2. Based upon information in Tables 3.1 and 3.2 what speculations are you able to make about representation and music video?

3. Drawing upon information in Tables 3.1 and 3.2 what speculations are you able to make about the nature of gender roles and their representation in film?

4. Are there any limitations in the information presented here? What are they?

5. How would you construct your own content analysis? What would be the basis of your analysis?

Social Age	Television characters (number)		Film characters* (number)		Commercials models (number)		Music videos people (number)		Mag. articles photographs (number)		Magazine ads models (number)	
	Women (109)	Men (133)	Women (26)	Men (45)	Women (195)	Men (270)	Women (14)	Men (50)	Women (262)	Men (110)	Women (288)	Men (64)
Child	1%	1%	0%	4%	10%	17%	0%	0%	0%	0%	2%	0%
Adolescent	16	11	19	7	8	4	0	6	58	30	32	22
Young Adult	41	50	42	36	39	27	79	64	39	69	42	61
Adult	38	34	27	47	19	23	21	12	0	1	0	2
Elderly	3	2	4	2	1	4	0	0	0	0	0	2
Cannot Code	2	2	8	4	24	26	0	18	0	0	24	14

*Note: Percents may not equal exactly 100% due to rounding.

Table 3.1   Percentage of women and men by perceived social age

Race/Ethnicity	Television characters (number)		Film characters* (number)		Commercials models (number)		Music videos people (number)		Mag. articles photographs (number)		Magazine ads models (number)	
	Women (109)	Men (133)	Women (26)	Men (45)	Women (195)	Men (270)	Women (14)	Men (50)	Women (262)	Men (110)	Women (288)	Men (64)
White	77%	71%	85%	84%	87%	54%	86%	58%	73%	80%	88%	88%
African-American	19	20	8	4	7	37	14	42	19	12	8	0
Asian	2	1	0	0	4	4	0	0	5	0	1	2
Hispanic	0	2	0	2	1	0	0	0	2	6	1	7
Native American	0	0	4	4	0	0	0	0	0	0	0	2
Other	0	0	0	1	0	2	0	0	0	0	0	0
Cannot Code	2	5	4	4	0	5	0	0	0	2	1	2

*Note: Percents may not equal exactly 100% due to rounding.

Table 3.2   Percentage of women and men by racial and ethnic category

Representations of individuality: stars, personalities, celebrities

We can now extend our concern with the symbolic meaning of the representation of social groups in media by turning our attention to the representations of individuals and individuality in the form of 'stars', 'personalities' and 'celebrities'. This is a potentially important extension of what we've done so far as you would probably agree that we live in a society where a great deal of worth is accorded to fame, its pursuit, attainment and attendant trappings in the form of wealth and privilege. It is often said that we live in a 'celebrity culture', and while not wholly new it seems to be a relatively recent intensification of long-standing media and consumer preoccupations. In this section we offer a way of approaching the meanings of such individuals and categories, how they are represented and what they represent. Much valuable work that will help us to make sense of this area has been done in the domain of film studies. This is not surprising given the importance and dominance of this medium across the world in the twentieth century and the way in which it set the agenda for the now all-pervasive TV. However, stardom and celebrity do pre-date the development of the film industry in the twentieth century and indeed success in other forms parallels and interacts with that form. For instance, music-hall 'turns' and theatre actors were well known before film arrived and during its ascendancy. Pop stars such as Elvis Presley and the Beatles arrived during the 1950s and 1960s when TV was usurping the status of film, but their star status, despite film and TV appearances, rests upon their achievements as recording artists and this sector itself has contributed to our understanding of these categories.

Defining stars

Media stars must be understood primarily as commodities 'produced' by media companies for consumption by audiences that will lead to profit. To the industry, stars and celebrities represent capital – they are 'owned' or paid for by studios, record companies, agencies or individuals. They represent 'investment' and an outlay of time and money in terms of development and promotion (the 'naturalness' of stars as talent and 'discoveries' obscures this investment and capital outlay). The status of stars relates also to market organisation and their economic function in terms of ensuring purchases of media texts, getting bums on seats at cinemas, getting audiences through the doors of concert halls and so on. However, this economic focus must also account for the way in which this function relates to the 'meanings' of stardom in general and of stars in particular and how that meaning is constructed. Why some people prefer to see Jack Black in films compared with Hugh Jackman, for instance, is not just about the money spent on their images or how much we pay for the privilege of seeing them at the cinema, on DVD or by download.

Stars can be defined in a number of ways but may be broadly understood in the words of theorist Christine Gledhill on film stardom: 'Actors become stars when their off-screen lifestyles and personalities equal or surpass acting ability in importance' (Gledhill, 1991). In addition, as John Ellis puts it: a star is 'a performer in a particular medium whose figure enters into subsidiary forms of circulation and then feeds back into future performances' (Ellis, 1992). The image of a star is not just made in a film or TV show or on record, but through all of the other materials in which they figure – guest appearances, publicity, gossip columns and so on. Therefore, a star's image occurs across a wide field of media texts.

The fame attained by film and television actors as well as TV and radio presenters, pop and sports stars, and contestants in reality TV shows is generated and supplemented by attention from journalistic organs such as prime-time TV news programmes to newspaper gossip columns, magazines filled with paparazzi photographs, websites, as well as newer forms of delivery such as telephone text information updates. Thus, stars and stardom are vital to media industries – TV, popular music and a whole sector centred upon newspapers, magazines and websites. In fact it now seems that one no longer has to be famous for something at all – one can just 'be' a celebrity. Consider the figure of the socialite – heirs and heiresses whose wealth has been inherited and renown unearned in terms of talent or physical, intellectual or creative achievement: for example, Paris Hilton or indeed any winner (or loser) of the many versions of *Big Brother* around the world. Such figures appear in media and may go on to make films, TV shows or pop music but this largely as a result of their celebrity rather than vice versa.

Stars as texts and signs

The fame of stars stretches beyond any one single text such as a film or video performance. Stars exist across a wide field of texts and their image accompanies them to any part that they play or any situation they find themselves in, in other media forms. So while the image of a star is accrued primarily around some defining text – a film, a photograph, a video – it is then developed, added to and complicated by other contexts, publicity materials and so on. But the success, failure and reception of stars, personalities and celebrities relates to audience responses and understanding of their meanings. When, as scholars, we think about stardom we are, by and large, unconcerned with the actual individual (and their biography) whom we will probably never meet or form a relationship with, and therefore cannot know as we know ourselves and others in our social fields. Thus, we are dealing with a star's *image* here – as a version of media output. All that we know of the star is their image. Therefore we must analyse stars not as real people but as signs and texts. This is why some writers, when dealing with stars, use quote marks (e.g. 'Marilyn Monroe') when writing about them. It is because they want to stress that what they are dealing with is a constructed image rather than a real person who is in any way able to determine their meaning in any fully controlling manner.

How do we know that stars *are* signs? Well, we could try the kind of commutation test that we introduced in Chapter 1. We could imagine replacing the Brad Pitt of *Troy* with Mackenzie Crook (*Pirates of the Caribbean, The Office*) for instance. Or we could substitute the Eminem of 'My name is . . .' with Chris Martin from Coldplay. Mackenzie Crook and Chris Martin would mean different things from Brad Pitt and Eminem. This suggests that these individuals have accrued meaning – both denotatively and connotatively – that is deployed in each media text, just as they assume roles and meanings in their performance in those texts. In other words, they can be considered to be signs.

Stars are rich in denotative meaning. We assume that they look like, or sound like (in popular music and in radio – if the latter can be considered to have stars), the person they represent and therefore they seem 'natural', which is perhaps why people often feel that they know what a star is *really* like. However natural a photographic (iconic) sign seems, for instance, it is always a re-presentation of its referent (in this case, the real person – whoever the star is), and therefore contains elements of choice and combination. The choice of a certain star for one film role and not another is meaningful as our previous commutation test confirms. By way of a further example, ageing film star Clint Eastwood would be unlikely to play the part of a male nurse, for instance. What does this tell us about this individual's meanings let alone our society's ideas about masculinity and gender? In terms of the combination of signs, Clint's screen appearance would strike us as strange if his snarling lips and firm chin were combined with short-sightedness and the wearing of glasses. Thus, we can begin to deconstruct a star's image in order to understand it better if we look more closely at issues of choice and combination. In order to do this, we must analyse, for instance, the *mise en scène* in films and stills, body language, voice – anything that is used to construct a certain set of meanings.

Construction of the image

In thinking of the manner of its construction, we can see how a star's image is made out of a range of primary and secondary elements. We break these down as follows. Secondary materials (e.g. posters, badges, T-shirts, web pages) consist of those generated by the processes of promotion and are the deliberate textual constructions of record companies, film studios, PR departments or fan clubs. In addition there is also 'publicity', i.e. material that is not – or doesn't seem to be – the result of deliberate manipulation or occasionally intention. Often this form of publicity seems more authentic because of this and may take the form of secrets the star 'lets slip' about their personal life, for instance, or the perspectives of paparazzi and gossip columnists. Primary elements in the construction of any image – the primary texts – are the films, videos, songs, TV programmes and so on of a star's portfolio. Nowadays, however, movies may not even be the most important element in a film star's image. A figure such as Angelina Jolie is, at the time of writing, a regular feature in tabloid newspapers and celebrity magazines largely for her relationship with Brad Pitt and their family life. Her performances in the movies she stars in are rarely 'news'. Finally we should add to the construction of image and the star as sign the criticism and commentary produced by contemporary and subsequent appreciation of figures as well as interpretations by writers and researchers such as ourselves.

Because a star's image occurs across such a wide field, it is characterised by polysemia (p. 61) or a multiplicity of meanings. Primary texts that define the star may work to limit or increase polysemia in order to anchor and impose 'preferred' readings. If an actor in film or TV 'immerses' themself in a role then they will go to great lengths to avoid their 'public' image and personality being an issue as it may impact upon the reading of their role. Others tend to reproduce those aspects of their identities and meanings that appeal to their audiences. The same may occur in popular music where songs may or may not play upon the reputation of the performer.

Rap music is one genre of popular culture where the persona of the performer can prove paramount. Songs may involve a high degree of self-reference and bragging about wealth, sexual prowess, 'authenticity' and general toughness, for instance.

We would suggest that stars are important identification figures for consumers. In order to identify with a star, audiences must therefore find points of contact. On the one hand a star must be 'typical' in some way – they must represent ideas that we have of what it is to be human. In this sense they must balance elements of the ordinary and extraordinary. On the other hand, if the star is too ordinary, they are no longer special enough to be a star. This is the typical–special balancing act necessary to the condition of stardom.

What stardom represents

The elevation of stars and celebrities tells us a great deal about society and how media are regarded and understood. It is demonstrably the case that the making, distribution and promotion of films, television programmes, videos, music and so on are a co-operative enterprise. And yet certain individuals are singled out as the focal point of many media forms, as if they were the originators of all of this effort. For instance, and allowing for the skills of performance and delivery, film stars are often treated as if they themselves are the originators of the dialogue delivered in their many appearances. Or, in other cases, they are treated as if they are actual, real-life dispensers of justice, great lovers, war heroes and so on, when in fact they are but one element in a process supported by scriptwriters, make-up artists, stuntmen and -women, directors and so on. Even newsreaders who, for the public, often become the object of trust are not themselves much more than just that: they *read* news from an autocue, news that is gathered by reporters and selected by editors, then written up, again, by scriptwriters. Sometimes, their sobriety, professionalism and stature are accentuated by make-up, wardrobe choices and direction as well as the coaching of their 'performance' according to tried and tested rules.

Ultimately the main point that we can tease out here is that this elevation of the individual attests to the sometimes 'mystifying' media processes. Whether in front of or behind the scenes, the rhetoric and language of media forms 'disguises' the collaborative process in its foregrounding and privileging of such individuals as part of a hierarchy. This is supported by a whole range of structures within and without media institutions – in terms of the salaries that stars have traditionally attracted to the interest afforded them across the rest of a range of media texts.

The other thing that this focus on the individual tells us about is just that – the validation of the individual in society in general. Of all the pop stars, news reporters, actors, voice-over artists, and indeed 'celebrities', who are available to the media some are deemed to be more valuable than others. At a level of talent and aptitude (which itself seems hard to define in any objective fashion) this may indeed be so. However, such individuals are singled out for critical and financial reward, their elevation and importance remaining relatively unquestioned and in fact deemed to be evidence of the validation of certain ideas about the primacy of the individual in our society. In fictional narratives the focus is upon the individual, but in realist media we also focus upon individuals. News reporters in war zones or famine-struck countries, as our representatives, are also individuals, distinguished from the anonymous multitude around them. We suggest therefore that stardom, celebrity and the elevation of the personality embody and promote the individualist ethos of our society as well as what it means to be a man, woman, American, French, working-class and so on.

Summary

Researching representation

We have explored the various meanings of representation as a general category for thinking about how media texts convey the world, or the worlds that they create, to us as audiences. Specifically we used representation as a label for thinking about how individuals and social groups defined by gender, sexuality, class, ethnicity, nationality and so on are depicted. We introduced the idea of the stereotype to explore the positive and negative ways in which individuals and groups were represented and how this process worked as a form of shorthand to tell us about the world that might in fact be inescapable in cultural depictions. As Tessa Perkins (Perkins, 1997) tells us, while we think of stereotypes as simple ideas and readily identified the concept is full of complexity, as evidenced in your exploration of new stereotypes.

We outlined the resulting 'politics of representation' which are suggested by some of the negative functions of stereotyping, addressing questions about the responsibilities of media producers regarding the demographics of media institutions and the access that different groups have to the means of representation. We introduced the method of content analysis as a way of investigating the 'proportionality' of representations across the media that, while limited, offers quantitative data with which to make sense of the balance of representation as a reflection of society's make-up. The complexity of the issues here were illustrated by the 'burden of representation' borne by minority groups who are stereotyped and who might have limited access to the means of cultural expression – for us media forms in all their variety.

We developed our exploration of representations of individuals in the final sections by exploring the concepts of 'stars', 'celebrities' and 'personalities'. Building upon the semiological work of theorists like Richard Dyer we saw how such representations in media forms work as signs, constructed by and within media texts. Importantly, and despite the attraction and connection we have with such apparently rounded individuals (who seem very different from stereotypes), we don't know them and will never know them, and as such we need to comprehend them as 'texts'. In this way we argued that stars in general tell us about individuality and we can conclude that individually and within the texts in which they are situated, stars etc. embody particular 'ways of being human' that convey ideas about what it means to be a man, or woman or so on. In this the star, celebrity and personality as text underlines the broad thrust of this chapter and the approaches introduced show that media representation is not transparent but a site and process of social meaning making.

If you have followed this chapter through and engaged with the activities and thought about the issues covered you should be able to:

- Identify and outline issues involved in thinking about representation and media. Go back and think through these key issues and what other ideas they raise for you. Take a look across media news and our suggested reading to consider further issues and how they are dealt with.

- Define the concepts of representation, stereotyping and associated subcategories. Are you clear about these ideas as we've introduced them? Can you extend our case studies and examples to areas that you know about?

- Deploy skills of rhetorical, semiological, genre and narrative to analysing media representations. As we did in the previous chapter, it is important to bring our tools and ideas together and to continue to use them to investigate media texts as an ongoing project.

- Engage with and respond to debates around the depiction of individuals and social groups in the media. As we've suggested, representation is a political issue when stereotyping is considered for instance. Representations matter because they speak to us about the world and guide our perceptions of it and social groups. Taking sensitivities into account and recognising why and how this matters is an important means of understanding the contexts for textual meaning.

Ultimately, then, what we have suggested is that all representations are 'selective abstractions' of a 'messy' reality and are worthy of investigation due to their distinct link to social contexts. How representations relate to ways of identifying people through categories of class, gender, race, sexuality, disability, nationality and so on have important things to tell us about the power of media texts and their meanings. Overall we should understand the nature of representation in general (the lessons of the previous chapters) and in particular – in conveying ideas about social groups, of majorities and minorities – as a political issue. Representation, at its most basic level, is an issue of power and how we look at the world: who gets to look and speak and what gets said is never innocent or devoid of interests. The task now is to keep going and explore these issues further in your own consumption and in tandem with the ideas introduced in other chapters in this book.

Doing media studies

Investigating representations

Identify any one individual who could be termed a star or celebrity as defined primarily through their role in media forms (sports stars, by and large are defined primarily through their field of expertise despite the ubiquity of some figures who might suggest otherwise). Then, identify primary and secondary texts that construct your chosen individual as a sign and produce a semiological reading of their image and the relationship between their persona in the roles they play or take in the media and supplementary biographical information.

The aim of this activity is first to track the range of materials available to you and the audience in 'knowing' this individual, what is known about them and the symbolic meanings they represent (what skills do they embody?, what ideas about being a man or woman?, etc.).

Are there problems in doing this analysis? To what extent are you able to divorce your sense of the 'individual' and what they represent as a sign? How might the meanings of your individual change with the choices they make in their media careers? How does your individual compare with other identifiable media representations such as some of the stereotypical figures you identified in earlier activities?

Further reading

Celebrity Studies (Taylor & Francis).

> A journal that focuses on the critical exploration of celebrity, stardom and fame. The journals takes an inter-disciplinary approach in assessing celebrity via various media forms, historical periods and national contexts. The journal explores issues in the production, circulation and consumption of fame.

Cottle, S. (ed.) (2000) *Ethnic Minorities and the Media*, London: Open University Press.

> A collection of articles that each study the representation of ethnic minorities in the mass media. A useful introductory section outlines recent developments in the field and topics such as ethnic minority television, image and the public sphere in multi-ethnic societies are explored in the book. Of particular worth is Teun van Dijk's discourse analysis of race in British newspapers. A most helpful discussion of key concepts and terms is also provided.

Craig, S. (ed.) (1992), *Men, Masculinity and the Media*, London: Sage.

> Femininity and the role of women in media texts is a commonly discussed subject in a range of academic work. However, the study of masculinity is, in comparison, a relatively new area. Craig's *Men, Masculinity and the Media* provides the reader with carefully selected articles ranging from studies on gender performance in heavy metal, male comic book heroes and men in sport. For those with a particular interest in the area, a thorough bibliography is provided that carefully surveys the field. Though there have been some recent developments in this area of study, this work is still a worthy introduction for scholars.

Dyer, R. (1997) *White*, London: Routledge.

> A seminal work in the field of representation. Dyer is interested in how 'white' people are labelled as such even though they are not physically that colour. In a series of essays Dyer uses numerous examples taken from film, photography and advertising for analysis. In these he tries to understand what different constructions of whiteness exist in the media and how these might shape people's perceptions. The section on the association of whiteness and death in horror films will be of worth to those who are interested in horror cinema.

Dyer, R. and McDonald, P. (1982) *Stars*, London: BFI Publishing.

> Another important work by Dyer and McDonald that is arguably the first true academic work devoted to the study of stardom. Particular attention is given to Hollywood film stars such as Marilyn Monroe, Jane Fonda and Al Pacino and the construction of image. Though some of these examples might seem a little outdated, the theories and observations still apply when relating them to the stars of today. The most recent edition of this work offers an additional chapter written by Paul McDonald that discusses recent developments in the field of stardom since this work was published.

Haskell, M. (1974) *From Reverence to Rape: The Treatment of Women in the Movies*, New York: Holt, Rinehart & Winston.

> An oft-cited and highly regarded feminist critique of the role of women in film, Haskell's accessible writing style makes this a useful starting point for those who are interested in the representation of women in Hollywood film. Though originally published in 1974, *From Reverence to Rape* offers numerous examples from well-known films such as *The Wizard of Oz* to look at how Hollywood film helped to marginalise women, providing them with role models that reinforced patriarchal values. Haskell does not just look at the role of women in film but also at how women use film. The most recent edition of the classic study includes a new chapter on recent developments of the role of women in film.

Tagg, J. (1988) *The Burden of Representation: Essays on Photographies and Histories*, Basingstoke: Macmillan.

> Disposing with the idea that photographs are purely used to document and merely capture reality Tagg draws on the work of Michel Foucault and uses semiotics to study how institutions have used photography to impose order. Using examples such as police mugshots, passport photographs and licences, Tagg argues that photography is more than just a secondary medium and should be considered a powerful ideological tool in power relations.

CHAPTER 4

Reality media

Images of the torture of prisoners in Iraq generated immense interest around the world when published in this UK newspaper. The revelation that they were fakes caused a scandal and drew attention to our ongoing concern with 'reality' and its portrayal.

Source: Getty Images

Thinking about 'reality media'

In 2004, a British tabloid newspaper, the *Daily Mirror*, published photographs of what it claimed was evidence of British troops torturing Iraqi prisoners. The images caused outrage, but were quickly proven to be fakes, and pretty poor ones at that. Uniforms, guns and what we'll call 'verisimilitude' were unconvincing. The *Guardian* newspaper's Eamonn McCabe, for instance, analysed the 'unconvincing' nature of the pictures noting that the pictures were stiffly posed; the soldier's uniform seemed remarkably clean considering that

these were scenes from the desert trouble spot; and the prisoner shown made no effort to protect himself by curling in a ball or turning away. It looked, in fact, like a 'set-up' (21 May 2004, www.guardian.co.uk/world/2004/may/03/iraq.military and www.guardian.co.uk/gall/0,1208623,00.html).

Even before their fabricated status was revealed, the very publication of the original photographs led to an outcry that evidence of such brutality would engender negative

reactions across the Muslim community and place British soldiers in danger. In the end, the one discernible effect was that Piers Morgan, the newspaper's editor, lost his job, and the reputation of the *Daily Mirror* was much reduced.

The furore surrounding this event illustrates the degree to which issues of honesty, accuracy, objectivity and fidelity to some sense of an empirically verifiable 'reality' are at the forefront of expectations of and debates around the media.

What we will do in this chapter

This chapter develops questions raised in the previous chapters on media texts by asking about the relationship between media forms, representation and reality. Do (or should) media 'mirror' the world, for instance, in some accurate manner or does it inevitably 'warp' it, intentionally or otherwise? On the other hand, as some have argued, do media, like all signifying systems, 'construct' reality and our perception of it?

On our way to developing a definition of realism, we will consider some political and philosophical questions presented in dealing with a range of 'reality media'. At heart here is a concept of the relative nature of 'realism' in media and other cultural forms. We will attempt to conceptualise the nature of the real and the way that media deal with the 'empirical' world, and then explore some of the historical developments that lie behind the aspiration to realism in media. We will explore the ideas of the British theorist Raymond Williams in order to better understand the qualities and expectations that mark out realism as it develops. We'll look at ways in which semiology can help us analyse and identify the construction of realism. Employing our tools of rhetoric, narrative and genre, we will identify some of the dominant ways of organising reality and how this functions. We'll pay particular attention to the privileged form of documentary in conveying the real, and the kinds of attention this genre attracts. This will allow us to explore the contemporary category of 'reality TV' and the way that the boundaries of media forms and expectations have become blurred in recent years. From this, we'll consider the ethical dimensions of 'reality media', concluding with some thoughts about realism and sound – particularly in relation to popular music.

By the end of this chapter you should be able to:

- Distinguish between different modes of representing reality within and across media forms.
- Outline a range of debates and issues around the relationship of media to 'reality' and realism.
- Identify different strategies in media representations of reality.

KEY TERMS: ▶ authenticity; documentary; empirical; ordinary people; phonologism; realism; reality; verisimilitude; virtual reality; witness.

Doing media studies

Getting started

In order to get to grips with some of the propositions about different media forms in this chapter it would be useful in getting started to work through this simple activity.

Brainstorm a list of texts from as many different media as possible that you consider to be in some way 'realistic'. Outline those features (rhetorical, content, contextual) that support your view.

Are there any similarities between features across media forms? Do some forms appear to be 'more' realistic than others? On what basis would you judge a media text to be *un*realistic?

Conceptualising reality and realism

Why do we need to 'conceptualise' reality? What could be more unproblematic than the real? There it is, right outside our door or through the window. You can hear it, see it, touch it, smell it, right? However, put three people in any one situation and ask them to describe what they see, feel and hear and we might end up with three rather different descriptions. Differences might arise from individual perceptions, positions and approaches, not to mention what happens if we don't specify exactly what it is we want our observers to describe. Such instances, and the potential conflicts and confusions – as well as consensus views – arise in the law courts every day of the week, when witnesses are called upon to testify to what they saw at potential crime scenes. Even if we ignore the lessons presented by this scenario about perspective, position and the way in which we might relay our descriptions (not to mention any individual person's psychological and cultural background, which might bear upon these matters), we can begin to appreciate what is at issue in the relationship of media to 'reality'.

Realism as an imperative, idea and concern, along with attendant concepts, can be found in debates about media representations everywhere. Collectively, we still seem to be obsessed with versions of 'reality TV', while computer games present an ever-heightened experience of the worlds they create – a 'virtual' reality – through rumble packs, enhanced graphics and surround-sound audio systems. Philosophers, too, continue to talk about our mediatised age as a 'hyperreal' one. Even concerns about media effects, we would argue, are in some way about the relation of media forms to reality. Realism then, is one of the most used of media studies concepts outside academic circles. Not everyone uses the term specifically but the concept is at the core of everyday evaluations of media texts and debates about the convincing (or otherwise) qualities of texts. It is at the heart of concerns about accuracy and balance in news reporting, objectivity, and certainly behind any reference to stereotyping and perceptions of certain social groups – issues which we dealt with in the previous chapter. We can see the scope of theories of the relation of the real, and its representation and allied concerns, if we consider a range of the senses comprised in any dictionary definition of the real:

> *existing or occurring in the physical world; not imaginary, fictitious, or theoretical; actual, true; not false* (p. 827 *of New Collins Dictionary* (1987)).

We can consider the kinds of issues that come up in everyday debates about the media through two very different examples (you should compile a compatible list from your own viewing, reading and discussion):

1. The films of American documentarist Michael Moore have generated much controversy in recent years for their criticisms of his country's gun culture (*Bowling for Columbine*, 2002), its war on terror (*Fahrenheit 9/11*, 2004) and, most recently, its health system (*Sicko*, 2007) and entire ethos in *Capitalism: A Love Story* (2009). Moore made his name and reputation with his first film, *Roger and Me* (1989), which explored the effect of the closure of the Ford motor car plant in Moore's home town of Flint, Michigan. The film revolves around Moore's ultimately unsuccessful attempts to gain an interview with Ford's director, Roger B. Smith. His critics have unearthed evidence to suggest that Moore did actually gain this interview and hid this fact in pursuit of a good story (e.g. in the film *Michael Moore Hates America* (dir. Wilson, 2004)).

2. Multi-millionaire songstress and actress Jennifer Lopez released a single in 2002 called *Jenny from the Block*. In this song she sought to assure her listeners that, despite her wealth and remove from 'ordinary' life and the ridiculousness of stories in the press about her excesses, she was to all intents and purposes the same old working-class

Latino girl in touch with her roots. These roots were the basis for her authenticity. We should note also that in the previous year Lopez had a big hit with the song 'I'm Real', releasing a further 'Murder Remix' which enlisted the help of rapper Ja Rule in order to 'add' authenticity.

We can see how these examples are based upon claims to and disputes about representation and the nature of the real. At issue are questions of accuracy, truth, fairness, authenticity and a fidelity to some sense of empirical reality. Such instances prompt questions about other media forms that we might consider in terms of 'reality'.

Defining 'reality media'

Empirical

Based on experience or observation, and verifiable by observation or experiment, without recourse to a scientific or philosophical theory or system.

Different media forms seem to access and represent the '**empirical**' world differently; some seem to be more effective in doing this than others, or by convention are accepted to be so. For instance, we tend to evaluate a documentary TV news report rather differently from a radio report, newspaper cartoon, soap opera or indeed 'reality TV' shows that are predicated on entertaining and highlighting characters in unusual situations.

Taking account of the issues we've considered in previous chapters, we can appreciate what is at stake here. The rhetorical repertoires available to different media forms, their differing generic conventions and narrative strategies – whether fictional or fact-based – all impact upon the way in which mediation between reality and textual expression works. However, a philosophical question arises here: what is reality anyway, can we agree on what it is and how can we know it? Likewise, if we accept that media are one way of accessing the 'real', it is worth asking: what exactly is the nature of that media reality itself? The logic of this line of reflection is compounded by the fact that most of us live in a highly mediatised world, with media forms being the primary source of our ideas about that world.

This philosophical digression belies the fact that, as suggested, we do tend to identify particular media forms and genres with particular representations of reality, and accept and trust them; and this is expressed in the various ways in which we describe them. In relation to photography, even in this digital age, we still sometimes hear the phrase 'the camera never lies'; television is still a 'window on the world', which provides us with 'documentary' and 'reality TV' forms; popular music still uses the term 'to record', while rappers

Key text

Niklas Luhmann: the reality of the mass media

The German theorist Niklas Luhmann has stated that 'Whatever we know about our society, or indeed about the world in which we live, we know through the mass media' (Luhmann, 2000: 1). In this provocative treatise, Luhmann argues that the functions of mass media systems are not determined by reference to values of truthfulness, objectivity or knowledge produced outside these systems. Instead, these systems are regulated by internal codes and their own criteria of what constitutes news, objectivity, reality and so on. It is through these systems that modern societies construct their own reality. This is not to suggest that the 'illusion' of reality is ultimately false or mendacious: 'one cannot comprehend the reality of the mass media' if one sees its task in providing relevant information about the world and measuring its failure, its distortion of reality, its manipulation of opinion against this' (Luhmann, 2000: 98). This construction has a function which is to process information without overburdening us as members of society and aiding in social stability.

'keep it real'; film shares TV's documentary form, while its history and scope encompass Soviet Realism, Italian neo-realism and *sur*realism, among other 'realist' modes.

We can make a working distinction between media forms that seek to represent (*re*-present, p. 103) the world as it is (or was) – through actually existing people or occurring events – and those which seek to represent the world or imaginary worlds in realistic and coherent fashion. This distinction is one media consumers implicitly recognise and usually make, although it presents us with a potential problem. While we might focus on realism in media as related to those forms that *re*-present the world, the term applies to fictional forms as much as to fact-based, documentary forms. Likewise, do note again that the concept of reality media encompasses all forms and cannot be reduced simply to audio-visual forms that present an analogue representation of the world and seem to be more effectively 'real' than others. Thus, any serious attention to reality media needs to account for written language in the form of journalism as much as for the spoken word of TV and radio news, webcams and the internet in general, and also for the 'virtual' realities of games and online environments. In addition it is important to consider popular music and how it has been understood in relation to validations of the real and authenticity.

Historical realisms

The different ways in which media forms convey and relate to the world illustrate what the Russian semiologist Roman Jacobson calls 'the extreme relativity of the concept of realism' (Jacobson, 1971: 42). Some attention to the historical roots and changes in the broad concept of realism underline this relativity but also indicate some of the common ground on which varying conceptions of the real rest. We'll explore some of these roots in order to understand reality media better.

The general concept of representational realism (across modes of cultural expression which incorporate the sciences, philosophy and the arts, too) is rooted in the classical Greek concept of *mimesis*, meaning imitation. It derives from the concerns of the works of Aristotle and Plato about whether or not art and the sciences imitate the world in its 'mere' surface appearances or in terms of its ideal 'truths'. Metaphors of 'windows' and 'mirrors' in representational discussion can be traced back to these ancient philosophers. Alongside mimesis, we have also inherited the term 'verisimilitude'. This term is usually used to describe the believability, likelihood or credible qualities of fictions in particular, and the way that individuals act in these fictions. This is not to say that one should dismiss fantastic tales as unreal. Instead, one should consider whether or not, within the logic of stories, characters act in ways related to their nature as sketched out, and whether or not plotlines unfold as a consequence of inevitability or probability within the 'diegesis' (p. 86).

Modern senses of realism can be traced through aspects of science, philosophy and specific literary developments, traditions and related usage in Western art and popular forms. In the nineteenth century, for instance, the term Realism (note the capital) was coined in order to describe a broad movement in literature, classical music and art. This Realism was conceived in opposition to romantic 'idealism' that was felt to inadequately attend to the contemporary world of modernity and the Industrial Revolution. Novels by French authors such as Honoré de Balzac and Gustave Flaubert, or George Eliot in England, for instance, sought to deal with the world as it 'really was', through recognisable, if 'typical', individuals and social situations. As historian Linda Nochlin relates, artworks sought 'to give a truthful, objective and impartial representation of the real world based on meticulous observation of contemporary life' (cited in Winston, 1996: 23).

Romantic works approached representation in a high-minded manner, particularly when they dealt with or portrayed sensitive matters (e.g. the naked body, human love), presenting things in idealised fashion – as they 'should' be. Intense new realist works elicited scandalised responses and were censured as immoral, or for wallowing in squalid and depressing subject matter. This is perhaps a burden that 'reality media' often still contends with in its claims to truth, as we'll see.

Similar things were happening in the world of theatre, with works such as Henrik Ibsen's *A Doll's House* (written in 1879), in which actors were required to take on the guise of the characters they played with more commitment and conviction than was usual – a trend later informing the 'method' developed by Konstantin Stanislavsky.

In the visual arts, the literal depiction or 'mirroring' of life had long been achievable through the use of lenses and refraction in devices such as the 'camera obscura'. As argued by David Hockney (2001), this was able to project 'live' images of the real world on to screens or walls and was used by painters such as Ingres and Van Eyck in their quest to accurately capture life, guiding the hand of artists and illustrators. However, of greatest significance to us, and of major importance to ideas of representational realism developed during the nineteenth century, was the invention of a device for capturing and reproducing images called the daguerreotype. The daguerreotype, despite its limitations, influenced the development of photography, which produced quicker and 'cleaner' images. Both had a major impact upon other 'realist' forms and the degree to which painting, for instance, was thought to be unable to depict reality any longer. From the very start, photography became the acme of 'reality media' for its apparent ability to 'capture' reality in analogue form, in ways not obviously involving the intercession of human hands, tools or interests.

What we should take from such brief historical detail is simply that any sense of the textual representation of reality – realism – has a history in which its changing nature and responses to it outline its relative qualities. Once we accept that 'realism' is not reducible to any simple mirror metaphor, an idea of an adequate, truthful or exhaustive relationship between a representational form or text and some objective empirical reality, then we can proceed. Thus, we can consider how realism can be thought of as a rhetorical strategy, the objective of which is to position the consumer of any text to understand the representation before them as in some way conveying the world in reliable fashion.

Thinking aloud

Acting and realism

Theatre directors Konstantin Stanislavsky (1863–1938) in Russia, and later Lee Strasberg (1902–82) in the USA, developed systems of training actors that were based on an actor's attention to detail and attempt to thoroughly 'get into character'. 'Method acting', as it has become known, is associated with actors such as Marlon Brando, James Dean, Robert de Niro, and, more recently, Christian Bale and Heath Ledger, and seeks a 'psychological realism' in terms of a truth about imaginary characters that has fed into perceptions of modern film and TV, providing a heightened realism. Acting style and commitment – de Niro acquired extra weight in order to portray the boxer Jake La Motta in *Raging Bull* (dir. Scorsese, 1980) – in tandem with the development of technologies such as handheld cameras and techniques such as location shooting, and the breaking of taboos over sex, violence and profanity, seem to provide us with forms that are very different from the melodramatic styles apparent in the early cinema.

Media scholars have not given the work of acting much attention, however, offering suggestive openings for us to think about what our expectations are in terms of performance and how we judge 'accuracy', 'truthfulness' and so on in this aspect of media texts.

Key thinker

Brian Winston

Brian Winston is a British media scholar and documentary film-maker. He was part of the influential Glasgow Media Group (see www._glasgowmediagroup._org/) and has written widely on documentary practice. His studies have included key works on documentary – *Lies, Damned Lies and Documentaries* (2001) and the earlier *Claiming the Real*. The latter work explores the history of documentary film in relation to technological changes and the differences between the way that this genre 'claims' the real in comparison to fiction film (Winston, 1995). In his book *Technologies of Seeing* (1996), Winston has argued that, since the Renaissance period, a series of aesthetic or stylistic strategies and preferences have become embedded in Western cultural taste. This trend amounts to what he calls a 'species of addiction – an addiction to realism. This addiction which produced Renaissance perspective painting also deeply affected the development of the Western theatre' (1996: 23). Furthermore, he sees this tradition as setting the foundations for cinema:

> The operation of this addiction to realism thus created in the social sphere a number of elements which were crucial to the cinema. Before the turn of the 19th century, the public was prepared to be entertained by being seated in rows in a darkened space to look at magic lantern slides. After the coming of the gaslamp, auditoria for live spectacles were also darkened. A taste for dumb show was in vogue. These live spectacles involved highly realistic effects and some entertainments consisted entirely of displays of realistic scenery, animated and augmented in various ways short of live acting. What characterises these last is an extreme verisimilitude, an expression of the sort of public pictorial taste that had dominated in the West for the previous several centuries. (Winston, 1996: 25)

Realism
is a rhetorical and signifying strategy (in media texts) for representing the worlds to which those texts refer. In this way it is best to think of 'realisms'.

We could, therefore, suggest several ways of making sense of **realism** based upon this definition and our thinking so far. First, realism is a matter of rhetorical or narrative intention and convention. Secondly, realism is a perception of the audience. Audiences can agree or differ over what constitutes the realistic qualities or otherwise of any text ('that was a bit far-fetched' someone might say after watching a movie). Finally, realism refers to specific periods in the history of media forms and competing forms and ideas. However, this is a relatively dry list that tends to ignore an important aspect of the nature of realism. It is often the *content* of media texts that is a determinant of how 'realistic' a form is in its representations and how audiences perceive its effectiveness. This is where the observations of the great British critic Raymond Williams are most useful (see p. 389).

Williams explored dramatic forms in theatre, and the historical development of the defining characteristics of theatre's attempts at realism (Williams, 1977, and in Burnett, 1991). He suggested that realism here was related to changes in the decorum of representation, i.e. the nature of what was fitting material for drama. Thus the accretion of 'realism' over the period he studied can be thought of in the following ways:

- First, a conscious movement towards social extension, i.e. the inclusion of groups hitherto excluded from the field of representations or represented in limited manner, usually at a distance rather than from 'within', upon their own or sympathetic terms. In the history of cinema many movements associated with realism have been labelled in this way due to shifting attention from the 'well- to- do' to groups such as the working classes. In fact, the hugely influential British Documentary Film Movement of the 1930s defined itself largely through dealing with social issues associated with the condition of the lower classes (see the discussion of John Grierson below). As we discuss below, in music 'realist' forms such as folk draw their associations with 'the people', while many genres of African-American music – soul or rap, for instance – are indexed as 'real' or authentic by the very race and culture of their originators. This relates to the long history of oppression and exclusion of people from this group in American society. In terms of social extension, we might well consider how the web and digital distribution – across blogs, social media and so on – have added to the textures of media realism.

■ Secondly, the development of realism involves a movement towards action conveying the present, i.e. contemporary social issues or matters of contemporary relevance. This has value for us in thinking about the way in which we value current affairs and journalism, for example, for being, by definition, up to date and in touch with the empirical world. Again, in relation to digital media, the immediacy of reports from Twitter, for instance, at key new moments – from within and without – accentuates the literal quality of representing the present and 'being present'.

■ Thirdly, Williams identified an emphasis on secular action – action depicted in human terms. In Williams's analysis of theatre, he notes how gods and fate played a part in much traditional drama, whereas realism was signalled and evinced in the turn from such sacred and supernatural aspects to those of more secular origin. On this note, it is worth recalling how much of contemporary popular media fantasies rely upon ideas of aristocracy to support the worlds that they present. From *Star Wars* (Princess Leia, Jedi knights, etc.), to the Harry Potter series (halfblood princes, Lord Voldemort, etc.), 'Narnia' adventures (the children become kings and queens) as well as *The Golden Compass* (dir. Weitz, 2007), the film version of Philip Pullman's book *Northern Lights*. In these texts, the notion of the everyday, of ordinary people and ordinary life, is importantly absent other than as something to be escaped.

Thinking aloud

New media and new realities?

With the advent of digitisation, computer gaming and the internet, online experiences have become much more detailed and convoluted, while aspects of new media usage have become integral to the everyday lives and self-definition of millions of people. A question for new scholars to address, therefore, is: how have new media forms challenged realism? Indeed, are there new realisms? Are these new or altered realisms qualitatively different experiences from what has come before?

It certainly seems rather old hat now to speak of virtual reality or VR – a contradictory term if ever there was one. It is a label for the fabricated worlds and environments created by computer technologies, which are realised in image, word, sound and sensation but distinct from the bodily or 'corporeal' reality presented to us outside such mediation and constructions. Whatever the realities and possibilities of a 'virtual' reality, it has appeared as an object of speculation in science fiction novels and Hollywood films, from Disney's *Tron* (dir. Lisberger, 1982) to, more recently, *The Cell* (dir. Singh, 2000) and *Tron Legacy* (dir. Kosinski, 2010).

Despite antecedents, VR was coined in 1986 by a computer developer by the name of Jaron Lanier. It has been most effectively dealt with in the work of Howard Rheingold (Rheingold, 1991, 1994), who has drawn attention to the online nature of sociability and community, alongside the more imaginative speculations based upon the immersive capabilities of internet and gaming environments and available technologies.

Furthermore, if we rely upon media for our access to the world at large, how has interactivity, for instance, inflected the nature of the honesty and truthfulness of the reporters and documentarists we have traditionally turned to? New scholars of media, who have grown up with the new media forms, will be well placed to reflect upon the realities of new media but also to learn from the abiding issues in the field touched upon in this chapter.

In tandem with the idea of social extension, we can adapt Williams's last idea of the secular here in two ways. One would relate to an increasing attention to and construction of the 'ordinary' in the media – in TV in particular but also across the web – by design or default (see below). Likewise, if we take the secular to be a move away from the sacred, it might be useful to consider the nature of its antonym, the profane, as relevant to realism. At a simplistic level this might, perhaps, relate to the manner in which language has been used in media across time. If we look back at the propriety with which language was regulated in the press, movies and TV of the past, not to mention in popular music, we can see how it did not, until recently, tend to reflect some of the more colourful aspects of expression – namely 'swearing' – or the direct way in which we tend to label the world nowadays (calling a spade a spade, as it were).

We can also add a fourth element to Williams's list for our purposes, which is that of technological development. We can see how the coming of a medium such as the daguerreotype, then the development of photography, later the moving picture, in black and white, then with sound and colour, indicates the manner in which technology has enhanced a sense of realism and its emulation, and added to the available armoury of representation. Of course, technology does not come to be used in forging representations without taking on or developing series of conventions and associated codes and is thus never 'innocent' or transparent. The development of handheld cine cameras, for instance, has given us a coded association of actuality through movement and altering focus, despite the subsequent invention of 'steadicam' and automatic focus, both designed to do away with the 'wobble' of images produced by handheld cameras. In the same way, and despite the long available association of colour photography, the black and white image often serves to 'connote' truth and realism, despite the fact that the colour image more adequately 'reflects' the nature of the world as most of us perceive it.

We can summarise our discussion thus far through the observations of film theorist Noël Carroll, in his writing on non-fiction film (Carroll, 1991, 1996). He argues that there can be no abiding transhistorical, and by implication transcultural, 'absolute' realism that works in a neutral manner for all people across all times and cultures in the same way. So, then, realism and its conventions change over time, and what looked 'real' to people of the past may be less convincing to us, and not just because the trappings of culture (dress, manners, etc.) have altered. Likewise, across the world, there are different ways of comprehending reality through cultural works and media conventions, each working adequately within its culture. To tie together the philosophical and media studies problem, this suggests, therefore, that reality and its depiction is not a constant and fixed category.

Realism is then, as Jakobson tells us, a relative concept. Nonetheless, realism as aspiration and expectation and its associated concepts continues to inform many of our debates about media forms and the social roles taken up by the different industries. We'll explore this further by looking at some specific instances of 'reality media' and realist forms, but

Doing media studies

Investigating technologies of the real

Research and produce a timeline of media technologies, giving their date of invention. Identify examples of where and how those technologies have been used in media forms. Use your timeline to answer the following questions.

What can we learn from such a list about the changing nature of realism and available technologies? Has the aspiration to realism become more effective or convincing? What other factors would we have to account for in evaluating the 'real' of 'reality media' in deploying such technologies?

in progressing let's consider a semiological perspective on the real in media texts that will aid our explorations further.

Semiology and the real

The explorations and suggestions of semiology in its attention to systems of signification and codes support our idea of realisms – historical and plural – rather than any single 'realism'. This, in turn, problematises any sense of an empirical, objective 'reality' that media convey. In his writings, Roland Barthes coined the term 'reality effect' (*effet de réel*) (1968) to describe the accumulation of details in texts which serve little more purpose than to signify 'reality'. Barthes was particularly interested in fictional forms in literature and noted how, in structural terms, some of the detail provided often appeared to be redundant and sometimes even served to potentially interrupt narrative flow. We might call these details 'colour' or aspects of 'scene setting', and Barthes suggests that reference to objects, furniture, landmarks and so on serves an indexical function in this way to announce 'we are real' – an effect supporting the verisimilitude of the text. These features, however redundant, locate the story in relation to our knowledge of reality as a guarantee of plausibility, even at the most basic level of establishing a viable background to a tale.

In fictional media forms such as Bollywood film, this seems fairly straightforward and is dealt with in the way that *mise en scène* will ensure that period or location detail is coherent and consistent. Motor cars and computers would be unlikely to feature in a film about the Middle Ages, for instance, while stories set in identifiable locations will take time to illustrate these by including views of landmarks in montage form or as a backdrop to events. However, documentary forms on TV and in film also tend to follow the same procedure in deliberately highlighting features of landscape, habitat and so on, in order to support their claims to truth. Likewise, journalistic writing and current affairs broadcasting feature elements in stories that, it could be said, serve to enhance truth claims in order to locate the story as 'real' and to enhance authenticity. We can see this every time a newsreader in a TV studio turns to a colleague who is out on location. The newsreader's 'bodily' turn, while literally unnecessary (it looks as if the broadcasters are talking to each other via images when they are, in fact, only listening to each other's words via earpieces), is part of a rhetorical 'realism' that constructs an implied and coherent relationship in time and space. Often, a reporter in the field might be standing outside a political location (the White House, Downing Street, the European Parliament) but without any literal purpose – i.e. they will not be interviewing anyone and it may be the case that the person or event to which they refer may not actually be at that location (the president is away, the debate is long since finished, MPs are actually in their constituencies). Sometimes these aspects of media practice and signification may actually strike us as obvious redundancies, as they have become habitual. Nonetheless, they serve to remind us of the range of factors working to construct and signify 'reality'.

Dominant practices and forms of reality media

Despite this attention to the codified nature of the real, in tandem with potential questions about how we know the nature of the empirically real, this should not lead us to a position of abstract inertia in our studies. Producers and consumers, as well as theorists, continue to rely upon media forms as indexes of the real for the way in which they investigate and tell us about it, sometimes with the purpose of affecting or altering that reality.

Thanks to the 'heightened' representational aspects of the moving image, many ideas attending to realism in media have concerned cinema and, more recently, television. From its inception in 1895 as *moving* pictures ('cinema' derives from *kinesis* meaning motion), subsequently acquiring sound and colour, cinema, when compared with print or still photography, has offered something that appears to be akin to our experience of the world. Early theorists such as André Bazin in France, Béla Bálazs in Hungary and Siegfried Kracauer in Germany emphasised the 'vocation for realism' presented by film. Aware of the variety of available techniques and the ways that they were used, they noted also the different ways in which film appeared to emulate perception of the empirical world. Deep-focus photography or long takes offered the ability to convey 'life as a continuum', for us as viewers to survey in much the same way that we do events and the world about us.

Interestingly, this appreciation related not to a belief that film was simply useful for documenting the world but that, in its dramatic shapes, it would produce insights into the greater realities of society and the human condition. This understanding, in part, derives from the critics' grounding in those forms of literature, drama and painting outlined earlier but also in the debt owed to those forms by cinema producers in the development of rhetorical and narrative practices and conventions. In short, cinema inherited from other forms particular conventions of conveying the real in coherent and convincing fashion in its storytelling.

Bazin was one of the first to talk of a 'classical' cinema, using the term in much the same way as one might when talking of classical music. In this usage the reference is to a series of principles, rules or practices through which texts are constructed. Others, such as David Bordwell (see p. 87), refer to the 'classical realist text' or, as Noël Burch does, an 'institutional mode of representation'. What all of these analysts are pointing to is a conventional way of representing stories (fact and fiction) in a coherent and believable manner that was dominant in Hollywood and other mainstream national/commercial cinemas from about 1915 to 1960. While this mode of telling was challenged by innovations from young film-makers in Italy, France, the UK and other countries, it continues to influence representational modes.

This classical form organises its rhetoric around narrative, to tell stories in as conventional and clear a manner as possible in order to engage and entertain the consumer. This produced a form of dominant realism, a set of conventions that, by virtue of the ubiquity of this practice, acquired a kind of naturalised and accepted mode of representation. Features of this way of representing worlds include:

- A cause and effect structure, i.e. one event would precipitate another in clear developmental fashion. In *I Am Legend* (dir. Lawrence, 2007) a plague wipes out most of the human race, leaving Will Smith to deal with the consequences.

- A focus on the centrality of human agency, i.e. individuals are the subject of stories, whatever their grandiose or banal nature. War films are thus not about war or politics but about the growth and problems of the individuals caught up in them, who incidentally happen to resolve such conflicts as a consequence – see Michael Bay's *Pearl Harbor* (2001), for instance.

- Verisimilitude conveyed through *mise en scène*, but also the marshalling of camera and editing techniques to convey conventionally coherent and consistent time and space. A series of rules about camera movement, matching eye-lines between cuts, all ensuring continuity, are employed in the service of coherence here.

- The effacement of all of these techniques and any sense of an individual style. The rhetorical and narrative organisation of this form thus convey a 'seamlessness' about it – we focus on being involved in the story rather than being presented with questions about how the story is being told. Viewers tend to notice this when watching films that experiment with form, such as art cinema and avant-garde works (see Chapter 12).

One thing to note here is that this structural mode of representing reality applies to both fantasies such as *Star Wars* (dir. Lucas, 1977) and historical recreations such as *Braveheart* (dir. Gibson, 1995), as well as many types of documentaries such as *Sicko* (dir. Moore, 2007). Thus we are presented, in classical narrative forms, with a repeated dominant mode of representation that disguises one version of reality as *the* reality because it attains the status of appearing to be natural or obvious. In this sense, this 'classical realism' can be considered to be a highly value-laden or 'ideological' way of presenting stories (see Chapter 12).

Truth, honesty and documenting the real

As outlined, then, classical realism has a role in ordering the dramatic and fictional, but it is also a mode that can be seen to be at work in those texts which we accept more readily as being about 'reality', namely documentaries. Documentary forms in television and film (and also in radio) have a privileged place in media that overlaps with our expectations of broadcast and print journalism. Traditionally, documentary film-makers (and radio programme makers) have been held in high regard for their commitment to exploring and exposing aspects of society otherwise ignored or overlooked. In this manner they fulfil one of the aspects of realism identified by Raymond Williams. At the same time, their work is subject to the kind of scrutiny about its rigour and reliability that both tests and endorses the ways in which we trust it to convey truth about the world.

The term documentary as applied to film – to document – was coined by the British film-maker John Grierson (1898–1972). The term was already familiar, however, from a tradition in photography. From Victorian times, photography had been used to accompany adventurers, anthropologists and colonists from the West on their explorations of 'darkest' Africa and other 'undiscovered' territories, recording the human, animal and geographical curiosities found there. Closer to home, in countries like the UK, France and Germany, photography was also used as a form of social investigation. The camera followed social reformers into slums and other 'dark places' closer to home, in documenting the lives of the impoverished or recording the faces of criminals and social types, and in producing visible data that could be used for understanding humanity or in support of attempts to improve social conditions. What developed was a close association between seeing, knowing and aspects of power, reflecting a will to philanthropic reform and control (Tagg, 1988).

From the advent of film in 1895, the medium was understood as one which 'documented'. Most early films presented records of everyday activities (train arriving at a station, boating, snowball fights), re-presented through this new medium as a novelty. The ordinary became extraordinary by virtue of a new mode of seeing it. At the start, there was no 'obvious' reason why film should be used for narrative and entertainment ends, and many suggestions and uses for film were offered that posited it as a relatively straightforward documenting device, i.e. it could be used to record written documents, images of the great and good for posterity.

Like photography before it, then, the medium offered enormous possibilities for 'recording' and re-presenting aspects of reality. Sometimes with scientific intent, sometimes purely commercial, moving images of faraway places could be put before interested audiences as objects of interest and scrutiny. Many histories of documentary in film locate its roots in this way of using film but identify its maturity with the work of British documentarists such as Robert Flaherty and John Grierson.

Flaherty's films, such as *Nanook of the North* (1922) on the Inuit people, *Moana* (1926) or *Man of Aran* (1935), were ethnographic explorations of places beyond the experiences of the urban audiences normal for cinema, and sought to capture an 'unseen' reality (on ethnography see p. 335). However, even in these early moments of consciously distinct documentary, issues around the fidelity of representation to reality arose in explicit fashion. Initially using pre-sound film equipment with all of its limitations (bulk, limited ability to capture natural light, etc.), Flaherty often had to encourage his subjects to re-stage events in their lives for the benefit of his camera. As he said, 'Sometimes you have to lie. One has to distort a thing to catch its spirit' (quoted in Heider, 2006). Grierson's work as director and producer, alongside his colleagues in the 1930s and 1940s (and later in television), also focused on the 'unknown' here in films such as *Housing Problems* (dir. Anstey and Elton, 1935), *Coal Face* (dir. Cavalcanti, 1935) and the renowned *Night Mail* (dir. Wright and Watt, 1936). Such productions concentrated on the under-represented social groups of the UK and afforded insights into how people lived and, indeed, the nature of the world of everyday work.

Between them, the two film-makers evinced two distinct tendencies in documentary film-making that indicate aspects of the rhetoric and address of the genre. These are known as expository and observational styles. Observational documentary is faithful to the empirical idea in observing the world as unobtrusively as possible. Documentaries in this style are presented very much as a series of 'found' scenes, linked together. Intimacy and access are usually gained and implied by an approach that seeks to let events unfold before the camera, and any organisation appears loose and naturalistic. This is, of course, only a rhetorical strategy – we see events where a camera and crew, however small, are an alien, if obscured, interlocutor to the world unfolding before us. However 'real' it appears and however much the subjects ignore the camera, we cannot but note that its presence has some impact upon that unfolding world.

Expository documentary does not rely upon the ability of the empirical world to make its meanings manifest. This label describes an active attempt to interpret and explain. What we encounter in texts of this kind is a narration that endorses an objective 'god-like' view of events. Generally through its narrative and the use of voice-overs, it offers what is usually a single, coherent, explanatory position, representing a view of 'them' or 'others' to the audience, which constitutes an implied 'us'. Interestingly, this kind of approach is still most explicit in documentaries about the natural world. In the tales of lions, birds, whales or wildebeest, we see not only all of the virtues of claims to the real but also all of its potential faults, in narrativising the natural cycle and reducing the complexity of the empirical to a manageable size – giving it a form that adheres rather closely to the classical text.

Examining how its originators spoke of documentary reveals some of the intriguing ways in which its relationship with the real was worked through. For John Grierson, the documentary form was *creative* in the same manner as music hall, ballet, Post-Impressionist painting or the blank verse of Shakespeare, but could claim something more as a result of its subject matter: 'When we come to documentary we come to the actual world, to the world of the streets, of the tenements and the factories, the living people and the observation of living people . . . We have to give creative shapes to it, we have to be profound about it before our documentary art is as good or better than the art of the studio' (quoted in Long, 2008, pp. 166–7). He wrote that it was important to make a distinction between 'a method which describes only the surface values of a subject' and that which 'more explosively reveals the reality of it. You photograph the natural life, but you also, by your own juxtaposition of detail, create an interpretation of it' (ibid.).

Such work was not about mere reproduction but about the correct kind of mediation and interpretation of the world. This was based upon the notion that the subject – i.e. 'ordinary people' and work, the fascination with essentially everyday things – was itself the guarantor of truth, qualifying a particularly prescriptive interpretation of the world. Grierson, in particular, was instrumental in insisting upon the responsibility of the documentary film-maker in using the form to encourage social awareness, built upon a responsibility to 'reality'. For him, in the UK context, film was something that could encourage the nation to communicate with itself and so aid community cohesion.

Some questions that we should tease out here on the back of this agenda – concerning documentary in particular, but also the other kinds of texts that claim a relationship to the real – are as follows:

■ Who is speaking, about whom and to whom?

■ What is the nature of the knowledge produced by the text?

Clearly these relate back to those issues identified in Chapter 3 on representation.

These instances and individuals are merely touchstones for the roots of documentary and its principles, which have been tested, have taken on many forms and have been pursued across media in photo-journalism, photo-documentary, new journalism, TV forms, radio and so on. Likewise, the two distinct and discrete types of documentary may be somewhat redundant nowadays: as documentarists continue to explore ways of investigating and conveying the real, 'hybridity' and cross-fertilisation has become the norm.

Ultimately, documentary as a genre exemplifies in its associations many of the features that Raymond Williams notes in the historical development of realism. It has traditionally dealt with the investigation of social issues and the extension of media coverage into the lives and thoughts of those neglected in traditional or contemporary representations. Here,

Thinking aloud

Contemporary TV documentary from the inside

Here's an insight on TV documentary from an insider, BBC TV film-maker Vanessa Jackson, who outlines her thoughts on contemporary documentary, how creatives define its various forms and how documentaries are made:

> I have worked in television production with the BBC for 20 years, in all roles from production secretary to series producer, and everything in-between. Over those years I have produced a range of factual series, but it is the documentary programmes that I have found most challenging and most rewarding to be involved in. It is a powerful genre with the ability to change lives and perceptions, a responsibility that programme makers must take very seriously. That responsibility does not end with transmission. Some of the contributors whose lives we have recorded I am still in touch with today.

In contemporary documentary there are several distinct subgenres, some more in vogue than others.

■ **Observational**, or 'fly on the wall', documentaries usually involve a self-shooting director recording a large quantity of material 'as it happens', without influencing events, and then picking out story threads in the edit. Often the director asks questions of the contributor off camera, which will usually be edited out, in order to get the contributor to articulate how they think or feel. Asking questions obviously does influence events, as does the actual presence of the production crew itself, so even this low-impact style of shooting does not capture reality as it really is. Observational documentaries are usually character led, and good access is crucial.

■ **Slice of life** documentaries concentrate on showing a particular aspect of life, but are not necessarily driven by a strong narrative thread. They are not as popular today as in previous decades. They have a tendency to be charming or whimsical but may lack the drama and concentration on character of some other forms. *Lido*, Lucy Blakstad's 1995 award-winning documentary, is an example.

■ **A constructed** documentary is one that has been largely shaped by the production team in pre-production; examples would include programmes like *Timewatch*, or *The Secret Life of Motorways*, which rely on extensive research. Contributors will be researched who can tell a particular part of the story, or to show a particular viewpoint. This type of documentary will often include first-hand testimony and archive footage, or other illustrative material.

■ **An authored** documentary is seen from the viewpoint of the 'author', who may be the reporter, presenter or producer; it is not pretending to be objective. This form often involves the 'author' setting out on a quest, such as in Nicky Taylor's documentaries (e.g *Face of a Binge Drinker, Should I Smoke Dope, How Dirty Can I Get?*), Adam Curtis's Power of Nightmares or Michael Moore's *Sicko*! or *Fahrenheit 9/11*.

No documentary is truly objective, nor does it accurately document real life, but all documentaries should be true to the story they depict. The vast majority of documentaries are shot on a single camera, so every shot change is a condensing of time and a break in the continuous action. The editing process is the making of most documentaries. The sequences recorded, even in an observational documentary, will be ordered in the most effective manner, no matter when they were chronologically recorded, as long as this doesn't break through the line of the story. Producers can do this and still be 'true to the story' as long as they do not distort cause and effect. The editing of *Monarchy: The Royal Family at Work* (dir. Reid, 2007), which caused such controversy by editing shots out of chronological order, failed to be 'true to the story' because the editing altered the cause and effect of events. All documentaries are constructed in the edit: the narrative arc must be satisfying for the viewer. Any pre-title sequence must hook the audience in, and then we need to know enough about the bare bones of the story for it to make sense. The majority of detail will be saved until later on, because we need to get to know and care about the characters before finding out additional facts. The narrative then needs to develop in interesting, unexpected and engaging ways, building to a denouement towards the end of the film. The vast majority of documentaries contain commentary. It is almost always quicker and easier to tell the viewer what they need to know in order to understand what is going on, or to move to the next scene, by voice-over, rather than via audio or synch from the contributor. But by having commentary the producer is giving a perspective or viewpoint to the film that will colour it, and further shape the reality it portrays.

Source: Vanessa Jackson, Degree Leader Television (BCU), former BBC Series Producer.

for instance, is a list of some of the films of one of the most renowned of contemporary documentarists, Nick Broomfield. The subject matter indicates how faithfully Broomfield has followed the terms of the genre but also how he has expanded its subject matter. His films also add to a tradition of challenging taboos about what can and cannot be represented in polite society, tracing a movement from the sacred to the profane:

■ *Behind the Rent Strike* (1979) (concerning a trade union dispute);

■ *Soldier Girls* (1981) – concerning women serving in the armed forces;

■ *Chicken Ranch* (1983) – concerning prostitution and other workers in the legalised brothels of Nevada;

■ *Aileen Wuornos: The Selling of a Serial Killer* (1992) – concerning an American female murderer on death row;

Nick Broomfield can be heard and often appears as a protagonist in his own documentary work.

Source: Mohamad Zaid/ Rex Features

- *Fetishes* (1996) – concerning people with unusual sexual preferences;
- *Kurt and Courtney* (1998) – concerning 'alternative' rock stars;
- *Biggie and Tupac* (2002) – concerning gangsta rappers.

Over time, the possibilities of the genre in accessing and conveying the real have been enhanced by technological developments and improvements that have made equipment cheaper, lighter and more unobtrusive. Aspects of the socially and politically committed qualities of traditional documentary endure, despite the cross-breeding of the genre with others in the form of 'mock-umentary', docudrama, docusoap and so on. These latter forms tend to undermine any sense of social responsibility, which is in any case merely

Case Study

The Queen 'storms' out

Some of the issues concerning the responsibility of documentary are illustrated in a recent scandal surrounding the BBC. In the UK and across the world, the BBC is often cited as one of a handful of non-government and non-commercial organisations with a reputation for scrupulous fairness and objectivity in its approach to current affairs. Across its television shows, radio broadcasts, and

publications, and increasingly in its web presence, it provides a trustworthy first port of call for those seeking information and balanced analysis of the world at large. In recent years, however, this organisation has had to deal with a series of scandals that have undermined its reputation. One of these scandals concerned the TV documentary *Monarchy: The Royal Family at Work*, which resulted in widespread debate, resignations, a full-scale investigation and parliamentary censure.

This five-part documentary series was produced for the BBC by independent company RDF, which claimed that it offered 'remarkable behind the scenes access . . . Never before have television cameras been allowed to observe so comprehensively the working life of Her Majesty the Queen and other members of the Royal Family . . .' One sequence in the series involved a photo shoot with Annie Leibowitz which is summarised in the BBC report as follows:

> A shot of the Queen striding towards the photo-shoot in which she is heard to say, obviously disgruntled, *'I'm not changing anything. . . . I've had enough . . .'* was moved from the beginning to the end of the sequence. (The Queen was uncharacteristically late after having to put on the Garter robes and was being briefed that there might have to be 'changes later.')' This shot was now placed after the Queen responding to the photographer's request that she remove the crown, to look 'less dressy', by saying, 'Less dressy! What do you think this is?' The clear impression created is that the Queen had walked out. She did not. In fact the rushes show that after her irritated response she paused, then chuckled and carried on with the photo shoot.

(You can read the BBC's own report on the investigation into *A Year with the Queen* at www.bbc.co.uk/pressoffice/pressreleases/stories/2007/10_october/05/investigation.pdf)

This rearranged sequence was used in a promotional video by RDF and through a series of events became part of BBC series publicity that played up the apparent scoop of the Queen 'storming out' of the shoot. In turn, the tabloid newspaper the *Sun*, whose editors saw a titillating instance of a royal tantrum, picked up this story. Quickly, however, once the 'truth' of the case came out, the story became one concerned with the sequencing and perspective of the events rather than the events themselves, raising questions about the reliability of the media.

conventional or even assertive rather than inbuilt. Even so, the particular status of documentary across media forms is such that it continues to attract special attention for its relationship with the world it portrays.

Reality media, democracy and ordinary people

As we saw above, one way in which 'reality' is signified in media forms like documentary is through the associations of certain types of content and depictions of social groups. One subject that has proven incredibly popular in recent years is accentuating realism, namely the lives and activities of 'real' or 'ordinary' people, a direct result of the social extension aspect of documentary film, which was carried forward into TV forms. This is notable in the rise of new pseudo-documentary formats and hybrid genres, such as docudrama or docusoap reality shows (*Making the Band, Airport*), reality game shows such as *Big Brother* or *Survivor* and 'clip' shows such as *America's Worst Drivers* or *You've Been Framed*. The format for shows such as *Big Brother* has been successfully sold by its parent company Endemol around the world, indicating the economic value of such shows. Likewise *FC Zulu* (2005–7), which originated in Denmark and involves training up a bunch of non-footballers to compete with professionals, has been translated as variants into *FC Nerds* for Australia, Belgium, Spain and Norway (as *Tufte IL*), Finland (as *FC Nörtit*), the Netherlands (*Atletico Ananas*) and Germany (*Borussia Banana*).

While taking some cues from the pre-existing documentary form and precursors as wide-ranging as the BBC's *The Family* (1974), the Australian *Sylvania Waters* (1992), and international practical joke programmes in the *Candid Camera* format (which began on US radio!), such shows are a relatively new phenomenon and have inherited little of the social agenda of documentary. We would argue that this concentration on 'ordinary' people is possibly evidence of a democratic trend in our media. 'Reality TV' often draws its stars from the ranks of the anonymous, is variously based around explorations, work or everyday experience and, in turn, works with and constructs ideas about these categories. Curiously,

Cast members from the UK scripted-reality show *The Only Way Is Essex* (commonly referred to as *TOWIE*).

Source: Rex Features

such programmes do rather rely upon extraordinary versions of the ordinary, rather than any respect for or fascination with the everyday. The discoveries of such programmes do tend to become celebrities in their own right, sometimes graduating to 'showbusiness' employment, despite displaying no discernible talent (the prerequisite of modern celebrity, perhaps).

If we were to compare UK TV schedules, for instance, from the last 10 years or so with the early 1980s or 1970s, we would be struck by a number of immediate differences. One of these would be the contemporary dominance of 'reality' genres (in this sense the term reality TV has reached a point where it now seems to mean everything and nothing) and the virtual disappearance of 'serious' documentary in tandem with current affairs programming or investigative journalism shows. More obvious, however, is the fact that there is simply more TV nowadays – whether terrestrial or digital, cable, satellite or online. The two points are not unconnected. Thus, the advent of digital technologies (smaller, cheaper production equipment, the internet, cable) and trends in TV deregulation around the world in the late 1980s and early 1990s can be seen to coincide with an increased demand for content and the efflorescence of a range of cheap programming based around the lives of ordinary people. This knowledge might undermine the potential celebration of the democratic social extension of representations in this manner but we should also note that such programmes exist and proliferate because they are popular with audiences, too. TV companies don't *just* make filler to pack schedules; the commercial imperative means that they have to attract audiences through meaningful and attractive product, and retain them so that they, in turn, are meaningful and attractive to advertisers.

Doing media studies

Analysing 'reality TV'

Using the principles of generic analysis, brainstorm the 'paradigmatic' features of the 'reality TV' category. Use a set of TV schedules or listings to itemise and name the variety of subgenres of reality TV (as well as measuring the frequency of the genre in the schedules).

To what degree is this genre identifiable and/or distinguishable from traditional documentary? What kinds of issues arise as a result of your findings under this question?

Case Study

'Ordinary' people, the real and *Take a Break* magazine

The biggest-selling women's magazine in the UK is the remarkable and long-running *Take a Break* (*TaB*), published by the German company Bauer Verlagsgruppe, which recently acquired the magazine and radio divisions of the British company EMAP. This magazine exhibits typical generic features of the broad field of women's magazines. There is some content organised around recipes, fashion features, entertainment, news items and so on. What makes it interesting, however, are its 'realist' claims and character that broadly parallels the rise and form of reality TV and, in fact, pre-dates it.

The main material in the magazine comprises a series of stories labelled as 'true' or 'real life', drawn from the experience of the magazine's readers. These stories – usually concerning some kind of domestic woe or crisis (a partner in peril or a perilous partner, illness, family misfortune and so on) – are in some respects 'excessive' and unusual in nature, in that they represent ruptures in the banality of everyday routine. However, the stories deal in the lives of recognisably 'ordinary' people, perhaps more specifically and accurately described as regularly white and working class in origin. The rhetorical presentation of the stories emphasises and signifies aspects of ordinariness through a number of aspects. Stories utilise aspects of vernacular speech (although never any profanity) and are often told from the perspective of those involved. Stories are usually illustrated and realism supported by the family snapshots of individuals involved.

The general 'true life' aspect of the magazine is enhanced by a range of other features, such as 'Readers' Reality', which is stamped with the strapline 'Real names, real addresses, real photos' alongside 'real life problems, real life relationships'. Generic women's magazine features on beauty are offered as solutions for 'real life'. The style here echoes the anecdotal 'over the garden fence' narrative stereotypically associated with housewives speaking to or 'gossiping' with each other. Readers with something to say are encouraged to write in following an itemised list of things to deal with. A typical template guide invites readers to 'Send us your Britain's Got Love Rats stories':

Do you want to expose a love rat? Use our on-line story form to send us your stories. You only need to send us a brief outline, although you can include more if you wish. It will come straight to the *Take a Break* features team who will then phone you to check the details.

Include as much detail such as:

Who is involved?

How does your story begin?

What crucial event happens next?

How does your story end?

All stories must be TRUE and exclusive to *Take a Break*.

Source: H. Bauer Publishing

Reality print media: *Take a Break* magazine

➡️ Every week *Take a Break* is enjoyed by over 3 million adults including 2.7 million women, a readership which puts all others in the shade. We like to think of it as a community which speaks up for ordinary people of all ages. We have lots of puzzles and competitions offering cash prizes, cars and holidays as well as pages on health and relationships, fashion and beauty and household tips. We hope you enjoy reading it as much as we enjoy putting it together.

Source: www.takeabreak.co.uk/, © H Bauer Publishing

Reality, truth, freedom, ethics and responsibility

Considerations of the fidelity of media texts to the real in the form of documentary or current affairs programming lead us to related issues of truth, responsibility and ethical problems in media. Specifically, these relate to ways in which media are considered to act in the role of a fourth estate within a public sphere, conditioned by rules of objectivity and rationality – issues taken up on page 183.

TV producer and theorist John Ellis (2000) has argued that the modern media have provided 'witness' to events in quite important ways, changing the nature of perception and our relationship with the world and reality. His argument is that 'witness' is a new mode of perception whereby, despite being removed from events (and maybe powerless), nevertheless 'we cannot say we did not know'. We witness things at a remove, in the intimacy of our own homes, often live and through a feeling of co-presence. While we may not be literally present at an event, collectively we have a knowledge of our times in more immediate and expansive terms than in any previous age. Perhaps this brings with it new collective responsibilities on behalf of producers and audiences.

A good example of 'witness' with positive results perhaps lies in the 'Band Aid' phenomena of the 1980s and the actions of pop star Bob Geldof. Spurred into action as a result of watching a BBC report on famine in Ethiopia in 1984, Geldof used his connections to launch a charity record to generate aid for the starving. This was followed by the globally broadcast concert 'Live Aid' in 1985, which generated tens of millions of dollars. Geldof repeatedly commented on his feelings at watching the original BBC report and how he felt about not acting in response to the news and reality of this tragedy brought directly to his living room. He regularly transmitted this paranoia about inaction to TV viewers in demanding their contributions to his charity fund-raising drive.

While the mass media, through institutions and forms generated by a few for the many, have provided testament for us, it is now possible for the mass witnesses (us) to provide their own testament to the nature of the world via the web. User-generated content encompasses a mass of material, from fiction to fact, but using the specific label 'citizen journalism' we can take account of the myriad ways in which blogs (web logs), personal websites, uploaded mobile phone images and footage, and audio textualise the available reportage. In fact, news-gathering organisations actively seek the input of 'eyewitnesses' with mobile phone footage. More and more, individuals who were once consigned to the consumption of media are part of its construction, indicating how responsibilities can be addressed in the age of 'witness'.

Ellis has also drawn attention to realism's ethical dimension. This ethical dimension is always at the core of ideas of integrity, closeness to truth and, indeed, the perceived desirability of knowing about the world. Ellis suggests that judgements about realism are often predicated upon judgements about the relation of object and referent – representation and what is represented – even when we may not have the empirical experience to satisfy our evaluation of this relation properly. The relation of empirical reality and its representation – in documentary and allied forms such as docudrama – has long been subject to a contract between the producer and the viewers and listeners about the reliability and purposes of these forms. This contract – whether explicit or implicit, foregrounded or obscured by rhetorical address – has functioned as a bond of trust and expectation of honesty. The nature of this contract emerges in some of the reactions to the use of documentary forms for rather frivolous ends, such as in the case of the BBC's *Ghostwatch*, where trust is perceived by some to have been 'betrayed'.

Case Study

Unreality media – the BBC's *Ghostwatch*

Ghostwatch was a cleverly constructed production that was part of the BBC's season of 'Screen One' dramas and was broadcast on Halloween night 1992. It attracted 11.1 million viewers, and some critical acclaim but also opprobrium, causing a scandal and adding to ongoing panics about media 'effects'. *Ghostwatch* was based on 'real' poltergeist activity in Enfield. The show's producers had decided that it would take place in a haunted house as part of a fictional 'live' broadcast. The show took its cues from contemporary BBC 'reality' programming such as *Crimewatch UK*, which was first premiered on the BBC in 1984, and *999*, which was first shown in 1990 – the latter mixing drama and documentary in popular form. Drama documentary used in such a 'frivolous' cause was relatively rare at the time and its use of recognisable personalities contributed to its affect. In order to create the 'illusion' of being live, producers adopted a telethon format and style.

Ghostwatch was never intended to be a *War of the Worlds*-style hoax; the use of a live broadcast was there to simply make it more effective. The producers thought that 'people might be puzzled for two, perhaps five minutes, but then they would surely "get" it, and enjoy it for what it was – a drama' (Volk and Sutton, 2003). The use of the

camera in *Ghostwatch* is coded as witnessing 'live' events – there to capture reality. We are told by presenter Sarah Greene and the supposed BBC audio-visual technicians that all variations of technology are being used in order to capture live footage of a ghost. Behind this aesthetic was a serious intent. It was producer Stephen Volk's belief that we 'could no longer trust what we were seeing, what we were being shown or told by TV' (Volk and Sutton, 2003). This view of trust was further questioned by Volk after he witnessed the CNN news reports from the Gulf War: he argued that even these reports 'felt suspect, somehow unreliable' (Volk and Sutton, 2003).

Lesley Manning, the director of *Ghostwatch*, used infrared footage to emulate the CNN footage, in order to illustrate this boundary between fact and fiction. It was this issue of trust that Volk wanted to raise in *Ghostwatch*, to get the audience to question whether what they were seeing was reality or a cleverly constructed drama, not to view the programme as a hoax and to attack the traditional conventions of television.

The producers used a range of available techniques associated with live broadcasting in order to make the show as believable as possible. There would also be a phone number on screen to encourage viewers to phone in and tell their own ghost stories and experiences of the programme. The number was fictional; callers reached an operator telling them that the show was fictional. Lines were overwhelmed with 20,000 phone calls, many having to go unanswered (Glover, 2001: 25). By emulating a live broadcast, with all the technical jitters complete,

Volk and Manning were able to comment on the falling boundaries between fictional and factual television that were occurring at the time.

In the notes of Stephen Volk's original *Ghostwatch* script, he proposed that real-life personalities should be used to host the programme. UK chat show host Michael Parkinson became the host of the show, real-life husband and wife TV presenters Mike Smith and Sarah Greene were enthusiastic about appearing in the programme and, finally, comedian Craig Charles was brought in to add comic relief to the proceedings. The rest of the cast was made up with non-actors and non-TV personalities, just as Volk wished. The use of the cast in *Ghostwatch* does add to the signs of 'reality' that are created, exploiting the viewer's trust of well-known celebrities and utilising unknown actors to further enhance the illusion of a live setting.

Such drama documentaries have often been associated with controversy. For example, the BBC's 1965 nuclear-war drama documentary *The War Game* was withheld from broadcast by Hugh Greene, the BBC chairman of the time. According to Volk, the BBC had considered withdrawing *Ghostwatch* from its schedules: 'Right up until the last minute, the transmission was threatened with being pulled due to corporate nervousness, but we made it by the skin of our teeth' (Volk and Sutton, 2003). Journalist Kim Newman believes that 'the controversy surrounding *Ghostwatch* led to it's suppression' (Newman, 2002): it was never repeated or mentioned by the BBC until 2002, when it was unearthed from the vaults and released by the British Film Institute on DVD and video.

While a cast list was published in advance in the *Radio Times*, outraged newspaper coverage ignored this as well as the 'Screen One' introduction that preceded the show. The press criticised the programme as a sick hoax. The situation became even more troublesome when the body of an 18-year-old boy was found hanging from a tree in Bestwood Lodge Park in Nottingham. He was reported to have watched the programme in a 'hypnotised'

state (Glover, 2001: 26). As in many press-led moral panics, the connections were 'obvious' and there for all to see. We must also note, however, that many viewers did not find *Ghostwatch* convincing at all, recognising fully its 'fabrications'.

Stephen Volk believes that the only thing *Ghostwatch* was guilty of was 'underestimating the power of the language of "live TV" to convince people that what they are watching was real' (Volk and Sutton, 2003). After all, Volk and Manning had successfully questioned the trust of the viewer, coining the phrase that you shouldn't always believe what you see on television.

Further reading and references

Buckingham, D. (1998) 'Electronic child abuse' in Barker, M. and Petley, J. (2001) *Ill Effects: The Media/Violence Debate*, second edition. London: Routledge.

Glover, J. (2001) 'Hunting Ghostwatch', *Headpress*, vol. 22: 13–26 (August).

Newman, K. (1993) 'Ghostwatch Review', *Sight and Sound*, January.

Newman, K. (2002) *Kim Newman on Ghostwatch*. Available from: www.bfi.org.uk/videocat/more/ghostwatch/newman.html. Accessed 4 November 2002.

Volk, S. and Sutton, D. (2003) *Faking It: Ghostwatch*. Available from: www.forteantimes.com/articles/166_ghostwatch.shtml. Accessed 10 April 2003.

Ghostwatch (1992) Film directed by Lesley Manning for the BBC. Available on BFI DVD 2002.

Ghostwatch is a highly effective example of contemporary reality media. Reactions to it in the UK demonstrate some of our expectations of the form. This was a highly complex production that attempted to blur the boundaries between the real and what can be considered fiction. Popular culture is now littered with all kinds of reality programming that reference the 'real' in this hybrid manner, whether it be *Big Brother* or films such as *Paranormal Activity* (dir. Peli, 2007) and the television shows *Most Haunted* and *Ghost Hunters*, for which *Ghostwatch* perhaps paved the way.

Ethical questions arise here, too, if we question whether some events are beyond the pale in terms of representation. Are some things so singular as to be impossible to deal with in realist terms and thus *un*-representable? Such issues and arguments arose around Steven Spielberg's film *Schindler's List* (1993) and its depiction of the Holocaust. In this film, Spielberg and his team went to great lengths to convey the nature of the experience of Polish Jews at the hands of the Nazis. Location shooting, gruesomely visceral special effects and bravura acting all conveyed the fear and brutality of the moment, albeit presented in a curious 'Thirties Hollywood' black-and-white aesthetic. As some suggested, however, Spielberg managed to extricate from this historical genocide his trademark motifs concerning the value of family, turning the whole episode into a kind of adventure story typical of the classical narrative. Serious objections arose around a particular scene in which a group of Jewish women were shipped to Auschwitz extermination camp and were sent to take a shower, which rather than the anticipated gas chamber turns out to be an actual shower. Whatever the intent, effectiveness or crassness of such a scene, critics objected to the very attempt to deal with the recreation of these moments and experiences. The experiences of the extermination camps have proven taboo, experiences so appalling as to be unrealisable and irreproducible, the truth residing only in the testimonies of those who survived to bear witness alongside the numbers – the millions – who died there. Spielberg was accused of being at worst exploitative and at best political, culturally and aesthetically naïve (Loshitzky, 1998).

In some reviews, the film was compared unfavourably with Claude Lanzmann's nine-hour documentary *Shoah* (1985), in which the sense of the *un*-representable aspect of this terrible reality was acknowledged. Lanzmann sought instead to present his account via unfolding eyewitness accounts and the memories of both victims and persecutors, showing locations as they are now and allowing the nature of events to be inferred from this combination. Of course, these films were produced within different forms but the nature of the reality they sought to depict is regarded in such a manner that it determined the evaluation of the integrity and seriousness of each film. Here was an example where 'witness' was provided solely by the witnesses themselves: nothing else was required.

Case Study

Snuff movies and the boundaries of the real

The mythical category of the snuff movie is an interesting place to consider how 'witness' is presented and played with for the thrill of audiences – again with highly controversial results. The term 'snuff' was coined by author Ed Sanders in his book *The Family* (2002) in relation to a series of murders in California in 1969 by the crazed killer Charles Manson and his followers. It was suggested in various reports that the 'Manson family' had, in fact, filmed their murders even though no footage has ever surfaced. The term received even further attention when a film entitled *Snuff* (dirs Findlay and Findlay, 1974) was released in America in 1976. Nothing more than a zero-budget feature, based loosely on the Manson Family and made in Argentina, the film derived its notoriety from a tacked-on ending shot by distributor Allan Shackleton. This ending featured what appeared to be behind-the-scenes footage of the film crew ceasing production then deciding to murder an actress 'for real'. Though it was 'clearly' staged, this addendum, when combined with the unique marketing of the film, generated both attention in audience figures and scandal in vocal public opposition. Thus the urban legend of snuff was born.

A simple definition of the term would be: a film in which a person is actually killed in front of a camera for the purpose of 'entertainment'. Such films are also known as 'white heat' films or 'the real thing'. Snuff is best thought of as a media construction, a moral panic (p. 290) or an urban myth rather than actual practice. The idea has been fuelled by being the subject of various Hollywood films, such as Paul Schrader's *Hardcore* (1979) and Joel Schumacher's *8 mm* (1999), as well as featuring in TV shows such as *Miami Vice*. In 2005, a commercial film called *Snuff Movie* (dir. Krabbe, 2005) was released to cinemas. Many independent horror features, such as the *August Underground* series of films, use the theme of the snuff movie as a narrative driver. A number of films labelled as 'video nasties' by the British tabloid press were incorrectly named as snuff films.

Some films have been labelled by the media as actual snuff films due to heightened realism in their portrayal of murder, leading to some curious confusions, a trend started by the Italian *Mondo* films of the late 1960s and 1970s. Ruggero Deodato, the director of *Cannibal Holocaust* (1980), found himself having to prove to Italian investigators that the actors in his film were not actually eaten by cannibals. The Japanese creators of the horror film series *Guinea Pig* also had to prove that their film *The Flower of Flesh and Blood*

(1985) did *not* feature a samurai-dressed serial killer dismembering a victim for real. The producers even went to the length of shooting a 'making of' film to prove their innocence when they were being investigated by the FBI. The infamous *Faces of Death* series has also fallen foul to such allegations due to many sequences pursuing realism.

Since 9/11, the term snuff has become synonymous with the videos of hostages being murdered by terrorist groups. These videos do not actually follow the definition of snuff as they are not produced for entertainment or titillation, but some would argue that the downloading and/or uploading of these videos on the internet suggests some form of thrill or sick gratification. Up until the publication of this work, despite numerous state investigations, there has been no evidence of a snuff film actually in existence.

Why are snuff movies more likely to be myth than reality? How can we tell?

Further reading

Goodall, M. (2006) *Sweet and Savage: The World Through the Shockumentary Films Lens*, London: Headpress.

Kerekes, D. and Slater, D. (1993) *Killing for Culture: An Illustrated History of Death Film from Mondo to Snuff*, London: Creation Books.

The sound of the real

As we have argued, different media forms deploy strategies and claim to access and present the real in different ways. It is common to think of visually based media, such as film, TV or web versions that combine the audio and visual within their pages, as having some superior claim to a relationship with the world because they seem more effectively real in their ability to emulate our sensual experience of empirical reality. Nonetheless, consideration of the real in such media representations needs to account for the particularities of the use and meanings of sound but also for the way in which specifically sound-based media – radio as well as pod-casting – echo some of the observations on the nature of realism in audio-visual media and enhance debates in this field. When we turn, in particular, to popular music, however, we are presented with some further ways in which the real is often cited and has meaning, notably around questions of authenticity and realism in performance and, indeed, in the musical form.

The first thing to do here is to note the way in which sound-based narrative or documentary forms – fiction or fact-based – share similar reference points with compatible conventions in film and TV. The coming of film sound in the 1920s enhanced cinematic realism and, for a long time, was a dominating rhetorical device in TV (often labelled 'radio with pictures' upon its emergence), which was bound to a relatively small-scale image for most of its history. Thus we speak of the 'small screen'. In fact, bigger TV screens are still an exception rather than the rule.

Whether as an aid to the image or working on its own in radio, sound has a variety of signifying and rhetorical functions. Denotatively, sounds are added or included in broadcasts to give colour and context to texts. A report from a beach will allow the sound of the sea; a character enters the room in a drama and the door can be heard opening and closing. Thus, sound adds a sense of space, location and ambience to increase the coherence of texts and to underwrite authenticity and realist claims. Sound can, likewise, also work connotatively – the sound of Big Ben striking on UK TV news broadcasts to emphasise a roll call of the day's news anchors stories with an indexical sign for the home of British government, from whence all of the primary UK political news usually originates.

A key aspect of the reality of sound resides in our attitude to the spoken word – with or without pictures to illustrate the speaker. Images work for us on the basis that 'seeing is believing'; the word works on the principle of 'hearing is believing'. The sound of the word, of spoken testimony, is also enhanced by some long-standing perceptions identified by a number of theorists. The first is of an assumption of 'organicism', which is a faith in an essential connection between speaker and utterance. The word spoken seems organically connected to the speaker in that, while we may not see them, voices are so apparently individual as to tie meaning to the nature of how we talk. This point can be further illustrated with reference to a curious if abiding prejudice common in Western thought. For instance, Jacques Derrida has explored the ways in which philosophers from Plato, through to Enlightenment thinkers like Jean-Jacques Rousseau, and onward to Friedrich Nietzsche and Ferdinand de Saussure, displayed their *phonologism* – i.e. privileging the spoken word at the expense of the reliability of writing. Rousseau, for instance, contended that writing is no more than incidental to speech, which has been accorded a veracity and sense of integrity denied to the book and literary culture. The suggestion here in this 'phonologism' is that in speech one is offered a moment of authenticity, a unity of word, thought and world. 'Somehow we think that what is said is more true or authentic if it is actually being said by someone we can see saying it. We think that speech offers transparent and unified meaning, whereas writing must be secondary, since it cannot offer such certainty' (Finlayson, 1999: 63).

We could explore how this phonologism works in a mostly unexamined manner throughout the media – in face-to-face interviews, in phone calls in news reports from 'on-the-spot' reporters, in the way in which visual documentaries sometimes support what we see, not necessarily with a narrator's analysis, but with the reiterative description of what we are seeing. If we cast our minds back to our analysis of stardom in the previous chapter, we can think this concept through in the way that many treat actors as if they themselves spontaneously thought up the witty one-liners and catchphrases they speak in their films. It is not just the skill of their acting but the way in which words and what they mean seem to organically spring from the speaker.

There are other ways in which this phonologism works, too, in relation to how we think about popular music. Concerns over the value of the real and authenticity abound in popular music – witness the relatively clichéd claim or promise of artists to 'keep it real'. As one of our first examples in this chapter suggested, even a jet-setting multi-millionaire such as Jennifer Lopez invests in this claim to authenticity. Certainly, genres such as soul, reggae, grime and R&B have been the locus of authenticity for many consumers, due not only to their associations with black culture but also through their rhetorical organisation. In soul music, this takes the form of a baring of emotions through (sometimes) shrieking and emotional vocal mannerisms designed to convey the deep and sincere feelings of the artist. In genres such as rap, it takes the form of the language and intonations of those claiming to be from 'the streets' (see Perry, 2004; Barker and Taylor, 2007). Often, perhaps rightly, we conflate the nature of what a song conveys and whether or not it is convincing with our experience of the singer's performance. Although singers may be interpreting the words and music of others, or merely narrating a tale about fictional characters and scenarios, our phonologic tendencies lead us to relate words and expression to them alone – as we tend to do with other dramatic performances.

We can see how 'realism' and authenticity operate in other ways, too, in popular music. A genre such as folk music, historically 'the music of the people', often unaccompanied or supported by acoustic and traditional instruments, has also been understood to connote realism in its narratives of social struggle and linking of voice and unalloyed expression. Folk music (as well as that music labelled 'world') is also traditionally important for perceptions of the form as untainted by the modern or commercialism.

As with the celebration of folk music's traditional sparseness, over-elaboration and 'technologisation' has sometimes been deemed to be the antithesis of authenticity. We can see this at work in the punk rock music movement of the late 1970s in the UK, for instance, and indeed in its various permutations around the world. What was important were a number of strategies to 'return' music, its practices and performance, to a connection with contemporary 'reality', in opposition to the fantasies and remoteness of commercial music or serious rock such as that produced by stadium-filling groups of the 1970s like Queen and Led Zeppelin.

Thus, in punk rock's construction of authenticity and realism, songs were stripped down to bare essentials – basic guitar chords, simple structures and band line-ups with barely more than guitars and drums. Likewise, elaborate or professional musicianship was eschewed in favour of 'expression', for example, shouted lyrics, use of feedback, simplicity (as above). Songs also dealt with what were perceived to be 'real' world issues rather than romantic love or fantasy subjects. Finally, barriers between band and audience were broken down in small venues and, again, by producing songs about issues pertinent to the audience and by conveying the sense that 'anyone can do it'. In this way, the rhetoric of the texts was highly conditioned by surrounding pronouncements and the contexts of production and performance.

We should note here that this discussion of sound and music seems a long way from the way that we tend to relate to audio-visual media. This does, however, offer us a broad sense of the various ways in which media forms relate to and convey the 'real', as well as related concepts. Likewise, we receive a similar sense of the way in which we respond to media forms and the kinds of expectations we have of them, which are surely in some way ordered in hierarchical fashion. It is difficult, of course, to compare our viewing of a scene from a live newsworthy event and the feelings we have when listening to music – which can be very intense and 'genuine' in its affect upon us. Nonetheless, we need to be aware of the continuum of realism and reality media which links these things, in order to comprehend the value of this aspect of media production and consumption.

Summary

Investigating reality media

In this chapter we have explored the relationship between media forms and 'reality', thinking of how the world is referred to and represented as well as the kinds of realities that those forms create. We began with a broad philosophical conceptualisation of what we mean by reality in order to problematise how media forms achieve realism and what this might mean. However, while underlining how evasive a definitive idea of reality and realism is, we saw how important these categories continue to be for us as consumers as well as in media debates.

In trying to work through what realism might mean we explored its historical dimensions in order to comprehend how context is important to any definition and aspiration to depictions of the real. We established therefore that we should think of realisms rather than any definitive and absolute sense of realism. Here, we drew upon the work of Raymond Williams in order to understand this position further in relation to the way in which certain types of content connote the real. Our contemporary example of a digital 'virtual reality' demonstrated how realism continues to change and develop.

We used semiology to explore the ways in which the real is signalled in media texts, exploring too the rhetorical strategies and particular aspects of the dominant forms of media realism. This led us to a consideration of the particularly privileged form of documentary in dealing with the world. We detailed how realist forms such as documentary had given birth to contemporary 'reality TV' which gave attention to the lives and presence of ordinary people. This raised questions about the democratic aspects of realism implied in Williams's work and the idea of social extension. As we saw, other issues arising in relation to our expectations around the real concern the ethical responsibilities of media producers. Our case studies showed that controversy was caused in many quarters regarding some of the perceived duplicity involved in presenting the 'truth'.

Finally, we explored realism and authenticity in relation to sound – the audio aspects of TV, film, radio and so on as well as how music works, or can work, as a realist form.

If you have followed this chapter through and engaged with the activities and thought about the issues covered you should be able to:

- Distinguish between different modes of representing reality within and across media forms. Do reflect upon the central challenge here that suggests that there is no media realism but a range of realisms. If you lack confidence in this idea go back to the discussions and examples in this chapter and give them some further attention.

- Recognise, outline and engage with a range of debates and issues around the relationship of media to 'reality' and realism. Here you can examine different media forms, as we have, to get to grips with and test out how realism and reality are important across media forms as well as attendant concepts such as truth, authenticity and integrity in media professionals.

- Identify different strategies in media representations of reality. As in previous chapters, we're building on our tools and range of ideas to get to grips with media meanings. Go back to the tools we've introduced throughout this section and use them all to analyse media texts in terms of the specialised questions and issues we've raised here.

Ultimately, we've suggested that realism is a saleable commodity in media production (people like the real, the authentic, truth as much as they like fantasy) and an aesthetic category that presents us with intriguing paradoxes, feeding into many of the popular and scholarly debates on the media. For this reason it demands continued scrutiny and a sophisticated awareness of the playful and sometimes life-or-death issues at stake in its depiction.

Doing media studies

Short essay writing

Research and outline a plan for a short essay exploring the nature of media realism from your perspective as a consumer. Address the following issues in your piece:

- What does the 'real' in media mean to us as consumers (you might ask around for answers to this)?

- How do we experience media realism? What are its pleasures?

- What kinds of appearances does realism have across different media? Does a comparison of forms make us more or less aware of the kinds of issues outlined in this chapter?

Think about how best to focus this work – on a text or genre. The specific detail will aid you greatly in thinking of the bigger issues that we've been considering in this chapter.

Further reading

Aitken, I. (2001) *European Film Theory and Cinema: A Critical Introduction*, Edinburgh: Edinburgh University Press.

This study examines the dominant approaches to realism as a concept in European film. Aitken looks at different forms of European cinema since the 1900s, such as the Soviet montage, Weimar cinema, *nouvelle vague* and the Italian neo-realism movement, and how they have been studied in academic work. The varied ideas of realism in film are discussed in detail and this serves as a challenging but rewarding introduction for studying realism in film.

Bignell, J. (2005) *Big Brother: Reality TV in the Twenty-first Century*, Basingstoke: Palgrave Macmillan.

Of all the current spate of works on the subject of *Big Brother* and reality television this one has particular value as it encompasses a range of pertinent issues surrounding this popular genre of programming. While providing a useful overview of the genre Bignell also considers *Big Brother* and its relation to the cult of celebrity and surveillance. Not just focusing on analysing the text, Bignell discusses how the popularity of reality television reflects changes in contemporary television production. Accessible and well written, this book is a worthy starting point for those interested in contemporary reality television.

Ellis, J. (2000) *Seeing Things: Television in the Age of Uncertainty*, London: I.B. Tauris.

Ellis argues that television, along with other media, has allowed the audience to be witnesses to events and offer us perspectives on how we might understand the world in which we live. He is also interested in how we use other programming to detract from the serious real-world content we consume. He sees there being three stages in the development of television programming: scarcity, availability and plenty. Now the viewer is faced with a wealth of programming, along with interactive capabilities, that, for them, means that television is taking on a new social role. At heart are important questions about how we experience 'real' events on television.

Perry, I. (2004) *Prophets of the Hood: Politics and Poetics in Hip Hop*, Durham, NC: Duke University Press.

Perry, both a scholar and a fan of hip hop music, analyses lyrics taken from songs by musicians such as Ice Cube, Public Enemy, Outkast, Tupak Shakur and Lauryn Hill to consider the cultural implications of this popular music genre. Even though she admits that some of the content contained in these songs can be found to be worrying by many, she believes that they offer a certain authenticity that has cultural importance for the consumers of hip hop music. This is a valuable source for those interested in realism in popular music.

Winston, B. (2000) *Lies, Damn Lies and Documentaries*, London: British Film Institute.

A study of ethics in contemporary documentary film-making, Winston takes the Griesonian perspective of documentary making and considers what the current ethical guidelines for documentary makers might be. Using the moral panic surrounding the faked scenes in the 1997 British television documentary *The Connection*, the catalyst for the book, Winston sees this as calling into question the freedom of expression for the documentary film-maker. The question of media ethics is a difficult area of study particularly in relation to artistic freedom and the compromises it might have on realism, yet Winston raises many interesting questions that are important for the thinking media student to consider. His earlier work *Claiming the Real: The Documentary Film Revisited* (1995) may also be of interest.

Appendix: Analysing texts

How to read this appendix

This appendix develops the textual analysis we've introduced in previous chapters as a whole, reiterating the meaning and rationale behind the tools employed. It combines an attention to the rhetorical address of media texts, their generic and narrative codes, exploring aspects of cultural signification understood through the tools of semiology. We deploy these tools extensively so you will need to have read the previous chapters closely in order to get to grips with the terms but also to comprehend why we've employed them.

The analysis echoes Roland Barthes's essay on his concept of mythology 'Myth today' (Barthes, 2000). In that essay he places himself in an everyday situation – at the barber's – and considers the image of a black soldier on the front of an issue of a popular magazine called *Paris Match*. In his reading, his aim was to make a point about the nature of texts and the ideas they present, how they are all around us in everyday life and so media messages are never-ending rather than reducible to any one instance. However, in this instance of media expression he finds something quite rich which is indicative of how media texts work on us to convey certain ways of seeing the world.

In Barthes's analysis of the cover of the magazine he argues that at the level of denotation – the 'obvious', agreed, iconic, analogous meaning – here is a black soldier saluting the flag. Do note that the flag is not seen but the pose, gaze and cultural convention of what we do see happening suggest it is an object beyond the cropped space of the image.

At the level of connotation we could appreciate that the image presents us with an association of good, upright 'soldierliness', notions of servitude and obedience perhaps. Already there is a symbolic aspect to this complex sign. However, if we consider the nature of myth, as suggested by the anthropological insight of Claude Lévi-Strauss, to be belief systems that magically resolve social contradictions, we are confronted by just such contradiction. In 1955, at the time of publication of this magazine, France, like many Western European societies, was much less visibly and physically multicultural than it is nowadays. It was largely white European in make-up. We could ask therefore: how has this young black man come to be saluting the French flag at all and why? One answer is that France, like the UK at that time, ruled over a vast array of overseas colonial territories that had been acquired by a mixture of diplomatic stealth and force. The question that arises from the contradiction presented by this image is exacerbated by the knowledge that such colonies – from Vietnam to Guiana – were generally in revolt, seeking independence from European rule.

Source: PARIS MATCH/SCOOP

'Whether naively or not, I see very well what it signifies to me: that France is a great Empire, that all her sons, without any colour discrimination, faithfully serve under her flag, and that there is no better answer to the detractors of an alleged colonialism than the zeal shown by this Negro in serving his so-called oppressors' (Barthes, 2000: 124).

Thus, the salute to the flag by this young African man becomes loaded with significance, but it is a significance that cannot be recognised as such. Any symbolic meaning is always tied to the literalness, the 'fact' of the denoted meaning. In this way the literalness of the image offers what Barthes calls an 'alibi' for any further interpretation or accusation that this is something more than an innocent scene. Barthes writes that:

> *it is again this duplicity of the signifier which determines the characters of the significa-tion . . . myth is a type of speech defined by its intention . . . much more than by its literal sense . . . and in spite of this, its intention is somehow frozen, purified, eternalized,* made absent *by this literal sense.* (The French Empire? It's just a fact: look at this good Negro who salutes like one of our boys.) *This constituent ambiguity of mythical speech has two consequences for the signification, which henceforth appears both like a notifica-tion and like a statement of fact.*

(Barthes, 2000: 124)

Such a mythological moment is one of a whole chain of signification in a culture (in this case France of the 1950s) and not an isolated case but part of a whole social context in which such meanings have value (see the discussion in Chapter 10 on this issue). It is an instance of what Barthes here calls a 'type of speech' in which 'culture' (our social ideas, born of historical moments and contingencies of tradition) is turned into 'nature'.

The analysis below deals with a series of reflections and arguments about the nature of this kind of approach. These digressions aim to support your own sense of how and why we do such work but of course your own analyses would not generally include such expla-nations. Where a technical term is introduced we've **emboldened** it and included page references for you to refer back to previous chapters if you are unsure of the concept used.

Analysis of Chanel advert

In any everyday situation we are likely to be confronted by thousands of signifying systems and instances of signifying output. We call these signs. These signifying systems include the language we use to commu-nicate with, the signs that direct us to destinations (on the road, a fire exit, a toilet), to the myriad of media texts that are presented to us or merge into the background of our everyday lives. Songs on an iPhone or radio and on an in-store PA system, newspaper headlines, web-sites, snippets of radio and TV shows as well as the many adverts that plaster our built environment and transport indicate our sub-mersion in such signs, all of them competing for our attention.

The Chanel advert here is one such media text that might appear on a billboard

Source: The Advertising Archives

A Chanel advert

or perhaps in a glossy magazine we might buy intentionally or pick up to pass the time while waiting at a doctor's surgery or barber's – just like Roland Barthes. We might pay it some close attention (it might catch our eye for particular reasons) or might pass by in an instant as we drive past it, turn a page in a magazine or close a website pop-up. This is an important observation as we rarely have to stop to pick up meaning – all of the factors in this complex text work together in their impact.

Where to start? Any analysis must begin with the text and what we make of it. The logic here is that for textual meaning to work we already *know* what it means; the object is to understand how it means what it does and how meaning is marshalled, organised and anchored in order to make a text effective. Our job is to explore the relationship between explicit and implicit claims that media texts are merely innocently functional – as manifested in their surface meanings – and the deeper social values they articulate, sometimes unthinkingly and certainly not in a conspiratorial manner (or at least not always). As our chapter on representations should have taught us, such images are never 'innocent' and may have an important relationship with social power and, possibly, oppression.

In starting, we could very well claim, as people often do, that the meanings of this advert are 'clear', 'obvious' and incontrovertible. But to do so is to obscure the efficiency and sophistication of **signifying meaning systems** (p. 54) such as advertisements, with their complex nuances, and to treat them as though they 'just' appear automatically in magazines and elsewhere as if they were a simple snapshot of a simply comprehended reality, treated almost as a part of nature.

Look at the collection of images and words shown in the picture as part of a greater text – a **combination of complex signs** (p. 55) – that is designed to sell a perfume and consider it, for a moment, as if it were a message. Nowhere at all does it 'say' or spell out anything directly or plainly for a reader. It does not say 'Here is Estella Warren [the name of the model], a supermodel who wears Chanel.' Nor does it say anything along the lines of 'Chanel smells nice, makes you feel good and attractive to men' etc. This, we could take to be one of the possible aims or intentions of this kind of advertisement but while it says or tells us none of these things it is loaded with significance in speaking about them.

The makers of the advert have constructed it and, we assume, intend it to have a certain **affect** (p. 36) and possibly effects. Adverts elevate brand recognition among a competitive market and so 'urge' us to buy the product presented instead of all of the other similarly available products. But exactly what does it mean to say so, and how *do* advertisements mean what they do, and exactly what does this advert mean if it is not 'saying' anything explicitly?

As students of the media we could examine this advert through several lenses of analysis in search of an explanation: **genre**, **rhetoric**, **semiology**, and to a lesser extent on this occasion – **narratology**. These tools should also enable a consideration of the mythological aspects of this text and tell us something about issues related to **representation** (see Chapter 3). For now, these are artificially separated approaches but ultimately interrelated, as we shall see. The point of emphasising each approach and attempting to be schematic in their use is that they allow us to order our thinking and analyses, supporting our interpretations with argument and evidence and a convincing demonstration of our understanding of each.

First, let's consider this advert in terms of its **rhetorical** devices and **genre conventions**. A **rhetorical** approach identifies the use of presentational, photographic devices, verbal communication, colour, etc. **Genre** is about identifying the *type* of media form this is, its conventions in terms of its construction, appearance and how it treats its subject matter. Thus, and as students and other, more casual, observers of the media often do, we could say that this is 'obviously' a perfume advert: but what does such complacency obscure?

Generically, the text belongs to the wider system of advertising, of perfume ads in particular and a subgenre of Chanel's publicity and what was a themed series featuring this model. But what are the conventions of this greater genre of perfume ads and what do we expect of it? At base, the conventional way of doing things or representing the world in evidence here is one in which we do not think twice about a naked woman lying down amidst a few bottles while being attacked by a swarm of butterflies. Likewise let's draw attention to some other 'obvious' features and make some really blunt points. Is this a snapshot of an actually occurring event? Is this Estelle Warren at play? Rhetorically, it is likely that some manipulation of the image has gone on here (using Photoshop and various digitised technologies). The butterflies are probably superimposed, as are the bottles (do Chanel make them in such sizes?) and it is unlikely that the model has posed in a studio alongside super-sized blown-up typeface arranged about her body (although she is in the artificial setting of a studio – an important point that we'll return to later). This image has been overlaid with some desktop publishing (DTP) devices. Thus, we can conclude that this is a managed, composed image and already comes coded in part through such devices and choices that, as we don't stop to question them, don't appear as such: we don't question the logic of this set-up.

To talk further of the **conventions** of such adverts would also point to how we don't question the logic of a woman lying around naked (although 'made-up' to an extent that belies any claim that she is in an entirely natural state – an important counterpoint to the observations that follow) in such a fashion. Here the intention is not, ostensibly, to create art, erotica or pornography although this image may bear the traces of and allude to such types of text, intentionally or otherwise. Such is the proliferation of objectified images of women in our society and in Western tradition that it is hard to avoid such connections.

It is **conventional** to use particular types of women in such advertisements (often, well-known models or personalities such as this one). They may be blonde or fair-haired, as this model is, or the dark-haired, stereotypical seductress. Rarely are they red-haired or dark-skinned but they are always young, slim and conventionally attractive: any exception you can think of is enough to prove the rule. Models who are exceptions are few enough in number for many people to be able to identify them and they function as a marker that demonstrates the supposed variety of models, but each has a 'burden of representation' for their category (p. 120).

To draw attention to such stylistic **conventions** begins to worry at the often unchallenged assumptions behind them: that they are not merely mechanical or innocent but that they convey habitual social attitudes, conventional ways of understanding the world. Imagine a substitution here – what we'd call a **commutation test** (p. 57) in semiology. This would involve imagining what would happen if we replaced this model with an older woman, or someone with (for an advert) *un*conventional looks, or a non-'perfect' or idealised body shape (for north European/Western culture at least!). The resulting image would seem apparently odd or *un*natural or even make 'us' uneasy, so disruptive would it be. The advert makers or commissioning company, if confronted by such an experiment, might suggest to each other that it 'doesn't work', depending upon how conventional and conservative they wish to appear.

A further **convention** that we should note is the primacy of the brand name, which sits across the bottom of the frame: an element of the linguistic signs in this text (No 5 and 'bath and body range' are the others). Of course, modern adverts for many products no longer exhibit anxieties about leaving out an identifying name or even an **iconic** (p. 59) logo to ensure that prospective customers or disciples are not confused. It is sometimes in the interests of generating curiosity rather than instant recognition and dismissal in advertising campaigns that a degree of **polysemia** (p. 61) *is* encouraged.

Campaigns for gaming systems such as Xbox have employed this kind of approach which encourages inquisitiveness and makes an advert a talking point. This involves an intentional flattering of certain audiences whose 'media literacy' is well developed and media creators have to address the sophistication and 'knowingness' with which such people regard the material they consume. Often, the associations and conventions of how particular campaigns are mounted are enough to establish their ongoing identity as a sort of subspecies of that particular **genre** (beer adverts for Heineken or Stella Artois come to mind, as do those for Oxo cubes, Fiat Punto, etc.). We would certainly want to draw attention to how this advert is one of a series for this product that are similar in presentation and theme.

We are accustomed to perfume ads conforming to such **conventions**, partly due to this fact that they have to convey something of a product that is difficult to represent literally and where a blunt instruction is something to be avoided when pitching such a sophisticated product (or one that is underwritten by appeals to sophistication). Compare this for instance with a car advert, where it is not unusual to state that it does 50 miles to the gallon or to show its capacity – that it holds up to five people – or to demonstrate its power, speed and safety. Adverts for aspirin are those in which doctors, facts or figures are deployed to convey the message directly that they get rid of headaches.

Such presentations are predicated very much on what products can *do* or allow you to do. In this case, how is it possible to convey the impression that a bunch of chemicals blended together have a pleasant smell in a sophisticated manner? Of course we would have to allow for novelty 'scratch and sniff' promotions maybe in some magazines but not on a billboard or on TV or radio.

Let's move on, however, to consider the **science of signs**: **semiology**. In doing so, we should not get bogged down with the conceptual detail of the make-up of each individual **sign** (comprising **signifier** and **signified** – the physical nature and associated concept respectively) (p. 53) but instead recognise that here is an amalgamation of **signs** – and quite **complex signs** at that. They are combined into a greater whole, a complex system of textual meaning.

What we need to be attentive to in our **semiology** are the **levels of signification** (p. 58) and the wider references that their combination draws upon and alludes to. First, the written text of the advert is **symbolic** (p. 60). The **sign** and **referent** in written and spoken language have an arbitrary relationship. The Roman alphabet, as is any other, is a series of invented shapes that we accept by convention to have meaning in relation to sounds (e.g. 'a', which might be the a of h*a*y or b*a*t; combined **syntagmatically** (p. 55), in linear fashion, they create words and thus more **complex signs**).

We can pause momentarily, however, to note the **significance** of the typeface as identified with the brand Chanel, as well as its trademark, suggesting that this works **symbolically** beyond the **denotative** (p. 58) announcement of the name. It also operates **indexically** (p. 60), evoking a **cause and effect relationship** between **sign**, wealth and taste – being able to afford and also choose Chanel. Alternatively we can say that this is also a **connotation** of the sign Chanel.

At the generally uncontroversial, **denotative** (p. 58) level we can state simply that here we have a naked woman lying belly down, shielded by some perfume bottles while butterflies flap about her and land upon her body. This is an image that, while not simple, **connotes** (p. 58) simplicity in many ways that rein in any vulgar tendencies we might indulge in over-reading its erotic appeal. The model's youth is striking and serves to underline the romantic impression of this advert, of sensuality rather than a musky sexuality. This is certainly convincing if the butterflies can be imagined as metaphorical petals falling on to the woman – one thinks of poetry, of 'Shall I compare thee to a summer's day' or 'My love is like a red, red rose' and so on.

Ads such as these that present products for women in such romantic ways can be usefully compared with those for men, where the overtly sexual intent involved in using the product is paramount. The idea of many aftershave or body wash ads aimed at men is that using the product will attract women, driving them crazy with lust with predictable results.

This woman (or girl perhaps) is youthful – in fact presents a youth and purity of spirit and physical nature worth preserving. Many of us do seek such preservation, with recourse to beauty products like those offered here. But to suggest that something so natural as unalloyed youth needs the enhancement of a concoction of chemicals would be to give the game away. And so, the deployment of evidence of and allusions to 'Nature' in the advert is not only to 'naturalise' the need for such a product as **necessary** but also to **connote** that it is, despite the facts of the potentially noxious ingredients that one would find listed on any bottle, a *fully* natural substance (urban myths have it that pig and horse urine provide a valuable source of pheromones in such concoctions). It is as fresh and essential as the vivacity of 'woman' as she is presented here in all of her **synecdochic** (p. 38) glory.

Of course, the butterflies serve a number of functions – they're not there by 'chance'. These signs are **'iconic'**, indisputably imitative images of actual living creatures (although acting metaphorically as falling rose petals perhaps). They are also **indexical** (p. 60). Butterflies are one of the symptoms of summer and so in the relationship of **cause and effect** serve to underwrite and cement a rather pleasant series of affective responses and **connotations** about a scene that with its abundance of white might have seemed rather chilly in aspect rather than simply 'pure'. This then is a way of **anchoring** meaning and preventing **polysemia**. The butterflies cling to the woman as they would to flowers – conveying something of the natural scent of the product (and the delicacy conferred upon the user). But their velvet wings, as they flap and rest on the ivory skin of the model, must feel rather like the luxurious product itself when applied directly to the skin through the relaxing waters of a bath. Nothing so vulgar as a rushed shower is cited here! How can one pamper oneself or prepare oneself to be the feminine incarnate through a mere *shower*? It is an important aspect of the **presentational rhetoric** (p. 39) that the model does not look *out* at us, narrowing down the sense that this might be an overtly sexual advert in which 'Woman', completed by her acquisition of Chanel and the desire imbued or elicited by the scent of the new body range, gives us a 'knowing' or 'come-on' look.

A sense of the **mythological** aspects of this advert would remind us of one of our initial observations about how we don't question the fact of a woman lying naked for our perusal as part of an advert for perfume. She is there ultimately in the role of Woman – to be looked at – in fact connoting 'to-be-looked-at-ness' (p. 93). Of course, to be naked in a Chanel advert might conjure up anecdotal references to a historically resonant version of the feminine, namely the figure of the actress and icon Marilyn Monroe. When once asked if she wore anything to bed, Monroe titillated and thrilled her fans by answering that she wore nothing but *Chanel No 5*!

Here, our woman is insouciant, caught unawares and as nature intended; **narratively** speaking, this would be a case of *in media res*. Here we want to suggest that the image digs deep into a tradition of possible images bequeathed by a Western tradition of representation. Thus, this image has distant, trace **connotations** of the deep structure of a whole tradition of religious iconography and Western paining (see Berger, 1972 for instance). This woman can be thought of as akin to 'Eve' – nude and innocent in a Garden of Eden, woman as virginal innocent rather than corrupting seductress – the binary other in that Madonna/whore trope which has been a perennial in the imagery and narrative of Western civilisation.

If we accept that the combined signs **connote** a situation, or the feelings associated with a situation, of a summer's day, of a young woman in her natural state, at one with nature, then she is perhaps glancing up at a benign and warming sky. Incidentally, although this is a planned incident, what is the object of her glance in the absence of any image of the sun (and by the way the **complex sign** set out here is **indexical** of the presence of a sun)? It is the benign 'No 5' itself, a fount of warmth and naturalness! The product assumes the place of that object which ensures life on earth, the object of religious and secular worship by turn! Like the sun that rises every day, the product is new and refreshing – enhanced by the metaphor of the butterflies in their role here, fresh from their pupae, reborn after their caterpillar stage.

Here then, at the level of **mythology**, nature is invoked in excess, but clearly not spoken about in an obvious way ('use our product to keep you young'). It presents the **product**, a manufactured, artificial good, and the need to have it and define oneself (as feminine, attractive, sensual) through it as if Chanel (or at least these products) and the feminine were indivisible. Here's a curious set of contradictions then in which the 'natural' is prized but is implicitly redeemed or preserved through the unnatural or manufactured.

Unremarkable and unremarked upon then, this image of the feminine, for all of its admirable and appreciable qualities, becomes a pawn of economic exchange. Not only desirable but also accessible through the market price of this perfume for all who can afford it. Humanity and its **essence** (p. 111) – if there could be such a thing – and all of this 'eternal', ineffable beauty, purity, humanity, is boiled up, reduced and available in a range of bottles of varying sizes. For the women and men who are the intended audience for this advert, they are asked to recognise this image as natural and desirable: the acme of feminine beauty.

Of course, there are many ways of expressing a rather limited set of **mythologies** of the feminine – some sophisticated, some less so. This one is just a little more sophisticated than a tabloid newspaper glamour shot or a posed image for a fashion shoot or publicity still. We could, perhaps, appreciate this image for its 'artistic' leanings (and connotations), convincing ourselves that it doesn't exploit women or represent them in brutal fashion as more vulgar forms do. But then, all adverts do the same thing in the end. Furthermore, we should not forget the **alibi** here that the **denotative** meanings confer upon the connotative aspects of signs. This is, after all, just an advert and just another image of a female model – Estelle Warren 'wears' Chanel. To rest upon such assertions, however – whether speaking as scholar or 'ordinary' consumer – is to be willingly ignorant in the face of the overwhelming evidence of media meanings in general.

We would argue that the approach we've set out here would be important to any one with an enquiring mind and desire to be aware of how ideas operate in society, that images are never obvious in their meanings, nor are they innocent of vested interests. Pragmatically speaking, such analyses are certainly useful to capable media workers of any kind – the kind that media studies students often aspire to be. Whether you are convinced by our argument about the meaning of this advert and how it means what it does, a lot of astute thought and effort has gone into it on behalf of the manufacturers of the perfume by advertisers and creative workers. Some of the resonances we've reached for in interpreting

Doing media studies

The process of analysis

Does this process of analysis and its outcomes convince you? To what degree would you endorse this reading? Is there something missing or does it offer an *over*-reading of the material?

We have not said much about the uses of 'Estelle Warren' and her function as a sign with its own associations. How would such attention aid our reading? What evidence would *you* present and how would you pursue an argument to support, develop or refute this reading?

Choose another advert and perform a thorough textual analysis using the tools of **rhetoric, semiology, genre** and **narrative**. Concentrate on the overall interpretation rather than explaining the method as we have done here. Use the tools to support your analysis and generate clear evidence in the form of textual readings. How do your text and your reading compare with this one?

Do *all* media texts present us with such myths? Are some more mythological and some more 'innocent' than others?

the image come from a shared cultural tradition of representation and views of the world. We would argue that the creators of this text and its meanings have reached for these too, almost automatically and unconsciously – so naturalised and conventional, so embroiled in the naturalised as **myth**, are they. Other ways of making and deploying meaning are more conscious of course and this advert presents a balance of both. However, the point is that such combinations work on us affectively and impressionistically, drawing upon our own cultural position and acquaintance with conventions in media and from society and culture at large. Students who aspire to be thinking media professionals, those who create and determine media texts, are the ones who understand this and are able to articulate their own ideas and readings of media meanings.

References

Barthes, R. (2000, first published 1957) *Mythologies*, translated by Annette Lavers in 1972, Vintage: London.

Berger, J. (1972) *Ways of Seeing*, London and Harmondsworth: British Broadcasting Corporation, Penguin.

PART TWO

PRODUCING MEDIA

We introduced the last part by considering the way that media industries are organised around basic linear principles in a process of production, distribution and consumption. Having explored the output of this process, as we encounter it in the form of texts and the meanings generated in that encounter, we now move on to consider how to make sense of the origin of those meanings, in the form of media production.

We begin in Chapter 5 with a broad consideration of the nature of media production as a business. This encompasses an exploration of the economic context for media businesses, the organisation of media companies and the culture of media workers, as well as aspects of the digital age which are challenging some of the established aspects of production and, indeed, the economic assumptions that have supported businesses.

The second chapter in this part (Chapter 6) explores aspects of media regulation which impact upon production, distribution and, ultimately, what, how and where we consume media products. Our objectives here are to discover why specific media regulation exists, the nature of wider, non-specific legal frameworks and the way that we might make sense of these.

Finally, we bring these two themes together (in Chapter 7) in a consideration of the increasingly global nature of media production. We'll outline some of the historical strands behind this development in order to comprehend the consequences of media production and meanings in an international context.

Chapters in this section:

Chapter 5: The business of media
Explores the economic contexts for media production and the resulting organisational structures and procedures of media companies

Chapter 6: Media regulation and policy
Examines the ways in which media production and output are conditioned by rules and regulations within media business and wider social contexts

Chapter 7: Media production in a global age
Explores the nature of media production and regulation in the context of a worldwide economy and interactions

The business of media

Thinking about media businesses

The business of the media is business. What we mean by this is that, with some exceptions, most media organisations seek to generate profits to cover investment costs and to produce a surplus for owners and shareholders.

This point can be illustrated with reference to the French company Vivendi which among its assets lists ownership of TV group Canal+, Universal Music Group, Vivendi Entertainment and controlling stakes in video games company Activision Blizzard and telecommunications companies Maroc Telecom, GVT and SFR. Here is an edited extract from Vivendi's 2010 Annual Report (available at www.vivendi.com/vivendi/IMG/pdf/03_01_2011_Annual_Report.pdf) which gives some sense of the scope of the meanings of its 'business' here and the nature of this for one particular media organisation.

Summary of the 2010, 2009 and 2008 main developments

Following the sale of Vivendi's stake in NBC Universal [. . .] Vivendi now controls alone all of its assets. More than ever, customers of digital content and services lie at the heart of Vivendi's focus. Vivendi will combine its investments in networks, platforms and content with sustained efforts to develop projects, to share expertise between its divisions and stimulate innovation to enhance Vivendi's organic growth. As a result, Vivendi is pursuing its profitable growth strategy, while maintaining an investment grade debt rating. The key elements of Vivendi's strategy remain unchanged: the buy-out of minority interests in France at a reasonable price, financial discipline and a high cash dividend with a distribution rate of at least 50% of Adjusted Net Income.

2010

- In January, SFR paid a €1 billion dividend (of which €440 million was paid to Vodafone) with respect to fiscal year 2009.

- On February 18, SFR and Réseau Ferré de France entered into a GSM-R public—private partnership agreement.

- On February 22, Vivendi/Canal+ Group acquired from M6 a 5.1% interest in the share capital of Canal+ France.

- On April 2, Activision Blizzard paid a $189 million dividend (of which $108 million was paid to Vivendi) with respect to fiscal year 2009.

- On April 15, Lagardère decided to exercise its liquidity rights regarding its 20% interest in the share capital of Canal+ France.

- On April 27, Vivendi held a 99.17% controlling interest in GVT.

- In May, Vivendi paid a cash dividend of €1.40 per share with respect to fiscal year 2009, representing a total distribution of €1,721 million.

- On June 11, Vivendi obtained a 100% controlling interest in GVT following the cancellation of GVT outstanding common shares.

- In June, SFR acquired additional 3G mobile telephony spectrum for €300 million.

- On August 26, La Poste Group and SFR entered into exclusive negotiations to form a partnership to develop a mobile telephony offering under the 'La Poste' brand.

- On September 26, Vivendi sold a 7.66% interest in NBC Universal to General Electric for $2 billion.

- On December 14, Vivendi, Deutsche Telekom, the main shareholder of Elektrim and the creditors of Elektrim entered into certain agreements (subject to conditions precedent) to end the telecommunications dispute in Poland.

- On December 23, Maroc Telcom completed the acquisition process of a 51% interest in Gabon Telecom Group.

- On December 30, Vivendi acquired a 65% interest in Digitick.

Overall, the net income for this group was €2698 million in 2010, an increase on €2585 million. While not all media activity generates such amounts of revenue, even organisations not governed by the incentive towards profit operate within the same economic system. Their existence is determined by an economic reality which governs all aspects of decision making, as well as the kind of organisation media companies adopt, impacting too on the possibilities, nature and meanings of product. What media products are available to us, when and where they are available, and whether we have to pay anything in exchange for them, is directly related to media markets, share prices, material costs and, indeed, the broader economy in which we're all involved. It is conceivable too that this situation has an impact also on the possible meanings of texts. This, then, is the background to the questions and approaches explored in this chapter.

What we will do in this chapter

In the preceding chapters we made a distinction between the production, distribution and consumption of media products. We looked at the different ways of framing the products of media as: artefact (the product as *physical* 'thing'); commodity (the *economic* or *exchange* value of the product); text (the symbolic, meaningful aspect of the product). What we want to do now is begin to explore a range of related issues that require us to step back from the meaningfulness of the 'output' of media (textuality) for a moment and consider it in the context and process of its *production*.

Of course, our distinction is a rather arbitrary one. When we hear that a film cost $200 million to make and subsequently flopped at the box office, or that a rock tour grossed €1 billion, it tends to impact upon the manner in which we look at the film or hear the band and think about their audiences. Nonetheless, the distinction is one worth making, if only to clarify some of the terms and concepts involved in thinking about the business of media as a business. Here, we will explore some key questions around media businesses and introduce a number of approaches that will aid us in making sense of the production end.

We'll start by considering some key questions concerning media businesses and where we can find information about who, or 'what', produced those things that we consume. We'll then outline one of the main approaches to studying media businesses in the form of 'political economy'. The political economy approach encompasses an exploration of the market conditions of media businesses and how they seek to generate profit and reduce costs – and with what kind of consequences. We'll look at a number of strategies that companies use in order to achieve their goals such as producing audiences, occupying the centre ground of taste, working on large scales and so on. All of these aspects also lead us to consider questions about the meanings that are produced under these strategies and how business objectives impact upon our expectations for the social role of media. This is discussed under the concept of the public sphere.

We'll consider too the nature of media organisations and how they operate and how we might make sense of them. In addition we'll go on to ask questions about media workers and how they can be understood as professionals and creative workers.

Finally, we will explore how the digital age is challenging the traditional ways in which media production has been organised and how some economic assumptions are changing. In particular, the distance between producer and consumer is closing. Throughout this chapter, new media scholars will note that this new domain presents new questions about media and offers interesting opportunities to produce original research.

By the end of this chapter you should be able to:

- Define and outline the key issues in 'political economy', 'organisational' and 'culture of production' approaches to the study of media.

- Apply these key concepts to research contemporary media businesses.

- Identify and engage with contemporary issues facing media businesses in the digital age.

- Discuss and draw conclusions about a series of key debates concerning media as business.

KEY TERMS: ▶ audience as commodity; commodity form; concentration; corporations; critical political economy; economies of scale; ethnography; fixed and marginal costs; free market; Hotelling effect; mass and niche audiences; media organisations; monopoly and oligopoly; political economy; professionals and professional culture; public service broadcasting (PSB); public sphere; scarcity and abundance; supply and demand; synergy; the long tail.

Doing media studies

Conceptualising media businesses

We've suggested elsewhere that an advantage for the new media scholar is that most of us are already familiar with a wide range of media products, forms and meanings thanks to the role that these play in our everyday lives. However, knowledge of the organisations and market conditions that originate, develop and deliver our films, websites, music and so on is usually less certain. On this basis, it is useful to do some quick work in advance of our discussion in order to get a broad grip on what we mean by the terrain of media businesses, by seeking out information on them and their share prices.

Shares are the parts into which the assets or 'stock' of a company is divided. The amount of available shares, their price when compared with others and their stability or fluctuation (increasing or decreasing in price) is an indicator of the economic worth and success of a business. This is especially important when profits are made and paid out per share to those who own them in the form of 'dividends'.

Access the financial pages of a newspaper, website or magazine. Look at the share listings for media. These might be listed as communications, or part of entertainments and leisure. If not, just look among the names in the top 100 shares.

- How many of the names listed here are familiar to you?

- How do the share prices of media and communication companies compare with other commodities and companies on sale?

- Can you find out more about any one company's finances and nature in your source? Where else would you look and what kinds of information are you able to find out about the expenditure and income of this company?

- To what extent do you contribute to the income of any of these companies, i.e. what products produced by the company do you consume – whether by direct purchase, subscription or otherwise?

Investigating media businesses

To some degree, perhaps to the naïve, inattentive or plain uncaring, the various media might appear to get to us as if by magic, simply because, in their various forms, they are 'just there', and we're rarely inclined to think about how they reached us and who brought them there. When we consume media products we are not always fully aware of the companies and organisations that made them; we're more interested in the details of the story – about what's happening at the Olympics for instance, or the moves and shapes of the dancers in Lady Gaga's latest video.

You can explore this point simply by examining the next few media products you consume and by noting also the 'obviousness' or relative obscurity of information about who or 'what' was responsible for your media choices. Think about the adverts on TV and radio, and in magazines, for instance. Do Coca-Cola, Gap, PlayStation, Nescafé, etc. produce these directly, or are they produced by some other agent? Who made the radio programmes and music that you listen to? Who owns tabloid newspapers such as the *Sun* (UK), *Das Bild* (Germany) and broadsheets such as the *Guardian* (UK), *Le Figaro* (France) and *El Pais* (Spain)? What kinds of organisations lie behind them? How can you find out? (By the way, did you pay for your music or 'rip' it from a friend's CD or online? Who paid for the music played on the radio? How is the wealth of material online paid for? Is it?)

There are, of course, many clues as to who, or 'what', produced any media product, the most obvious of which are perhaps the title and credit sequences of the TV programmes or films that we watch. These give us lists of personnel and companies involved in the production of such work. Of course, many of us are aware of and recognise the large media organisations like Canal+, MTV Sweden, the BBC, Sony or Time Warner that provide so much of our entertainment. Indeed, we may get a thrill when the music and searchlights to a 20th Century Fox film start up, for instance, or when the crackle and fizz of the HBO logo comes up on TV or a DVD. Newspapers and magazines also use brands to promote their publications which, we are aware, have something to do with the company that produced our daily or monthly copy. Looking at the small print inside also reveals that companies like Emap, Time Inc., Hello Ltd or Bauer produce quite a lot of these publications. Popular music has equivalents in the labels on CD inserts (and vinyl if you use that format), websites in their corporate brands, and radio in the station names repeated in different parts of the country, as well as in the announcements over credits.

Often, the names in production credits – the who (individual) and what (company) – will guide our viewing, reading and listening preferences. If you aspire to work in media, you may imagine yourself in a TV newsroom, a particular radio station, or as the creator of a well-known website, as one of the names on those credit lists.

Media studies students (among others) sometimes have romantic ideas of how media products are produced, imagining that media employees follow their instincts or muse in order to produce creative and stimulating media texts. In reality, although media workers *are* privileged enough to get these sorts of creative opportunities, media as highly organised businesses are those in which creative and managerial staff have a responsibility to create content for specific audiences, on a regular cycle and to a certain budget. Often this is done within strict internal and external guidelines and conventions – institutional, professional, social and cultural. Understanding *why* this is, and what it means for media, is a central part of our study.

The significance of media organisations as organisations and as businesses with an important place in the wider economy is signalled by the fact that they are often the subject of news stories themselves. Reading through the headlines below you will see that the way in which these companies operate, the type of content that they supply us with, who they employ, and who owns them are important enough matters for them to be given prominence on the inside pages of broadsheet newspapers.

- 'Media's losses in social networking top $1.5b' (AsiaMedia.Net, 21 June 2010) (www. telecomasia.net/content/medias-losses-social-networking-top-15b)
- 'Watchdog accuses BBC chiefs of breaching licence as website overspend hits £36m' (*Guardian*, 30 May 2008)
- 'Warner tries a new tactic to revive its DVD sales' (*New York Times*, 30 May 2008)(www. nytimes.com/2008/05/26/business/media/26retail.html?_r=1&scp=1&sq=%91Warner% 20tries%20a%20new%20tactic%20to%20revive%20its%20DVD%20sales%92% 20&st=cse&oref=slogin)
- 'Television magazine successes slow erosion of press sales' (*Le Figaro*, 30 May 2008).

In proceeding, we should recognise that the current organisation of media is neither obvious nor inevitable. It is not obvious in two senses: there is substantial variety in the nature of organisations that produce media products, and it is not always clear who actually made any given media product. Single individuals working as freelancers create some products, others are produced by small youthful companies, and other products by organisations that have existed for over a century. In some cases media organisations are very local to us (nationally, regionally), in others people from all over the world produce aspects of the same programme, website, song or publication. It is not always clear why one media organisation is the way it is or what such an organisation seeks to do. Sometimes, debates about the way in which media *should* be organised have resulted in the form that they have taken. Furthermore, although media products are often heavily branded, those brands sometimes disguise who actually produced or distributed them to us – whether at an individual, collective or company level.

To reiterate: all media organisations are businesses involved in a commercial sphere of exchange, of income generation, of profit and loss. Even the UK's BBC, as well as any listener-supported or bedroom radio station, costs money to maintain, as does programming, and all have to get income from somewhere in order to sustain themselves. The economics of media, though, apply just as much to the not-for-profit organisation as to the profit-maximising firm; it is just that, for the former, the contemporary economic system represents the reality in which it has to work, while for the latter it is the very reason it exists. So, although all forms of media organisation operate in a similar economic environment, they will respond to this environment in different ways. As we work through some key concepts set out below, then, we need to think about the economics of the environment in which organisations operate, how different forms of organisation will respond, and what the implications of this are.

There are three main approaches that have been developed to study the three different levels at which we can understand media organisations operating, and it is these approaches which we now move on to outline. The first looks at the place of media business in the wider world of economics and politics, and so is called 'political economy'. The second is interested in the detailed structure and objectives of the organisation, and so is called 'organisational study'. The final approach looks at the culture of media workers in their organisation, exploring the ideas of professionalism, skill, creativity and views of audiences they operate with, and uses a method called 'workplace ethnography'.

Political economy of media

The term 'political economy' is associated with thinkers such as John Locke, Adam Smith and later Karl Marx (see Chapter 10), and in essence concerns the nature of production and the wider social conditions under which it takes place. It emerged as a term in the eighteenth century, as a label for the study of new market relations that emerged in the modern age, namely the buying and selling of things in relation to the means of production, organisation and cost of those things. It relates to questions about where economic value lies and where it is generated, whether in the ownership of things, for instance, or in the skills and availability of the workforce. The political element of the term 'political economy' relates to the way in which thinkers were concerned with nation states, of the way that economic markets were (or were not) managed, whether they were supported or hindered by the policies and attentions of elected politicians and non-elected rulers such as kings and queens and, indeed, how the vested interests of such individuals and groups impacted upon economies.

Useful for our purposes, the sociologist of communication, Vincent Mosco, has defined political economy as 'the study of the social relations, particularly the power relations, that mutually constitute the production, distribution, and consumption of resources' (Mosco, 1996: 25). Mosco's definition points to the need to study the ways in which media products are made, circulated and experienced, and how powerful the different people involved are and what role they play in these processes. Therefore, political economy approaches, when brought to bear upon media, have sought to investigate the conditions under which media institutions and organisations are formed and work, as well as the incentives and constraints under which they operate. A blunt example here that would illustrate the issues and concerns of a political economy approach would be the rise of News Corporation's STAR TV (Satellite Television for the Asian Region) and its move into the burgeoning and lucrative market of the People's Republic of China in the 1990s. That country's government was dissatisfied with the coverage offered by the BBC on one of the channels on STAR's delivery platform and threatened to block STAR transmission to China as a whole unless the BBC was removed (Weber, 2003; Chang, 2007).

Historically, the political economy approach has been concerned with exploring the relationship between the range of meanings available in media and the underpinning economic interests and ownership patterns across the different media spheres – press, music, TV, film, radio, advertising and lately the internet. The focus is, therefore, on questions such as: who pays for media at the point of production? What is the primary commodity of any medium? And how do consumers pay for this commodity and for the different economic activities of media? As a result, many media researchers have explored questions of power within the framework of what has been called a *critical* political economy'. The critical aspect of critical political economy is brought to bear upon the nature of states and governments and the way that they oversee media management and regulation, and, indeed, the nature of the wider capitalist economy which underwrites the profit impulse of media businesses in relation to wider participatory politics. For Peter Golding and Graham Murdock, this constitutes an approach in which we must engage with basic *moral* questions of justice, equality and the public good (Golding and Murdock, 2000). For such media theorists, fundamental questions arise from an acceptance of the centrality of media in modern societies and concern the concentration of media ownership, the way that media are organised and the degree to which such factors impact upon the management of society in general, and upon us all as individuals. Some of these ideas are explored below in our discussion of the public sphere, and also in our chapters on power and ideology and mass society (Chapters 10 and 11), all of which extend the basic terms of a political economy approach outlined here. Within the aegis of this political economy approach, we shall now move on to consider the nature of media organisations in the context of the free market, the exchange of the commodity goods that they produce and the curious relations that they enter into.

Media organisations in the free market

One of the features of the landscape of media businesses in a capitalist economy is that of competition. Media organisations compete with each other for audiences, sales and other revenue streams, such as advertising, in order to generate return on their investment and in order to maximise and deliver profits to shareholders. They compete by sometimes

Thinking aloud

When we examine the deployment of labour resources and what we all get paid for the work we do, you might reflect upon how we might explain the mega-salaries afforded some media producers (e.g. pop singers such as Lady Gaga and movie stars such as Jack Black). While 'stars' can be considered to have an existence as signs and commodities (see p. 124–127), how might supply and demand explain their status and rewards when compared with the meagre pay of a textbook author, for instance, or, better still, for those 'behind the scenes' in media enterprises, who are ultimately responsible for making the stars 'look good'?

Free market
The term 'free market' describes a condition where business is governed by laws of supply and demand, rather than by government interference, regulations or subsidies.

Supply and demand suggests a relational and dynamic model where the price of a 'good' (commodity, service — a media product) in a competitive market will impact upon the degree of demand from consumers (how many can afford and want the good) and the response of producers (how much of the good is worth producing in order to return investment and maximise profit).

offering varieties of the same thing (*Corriere dello Sport*, *Gazzetta dello Sport*, heavy metal music across radio, reality TV shows on different channels, etc.), the same thing again and again (*Saw V*, *Big Brother 2011*), or attempting to innovate (or offer a semblance of innovation) and forge new audiences, attracting them away from their habitual pleasures and habits: 'Like MSN? Try 'Chat Roulette'!

The wider economy in which media operate is, by and large, global in nature (see Chapter 7). In this context, media products and services are comparable to others, such as cars, food or insurance provision, in an economy where rules and regulations governing competition have been reduced to a minimum in order to encourage variety, exchange and competition. This is known as a 'free market' economy.

Free market competition (also called laissez-faire competition) is claimed by its supporters to be the engine of capitalism – keeping prices low and product quality high, and giving people what they want as a result of offering a choice of goods. In a free market economy, scarcities of commodities – media products for instance – are resolved through changes in relative prices. If a commodity is in short supply relative to the number of people who want to buy it, its price will rise, producers and sellers will make more profit and production will tend to rise to meet the excess demand. If there is an over-supply of a commodity – a glut – the price will tend to fall, thereby both attracting additional buyers and discouraging producers and sellers from entering the market. Theoretically, in a free market, buyers and sellers come together voluntarily to decide on what products to produce, sell and buy, and how resources such as capital and labour should be used and rewarded. In the last instance, we're talking about how we get paid and how much we get paid.

Commodity relations

Although most people who work in media concentrate in producing programmes or publications to ensure they are of a good technical quality and meaningful to their audience, they are also producing things that will be economically valuable to the company that employs them. Economic value defines the commodity form of any medium and its outputs (recordings, newspapers, TV programmes), and these outputs cost money to produce and, in turn, are used to create revenue for the companies that produce them. Even a broadcaster like the BBC in the UK, which is publicly funded to the tune of £3.5 billion, generates over £1.4 billion of income in its commercial operations through sales of its content and services, with profits of over £100 million (BBC Full Financial Statements 2010/11, p. F5 at www.bbc.co.uk/annualreport/). Nonetheless, media products are different from other products because of the combination of the way that they generate revenue and the way they are consumed. Revenue can come from two sources. The first is directly from the final consumers, made in some form of payment for a physical artefact, like a newspaper, or a subscription for a broadcast programme or web access. The second is by selling some of the space in the physical artefact to advertisers, who wish to communicate with the audience: this happens in commercial radio, free-to-view television, websites, free sheet newspapers and so on. In addition, media products are not usually characterised by repeat purchases. That is, once we have bought an edition of a newspaper, or a copy of a recording (on vinyl, in MP3 form), we are unlikely to buy the same thing again – they are used up as commodities even if their textual meanings go on and on (we play songs *ad infinitum*). Contrast this with other consumer goods such as branded food; if we like one tin of beans we will go back and buy more, as we will have eaten the first tin.

Balancing revenue indirectly from advertising and directly from consumers creates a distinctive media landscape and benefits larger companies. For a start, the revenue from advertising can offset that from sales, which may or may not be great enough to cover costs. In the case of publications, this often means the cover price is far less than the cost of production, despite the fact that circulation alone doesn't always return retail sales revenue that justifies the cover price. In the case of over-the-air broadcasting, this makes many programmes ostensibly free to viewers and listeners (unless you are paying to view or are required to pay for a licence to view). The peculiar economics of media products leads to the distinctive strategies followed by media organisations.

Audience as commodity

The importance of advertising to underwriting the commodity form of media products has led theorist Dallas Smythe (Smythe, 1981) to argue that we should not think of media organisations as producing products like newspapers, websites or broadcast programmes at all. Rather, he suggests that they produce audiences. This is a very interesting idea that allows us to understand the importance of particular audiences to media. From this perspective, the news stories, websites and broadcast programmes are the way that they are because they are aimed at attracting the particular audience that a group of advertisers want. Likewise, many Hollywood blockbusters are constructed, promoted and distributed in order to appeal to a particular demographic, impacting upon what stories are told, how they are told and when films appear. For the blockbuster, this is most usually around key annual holidays when the core audience is freed up from kindergarten, school, college and university commitments (Biskind, 1999; Shone, 2005). For further discussion of media businesses and the production of audiences, see Chapter 8.

It is possible to construct an optimistic and a pessimistic conclusion from this observation. Optimistically, this should ensure that different groups of people get products targeted at their tastes and interests. Pessimistically, this could mean that we get lumped together with a broad group that is attractive to an advertiser and that the media producer finds has the lowest common range of interests or, even worse, we get nothing because we are not attractive enough to advertisers. It is possible to see this at work in any local commercial radio provision. If a city has only one commercial station wanting to maximise its profits, that station will most likely produce general pop music programming in the belief that it can attract the largest and wealthiest audience through this strategy. As other stations join the original broadcaster, they will try to attract either some of the current listeners or others who do not like the first station. However, it is likely that these stations will be based upon variations on

Doing media studies

Your local radio

Look into the development of radio in your city or region (station websites will often give potted histories of their own progress and change). This task should also encompass online radio stations which, while addressing the global digital audience in principle, are also often addressed to a locality.

To what degree did the development follow our model? What provision exists across your location? If there are differences from our descriptions of media business, what could explain them? Are there forces at work here other than the economics of advertising markets?

Public-service broadcasting (PSB) is a system whereby the broadcast media receive some or all of their funding from the public, usually through state sub-sidies or specific taxes, such as com-pulsory licence fees on radio or television receivers, collected by the broadcaster.

Public broadcasters normally use this money to achieve the following goals: geographic universal-ity (i.e. widespread reach or cover-age); catering for a plurality of cultural interests, tastes and minorities; address to national iden-tity and community; detachment from vested interests and government; and competition in 'qual-ity' programming rather than numbers. (A more detailed discussion is offered in Chapter 6.)

a pop format, as whoever attracts the largest audience will make the most money. As more stations start broadcasting, they may now try to attract more specialist audiences, but only if they are fairly wealthy. Young, middle-class people may be attracted to a dance or rock station, and so these will be the next formats to be created. However, their playlist will mostly feature well-known artists who have had some pop success, and more underground music may only get played in the evening, when listenership is lower.

Mass and niche audiences, and the Hotelling effect

We can begin to see that profit-maximising companies are likely to produce media prod-ucts that will appeal to mass or niche (smaller, specialised) audiences. Niche audiences are only likely to be economically worthwhile if they are made up of relatively more affluent consumers for whom an advertiser will be willing to pay more per thousand listeners. When trying to attract wide audiences, producers will try to produce common denomina-tor programming, or content that will not alienate or offend anyone in particular but will have as wide an appeal as possible. Most importantly, some people will not be attractive to advertisers because they do not have high spending power and are unable to afford expen-sive cover prices or subscriptions.

These phenomena were explained by economic theorist Harold Hotelling in the 1920s (Hotelling, 1929: 41–57). Hotelling posited that profit-maximising companies always position themselves closest to a market's geographic centre so as to be equally available to all potential customers. By extension, all other factors being equal, media companies will 'play safe' and place their products in close proximity to the centre of 'taste' within any market. Anecdotally, the authors of this book, in their research interviews, have encoun-tered media producers who make direct reference to Hotelling's ideas as the basis for their strategies. One result of this tendency identified by Hotelling, therefore, is that it militates against innovation and variety.

On the other hand, media organisations that are not ostensibly organised to seek profit maximisation – because they are publicly funded like the BBC in the UK, PBS in the USA or NHK in Japan, or have cultural aims like community radio or community newspapers – may purposely target groups not supported by profit-maximising compa-nies seeking a niche audience, or those neglected by lowest-common-denominator pro-gramming or editorial policy. This has been the basis for arguments for the use of public funds for certain forms of public service media or for the regulation of profit-maximising companies to ensure that they consider the types of content and audiences neglected by a free market.

Doing media studies

PSB in your own country

Do national broadcasters in your country have a PSB remit? Find out who they are and what this remit is and where it is expressed. How is the PSB remit defined? How is it supported (legislation, taxation, voluntary donations)? How much funding does your PSB use up to sustain production and its services? Does your PSB generate revenue through sales or carry any form of advertising and, if so, do you think this is a good thing or a bad thing? Why?

Controlling uncertainty

The combination of audience commodifica-tion and the 'non-repeat purchase' of media products leads to a high degree of uncertainty in media production. Even though there is a tendency to play safe in some aspects of pro-duction, the fact that fashions for products are often fast-changing (and increasingly so) makes it very difficult for media organisations to predict what is likely to appeal next, and to plan accordingly. To combat this, media use various strategies, via forms of branding for instance, in order to encourage more predict-able consumption. This is most obvious in the publication or broadcast industries. Here, the very means of distribution is turned into a brand. A heavy emphasis is given to the name of a radio station or publication title, and although the content will alter, the branding may encourage the consumer to buy, listen or view regularly on the basis of association and predictability. A useful example here would be the various spin-offs from MTV, the American music station which began on cable in 1981. MTV has diversified (and spread globally) to such a degree that it offers niche stations such as MTV Base, MTV Hits, MTV Dance as well as VH1. Such strategies will no doubt resonate with you in relation to the concept of genre (see Chapter 2).

It is possible to encourage repeat purchases of media products through the development of star names and the exploitation of genres that will encourage audiences to consume similar products. We may know nothing about a new film but, if it stars an actor we like, we will be more inclined to go and watch it at the cinema, or even to buy the DVD release or purchase the film via cable TV delivery. The same is true of popular music, where genres are also important. If we like a particular R&B artist, we will be more likely to buy their records and, if our tastes are heavily oriented to that genre, we will be more likely to continue consuming further products by the same artist or others like them. We'll also seek out radio stations that play such music, as well as visiting websites and reading magazines devoted to our genres of choice. Indeed, we may find that a variety of magazines and other products are promoted and are attractive to us because they have features on stars we like. Such operations across different media forms can be described as synergistic.

Synergy

is a number of processes working together within a system for greater benefit than they could achieve individually.

Synergy derives from a combination of the Greek *syn* (together) and *ergon* (work). For us this refers to how media and other entertainment industries work together to generate greater (or more precisely targeted) audiences, publicity, sales and thus profits. In this way, costs of promotion, for instance – as well as some of the risks – can be spread and shared. So, when radio stations play music made available from music companies, the station and company form a synergy (or are in a synergistic relationship), engaging in activities that together create a greater benefit for both partners. However, synergies can exist independently of any conscious or co-ordinated plan or activity of the company.

The nature and extent of media synergies is most apparent when new media releases are upon us, and this is most noticeable upon the occasion of a new film release. Songs from the film are promoted by record companies, using videos of the artist and scenes from the film, which in turn appear on music TV shows and channels, which in turn feature advertisements in their breaks for the film (which partly pay for the shows). Magazines feature the stars from the film and maybe even clothes and equipment (think of the ads for expensive watches and cars every time a new James Bond movie appears!). Stars will also do the rounds of chat and review shows, feeding the content-hungry editorial. Let us not forget, either, the franchise tie-ins for some films – in fast food, cereals, novelisations, comic book adaptations, video games, posters and so on. The key issue here, perhaps, is to understand when and how all of this is (or is not) planned and co-ordinated and by whom, on whose behalf and with what kind of financial result.

Cost structure and managing risk

Of course, the revenue achieved from a commodity is not the only factor to consider in media businesses. Of equal importance in balancing income and outgoings, in order to post profits, are the costs of production. Until recently, all media organisations tended to face a very distinctive cost structure. It was very expensive to set up a media business, but relatively cheap (or often entirely cost-free) to make extra versions of a media product for additional consumers. In economic terminology, therefore, media usually have high fixed costs and low marginal costs.

Just think how expensive it is to set up a television production company: the cost of all the studios and equipment, of employing all the highly skilled staff, managers and

Doing media studies

Tracking synergies

Identify a current film or pop album coming up for release (sites such as IMDB. com have information on the former, Amazon on the latter and, indeed, new music releases are often heavily premiered on radio and in new release sections of magazines, newspaper reviews, etc.).

Establish the names of the company or companies behind these releases. Then look for all of the different 'platforms' across the media and other areas in which the product, or related products, are featured during the week preceding and the week after the release date. Establish which companies are behind these media forms (or cereals, burger bars, MP3 players, live events, tours and so on).

Produce a 'mind-map' that allows you to visualise the relationship between these platforms, with your film or CD at the centre of the map, listing the companies involved in this relationship. Which of these do you think have had to 'pay' to participate in this synergy? Which ones have not? Why not?

After a week or so, look for 'top 10' chart listings for film or CD and information on revenue, and consider the extent to which the central product, as well as the related platforms, has benefited from this cross-promotion.

Finally, what are the likely benefits and consequences of this synergy?

producers for such a complex production base. Even before a single programme has been produced the costs are enormous (even in the age of digitisation). If no one watched, the costs would still be the same. However, once made, a programme can be broadcast, and it does not really cost any more for one million people to watch it in an available broadcast area than it does for one person to do so. This is just as true for companies running radio stations and, hitherto, almost as true for record companies or newspaper or magazine publishers. There are some extra costs for the blank CD and artwork, or the paper and ink, but these are very low compared with the other costs incurred. This gives enormous benefit to existing or large media companies with large numbers of consumers. If you *already* make television programmes, you already have the equipment, buildings and staff to make others, and the more programmes you make, the less it costs, as the total costs are shared across all the programmes. Likewise, the larger the audience, the lower the costs for each one of them – if there is a charge. When combined with the extra revenue created by a mass audience and advertising, this results in far greater profits for the larger company than for the smaller one, which may produce fewer programmes and attract smaller audiences.

While this state of affairs is still generally true, recent technological changes have made a major difference to these basic economics. Initially, we can see this change in two main areas: new production technologies and new distribution technologies. Computers in newsrooms and magazine offices have cut the costs of production dramatically. This means that the point at which a publication can break even through individual sales has fallen. You can attract fewer readers and still make a profit, or attract many more and make even more money. It is possible to see this in the profit-maximising magazine and newspaper sector. The number of niche magazines has risen enormously, while the circulation of some mass titles has been encouraged by real cuts in their cover prices. In recent years, in fact, the appearance of numerous magazines (listings, entertainment, lifestyle) and newspapers with no cover price, relying entirely upon advertising revenue, have proliferated across the world. Titles such as *20 Minutos* in Spain, *Bladid* in Iceland, *Metro* in the UK, Holland, Czech Republic and elsewhere, contribute to the 44 million copies of freesheets distributed every day in over 56 countries across the world (www._newspaperin novation._com/_index._php/_about-free-dailies/). Similar developments have taken place in broadcasting, photography and other forms of print, as well as in the music industry. We'll return to these issues in more detail towards the end of this chapter.

Size, concentration and media corporations

Above we saw how the costs of media production traditionally gave larger firms a market advantage. First, they could share the high fixed costs of technology across a large number of productions, and secondly they had the capital resources to buy expensive equipment at the outset. These advantages have been one of the key reasons that media production has been increasingly dominated by an ever-decreasing number of larger and larger companies. For instance, the worldwide recording industry is dominated by four big companies – Sony BMG Music Entertainment Inc., Warner Music Group, EMI Group and Universal Music Group, and these share around 71 per cent of global retail sales (www. ifpi.org/). The tendency towards largeness happens because corporations, in their search for ever-increasing profits, seek to lower their costs, and an effective way to lower costs is through what economists call '**economies of scale**'.

Size gives advantage, offering the chance to improve profit margins, or the difference between cost of production to the company and purchase price of product for the consumer. This can be achieved, for instance, by purchasing raw materials on a large scale (CDs for copying, land for offices, electronic equipment, paper, computers, etc.), and thereby getting preferential prices, sometimes passed on as lower cost prices for the consumer; or by keeping staff numbers low (by eliminating duplications in management), through vertical integration processes and so on. The quickest way to achieve economies of scale is to merge with, or take over, other companies. Such mergers then create what economists call 'barriers to entry', as smaller firms struggle to start up in a market already dominated by a few big players. An impetus to go large not only at the national level but internationally happens when local markets become saturated, spurring large corporations to seek new markets around the world to maintain or increase profits. When a particular area is dominated by a small number of companies, control of that area is concentrated in the hands of a small number of organisations and their owners or bosses. If one firm controlled almost all the money being made in a particular area of business, they would have monopoly control. When a handful of firms control over half of an area of business there is an oligopoly. Most media sectors are dominated by oligopolies.

It is ironic that the free market, which in theory generates a level playing field, encouraging variety and competition, rarely leads to such a situation. In fact, the market often leads to a condition of monopolisation and cartels, with big conglomerates exploiting their monopolistic or oligopolistic power to maximise their profits, regardless of the wider social implications of such domination of mass communications. As a result, there have always been widespread concerns about having far too few firms providing media products. These would range from the fear that a small number of media companies could control the information we receive (and which we use to make political decisions in a democracy), through the view that, when large firms dominate, the products they produce are formulaic and uninteresting, to the deep anxiety that such **concentration** will give some individuals control over what we think (for a discussion of power see Chapter 10). The issue of dominance in media production is not just restricted to issues of concentration. Not only do a small number of companies control the majority of revenue in individual sectors, these companies also tend to operate across sectors, and operate in different countries: they are multi-sector, transnational corporations (see Chapter 7).

The term 'corporation' describes any group of people with a common purpose. It has also come to mean those particularly large businesses that we are thinking of here. The

Economies of scale are all the ways that a corporation can save money through size – being big, buying big and acting big in terms of sales and profits.

Concentration measures the degree to which control of a particular sector of media (or any other economic sector) is in the hands of the most dominant firms. It is usually measured as the percentage of the revenue received by the largest 5 or 10 firms.

Monopoly and oligopoly Monopoly describes a condition in which one company or seller has control over the entire market. An oligopoly describes a market condition in which sellers (i.e. businesses) are few. The result is that the actions of any one of them will affect the market price as well as their competitors.

legal status primarily refers to the arrangement of ownership, with a large number of people owning a share in the company. These are the shares that are sold and bought on the stock exchange. The term corporation, though, is most often used to describe those companies that became large by buying enough shares in other companies to take them over. Sometimes companies grow by taking over other firms who do the same thing. This is called horizontal integration, because the takeover is understood to have taken place at the same level of production. On other occasions a company will take over a firm involved in another level of production – vertical integration – or one involved in another media sector – lateral integration (see p. 247).

So, a TV production company may grow bigger and control more revenue in a sector through horizontal integration – by buying another TV production company. It may buy a facilities house that supplies equipment, or a broadcaster, through vertical integration. In addition, it may grow laterally, by buying a radio station or newspaper business. This integration also happens across countries, so that the ownership of major parts of one country's media can become part of corporations based, owned and controlled in another country. This characteristic of modern media conglomerates encourages the synergies and cross-platform promotions we outlined above and, potentially, an exacerbation of the effects suggested by the ideas of Harold Hotelling.

You will be able to see that this tendency raises the anxiety about corporate influence further. If a corporation owns a high proportion of the largest TV companies and broadcast networks plus several newspapers and radio stations, its influence is potentially dangerous to the pluralism one expects of democratic systems.

Having suggested that each media sector is very concentrated, we also need to note that, for every large firm with a lion's share of the revenue in the sector, there are also many smaller companies at large working on a much more reduced scale. These companies are often called independents because they are perceived to work separately from the kinds of transnational corporations discussed above, which contain many smaller brands within their overall control. Many of these independent companies remain short-lived. They often target small niche markets, and are often very successful by being very specialised, or because of the commitment or expertise of the people who work for them. When successful, they are often targeted for takeover by big corporations, and their lack of access to resources to launch new ventures often means they cannot make a profit when competing with corporations. Many of the longer-running independent companies survive because they do not aim to make immense profits, are staffed by unpaid volunteers or have strong social and cultural agendas.

Distribution

One of the biggest fears expressed about the dominance of corporations is that they control *access* to audiences and of audiences to media through their success at vertical integration. If a corporation owns both TV production companies and broadcast networks, it will make more profit from broadcasting its own television programmes. A small, independent TV production company may make interesting television that could attract an audience, but it relies on a larger corporation to allow the programme to be broadcast. All traditional media still rely on expensive forms of distribution, which are often owned by oligopolistic transnational corporations, where regulation does not intervene to prevent ownership. This is the reason that state intervention and regulation has most often been focused on channels of distribution, for instance over broadband or over other physical avenues, for access to media product. This could range from establishing a semi-independent public body (such as the BBC in the UK in 1927), through a French experiment in the 1970s to allow all publishers the right to have their magazines available in newsagents, to the controls on cross-media or concentrated ownership that most European countries had from the 1950s to the 1980s. We expand upon the specific area of media regulation in the next chapter.

Case Study

Time Warner

As the conglomerate that underwent one of the biggest mergers in history, Time Warner is worth a closer look for the way that its progress is typical of other media conglomerates. This is not the whole story, of course, but a useful résumé of some aspects that have made it such a news item in recent years.

Time magazine was launched in 1923 by Henry Luce and Briton Hadden. It was targeted at conservative, middle-class people who were offered an efficient and appealing way to consume news. Its formula – of condensing and compartmentalising news each week under headings like business, science and religion, and focusing on human interest – was extremely successful. The Time Inc. empire grew, in 1973, by acquiring control of Home Box Office (HBO) – a pay channel offering movies and sport. In 1989,

under threat of a takeover bid, Time Inc. took over Warner Communications Inc. The resulting Time Warner operations now included magazine and book publication, cable TV systems, films and TV programming, videos, music labels, cinema chains and theme parks (Warner Communications Inc. had, itself, been a highly diversified entertainment company). In 1996, the US Congress deregulated the telecommunications industry, which allowed Time Warner to acquire Ted Turner's Turner Broadcasting System (TBS), which already owned the CNN news channel – itself a global operation reaching 212 countries. Meanwhile, another communications company called AOL had grown from a computer games supplier, formed in 1983, to become the world's leading internet service provider (ISP), when it acquired rival company CompuServe in 1998. By 2000, AOL had over 22 million subscribers worldwide – a quarter of the world's internet households.

In 2000, AOL and Time Warner announced their intention to merge – the biggest merger in history, as the deal was worth $160 billion. More accurately, as Demers (2002) points out, this merger was an acquisition: AOL, which had a lot of capital available because market speculation had driven up its stock price and worth, purchased Time Warner. From AOL's perspective, this purchase allowed it to combine home information with home entertainment – which would be supplied by Time Warner's huge back catalogue of film, music and the like (Balnaves *et al.*, 2008; Demers, 2002).

As AOL Time Warner (as they were then called) announced in a press release on the merger, it was envisaged that this would 'fundamentally change the way people get information, communicate with others, buy products and are entertained – providing far-reaching benefits for our customers and shareholders' (Demers, 2002: 30). Interestingly, the 'merger' was approved by the US Federal Trade Commission (which seeks to prevent markets narrowing through monopolisation or unfair practices that skew the market and competition) only

Source: Alamy Images

The Time Warner HQ, New York City. Time Warner is worth a closer look for the way that its progress is typical of other media conglomerates. The Music Group, with its many labels and companies, is but one arm of a global corporation.

after AOL Time Warner agreed to open its cable TV lines to internet rivals, thereby turning the cable lines into a public channel for delivery of information on the internet.

After the merger, the profitability of AOL decreased, in tandem with a downturn in the fortunes and value of similar independent internet companies, significantly devaluing the AOL division. In 2003, the company dropped 'AOL' from its name. Given that AOL's dial-up internet service lost 3.8 million subscribers over 2007, in 2008 it prepared to strip away its waning dial-up business, focusing instead on nurturing its advertising business by investing in the still infant social media space. With an eye towards the future, in March 2008 AOL announced that it was purchasing Bebo, the British social networking site, with more than 40 million members worldwide – the third-largest audience of social networks in the USA, behind only Myspace and Facebook. In the words of AOL Chairman and CEO Randy Falco: 'Bebo is the perfect complement to AOL's personal communications network and puts us in a leading position in social media.'

This acquisition gives AOL a global social media network of about 80 million unique users. Given that, with an average of about 40 minutes per visit, Bebo promises advertisers a highly engaged audience, this puts Bebo at the cornerstone of AOL's efforts to become a 'social media powerhouse', pairing Bebo's reach and engagement with AOL's advertising network (Corbin, 2008). Whether this places AOL in competition, or in alliance, with the other main online advertiser, Google, depends upon your point of view, as Google already owns 5 per cent of AOL (Corbin, 2008)! There are various other synergies of Time Warner allying with Bebo as, in November 2007, Bebo launched its Open Media programme, allowing its members to embed content from CBS, Entertainment and Sports Programming Network (ESPN), MTV Networks and other partners into their profiles (Corbin, 2008).

Ultimately, then, this case study serves to illuminate the impulse of media companies to grow, and their pursuit of profit through new markets and innovations. It also indicates something of the potential difficulties and uncertainties they face as media companies: despite incredible size and assets, things don't always go to plan.

Source: Vian Bakir

Case Study

Media business in the business downturn

In spite of the stories of amalgamation and super-profits generated by international conglomerates the business of media is a difficult one in the best of times. In the context of the challenge of digitisation (see below) as well as a global recession this is an unusually tough time. Consider, for instance, the parlous state of the local press. Typically, journalists work long and unsocial hours and receive relatively low wages, certainly incomers can expect to earn considerably less than the average national wage should they be fortunate enough to land a position as a reporter on a regional title. That situation is unlikely to improve in coming years as the industry continues to make cuts, following the onset of digitisation. We can understand aspects of the situation with reference to two West Midlands titles as case studies.

The *Express & Star* and *Shropshire Star*, which are based in the West Midlands, are two of the UK's best-selling local newspapers. However, they have not been immune to changes caused by digitisation and a general economic downturn.

In April 2011, the titles, which form part of the Midlands News Association, announced a 10 per cent reduction in their 900 staff. The cuts followed a similar programme that had been implemented two years earlier. The *Express & Star* formerly enjoyed a circulation of around 250,000 copies per edition – today that figure has more than halved. The *Shropshire Star* formerly enjoyed a circulation of around 100,000 per day – now the figure is closer to 60,000.

Alan Harris, MNA managing director, has said that: 'Like every other publisher, the MNA is facing very difficult trading conditions and there seems to be no sign of improvement. If we are to continue to invest for the future in our publications, both in print and online, then we must make some cost savings.'

There have been other effects. At *Shropshire Star*, the title has cut back the number of editions that it publishes. In recent times it has merged a number of editions, so that the former stand-alone Midday, South, Bridgnorth and Powys editions are among those that are no longer published. There have also been sharp declines in advertising revenue, caused by a reduction in motoring, classifieds and property. The advent of successful websites to market homes for sale online has hastened the decline.

The print media industry has opted for an extensive programme of rationalisations so as to cut high fixed costs. Print media have been further hit by rises in the cost of newsprint and fuel.

Should students be fortunate to find employment – and given the above, scarce new opportunities are fiercely fought over – they will find themselves in an industry where operatives have little flexibility. News editors manage reporters' time, telling them what stories to write and how best to write them. Reporters are governed also by strict editorial policies and media law, including defamation, contempt, libel and similar. Reporters can expect to be dispatched to local council meetings, to the scenes of fires and accidents and then have to work under pressure to strict and immovable deadlines. It is not a profession for the faint-hearted.

Source: Andrew Richardson

Key theory

The public sphere

Beyond contributing to the economic good, what is the social role of media, given the communicative reach and potential power of TV and radio, for instance? What, if any, obligations do media companies have beyond obtaining a return on their investment, their employees ensuring that audiences tune in to more of the same next week? Within media studies, and the concerns of critical political economy that raise political, moral and ethical questions about the social role of the media, this is often dealt with by debates concerned with the role of media as a public sphere.

Our use of the concept of the public sphere is derived from the work of a German theorist by the name of Jürgen Habermas and his 1962 publication *The Structural Transformation of the Public Sphere*. The 'public sphere' is used by Habermas to describe a conceptual rather than literal space in which democratic public debate can take place. It is the space in which a collective 'public opinion' is formed and where collective interests are articulated. This space is one where individuals as social beings argue about the nature and direction of that society, as befitting a proper democracy in which everyone is supposed to have some power to say how things are done. Ideally, this sphere, as a public space, is open to all, on the basis that participants come to discuss and argue as rational beings in the interests of the greater social good.

Habermas traces the historical development of the idea of the public sphere as deriving from the appearance of literally physical places and activities, locating its rise in eighteenth-century European 'bourgeois' society, in the appearance of salons, coffee houses, newspapers, learned societies and so on. These were places where modern democratic ideas were partly formed, as was the notion of a public itself, comprising individuals with entitlement to rights, liberty and self-determination, as opposed to rule by monarchs and the Church. Whether or not Habermas's conceptualisation of the public sphere is an idealised notion, as has been suggested – particularly for the way that it is a rather gendered notion (Scott, 1999) – it raises important issues that have been taken up when thinking of the nature and role of media in society.

Theoretically, the mass communication afforded by modern media offers an opportunity for the operation of a proxy public sphere (the opportunity for genuine and widespread participation having been limited until relatively recently). However, how does this potential sit with the fact that media institutions seek primarily to generate a profit, positioning audiences as consumers? Do they really have some responsibility and role to play in the maintenance of democracy and should they treat audiences as citizens instead?

Citizenship is, in short, the broadly political identity that individuals with a say in society inhabit, one underwritten by social rights and obligations in relation to the political organisation and governance of society. Exactly what rights and obligations we have can shift depending upon the perspective we have on these very terms. Media theorist Graham Murdock proves helpful in arguing for a general definition of citizenship, which identifies it with 'the right to participate fully in existing patterns of social life and to help shape the forms that they may take in future' (Murdock, 1994: 158; Murdock, 2004). His idea of rights relates to further guarantees: civil rights, political rights, social and economic rights and, finally, cultural rights. It is the last one that concerns us, in its relation to the media in particular, and this, for

Murdock, entails rights in four main areas: information, knowledge, representation and communication. The argument is that these areas should by served by media so as to enable an active and participating citizenship, rather than just to construct individuals as consumers, defined by an ability to select from a menu of desires.

The free market in which media operate serves to give people what they demand or apparently want, in turn generating entrepreneurial and economic dynamism. There are, however, a number of significant problems with its operation in relation to the kinds of expectations set out above. Can a proper public sphere, or its media proxy, exist or operate when in thrall to the national, if not global, financial system? As Bagdikian (2002) observed, an increasing proportion of the huge corporations dominating the US media spectrum appear on the well-known list of the 500 largest corporations, compiled annually by business magazine *Fortune*. These corporations sometimes share directors, as well as considerable financial interests. Bagdikian documents cases of repeated corporate interference with editorial policies, with a tendency to deflect critical attention from the corporate world, focusing it instead on various forms of government 'interference' in the media. This serves in part to locate political questions around the media at the door of 'formal' political institutions and individuals (governments and elected representatives), when it is equally an issue for the business world, where the powerful are overseen primarily by share prices and a limited pool of investors.

Perhaps the potential for a genuine public sphere in the modern age lies in the advent of digital technologies and the internet. As we discuss below, patterns of ownership, creativity, distribution and exchange are all subject to challenge and change now that anyone with online access can reach the rest of the online world.

By contrast, the internet sets up a fascinating space for thinking about issues of distribution. In its origin, it was not a form of distribution owned by any one group, and it developed in large part outside the activities of the great media corporations, and direct nation-state control. Although there have been proposals more recently to control, or take ownership of, parts of the internet, there is a continuing debate on the idea of the internet as a common carrier for content (on questions concerning the internet see Chapter 7).

Thinking aloud

It would be easy to move from the observation that media are concentrated markets, dominated by multisector, transnational corporations, which often also control the main distribution outlets, to a pessimistic view that we are heading for the unified control of our entertainment, information and culture, with detrimental effects.

The most dystopian view suggests that those individuals who own, or have most control within, a corporation have a major influence over our lives. However, such pessimism might be tempered by other factors that we outline elsewhere in this chapter and throughout this book. Negative tendencies in the operations of media companies as organisations may be exacerbated but also tempered by the role of media producers – individuals with their own particular sense of professionalism and mission. For instance, in June 2007, US TV news anchor Mika Brzezinski refused to read a story on hotel heiress Paris Hilton's release from jail after serving time for violating probation, which editors had prioritised over news from Iraq. In the previous year, too, employees of the US Fox TV network refused to publicise a book by O. J. Simpson which exploited suspicions that he had actually murdered his wife and her lover, despite his acquittal in a trial for that crime. The publisher of the book was itself an arm of Fox's parent company, News International.

Likewise, we should not neglect the power of consumers, who do not always act in ways that suit media conglomerates, a factor exacerbated by the nature and uses that people have found for the internet. This is especially important given the wide-ranging filesharing and duplication of music, films and TV programmes that has been facilitated by new technology. That much of this activity is highly illegal and threatens profits considerably has presented enormous challenges to companies and, indeed, the very models and 'laws' of production set out above.

Organisational studies

We can now pursue a further way in which we can study media businesses – in terms of their internal organisation. The primary purpose of this is that it leads us to consider the practices and decisions that lie behind the origination, development and delivery of media products, both as commodities in search of profit and as texts that have meaning for us. This approach involves examining the way that staff roles and production processes are arranged within a single company, and possibly the way that they relate to different parts of other companies in terms of the kinds of practices and roles which characterise particular sectors. This approach is not discrete from the political economy foundations we have just been examining because issues of organisation overlap strongly with questions of ownership and control, the power relations they reveal and the way that these are played out along the line from producer to consumer.

A useful way of beginning to study media businesses as organisations is by trying to map out the different divisions, groupings of staff and production activities, and functional roles within a specific business. In this way we can focus on individual companies and their distinctive arrangements, in order to examine the part that they play in the wider analyses presented by political economy approaches. The value of organisational studies, then, is that they allow us to map out the day-to-day operations of media business, theoretically allowing us to get at the concrete processes behind production that we so often overlook as consumers. Indeed, it is not only consumers who are perhaps less interested in this area; academics also have not given much attention to these issues.

Here, we will explore the way that we acquire the information about an organisation that we need, and the process of mapping the structure, staff and processes of media organisations. Information about any media business is often more readily available than is apparent at first glance. If you have followed some of the activities directing you to explore media companies so far, you'll have identified documentation produced by the organisations themselves, much of which is now available online. These are valuable sources for analysis. While it is not impossible to find a document that actually maps an organisation, produced by the firm itself, most often we have to piece together information from a number of places to produce a fairly accurate analysis. This process does involve some perseverance, in large part because media companies produce vast quantities of promotional material that tries to create a particular image, and we want to get behind this façade to the structure that supports it. By following a series of stages in understanding organisations, we can begin to see how much insight we gain into media company operations, and begin to develop an analytical understanding of the way in which media production is achieved.

Mapping divisions, departments and executive control

As soon as a media company has more than a few employees, those employees begin to take on specialist roles, which become cemented as defined jobs with salaries attached to reflect their status in the organisational hierarchy. As numbers grow, they form departments around shared activities, and when a company reaches the scale of a transnational, multimedia corporation wholly distinct divisions will have been formed to deal with particular parts of the company's business.

Mapping staff, role and function

Just as we can find out information and map the key organisational parts of a media organisation, we can identify key staff within an organisation, and then map the relationships between them. Again, we can learn about the value placed upon particular roles and individuals, and what skills they bring to media companies, exploring the part that they play in the enterprise of producing media. Like the structural map, this will implicitly unwrap the power relationships between staff – who gets to do what, who has a say and at what stage over intellectual and creative work. Most organisations are structured around hierarchies, with key staff making general policy at the top, and others directed to carry out specific functions to implement the organisation's purposes.

Elsewhere in this chapter, we mentioned the romantic notion that some have about the independence, creativity and glamour of media workers. In fact, the modern media worker is a blend of creative individual, manager and industrial labourer. We can trace the changing role of the creative communications worker through the three eras of cultural production identified by the British cultural theorist Raymond Williams (Williams, 1981: 38–56). The first stage in Williams's three eras is what he labels the 'era of patronage', describing the pre-industrial period. This was the era of patronage due to the fact that creative people worked under the sponsorship of the rich and powerful. By the nineteenth century, creativity and communication became organised into markets, and workers became professionalised, to provide for distinctive audiences who would pay to be entertained. As they developed, the professional roles often split between the creative worker, paid by royalties, and the technical and managerial staff, who organised production around creative ideas and made them available to audiences. In the twentieth century, what we now call mass media joined the visual arts, public performance and publishing as forms involving creative communication work, although not all media producers are thought of as creative in the same way in this tradition, if at all (compare the journalist and the film director for instance). Williams called this third phase the 'era of the corporate professional', in order to emphasise the way that workers were now organised as groups, rather than individuals. By the 1950s, most people employed to produce creative communication worked as parts of large organisations in rationalised production-line processes. As we can see from our discussions of the contemporary consequences of this organisation, these workers were now also corporate professionals in another sense, in that they worked for large commercial companies whose managers paid close attention to costs, and sought to produce a high volume of content that involved as little risk as possible. In this context, successful formulae could be reproduced and workers trained in specific skills.

Case Study

Mapping the BBC

We chose the UK's BBC here for a case study because, as a public-service broadcaster, its resources are quite transparent. In turn, it provides a model for the way in which you can then actively consider and research the nature of other, more obviously commercial, organisations in other media sectors. Undertaking a web search produced several web pages on the BBC's own website. Drawing on just part of the information, we can produce a basic organisational structure as follows.

The BBC was established under Royal Charter, which was renewed in 2007 and runs until 2016. It is run in the interests of its viewers and listeners. It is run by a trust which consists of a Chairman, Vice-Chairman and a further 10 members (or 'trustees') who act on behalf of the public interest and regulate the BBC. They are appointed by the Queen on advice from ministers.

Day-to-day operational responsibility for the BBC rests with an executive board which oversees delivery of BBC services in accordance with strategy as set out by the trust. The board is chaired by the director-general who is the chief executive and editor-in-chief

of the BBC, appointed by the BBC trust chairman. The board is made up of executive directors from within the BBC itself as well as five non-executive directors from outside.

The board delegates some of its responsibilities to four subcommittees: audit, fair trading, nominations and remuneration. The board also delegates the BBC Direction Group (BDG) with responsibility for managing pan-BBC issues and reaching its overall objectives.

Under this upper managerial level are six operational areas:

Vision. BBC Vision is responsible for all of the BBC's television channels.

Audio and Music. BBC Audio & Music is responsible for all of the BBC's national radio networks.

News Group. The News Group is responsible for all the BBC's news, current affairs and sport output. It comprises BBC News, English Regions and BBC Global News.

Future Media. Future Media is responsible for all of the BBC's digital media services.

BBC North. The BBC North Group includes BBC Sport, Children's and 5 Live.

Operations. The Operations Group is responsible for strategy, policy, distribution, property, legal affairs, fair trading and business continuity, including managing BBC buildings and major infrastructure projects.

Finance and Business: Finance & Business division manages all aspects of the BBC's finances.

The BBC also has three commercial subsidiaries: BBC Worldwide, BBC Studios and Post Production, and BBC World News.

From this information we could produce an organisational map.

You can see how this mapping produces a sense of the hierarchical structure of the company. Such a map could help us to explore usefully some further details of the organisation – around questions of its financial management, for instance. Income and expenditure information is sometimes relatively easy to come by since the advent of the internet, as the citation at the beginning of this chapter indicates. In this case study, in tandem with available details of the BBC's revenue from licence fees and other income (available at www.bbc.co.uk/foi/docs/annual_reports_and_reviews.s html), we could pursue an analysis of how the Corporation's budget is spent and how it is balanced between divisions and programming departments, impacting upon the kinds of radio and TV it produces. This might tell us something about where 'value' lies in such media organisations, but also about where investment is leading and, indeed, where reductions in expenditure are rolling back particular types of service and production.

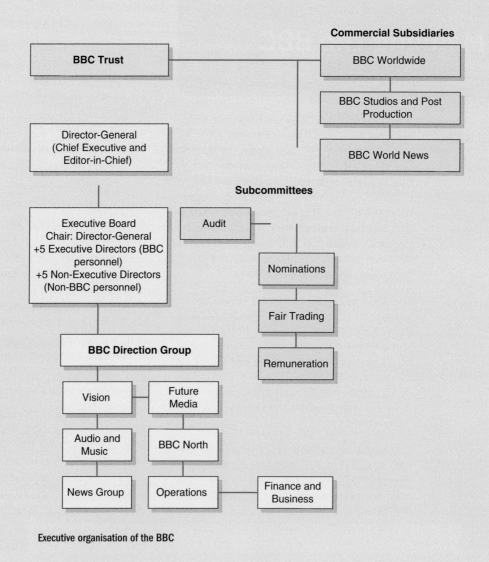

Executive organisation of the BBC

Thinking aloud

The value of organisational mapping is useful in aiding understanding of a topic that, at the time of writing, was a major issue in international news production. Revelations that reporters at the UK newspaper *News of the World* had 'hacked' into the telephone voicemail of celebrities and politicians as well as many ordinary people in the news, including murder victims and their relatives. The ongoing scandal led directly to the closure of the newspaper and investigations in which Rupert Murdoch, the CEO of the newspaper's parent company News Corporation, was called before a parliamentary committee. The proximity of CEO and 'local' staff can be traced by mapping the organisational structure of this company which can be teased out from corporate information at www.newscorp.com/.

If you produce a map of the organisational structure of the company you will be able to ponder the nature of the relationship of those who are ultimately in charge of such mega-corporations and those who produce the media output. How far are scandals such as 'phone-hacking' issues to be addressed in the responsibilities of senior executives?

There are a number of classic studies of staff hierarchies, and they offer good guides to how to present and interpret organisational structures of this sort. Often they originated in wider sociological attempts to look at media work and the dispositions and practices of those involved. Jeremy Tunstall, for instance, provided a study of British journalists, *Journalists at Work* (Tunstall, 1971), which influenced the work of Michael Tracey, Philip Schlesinger and Steve Chibnall (see also Ettema and Whitney, 1982 and Bantz, 1985). Likewise Tom Burns's 1977 study *The BBC: Public Institution and Private World* is echoed most recently in Georgina Born's *Uncertain Vision: Birt, Dyke and the Reinvention of the BBC* (2004) in exploring this most influential of cultural organisations.

Peter Golding and Philip Elliot (1980) provide us with a useful example of how to map out roles and relationships within a media organisation, but we should be aware that they were primarily interested in understanding how the hierarchy of roles operated within a newsroom. In particular, they showed that, by mapping out the power relationships between different members of staff, they could understand how decisions about newspaper content and news angles were made. In effect, like so much media research into journalism, this challenged the nature of the professional culture of journalism and the terms of 'objectivity', and some of the unexamined assumptions about how news appeared and came to be made.

Golding and Elliot's work was based upon a comparative examination of the newsroom in broadcasting organisations in Sweden, Ireland and Nigeria. The fact that this study is now 25 years old allows us to make comparisons with contemporary newsrooms. It was carried out before the major technological innovations in news gathering and editorial control, such as satellite, the 'net' and so on. Most of these changes led to a reduction in the size

Doing media studies

Mapping media organisations

Repeat the process shown above for one of the BBC's broadcast divisions. Try to identify the names of individuals responsible for actual roles.

Repeat this process for one of the following major organisations: Bauer; Sony; Rockstar Games; Bertelsman; Canal+.

What kind of information is available, how readily, and how useful is it in comparison between the organisations? What kinds of observations arise?

Doing media studies

Organisational studies

If you have access to a newsroom (or any other media production unit) through an internship or job placement, you can research the way in which a modern newsroom is organised, mapping out the relationships of role and function between the different staff. Access is not easy, but you could possibly ask a local editor visiting your department, a journalism tutor or a fellow student who has been on placement in a local newsroom to aid you in this task. Such work is relatively under-explored by media scholars and thus organisational study is an area in which the newcomer to the field can chance their hand a little.

of newsrooms and changes in the roles of staff. They also allowed for a growth in newspapers with smaller circulations, which could be produced by smaller news teams at lower costs.

The mapping processes that we have looked at so far have involved looking for specific jobs in specific organisations. However, it is also possible to create a series of broad categories of media workers that we can apply generally to all media activity. Theorist David Hesmondhalgh (2002) offers four types of media workers

1. primary creative personnel,

2. technical craft workers,

3. creative managers,

4. owners and executives.

Hesmondhalgh uses these categories in a political-economic analysis of the different ways staff are rewarded for their work, and to look at the way that creative personnel have more prominence and freedom in certain parts of the production process. However, the list is also useful in organisational analyses in a number of ways. First, it ensures that we take account of all staff within a firm, and don't just concentrate on particular individuals or roles, some of which may seem minor or incidental within a hierarchy and in the creative production process. Secondly, it allows us to make contrasts between different forms of media, different companies or different points in time. Finally, if we interpret these categories as roles and functions, and not single labels to apply to specific workers, we can understand the degree to which these functions are combined within the role of individuals in different organisations.

On this basis we could turn back to a study such as Golding and Elliot's and note that it focused on primary creative personnel and creative managers. It neglected the technical craft workers who supported the journalists and transformed their typed words into published newsprint, and the owners and executives who set general policy for the publication Golding and Elliot studied, not to mention allocating budgets for what work could be done and where.

Mapping production processes, gatekeeping points and transformations

As we have seen from Williams's argument from the 1950s, creativity in communication came under increasing managerial control, and formulae, work routines and cycles became central to media production. By the start of the twenty-first century, though, new technologies have made many of the former rigid demarcations and rationalisation of role less fundamental to keeping costs down and ensuring a regular supply of content. For instance, media news teams 'in the field' are much smaller now, thanks to digitisation and the relative de-skilling of camera and sound work, which has become much more automated. Thus, many reporters are required to train to do work that once required several people.

Here, then, we can examine some of the key concepts used to map and make sense of media production processes, as well as compare the ways in which they can differ between organisations and have changed over time. At the simple level, a map of any production process will identify a series of different stages that production will go through. This sort of analysis really requires some direct observation (how people work, what they do, time spent and so on), although the basic process can often be understood through interviews with media workers, if available. The production process for a radio news programme might therefore be constructed as follows:

> Identify news stories → write stories → create running order → subedit stories for broadcast → read stories live, or record and play back for broadcast.

However, there is far more to the process than there initially appears. In particular, media production processes are built on routines, and on key points of decision making regarding what should be included as content in a single publication or broadcast. Any mapping of the process, then, should identify these routines and the key decision makers. To do so, media theorists have developed a series of concepts that we can use in our analysis. The first of these concerns the idea of gatekeeping and production routines.

Gatekeeping and routine in production

David White established this concept early on in the development of media studies, through his analysis of news selection (White, 1950). The concept conceives of the process of creating content for news publications or broadcasts as one of selection, in which a flow of information passes through a gate to be opened for the chosen information and closed for the rejected. On any news day, for instance, editors receive a range of stories in their in-boxes and in-trays, some of which will make the news, others of which will be rejected as either 'un newsworthy' or simply due to the fact that there is not enough space in the bulletin. Each 'gate', therefore, is understood to be operated by a key member of the editorial staff. While this model has been criticised in journalism studies as assuming that news is simply a flow of information, rather than a more complex process of interpretation, pursuit and investigation (see White, 1950; Fishman, 1980; Shoemaker, 1991), the idea is important in highlighting the power of key personnel in a media organisation, and revealing that news is neither obvious nor natural, but dependent on the values used by media workers, who choose between alternative possibilities.

Critics of the gatekeeper idea applied to journalistic practices have also pointed out that news is not selected, but 'manufactured' (Fishman, 1980). As such, we need to see media production as a process of transformation. In news, social facts and comment are turned into news stories by journalists using the styles of the publication or broadcaster they work for. Although tens of journalists will write in a newsroom, their written style will be broadly similar, following both the general professional conventions of media and also the distinctive 'house style' (see p. 39–40). These conventions are often related to formulae that are widely held to have been the basis of proven success in the past. Sometimes these formulae become codified as a particular genre (see Chapter 2).

An emphasis on the routines that media professionals undertake as part of their cycle of work reveals other aspects of production processes. In news, like other media activities, media workers repeat the same tasks on a cyclical basis. Manheim (Kettler and Loader, 2002) has identified a process of 'cultivation' in news generation, through which journalists establish contacts with people who may supply details of events and with whom they speak on a daily or weekly basis, and another of 'hunter–gathering', where journalists visit places like courts, or collect together information from press releases, which are most likely to provide useful facts for stories of interest.

These ideas also have a wider use in analyses of media production processes which involve choosing from available material or where decisions of creative control are primary. Prominent examples would include music radio and the music industry, as well as photography and publishing. You can explore the issue of gatekeeping here, for instance, by taking a look at playlists for radio stations and considering the release schedules for music companies, thinking about what kinds of music and bands get played and signed at any one time in relation to the vast wealth of releases and activity in both areas. On the other hand, of course, music companies (as well as film and TV companies) also cultivate acts: the international success of varieties of *Pop Idol*, *X Factor* and *Making the Band* have made this explicit.

The culture of production – media professionals, creative workers

The approaches we have examined so far emphasise the economic imperatives and structural relationships that characterise media production. However, we should not lose sight of the fact that media organisations are staffed by individuals, and the way they work together and the values they hold have a significant influence on the production process, and thus on media products and their meanings. These factors, then, are the focus of studies of the culture of production. Paul du Gay *et al.* (working on the Open University's *Doing Cultural Studies* project (du Gay, 1997) define the culture of production as: 'the distinctive practices used in the production of the [artefact] and the way that such widespread practices are represented in terms of specific values, beliefs and patterns of working' (1997: 43). They highlight the importance of routine tasks within a media organisation that create its atmosphere and working conditions, the naming of the company and its products, the creation of an imagined consumer in the process and objectives of production (see also Chapters 1 and 8) and in the minds of creative workers, and the monitoring of the way that these products are incorporated into the consumer's cultural life.

The study of the culture of production, as an extension of organisational studies, is a rather underdeveloped area. This is understandable, as getting access to the production process has traditionally been one of the greatest challenges for media scholarship. Even if media organisations are willing to let researchers in, they may be guarded for a variety of reasons – perhaps due to intellectual property issues (p. 225–229), or to sensitivities about opinions, personalities and so on, not to mention guarding against the attentions of competitors. In addition, such research can be time-consuming. However, when built on the insights of political economy and organisational studies, the study of culture offers rich data for understanding media organisations.

In proceeding, it is useful, then, to focus on media professionals and to ask questions that are likely to illuminate their worldview and their sense of themselves as workers, as well as getting at what they do and why they do it. Questions might be attuned to the different ways in which creative work is validated and privileged in society – writers, actors and presenters, for instance, are often viewed with envy and affection – but also to the variable standing that certain jobs and roles have. Certain types of pop star can be seen as 'rebellious' or 'dangerous', while journalism and journalists are sometimes viewed with suspicion. Thus, questions might focus on how they are categorised from without, and from within by themselves. How are they trained (if at all) and in what ways can they be conceptualised as professionals, as creative workers?

We should be attentive to the overt culture of any sector – both the written and unwritten guidelines on how things are done, and the cultural aspects within a sector. For instance, Paul Espinosa's (1982) analysis of the discourse of one meeting of TV programme makers offers us a good model of how a cultural study could be conducted. His focus was on the nature of how workers conducted themselves in their day-to-day interactions and activities. Espinosa explored the interactions of members of a programme-planning conference. He found that their conception of the audience, and their knowledge and expectations, create rules that govern the discussion of what should happen next on the show in production. Espinosa's research could be broadly categorised as workplace ethnography.

Ethnography
literally means 'writing culture'. So it is a study that involves observing and writing a description and analysis of some form of cultural practice and orientation.

Ethnography is a method derived from anthropology, where researchers go to live in a culture other than their own to understand the rules and concepts that govern that world (see also p. 335). Most often, the techniques employed in order to obtain data use observation of the culture being studied, sometimes incorporating unstructured interviews (p. 331) and participation by the researcher in the culture under observation. Unlike anthropologists venturing into sometimes very unfamiliar cultures and societies outside of their experience, media scholars have some kind of purchase on the worlds that they seek to explore – i.e. they are, by and large, dealing with the production and consumption of mass media forms among people who, usually, share the researcher's broader cultural contexts. However, this can create problems. Thus, cultural researcher Paul Willis has suggested that we should conduct ethnographies with the intent of accepting a 'possibility of being surprised', rather than importing to the research our existing experiences and assumptions (Willis, 1976).

Overall, then, we should approach the culture of media producers, as far as possible, as if it is an 'unknown' world. We should 'make it strange', attuned to the potential significance of all aspects of activity, so that we can understand it better on its own terms. Within cultures, why things are how they are, why they are so done and so labelled, then becomes conventional or 'obvious'. In a very simple way, we can see this at work in the credits for films which contain unusual job titles – 'gaffer' (electrical head), 'best boy' (assistant to the gaffer), 'grip' (lighting and rigging) and 'foley artist' (person responsible for sound effects), for example. Getting to grips with such terminology is not only a job of translation but also one of understanding. Anthropologist Clifford Geertz coined the phrase 'thick description' to suggest what ethnographers are trying to achieve in portraying a world in detail, including its values and meaningfulness to participants. We do not just seek to say who does what and what went on, but to get beneath this, perhaps, as Espinosa did, to work out a set of rules that govern the cultural practices. Based upon Espinosa's work, and that of theorists like du Gay, we can develop, therefore, a series of useful points of focus for thinking about how we might study the culture of production. These involve:

- exploring the brand and identity of the product the media workers produce (how one sees the work of a shopping channel compared with a European art film might have an impact);

- identifying and analysing the routine tasks that media workers undertake to produce it (journalists in the field write their copy within particular structural conventions; this is then reviewed and revised by copy and desk editors in order to fit final publications);

- contextualising individual contributions by placing them in the hierarchy of the organisation (those responsible for finding talent on behalf of recording companies are not always those who record and package them for the consumer – each has a particular role and investment in the final outcome of the process of production);

- identifying and analysing the different ideas of audiences used by media workers and the ways they find out about audiences;

- exploring the ethos of craft, creativity, professionalism (or otherwise) that informs the particular job, but that might be shared across a media sector (journalists might think of themselves as Journalists, with all that entails, just as much as they might see that identity embroiled in their role as a freelancer, or on the staff roll of CNN, or the *Shanghai Post*, for instance, in tandem with the kinds of material they are tasked with covering).

When we think of media companies as businesses, we should recall that their primary object, of producing pleasure and information in the form of symbolic, meaningful texts, makes them qualitatively different from, say, tin can manufacturers or insurance companies (although tin cans and insurance also have symbolic meanings, they have a more directly functional and mechanical purpose). Behind these products are media workers, who are, therefore, clearly creative workers of a particular sort, even though, as we point out above and elsewhere, they work under certain constraints. However, while the business environment, budget management and profit motive might mitigate against the romantic image of the 'artist', as Negus and Pickering (2004) point out, the relationship between organisation and creative individual is a productive one. Organisations nurture, support and finance creative workers, even when they impose limitations upon them. One thing that they do impose, for instance, is deadlines – ensuring that creatives do deliver, rather than slouch around as some feckless artists are wont to do. Likewise, of course, creative workers bring innovation to organisations, offering new ideas that might provide new ways to generate audiences and revenue. However, despite the limits and demands they make (and the rewards that they reap), organisations also ensure that the work of creatives in media industries gets to wider audiences than they do in other creative sectors: rarely would the author of a novel or a fine artist reach the kind of numbers addressed by one nationally broadcast radio show, for instance.

Certainly, the professional world of the media accords great respect to 'the talent' in particular (think about how we hear about the rewards for big-name stars at awards events) and demarcates in a hierarchical way between particular types of creativity and those areas that are defined as simply being about technical skill. All of these areas are defined by their own sense of professionalism, duty and accomplishment, which inflects both the way in which cultures of production work and the view that media workers have of their responsibilities to their employers, themselves, each other and the wider contexts in which their work takes place. While the culture of a workplace is likely to be very rich and nuanced (even when media workers seem blasé or uncaring about what they do, this is itself revealing) and perhaps very hard to make sense of, it deserves our attention in order to understand how media products are originated, how they come to us as consumers and how they take the form that they do as a result of, usually, collective toil.

Source: David James/New Line/Kobal Collection Ltd

The culture of production (behind the scenes etc.) of media production and the nature of individual roles and routines merits our attention in order to understand media businesses.

Thinking aloud

Although it takes different forms in different media industries, the role of creative workers is often a very privileged one (even though identification and reward can be very uneven). This regard accords with wider values in many modern societies. Think, for instance, of the esteem in which we hold the artistic 'greats' of history, from Leonardo da Vinci to Shakespeare. In addition, creative work (is it 'work' as such?) is often seen as a highly desirable pursuit, offering individual satisfaction and expression – even if some of the frameworks we outline here might militate against the extremes of such romantic notions. Nonetheless, and in spite of this regard, it could be argued that, traditionally, creative work has been a rather secondary, inessential part of society.

In recent years, as Western economies have seen a decline in traditional manufacturing and a turn towards the development of lighter, 'knowledge-based' industries (computer technologies, software, tertiary services), the role and importance of the creative has also changed. The influential commentator Richard Florida (Florida, 2004) has suggested

that the creative economy is paramount in modern economies, and that cities, in particular, are better places to live when there is a vibrant 'creative class' at work there (Florida, 2008). Furthermore, cities faced with the decline of traditional industries and in need of rejuvenation are advised to set out to make themselves attractive to this creative class, due to the benefits they bring.

You will have your own ideas about the value of creative work but some final questions are worth asking here, to underline our work on the kinds of approaches we might bring to bear upon an investigation of media workers.

- What is creativity?
- What does it mean to media workers themselves as a motivating and defining part of their identity?
- Where exactly can it be found and what counts as creative work?
- Why exactly is creativity so privileged – in comparison, for instance, with the work of nurses, garbage disposal men and so on, whose social roles are indispensable?

Case Study

The life of a freelance writer

→ The stereotypical image of a freelance writer is of a freewheeling dandy who rises late to browse the day's broadsheets while devouring *pain au chocolat* and quaffing *café au lait*. Truth is, it is none of those things. The life of a freelance writer involves absurdly long hours, inordinate levels of self-exploitation, an inability to switch off from the rigours of work and typically low rates of pay. Precarious relations with newspapers, magazines and other forms of media outlet that are in a constant state of flux means the freelance has little, or no, job security.

Freelancers are idea finders, who are constantly in search of zeitgeist-defining articles; salespeople, who pitch their wares to fraught commissioning editors; accountants, who chase companies who are slow to pay; and social networkers, who invest endless social and emotional capital into promoting themselves as indispensable adjuncts to assorted media empires . . . and that's before they start writing.

Demystifying the life of a freelance writer is relatively easy. A third of their life is spent chasing work, a third is spent chained to a laptop doing the work and a third is spent worrying about where the next work is coming from.

Freelancers cannot survive by simply being good, or simply having a great idea. They have to be flexible, multitasking, self-motivated and driven, if they are to succeed. They must develop contacts with the movers and shakers who decide which articles are going to be published. That might involve visiting commissioning

→

→ editors at high-rise office blocks, taking bosses out for lunch or finding other ways to inveigle themselves into the lives of their paymasters.

Social networking tools like Twitter have fast become an essential part of the freelancers' armoury. They are able to spot messages that can give them leads, observe trends that might lead to articles and find new ways of improving their social relationships with commissioning editors.

Freelancers also have to learn not to give up. When an article falls through – for instance, for a freelance travel writer who returns from a becalmed Middle Eastern nation only to see it go up in flames two weeks later – he or she must bide their time until it is feasible to submit an article for use.

Timing is everything to do with the freelancer. Knowing when an article is hot and when it will sink like a stone is the difference between receiving a pay cheque and going hungry. While salaried writers might be able to easily flick the switch between work life and domestic life, freelancers have no such luxury. Their phone can ring at any time and their antennae are finely tuned so that they are alert to potential stories or new contacts – regardless of when, where, how or why.

The freelancer will spend long hours writing on a laptop, discussing ideas or nurturing contacts on the telephone, pitching ideas, networking with potential clients and finally chasing payment – not to mention the time spent worrying about all of the above. They will, however, spend very little time at rest.

Source: Andrew Richardson, freelance journalist

New media, new media studies

New media, new work?

For many employed in contemporary modes of media production, the way in which they work seems indicative of new patterns of labour in evidence in many other sectors of employment. Working freelance and across organisations or sectors, on short-term contracts, with low pay, long hours and uncertain benefits, many media workers find themselves in a position that can be characterised by 'precariousness'.

This is certainly the case for those involved in new media production as described in the research of Rosalind Gill. She interviewed over 30 such workers located in Holland whose responses and self-definition revealed the various ways in which their work could be labelled: programmers, copy writers, designers, illustrators, etc. They collectively described the precarious nature of the work that most of them did or had experience of. For many respondents there was a worry about the boundaries between work and pleasure, meaning that when they reflected on time spent net surfing, they found themselves wondering whether that was time well spent (whether discussed as simple pleasure or 'research') or whether the time was lost 'labour' that might have been better deployed in a never-ending roster of production, networking and searching for new work.

A particularly interesting thing about such accounts (which never fail to depress students who are planning for work in these fields) is the degree of 'complicity' that many have in their own 'self-exploitation'. The casual, informal, self-directed nature of much of this 'precarious' labour is what also gives it its appeal. Indeed, the overriding factor for many is the opportunity, in the midst of all of the challenges they face simply to maintain a living, is that creative work is rewarding in ways that are not simply reducible to the offer of a salary. Working in the new media sector is where perceived freedoms balance the limitations of such work and 'employment' structures.

Ultimately, we don't have enough accounts of how and why this kind of balance is achieved and what it means to individual media creatives. Nor do we have enough accounts of all of the different levels of work along the production chain of media production, particularly in the area of new media work. Here then are interesting and provocative opportunities for new scholars to engage with media studies and also with those areas in which they themselves might have ambitions.

Source: Gill (2009: 161–78)

Ultimately, then, our approach to understanding media – in terms of textual meanings, audience responses and social contexts – is richer for any attention afforded to the economic aspects of production and the associated concepts set out so far. The dynamic between economic imperatives, aspects of organisation and the nature of professionals, the culture that they make and which defines their work, is still a largely under-researched aspect of the field of media studies. Clearly, all of those things that lie under the label of media business determine what gets made and, to a great degree, who produces media texts and aspects of their meaning. As media analysts, we need to be attuned to such questions in relation to how we think about the social role of media, our expectations of media forms and indeed of the people who own and produce media, whose responsibilities may be about more than adding to financial turnover and share price. We can think about the potential for the media to act as a public sphere as suggested above, especially as media businesses face challenges of an unprecedented order to their very principles and existence. This challenge is presented by the development of digitised technologies and, of course, the internet, which we consider next.

Media business in the digital age

What is happening to the media economy and organisation, and the skills, status and culture of media workers? To some extent, the coming of technologies and techniques of digitisation, the year-on-year reduction in equipment costs and size (computer processors, cameras, microphones, software), as well as the communicative and distribution possibilities of the internet, have challenged media start-up costs, not to mention, in some important cases, the preserve and culture of professionals. Concepts such as 'the citizen journalist' and 'interactivity', alongside processes such as blogging, social networking and file uploading, sharing sites such as 'RapidShare' and 'YouTube', podcasting and, of course, the ease with which one can acquire a domain name and design and manage a web page have, to some degree, challenged the preserve of media organisations and the traditional models of practice and control outlined above.

Podcasts such as 'The Dawn and Drew Show' (http://dawnanddrewwp.mevio.com) or 'Brumcast' (http://brumcast.podomatic.com), and sites such as 'Perez Hilton' (http://perezhilton.com), 'Ain't It Cool News' (http://www.aintitcool.com) and so on attract visitors and attention, actually and potentially generating income in new ways, independent of traditional structural and operational modes. On the other hand, the effects of new media, changing distribution landscape and creative, democratic opportunities can sometimes be overstated to the point of hyperbole. For instance, in recent years musical artists such as Sandi Thom, the Arctic Monkeys and Lily Allen have all been described as achieving fame and success through independent use of live performances online, social networking allegiances and so on. However, they are not super-famous, rich and successful just because of Myspace, nor because they miraculously drew a crowd of thousands to their homegrown webcast. PR, traditional media, record labels and money were all involved.

When we hear that bands are making it big because of Myspace or Twitter, it would be wise to consider what such claims mean and what is at stake if such claims are true. What sells a pop band is a great story. The more that story is about them being genuinely great and a real discovery, rather than simply marketing blurb (every release is a classic, everyone a legend nowadays), the more successful that sell becomes. You might even consider the fact that Rupert Murdoch, who owns Fox News, Sky, STAR, *The Times*, the *Sun* and many other media outlets, is also the man who owns Myspace. So, when we recall the buzz around the fact that musician Sandi Thom was signed to Sony because 100,000 people were tuning in to her nightly live webstream from her flat in London, we should note that story actually emerged *after* she had signed to Sony. Think about the fact that internet bandwidth costs money, and that there are considerable technical limitations on streaming from home connections. If Sandi Thom had so many listeners and viewers without corporate support, she was pretty much running her own ISP with outgoings in the thousands of pounds, and no income of which to speak.

Nonetheless, we find ourselves in what looks like a new terrain, where these examples tell us about the huge range of possibilities open to media entrepreneurs and the challenges facing existing media organisations. This is partly due to the fact that we appear to have moved from an age of control and scarcity to one of pluralism and plenty. The first thing to recognise is that the economics of the internet are different from the economics of the offline world and the traditional ways in which the business of media has been organised. The ways in which it is different are still being determined, but the most well-known and now established principle is that of 'the long tail'.

The long tail

Originally an article by *Wired* magazine editor Chris Anderson, then a blog and then a very successful book (2006), the long tail presents a very simple concept. It is a model for describing an important characteristic of the online environment and the way in which the economics of media businesses (alongside many other businesses) are being challenged and changed. The model discussed here relates to ways of thinking about online retail and delivery or distribution businesses such as Amazon and iTunes, but also dial-up movie rentals, pay TV and so on. The top left of our graph represents a very small number of popular items that have a very high number of sales. These are the hits. The tail towards the bottom right represents the vast number of items that sell in smaller quantities.

The main point of Anderson's argument is that the internet enables the large number of non-hits to expand to the extent that they economically outweigh the hits. And, he argues, this is exactly what's happened in recent years and, in a sense, it is to do with physical space. In the offline environment, there's only a certain amount of shelf space, audience space or broadcast reach, for instance. Online, storage is less of a problem – not only in terms of digitised material but for distributors and retailers operating between producer and consumer demand for hardware. In traditional record shops and bookstores, only the most popular items can be offered. Online, far more things can be made available, and that raises some issues.

The first issue is that the more things producers make available, the more people will explore the non-hits. The repercussion of this is that the sales of the most popular items suffer. If 100 things are available for sale, those 100 things will enjoy sales success. If a million things are available for sale, the 100 most popular things will still enjoy sales success, but a greater proportion of people will explore the tail instead of consuming the hits. The second issue is that the more things you make available, the more things people will consume overall. Amazon.com sells a greater quantity of books and music than any other book or music store because it offers a greater range than any other book or music store. The third, and perhaps most important aspect, is that the long tail provides not only greater potential for mass-market retailers moving online by reducing the problem of shelf space, but also a route to market for a wide range of niche products that might not otherwise have been made available by more traditional means.

Anderson's book on the long tail has had two subtitles (in the American and UK versions), each with a different emphasis. The first is: 'Why the future of business is selling less of more'. This suggests that the trick is to make everything available, and sell a small quantity of a large number of items, rather than the other way around. Of course, this challenges the supremacy and dominance

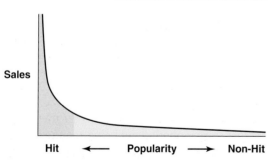

The long tail in graph form. The number of 'hits' are few but achieve high sales. The non-hits are more in number but sell less per item. However, the range of the non-hits is infinite, thus causing the 'long tail' of exploitable sales.

afforded by the economies of scale achieved by big media companies. It does not replace this advantage, but it does suggest that it is not the only way of doing business and, perhaps, that it may even no longer be sustainable. The second subtitle of Anderson's book is: 'How endless choice is creating unlimited demand' – a slightly more problematic assertion. This suggests a domain completely untainted by economic considerations for producer and consumer, but it does alert us to the growing importance of niche businesses in the online environment, particularly for the media.

The simple fact is that economics are transformed online, particularly when product is available in digital form. An online music retailer of digitised product, such as iTunes, will never sell out of a record. They will never have to stop stocking an item in order to stock another. There is no reason for labels to delete from their catalogue and every reason to reissue everything. Movie companies that deliver digitally to cinemas, through cable or online, no longer have to pay for expensive celluloid prints (which also incur transport, security and preservation costs) when they own a digital master. When you request a movie via cable it will always be in stock, unlike at the DVD rental store. The model is already there in the guise of YouTube and its imitators – everything is available all the time to everyone who wants it. Indeed, anyone can offer the work on an ostensibly equal platform. The problem such innovations present to traditionally configured industries is that it is not immediately obvious how to make money from such openness and how to sustain and grow business.

The real reason the major record labels (as well as film companies and DVD distributors, newspapers, magazines, TV companies, etc.) have been experiencing problems is not the issue of piracy or file sharing, as they claim. It's that they no longer only have to compete with other hits. Now they have to compete with a range of choice that is exponentially greater than anything they've ever come across. The age of the hit is over. The simple, powerful fact is this: for the first time in history, the sum total of the economic value of the tail is now greater than the sum total of the economic value of the head. Amazon sells more books overall that are not in the top-100 bestseller list than those 100 combined. Probably more outside the top 1000 than in it! Add all the sales of all the records that made it into the charts in the last year, and the economic value of everything that never made it close to eclipses it. All of this challenges the traditional nature of how media companies work, not just at the point of sale!

Source: Getty Images

The death of scarcity: digital distribution potentially offers media consumers endless variety instantly – as evidenced by sites such as YouTube and retailers such as Amazon.com

The death of scarcity

The coming of digitisation, along with the internet, has challenged some of the apparently immutable laws of economics and the way that these affect media businesses. The first is the law of supply and demand that we discussed above, and this law relates to scarcity: the notion that there's a limited amount of product available. Stuff is scarce. If there are three packets of cornflakes on the supermarket shelf, and the supermarket sells three packets of cornflakes, then there are no more cornflakes. If nobody buys the three packets of cornflakes, then the supermarket is stuck with the cornflakes. If cornflakes are really popular, the supermarket can put the price of cornflakes up. If the price of cornflakes is too high, people won't want the cornflakes as much. If the cornflakes aren't moving off the shelf, you can create more of a demand for cornflakes by cutting the price. These were the natural laws of economics in simpler times.

Enter the internet, where the law breaks down. If an online music store wants to sell a song, it keeps one digital instance of that song 'in stock' from which all 'copies' are derived (these are copies with no reduction in quality produced by the copying process, as there would be in an audio or video tape-recording). If they sell one copy or a million, they still only ever have one copy of that song in stock. It's like a magical packet of cornflakes. There is no need to worry about being stuck with the leftover shelf space, and nor is there concern about ever running out. There is no scarcity of that song. So, for someone who makes a living through the business of music, or any other digitally available medium – film for instance, where distribution has been governed by available prints and exhibition space, i.e. cinema screens – it means everything changes.

The death of scarcity in the online environment also means that the super-serving of niches by media companies is potentially now a better market strategy than banking on hits and mass audiences – as per Chris Anderson's proposition that the future of business is selling less of more. In fact, Anderson has taken his ideas a step further and has introduced the phrase 'the economics of abundance'. In terms of access to the means of production and the market for aspiring producers, abundance means that the tools of production and distribution are far more widely distributed and available: anyone can make a movie or radio show and upload it so as to be available to anyone online. This is not to suggest that we live in a utopian media landscape where all messages are equally conveyed and weighted, but the balance is shifting away from the kinds of **big** organisations that have hitherto characterised the business.

Consider the example of broadcasting. There is a scarcity of broadcast spectrum over the conventional airwaves, so the way to become a radio or television broadcaster has always been either to be a heavily capitalised major corporation or a government (or unlicensed and a 'criminal' or pirate, so called). Leaving aside arguments about whether streaming audio online is actually akin to 'radio' as we know it or not, there are certainly far more channels available to far more people than ever before – simply because there is an abundance of 'space' online, and so the price of entry is considerably lower. The maximum capacity for FM stations in any given town is probably about 50, while the maximum number of online audio streams available for reception in that same town is practically infinite. And not only are things abundant by nature online, they are increasingly abundant. Look at hard drive space and bandwidth. The 14.4 kbps dial-up modem was a revelation. Now, it's unthinkably slow to the point where readers of this book would probably laugh at the idea, let alone actually use it.

As Michael Goldhaber (1997) points out, the basis for economics online shifts from a concern with the scarcity of goods and services to an economy primarily centred around attention. Attention is the basis on which success is measured online in the digital age, because there is no shortage of digital goods and services. But this is not to say that money is not part of the equation: money now flows along with attention or, to put this in more general terms, when there is a transition between economies, the old kind of wealth easily flows to the holders of the new. It is no accident that Google spent in excess of US$1.5 billion on YouTube – and more than twice as much on its acquisition of DoubleClick (www.nytimes.com/2007/04/14/technology/14DoubleClick.html). Money flows to attention – and both of these services, while providing no actual content themselves, generate masses of attention. Google itself is the most looked-at site online. That's not to say that money will automatically turn up in the pockets of whoever gets the most eyeballs (or ears)!

Anyone who's ever used Myspace, Facebook, Mog, Last.FM, iLike, Twitter, Skype, Second Life, Tumblr, Vox, Blogger, Live Messenger, Yahoo! Groups, Flickr or Bloglines could tell the big media companies that such places are about conversation, connectivity and relationship. Such sites do not offer a top-down, one-to-many distribution model, nor do they offer a model of 'customer off the street happening by and exchanging money for a product'. What such places are built upon is trust, recommendation and reputation. This is a many-to-many dialogue and the money goes where the attention lies.

In this sense, this relatively new terrain offers enormous possibilities and challenges to all that we've considered hitherto, to the very terms considered in political economy and business as traditionally conceived. Of course, while things change, the power and reach of media corporations is such that they are unlikely to be left behind or to let control slip from their grasp, so high are the stakes. Nonetheless, new media scholars are well placed to explore this moment and its meanings as they – you – are already deeply immersed in it and understand its culture and conventions at the border between habit and innovation. This, then, should be a basis for exciting new work, building upon the approaches and ideas outlined here.

Summary

Studying the business of media

In this chapter, we have explored the ways of making sense of the assertion that the business of media is business. We started by setting up a context for thinking about the economics that govern all aspects of media production and consumption, whether companies seek profit as a rationale or not. In order to make sense of media business we explored three related approaches.

The first approach was labelled 'political economy', within which we considered questions of the economic market for media organisations and the particular ways in which media products or commodities generate revenue. A major way in which revenue is generated is through the organisation and sale of audiences for media products and services to advertisers. We considered the distinctions between mass and niche audiences with regard to the economic ideas of Harold Hotelling, who suggested that companies will always seek profit maximisation by occupying the centre ground of taste. We can see this as a way of controlling the uncertainty of markets, which actually tend to militate against diversity and risk taking. In search of profits, therefore, media companies seek alignments across different platforms in order to sell products via synergies, benefiting from the fact that, while initial start-up costs have tended to be high, once established, media companies incur low marginal costs. As with other economic activity, we saw how there are benefits to be gained from size and, therefore, the tendency is for media companies to converge, amalgamate and concentrate. One key example here was presented in a glimpse of the recent history of Time Warner. The consequences of the character of media companies in search of profit, and their resultant strategies and tendencies, have an impact upon the way that we think about their role

and responsibilities. The concept of the public sphere was enlisted here to consider the ways in which we, as consumers, are positioned in a media landscape, in which companies have a determining responsibility towards owners and shareholders.

The second approach we introduced focused on the structure and operations of media businesses as organisations. We looked at ways of mapping structures and roles within media companies using the BBC as an example, partly due to its transparency and the availability of instructive in-house documentation. In thinking of the distinct roles of individuals within organisations, we also began to consider media practices in the process of production. Here we thought about the concepts of gatekeeping and transformation and the routines that govern and direct these processes.

In turning to the final related approach to the business of media – the culture of production – we considered media workers as professionals and the nature of creative work. Both of these frames exist in tension with the more limiting aspects of media organisation, such as routine and commercial pressure. Here we introduced the method of ethnography as a means of making sense of the activities and meanings of the culture of production, of why things are done in a particular way and the values that professionals hold as employees in a particular sector, of particular companies and engaged in the production of meaningful output – media texts.

In our final section, we turned to consider some broad challenges presented to the media economy by new media and the digital age. Based upon the ideas of Chris Anderson we considered the concept of the long tail that is transforming traditional models of supply and demand. In fact, and as we suggested, with the advent of digital production, storage and delivery, we have moved from an age of scarcity to one of abundance. Whether or not this is a new condition is in need of closer examination, and new researchers in their guise as consumers are making sense of this new era and, indeed, challenging media companies through their activities.

You should now evaluate what you are able to do as a result of this chapter. If you have followed this chapter through, engaged with the activities and thought about the issues covered, you should be able to:

■ Define and outline the key issues in 'political economy', 'organisational' and 'culture of production' approaches to the study of the media. If you are not sure about these ideas, go back or follow up on some of the further reading suggestions. We've only touched upon the basics here and there is a lot more to learn about the way in which researchers have gone about defining and applying ideas.

■ Apply these key concepts to research contemporary media businesses. If you've followed the activities set out and thought more widely about media businesses, you'll be testing and exploring the concepts we've introduced. Do remember that by application, exploration and the formulation of your own questions – about our approaches and media – you'll advance your ability as a media scholar.

■ Identify and engage with contemporary issues facing media businesses in the digital age. How are some of the issues touched upon here manifested? Follow up these ideas by reading the media pages in your newspaper, or by tracking down those industry bodies in your area of interest which are effective in co-ordinating debates concerning their members.

■ Discuss and draw conclusions about a series of key debates concerning media as business. You'll do this by continuing to engage with the approaches set out here, and by becoming confident in the use of the ideas explored and in locating what goes on in the world of media businesses. Keep an eye on what is going on in the sectors that you're interested in. If you're the kind of media student who wishes to work for a media company, pursue an internship, try to find out about what is happening from media professionals and, of course, make them and their culture the object of your study.

The task now is to keep going and explore these issues further, along with the ideas introduced in the other chapters in this book.

Doing media studies

Investigating the business of media

Outline brief answers to the following questions by locating specific sources and details about how and where your answers were found.

■ What would a political economy approach entail for the following areas of interest: journalism, photography, music industries, public relations, radio, television, the web and new media?

■ What organisations are your able to identify within each category and what information is available to aid your study of them? What kinds of professional culture would you expect to characterise your choices?

■ Are some areas potentially more obvious and easier to research than others through this approach? Why do you think this is so and what does it tell you about the differences between media sectors?

Further reading

Some of the most useful reading on media businesses, the nature of organisations and professional culture is to be found in the reports produced by companies themselves, and also in the autobiographies of media workers. The last category, while often written at the end of a career, and by nature highly subjective, affords insight for those very reasons. However, here are a number of works that new researchers will find informative for the insights they offer, as well as for the particular approaches that have been brought to bear on the study of media operations.

Biskind, P. (2005) *Down and Dirty Pictures*, London: Bloomsbury.
A non-academic work and not for the nervous, but one built upon rigorous research, detail and access to the contemporary American (and thus global) movie business. It offers a historical narrative of the independent film movement and, in particular, the role of film festivals such as Sundance and Cannes and the organisation, practice and culture of companies such as Miramax in relation to the dominant studio system and wider economy.

Caldwell, J. (2008) *Production Cultures: Industrial Reflexivity and Critical Practice in Film and Television (Console-ing Passions*, Durham, NC: Duke University Press.
Caldwell investigates the cultural practices and belief systems of Los Angeles-based film and video production workers, not only those in prestigious positions, such as producers and directors, but also many 'below-the-line' labourers, including gaffers, editors and camera operators. Caldwell analyses the narratives and rituals through which workers make sense of their labour and critique the film and TV industry, as well as the culture writ large. The research draws on interviews, studies of sets and workplaces, and analyses of TV shows, industry documents, economic data and promotional materials, The context for the study is a changing industry of convergence, outsourcing, new production technologies, corporate conglomeration and the challenge of user-generated content.

de Burgh, H. (2005) *Making Journalists: Diverse Models, Global Issues*, London: Routledge.
This edited collection takes a critical political economy approach to the evaluation of the way that journalists can affect public discourse on politics, economy and society at large. The various chapters consider journalism education, training, practice and professionalism in various countries, including Saudi Arabia, India, the USA, the UK and across Africa. The book considers questions about the nature of journalism, how education makes journalists and the news, and the ethical implications of this process.

Dubber, A. (2007) *The 20 Things you Must Know about Music Online* e-book available at 'New Music Strategies', http:/_/newmusicstrategies._com/_ebook/
Academic and practitioner Andrew Dubber, who contributed to this chapter, has studied the way in which new media forms and practices are affecting media economics and, in particular, the music business. His weblog offers a free e-book, which is mainly aimed at media professionals but has a lot to offer the new researcher wishing to make sense of technologies, traditional practices and the kinds of innovations that are changing the music business.

Gitlin, T. (1994) *Inside Prime Time (Communication and Society)*, London: Routledge.
Gitlin's work was first published in 1983 and produces an ethnographic study of US commercial TV using participant observation and interviews with TV production personnel, as well as those working for the wider TV network. Gitlin began with suspicion of the way in which TV professionals rely upon obscure ideas of 'intuition' or 'instinct' in order to explain how they do things and their creative decisions. He explores the system of values and cultural preferences underlining the context of production and the place of professionals within it, teasing out the conservatism of the network and the commercial pressures under which it operates.

Hesmondhalgh, D. (2002) *The Cultural Industries: An Introduction*, London: Sage Publications.
Hesmondhalgh's is a wide-ranging study, which takes on a political economy approach that engages in detail with the organisational and productive character of the entertainment and information sectors of media and other, related industries. For new researchers interested in developing approaches to this area, it is probably the most useful starting point. He gives a sense of the historical background to the organisation of media industries, exploring political, economic, organisational, technological and cultural changes.

Negus, K. (1999) *Music Genres and Corporate Cultures*, London and New York: Routledge.
Negus explores the contemporary music industry in terms of the relationship of entertainment corporations and artists. He examines the strategies of labels such as Song and Universal in managing staff, artists and musical genres. The research covers the work of personnel in Japan, America and the UK and, while the industry continues to change thanks to the unnerving takeovers and mergers Negus describes, this offers an ambitious approach to integrating a variety of perspectives linking textual meaning with industrial practice and culture.

CHAPTER 6

Media regulation and policy

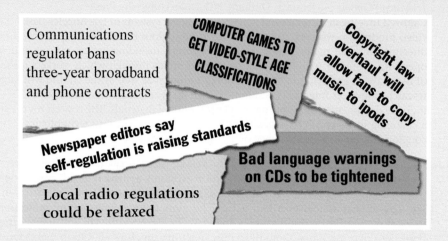

Communications regulator bans three-year broadband and phone contracts

COMPUTER GAMES TO GET VIDEO-STYLE AGE CLASSIFICATIONS

Copyright law overhaul 'will allow fans to copy music to ipods

Newspaper editors say self-regulation is raising standards

Bad language warnings on CDs to be tightened

Local radio regulations could be relaxed

Thinking about media regulation and policy

These are a few headlines that we have adapted from real news stories from different countries over the past five years.

Headlines like these indicate that the organisations that produce media products cannot simply produce what they like, but are often subject to control by the law courts, by other organisations set up by the state or by media organisations themselves. In other words there is some form of regulation of their activities. News reports like these show that some media are regulated differently from others, but the reports do not explain why this is. If we took a range of headlines from different countries we would also see that each country regulated their national media in quite distinct ways, but there are very few discussions of the relative merits of the different approaches. The different regulations in different countries are a result of different government policies. These policies reflect what people think about the impact of media in society, and what they think can be done to make media organisations behave in the ways they want.

Regulation clearly has a major impact on the sorts of media we can watch, read and listen to, and so to understand this impact we need a set of skills that allow us to investigate the policies developed in societies, the regulations themselves and what happens when they are applied.

What we will do in this chapter

The issues we will explore in this chapter lead on from our examination of the business and organisation of media covered in the last chapter. They lead directly into concerns about production practices and cultures, as well as questions about textual meanings and the relationship of media output to its audiences that we study in other chapters. We can see this link between production, texts and audiences most obviously in one of the central concerns of media studies: the power of media in modern societies (see Chapter 10). This concern is widespread outside the subject as well. People will often ask questions about media influence and effects or about the control that individuals or corporations have if they own a substantial number of media producers. The extent of this concern is indicated by the vast number of laws, rules and statements of guidance which exist for media organisations.

If we were to take into account all the laws and organisations, across all the nations of the world, over the whole of the past 100 years, there would be far too many facts to be mastered, and it takes an expert in the area of media of individual countries to understand all the detail of just one system of regulation. It is, however, possible for you to grasp some key ideas, and then to apply them to individual instances when you want to find out and understand something specific about a medium, a single country or a point in media history.

By the end of this chapter you should be able to:

- Define the concepts of policy and regulation.

- Research and analyse policy in at least one media sector, including identifying primary policy documents, policy objectives and relevant regulatory bodies.

- Research and analyse regulatory practice in at least one media sector, including identifying regulatory objectives, examples of external and internal regulation, and examples of unintended regulatory consequences.

- Evaluate the degree to which a particular media sector is regulated, and make comparisons with other countries, time periods and media.

- Engage with debates that highlight issues at the heart of regulation of media.

KEY TERMS: ▶ controls; copyright; creative commons; deregulation; economic intervention; external regulation; intellectual property; internal (self-) regulation; policy; policy documents; public-service broadcasting; regulation; regulator; rules; unregulated.

Evaluating the degree of regulation

A useful way to get to grips with how control works and the issues that we'll deal with here is to assess how much you already know, or can deduce, about the amount of regulation each of the media is subject to.

Create a table like the one below with the different media listed in the rows, and headings for the associated regulator(s), what they regulate in that media, and a rating out of 10 for the degree that each medium is regulated (10 = strong, 0 = weak).

Medium	Regulator(s)	What they regulate	Strength of regulation
Television			
Radio			
Press			
Internet/ new media			
Music			
PR and advertising			
Photography			

Then give some thought to these key questions:

- How much did you know about regulation?
- How did you come to know this information?
- How widely known do you think this information is?
- How much similarity is there in the degree to which different media are regulated?
- Are all organisations in a particular medium regulated in the same way?
- Can you see any patterns in this regulation? Are broadcast, print and internet media similarly regulated for instance?
- Could you make any initial speculations for any differences?
- What areas do you not know about?
- Are there other questions about regulation that you need answered?

Regulation and public policy

The development of each new media form has been accompanied by concerns about the impact the medium will have. This is as true of the internet as it was in earlier times for video tapes, television, radio, cinema, photography, commercial music and the press. As each medium has emerged, it has usually been accompanied by demands for its regulation, and the development of new legal controls, regulatory bodies or rules and guidelines. We will look at some specific examples that are useful in highlighting issues and debates, and in indicating how the issues have played out in different media, in different places at different times.

Why do we have regulation?

As we will see, the regulation of media that we can observe in practice is almost always a manifestation of policies decided upon by governments, and these in turn are based upon political or moral philosophies about the role of various media in society. For this reason we need to relate issues of regulation directly to the issues of political economy that we dealt with in the previous chapter, but also to questions about the nature of the society we believe we should live in, and our view of the power of media.

Different societies have also taken different approaches to regulating media, some placing the various forms and organisations under the direct control of the state, while others allow considerable freedom to publish or broadcast, even guaranteeing these freedoms in the country's constitution. You will not be surprised to know that the more authoritarian the society, the more control is exercised over the operation of media. This inevitably means that this discussion relates to the degree to which democracy and freedom are conditioned or guaranteed by the freedom of media and access to information by people in society. In fact, it is commonly argued that the freedom of media workers or organisations is an important part of democracy. Nevertheless, the matter is more complex than this. Unrestricted media do not always contribute to democracy, and it is often argued that the prevalence of profit-maximising companies leads to unacceptable social outcomes, as these companies put profit before what is best for society.

When people do discuss regulation, it is most often considered in relation to overt acts of censorship. In liberal societies restrictions on free speech are major issues of debate. At the same time as mass media forms developed, many people were anxious about the impact of these media, and they argued that, either to protect vulnerable individuals or to promote a good society, we needed to control media in some way. However, direct and overt censorship constitutes only a small part of the regulatory activity carried out in society. It is harder to see what impact these other regulations have on the various media forms

Thinking aloud

There are far more justifications for regulation than there are regulated media. How many reasons for regulating the media can you think of? Could we just let media organisations operate as their owners and operatives thought best? Is it a restriction on freedom to regulate a media worker or the organisation they work for? Given that so many people criticise regulation in media, why do you think some are still so strongly regulated? Do you have any sense that what you watch, read or listen to is restricted because of media regulation?

Key thinker

Tony Bennett (1947–)

Tony Bennett is one scholar who contributed to debates in the 1990s around media and cultural policy and its place in the field of media studies. In his work he argued that culture and media are 'intrinsically governmental'. That is, that some form of governance, regulation or control is at the heart of how they operate. This is because issues of governance etc. are tied to the role of citizenship in contemporary society, and they develop and interact in the fields of education and culture. Over 15 years ago, Bennett suggested that policy had hitherto played a minor role in media and cultural studies, and that interpretation of media texts and audience activities tended to have privileged positions. This tendency is possibly even stronger today. Bennett argued that the study of cultural policy (in which we should include media policy) should become 'central to the definition and constitution of culture' (1991: 397).

and organisations, and on our consumption, because they are less direct and usually create less controversy and media coverage. This has led to a neglect of the ideas behind media regulation: government **policy**.

Policy

is government objectives or plans of action which set rational goals to be achieved by directing or influencing decisions that are made by media companies or consumers.

Defining policy and regulation

Regulations have almost always been introduced as a way of achieving a policy goal. Policies are those deliberate plans of action that set out what is to be achieved in directing or influencing decisions that are made by media companies. Every organisation will have its own policies, but here we are interested in the policies of the governments which control the state, and the organisations that have been set up as part of the infrastructure of the state.

When something is regulated it is controlled or restricted in some way. Modern states have always been active in trying to control media organisations and the texts they produce to achieve a set of policy goals. You should be able to see that some of our opening examples – like controls on commercial television, radio companies or newspapers – involve the regulation of organisations, while others – like age classifications for computer games or stickers on records – involve controlling media texts. Some, like the direction of internet providers to filter music downloads, aim to control organisations as a means of controlling consumption of texts.

Regulations try to ensure that something happens or is prevented from happening. It may be that the rules *authorise* some groups to be able to do something, or they may *prohibit* some or all from doing something. The press, for instance, was the first medium in the UK to be regulated, and from the sixteenth century copyright law authorised only selected individuals to print books and pamphlets. Likewise, when radio and then television became key media from the 1920s through to the 1950s, there were restrictions on who could and could not broadcast. Equally, the rules may simply try to direct or *inflect* the actions of people involved in media production. Modern broadcasters have to work in a framework of laws and rules which insist that they

Source: Rex Features

Ofcom or the Office of Communications is an independent organisation which regulates the UK's broadcasting, telecommunications and wireless communications sectors. It sets and enforces rules on fair competition between companies in these industries.

do things like broadcast to certain technical standards and produce public service material. The regulator may also try to *promote* certain technical or economic developments within an industry. The broadcasting regulators also try to encourage broadcasters to think about children watching in the early evening, or to try to provide content that represents the diverse population of a country or region.

Regulations may focus on the actual *production* process, determining who can own a production company, what equipment is used and who is employed. Broadcasting has been most typically regulated in this way. Alternatively the *content* of media may be limited in some way. You may well be most aware of this in film, computer games or advertising. Finally, rules may *restrict* some or all people in a society from being able to *access* certain content. We most often associate this with issues of censorship.

The different sorts of **regulation**, aimed at different aspects of media, can also be achieved in a range of ways. There may be *rules* which have to be followed by producers, or *controls* on production or access, or regulators may use *economic intervention* in terms of taxes, licence fees or subsidies to achieve a particular end. Based upon these terms and the parameters of action outlined above then we can now give a pithy definition of regulation as well as some real world examples of the ways in which regulation is actually formulated, which prompt further questions.

Regulation
Concerns legal or self-imposed controls or restrictions on media organisations, involving their ownership, production processes and output, as a means to achieve a policy goal.

Example 1: Regulating ownership

Rules of the UK Office of Communication (Ofcom)
In accordance with paragraph 2(1A) of Part 2 of Schedule 2 to the Broadcasting Act 1990 (as amended by the Communications Act 2003), religious bodies are not eligible to hold the following licences:
1. a Channel 3 licence;
2. a Channel 5 licence;
3. a national sound broadcasting licence;
4. a public teletext licence;
5. an additional television service licence;
6. a television multiplex licence; or
7. a radio multiplex licence.

Source: www.ofcom.org.uk/tv/ifi/tvlicensing/guidance_notes_and_apps/guide_rel_bod/

Why do you think this long-running rule about religious bodies and broadcasting was introduced? Why does it still survive in UK regulation? Is it acceptable that faith groups cannot use mainstream television and national radio to propagate their faith? Are there examples from elsewhere in the world where such regulation exists as well as where more freedom is allowed?

Example 2: Regulating output

The French 1994 Broadcasting Reform Act
This act sets a minimum quota of 40 per cent of French-language songs on popular music radio stations in peak-time listening (between 6.30 am and 10.30 pm) each day. Half of the quota also had to be '*nouveaux talents*' or '*nouvelles productions*' (new artists or releases) (Hare, 2003: 62).

Why do you think the French government imposed these quotas? Would they be necessary in the country you live in? What do you imagine the impact of the regulation would be on the output of radio and the patterns of music consumption of French citizens? Is this is an undue restriction on the radio stations to conduct their business as they see fit?

Example 3: Regulating consumption

In a series of judgements in the mid- to late 2000s Spanish courts have established that under Spanish law its citizens could not be penalised for downloading music or films for their own private purposes. From 2004, the Spanish Data Protection Agency (AEPD) has argued that IP addresses were 'personal data' and so protected under the country's Data Protection Act. Unlike most other European countries, then, it was not possible for record companies to request such information on internet users they suspected of downloading audio-visual files where they held copyright (www. mondaq.com 9/10/2008). In a judgement in 2006, according to the *Guardian* newspaper, a judge ruled that 'That would imply criminalising socially admitted and widely practised behaviour where the aim is not to gain wealth illegally but to obtain private copies' (3/11/2006). In 2009 another judge found that an internet user had downloaded films 'without consent of the holders of copyright' but that this was acceptable because they were for 'personal use' or 'exchange with other Internet users' (www.20minutos. es, 29/05/2009).

However, at the time of writing the Spanish government was attempting to change the law in line with other European countries (www.depepi.com/2011).

At this time a Bill for a Sustainable Economy included provisions to remove websites offering downloads or P2P links without the need to go to a Spanish court for a decision. The proposed legislation came after extensive lobbying on behalf of the Sociedad General de Autores y Editores (SGAE), which is the main collecting agency for songwriters and publishers in Spain.

It would be very interesting for you to do some research to find out how this attempt to regulate the consumption of downloads was settled. It also illustrates the claims of other nations' copyright holders that downloading is unambiguously illegal.

Policy and regulation analysis

The aim of regulation and policy analysis is to understand both how any control works and what it aims to achieve. The degree to which governments manage to control the practices of media organisations or the content and consumption of media texts, and the degree to which the control achieves the policy objective, are both central debates about media regulation.

Policy analysis: identifying policy

Although the news often covers government policy, it is more likely that the headlines are focused on economic or social policy, rather than cultural or media policy. Policy also comes from quite a large range of bodies which would include government departments, independent or autonomous regulators, or even professional or industry bodies. The ideas are often published in long and technical documents which require some understanding of the issues and language of regulation to be able to decipher them. Although you will be able to find summaries of the policy, these shorter and more accessible documents are usually written by people or organisations with vested interests. When media report on media policy, the owners and workers who produce the analysis often have a strong vested interest, and their reports may well represent this perspective. As academics, the authors of this and other books and articles are often involved in writing or commenting upon media policy, and we often take strong positions about what should be achieved, or view that more (or less) regulation in a certain area would be beneficial for society.

Policy on issues relating to media and culture has not been consistent or even around the world. At different times and places there has been a greater emphasis on control than at others, and so different media have been treated differently. Accordingly, you will find information on the regulation of different media in diverse places, and you will need to try to understand the practices in their own distinct forms. The history and practice of policy on the press is very different from broadcasting. The press in Europe and North America tended to benefit from a general political and social liberalisation at the end of the nineteenth century and, as a consequence, many regulations on press action and ownership were relaxed (see Curran and Seaton, 1981/1997; Williams, 1997; Briggs and Burke, 2001).

Beyond issues of taste and decency, and some political censorship, most regulation has been self-administered. By contrast, broadcasting has been the most regulated of all media, reflecting concerns in the early twentieth century that the geographical reach and power of broadcasting produced a mass culture which needed controlling (see Chapter 11). In some countries (e.g. Japan and the UK) radio regulation was simply extended to television but there are crucial differences between the two in terms of their use of available resources (bandwidth) and of course their rhetorical scope (what you can see or hear). Film and video, advertising and PR, and the music industries have tended to be dealt with

Case Study

Media academics involved in policy consultation

➡ The Media, Communication and Cultural Studies Association (MeCCSA), which incorporates the Association of Media Practitioners in Education, is the subject association for those of us who teach and research in these and related areas in the UK (see www.meccsa. org.uk/). One of its subgroups is the Policy Network which has the aim of joining with non-government organisations (NGOs), media workers' organisations, press freedom campaigns, consumer groups and so on in their debates with the regulators, the broadcasters and the government. In recent years it has been engaged with the role of the UK media regulator, Ofcom, established as a result of the Communications Act 2003. The Policy Network has issued this statement on its aims in this area:

MeCCSA welcomes the increasing recognition of the importance of the role of

the media in all its forms in modern societies and in particular the emphasis on the concept of media literacy and Ofcom's role in promoting it. We endorse the evidence-based approach to policy and recommend partnership with media experts in the higher education sector as a cost-effective way of identifying research already in the public domain and areas where more research is required to address fully the complex of issues, problems and practice-based solutions to media literacy.

The Communications Act proposes more deregulation of the media, promising access to increasing layers of mediated information and entertainment and shifting responsibility for media content from the government to the home. MeCCSA acknowledges that the role of Ofcom is to attempt to ensure that this shift is as inclusive as possible while also equipping people with the skills to filter content where it is perceived necessary.

Source: www.meccsa.org.uk/papers/ofcom-response.html

Whether or not media academics can make a difference to policy is a moot point. However, they are able to use their skills and insights to engage with the issues and at least attempt to contribute to debates in this area.

individually, with most regulation focused on their output. New forms of media, like the internet, have been the least regulated, but the idea that the internet is bringing together media through 'convergence' has led to attempts to bring together the regulation of telecoms, broadcasting and the internet (see www.ofcom.org.uk/static/archive/bsc/pdfs/research/Update4RegulatingtheInternet.pdf; Livingstone and Bober, 2006; Wall, 2000).

It is also surprisingly hard to interpret policy from the regulation that is intended to enact the policy. There may be unintended consequences when regulation is put into action, or policy may be ignored, unenforced or unenforceable. Broadcasting companies have tended to follow the letter of regulation, rather than the spirit, and often the intentions of the policy makers were therefore not achieved. Copying of music is often presented as an illegal act, but it is still widespread in practice even though record companies have won cases in court against individuals around the world. Likewise, in Japan, the television licence fee which supports the state broadcaster is regularly ignored by large sections of the population.

In spite of this, the widespread availability of policy statements by governments and statutory bodies online has made researching policy far easier. It does not take long to track down full documents or useful summaries of government policy on a range of media. You will also be able to find a range of responses to these policy statements. Governments usually undertake some form of consultation and interested parties often make submissions in support or argue against part or all of the policy. If you use just one of these sources you will only understand part of the argument, but by reading a range of submissions or other media commentary, you can build up a very good idea of the policy, its advocates and its opponents.

Almost all policy is still produced by nation states. So each country will have its own rules, regulations and governing bodies. There may be some international agreements, especially among neighbouring countries, or when they belong to confederations or international unions like the European Union (EU). For instance the EU has been trying to co-ordinate media, and especially broadcasting and telecoms policy, among member states. The most recent initiative is the Audiovisual Media Services Directive (AVMSD) which directs each nation to change its laws regulating audio-visual media by the end of 2009. The directive builds upon the 1989 'Television without Frontiers Directive', to include digital and internet media. These directives promote a dual policy of promoting economic competition within the EU, and so reduce national regulation, while at the same time trying to ensure that important social and cultural goals are met. There are therefore conditions set around television advertising and sponsorship, production, the protection of children, social access to major sporting events and a guaranteed right of reply for citizens. In practice EU nations have applied the directives unevenly, depending on the political complexion of the countries' governments (see http://ec.europa.eu/information_society/newsroom/cf/itemdetail.cfm?item_id=2343).

We have discussed these factors because they provide a basis to approach policy analysis. This sort of analysis focuses on looking at the bigger picture in which individual regulations are introduced. It is not possible to understand fully why a certain law or rule is introduced without a sense of the arguments that have been made in relation to the medium concerned, what the national government or international body tried to achieve, and what means it chose to achieve these ends. For that reason we need a series of stages that can act as a guide to doing policy analysis. That's what we offer below.

Getting the big picture – surveying government media and cultural policy

From what has been said so far, you should be able to see that we can look for specific aspects of policy, both in how it is expressed and in how it is put into action. To produce an overview we need to undertake some primary research. You will often find that information like this is available to you through secondary research, but books and articles on policy and regulation often become out of date as new governments take office, new laws are introduced and new bodies set up. Anything over five years old is likely to be limited in contemporary accuracy, even if it will be good for a historical study. You should look at each individual medium, and for each one be aware of some key government statements of current media policy, the key regulatory bodies and the main activities they undertake.

At the beginning of this chapter you were asked to produce an audit of what you already know. Now it is time to be much more systematic by thinking through the following steps, which will aid your policy research.

1. Decide on one or more medium to investigate

Your decision in doing such research will really depend on the focus of your particular study. If you are following a specialist media course, for instance, the matter will be decided for you. If you have a wider choice it will be easier to examine a medium that is more tightly regulated. Although this tends to vary between different nations, the broadcast media tend to be most heavily regulated, while still images tend only to be governed by laws relating to taste and decency. In newer media, like the internet, concerns relate more strongly to content than channel, while music, PR and advertising tend to be lightly regulated. The press varies quite significantly depending upon the country you are looking at.

2. Identify policy documents

A simple online search that strings together the medium, the country and 'policy document' will give you a good starting point. Searches we conducted at the time of writing gave us several million documents on radio regulation for the USA, and 250,000 for both the UK and for South Africa, and about a fifth less for Singapore. In the UK it is possible to identify three types of governmental policy document: green papers, white papers and acts of Parliament. The first two are documents that seek discussion and debate, and propose policy; the last obviously enacts laws. You will find the equivalent of all three in most democratic countries. Through this process it is quite easy to identify a range of important documents and details of the names of the regulatory bodies that we discuss below.

3. Identify policy objectives

The documents then usually set out policy objectives or aims. These are statements of what a government or statutory body hopes to achieve. Although such documents can often go on for hundreds of pages they usually contain executive summaries from which you can abstract some straightforward statements.

4. Identify the regulatory bodies

As we just noted, you will often find details of the relevant regulatory body, or bodies, when you search for policy documents. They almost always have institutional websites which set out straightforward statements of what they aim to do, and how they aim to do it. Often these are called mission statements. It will usually be possible to work out from what they say some important information about a body's status and objectives. In particular you should be interested in:

- a body's degree of independence from government;
- the amount of involvement of the media organisations it regulates;
- the extent of its regulatory powers;
- if it focuses on production, texts or access.

5. Map changes in policy

It is often useful to place the current policy and regulatory system in context by making sure you know a few of the key regulatory bodies which existed before the current one, and some of the policies they sought to enact. Secondary sources can be very useful here as long as you pay particular attention to the dates they were produced. Primary work is still useful, though, particularly when you want to explore the recent past (for a discussion of sources see Chapter 14). Look for exactly the same things as you did in your contemporary analysis: documents, objectives, bodies and their missions.

Applying the process

The five-stage process of analysis offered here can be applied to almost all examples of media policy. Keeping to each stage will allow you to be systematic, ensure you draw on a range of material and can produce a comprehensive analysis. As always, an example will show you how that can be done.

Radio policy in the UK and the USA

Following the approach outlined above we researched the policy and regulatory context for radio in the UK and the USA.

United Kingdom

The most recent major law relating to radio in Britain is the 2003 Communications Act, the central part of which defines the roles and responsibilities of the key regulator, Ofcom (the Office of Communication).

The act spells out the policy of the then government as far as Ofcom was concerned. The act states:

It shall be the principal duty of Ofcom, in carrying out their functions:

a. to further the interests of citizens in relation to communications matters; and

b. to further the interests of consumers in relevant markets, where appropriate by promoting competition.

(Communications Act 2003, Section 3(1))

Clearly, as far as stated government policy was concerned, the regulator was needed in relation to people in the UK as citizens and consumers. By looking at earlier laws relating to radio, it is possible to see that the idea of people conceived as citizens addressed by broadcasting is fairly

long-standing; the idea that they are consumers of the media as an economic good is fairly new.

Looking at Ofcom's statements about itself it says:

We are an independent organisation which regulates the UK's broadcasting, telecommunications and wireless communications sectors. We also set and enforce rules on fair competition between companies in these industries.

(www.ofcom.org.uk/consumeradvice/guide)

Here the emphasis seems to be far more on the technology of communication covered by the regulator and the media organisations as economic entities. It emphasises what it controls, rather than the purposes it controls them for.

United States of America

The most recent major law relating to radio in the USA is the 1996 Telecommunications Act. Its stated function is:

To promote competition and reduce regulation in order to secure lower prices and higher quality services for American telecommunications consumers and encourage the rapid deployment of new telecommunications technologies.

(Telecommunications Act of 1996, Section 1)

In comparison with the UK act there is no emphasis on individuals as citizens, but only on their role as consumers in a situation of competition between broadcasters. Equal importance is given to promoting technological developments. Looking back to the original act in the USA, which established broadcasting regulation, we can see a very different emphasis. The 1934 Act states that it exists:

> For the purpose of regulating interstate and foreign commerce in communication by wire and radio so as to make available, so far as possible, to all the people of the United States, without discrimination on the basis of race, color, religion, national origin, or sex, a rapid, efficient, nation-wide, and world-wide wire and radio communication service with adequate facilities at reasonable charges, for the purpose of the national defense.

It now seems strange that regulation of radio was required for civil and national defence, but radio at this time was thought of primarily in military terms. The 1934 Act also set up a regulator, the Federal Communications Commission (FCC), which today states that it is:

> an independent United States government agency . . . charged with regulating interstate and international communications by radio, television, wire, satellite and cable.

(www.fcc.gov/aboutus)

Comparing these extracts from the UK and US laws and regulator statements one would expect a radically different radio system in each country. However, anyone familiar with both countries would be able to identify as many striking similarities as they could point to differences, and those differences would not necessarily seem to be the result of differences in policy and stated regulatory aims. Of course this is a fairly basic analysis, and if you were working on this for an assignment you would look at a larger range of documents and statements. They would reveal a more sophisticated statement of policy and regulatory purpose, and far more similarities. However, the features of each national radio system are as much to do with the working of the regulation as they are to do with the policy and stated aims of the regulator. Understanding policy is not sufficient, we also need to understand regulatory practice.

Identifying regulatory practice

As we have seen, regulation is the act of the governance of media (or occasionally the absence of governance) as well as any rules or principles that determine the procedures and behaviour as well as aspects of what is delivered to consumers and the forms it takes. As we explore what actually happens we must move beyond statements of media and cultural policy to the complex sets of determinants that constitute actual regulatory practice.

First, we must make sure that we include all the sorts of regulatory activity going on. As well as *external regulation* from outside the activities of media production, it is also common to find *internal regulation* within the production process, in the form of *self-regulation* where companies or industries regulate their own affairs. Having said that, the systematic analysis we set up above in order to analyse policy and the statutory regulatory bodies established by law can also be used to study the bodies charged with organising self-regulation.

As the least regulated medium, in most countries the internet tends only to have self-regulatory bodies, and as an international phenomenon most are part of one industry association, ISPA (the Internet Services Providers' Association). According to the UK industry association ISPA UK it was:

> *established in 1995 and promotes competition, self-regulation and the development of the Internet industry.*

(www.ispa.org.uk/)

Doing media studies

Identifying internal or self-regulatory bodies

Again, these bodies tend to make lots of information available online. This includes mission statements for the organisations, policy statements, voluntary guidelines for their members and contributions to debates about policy. However, there are no straightforward search terms to use to track down information on organisations like these among the hundreds and sometimes thousands of other organisations in a media sector. You will need to be more imaginative in the search terms as 'internal' and 'self-regulator' are

not terms likely to be used by these organisations. 'Self-regulation', 'trade association', 'industry-led body' are useful search terms when combined with the name of the industry and the country you are interested in.

Based upon this advice, now try to identify bodies relating to the following media areas in your country: press, advertising, film and PR. What are the terms of this body – does it have a regulatory remit? If so, what are its powers? Does it provide evidence or case studies of how it has exercised its powers?

Members agree to abide by the ISPA UK Code and represent the industry in matters of policy.

There is another important sense of self-regulation which operates, not at an industry level, but at a professional level. Most often this relates to the professional values of a group of people and the ethics which govern the way they do their jobs. These ideas are found at their most developed in the work of news journalists, and their trade unions often have well-developed statements of ethics. So, although newspapers almost always operate in a competitive market where money could be made on the back of stories acquired by underhand means, or representing people or events in a less than truthful manner, journalists often talk in terms of their duty or responsibility to report fairly and accurately.

The ethical principles that guide the creative decisions of media producers may be explicitly codified by their professional organisations or unions or by the organisations that they work for. On the one hand these may be important and necessary guidelines for conditioning rights and responsibilities, as is set out in the NUJ code of conduct reproduced here. You will be able to find codes of conduct or ethical guides for other countries and other media professions, but where none seems to obviously exist, ask why this is so.

The second aspect of regulatory practice we need to be aware of is that certain regulatory actions may even undermine the policy objective it was designed to achieve. A historical example makes this clear. In the early UK film sector, the Cinematographic Film Act of 1927 aimed to stimulate film production. Principal distribution companies were US-owned and, as one might expect, tended to favour North American product at the expense of the home-grown. The Act imposed an obligation upon the distribution companies to fund a rising percentage of British and Commonwealth films. Effective for 10 years the act resulted in a range of 'quota quickies' that, as Rachel Low has argued, 'had a profound and damaging effect upon the structure of the British film industry . . . British production was swamped by the boring, badly made and routine work of the quota producers . . . harm[ing] the reputation of the British film' (quoted in Sweet, 2005: 104). See also Williams (1997).

The third factor to keep in mind is that production companies that are being regulated or consumers who are being managed do not necessarily comply or may only pretend that they are compliant. This may include a youngster watching a video that the video

UK National Union of Journalists Code of Conduct

The NUJ's Code of Conduct has set out the main principles of British and Irish journalism since 1936. It is part of the rules that all journalists joining the union must sign that they will strive to adhere to it.

Members of the National Union of Journalists are expected to abide by the following professional principles:

A journalist:

1. At all times upholds and defends the principle of media freedom, the right of freedom of expression and the right of the public to be informed
2. Strives to ensure that information disseminated is honestly conveyed, accurate and fair
3. Does her/his utmost to correct harmful inaccuracies
4. Differentiates between fact and opinion
5. Obtains material by honest, straightforward and open means, with the exception of investigations that are both overwhelmingly in the public interest and which involve evidence that cannot be obtained by straightforward means

6. Does nothing to intrude into anybody's private life, grief or distress unless justified by overriding consideration of the public interest
7. Protects the identity of sources who supply information in confidence and material gathered in the course of her/his work
8. Resists threats or any other inducements to influence, distort or suppress information
9. Takes no unfair personal advantage of information gained in the course of her/his duties before the information is public knowledge
10. Produces no material likely to lead to hatred or discrimination on the grounds of a person's age, gender, race, colour, creed, legal status, disability, marital status, or sexual orientation
11. Does not by way of statement, voice or appearance endorse by advertisement any commercial product or service save for the promotion of her/his own work or of the medium by which she/he is employed
12. Avoids plagiarism.

Source: www.nuj.org.uk/

classification board has indicated is for adults only, or a newspaper consciously breaking the rules of its industry body on reporting because it calculates it will make more money from printing a particular story than it will lose in a fine or admonishment, through to a radio station reinterpreting the licence guidance on what type of music can be played so that it can attract a larger or richer audience than the one it is licensed to broadcast to.

The changing landscape of regulation

You will get the most rounded understanding of regulation if you think about it beyond a simple sense of restricting people and companies. Regulation has often been used to enable marginalised groups to access media representation, or to promote aspects of society or culture that are not well served by unregulated media. For instance the Portuguese classification system for films and games aims to protect young children; the French Fonds de Soutien à l'Expression Radiophonique (Radio Expression Support Fund (FSER)) promotes local radio broadcasters by reducing an individual station's reliance on advertising funding using state subsidy; and Singapore's Media Development Authority (MDA) merged commissions for film and for broadcasting, and charged them with an enabling mission 'to develop Singapore into a vibrant global media city so as to foster a creative economy and connected society' (www.mica.gov.sg/mica_business/b_media.html).

Thinking aloud

The nature and extent of regulation is neither *obvious* – it is not restricted to those things labelled 'media regulation' – nor is it inevitable. Conscious decisions have been taken to regulate particular industries in particular ways. However, the actual regulatory practices are very much the product of the history of those media, and usually say something about the attitudes of powerful people at the time that the medium came into being. In the early to mid nineteenth century, UK newspapers, for instance, were aimed at the newly powerful middle classes and were encouraged and left free to develop as their proprietors felt fit, while news-sheets aimed at the working class (who at the time could not vote) were banned or highly taxed. When radio developed great fears were expressed about its power to influence people, and in many countries radio was controlled closely by the state. The internet is technically very difficult to regulate, and it takes a major effort of a centralised state like China to even contemplate doing so.

These observations invite a series of questions. On what basis is regulation decided upon and why? Who decides? Do we *need* regulation and for what purposes?

Any consideration of the grounds of regulation must also deal with its opposite – an unregulated media – and be aware that over the last half-century there has been a trend towards deregulation. For our purposes, 'unregulated' describes the ways in which media sectors are not subject to direct bodies or legislation written for them. However, as we have seen, this does not necessarily mean that they are entirely free. It has become passé now to compare the internet to the 'Wild West' as a space in which there is a virtual free-for-all. However, there are many forms of regulation outside any direct injunction which suggest that such characterisations are inaccurate. It is perhaps better to think of unregulated media as being at one polar position, with completely state-controlled media at the other end. Both these polar positions are found less and less within modern societies. Where regulation has existed for a number of years there has been a trend to loosen the controls and rules. Where media organisations were directly controlled by the state, there has been a trend towards privatisation, and to some independence of the editorial control. These are usually called processes of deregulation.

Here 'deregulation' describes a process of restructuring of the media (as well as other industries) commencing in the USA in the 1980s under the Reagan administration and the influence of monetarism, and then taken up in first Europe and then Asia, Australasia, Africa and South America. It relates to an ongoing *privatisation* programme, transferring areas such as public-service media and others to commercial interests. The process is one of rolling back paternalist structures, assumptions and state controls in order to allow the emergence of the market and competition. While the hand of the state may be undesirable, as we will see when we discuss ideas of the public sphere and issues of participation in democracy later on, claims that market freedoms are the only form of freedom are usually an expression of industry interests rather than a developed perspective (McChesney, 2004).

Issues in policy and regulation

As you can imagine, the control of media generates a whole range of issues and debates. In the rest of this chapter we want to take you through two that are particularly pertinent: the idea of public-service broadcasting and the issue of intellectual property rights. These will act as case studies of the way to conduct an analysis of policy and regulation in a particular area, but also of the way that they bring out major debates about culture and society. In doing so we want to foreground the idea that a form of regulation is not inevitable, and that any particular regulatory structure is the product of distinct historical and social factors. As your own studies develop you will come across others that may well be equally important, particularly if you are focusing on a single medium, or particular places or times. The value of the studies outlined below is that they remain of considerable contemporary significance, they get to the very heart of the debates about regulation, and they allow us to draw on all the ideas we have developed so far and apply them as you might in an assignment.

In the preceding pages we have set out an approach to studying policy and regulation. It is simplest to set this out as a set of prompts which can tell you what to do in a systematic way. There are six prompts. We have looked at some of the detail of the essential parts of a regulatory system (its elements); the active things that the regulator seeks to do (the regulatory verbs, so to speak); and the points at which regulation is directed (the regulatory focus). We have also briefly examined how the regulation could be managed (its possible forms); what is actually achieved (the outcomes); and accordingly where we end up (status and change).

We could summarise and set these out as follows:

1. **elements** (the essential parts of a regulatory system): philosophy, government policy, regulatory bodies, regulatory practice;

2. **regulatory verbs** (what regulation seeks to do): authorise, prohibit, direct, inflect, promote;

3. **regulatory focus** (where regulation is directed): production, content, access;

4. **form** (who manages the regulation): external or internal (self-)regulation;

5. **outcomes** (what is achieved): compliance, non-compliance, avoidance, unintended consequences;

6. **status and change** (where we end up): regulated, unregulated, deregulated.

For each example below we have combined some primary analysis of the policy, regulatory documents and historical events with the secondary material on the subjects concerned. What you will not find is any explicit evidence of this six-prompt system of analysis. This is because schemata like these are very good for undertaking analysis, but they produce rather dry lists of findings. As we imagined ourselves undertaking the sort of assignment you are

Doing media studies

Identifying analytical frameworks

Although when we created the two examples below we used the schema mapped out above, it will not be immediately apparent in the discussions. As this is usually the case when you read academic writing, a very useful skill to develop is the ability to deduce an analytical framework from a piece of scholarship. By going through each example you should be able to see that we have systematically used the six-prompt schema of elements, verbs, focus, form, outcomes and status. So, you should first read through the example to find out something about the regulatory approaches to achieve public-service broadcasting, and the way the idea of intellectual property regulates music. After each example, though, go back and identify the elements, verbs, focus, form, outcomes and regulatory status. By doing so, you will apply and practise these analytical skills, setting yourself up to be able to do an analysis of your own.

likely to face in your course we have written up our findings in the form of an assignment report paper. Media academics tend to do this when they write up their research as well. Even though they used a schema to guide their analysis they will often write up their findings in a way that makes them more interesting to read.

Example 1: Public-service broadcasting and the regulation of radio

Historically, it has been media sectors such as radio and television which have been subject to the most overt regulation in democracies. In debates (if not always in practice) this regulation is tied to the idea of public-service broadcasting (PSB): the notion that the purpose of broadcasting should not primarily be the pursuit of maximum profit, but of some cultural goal. Most often these debates focus on the UK, the British Broadcasting Corporation, its first Director-General, John Reith, and the phrase often attributed to him and expressing his apparent mission for the BBC that it would (in this order) 'inform, educate, entertain'.

Countries with historical links to the UK usually adopted similar structures to those applied in the UK, and even when radio developed in very different ways (for instance in the USA) the BBC became a totem in the debate about the purposes of broadcasting. However, there is a much richer and more interesting investigation to initiate than the one usually offered up.

We introduced the idea of public-service broadcasting in Chapter 5 and here we extend those initial points by discussing the ways in which we can understand PSB as a form of debate about the aims and ideals of broadcasting. Although it is possible to produce a broad definition of public-service broadcasting, one of the main difficulties in talking about the development and application of public-service broadcasting policy is that the idea has meant slightly different things to different people at various times.

As the name suggests, ideas of PSB normally try to associate programme production and the types of programmes with meeting the perceived needs of the public. In this context 'service' is the key word, as it derives from the idea of a selfless commitment to doing good for people. For this reason it is normally set against the idea of profit maximisation which is seen as self-serving. However, commercial broadcasters tend to argue that in order to be profitable they have to provide what people like, and through these means they serve the public good. They set themselves against programme makers in subsidised organisations whom they characterise as being out of touch with the lives and tastes of normal people.

For this reason advocates of PSB usually call on one or more external ideas to justify their existence. Sometimes this will involve the notion that there is a hierarchy of culture, that people's lives and society as a whole are enriched when people are involved with the 'best' of culture, and that when exposed to the most valuable things people learn to appreciate them. At other times it is argued that commercial media organisations are too strongly linked with the powerful in society and if we want to have a developed democracy we need impartial information and a public space in which to discuss things. Finally, advocates of PSB assert that culture is a social good and that free economic activity does not allocate resources for cultural production effectively. We can see these as the cultural, democratic and economic justifications of a public-service system.

In this discussion we will concentrate on radio, which allows us to look at over 80 years of regulations, and gives us a focused example of broadcasting regulation.

For a start, although the UK's BBC (as a public corporation) came into existence in 1927 as a result of a fairly draconian piece of legislation which gave it a monopoly to broadcast in the UK, there were few directives about how it should behave, and although a number of the government commissions which looked at the issue of broadcasting promoted particular ideals, the actual regulation of the BBC was very light both as written and as practised. The BBC's distinctive qualities, which are signalled by the idea that its purpose is to serve the public, come primarily from internal regulatory systems established within the Corporation

Thinking aloud

The central question for this discussion is whether the normative, agreed or universally accepted ideas of cultural value, impartiality or participation actually exist, and whether some form of regulation is required to ensure they survive? The first part of the question is more philosophical, and depends on the values that you hold as a citizen and consumer. The second part is more open to analysis, as we can actually look at how the media developed, and compare countries with greater intervention with those who had a less regulated environment.

Even among advocates of public-service broadcasting, and public-service broadcasters themselves, there has been a long-running debate about how best the aspiration can be met, and how much regulation is required to achieve it. At the same time, PSB organisations have had to work in contexts of changing media, social, economic and cultural environments where they have had to argue for ever-increasing funding when the advertising-based model of commercial radio and television funding appears to people to provide entertainment for free or for relatively cheap subscriptions compared with taxes and licences.

There have certainly been shifts in what 'public service' means, and it has moved from a strongly paternalist model defined in the early part of the twentieth century where knowledgeable professionals were considered best placed to serve the public, to ideas that diversity and plurality in provision is important, and that the purpose of regulation is to intervene when mainly commercial media fail to ensure the widest and best programming. At its furthest extent this has become an argument for citizen or community media, based on giving everyone access to production broadcast technology, and developing the broadcast skills of individuals and communities.

There is an important place for careful study and analysis in all this, therefore. It is not just where you stand on the ideals of public service, but how regulation can help or hinder the goals we set for our society.

itself. The BBC was given a monopoly because radio waves were seen as both scarce and not subject to international boundaries, radio communication was viewed as a potentially dangerous medium if in the hands of 'the wrong people', and broadcasting was perceived as a sphere that needed order. When you understand that Britain was in the middle of a general workers' strike at a time of economic strife and class division, as the deliberations went on you will get some idea of the context in which the decision was made (Briggs, 1961).

Beyond the monopoly to broadcast, though, most of the distinctive features of the BBC were determined by the wider philosophy of the powerful people of the time through internal regulatory processes. To achieve this the BBC was nationalised. By this we mean that what had been a commercial company – the British Broadcasting Company, established in 1922 – was turned into a public corporation like those which supplied other essential utilities like power and water. In tandem, the Company's earlier regional structure was centralised in London, but developed as a universal service for everyone in the nation. This centralised organisation, but universal service, meant that the internal regulatory systems could be very effective in determining the values of the new organisation (see Scannell and Cardiff, 1991).

Most prominent among them was that this new medium should be used as a means of 'cultural up-lift'. Although this is not such a widely used term today it was a strong philosophical idea in the early part of the twentieth century (see also Chapter 11). In essence the idea was that people needed to be exposed to important works of culture in music, drama and the arts, and that the programmes made by media producers should demonstrate similar high cultural values. For instance, scholar Paddy Scannell (Scannell and Cardiff, 1991) has pointed to the BBC's significant achievements in developing art music performance in Britain. We should note too that scheduling in the early days of BBC radio was very imprecise, based upon the notion that listeners would be stopping to pay serious attention to broadcasts rather than treating them as a background support to other activities. It is possible to see, in the accusations of 'dumbing down' that are made about contemporary BBC television, the remnants of this 'cultural up-lift' ideal.

It would be mistaken, though, to attribute this ideal solely to British broadcasting, as it was just as strong throughout the world. It is a little observed fact that the most common types of station in early US radio were ones based at universities, and many churches and political parties also set up stations for educational purposes (Barnouw, 1966; Wall, 2007). In spite of this, though, UK broadcasting developed differently from US broadcasting because in the UK external regulation gave a monopoly to the BBC, while in the USA, which covers a massively larger geographic area, it focused mainly on ordering transmissions among competing demands for radio frequencies. Michele Hilmes (2003) has traced some of the important links between the developing broadcasting institutions in the UK and the USA through the 1920s and 1930s.

Radio changed rapidly in the developed nations through the 1930s and 1940s, in part because of the economic and social changes which took place through the depression and war years. In the USA the diversity of radio programming became concentrated in the hands of a few companies which distributed centrally produced, entertainment-led programming through systems of networks to overcome the problem of broadcasting in a nation that spread across a continent (Barnouw, 1966). Much of the entertainment was based upon dance music, comedy and popular drama. In the UK the BBC's monopoly did not prevent people from listening to the sorts of programmes that were broadcast in the USA, and commercial companies broadcast English-language services from the European mainland and, in the 1960s, from ships at sea. The BBC made attempts to accommodate these forms of radio in the early 1940s through tripartism, the pursuit of relaxation and a philosophy of 'culture light'. Licensed British radio was reorganised around three services (one for art culture, one for drama, news and current affairs, and one – the Light Programme – for relaxing music and entertainment). Jean Seaton (Curran and Seaton, 1981/1997) has drawn attention to the way that this ordering reflected the organisation of other parts of British society as a way of accommodating rising equality and democratic participation, while Frith (1988) has examined the idea of non-threatening and non-rousing music and culture as part of a new suburban British middle class.

In America, the progressive mission of some early broadcasters did survive the initial decline of the university stations, and can be understood to have developed within the campaigns of the broadcast reform movement of the 1930s, and in the establishment of National Public Radio (NPR) in 1967 (Engelman, 1996; Mitchell, 2005). NPR has to some extent modelled itself on some aspects of the BBC, but again it is merely authorised by the US regulatory system, rather than promoted by it. Today NPR stations are listener-supported, and the regulation relates only to the right to own a licence, statements of public radio's not-for-profit status, and the definitions which distinguish supporters' messages from paid-for advertising.

NPR's mission statement

The mission of NPR is to work in partnership with member stations to create a more informed public – one challenged and invigorated by a deeper understanding and appreciation of events, ideas and cultures. To accomplish our mission, we produce, acquire, and distribute programming that meets the highest standards of public service in journalism and cultural expression; we represent our members in matters of their mutual interest; and we provide satellite interconnection for the entire public radio system.

Source: www.npr.org/about/nprworks.html

From the 1950s radio in the USA underwent a radical reordering. Rothenbuhler and McCourt (2002) have analysed both the resultant characteristics and the key events and determinants which initiated the transition. By the early 1970s the networks had lost significant influence and the independent sector was dominant. This allowed for greater diversity in radio, and a wider range of types of stations, in terms of both ownership and audience, were established. Again, though, while these characteristics can be understood to be valuable to citizens in a national culture, they were authorised, but not promoted, by policy or regulatory practice. The most noticeable change during this period was the gradual replacement of mixed programming radio with music radio formats. It took well over 15 years more until licensed music radio arrived in the UK when Radio 1 and Radio 2 were formed out of the Light Programme in 1967 (and by a nice irony this occurred in the same year that NPR was established in the USA).

The period from 1970 onwards has mainly been characterised by the deregulation of radio. In 1972 commercial radio was allowed for the first time in the UK, and increasingly in the USA any regulatory encouragement for public service content was removed, and legislation focused on promoting economic competition and utilising new forms of transmission including FM, digital terrestrial, satellite, and then internet communications. By contrast, UK regulators held the new commercial stations to quite strong public service obligations. They were committed to provide local, mainly music, services with sizeable quotas of news and local content (Wall, 2000). The 1972 Act also set out stringent controls on who could own a radio station. This prevented people who were based outside the UK from owning commercial radio stations, restricting ownership to single stations so that control did not become concentrated in the hands of a few companies, and placed clear rules on cross-media ownership so that people who already had interests in newspapers, music companies or television could not also own a radio station. In the 30 years that followed, through a sequence of regulators (the Independent Broadcast Authority, the Radio Authority, and lately Ofcom) new stations were licensed to offer alternatives to existing provision.

Nevertheless, over this same period policy moved away from tight controls to deregulation of radio. The regulatory bodies moved towards what is called a 'lighter touch' regime for overseeing commercial radio stations. Ownership controls were systematically removed, the need to provide local content, or even to be based in the locality, were dispensed with incrementally, and the regulator only responded to complaints, rather than investigating compliance. In this more 'deregulated' context stations found ways to avoid many of the regulatory obligations that were left (Wall, 2006), and British commercial radio continued to lack much of the diversity apparent in the USA. Unlicensed broadcasters (misleadingly labelled 'pirates') tended to fill the gaps, and most of these stations tended to serve minority groups, either with programming targeted at particular cultural groups, or for minority music tastes. At the same time deregulation was far more radical in other nations. In New Zealand, for instance, the national radio system moved from one based strongly on the BBC to one far more similar to the US system and largely owned by US corporations (Neill and Shanahan, 2005).

British radio grew considerably from the four BBC national stations of the late 1960s to a complex system of over 400 over-the-air radio stations. By 2004 the public, commercial and unlicensed sectors were enhanced by new 'third tier' broadcasters (regulators do not recognise unlicensed broadcasters for obvious reasons) who attempted to build a model of community radio which had blossomed in less regulated environments (Lewis and Booth, 1989).

This issue perhaps gets to the nub of the matter of regulation for public service principles in radio. In perusing the objectives of cultural improvement, the advocates of the BBC had neglected the idea that radio could serve more democratic impulses. Although there were champions for a decentralised BBC, and the development of local radio in the early 1970s is one of their best achievements, ideas of paternalism and professionalism often

Doing media studies

Researching public-service broadcasting

In the example above we focused on radio in the UK and the USA. Of course a full analysis of public-service broadcasting as media policy and regulatory practice needs to include television, a wider international study, and more detail of each of the events discussed here. This suggests three areas where you could repeat the example we have outlined, but with a different focus:

■ a policy and regulatory practice study of television as public service in a single country;

■ a policy and regulatory practice study of radio as public service outside the UK or the USA;

■ a detailed policy and regulatory practice study of radio as public service in the UK or the USA at one point in time.

You could just undertake such a selective study as an individual to develop your analytical skills, or as a way of responding to an assignment. Alternatively, as part of a study group, or as a whole class, you could each take a part of the wider project suggested above, and then meet up and compare and contrast what you have found, as well as discuss the successes you achieved and difficulties you faced.

got in the way of encouraging participation (Barnard, 1989: 65–8). By contrast the regulators of commercial radio had pursued a policy of trying to extend the range of programming available to listeners, although the chronology of experiments in types of licensing arrangements, and the dominance of mainstream pop music radio, suggest they were not always successful in their aims (Wall, 2000).

By the late 1990s both the BBC and the commercial radio regulator were attempting to produce a mutual radio system where the practices of the one complemented that of the other. Most radical here was the move by the BBC's music radio stations to lead, rather than follow, music taste (Hendy, 2000), and to develop a series of digital over-the-air stations targeted at distinct cultural groups within British society – young Afro-Caribbean, British Asian, older music fans and sports enthusiasts – who were felt to be neglected by the main BBC stations, and by commercial radio. At the same time the commercial regulator dispensed with the 'cultural up-lift' argument completely, and focused more centrally on the economic ideas of rectifying market failure, broadcasting as a public good, and the pursuit of distinctiveness and diversity. This new focus led to an even greater deregulation of the production of radio, and a new interest in the output of stations. The commercial stations were made responsible for reporting on their success in meeting PSB commitments, and carefully defined community stations with clear social agendas were allowed to broadcast for the first time on a scale found widely in the rest of the world.

Thinking aloud

There are interesting challenges to think through about the extension of PSB activities to online spaces and, in the case of the BBC for instance, across the world to non-licence-fee payers. Why have PSB organisations moved into digital activity and in what ways? What happens to the cultural remit of a broadcaster that is geographically specific (in Catalonia, Spain, for instance) when it becomes available to and gains an audience in other, more diffuse places? What benefits are there to broadcasters for extending their brief in this manner?

Example 2: Regulating popular music

At first glance, it would seem that, of all the media forms that exist in today's world, the music industries are the least regulated. There appear to be no regulatory bodies like those that accompany the worlds of broadcasting. Likewise there is very little in the way of policy in terms of what you can and cannot do or say – or the ways in which a business can be organised. But in fact, and although it is of quite a different nature from those regulatory forms that guide and constrain other media, copyright law and the notion of intellectual property (IP) can be understood as the mechanism through which the music industries are regulated.

Most people are aware that copyright relates to the law, and you may well have heard about cases when one artist has taken another to court for infringement of their copyright (see www.superswell.com/samplelaw/horror.html#verve), or where a record company has threatened legal action against individuals for downloading digital audio files without payment. However, both the legal idea of copyright and the broader concept of intellectual property are widely misunderstood. The close association of copyright with issues of first taping music from records and then sharing digital audio files over the internet has somewhat confused the issue as well.

Many people assume that copyright implies laws that forbid copying music through taping or sharing music files, when this is not really the case. That is why it is useful to think about copyright as a means of regulating publishing in general, and, for our example here, music publishing specifically. The matter is not made any easier to understand by the fact that what copyright is, and how the laws of copyright are applied, has changed since it was initially introduced in the UK in 1710 through the 'Statute of Anne' (Kretschmer and Kawol, 2004: 26), thus informing the legislation of other developing countries. Significant reciprocal international agreement came in the Berne Convention of 1886, and hereafter our discussion is focused upon the common core ideas shared across legal frameworks in different countries as there are some important distinctions around the world.

Change has been quite rapid in the past hundred years. Initially copyrights were the means by which monarchs decided who could publish printed books in their realm, and this idea was later extended to printed music. Later, as democratic movements established more liberal principles by which societies were governed, the idea moved from the attempt by kings to control what ideas could be published, to questions about the ownership of the ideas contained in literature and music. What this means then is that, legally, you cannot 'copyright' a song or a recording; copyright is not something that can be added to a work, nor does copyright exist in an idea, and (in spite of the name) copyright is not even really 'the right to copy' in the sense that most people think.

In contemporary law, copyright is first a form of ownership, and that is why it is often associated with the concept of intellectual property (IP). Just as you can own a house, a car or a media company (or any object created through manufacture) people started to argue that when someone created a cultural or media text they owned the idea that lay behind it. Equally, just as the car, house or media company you own has to have been made before you can own it, so the film, book, or in the case here, a song, has to have been made before its intellectual property can be owned.

The creator of a work automatically owns the copyright within a work when they make it. So copyright is something that is created when a creative work (such as a song) is put into some concrete form. In fact, copyright does not exist separately from the work itself. Legally, it is said to 'subsist' within a work.

Another person who wishes to make use of that work – whether for public performance, to replicate it for sale, to synchronise it to pictures (e.g. in a movie soundtrack) or to create some sort of derivative work – must ask permission of the copyright holder, who can give or deny permission, and ask for payment for that permission to be granted. In that respect, copyright can be said to be a 'property right'. By law, it belongs to somebody, and they have a say over the ways in which that owned thing can be used.

A second aspect of copyright is that of the 'moral right' of the author. This means that someone who, for example, writes a song, has the right to be attributed as the creator of that work. That may not seem like a particularly important principle, but in fact it is one of the key aspects of copyright. This moral right is less a driver of economic gain for the artist than the principled right not to have other people pass off the artist's creative work as their own, or use the work in a way that is derogatory to the artist.

The third, and perhaps most important, aspect of copyright is as an incentive to creativity. This is one of the key factors that drove legislators to adapt copyright as a property right in the nineteenth century in industrialising countries such as France, Germany and the USA. It was seen as a public good that artistic and scientific works were being created for the promotion and advancement of culture, and so law makers put in place ownership laws that allowed for artists to earn money from their creations, as a way to encourage more people to create more works. Originally, the idea was that the ownership would last for several years, and then the works would become part of the public domain: that is, the songs would simply become part of the culture over time, and that everyone would 'own' them. However, throughout the course of music business history, the length of the copyright period has been extended time and again, due to the value that those copyrights have acquired because of contemporary music business (and other media business) practice.

In fact, in a profound sense, copyright enabled the development of all mass media, but especially the music industry. In legal terms songwriters are agreeing to allow music companies to use their songs in return for a share in any revenue that flows to the company when the song is used. So if the song is sung in public, or recorded and sold, or made into part of an advert or television programme, the user has to pay, and a share goes to the songwriter. As the music industries have developed over time, and recording and distribution technologies have been invented, notions of copyright have changed, both in the realm of law and in terms of the way that music businesses and processes are organised. However, these ideas of granting or withholding permission, the moral

How long does copyright protection endure?

From the US Copyright Office

Works Originally Created On or After January 1, 1978

A work that was created (fixed in tangible form for the first time) on or after January 1, 1978, is automatically protected from the moment of its creation and is ordinarily given a term enduring for the author's life plus an additional 70 years after the author's death. In the case of 'a joint work prepared by two or more authors who did not work for hire,' the term lasts for 70 years after the last surviving author's death. For works made for hire, and for anonymous and pseudonymous works (unless the author's identity is revealed in Copyright Office records), the duration of copyright will be 95 years from publication or 120 years from creation, whichever is shorter.

Works Originally Created Before January 1, 1978, But Not Published or Registered by That Date

These works have been automatically brought under the statute and are now given federal copyright protection. The duration of copyright in these works is generally computed in the same way as for works created on or after January 1, 1978: the life-plus-0 or 95/120-year terms apply to them as well. The law provides that in no case would the term of copyright for works in this category expire before December 31, 2002, and for works published on or before December 31, 2002, the term of copyright will not expire before December 31, 2047.

Source: www.copyright.gov/circs/circ1.pdf

Copyright

The ownership rights that subsist within a creative work to be recognised as its creator, to decide how the work will be used, and to derive income from that use.

right of the author and the incentives for creativity have remained central – at least in principle.

Copyright is, therefore, in essence a way of regulating the production and use of music. Just imagine another situation, in which the person who created a piece of music did not have a copyright. They could not earn a living from having created that music; anyone could use it for free. This is the reason songwriters and composers usually support some form of copyright, and are keen to assert their intellectual property rights over the music. The media and music companies that make a legal agreement with the creator to control or use the latter's property are also very keen on these rights. As they collect the revenue and then share it with the copyright holder they aim to ensure the music is only used in ways that will benefit them financially. For over 60 years the greatest revenue stream for music has been through the sale of records that contain that music. This, of course, is the reason why such companies are so keen that you can only listen to music which they have a legal agreement over in ways that add to their revenue.

In the case of a record or audio file there are actually three copyrights, which are usually owned by different people. When composers make legal agreements with music companies they will be paid a royalty. The royalty is a share in the revenue that accrues from the use of the recording. There are three main types of copyright within a piece of music:

1. the music itself (its melody, harmony, etc. and other compositional elements);

2. the lyrics;

3. the sound recording.

Generally speaking, the composition (music and lyrics) is owned by the composer (unless it was composed as part of their employment), and the sound recordings are owned by whoever paid for those recordings to be made – usually a record company. It is helpful therefore to think of the distinction between a 'song' (which can be performed by different people in different ways) and a 'recording' (which is the capturing of a specific performance of that song).

You should be able to see that who owns and controls the music, who can make money from it, and who can listen to it through what means, are therefore regulated by copyright. Having said all that, however, the general sense of intellectual property rights, and the actual copyright laws, are only part of the regulation of music within modern mass media. Looking back over past years we can see that the regulation of music as a medium has related to the relationship between the different media companies that try to use music to make money, and the consumers of music who pay to listen to this music through different means. Each company, or sector of companies, tries to make sure that arrangements maximise their revenue, and that copyright relationships benefit their activities. Just think about some of the ways you listen to music and the ways you pay for it. This is actually different when listening at a concert, on a digital audio or CD player, on an advert, on a film or TV programme, or on the radio. Until recently music industry companies did not make much money from music on radio or screen media because they learnt that listening to music in this way encouraged people to buy recordings, enabling the companies to make a lot of money. Broadcasters were therefore able to make programmes far more cheaply than if they had to pay the intellectual property holder directly.

There is no absolute or fixed relationship between these different companies, however. As music companies make less money from record sales as we buy less, they have focused on ways of making more money from the use of recordings in other media. This change in regulatory activity is carried out by the bodies that represent the different media sectors. While there may not be regulatory bodies in the same way that there are in other media industries, there are many organisations that use the legal parameters of copyright to regulate their industry. These fall into two main areas.

First, there are a number of rights organisations which protect the interests of copyright holders. Over time copyright has become more and more complicated as different interest groups within the music businesses have successfully argued for protection over intellectual property rights and payments for different uses of music. For instance, composers are entitled to payment when their compositions are performed publicly, transcribed or used in another medium. Owners of sound recordings are entitled to payment when physical copying of that recording takes place, and when public performances of that recording (as opposed to live performances of a different version of the song itself) take place. These organisations are sometimes called collecting societies because their role is to collect bulk payments from broadcasters and other businesses that use music, and distribute those payments to the rights holders in the correct proportion. Without collection agencies, individual rights holders would have to approach broadcasters and invoice individually for the use of their music.

Secondly, there is a whole raft of industry bodies which promote, advocate and lobby on behalf of a single sector of the music media industry. Examples of these organisations include recording industry bodies such as the BPI (British Phonographic Institute) and the RIAA (Recording Industry Association of America), and advocacy organisations such as musicians' unions and music publishers' associations. These organisations are engaged in activities such as:

- lobbying on behalf of their members for incrementally advantageous copyright and royalty payment protection;

- using copyright law to enforce and punish copyright infringement;

- advancing campaigns to encourage certain behaviours among music consumers (a 'Home Taping is Killing Music' campaign in the 1980s was a good – though unsuccessful – example of this).

It can be argued that music has been more altered by the move to digital forms of distribution, and more recently the role of the internet, than any other media sector. It should come as no surprise, then, that this medium is also the area where changes in regulation through copyright have developed far more quickly. We have already touched on some of them. Companies have been looking for new ways to ensure that their traditional sources of income are protected, and to develop new ways to make money. The catalogues of music and songs, and of recordings of this music, have become a central focus of both ownership and control, copyright law, and the relationships between companies and the audience. Companies have bought up others just to own a large 'back catalogue'. At the same time they have developed technologies which control the way we can share digital files. This process is called digital rights management (DRM). (See, for instance, www._ microsoft._com for details on the technology and principles of DRM as well as http://drm. info/ for expressions of protest about this development.)

Industry bodies have also been successful in getting changes in the law so that larger payments have to be made to use music on the radio and screen media, particularly when digital technologies will be used to distribute them. This is particularly the case in the USA where the Digital Millennium Copyright Act made it illegal to manufacture technologies which can circumvent DRM (Litman, 2001).

The wider debate generated by these changes has led to a wholesale evaluation of the role of existing media companies, and of the role of copyright. These ideas have tended to come from writers and thinkers who believe the internet offers an opportunity for more democratic media, and a wider access to the vast wealth of media texts that have been produced over the decades. There have also been some radical suggestions, and actions, to change copyright law, and to alter the regulated relationships between creative producers, media companies and audiences.

Key thinker

Lawrence Lessig (1961–)

Professor Lawrence Lessig is a significant figure in the area of music copyright. His idea of the 'Creative Commons' has changed how many musicians and music industry enterprises relate to copyright. More importantly, Creative Commons Licensing has challenged and transformed the way in which copyright acts as a form of regulation for the music industry. Lessig's book *Free Culture* (2004) discusses the difference between strict copyright (all rights reserved) and the public domain (no rights reserved). As copyright is essentially a system of granting and withholding permission for certain uses of a creative work, this has led to the idea of a middle ground – some rights reserved – allowing rights holders to pre-allow certain types of usage of their work. The Creative Commons framework developed by Professor Lessig allows for creators and rights holders to grant certain types of permission in advance of their use, and to reserve the right to withhold other types of permission.

For instance, some musicians may decide that their compositions can be used by anyone for private use, as long as they are not exploited commercially, and as long as the work is attributed to them as the author. In this case, the author of the work would choose an Attribution-Non-Commercial Creative Commons Licence. Another author may decide that derivative works may be made only if the creator of those derivative works shares their music on the same terms (a Share-Alike Creative Commons Licence).

With the rapid explosion of music availability (and music remixing) on the internet, Creative Commons Licensing both allows for creative use of an original work by a third party and simultaneously provides a regulatory framework for certain types of usage to occur without individual prior consent.

It is important to think of copyright as a noun not a verb. Although it is common for people to talk about someone 'copyrighting' an idea, this is not how the legal statutes set out intellectual property rights. As we have seen, the copyright resides or subsists in the media text, and the creator of that text can give permission for their text to be used by a media or music company or organisation, usually in return for a royalty. The bodies which set the standards for these relationships between copyright owners and users effectively regulate music as a media form. These relationships shift over time, and one of the fascinating things about studying this area at the moment is that it is going through its most significant period of change. This should provide you with many opportunities for research topics.

Copyright regulates so many of the production and consumption activities of the media, and the implications of copyright ownership are significant in almost all areas of music use. Given the discussion above we can identify three main states of regulation through copyright:

1. those activities of production or consumption that are regulated through compliance with existing copyright;

2. those unregulated because of the non-compliance of existing copyright arrangements by individual producers or consumers; and

3. a new set of relationships where regulation is negotiated through Creative Commons Licences.

Although most attention is given to the issues of unregulated music file downloading, copyright remains a powerful force. It is likely that the relationship between copyright holders, media organisations and consumers will have to change significantly and it will be interesting to see how important Creative Commons Licences will be in the new settlement.

Doing media studies

Exploring copyright

Choose a series of situations where music is incorporated into another media product, distributed or consumed, and then work out which aspect of copyright would be involved, which organisations are likely to be regulating relationships, and how copyright holders derive revenue (if any) from the particular regulatory arrangements. These situations could include:

■ a radio station plays music in a programme on its over-the-air FM service;

■ a product manufacturer uses music as a soundtrack to a cinema advert;

■ you listen to music through a social network like LastFM;

■ someone you know downloads music from iTunes;

■ another person you know downloads music from a music share blog;

■ a band puts its video on Myspace;

■ a computer game soundtracks its action with recent pop tunes.

Think of further situations and work through this analysis yourself.

Summary

Investigating media regulation and policy

In this chapter we defined policy as those deliberate plans of action, made usually by governments, which set out what is to be achieved in directing or influencing the decisions that are made by media companies. We investigated the way that these policies were rooted in philosophical positions and resulted in regulation. We defined regulation as the controls or restrictions that authorise, prohibit, direct or inflect the activities of media companies in their production work, the content or nature of media texts, or the access to them.

We outlined ways to research and analyse both policy and regulatory practice through primary documents and the work of regulatory bodies, and discussed the extent to which regulation actually achieved policy goals. We also outlined the difference between regulated and unregulated media sectors, and noted the general process in modern societies of deregulation, where existing controls are lightened, and the role of public bodies in the media are reduced or removed.

In the later part of the chapter we examined some key issues in regulation, exploring them through two examples of public-service broadcasting, and intellectual property and copyright in popular music. To do so we applied the forms of research and analysis we had outlined before, identifying the main policy and regulatory practices which were apparent in different countries, as well as highlighting the general processes of deregulation, the debates about the value and likely success of regulation, and linked the regulatory practice back to the philosophies which guide them.

You should now evaluate what you are able to do as a result of this chapter. If you have followed this chapter through and engaged with the activities and thought about the issues covered you should be able to do the following:

■ Define the concepts of policy and regulation. If you are uncertain of these core concepts and their meaning, go back and explore our definitions and explanations again. Research and analyse policy in at least one media sector, including identifying primary policy documents, policy objectives and relevant regulatory bodies. (We gave some pointers on how to do this in tandem with directions about where to look and what to look for in order to develop your skills.)

■ Research and analyse regulatory practice in at least one media sector, including identifying regulatory objectives, examples of external and internal regulation, and examples of unintended regulatory consequences. While our discussion was broadly based in order to outline ways to go about such an analysis our two examples offer models of what to do. You can explore any one media sector in order to develop your skills. Do try to focus by identifying individual case studies where policy and regulation have impacted on media businesses, texts and audience.

■ Evaluate the degree to which a particular media sector is regulated, and make comparisons with other countries, time periods and media, engaging with debates that highlight issues at the heart of regulation of the media. Any comparative study will throw up questions about the regulatory systems that you live under and prompt questions about why regulation exists. Should media be regulated? How? For what purpose? These are core questions informing any exploration of the areas in this chapter, and your engagement with them, supported by systematic research, will aid your ability to make a contribution to debates.

Doing media studies

Studying regulation in a single medium

For more developed work you should be able to use primary research to find policy documents and details of relevant regulatory bodies for at least one media sector. Outline how you would do this. Where do you think you could find a statement of the most recent policy objectives for this medium?

Next you need to move on to the actual regulatory practice. Can you explain in writing what is the difference between the policy objectives and the regulatory practice? Could you define the difference between external and internal regulation? Are there examples of each in the media sector you have chosen? How could you judge if the policy objectives had been met by the regulatory practice? Can you see any unintended consequences of the regulatory regime?

How easy do you think it would be to compare regulation and policy in the country you live in with the practices in other countries? How would you compare what happens today with what happened in the past?

How useful do you think media coverage of regulatory issues is as a basis for identifying areas that are worth studying? What issues are most likely to be covered, and which ones less likely to be covered?

Further reading

Much of the reading around policy and regulation relates to specific countries and cultures and you can explore some of this work by looking at the bibliography at the end of this book. However, there are some engaging studies in this area that new scholars will find useful as evidence of how to proceed.

Curran, J. and Seaton, J. (2003) *Power without Responsibility*, sixth edition, London: Routledge. A classic study that relates detailed threads of policy and regulation to historical contexts and the broader field of various media forms and organisations. It draws upon the UK context in particular via a sociological and political science approach but this most recent edition explores the wider, global issues pertaining to our expectations for the press and other media forms.

Feintuck, M. (1999) *Media Regulation, Public Interest and the Law*, Edinburgh: Edinburgh University Press.

Feintuck writes from the perspective of a legal scholar, dealing with some of the issues behind the claims to act in the 'public interest' which lie behind much policy and regulation. He explores terms involved in debates around 'citizenship' in the tensions between public service and marketisation and evaluates the actual legal mechanisms involved in policy and resulatant regulation.

Tunstall, J. and Machin, D. (1999) *The Anglo-American Media Connection*, Oxford: Oxford University Press.

This book is a useful one for understanding the context of calls for media policy and regulation and how academics contribute to the debate. It explores the media in the UK as well as the USA as a source of global influence and media imperialism (see Chapter 8). It focuses on Britain's efforts to remain an internationally significant player in the world's media, documenting its successes (for instance in globally promoting PSB, and purveying elite news and popular music) and its subservience to the USA (such as in film, television and the press). It ends with a series of recommendations for UK media policy.

Vaidhyanathan, S. (2001), *Copyrights and Copywrongs: The Rise of Intellectual Property and How It Threatens Creativity*, New York and London: New York University Press.

Vaidhyanathan explores the history of copyright law from an American perspective, moving through the twentieth century and the rise of mass media. His case studies encompass recent lawsuits over sampling in rap music as well as the coming of filesharing in the form of MP3 technologies and platforms such as Napster. The author is an advocate of relaxed laws of copyright in tandem with clarity over what the law entails and so there is a project to be aware of here. Nonetheless, in engaging with the changing environment we've sketched out above, this is a useful guide.

Media production in a global age

Source: Alamy Images

Thinking about global media production

In March 2010, China's state-run Xinhua news agency began an attack on Google Inc., complaining that the company had broken Chinese law by reneging on promises to support the state's censorship of its search results and services such as YouTube.

Google had abided by this rule since the establishment of its China facility in 2005 and prior to this access to its platforms outside of the country were heavily censored anyway, partly facilitated by the then limited size of the internet user community. By 2010 the size of the user community reached 420m — the largest community in the world, albeit still representing a relatively small penetration of the overall population ('China Internet population hits 420m', *China Daily*, 18 July 2010).

Just as other Western media companies had discovered, China's opening up to the free market since the 1980s had created a potentially lucrative market for exploitation, albeit one fraught with dangers and difficulties.

Google's dealings in China presented it with enormous problems, particularly in its acquiescence to censorship by a repressive and anti-democratic regime. This compromise seemed at odds with the company's unofficial motto of 'Don't be evil'. On the other hand, however, and as many CEOs of Western companies would argue, business is an augur of democracy for, if a country like China embraces capitalism in order to prosper, it must embrace social and political freedoms to allow it to function effectively.

In the contemporary globalised world, companies like Google appear to be more powerful in some respects than many nation states, even as they place their interests above and beyond such limited and limiting concepts. However, in this instance, the company found itself involved in global political struggles and a co-ordinated and chauvinistic reaction to complaints of 'cultural imperialism' in its actions. As Reuters reported:

Joseph Cheng, a City University of Hong Kong politics professor, said China's ruling Communist Party was deploying nationalism to stifle debate about censorship.

'The criticism of cultural exports, or cultural imperialism, is a kind of defence to justify the Chinese authorities' censorship controls,' said Cheng.

'In dealing with the American government, the Chinese authorities will try to emphasise that this is only a commercial dispute and has nothing to do with Sino-American relations.'

A *Global Times* editorial cited online surveys as showing 80 per cent of respondents saying they could not care less if Google withdrew from China, the world's largest Internet market with an estimated 384 million users.

Though Google has remained mum on the progress of talks, the firm's chief executive said earlier this month that an outcome is expected 'soon'.

The Google case has spread beyond censorship and hacking and has become a diplomatic knot in Sino-US relations, already being challenged by spats over Taiwan, Tibet and the value of the Chinese currency.

The United States is studying whether it can legally challenge Chinese Internet restrictions, a top US trade official said recently.

Ben Blanchard and Melanie Lee, 'WRAPUP 2-Chinese media launches new attack on Google', Reuters US, 2 March 2010 (www.reuters.com/article/2010/03/22/china-google-idUSTOE62L03V20100322?type=marketsNews).

Whatever the socio-cultural politics, Google's threat to withdraw promised to open a $1 billion search market to local firms, such as Baidu Inc.

This story illustrates a conjunction of issues for the modern world. The business of media, the attendant meanings of media texts, and the actions of producers as well as consumers, are now global concerns. The operations of Google or the release of music and films such as *Kung Fu Panda* are planned with a worldwide audience in mind (releases are simultaneous, for instance, so as to avoid pirate distributors trumping the producers), in order to cultivate new territories and to maximise profits. A market like that of China, with one billion individuals, until recently off limits to global capital, cannot be ignored, whatever compromises might be necessary. We can see, however, that the exchange of cultural meanings and messages, in tandem with the exchange of goods, saturates this network with interesting consequences that demand the attention of media scholars.

What we will do in this chapter

This chapter focuses on the production and distribution of the media at a global level – extending the approaches to business and regulation. We will explore the realms of information and entertainment, examining a range of media content and platforms. We shall address questions of how certain media forms became globally dominant, who owns global media companies, how global media are regulated, and patterns of global access to global media. Importantly, we address why these questions are significant.

As we will see, however, the debates concerning global media are complex, encompassing the thorny question of media effects and influence (see also Chapters 8 and 10). In particular, this concerns issues of media imperialism and cultural imperialism – namely, the domination of the global production and distribution of media and cultural products by a few, select, rich nations.

However, against this backdrop, we must not forget the relative merits of global media. Proponents of global media corporations point out that they satisfy a demand, asking whether global media would even have emerged if national media were capable of satisfying the information and entertainment demands of an increasingly complex and interdependent world. The emergence of pan-Arab satellite news stations since the mid-1990s, in the face of repressive Arab state media systems, is a case in point. Arguably, global media have the resources to produce high-quality, content-diverse products and services, and thereby have the capacity to enhance the public sphere and democracy. And finally, given that global media are largely products of, or are heavily influenced by, Western life, they spread values like representative democracy, free speech, equality for women and minorities, and the notion that diversity of ideas is important (see Demers, 2002).

After reading this chapter, you will be in a position to evaluate the relative pros and cons of the global media system yourself.

By the end of this chapter you should be able to:

- Demonstrate an understanding of the historical development and political economy of certain global media companies and global media forms.

- Comprehend the role and complexity of the free market and national and international regulation in generating the global media landscape.

- Understand and engage with key academic debates on the cultural, political and economic significance of global media.

- Apply key concepts concerning global media to research into global media companies and media forms.

KEY TERMS: ▶ cartel; CNN effect; conglomerates; convergence; free market; global media; global media forms; global media impacts; globalisation; media imperialism; new world information and communication order (NWICO); political economy of global media; vertical integration.

Doing media studies

Getting started

Make a list of all media you consumed yesterday – on- and offline. Do you know which company is responsible for the production of each of these media products, and which nations these companies are based in? Do you think it matters and, if so, why?

It would be useful for you to attempt this activity both before reading any further, and then again, once you have finished this chapter. See if your answer to the question 'Do you think it matters?' changes on your second attempt.

What's global about global media?

What comes to mind when you hear the term 'global media'? Is it the BBC World Service? After all, it has been broadcasting radio programmes around the world since 1932, in 32 languages and is available on FM, AM and shortwave, online and via mobile phone (as of 2011). Its stated aim is:

> to inspire and illuminate the lives of its audience by bringing the world together, making connections and helping listeners to make sense of the world. Its programmes – which range from news, education and entertainment – have a reputation for being authoritative, impartial and accurate.

(www.bbc.co.uk/worldservice/institutional/2009/03/000000_about_ws.shtml)

Alternatively, 'global media' may well evoke the monied media conglomerates with global presence, such as American companies Time Warner (whose revenue in 2009 was $26 billion) and the Walt Disney Company ($38 billion net revenue in 2010); 'American' (originally Australian) company News Corporation ($30 billion revenue in 2009); French company Vivendi SA (€27 billion revenue in 2009); German company Bertelsmann ($15 billion revenue in 2009) and Japanese company Sony ($88 billion revenue in 2010). (These figures were retrieved from the 2009 or 2010 annual reports of these media conglomerates, all available online on their home pages.)

Perhaps even more likely, the term 'global media' will evoke American company Google. Founded in 1998 by Sergey Brin and Lawrence Page, Google is not only big in terms of revenue (it earned $24 billion in 2009), but is the most frequently used and largest search engine. It searches not only across websites, but maps of the earth and sky (Google Maps, Google Earth), videos (YouTube), images (Google Image Search), academic writing (Google Scholar), complex financial data (Google Finance), news (Google News) and the 'mobile web', consisting of pages specifically designed for mobile devices (Google Mobile). With Google's new translation tool, Google Translate, you can search the web and read the results even in languages you don't speak (Google Annual Report, 2009).

Alternatively, perhaps 'global media' evokes American company Facebook – originally the social networking site of university students (although its user base has much widened). Facebook builds communities through the internet, and is, in its own words, 'helping people communicate more efficiently with their friends, family and co-workers' (www.facebook.com). Launched in 2004 by Mark Zuckerberg, Dustin Moskovitz, Eduardo Saverin and Chris Hughes from their Harvard University dormitory room, it has exploded in popularity. Two years later, in 2006, it had 12 million active users (users who have returned to the site in the last 30 days); by 2008 this had increased over fivefold to 67 million; and by 2010, it had more than 500 million active users with 50 per cent logging into Facebook on any given day. (Are you one of the converted?) By 2010 Facebook's penetration into regional internet markets was highest in North America (at 69 per cent) and Middle East and Africa (at 67 per cent), with lower figures for Latin America (58 per cent) and Europe (57 per cent). These lower penetration rates are explained by competition from other social networking sites that have loyal user bases due to factors like language (Facebook's translations rolled out relatively slowly, starting in February 2008 with Spanish and French) (McCarthy, 2010). Nonetheless, in 2011, Facebook was one of the most trafficked websites in the world (Facebook press room, 2011).

More fundamentally, for many readers, it will be the internet that comes to mind – a global media platform – as synonymous with the term 'global media'. This would hardly be surprising given that, within a generation, the internet has become widespread across the globe, largely as a result of the development of the World Wide Web (the web, for

Continent	Proportion of population using Internet
North America	77%
Oceania/Australia	61%
Europe	58%
Latin America/Caribbean	35%
Middle East	30%
Asia	22%
Africa	11%

Source: Internet World Stats (2010a)

Table 7.1 Internet penetration by continent (2010)

short). However, while the last unconnected country joined the internet in 1998 (Balnaves *et al.*, 2008), the internet is far more accessible in some nations than others.

As Table 7.1 shows, as of 2010, the continent with greatest internet penetration was North America, where 77 per cent of the population used it, whereas Africa had the smallest internet penetration, with only 11 per cent being users. Also, even within developed nations, the rich and highly educated have far more access to the internet at home than the poor and the less educated (Balnaves *et al.*, 2008). This state of affairs has led to the term 'the Digital Divide', and this theme of unequal access to global media is one that runs throughout this chapter.

Global information – roots of global media businesses and forms

While the internet is perhaps the most instantly recognisable of global media forms, in fact it was news production that was the first truly global media enterprise. News not only deals with the events of the world, connecting the local with the global, but it also adopts a global form, being remarkably similar in style regardless of where in the world it is propagated. This is largely a result of the commodification of news, exchangeable between news outlets around the world and ultimately, of course, to consumers (for a discussion of commodification see Chapter 13). While early nineteenth-century newspapers did not separate fact from comment, openly taking sides on political issues, and carrying editorials on front pages where they conducted long-running arguments with their own 'correspondents', this changed with the development of news agencies (Machin and van Leeuwen, 2007). There are a number of important news agencies which dominate global media and we can now turn to examine what they do and how they developed as important global players.

The forerunner of French national news agency Agence France Press (AFP) was founded by Charles Havas in 1835; the forerunner of German national news agency Deutsche Presse Agentur (DPA) was founded by Bernard Wolff in 1849; and the forerunner of British national news agency Reuters was founded by Julius Reuter in 1851. These European news agencies came from, and primarily catered for, the financial world, and they monopolised the news flow in a European cartel, collaborating closely with national press associations and newspaper chains. With Reuters, this collaboration extended to newspaper groups from white-dominated settler states like Australia, New Zealand and South Africa. These three European news agencies explicitly divided the world among themselves in 1859, often serving the politics of their respective empires, with their government institutions reciprocating by ordering large numbers of valuable subscriptions.

News agencies also emerged in the USA. The forerunner of Associated Press (AP) was founded in 1848 by half a dozen New York daily newspapers, and the forerunner of United Press International (UPI) – United Press Associations (UPA) – was founded in 1907 by newspaper tycoon Edward Willis Scripps (van Ginneken, 1998). As these news agencies started to supply national newspapers with stories from across the world, information became a commodity, presented in a neutral style to be saleable to editors of different political persuasion to do with what they would. In this way, the news agencies built a wide market for their news items. In developing this neutral style, news agencies pioneered a 'journalism of information' (Boyd-Barrett, 1998) that has since become dominant. Here, the stress is not on opinion but on 'facticity', including specific times and places, and mentioning sources for anything open to interpretation. Alongside this, news agencies drove forward the importance of the speed of delivery – the 'newness' of news – helped by the new technology of the telegraph. This format of facticity and speed was important in terms of developing global standards for news (Machin and van Leeuwen, 2007).

In the run-up to the First World War (which occurred 1914–18), and then again in the run-up to the Second World War (which occurred 1939–45), the USA openly came to resent the prejudicial presentation of world news – especially news about the USA – by the European news agencies (van Ginneken, 1998). As such, the **cartel** of European news agencies collapsed, in 1934, when American news agency, UPA, refused to join them and instead began its own global operations, followed by AP.

Cartel
a formal agreement among firms in an oligopolistic industry.

> *Cartel members may agree (collude) on such matters as prices, total industry output, market shares, allocation of customers, allocation of territories, bid-rigging, establishment of common sales agencies, and the division of profits or combination of these.*

> (OECD, 2002)

From 1934, the major news agencies competed rather than colluded with each other, and the major player became the USA rather than Europe, the new global news agencies that started in the late twentieth century all being American (namely Bloomberg, Knight Ridder and Dow Jones) (Machin and van Leeuwen, 2007).

For many of us, television news is our primary source of information, and television, of course, is dominated by visuals. This raises the interesting question of which nation produces the news footage for the world's broadcasters to edit. Again, we find North American dominance in the emergence of the global news-film agencies of the late twentieth century, although here the British also have a large part to play.

- The UK's Reuters took a major stake in the Visnews news-film agency in 1992, alongside the British public-service broadcaster, the BBC, with Visnews changing its name to Reuters Television in 1993. In 2007–8, Canadian information company Thompson bought Reuters to form Thomson-Reuters (*Financial News*, 2008).

- The UK's Associated Press Television News Ltd (APTN) is owned and controlled by the American news agency, Associated Press. It was formed from a merger between Associated Press Television and Worldwide TV News (WTN) in 1998. In turn, WTN had been formed by a merger between America's UPI and the UK's commercial broadcaster, Independent Television News (ITN). Since its rebranding in 2005, the APTN name and logo have been dropped in favour of 'AP Television News'.

While other commercial satellite broadcasters sell their film abroad (for instance, Qatar's Al Jazeera or the USA's CBS Broadcasting Inc. (CBS)), the concentration of international TV newsgathering into the hands of so few organisations results in the same TV stories being broadcast on most TV stations across the world. There is a big demand from national television stations for such footage because it is cheaper to buy in the footage than generate it independently, due to the rising costs of sending out news crews, together with TV stations' financial cutbacks in maintaining international correspondents.

With the rise of the internet in the 1990s, newspapers and television news lost their stranglehold on information, and even the well-established global form of news is undergoing challenges, given the millions of bloggers distributed globally. News now seems democratically distributed and infinitely local, as millions subscribe to hear directly from residents on the spot at local events, through their blogs, social network sites, or citizen

Case Study

Blogging and global media

Internationally renowned journalism blogger Paul Bradshaw writes about why he blogs, blogging's global nature and the changes faced by journalists.

Blogging is enormously important, it's become really one of the most important aspects of my professional life, it has taken me to places that I otherwise wouldn't have been, and it has introduced me to people who I otherwise wouldn't have met. And it has completely transformed my knowledge and experience, and my opinion on how you do things journalistically. Organisationally, things are changing enormously, and I think you need to be doing it in order to understand what is changing.

Culturally, the exchange between journalists and readers has changed . . . 'from a lecture to a conversation'. Journalists really need to get to grips with that or they are going to lose their audiences. There has been a massive power shift in terms of distribution; it is predominately (sic) readers and, to a lesser extent, journalists themselves, who distribute the news. You don't have the distribution network that you did with print newspapers. In that sense having a blog is a vital part of your distribution strategy, it's very important because it is not only you as a journalist who is distributing the news but your readers who distribute it as well. Blogging is crucial, or at least being part of the conversation is.

My role as a journalist has become very much one of knowing how to use certain online tools: when the Chinese earthquake happened knowing where to go to find that information, knowing how to translate this information from local blogs from Chinese into English, all these things were really important in terms of news gathering. Another key thing has been learning how to filter that information so that you only gather the most important information. Also, I think that my role as a journalist has changed, it's really more of a social role now, and I think that's really key, and to focus so much on the technology can be misleading. Because as a result, or partly through that technology, we have been able to develop different relations with people, we have been able to organise better, and that's why I have made my online journalism blog a group blog, because I think as a network we are more powerful, in terms of what we can achieve. We have got a combination of skills, experiences and knowledge and contacts that we can tap into. I have a Facebook group, and the way that the Facebook group taps into what we do as well is really interesting, so that [Facebook] has really changed my role as a journalist, and I find myself being a conduit, as much as a seeker of information. The agenda is not necessarily set by me, and that is really important.

Source: http://onlinejournalismblog.com/ and www.paulbradshaw.co.uk/ See also Rohumaa and Bradshaw (2011).

journalism sites. Of course, anxious to retain their audiences (and profits), mainstream news organisations have adapted to the role of the internet, with a significant online presence, often incorporating their own blogs and Twitter feeds. (Twitter is a social networking site that emerged in 2006, enabling people to micro-blog or 'Tweet' short messages in real time to the internet and mobile phones.) Increasingly, across the past decade, news organisations routinely solicit user-generated content from the 'audience' – be this video or photographic evidence, or the audience's own analytical skills, and generating what has been called 'collaborative journalism' (Rusbridger, 2009).

Case Study

Collaborative journalism

A prime example of collaborative journalism was the reporting of the death of Ian Tomlinson at the G20 protests that took place in London from 28 March to April 2009. On 1 April, Tomlinson was walking through the demonstration (he wasn't part of it) and was struck from behind by the police and pushed to the ground, dying hours later. A police statement released three hours afterwards read: '*The officers took the decision to move him as during this time a number of missiles – believed to be bottles – were being thrown at them.*' The next day, the police named Ian Tomlinson as the dead man, telling reporters that he had pre-existing health problems and that his family were 'not surprised' by his death. However, a few days later, across 3–6 April, witnesses began to come forward saying they saw Tomlinson assaulted by the police. These witnesses came forward because of a piece of sustained reporting by Paul Lewis, a young journalist working for the British broadsheet, the *Guardian*. Lewis used the micro-blogging site Twitter to reach an audience way beyond the *Guardian* to try to gather evidence of what happened to Tomlinson at the G20. Eventually, scores of people who had been in the crowd that day started searching through their own digital records and sending their evidence to Lewis. A New York-based fund manager found he had captured the moment on video when a policeman wielding a baton assaulted Tomlinson just minutes before he collapsed and died. He sent it to Lewis at the *Guardian* on 7 April. The next day, after watching the footage, Tomlinson's family broke their silence and called for justice. The Independent Police Complaints Commission reversed its decision to allow police to investigate the death, taking over the inquiry and ordering a second post-mortem, which found that Tomlinson died of an abdominal haemorrhage, causing the officer who hit him to be questioned on suspicion of manslaughter (Gillan, 2009; Rusbridger, 2009). In May 2011, an inquest jury found that Tomlinson had been 'unlawfully killed' by the police officer (Lewis, 2011).

While most newspapers now have an online version, many deliberately appealing to international audiences (Thurman, 2007), search engine companies like Google and Yahoo play an increasingly powerful role in determining what information is internationally available, and the paths by which we can reach it (Balnaves *et al.*, 2008), both in their general search engines and in their news-specific search engines (like Google News, launched in 2002, www.news.google.com).

New 'global' media environments, search engines and information access

It is estimated that several million web pages are added to the internet daily, creating an explosion in available content at a global level, but this content must be classified in order to be accessible, and classification inevitably involves selection (Ó Siochrú and Girard, 2002). Search engines perform a vital function in that they catalogue the web, and these catalogues are updated continuously to keep them current.

In January 2010 alone (13 years after it was launched), Google captured 64 per cent of worldwide market share among search engines (Krazit, 2010). Furthermore, Google runs a news-based search engine, Google News, which relies on an entirely automated news system that collects headline links from over 4500 websites every 15 minutes, so selecting news sources without regard to political stance or ideology. This process raises issues of credibility, as automation means that it cannot detect deliberate disinformation and propaganda. Potentially, this radically expands access to diverse viewpoints on any issue, thereby standing in opposition to traditional journalism, which values creating a finite, ordered, authoritative news product (Carlson, 2007). By way of illustration, and underwriting the potential of a media public sphere, in 2007 Google, and its subsidiary, YouTube (the world's most powerful online video service), co-sponsored with Cable News Network (CNN) debates in which ordinary citizens directly engaged with American presidential candidates (see www.youtube.com/debates and www.thenation.com/doc/20071015/chester).

Our increasing reliance on search engines and their challenge to the status of traditional information outlets (like print newspapers) raises a crucial question: how do search engines find and order our information for us? Different search engines function differently. While the precise details are commercial secrets, we know that Google uses a technique called 'link-based crawling' to update its database, whereas AltaVista uses 'keyword-based crawling' (see www.searchengineshowdown.com/features/google/review.html). Moving beyond these technical details, however, there are a number of structural features that generate problems from the point of view of global access to information.

First, ordinary search engines, which typically index only a small proportion of available pages, tend to give a much higher profile to commercial sites due to the latter's marketing and technical savvyness. There is therefore an argument to increase the visibility of non-commercial sites and content on the web (Ó Siochrú and Girard, 2002).

Secondly, those who are not searching in English are disadvantaged, given that English has been, and remains, the lingua franca of the web. As of 2005, less than 30 per cent of the world's internet users were native English-speakers (Bytelevel Research, 2010), yet around 45 per cent of web pages were written in English (see http://funredes.org/lc/english/medidas/sintesis.htm). Furthermore, search engines were not geared up to non-English languages. For instance, an examination of services provided by Google, AltaVista and FAST in the early 2000s found that they ignored the structure and special characteristics of non-English languages (specifically, Hebrew, Russian, French and Hungarian, which are more complex than English in the variety of characters used, for instance). This was disturbing given the popularity of Google in non-English-speaking countries, where users are either not aware of what they miss when using such search tools or have no alternative to these search engines (Bar-Ilan and Gutman, 2005). However, this situation is changing as emerging markets such as China, Russia and Brazil drive millions of non-English-speaking people to the internet, causing global companies – including search engines – to communicate in the language of its new markets. For instance, a study of 225 company websites showed that whereas in 2005 Russian was found on only 35 per cent of websites, in 2010, it was one of the core languages that companies select when going global (Bytelevel Research, 2010). Indeed, as of 2010, while English was still the most used language on the web, with an estimated 537 million users, this was closely followed by Chinese (445 million users), and then, in descending order, Spanish (153 million), Japanese (99 million), Portuguese (83 million), German (75 million), Arabic (65 million), French (60 million), Russian (60 million) and Korean (40 million) (Internet World Stats, 2010b).

Thirdly, if we turn our attention to news search engines, the question of what sort of information we are accessing arises. For instance, all news aggregator websites – like America Online (AOL), Yahoo! News or Google News – rely on the online version of traditional media outlets for content. Therefore, these news search engines are ultimately dependent on the selection processes made by the normal institutional gatekeepers of news. With most of these news aggregators, another editorial process occurs in that they use human editors to sift the aggregated news. This means that the news items have been sifted through editorial procedures, both in the source news outlet and by the editors at the news aggregators. While this may enhance the credibility of the news on offer by the news aggregator, it hardly equates to unlimited access to all information (Carlson, 2007).

While search engines like Google, with their paid-for advertising and sponsored links (see Chapter 13), now dominate the internet, and play an increasingly important role in internet marketing and commerce (Green, 2003), in the early 1990s, the internet was still mainly non-commercial, and much speculation focused on how it would be paid for. It was transformed in the USA in 1994 from a small publicly owned academic, informally self-regulated, text-based network to a fast-growing, primarily commercial one, used from the outset for national communication. Given the USA's leadership in adopting the internet, this meant that, as the protocol and rules for global internet governance and management were formulated, they were inescapably shaped by the USA's early decision to liberalise, privatise and commercialise the new medium. This means that it could have been very different if it had developed elsewhere or on other principles.

There are a large number of organisations concerned with different aspects of internet management and functioning – such as the Internet Corporation for Assigned Names and Numbers (ICANN – established in 1998, located in California, USA) and the World Intellectual Property Organization (WIPO – a specialised United Nations agency established in 1967) – and the internet has some way to go before its governance structures stabilise (Ó Siochrú and Girard, 2002; McStay and Bakir, 2006). For up-to-date information on emergent internet governance structures, look at the websites of the internet Governance Project (www.internetgovernance.org/) and the World Wide Web Consortium (W3C) (www.w3.org/).

Regulating global media

Can a global medium like the internet be regulated effectively? If it can be regulated, where does the balance lie between being able freely to access and transmit information, on the one hand, and securing our rights to privacy, security and intellectual property, on the other? This is an increasingly problematic question in the age of new terrorism, ushered in by President George Bush (Junior)'s declaration of a War on Terror after al-Qaeda's terrorist attacks on the World Trade Center and the Pentagon in 2001 ('9/11').

The key sites of internet regulation are our own points of access to it. To gain access to the internet, we first have to subscribe to an internet service provider (ISP) like AOL or BT Internet. However, this raises the question of whether the entities performing the regulation should be private companies, or national governments and international organisations. The issues here are complex. In a global environment, where computer viruses originating in one country may cause widespread damage in others, or where the global distribution of culturally specific products (such as pornography, violence and religious parody) may cause widespread offence, legality becomes less clear-cut than it does within national boundaries.

The controversy over the Mohammed cartoons published by Danish newspaper *Jyllands-Posten* in 2005 is a case in point. While national press and broadcasting institutions deliberated long and hard over publishing these cartoons, they are today freely available on the internet (for instance, Human Events.com (2006) and Mohammed Image Archive (n.d.)). Thus, the internet makes it virtually impossible to regulate and censor content (Ó Siochrú and Girard, 2002). Nonetheless, censorship efforts are continued by offended governments. For instance, on 19 May 2010, the Pakistani Telecommunication Authority blocked access to Facebook on its government's orders. The ban was in response to the 'Everybody Draw Mohammed Day' page on the site, which encouraged members to upload images of the prophet Mohammed (Warburton, 2010)

As well as evading nationally specific cultural norms and regulations, internet regulation is problematic when oppressive or paranoid governments use the pretext of protecting citizens from 'subversive ideas' or defending 'national security' or 'national cohesion' to deny them access to the internet, usually by forcing them to subscribe to a state-run ISP

Case Study

The 'cartoon intifada'

Twelve editorial cartoons, most of which caricatured the Islamic Prophet Mohammed, were published in the Danish newspaper *Jyllands-Posten* on 30 September 2005, and then reprinted in newspapers in more than 50 other countries. Some of the pictures were particularly demeaning, pandering to stereotypes about Arabs, for instance: one depicted Mohammed wearing a turban shaped like a bomb with a lit fuse. This immediately angered Muslims, as any depictions of their prophets are idolatrous and thus blasphemous, and they publicly protested for weeks, first in Denmark and then across the Muslim world, leading to the torching of Danish and Norwegian embassies, the issuing of death threats by some radical Muslim leaders (resulting in the cartoonists going into hiding), dozens of deaths as police fired on protesters (see www.spiegel.de/international/0,1518,399177,00.html), and boycotts of Danish produce in some Middle Eastern countries.

While the Danish government and *Jyllands-Posten* apologised, the newspaper proclaimed that it was attempting to further the debate regarding criticism of Islam and self-censorship (see www.cnn.com/2006/WORLD/meast/02/04/syria.cartoon/index.html).

Several years later, on 12 February 2008, the Danish police arrested three men suspected of planning to assassinate the cartoonist who had drawn the 'Bomb in the Turban' cartoon, Kurt Westergaard. The next day, *Jyllands-Posten* and many other Danish newspapers reprinted Westergaard's 'Bomb in the Turban' cartoon, and it was also broadcast on Danish national television, as a statement of commitment to freedom of speech (see http://news.bbc.co.uk/1/hi/world/europe/7242258.stm).

Source: Getty Images
Protests against the *Jyllands-Posten* cartoons

(Balnaves *et al.*, 2008). For example, Iran's main ISP belongs to the Revolutionary Guards (Morozov, 2011). To take another example, the Chinese government operates censorship of the internet on a sophisticated and grand scale, cutting off searches and blocking specific sites and, when people manage to connect to prohibited sites, interrupting and ending streams. This censorship has prompted an organised response. The greatfirewallofchina is a non-profit group of media workers who aim to make the Chinese censorship system transparent. As such, their website keeps track of which and how many, or how many times, websites are censored in China (see www.greatfirewallofchina.org/).

Even on global issues that most nations agree upon – such as the need to combat international terrorism – enforcing regulation of the internet can be problematic, encompassing issues of technological change, negative financial impact on commercial media operators, and different regulations in different countries, as the case study on internet wiretapping shows.

From these examples, you can see that who produces and distributes our global information, and the extent to which national governments can control and monitor this, are important issues, reaching to the heart of democracy, security and identity. From this perspective, it is obvious, perhaps, that if information production and distribution are dominated by global media conglomerates from a limited number of countries (Eurocentric, Anglo-American, Judaeo-Christian, white, etc.), or dominated by regulation emanating from specific countries, then this is likely to colour the points of view with which that information is selected, presented, distributed and regulated.

Global entertainment

While the use of home computing for entertainment has been accelerated by falling costs since the 1980s (Balnaves *et al.*, 2008), this is a comparatively new development, and for most of the twentieth century media entertainment largely meant movies, TV and popular music. Here, again, we can see patterns of skewed global dominance by examining the movie industry more closely, by way of example. Until 1918, most movies and movie equipment were produced in Europe, and France in particular. In 1918, the US Congress passed an act that allowed the Motion Picture Export Association (MPEA) to set or fix the price of exports, imposing conditions on overseas sales that were not allowed on the home market, so making foreign sales a more important part of the film industry's revenue. This was part of the US government's recognition that Hollywood was an important driver of the nation's ideals and ideologies (such as family, church, community, and the 'American dream'), spreading the American way of life. Often profit was forgone in favour of ensuring worldwide access – as with the free distribution of Donald Duck movies and materials in the Netherlands (Machin and van Leeuwen, 2007). Indeed, early movie pioneers quickly spotted the potential for what has come to be known as '**globalisation**' and developed the organisational structures and marketing techniques to capitalise on it (Balnaves *et al.*, 2008).

Globalisation

is a term that has been much debated from a variety of academic disciplines (especially sociology and geography), and is frequently used by politicians, economists and the like. While there are many definitions of globalisation, perhaps the most neutral is from sociologist Anthony Giddens – 'the intensification of world-wide social relations, which link distinct localities in such a way that local happenings are shaped by events occurring many miles away and vice versa' (Giddens, 1990).

In terms of media globalisation, it refers to phenomena like the worldwide distribution of identical programme content or globally interchangeable programme formats, and the distribution of special interest information targeting a globally dispersed minority (in any one nation) audience.

Case Study

Internet wiretapping and state surveillance

The internet originated in the US, and was at first seen as little more than a commercial platform. As such, early designs of internet infrastructure sought to optimise business innovation by providing secure communications with no 'back doors' built in. This was seen as more important than enabling law enforcement agencies to listen in on conversations conducted online. However, internet wiretapping is a function much desired by the US and UK governments, particularly since 9/11. In the old world of telecoms, the path of a call was easy to trace: a continuous analogue or digital connection was established between the two parties so it was easy for investigators to select a point along the line (such as at the telephone exchange nearest to the caller) to tap the call. By contrast, on the internet, all information is chopped up into small packets of data and fired off across the network. The path one packet takes may well be different from the path of the next, and packets may arrive at their destination out of order. Intercepting a phone call made over the internet, therefore, is logistically very complex. Furthermore, internet tapping is recognisable by the person being tapped, and therefore, arguably, useless. Tapping can be recognised by sophisticated users (and, let's face it, terrorists are likely to be sophisticated users) by measuring the 'latency' of the connection – namely the time taken for a single data packet to travel from a local machine to a computer elsewhere on the internet (inserting bugging equipment into the chain can increase the latency).

In the USA, the law governing lawful interception of information is the Communications Assistance for Law Enforcement Act (CALEA), introduced in 1994 when most internet connections were too slow to be used for voice traffic. It obliged all telecoms carriers to enable interception. Similar European Union legislation followed in 1995 (Resolution on Lawful Interception of Telecommunications), and has since been adopted and strengthened by national governments. By 2004, American law enforcement agencies were calling for new powers in response to the emergence of new forms of internet communication, such as Voice-Over-Internet-Protocol (VOIP, allowing exchange of speech like a telephone), and successfully lobbied the Federal Communications Commission – the regulatory body that oversees the implementation of CALEA – to extend the rules to cover ISPs. This move provoked an outcry both from civil liberties groups and from ISPs. The latter objected partly because of the financial cost, and partly because of the practical difficulties involved in setting up and implementing such monitoring. For instance, under CALEA, it is the internet company's fault if the people being tapped realise that they are under surveillance. However, these objections were overruled on the grounds that extending the CALEA to the internet was necessary to fight terrorism. All broadband internet and VOIP providers were ordered to comply with the new rules by May 2007. Given that it is the responsibility of internet companies to ensure that tapped suspects do not realise that they are being tapped, American internet companies have agreed with regulators to leave lawful intercept equipment permanently in place so that it can be activated on an individual's connection if required.

Across 2008, the European Telecommunications Standards Institute (ETSI), a non-profit industry body, established procedures to allow the CALEA extension to be echoed in Europe. Indeed, although Europe leads the world on privacy rights, there are inconsistencies across the EU in terms of implementing its directive on Data Protection, while surveillance harmonisation is in disarray. As a study published in 2011 and funded by the European Commission's Special Programme 'Fundamental Rights and Citizenship', 2007–13 finds, numerous loopholes and exemptions make it hard to get a full understanding of the privacy situation in European countries, particularly given the cloak of 'national security'. One indicator of excessive surveillance by member states is their inability to build safeguards into processes to gain access to information over new services. For instance, France, Germany and Switzerland are seeking powers to conduct secret searches of computers; Ireland has ambiguous powers for unwarrranted interception of VOIP; Italy is building 'back doors' into systems; and Bulgaria has 'black boxes' at ISPs.

Sources: www.economist.com/search/display-story. cfm?story_id=10789393. © The Economist Newspaper Limited, London (2008)
European Privacy and Human Rights (EPHR) (2011)
Morozov (2011).

Vertical integration

is the organisation of production whereby one business entity controls or owns all stages of the production and distribution of goods or services. This allows the business to collect profits from all aspects related to the media content.

A vertically integrated corporation, for instance, can produce movies, show them worldwide in their own cinemas and TV channels, promote them on other media they own and rent them out in their global chain of video stores.

By the 1920s, partly due to the devastation of European cinema caused by the First World War, US companies were setting up a worldwide network of partnerships and franchises through which to control international distribution – prompting warnings from across the European political spectrum against the 'Hollywood octopus' and its perceived dire cultural consequences (Balnaves *et al.*, 2008). By the 1930s, the Hollywood studio system was firmly in place – allowing the five major studios (MGM, Paramount, Twentieth Century Fox, Universal and Warner Brothers) to become a cartel that controlled all aspects of production, distribution and exhibition. This is a process called '**vertical integration**', applying the same principles of mass production and time-and-motion efficiency to film as the Ford Motor Company did to producing cars.

The chaos of European cinema after the Second World War consolidated Hollywood's global dominance – a position it has never lost, despite attempts by European governments to impose quotas on imports of US films or encouraging domestic production through subsidies (Balnaves *et al.*, 2008). After the war, Hollywood giants had become part of large conglomerates that both produced the films and owned the cinemas in which they would be shown. By the end of the twentieth century, the leading Hollywood movie distributors took 83 per cent of the market in Latin America and 70 per cent of the revenue in Europe. Adapting to the spread of television as a mass medium since the late 1940s (which was first seen as a threat), the major studios moved into TV production, buying TV networks, and acting as distributors and investors rather than producers as such, allowing independent companies to assemble production packages and teams for the new medium (Balnaves *et al.*, 2008).

As of 2010, there were six big Hollywood studios – namely Walt Disney Studios Motion Pictures (owned by the Walt Disney Company), Sony Pictures Entertainment Inc., Paramount Pictures Corporation (owned by Viacom), Twentieth Century Fox Film Corporation (owned by News Corporation), Universal City Studios LLC (owned by NBC Universal) and Warner Bros Entertainment Inc. (owned by Time Warner) (MPAA, 2010). These companies are members of the non-profit business and trade association Motion Picture Association of America (MPAA), itself part of the international body, the Motion Picture Association (MPA) (and confusingly, this being the new name since 1994 for the Motion Picture Export Association of America). Interestingly, the big six's interests are routinely advanced by this organisation, not least in areas of copyright and digital rights management.

Unfortunately for the movie industry (as with other media sectors), with the advent of digitisation and media convergence in the 1990s intellectual property rights (IPRs) were severely challenged, as entertainment content and other digitisable products could be duplicated and shared over the internet virtually free.

The MPAA has taken strong – yet largely ineffectual – steps to reduce the number of file-sharing sites online where copyrighted films are available for download. (As an indication of how seriously they take these issues, just look at their home page, www.mpaa. org/.) A similar stance has been taken by the trade group of the US recording industry – the

Convergence

Two definitions of this much-used term are given below, each with quite different inflections. The first suggests integration whereas the second suggests divergence.

Convergence is the term for the merging of different technologies and industries to create new forms of cultural product and new modes for their production and delivery (Ó Siochrú and Girard, 2002). A good example would be current developments in mobile telephones, which offer MP3, internet access and digital cameras, as well as the usual calls. Gaming technologies, such as games consoles which operate as home entertainment systems, also serve to illustrate this idea.

Convergence is the flow of content across multiple media platforms, the co-operation between multiple media industries, and the migratory behaviour of media audiences, who will go almost anywhere in search of the kinds of entertainment experiences they want (Jenkins, 2006). TV viewing for many people nowadays for instance can take place via TV, DVD, downloads and so on, at any time, at the consumer's convenience.

Doing media studies

Exploring vertical integration in your local cinema

Look at the list of films on at your local cinema this week. Find out who their parent companies are and who they have been distributed by.

Have any of these films generated spin-offs, like books, video games, television series, toys, music downloads? Who gets the money from these various products?

Recording Industry Association of America (RIAA) (see www.riaa.com/index.php). For instance, the music industry was challenged by Napster, a piece of file-swapping software created in 1999 by a 19-year-old college student, which allowed people anywhere in the world to share music between their computers. A US lawsuit, initiated by the rock band Metallica and a number of major labels, for copyright infringement was issued against Napster in 2000 by the RIAA. It culminated in a 2001 order that Napster must prevent its subscribers from gaining access to content on its search index that could infringe copyrights. This ruling meant that music consumers, via Napster, had altered the distribution, form and access to a cultural product and demonstrated to industry that there was a significant market for different forms of consumption of individual tracks, especially if instantly available, rather than via a unique compact disc purchase (Ó Siochrú and Girard, 2002).

Television and globalisation

The global reach of television is undisputed as, by the end of the twentieth century, television had reached over 90 per cent of people in all developed countries and over 80 per cent of them in many developing countries (Balnaves *et al.*, 2008). While nations retain control over their state broadcasting institutions, each coloured by the nation state's cultural and sometimes political priorities, all the main television formats (news, soaps, drama, game shows, advertising) were first invented in the USA (Machin and van Leeuwen, 2007) in radio.

The first national broadcasting companies in the USA (the National Broadcasting Company (NBC)) and in the UK (the BBC), both founded in the 1920s, took their public responsibility very seriously, seeing the radio as a tool of education, entertainment and national consciousness raising, with responsibility for the moral health of the nation (Balnaves *et al.*, 2008). After the Second World War, the state-controlled public-service TV channels that most other countries had established gradually weakened under the pressures of commercial broadcasting. This was intensified by the arrival of commercial satellite broadcasting in the 1980s, providing both legal regulations and technical

Thinking aloud

A global public sphere?

The scheduled slots for the satellites which deliver TV or aid other communications in transmission around the world are a global public resource that is limited in supply. As public resources, governments are obliged to use them optimally in the interests of the public rather than selling them off to private enterprises. On the same basis as debates around the public sphere and arguments that place obligations on the broadcasters who use such resources, should certain frequencies be reserved to develop a global public sphere by transmitting global public service media? Should some of the profits derived from the use of such public property by private interests be diverted for public use on a global scale? (On the Public Sphere see pp. 183–4).

facilities for worldwide programme exchange (Volkmer, 1999). This forced even the strictest government-controlled channels – such as those of Egypt – to shift towards more entertainment-based programming (Machin and van Leeuwen, 2007).

Today, television disseminates around the globe issues that affect policy making, economics and culture, affecting the social agenda of societies and their public sphere (Volkmer, 1999). For instance, a number of US cable channels carrying news programming – such as NBC/MSNBC, CNN International, Bloomberg and CNBC – have expanded internationally into Europe and Southeast Asia. Another globally influential dimension of television is its 24/7 coverage and liveness (usually referred to as rolling news), and its resulting capacity to influence government policy on the hoof – known as the CNN effect.

The CNN effect

is a name for the process by which media influence government political policy at home and abroad. Real-time coverage and extensive rolling news present events taking place, evoking responses in audiences, through concentrated and emotionally based coverage (especially of events like war or disasters). Audiences in turn apply pressure on governments to respond to these events. What matters is swift action rather than evaluation, analysis and a measured response. While the CNN effect may have positive as well as negative effects (galvanising aid in time of international disaster for instance), its influence has been disputed (Hawkins, 2002; Robinson, 2002).

Case Study

CNN

Cable News Network (CNN) was founded in the USA in 1980, its producers bragging from the outset that it could go live from anywhere in the country, which, indeed, it could do (although not with ease) by trundling its 18-foot-diameter satellite dish around on a trailer (Loory, 2005). (It later pioneered the use of satellite telephones and suitcase-sized uplinking equipment.)

It was soon decided to take the station international, with an original intent to make CNN available to American travellers abroad. However, it became obvious that there was a wider global appetite for CNN, particularly after the 1990–1 Gulf War, in which Iraq invaded Kuwait, which made the station into an internationally known brand due to its live coverage of the events in Iraq. The impact of the live televised wartime image in 1991 has been extensively commented upon (Baudrillard, 1995; Hoskins, 2001; Virilio, 2002).

➡ Many feared that such globalising tendencies would lead to homogenisation. However, in the 1980s satellite broadcasters saw that localisation and diversification were profitable, as audiences demonstrated their preferences – not least determined by their local, regional or national language (Machin and van Leeuwen, 2007). For instance, as Volkmer (1999) documents, CNN strategically structures global, multilevel, audio-visual communication by creating its own specific notions of localities and their needs, in the interests of expanding its business. These include producing continental and regional programmes by exercising differentiated models of journalism and marketing strategies; and diversifying their global operations in other economically effective ways, such as time-slot placement of 'carrier' programmes, which are rebroadcast on national channels, and special interest programmes. Such global 'fragmentation' was, in fact, invented with the launch of internationally distributed commercial channels like CNN.

While global fragmentation may mitigate the worst excesses of homogenisation processes in TV, it remains the case that local and global TV producers use American formats as their 'best practice' models, adopting Western broadcasting structures (commercialisation, management hierarchies, broadcasting schedules, and so on). Furthermore, all commercial broadcasting systems depend upon advertising, causing programme makers to make programmes and generate news for audiences favoured by advertisers (Machin and van Leeuwen, 2007) (see Chapter 5).

Global media, free markets and regulation

The basic ownership and financing models that were to dominate broadcasting for much of the twentieth century emerged only several years after the 1920s introduction of broadcast radio in the USA and across Europe. These models then largely determined the possibilities for media organisation around the world. In the USA, the Radio Act of 1927 regulated broadcast radio as a primarily commercial enterprise supported by advertising. This was a policy that promoted the free market economy and was distrustful of government's intentions that might use the medium as a propagandist device. Even today US law prohibits the government broadcasting in its own territory to its own citizens. In Europe, the main trend has been towards public broadcasting or public-service broadcasting (PSB), intended to serve the diverse needs of the viewing or listening public. As Europe's colonies gained their independence throughout the twentieth century, they generally adopted the public broadcasting model favoured by their former colonial power, albeit with more rather than less government influence. Countries more influenced by the USA, such as those of Latin America, opted for private-sector ownership, although usually with some public broadcasting presence, and with a strong state presence in the form of licensing and regulatory bodies with the power to impose public service obligations on private broadcasters, to restrict anti-competitive practices, and to limit foreign ownership of national media (Ó Siochrú and Girard, 2002).

However, by the 1980s and 1990s, both European public broadcasting and US-style regulation for public-service broadcasting were weakened in the face of the forces of globalisation. While all commercial media systems are influenced in some way by the global financial system, *global* media are seen as particularly in thrall, given that they are more likely to be owned by international shareholders, and therefore must be constantly oriented towards profits in order to keep their shareholders happy and investment funds flowing in. Furthermore, given that their owners and managers are rarely involved in the

The United Nations (UN)

The UN was established immediately after the Second World War, in 1945, to mitigate the recurrence of major war. Its formation – the 50 original member states have grown to 193 currently – launched the current era of global governance. The UN adopted a co-ordinating role in international media regulation, bringing existing bodies such as the International Telecommunication Union (ITU) into the UN system as independent, specialised agencies linked through co-operative agreements. This initiative sits alongside other specialised agencies, such as the World Bank and the International Monetary Fund.

Corresponding efforts to establish an international trade organisation failed but resulted in the General Agreement on Tariffs and Trade (GATT) (Ó Siochrú and Girard, 2002), itself replaced in 1995 by the World Trade Organization (WTO). These initiatives were established so as to aid free trade and to counter import restrictions to individual countries – tariffs, quantity restrictions and so on. While GATT provided a set of rules, the WTO is an actual institution that has extended coverage beyond the overview of manufactured goods to include service sectors and the guarantee of intellectual property rights (IPR).

All of these bodies have a role to play in the exchange of media commodities across the globe and the regulation, or otherwise, of global media businesses.

local community in which the global media have an impact, again profits rather than the community's social and moral concerns will be paramount (Demers, 2002).

Indeed, in countries where public-service broadcasting prevails – Europe, Canada, Australia – regulation of the media is seen as a good thing, counterbalancing the drives towards monopoly and cartel that deregulation has delivered (Balnaves *et al.*, 2008). As we have seen so far, nation states – the European powers in the nineteenth century and latterly the USA – have played an important part in establishing one country or another's dominance across different global media forms. Having set the scene, it is important now to delve deeper into the historical role of regulation in creating the globalised media landscape that we know today.

For well over a century, the problems of mass mediated information and communication have been on the agenda in international multilateral negotiations. Examples include the first International Telecommunication Convention in 1865, the League of Nations negotiations on the role of the mass media in the 1920s that led to the Geneva Convention Concerning the Use of Broadcasting in the Cause of Peace in 1936, and the United Nations Conference on Freedom of Information that produced three draft conventions on communication problems in 1948 (Kleinwatcher, 1993).

There are several key institutions in the area of international communication regulation: the International Telecommunication Union (ITU – formed in 1865 and located in Geneva, Switzerland) and the United Nations Educational, Scientific and Cultural Organization (UNESCO – formed in 1945 and located in Paris, France). The ITU's role is to regulate world and regional telecommunication frequencies, forecasting demand and supply, studying technical problems, co-ordinating national plans and allocating radio frequencies (Volkmer, 1999; Ó Siochrú and Girard, 2002). It defines its areas of responsibility as technological in sphere – the exploitation, allocation, registration and utilisation of telecommunication resources (Rahim, 1984). In comparison with the ITU, UNESCO's aims are loftier: to contribute to world peace by promoting international collaboration in education, science, culture and communication (Ó Siochrú and Girard, 2002). In its founding constitution it proclaims that:

> since wars begin in the minds of men, it is in the minds of men that the defences of peace must be constructed . . . A peace based exclusively upon the political and economic arrangements of governments would not be a peace which could secure the unanimous, lasting and sincere support of the peoples of the world, and the peace must therefore be founded, if it is not to fail, upon the intellectual and moral solidarity of mankind.

(UNESCO Constitution, 2002: 7)

As such, UNESCO is in charge of UN communication projects designed to promote a free and balanced flow of information – the former aim made explicit in its constitution written in 1946 (MacBride and Roach, 1993). It sets up radio stations in underdeveloped countries, for instance, so as to aid the spread of health information and education. Interestingly, after the Second World War it was the USA that took the initiative in UNESCO to support the freedom of media to gather, transmit and sell information throughout the world, making it a principal international policy objective – initially mostly at the expense of the British, who objected, albeit unsuccessfully, to their loss of privilege (Gerbner *et al.*, 1993; MacBride and Roach, 1993). The resulting 'free flow' doctrine, which had ties with other Western libertarian principles such as freedom of the press, was seen as a means of promoting peace and understanding and spreading technical advances (MacBride and Roach, 1993).

As UNESCO's membership changed over time, to encompass countries from Africa, Asia, Latin America and the Middle East, the Third World and former socialist countries sought to oppose unrestricted freedom for the privatised information and media companies (Gerbner *et al.*, 1993), and to push for a more *balanced* flow of information (MacBride and Roach, 1993). (See http://erc.unesco.org/cp/MSList_alpha.asp?lg=E for a list of countries belonging to UNESCO, and when they joined.) Interestingly, this call sounded very similar to the complaints made by American press agencies against the European news agencies in the early twentieth century (van Ginneken, 1998). The aim of UNESCO is now to ensure that the mass media promote a fair and wide distribution of information on the goals, aspirations and needs of all nations and cultural groups, particularly those struggling against imperialism, neo-colonialism and racism. However, international agreements generally function only to the extent that individual states ratify them and incorporate them into their own laws and regulations (McQuail and Siune, 1986).

The World Trade Organization (WTO) and the World Bank are the institutions that control the world's media market, and underwriting their approach is a free market philosophy (Machin and van Leeuwen, 2007). The WTO was set up in 1995 to replace the GATT, which was itself a temporary agreement set up after the Second World War to reduce tariffs on trade in manufactured goods. This agreement actually worked in favour of the world's dominant country which desired large export markets – the USA (Ó Siochrú and Girard, 2002; Machin and van Leeuwen, 2007). As an institution, the WTO takes a much broader view of trade than GATT, which focused on manufactured goods. The WTO's purview includes trade in ideas (IPRs), telecommunications and mass media, allowing established media conglomerates to exploit the new markets (Ó Siochrú and Girard, 2002).

We should note that EU cultural commissioners hotly contested the establishment of WTO powers, guaranteeing the trade of media and other cultural goods. EU representatives remained particularly passionate about preserving cultural diversity and national identities in the face of global forces that seemed to presage homogenisation. The Europeans, led by the French, took negotiations for WTO powers to the point of collapse by insisting that cinema and TV should be treated mainly as cultural issues rather than as just another industry. This was an argument rejected by US negotiators, who expressed outrage at the very idea that Hollywood's worldwide domination might have cultural implications (Balnaves *et al.*, 2008)! The *New York Times* reported from the US perspective that a significant issue concerned the export of homegrown entertainment products: movies, TV programmes as well as accompanying technologies. Based in the free-market ideology of US business – underwritten by the then President Clinton – the representatives of the US entertainment sector expected and asked for open access to potentially lucrative overseas markets. As the newspaper reported, the film industry was second only to aviation manufacturing in the USA in producing a trade surplus. The European position, which demanded maintaining restrictions on imports, was perceived as a threat to US profits and employment. The former chairman of Columbia and Universal, Frank Price complained that the European stance was protectionist, arrogant and simply anti-America *'What they don't like is that audiences find American entertainment desirable. They want to prevent that.'* This opinion was common amongst US producers and executives who noted that the home market had few barriers to entry from outside, although audiences for foreign-language films were limited. In contrast, US blockbusters were as successful overseas as at home.

The *New York Times* quoted the chairman of New Line Cinema Robert Shaye, who complained of the ludicrous attitude of the French: *'Entertainment is one of the purest marketplaces in the world,'* he said. *'If people don't like a movie or record they won't see it or buy it. The fact that the American entertainment industry has been so successful on a worldwide basis speaks to the quality and attractiveness of what we're creating.'* (Weinraub, B. (1993) 'Directors Battle Over GATT's Final Cut and Print', *New York Times*, 12 December).

Case Study

WTO and Miles versus Anu Malik

A useful example of the operations of the WTO is sketched in a case study from Asia by Abul Kalam Azad of the University of Chittagong.

His report concerns an apparent act of media piracy. In 2004, the long-established Bangladeshi music band Miles accused an Indian film-maker – Anu Malik – of copying their song *'Phiriye Dao Amar Prem'* ('Give Me Back My Love') for the soundtrack of the Mumbai film *Murder*. A resulting court case found in favour of the band and the Indian judge ruled that the film-makers should remove the song from the film soundtrack and all associated products. Essentially, the reason that this resolution was reached was not down to agreements between the two countries but due to the fact that they were signatories to the WTO and a greater, global framework – an agreement called 'TRIPS' or trade-related aspects of intellectual property rights. As Azad writes:

The verdict of the Calcutta High Court in the *Miles* case was a triumph of the rule-based international trade regime. Previously, intellectual property right (IPR) laws were applicable mainly within national boundaries, and only the nationals of a country could benefit from such laws; India was no exception to such practice. The Indian Copyright Act empowered the government to extend the benefits of the Act to the nationals of other countries (i) if India had entered a bilateral treaty with that country; (ii) if India and the country concerned had been parties to a

→ common international convention guaranteeing protection to intellectual property rights; or (iii) if the Indian government was satisfied that the country concerned had adopted measures to reciprocate similar protection to the works of Indian nationals.

But Bangladesh and India had neither signed any bilateral agreement nor been parties to any common international convention related to the protection of property rights in literary and artistic works before 1995. So, according to the provisions of the Indian Copyright Act, Bangladesh would not have the right to claim IPR protection for its citizens' works in India before 1995.

However, both Bangladesh and India became members of the WTO on its formation in 1995, and the Indian Copyright Act was amended accordingly to make it compatible with the TRIPS Agreement.

Source: www.wto.org/english/res_e/booksp_e/ casestudies_e/case3_e.htm. World Trade Organization, 'Managing the Challenge of WTO Participation: 45 Case Studies', Cambridge University Press

On the other hand, European directors, including Pedro Almodóvar of Spain, Bernardo Bertolucci of Italy, Stephen Frears of the UK and Wim Wenders of Germany, responded: 'We are only desperately defending the tiny margin of freedom left to us. We are trying to protect European cinema against its complete annihilation' (Weinraub, 1993). The European directors said American films and television programmes had the potential to overwhelm local productions. If the Motion Picture Association succeeds with its demands, they said, 'there will be no more European film industry left by the year 2000' (Weinraub, 1993).

Clearly, those who wanted the WTO to oversee such matters got their way and it now plays a major role in the global governance of telecommunications equipment, infrastructure and services. Combined with its decisive influence over IPRs (such as patents and copyrights), it can reasonably be identified as the most powerful player in media and communications governance globally. However, the WTO is not a neutral force. Transnational corporations (i.e. companies which are financed and owned, and operate, across borders), which are understandably very concerned about the rules of trade, are very influential on the WTO, pursuing their interests through highly organised and well-resourced lobby groups, where normally competing corporations come together in long-term co-operation to influence the agendas of the various trade rounds (Ó Siochrú and Girard, 2002).

While transnational institutions dealing with media are important players, this is not to suggest that the nation state – the country in which you live, for instance – no longer has a role or say in regulation. Various studies show that the nation state and its internal politics are pivotal to the final contours of both national and global media landscapes (Semati, 2004; Steven, 2004). For instance, the nation state has been central in reregulating and facilitating the globalisation of free market capitalism, removing barriers to international production, distribution and consumption of media products (Artz and Kamalipour, 2003). This reregulation is often, and confusingly, called 'deregulation', to capture the somewhat mythical neo-liberal idea that free markets are naturally free and exist without state intervention.

The importance of national politics in determining the shape of the global media landscape is illustrated by the following example. In 1996, pushed by media lobbying, the US Congress introduced the Telecommunications Act. Previously, ownership across media sectors had been limited by law, partly in order to curb the power of media moguls and, indeed, theoretically to aid competition. As we have seen in our study of the thrust of media business towards economies of scale and in pursuing strategies such as synergies in order to minimise risk and maximise profit, cross-media ownership has huge money-making potential, especially when viewed globally. This US Act abolished boundaries between different media, allowing companies to make acquisitions and mergers across a range of media – so that one company could now own many different broadcasting and print media (whereas, historically, newspaper companies tended to own just newspapers and broadcast companies just radio and TV companies). The Act also lifted all restrictions on radio station ownership, and restrictions on TV station ownership as long as a company's holdings reached no more than 35 per cent of the national audience. As a result, there were 185 acquisitions and mergers in the broadcasting industry in 1996 (Demers, 2002). The spirit of this Act was exported globally, starting with Europe and Latin America, as national governments were obliged to relinquish restrictions and control over ownership of their media resources and institutions if they wanted to participate in world trade and subscribe to the agreements that inaugurated the WTO (Machin and van Leeuwen, 2007).

This regulatory environment led to the creation of massive media conglomerates in the 1990s, like Viacom, Disney and News Corporation, as they bought out other companies across the globe. For instance, in terms of American networks, Disney bought up the American Broadcasting Company (ABC) network, Viacom bought up CBS, and General Electric bought up NBC (Machin and van Leeuwen, 2007). Such conglomerates are among the biggest companies in the world, with interests across a range of other industries (Herman and Chomsky, 2002). The fact that such conglomerates readily and often aggressively absorb smaller media companies has created a situation where an extremely wide range of media forms, genres and their distribution channels are owned by just a handful of media conglomerates.

Evaluating and resisting globalisation

So, does it matter? Why shouldn't we all have access to glossy, entertaining movies, DVDs and computer games with high production values, and news provided by 24/7 TV news and professional internet outlets? Isn't it a good thing that big conglomerates exist, so that entertainment and information can be made globally available, across multiple media platforms? Wouldn't the world of mass mediated reality and representations be a little dull without Hollywood, CNN, Facebook and the like? However, there are at least three arguments that suggest that it does matter.

1. Many argue that such corporations are unlikely to be critical of free market policies and of capitalism, as they are dependent on the global advertising industry, which in turn is dominated by a few Japanese and American corporations. Critics, such as McChesney (2004 and www.thenation.com/doc/19991129/mcchesney) and Herman and McChesney (2001) further contend that global media are less likely to publish information that offends powerful groups and elites because such content could alienate advertisers, news sources or consumers, damaging profits. Thus, news and entertainment become 'corporatised', privileging entertainment over news, public affairs and educational programmes (McKenna *et al.*, 1997), avoiding controversy, featuring minimal public participation, producing less overall diversity in the so-called marketplace of ideas, and thereby eroding the possibilities of the public sphere. Thus, commercialisation and globalisation, while proliferating the *amount* of information on offer, may have narrowed the *range* of information.

2. Is it a problem when we find ourselves watching an action film where an American hero fights against evil cyber-terrorists, for instance, *Die Hard 4* (dir. Wiseman, 2007), distributed by 20th Century Fox, echoing stories and editorial positions concerning the war on terror broadcast on Fox News? Both media outlets are subsidiaries of Rupert Murdoch's media conglomerate, News Corporation. (Incidentally, *Die Hard 4* was initially stalled due to 9/11.) Regardless of the narrative details of

Case Study

VIACOM – media conglomerate

→ In the early 1990s, Viacom took over the Hollywood giant, Paramount, allowing Viacom to then control not only Paramount's catalogue of 50,000 films, but also Simon & Schuster's 300,000 book titles, Blockbuster's video and music stores, the Nickelodeon and Music Television (MTV) cable networks, and a number of theme parks, TV and radio stations, and cinema chains (Balnaves *et al.*, 2008).

When, in 1999, the US media regulator relaxed its rules on television ownership, Viacom took over CBS's TV and radio networks (Balnaves *et al.*, 2008). This merger was undone in 2005, with the original Viacom changing its name to CBS Corporation and a new company, the present Viacom, being spun off (the latter to include the MTV networks, Paramount's movie studio and Paramount Pictures home entertainment options). Seventy-one per cent of the voting stock of both companies (CBS Corporation and Viacom) is controlled by Sumner Redstone, who, through privately owned media and entertainment company National Amusements Inc., is the chairman of both companies (see www.viacom.com/investorrelations/Investor_Relations_Docs/Form%2010K.pdf).

Such a snapshot presents us with a sense of the size and the complexity of media conglomerates, and gives us some idea of how we might make sense of their operations.

Die Hard 4, its very existence arguably raises the profile of terrorism as a potential threat, and when this is reinforced by repeated news items on the same topic, it may well lead to unwarranted fear and heightened public perception of risk (Altheide, 2006, 2007). The use of entertainment as a vehicle for propaganda is a tried and tested formula that goes back at least as far as the 1930s, when Josef Goebbels looked towards popular song, humour and movies as key propagandistic tools in Nazi Germany (Machin and van Leeuwen, 2007). With media conglomerates now owning and controlling both entertainment and news outlets, the dividing line between fact and propaganda becomes harder to distinguish. Perhaps as a media-literate audience today, we would be aware of any such propagandistic attempts, and assess them for what they are. However, the elision of propaganda and factual information is dangerous if we do not understand whose interests are being propagated here, or if we uncritically accept all we see on the news as the whole truth rather than the partial and restricted representation of reality that it constitutes (for a further discussion of propaganda see p. 286).

3. What about the impact on local media? As more new countries enter the global trade networks, the larger corporations move in, introducing their own media products, buying up local media or creating trading relationships with existing large media organisations to bring them into the global system (Machin and van Leeuwen, 2007). This has negative implications for diversity and the encouragement of local creativity. It has long led to accusations of media imperialism and cultural imperialism, or, less extremely, to media hegemony and maintenance of the status quo. Studies show that global media, like all mainstream media, reinforce dominant institutions and value systems – such as responsible capitalism and representative democracy (as opposed to alternative economic and political systems) (Demers, 2002). Of course, the negative connotations of media, and of cultural imperialism and hegemony, may be lost when looking at some countries that resist such cultural contamination.

For instance, in Iran, the desire to exclude politically inappropriate content – especially that contradicting Iran's religious and moral beliefs – informs strong regulatory decisions against satellite TV (although satellite dishes are bought on the black market) (Balnaves *et al.*, 2008). Given that homosexuality is illegal in Iran, you can see the state's desire to prevent homosexually oriented programmes (*Queer Eye for the Straight Guy, Will and Grace, Ellen* and so on) from reaching its populace.

Clearly, these processes do matter and are not simply neutral or benign in their outcomes. Indeed, debate about the process of globalisation has resulted in vocal and physical responses and rejections. As early as 1973, the President of Finland, in an address to a UNESCO symposium of media experts, focused attention on the growing disparities between the meanings of freedom to rich and poor countries. He suggested that, for those in the West, freedom amounted simply to an obligation on behalf of states to guarantee free trade and the generation of profit. Thus, 'In this way freedom of speech has in practice become the freedom of the well-to-do . . . Globally the flow of information between states – not least the material pumped out by television – is to a very great extent a one-way, unbalanced traffic, and in no way possesses the depth and range which the principles of freedom of speech require' (quoted in Gerbner *et al.*, 1993: xi).

Spurred on by recognition of this global inequality, in the late 1970s and 1980s there was a move to try to create a 'new world information and communication order' (NWICO). This movement was fuelled by a report written under the chairmanship of Irish poet laureate Seán MacBride (MacBride, 1980). *Many Voices, One World* (otherwise known as the MacBride Report) was a UNESCO publication that aimed to study the totality of communication problems in modern societies. Enshrined in a 1983 report by UNESCO, the NWICO endorsed the concept of pluralism (social, cultural, political, etc.), free press and respect for human rights. It explored the nature and consequences of the monopoly of the news agencies, the one-way traffic in media entertainment and the spread of advertising, which the report said propagated Western materialistic values. The debate initially centred on the flow of news, accusing the Western international news services (AP and UPI of the USA, France's Agence France-Presse and the UK's Reuters) of monopolising news flow to and from developing countries, presenting information from a limited perspective, reflecting the economic and cultural interests of the industrialised nations, and reducing reports about the Third World to stories about coups, crises and earthquakes (MacBride and Roach, 1993). The flow of TV programming, including entertainment, was also debated, since a UNESCO study by Nordenstreng and Varis (1974) showed that the international flow of TV programming was dominated by the USA, the UK, France and the Federal Republic of Germany.

However, Western (especially US) press reaction to the idea of the NWICO was fiercely oppositional, as it threatened entrenched, privatised Western media interests. These interests, in turn, painted the idea of the NWICO as a front for totalitarian government control of the media, suggesting that this, in turn, would be hostile to freedom and democracy (Gerbner *et al.*, 1993; Kleinwatcher, 1993). The context for the terms in this argument was that of the Cold War (1945–89), which pitted Western consumerist and free market ideologies against collectivist Socialist or Communist ideologies. The collapse of the old Communist Bloc, signalled in the breaching of the Berlin Wall in 1989, is one of the reasons for the inexorable and triumphant advance of global free trade and attendant values.

Under the Republican government led by Ronald Reagan, the USA withdrew from UNESCO in the same year that the 1983 report was published. This withdrawal was not only because of the NWICO, but because of UNESCO's examination of peace, disarmament, people's rights and disputes regarding Israel, and for financial and organisational reasons. In the ensuing climate of deregulation and privatisation, the movement lost impetus (Machin and van Leeuwen, 2007). Allied with US policy, the UK withdrew from UNESCO in 1984 (although returning in 1997 under the Blair government) (Ó Siochrú and Girard, 2002). Faced with such opposition from such powerful members, in 1989,

Key theory

Media imperialism and cultural imperialism

Cultural imperialism concerns how the way of life – values, beliefs, moral structures – of a society is dominated by the 'way of life' of another. This can be understood in relation to the idea that the world system consists of societies holding different amounts of power and so can be divided into 'core' (the powerful, 'modern', often Western countries) and 'peripheral' (the marginal, less powerful, economically developing or Third World countries). Cultural imperialism refers to the sum of the processes by which a peripheral society is attracted, pressured, forced and sometimes bribed into shaping social institutions to correspond to, or even promote, the value and structures of the dominating, 'modern' world system (capitalist, free market, westernised) (Schiller, 1976).

Media imperialism refers to the processes whereby the ownership, distribution and content of media in any one country are subject to substantial external pressures from the media interests of any other country. These processes are tied to a power imbalance, where the country affected does not have a proportionally reciprocal influence (Boyd-Barrett *et al.*, 1977). Clearly, media companies have an important role to play in the spread of culture and the process of cultural imperialism.

A seminal study in establishing the concept of media imperialism was Galtung and Ruge's (1965) study of how major crises in Third World 'peripheral' nations (the Congo, Cyprus and Cuba) were reported in a First World 'peripheral' nation (Norway). They showed that peripheral countries do not communicate with each other directly: rather, communication flows from a peripheral country to a core country and then to another peripheral country. Thus, peripheral countries only ever get to know about each other's affairs according to the interests (and audiences) of media in the core country.

UNESCO formally retreated from its NWICO strategy (Gerbner *et al.*, 1993). Interestingly, as the NWICO fell off the agenda at UNESCO, other transnational groupings embraced the debates for themselves. For instance, the European Economic Community (EEC) (now the EU), following discussions about how to protect and develop European cultural identity in a global communication environment, produced a 1989 EEC Directive on Television to strengthen Europe's own TV production, while implementing a quota system to reduce the influence of imported media (Bakir, 2001).

The UK and USA still dominate the global export market for television – the USA in finished, made-for-TV programmes, from *Oprah* to *The Wire*, *Lost*, etc., and the UK in international TV formats like *Pop Idol*, *Who Wants to be a Millionaire?*, *The Weakest Link* and *Changing Rooms* (Colwell and Price, 2004; www.pact.co.uk/uploads/file_bank/1698. pdf). Nonetheless, the global flow of entertainment media has become more complex, and other countries have emerged as global exporters in certain niche products. For instance, Australia exports the popular TV soap opera *Neighbours* to the UK. A number of nations other than the UK have successfully exported international TV formats, including the Netherlands, France, Spain, New Zealand, Australia and Argentina. The highly successful *Big Brother*, *Masterplan* and *Test the Nation* are Dutch formats (Colwell and Price, 2004; www.pact.co.uk/uploads/file_bank/1698.pdf). However, outside the nationally customisable form of international TV formats, most local products do not travel well, and often rely on government subsidies to sustain them. Alternatively, local products may find a global market through a dispersed ethnic diaspora – the 'Bollywood' films out of India being a prime example (Machin and van Leeuwen, 2007). In terms of other global media forms, such as the internet, there are some interesting developments. For instance, open source software, which is free and available to all to refine and develop further, such as Linux platforms, challenges the grip of corporate giants like Microsoft (see www.linux.org/).

UNESCO continues to support media and communications initiatives in practical ways, aiming to ensure that free flow does not mean a free hand for corporate and private interests, but that it progresses societies and their democratic functioning. For instance, it promotes a non-partisan press through the International Freedom of Expression Clearing House (IFEX – www.ifex.org/), a mechanism to mobilise rapid international response to violations of press freedom. The main component of IFEX is the Action Alert Network (AAN). Member organisations report instances of the abuse of freedom of expression in their geographic region to a 'clearing house'. In turn this circulates reports and information to other members and interested organisations all over the world. The AAN organises rapid, worldwide and co-ordinated responses to violations of press freedom and freedom of expression – pinpointing those deemed responsible.

Some of the objectives in communication development forwarded by the NWICO included the idea of stimulating indigenous media production and more participatory communication institutions within developing nations. For instance, this could mean encompassing peasant and urban worker organisations, women's movements, and so on, countering the widening gap between a highly developed, urban industrial centre and a mass of rural peasants or underemployed immigrants (White, 1993). The use of such alternative lines of media production has intensified in the era of digitisation and interactivity and its spread of participatory media – where consumers have the means of making and distributing media, often unfettered by traditional gatekeepers or mainstream media regulation. As such, global media scholars have also turned their attention to the spread of participatory, horizontal communications and the way that consumer and participant power has battled against global corporations (Beaton and Wajcman, 2004) and state-controlled media in authoritarian regimes (Alterman, 2004, Lynch, 2006). For instance, collectively orchestrated, individual contributions are apparent in citizen journalism online.

A prime example of citizen journalism is Indymedia (or Independent Media Center) – an online, global network of collectively run news websites. It was established by various independent and alternative media organisations and activists in 1999 to provide grassroots coverage of the World Trade Organization (WTO) protests in Seattle. The centre acted as a clearing house of information for journalists. The site uses a democratic open-publishing system (although see Jones (2007) for a discussion of how democratic it actually is). Open publishing allows contributions from anyone wishing to add stories, which can be seen immediately and also peer-reviewed (this is not unlike a system such as Wikipedia). Through a decentralised and autonomous network of communication, hundreds of affiliated media activists set up independent media centres in countries in every continent (www.indymedia.org). For instance, the mission statement of the Los Angeles Independent Media Center explicitly addresses the dominance of news by global conglomerates, and includes the following:

> To encourage a world where globalization is not about homogeneity and exploitation, but rather about diversity and cooperation.

> To cover local events that are ignored or poorly covered by corporate media. . . .

> To seek out and provide coverage underscoring the global nature of people's struggles for social, economic, and environmental justice directly from their perspective . . .

> To encourage, facilitate, and support the creation of independent news gathering and organizations.

(Los Angeles Independent Media Center, 2008, http://la.indymedia.org/process/about.php)

Case Study

Illustrating the 'free flow of ideas': Al Jazeera

Al Jazeera was launched in Doha, Qatar, in 1996, as an Arab satellite news and current affairs outlet – one of around 100 Arab satellite TV channels that appeared in the 1990s (Cherribi, 2006). Al Jazeera's sponsor, the Emir of Qatar, Shaikh Hamad bin Khalifa al Thani, on coming to power in 1995, committed to transforming Qatar into a liberal constitutional monarchy and announced the end of media censorship, abolishing the Ministry of Information and Culture as a branch of government, granting start-up funds for Al Jazeera, and staffing the station with BBC-trained professionals who had been rendered jobless by the recent closure of the BBC Arabic service (Sakr, 2002).

By 2000, Al Jazeera had become a 24/7 news channel (Cherribi, 2006), and, just as CNN became the face of the 1991 Iraq War, so Al Jazeera's coverage defined the initial conflicts of the twenty-first century, being the only broadcaster sanctioned by the Taliban in Afghanistan, and becoming a major force during the 2003 Iraq War. Given minimal access as embedded correspondents with British and American forces in the 2003 Iraq War, Al Jazeera instead focused its coverage on the effects of the war on the Iraqi civilian community, producing images of dead civilians and coalition troops that enraged Western governments (Seib, 2004; Tatham, 2005) who were used to being able to tightly control war-time news (Bakir and McStay, 2008; Bakir, 2010).

Al Jazeera attracts an audience of between 35 and 50 million viewers, not just in the Middle East but also in South Africa, Indonesia (serving the world's largest Muslim population), Europe and the USA (Tatham, 2005). It was the second most watched network in the Arab region in 2003 (the first being the Lebanese Broadcasting Corporation's satellite station, launched in 1996). Its main competitor was Al Arabiya, another 24-hour news channel, launched by Middle East Broadcasting in 2003 (Quinn and Walters, 2004). However, in March 2008, the BBC launched its free Arabic-language TV channel, BBC Arabic television.

Source: Rex Features
Al Jazeera broadcasting

This is likely to present stiff competition as it will draw on the BBC's extensive newsgathering resources of over 250 correspondents reporting from 72 international bureaux – the biggest newsgathering team in the world (see www.bbc.co.uk/pressoffice/pressreleases/stories/2008/03_march/11/arabic.shtml). Competition aside, Al Jazeera is respected by journalists (Tatham, 2005), holding agreements to share material with CNN, ABC, NBC, Fox, BBC, Japan's Broadcasting Corporation, Nippon Hoso Kyokai (NHK), and Germany's public television corporation, Zweites Deutsches Fernsehen (ZDF).

In 2006, 10 years after its initial launch, Al Jazeera went global with the launch of a sister channel, Al Jazeera International (AJI), directly competing with BBC World and CNN for the world's English-speaking audience of over a billion people (see Miles, 2005, 2006; www.foreignpolicy.com/story/cms.php?story_id=3497). AJI brings a different news agenda to the West from that offered by Western-based global news channels, focusing on developing world issues and using more indigenous reporters and freelancers than other channels.

Given that satellite channels have relative freedom from domestic regulation, on its launch in 1996, Al Jazeera pledged to present all viewpoints. This was distinct from most media in the Middle East, which historically have been heavily state-controlled and sycophantic, with taboos on promoting the views of political opposition, particularly Islamic opposition; criticising their country's rulers or their families; religious writing that might cause undue dissension in a country; and social and sexual mores (Alterman, 1998).

Consequently, Al Jazeera has given air time to political extremists, including prominent members of al-Qaeda such as Osama bin Laden, and has received videotapes from insurgent groups in Iraq, Afghan warlords and the London suicide bombers. As such, it has been much reviled by outspoken critics, including former US Defense Secretary, Donald Rumsfeld, who has referred to Al Jazeera's coverage of US-led wars in Afghanistan (2001) and Iraq (2003) as inaccurate and inexcusable (see Miles, 2006; www.foreignpolicy.com/story/cms.php?story_id=3497). Western critics have accused Al Jazeera of covering uncontextualised violence, torture and death, of hampering democratisation efforts in Iraq after the toppling of Saddam Hussein's regime in 2003, and of causing the rise of insurgency and kidnapping incidents (Wojcieszak, 2007). As such, AJI had problems in getting American cable channels to distribute it, with the few that do generating hysterical complaints and allegations (for instance, from the media watchdog group Accuracy in Media (AIM)) that it is essentially a recruitment vehicle for terrorist groups and should not be allowed to broadcast in times of war (see Moss, 2007; www.multichannel.com/article/CA6439356.html).

Obviously, such an image is problematic in a commercial media system that needs to pander to consumers' tastes and prejudices. Yet Al Jazeera is also criticised by Arabs for giving regular air time to Israeli affairs and allowing Israelis to present their case in their own words – the first Arab channel to do so. This was a major departure from past practices and, as such, shocked the Arab world, leading many Arabs to believe that Al Jazeera was funded by Mossad, MI5 or the CIA. Supporters of Al Jazeera point to its programmes about Western politics, which have done more to inform Arabs about democracy than any other nation or station. For instance, after 9/11, Al Jazeera's Washington bureau started two weekly talk shows to illuminate American democracy for a foreign audience. Al Jazeera established the tradition of investigative reporting in the Arab world and rolled back the boundaries of debate in Arab families, breaking all sorts of taboos about what could be discussed on TV (see www.multichannel.com).

From UNESCO's perspective, Al Jazeera is an important tool in the free flow of ideas, which should then also inculcate democracy in the Arab region. With few exceptions, the state controls production and dissemination of information in the Middle East (Wojcieszak, 2007). Television is particularly controlled by government because of its power to reach both literate and illiterate audiences (in the Arab world, the average literacy rate in 2000 was 39 per cent (Sakr, 2002)). National news services were therefore more government propaganda machines than independent sources of information (Ayish, 2002). As such, many consider Al Jazeera to be a counter-hegemonic force in the Arab world that challenges its dominant social discourse and the existing political order (Lynch, 2006; Wojcieszak, 2007). The knock-on impact of Al Jazeera on other Arab media has also been observed, with many abandoning their parroting of the government line (Alterman, 1998).

However, free speech is no substitute for political reform. Just because a woman in Saudi Arabia can contribute to a debate on TV in real time does not mean she can go and vote in a national election. Arab autocrats know that, although information cannot be packaged on Al Jazeera as it can on national TV, they can still ban Al Jazeera from opening a bureau, as has happened in Saudi Arabia, Tunisia, Iraq, Bahrain and Qatar, or evoke emergency laws to confiscate equipment and arrest journalists, as in Egypt. Arab press unions, like Arab opposition political parties, are prevented from growing strong.

Information deficits are not the cause of the state of affairs in the Arab world: except in the most authoritarian Arab countries, news has long been accessible to determined citizens via the BBC World Service or Voice of America radio (www.foreignpolicy.com/story/cms.php?story_id=3497; Miles, 2005). Thus, free speech alone does not equate to democracy. Indeed, given the launch of AJI, and given that Al Jazeera's sponsor, the Emir of Qatar, on coming to power in 1995 calculated that hosting a popular TV network would help Qatar shore up Western support in the event that its neighbours should decide to invade (www.foreignpolicy.com/story/cms.php?story_id=3497), it would seem that Al Jazeera's aim is not so much reform in the Arab world, but more to act as a beacon to encourage the free flow of information about the Arab world for the West! Other interpretations are that the Emir showcases Al Jazeera as evidence of his commitment to making Qatar a *progressive* Islamic state that welcomes Western investment (Seib, 2004). Yet another interpretation is that Al Jazeera's real aim is to build a global Muslim identity and transnational Muslim 'imagined community', evidenced by its daily transmission of monodenominational religious messages (such as pro-veil advertising) and, in particular, its battle against the French ban in 2004 on wearing headscarves in state schools (Cherribi, 2006).

While pan-Arab satellite TV news stations like Al Jazeera provided the first real populist challenge to Arab regimes' state-controlled media, it is the internet that has proven ultimately the greatest challenge. In terms of horizontal communication circumventing state-controlled media in authoritarian regimes, we can do no better than look to the swathe of Facebook-organised and tweeted demonstrations across the Middle East from December 2010 to May 2011, some of which led to the ousting of long-standing regime leaders and promises of democracy – as in Tunisia and Egypt. Initially sparked in Tunisia, with the self-immolation of Mohamed Bouazizi on 17 December 2010, demonstrations and riots spread throughout the country over long-standing issues of unemployment, food inflation, corruption, poor living conditions and freedom of speech. They led to the ousting of President Zine El Abidine Ben Ali 28 days later on 15 January 2011, when he officially resigned after fleeing to Saudi Arabia, ending 23 years in power. Al Jazeera English said of the action that it was 'suicidal protests of despair by Tunisia's youth' and reported that Tunisian activists were amongst the most outspoken in its part of the world with various messages of support being posted on Twitter for Bouazizi (Sadiki, 2010). Another cause for the uprising was attributed to the inability of the Tunisian government to censor information reaching the Tunisian people, such as information posted on whistle-blowing website Wikileaks (founded December 2006) describing rampant corruption in the Tunisian government. The role of user-generated content is highlighted further by blogger LaTulipe, who describes himself as a physician and a long-time libertarian writer and activist, and also an officer in the United States Air Force for 13 years:

> *Unfortunately for President Ben Ali, Julian Assange's Wikileaks had recently released an American diplomatic cable that described, in chapter and verse, the rampant corruption rotting its way through Tunisia. And, unfortunately for President Ben Ali, his people read all about it on the Web. . . . President Ben Ali's luck took another bad turn when Tunisian youths published accounts of Bouazizi's self-immolation on Facebook. And they didn't stop there. They proceeded to organize street protests using a variety of social network sites. The demonstrations spread like wildfire, morphing into a revolution that eventually forced Ben Ali to flee the country.*
> *(LaTulippe, 2011)*

Such protests quickly spread to other Middle Eastern countries, with calls for a 'day of rage' or 'day of anger' proliferating on Facebook in countries such as Iran, Syria, Yemen, Bahrain, Libya and Egypt – with varying impacts, depending upon the regime's ability to stamp out the protesters. The most successful protests were in Egypt, the people angry over high poverty, corruption, and fake parliamentary elections in November and December 2010 which virtually shut out any opposition players. Although the protesters were from all classes, the vanguard was the thousands of urban professionals, and university students – people that have typically shunned politics, seeing Egypt's stage-managed version as a waste of time. President Hosni Mubarak, in power since 1981, blamed the protests on agitators, and said that the protests had grown so loud only because he himself had magnanimously granted rights to free expression. However, in reality, the free expression was the result of new global information technologies such as satellite TV and the internet, that made it impossible for states such as Egypt to retain the information monopolies they once enjoyed. Certainly, as internet access in Egypt increased over the past decade, loosely related groups pressing for reform on issues such as labour rights, human rights and academic freedom emerged, run through the internet by youths of generally secular outlook, but no particular ideology. Some of these groups began studying other people-power movements – such as Serbia's – and began quietly organising for a similar campaign. When, in June 2010, plain-clothes agents in the Eygptian coastal city of Alexandria beat to death a young internet user, Khaled Said, a Facebook campaign prompted silent vigils across Egypt, drawing a wide audience for a 'day of rage' or 'day of anger' held on 25 January 2011. Tunisia's speedy and successful revolt had concentrated Egypt's dissident minds on one thing they could all agree on – that Mubarak should go (The *Economist*, 2011). As tens of thousands peacefully and continuously demonstrated in Cairo and Alexandria, on 30 January Mubarak shut down the internet, BlackBerry and mobile phone access in Egypt for five days, as well as closing down Al Jazeera. However, this did not stem the protests. Al Jazeera continued to tweet about developments on the ground and provide a live stream at its website, curating the social

Doing media studies

Analysing and evaluating your Indymedia

Find out your closest Indymedia website. (Look on Indymedia's home page (www.indymedia.org) for your country and city.)

Browse the website on a topic of your interest (e.g. globalisation), making a list of the number of stories in the past month, and also noting the source of the story.

Now go to the website of any corporate media news outlet. See how many stories there are on your selected topic over the same time period, and note the sources.

Based on your analysis, which of these news websites is the most informative and credible? What is the basis for your judgement?

media (Al Jazeera, 2011). By 11 February, Mubarak had resigned. Interestingly, other authoritarian regimes, such as China's, tried to prevent the dissemination of information regarding the Egyptian protests: China's state-run media has largely avoided commenting on the turmoil sweeping Egypt, and from January 2011, Chinese who search for 'Egypt' on micro-blogging websites were met with error messages (Couts, 2011; Schafer, 2011).

Studying the impact of global media – further themes and ideas

As you can now appreciate, scholars have taken a range of approaches to studying global media. This chapter has focused in particular on illustrative histories, taking a political-economy approach to global communication. There are many scholars, however, who focus more on the various impacts of global media, rather than on its production process, contexts and economics, some of which you have already been introduced to earlier in this chapter. To aid conceptual clarity, some of the main approaches and themes in studying and characterising the impact of global media are outlined below, and may provide inspiration for you in devising your own studies of the global media landscape.

A spur to development

Early studies explored the modernising role of Western media on agrarian, traditional societies, of the way that they stimulated 'development' through spreading literacy, communications skills and 'progressive' ideas and values (Lerner 1958; Lerner and Schramm, 1967). This role was often enshrined in UN communications programmes, such as the International Programme for the Development of Communication, established in 1980 to increase co-operation and help for developing communication infrastructures, so reducing the gaps between countries in the communication field (Volkmer, 1999).

Scholars have evaluated and criticised the assumption of the 'spur to development' – both morally for its disintegrative impact on national culture, and practically for the fact that it would impact upon the elite of developing countries without trickling down to the rest of the population.

The media and cultural imperialism of global conglomerates

Following the Second World War decolonisation processes produced a wave of interest from colonies in independence built upon home-grown nationalism. They sought independence not only in their political-economic structures but in their communication structures. Subsequently, and as we've seen, such countries have found themselves subjected to a new process of cultural colonisation through global media corporations. Here, classic studies include Schiller (1976, 1979) and Boyd (1977). Such studies argue that media conglomerates transform national media structures, as the heavy international traffic of commercial media products flowing from the centre to the periphery are the 'most prominent means by which weaker societies are absorbed culturally into the modern world system' (Schiller, 1979: 25).

The political effects of internationally or globally transmitted media productions

Approaches focusing on the political content of international communication originate from the enforcement of US foreign policy via the media (Volkmer, 1999). Here, analysis of stations like Radio Free Europe (www.rferl.org/) and Radio Marti (www.martinoticias. com/) explore the USA's attempts to convert the populations of nations with what appear to be particularly entrenched or objectionable values (communistic, religious, etc.) to the American way of life (Horten, 2002; Wood, 1992) – what Nye (2004) refers to as the exertion of 'soft power'.

Studies of large totalitarian nations (such as the USSR and China) focus on the propagandistic nature of their communications, designed to quell dissent and integrate diverse ethnicities and formerly separate nations into a particular national mould (Donald and Evans, 1999). The role of the BBC World Service has also been studied – although normally focusing on the impact of its status as a widely trusted broadcaster (Boyd, 1977; Skuse, 2002). For instance, Skuse's (2002) study of the sociohistorical role of radio in Afghanistan shows that the BBC's World Service is seen as far more trustworthy by the general population than the national radio station, Radio Afghanistan (which was tainted by the propagandistic media of the Communist era, ushered in by the revolution in 1978 that attempted to inculcate socialist nationalist unification), or the Taliban's Voice of Radio Shari'at. (The Taliban, having seized power in 1996, used radio to explain their policy, Shari'at law and the moral propriety expected of the public.)

The globalising cultural and social effects of globally transmitted media productions

Studies analyse and theorise the transnationality of media images in global and local terms. For instance, Barber's (1996) juxtaposition of McWorld versus Jihad illustrates two polar opposite types of impact. 'McWorld' is a label for the global economic bond in which we all participate through, for instance, consumption of global icons (like Princess Diana, whose funeral in 1997 was watched by 30 million in the USA alone), brands (McDonald's, Coca-Cola), and entertainment and information (such as the various global media forms we have looked at in this chapter). 'Jihad' consists of new and revived forms of nationalism and emotionally led collectivities, focused on things like political or religious ideologies, local territories or ethnic groups. Barber sees these two worlds as distinctive but interwoven in particular ways, shaping global reality in short bursts.

Other studies examine the role of global media in creating global ways of thinking and acting. Undoubtedly the most famous theorisation about the impact of global media comes from 1960s visionary Marshall McLuhan. Writing at a time when America had just experienced its first television war – Vietnam – McLuhan argues that the technical 'evolution' of media structures has extended the human nervous system. One of McLuhan's now famous metaphors is that of the 'global village' which expresses an idea of global togetherness and community, and is often cited in popular culture. In this quotation he alludes to the way in which media have challenged the limits of space and time through instant global communication, allowing a utopian moment for humanity to rethink itself beyond the blinkers of nations' geographical and cultural boundaries:

> *Ours is a brand-new world of allatonceness. 'Time' has ceased, 'space' has vanished. We now live in a global village . . . a simultaneous happening. We are back in acoustic space. We have begun again to structure the primordial feeling, the tribal emotions from which a few centuries of literacy divorced us.*

(McLuhan and Fiore, 1967: 63)

This utopianism became more pronounced, and by the 1980s McLuhan viewed the satellite era as one in which more and more people were able to enter the market of information exchange, losing their established (national) identities in the process, and emerging with the ability to interact with anyone in the world (McLuhan and Powers, 1989). Such ideas are suggestive of a global public sphere and, indeed, Volkmer's (1999) study of CNN finds structures that support the emergence of such a space. Volkmer posits an idea of a global human condition ('globality') and a new field of political action practised through global institutions like the UN and international non-governmental organisations (like Human Rights Watch). According to Volkmer (1999), this global civil society emerges from the availability of a worldwide audio-visual, satellite-transmitted 'communication platform', such as that delivered by CNN. This model, in tandem with a new human condition, implies international co-operation, affiliation and syndication structures, and news exchange systems (like globally operating news agencies), as well as a certain style of news language and presentation routines, which involve avoiding national stereotypes and placing news events in a larger regional, continental or global context. The internet, of course, moves forward the ideal of global civil society, still further. The social media-facilitated 'Arab Spring' of 2011, as a swathe of people from different Arab countries repeatedly organised themselves and demonstrated for democracy in their own countries, often in the face of harsh repression from their own leaders, suggests the potency of internet-based global media forms in generating a functioning global public sphere.

Heterogenerisation

Academics from the fields of anthropology and cultural studies, whose research is characterised by fieldwork and interviews, note the diverse results in how people use and interpret global media. This diversity occurs through hybridisation or, in other words, the ways in which media forms become separated from existing practices and recombine with new forms in new practices (Artz and Kamalipour, 2003; Lull, 1995; Pieterse, 1995; Semati, 2004).

Here, concepts like 'de-territorialisation' (Morley and Robins, 1995: 87) have been formulated. This described how individuals lose the sense of their 'natural' relation (through their identity, for instance) to the geographic and social territories where they originate or spend their lives. In a similar vein, 're-territorialisation' is where people try to re-establish a new cultural home wherever they go (Tomlinson, 1999: 148), or fuse imported traditions with resources in the new territory to create local versions of distant cultures (Lull, 1995).

Another relevant concept is 'indigenisation' (Appadurai, 1996), where globalised products are made or adjusted to fit the specificity of local places. For example, global media companies may indiginise their own products by hiring people with multicultural backgrounds and/or knowledge of the markets at which the products are targeted, so generating already-indiginised products when they enter the market; or by indiginising global products, such as certain TV formats, by using domestic actors – as with *Big Brother* (Rantanen, 2004).

All of these concepts are worth following up and thinking about as aids for making sense of the processes and consequences of globalisation. Among these approaches, we can discern elements of optimism and pessimism about what it means to live in a global economy, where cultures become more diffuse and shared. Behind any consideration you might give to these issues will be your own perspective and opinion, as consumer and citizen, of both the local and also the wider global community. Whatever the size of the scale presented to us when thinking about the global machinations of media companies and their impact, always bear in mind the local and the human.

Summary

Studying media production in a global age

In this chapter, we considered the global nature of media businesses and what it means to operate on a worldwide scale. We unpicked the historical development and political economy of certain key modes of global information, focusing on news, news-film, satellite news, online news, search engines, ISPs and global entertainment in the form of TV, radio, movies, music and social networking sites. We explored the ideals and reality of the free market economy in global media products, evaluating how national and international regulation and self-regulation impact on the global media landscape. Of particular importance here in illustrating this point was the controversy over the cartoons of the Muslim prophet Mohammed published in the Danish newspaper *Jyllands-Posten*. The consequences of one action in one society ordered by certain principles caused almost immediate ructions around the globe, although, if anything, this case presented us with the virtual impossibility of censoring material on the internet. Nonetheless, and as we saw, this has not stopped countries such as China, Pakistan and Egypt taking a variety of measures to halt the exchange of information online, undermining the sense of the internet as a global public sphere.

We explored and engaged with key academic debates on the cultural, political and economic significance of global media. We looked at the various forces and institutions effecting globalisation, looking into the CNN effect and how the rise of transnational satellite TV, for instance, exemplifies a tension between homogenisation (or a move towards sameness) and the maintenance of local character in global trends. Other institutions that we looked at are also sites for examining the dynamics of global production in the tensions between the mission of organisations such as UNESCO and those such as the WTO, that seek to liberalise markets in order to benefit companies in the pursuit of profit. Both promote visions of freedom in which the media play an important role. However, as we saw, while ideas such as freedom and democracy may be exportable in the global age, how they are manifested in the actions of transnational media companies and the forms and content they bring with their practices and values also raises concerns over cultural imperialism.

We looked at the flow of ideas around the world by examining the case of the Arabic TV station Al Jazeera in detail, looking at the role it plays in contemporary representations and the dissemination of a non-Western viewpoint of global events. Likewise, we considered the global phenomenon of Indymedia, which, with its democratic, collective character, offers alternative models of exchange and media activity in comparison with the great global media corporations. The role of the social networking site Facebook in organising radical social change in the Middle East perhaps best exemplifies the potential of the internet in the free flow of ideas.

We rounded up by itemising a number of themes that scholars have identified in making sense of the global nature of contemporary media production. These are all provocative and usable ideas that will aid you in making sense of global media production.

You should now evaluate what you are able to do as a result of this chapter. If you have followed the chapter through and engaged with the activities and thought about the issues covered, you should be able to do the following:

■ Demonstrate an understanding of the historical development and political economy of certain global media companies and global media forms. Of course, we have not covered and cannot cover everything and all detail. You yourself must continue to build your knowledge in this area. Look for other accounts and consider the sources we've drawn upon, as well as our narratives and perspectives: are they convincing?

■ Comprehend the role and complexity of the free market and national and international regulation in generating the global media landscape. These are complex ideas, and further information and insight can be gained outside our field. If you have an interest in these matters, go to the web addresses that appear throughout this chapter and read the financial pages and international affairs sections of newspapers or current affairs websites.

■ Understand and engage with key academic debates on the cultural, political and economic significance of global media. Understanding comes from engagement: where do you stand on these pressing issues? What are the arguments for and against globalisation? How can you find out about what others, around the world, are thinking about these issues – not just in the academic world?

■ Apply key concepts concerning global media to research into global media companies and media forms. Your ability to apply these ideas will depend upon your confident familiarity with the other points above and the degree to which you continue to ask questions of global media, formulating and following through your own research.

The issue is now to continue to explore the ideas and approaches presented in this chapter in your practice of media studies. Continue to think about how you might utilise and apply the various resources you are building up and how you might develop your own investigations into global media production.

Doing media studies

Investigating global media perspectives

Some of the means by which we are presented with the global character of the modern media industries and forms offer us a way of exploring its reach, meaning and value to the various communities it affects. Social networking sites such as Facebook offer a means of communicating with a global audience and asking questions about perspectives from the opposite side of the world on the use and dominance of such forms (and whether or not individuals are bothered about such things as global media ownership). Likewise, a site such as the Internet Movie Database (www.imdb.com/), while conducted in English, has contributions from moviegoers and TV viewers from across the world.

Such places offer ways of communicating with others and asking direct questions about the issues raised in this chapter. Does globalisation matter to you? What kinds of issues arise when media you think are local (offering local meanings, jobs, contributions to the economy) are owned and controlled by individuals across the globe?

Identify a media product, form or company and, using one of the sites mentioned above (or others), seek out perspectives on it from around the world, framed by these very questions. Raise questions about your media product and these processes in forums. Use your findings to map out a response to the issue of 'Does the globalised nature of the media matter?' Think about the kinds of impact such responses have on your view of these issues.

Further reading

De Jong, W., Shaw, M. and Stammers, N. (eds) (2005) *Global Activism. Global Media*, London: Pluto Press.

This edited book examines mediated communication related to social movements in the current era of cross-cultural contact. It offers an introduction to the way in which new social movements contribute to a global public sphere, and how they make use of mainstream and alternative media. It stands out from other books in that it puts the concerns of global media and global activism into a common frame of reference, and it encourages activism on the part of the reader.

Dorfman, A. and Mattelart, A. (1984) *How to Read Donald Duck: Imperialist Ideology in the Disney Comic* (2nd edn), New York: International General.

This, now classic, study shows how Disney's most profound political effect lies in the humorous, seemingly innocent way in which it constantly reaffirms American superiority and hegemony by representing the rest of the world as comical, backward stereotypes – similar to those used in an earlier age to justify colonialism.

Gerbner, G., Mowlana, H. and Nordenstreng, K. (eds) (1993) *The Global Media Debate: Its Rise, Fall and Renewal*, Norwood, NJ: Ablex.

This historically important book examines the debate about the role of the media in social, political and economic developments around the world – especially the Third World of Africa, Asia and Latin America. It looks at the debate's history, key documents (such as the Mass Media Declaration of UNESCO from 1978, resolutions of the UN Conference on Freedom of Information from 1948 and the resolution of the League of Nations from 1925) and interpretations across political, professional and academic circles.

Hackett, R.A. and Zhoa, Y. (eds) (2005) *Democratizing Global Media: One World, Many Struggles*, Lanham, MD: Rowman & Littlefield.

This edited book has contributions from both media researchers and journalists, and provides a wide range of empirical material on the processes and obstacles in media democratisation in different continents. There are three sections: media globalisation and democratic deficits (covering Eastern Europe, China, India, Africa and Latin America); media and democracy in global sites and conflicts (covering Israel, the USA and the role of advocacy groups in global media governance forums); and modalities of democratisation (including media reform in the USA, feminist activists, peace journalism and transnational advocacy for media reform).

Herman, E.S. and McChesney, R.W. (1997) *The Global Media: the New Missionaries of Corporate Capitalism*, London, Washington, DC: Cassell.

This book documents the origins and rise of global media, analysing the strategies and dynamics of the 10 largest transnational media conglomerates of the mid-1990s, and also evaluating alternative media of the era. It details the following points: that the accelerated development of global media increasingly shapes national media systems; that transnational media conglomerates (mostly US-based) dominate global media; that global media are pivotal to a globalising market economy by centralising media control in a narrow business elite whose offerings are shaped by advertisers' interests; and that these offerings erode the public sphere.

Lynch, M. (2006) *Voices of the New Arab Public: Iraq, al-Jazeera, and Middle East Politics Today*. New York: Columbia University Press.

Since the mid-1990s, Al Jazeera and other pan-Arab satellite television stations have transformed Arab politics. By shattering state control over information and giving a platform to long-stifled voices, these global Arab media forms have challenged the status quo by encouraging open debate about Iraq, Palestine, Islamism, Arab identity, and other vital political and social issues. Focusing on transnational media forms such as the pan-Arab press and pan-Arab satellite TV, Lynch addresses the intersection between the media and the prospects for social change. In an engaging and authoritative discussion of the true nature of the Arab media and opinion, Lynch asks whether an Arab public sphere can now be said to truly exist.

Ó Siochrú, S. and Girard, B. (2002) *Global Media Governance: a Beginner's Guide*, Oxford: Rowman & Littlefield.

This book discusses the need for global media regulation, and provides a cogent introduction to the various institutions that enable global media governance, including the UN, the ITU, the WTO (focusing on trade in media products), UNESCO, the WIPO and ICANN. The authors maintain a careful balance between dry, but necessary, institutional analysis and more engaging, critical, political analysis. While it lacks explicit theory to drive the analysis forward, it implicitly relies on a pluralist model of bargaining among powerful players.

Rantanen, T. (2005) *The Media and Globalisation*, London: Sage.

This is a brief but critical overview of theories of globalisation and the role of the media therein. It addresses the lack of attention to media, both theoretically and empirically, in academic discussions about globalisation, looking at both the production and consumption of media. It also introduces a new methodology for studying the role of individuals in mediated globalisation – 'global mediagraphy'. It develops the idea that individuals contribute to globalisation, through individual media activities which become social practices.

Thomas, P.N. and Nain, Z. (eds) (2004) *Who Owns the Media? Global Trends and Local Resistances,* London and New York: Zed Books.

This edited collection focuses on the political economy of communications, discussing national and global trends within a framework of deregulation, reregulation and privatisation. The book discusses key institutions, such as global media governance structures and IPR regimes; the role of the media in the global economy and in political democracy; neo-liberal policies; the impact of media industry regulation in a market economy; the role of transnational advocacy groups; and research priorities, here illuminating some of the blind spots in mainstream media analysis. Most of the book is devoted to detailed regional and national case studies of media ownership across a range of continents.

Volkmer, I. (1999) *News in the Global Sphere: a Study of CNN and its Impact on Global Communication,* Luton: University of Luton Press.

This study usefully distinguishes between transnational media and global media, elucidating a range of theories therein. It offers a history of satellite broadcasting and an in-depth analysis of CNN in particular, through interviews with CNN staff and content analysis of CNN programming. Through this case study, it posits that global communication enables a global, as opposed to a national, civil society. For instance, the particular becomes universal, in that different 'local' stories (such as human rights abuses) become global concerns.

PART THREE

MEDIA
AUDIENCES

In the previous parts of this book, we considered media output in terms of textual meanings and how to make sense of these meanings, as well as aspects of production and the frameworks of regulation that impact upon media businesses in a global context. We now turn to consider the nature of media audiences who are the object of media businesses and who make sense of media meanings.

The first chapter in this part considers the proposition that audiences are a product of media businesses, a conceptual and economic object of economic interest and marketing strategies. In that audiences are therefore objects of media attention upon which businesses seek to act, we consider also the assumptions, roots and theoretical underpinnings behind fears that media produce effects in their consumers. This, then, is broadly an approach that sees media as doing things to people.

The second chapter investigates how audiences have been studied in terms of what they do with media and the meanings and resources that they take from the various forms. In this exploration, we will therefore outline a series of methods and considerations that will be useful in pursuing your own research into what we call the active audience.

Chapters in this part:

Chapter 8: Producing audiences: what do media do to people?

Examines ways of thinking about how audiences are produced by media organisations and how theorists have thought about the effects of media meanings on groups and individuals

Chapter 9: Investigating audiences: what do people do with media?

Extends the approach of the previous chapter to consider how people make use of media and media meanings in ways beyond the allotted role of audiences as consumers

CHAPTER 8

Producing audiences: what do media do to people?

Thinking about audiences

From the National Institute on Media and the Family (www.mediafamily.org/facts/facts_mediaeffect.shtml).

Media's effect on girls: body image and gender identity

Did you know? Gender identity begins in toddlerhood (identifying self as a girl or boy), with gender roles being assigned to tasks early in the preschool years (Durkin and Nugent, 1998).

[...]

Media's effect on body image

The popular media (television, movies, magazines, etc.) have, since the Second World War, increasingly held up a thinner and thinner body (and now ever more physically fit) image as the ideal for women. The ideal man is also presented as trim, but muscular.

- In a survey of girls 9 and 10 years old, 40 per cent have tried to lose weight, according to an ongoing study funded by the National Heart, Lung and Blood Institute (*USA Today*, 1996).
- A 1996 study found that the amount of time an adolescent watches soaps, movies and music videos is associated with their degree of body dissatisfaction and desire to be thin (Tiggemann and Pickering, 1996).

- One author reports that, at age 13, 53 per cent of American girls are 'unhappy with their bodies'. This grows to 78 per cent by the time girls reach 17 (Brumberg, 1997).
- In a study among undergraduates, media consumption was positively associated with a drive for thinness among men and body dissatisfaction among women (Harrison and Cantor, 1997).
- Teenage girls who viewed commercials depicting women who modelled the unrealistically thin-ideal type of beauty felt less confident, more angry and more dissatisfied with their weight and appearance (Hargreaves, 2002).
- In a study on fifth-graders, 10-year-old girls and boys told researchers they were dissatisfied with their own bodies after watching a music video by Britney Spears or a clip from the TV show *Friends* (Mundell, 2002).
- In another recent study on media's impact on adolescent body dissatisfaction, two researchers found that:

  1. Teens who watched soaps and TV shows that emphasised the ideal body types reported a higher sense of body dissatisfaction. This was also true for girls who watched music videos.

  2. Reading magazines for teen girls or women also correlated with body dissatisfaction for girls.

  3. Identification with TV stars (for girls and boys), and models (girls) or athletes (boys), positively correlated with body dissatisfaction (Hofschire and Greenberg, 2002).

Sources: Brumberg, J.J. (1997) *The Body Project: an Intimate History of American Girls*. New York: Random House; Durkin, K. and Nugent, B. (1998) 'Kindergarten children's gender-role expectations for television actors', *Sex Roles: A Journal of Research*, 38, 387–403; Hargreaves, D. (2002) 'Idealized women in TV ads make girls feel bad', *Journal of Social and Clinical Psychology*, 21, 287–308; Harrison, K. and Cantor, J. (1997) 'The relationship between media consumption and eating disorders', *Journal of Communication*, 47, 40–67; Hofschire, L.J. and Greenberg, B.S. (2002) 'Media's impact on adolescents' body dissatisfaction', in J.D. Brown, J.R. Steele, and K. Walsh-Childers (eds) *Sexual Teens, Sexual Media*. NJ: Lawrence Erlbaum Associates, Inc; Mundell, E.J. (2002) 'Sitcoms, Videos Make Even Fifth-Graders Feel Fat', Reuters Health (visited 16 September 2002); Signorielli, N. (1997) 'Reflections of girls in the media: a two-part study on gender and media', Kaiser Family Foundation and Children NOW (visited 6 September 2002); Sobieraj, S. (1996) 'Beauty and the beast: toy commercials and the social construction of gender', *Sociological Abstracts*, 044, American Sociological Association; Thompson, T. and Zerbinos, E. (1997)

'Television cartoons: do children notice it's a boy's world?', *Sex Roles: A Journal of Research*, 37, 415–33; Tiggemann, M. and Pickering, A.S. (1996) 'Role of television in adolescent women's body dissatisfaction and drive for thinness', *International Journal of Eating Disorders*, 20, 199–203; *USA Today* (1996) 12 August, p. 01D.

This extract and the survey of work it presents is indicative of a range of ideas for thinking about media that go way beyond the confines of academia. Discussing media and its audiences in terms of 'effects', 'influence', 'behaviour' and so on has a rich and influential history, with its own approaches and assumptions. Many of the assumptions are clearly based in worries about those who consume media, for instance, those '10-year-old girls and boys' who 'told researchers they were dissatisfied with their own bodies after watching a music video by Britney Spears or a clip from the TV show *Friends*'. However, what does it mean to conduct such research? What precedents inform such instances and what ideas about audiences do they work with and produce?

What we will do in this chapter

Drawing upon ideas developed elsewhere in this book, on textual address, meaning and institutions, we will concentrate here on an exploration of how media produce audiences. We also look at the way that the ideas of some of those who have studied media also produced another sense of the audience, as the subject of media messages and manipulations. That is, they focused on the idea that media 'do' things to their consumers or audiences.

It is certainly unusual in media studies textbooks to combine these two senses of audience but it allows us to break down the obviousness of the concept of the audience, and to unpack many of the assumptions made about the relationship between media and the people who consume their texts. By considering some of the ways in which audiences are conceptualised and researched by media companies initially, we will be able to tease out the 'constructedness' of this idea. Right from the start, we will explore the idea that audiences are themselves products of media operations and texts. We will also address a preoccupation with 'media effects' and 'influence' that is often found at the heart of discussions of the role of media in our societies. We will suggest that these are a 'construction' of earlier attempts to understand media and audience relations.

Once we have unpicked these ideas, and their 'common sense' assumptions about the passive qualities of media audiences, we can move on to what we consider to be a more sophisticated and fruitful understanding of the relationship of media and society, as well as asking the more active question: what do people do with media?

By the end of this chapter you should be able to:

■ Discuss and critique common sense ideas of the audience.

■ Identify ways in which it can be said media organisations produce audiences.

■ Identify ways in which it can be said media scholars produce media audiences.

■ Discuss and critique the ways in which propaganda and media violence have been addressed in both media and media scholarship.

■ Explore the extent to which ideas of the audience and of media effects are linked to 'moral panics'.

KEY TERMS: ▶ audience; hypodermic model; media effects and influence; moral panic; passivity; propaganda; social and historical position.

What is an audience?

In proceeding we should note that, for our purposes, audience is used here as a synonym for viewers of TV shows, photographs and film, readers of the press, listeners to radio and podcasts, online media users, video gamers and so on. We should, of course, bear in mind both the differences and the similarities between these different ways of being an audience. Media audiences and their experiences as audiences, while being an object of research for media scholars, are equally an object of speculation, opinion and, indeed, research by, among others, educationalists, pressure groups, politicians, media commentators and audience members themselves, as well as, importantly, media institutions in their role as businesses. The mass communication theorist Dennis McQuail has even gone as far as to suggest that the very consumption and interaction with mass media constitutes 'a mark, and possibly even a requirement of membership of modern society' (McQuail, 1969: 163). This consumption and interaction is so significant that it has merited varied investigations and speculations, which have produced a wide range of traditions and approaches.

What an audience is might seem very obvious; common sense, in fact. As we have done elsewhere in this book, however, we need to rethink the 'common-sense' quality of so much that we take for granted in discussions about media. Here, we need to think about the nature of audiences as audiences, the literalness and quality of being 'in the act' of consuming media products, the ways in which we are invited to consume, and why we seek out various forms of television, radio, music, journalism and so on. The act of consuming media presents us with observable actions, feelings and relationships with media forms, at the individual and group levels, which we can understand in conceptual and theoretical terms.

Often – at a music concert, for instance, or at the movies – the quality of being part of an audience is a tangible thing due to the presence of all of the other living, breathing members around us. Our sense of being an audience member is usually equally 'obvious' when we are part of the viewing public for a TV show or listeners to radio because the rhetoric of so much media output appears to address us directly. Presenters will sometimes speak 'to all of our listeners', or appeal to 'you lot at home', for instance.

On the other hand, this obviousness becomes problematic when we give some thought to how and when we are *not* part of an audience. Our non-audience status is most noticeable when we are turned *off* by particular content ('Science fiction? Ugh?'), or when there is a direct address from media to 'us' ('Streaming video of hunky guys for fun girls!'), but when this address does not seem to include us, and may in fact exclude and alienate us (sometimes intentionally). On these occasions, we seem aware of not being addressed and encompassed in the audience.

Media output and consumption

Based on your thoughts about our case study of the Wonderbra advert, you can see that we can start to make distinctions between senses of our place in an audience depending upon whether we are talking about what a media product means, how we are exposed to it or what financial relationship we may have to it.

We can categorise these different senses of the nature of the audience by returning to the categories of media products we set out previously, in the guise of artefact, commodity and text.

Media product	Media audience (defined as)
As artefact	Owner, purchaser, subscriber, listener, viewer, spectator, reader, user, player
As commodity	Market, consumer
As text	Receiver, reader, interpreter, spectator, respondent

We can recognise that some terms used here cross over categories but the relationship they describe and demarcate is very specific and separate in this outline. However, as we have suggested in earlier discussions of this three-tiered model, the separation is functional so as to aid initial understanding (p. 30). As media users, we may simultaneously relate to a media product in terms of its meaning, financial value and physical properties, or we may be excluded at one or more of these levels. Everyone who looks at the Wonderbra advert experiences it as a spectator, and most of us will read the image and the writing, but it is possible that we will interpret it in different ways. Only a small proportion of us will be addressed as a consumer of the product advertised, however. Collectively, those of us addressed as the consumers of the product will constitute its market.

We should briefly explore what the categories above mean for thinking about the relationship of media products and audiences in order to identify where and why the focus of scholars lies. Media studies scholars have tended not to concentrate on the relationship of the audience with the artefactual aspect of media products. This is perhaps owing to the apparent banality of the status and 'process' of owning, acquiring or apprehending physical things as things. We can own a media product as record collectors, see a TV show or webcast that exists in time and space as viewers, listen to radio and so on. However, it seems that, without address to textual meaning, this 'ownership' and physical engagement offer us little insight other than noting that some consumers own lots of media artefacts, and are particularly attached to them as artefacts (see the discussion of fans in the next chapter), while others consume and discard media artefacts without any particular allegiance or desire for permanence – thus demonstrating the ephemeral aspects of media. I might buy a newspaper, read it and then throw it away or buy a CD, listen to it for several days and then barely bother with it again. That said, of course, our relationship with the physicality of media artefacts does have some direct pertinence to our actions and behaviour as consumers. For instance, we find ourselves in particular places in order to consume media forms (cinemas, dance clubs, etc.), adhering to regimented habits in order to consume or 'fit' certain media forms into our lives (e.g. listening to live morning radio shows with our breakfast, getting a free newspaper on the way to college or work).

Relations with the economic or commodity form of media products have proven to be of more interest to scholars in making sense of audiences. We might pinpoint the range of charges and costs for goods or, indeed, the avoidance of costs and charges – witness file sharing and 'piracy' of digital music. Likewise, we can explore the popularity of goods as expressed through widespread purchase – box office or chart hits, for instance – or, conversely, we might consider mass rejection of media products expressed in economic terms – box office disasters, failing newspapers, bankrupt rock stars and so on. Similarly, we can consider how audiences are targeted as part of specific markets, mass or niche, defined through geography, ethnicity, gender and so on. All of these ideas are part and parcel of what makes this an area of interest. As we asserted in Chapter 5, media institutions are first and foremost businesses that contribute to economies through their relationship with audiences, and the size and nature of this aspect of economic activity demands our attention. That said, this area is also of significance and of more interest than the economy of, say, sales of socks, because of the wealth of symbolic meanings involved in our purchase and consumption of media products.

As we have seen in our earlier chapters, the primary focus of media studies has been with textual meanings and this focus thus conceives of the audience as receiver, reader or interpreter of those meanings. We can identify two broad assumptions about the relationship of media and audience texts, therefore. We can think of what media forms do to people through their meanings and what people do with these forms and meanings.

The first idea is based upon a model in which media forms operate as intervening vessels in getting messages and meaning from sender to receiver, producing results or effects determined by the message. The second, very broadly related to semiological and rhetorical models, is one in which the medium itself is important in inflecting the message,

Doing media studies

Conceptualising the audience

Sometimes it is just not immediately obvious who is supposed to be the audience. Consider, for instance, the famous (perhaps infamous) advertisement for the 1994 'Wonderbra' campaign. This advert seems to have been consciously constructed to confuse if one asks, 'Who is being addressed by whom?' At one level it captures the image of a woman in her underwear looking down, and the writing by the side seems to suggest that either the woman or the advert (or both) is speaking. It is less clear who is being spoken to. Is the woman talking to herself, exclaiming at the prominence of her uplifted cleavage? Is the advert talking to a male onlooker, expressing the conventional attractiveness of the woman to a male gaze (Gill, 2008)? Because it is an advert, we know it is ultimately addressing the target consumers for the products being promoted. In this case, the advert addresses women, to whom the advertiser wants to sell bras. Is it that this is a clever, ironic ploy? Does the advert play to women's vanity? Or is it an expression of *this* woman's confidence, as she presents herself in this sexualised manner?

Just in case you were in doubt, the 'wit' of the advert is based upon the focus on the model's breasts. She speaks to us, but of course the model is not the author of her own words, state of undress, posture or pose. We may actually read the advert in many different ways, making explicit value judgements about the product offered for sale, or the woman depicted, or the sexual politics that allowed it to be made. We actually know very little about who actually looked at this advert, or how they interpreted it, and indeed how, if at all, they acted upon it.

It is helpful to jot down your own reactions to this advert in bullet-point form, based upon the following questions:

- Allowing for its dated quality, is the advert aimed at you?
- If not, why not?
- Is your particular response down to your gender?
- What kinds of response does it 'produce' in you – does it elicit any reaction at all?
- What other instances are you able to identify in your media consumption of feeling 'in' or part of the intended audience or otherwise?
- Does it matter when you are not?

Source: Advertising Archives

Who is this advert aimed at? What is its audience?

one where the audience has a role, implying some kind of interpretative act and guise as 'reader'.

The first model tends to relate to what we describe as 'mass society' perspectives and approaches, in which **audience** members are often understood (intentionally or by default) as the passive receptacles for these messages and the kinds of beliefs, activities and behaviour that they engender (see Chapter 11). In fact, you will often find that audiences are referred to in such perspectives as if the constituent individuals were undifferentiated, a singular body – a 'mass' – or a product of the broad address of media texts themselves. Such perspectives tend to expose assumptions and value judgements of audiences. Thus, when we hear of 'couch potatoes', 'dittoheads' or 'TV addicts', or when commentators opine on the screaming crowds at boy band gigs or 'mindless' clubbers or 'gameboy addicts' we are in the same territory.

The second model, which forms the basis of the next chapter, informs the manner in which researchers have pursued evidence of audience 'activity'. This model takes a broad view of media products and their meanings as in some way determined by consumers themselves, rather than being products full of meanings simply imposed on them externally. As we will see, the supposition here is that, even if media products were simply formulated by producers without a thought about the needs and preferences of the individuals who make up the audience, 'we' do not always do what we are supposed to do with these texts!

Media organisations produce audiences

At some times then, we all find ourselves to be part of an audience, even if we do not necessarily think of ourselves as a member of any one audience specifically. The latter point is particularly important as, in many moments of media consumption, we are blissfully unaware of all of those other individuals – who may number millions, perhaps billions on occasion (televised opening ceremonies for the Olympic Games or football world cup for instance) – who have shared, will share, or simultaneously are sharing our experience of engaging with the media. Sometimes we are addressed and positioned by media organs as a member of a group – the radio DJ's 'Hello, listeners', the tabloid newspaper's 'To all of our readers' – and sometimes, implicitly or explicitly, as an individual – again, the DJ's intimate and rhetorical 'Hi! How are YOU doing?'

Dennis McQuail has written of the 'duality' of audiences as both a 'response' to media and an entity that corresponds to an existing social group or category (McQuail, 1997). McQuail's idea of 'response' here is something more than the kind of rhetorical one we have explored elsewhere; for example, the thrills, laughter and emotion we express in the hands of texts and the pleasures they give us. McQuail talks of the audience as a 'temporary aggregate', a collection of individuals whose position is momentarily determined by a common experience of a media form and 'event'. This, in turn, raises questions about how we think about the nature of the audience as a collective in terms of its location and behaviour during the said 'event'. For instance, during a pop concert individuals within a venue are bonded in one physical space, experiencing the same 'performance' (live) during the same time, but they may react in a variety of ways. Other audiences may be harder to locate; for example, 'YouTube' viewers, across the globe, logging on at different times and dates offer a different spatial and temporal dimension of the shared experience of being an audience. When millions of people watch television at the same time, they are 'together' in terms of their experience of viewing but are diffusely spread out in the locations where viewing takes place.

When we think of the audience in terms of an existing social group or category, we identify its members in terms of how race, gender, ethnicity, nation, class or religion may be a factor in responding to the address of a text. By way of example, we can think of the titles

Audience

For our purposes an audience can be defined as an anonymous and variable collective of individuals addressed, as a group and as individuals, by the organs of 'mass' media communication.

given to magazines and newspapers – *Gay Times, Woman's Own, Elle, Asian Bride, Daily Worker, Ebony, Deutsche Zeitung, Playboy* and so on. You don't have to be gay, a woman, a betrothed Asian woman, a 'worker', a black woman, German or a 'playboy' in order to read these, but there is a sense in which a specific yet broadly defined group is mobilised by each title.

As we have seen in our chapter on media businesses, one claim put forward by theorist Dallas Smythe (p. 175) suggests that media companies are best thought of not as producers of artefacts but as producers of audiences. The theorist and TV researcher Ien Ang has offered a useful way of understanding the consequences of this idea, arguing that the audience is primarily a concept born of media institutions. She points out that before the existence of the press, television, cinema, etc. there were no newspaper readers, TV viewers or cinema-goers! Even though people were sometimes constituted as part of some form of audience for other pre-media events, such as being part of a religious congregation, for instance, or as part of an audience for theatrical performances or sporting events, their constitution, activities and preferences *as* media audiences were not preordained, 'awaiting' the invention of television, film, radio and so on.

Ang offers a definition of the audience that makes a distinction between the sense of a literal body of individuals who all engage in a common pursuit around media consumption and a conceptual category, 'an imaginary entity, an abstraction constructed from the vantage point of the institutions' (Ang, 1990: 4). This idea itself is derived from the way in which media institutions operate. The measurement and conceptualisation of the who, what and why of audiences is vital to the business of media, in order that they might be delivered to advertisers. In the case of public service companies like NRK in Norway or ORF in Austria, audiences are also conceptualised as a means of justifying the input of funds or the levying of supporting taxes.

By way of illustration, here is an extract from a research report presented for the benefit of potential advertisers seeking to reach audiences via the Microsoft website (msn.com). It enlists the imaginary entity of 'digital families' in order to map out generalised online consumption activity.

Children boost their parents' web use

The internet is taking an increasingly central role in family life across Europe, with families going online more often and exploring a far broader range of web activities than those without children. The report makes it clear that internet marketing solutions should take account of children's influence when targeting campaigns at their parents.

The 'Digital Families' report from the European Interactive Advertising Association's Mediascope survey shows that 73 per cent of those living with children log onto the internet each week, versus 52 per cent for those living without. These 'digital parents' are also rapidly increasing the amount of time they spend online, with the European average now standing at 11.6 hours per week. Over a quarter (27 per cent) are now classed as 'heavy' web users, spending over 16 hours each week online.

Key thinker

Ien Ang (1954–)

Ien Ang is a Dutch scholar now based in Australia. The works which established her reputation explored the nature of TV audiences in two contrasting ways. First, through their qualities as 'products' of institutions. Secondly, in the way in which direct exploration of their responses as individuals reveals people engaged in active, responsive viewing. Our own approach to conceptualising the audience as something more than a 'common-sense' entity is directed by her suggestively titled study *Desperately Seeking the Audience* (Ang, 1990). See also *Watching Dallas: Soap Opera and the Melodramatic Imagination* (Ang, 1985) and *Living Room Wars: Rethinking Media Audiences for a Postmodern World* (Ang, 1996).

The sites and activities prioritised by digital families vary considerably with the age of their children, a key finding for those planning internet marketing solutions. Those with younger families are heavy users of health-related websites, whilst gaming sites become more important for those with children aged between five and nine. Older children have a substantial impact on their parents' web use, leading to increased use of services such as instant messenger and video sites. Of those living with children aged 16–18, 47 per cent used instant messaging, whilst 40 per cent watched TV, movie or video clips online.

Source: http://advertising.microsoft.com/uk/internet-research-children-boost-parents-web-use,
Research Report, 5 January 2008

Of course, audiences are more than a 'concept', and media institutions therefore depend upon the actual individuals who make up their audiences. In this recognition lies the fact that they need them and need to know about them. In exploring this point, Ang enlists ideas put forward by John Hartley who, in thinking of television in particular, writes that media institutions do not just determine and order audiences by their operations but are 'obliged not only to speak *about* an audience but – crucially, for them – to talk *to* one as well: they need not only to represent audiences but to enter into *relations* with them' (Hartley, 1987: 127).

Case Study

The audience as 'abstraction'

→ By way of illustration of the audience envisaged as a product of media institutions, as a generalised 'abstraction' to be sold to advertisers, here is an extract from the website of the men's magazine *Playboy*. This gives a sense of how the magazine's managers envisage its audience via a demographic breakdown.

Reflect for a moment on this information. A traditional stereotype of readers of pornography is that of 'dirty old men' but Hugh Hefner's magazine was instrumental in making this genre widely acceptable, respectable even, by couching the consumption of its core material in ideas of sophisticated masculinity. The magazine presents its advertisers with evidence to support its image and needs particular kinds of advertisers to maintain that image, claiming that '*Playboy* is a lifestyle, an aspiration, a state of mind and a platform of ideas shared by great thinkers and regular guys alike.'

Based upon this outline we could ask what kinds of advertisers are likely to be interested in this readership? What other kinds of information would be required by advertisers in order to support such claims? Are all *Playboy* readers likely to be captured by these descriptions (being a 'regular guy' doesn't seem to encompass the 19% of readers who are women)? What kinds of limitations are presented by this list or what kinds of reservations might present themselves to advertisers interested in reaching the *Playboy* demographic?

Male	81%		
Female	19%		
age 18-34	50%		
age 35+	50%		
Median age	36		
HHi $50,000 +	56%		
HHi $75,000 +	35%		
HHi $100,000 +	22%		
Median HHi	$55,620		
Married	38%	*Single*	46%
Employed	65%	*Student**	7%

*Currently attending college/university
Source: MRI, Spring 2011
HHI = household income.

Source: www.playboy.com/advertise

Table 8.1 Playboy magazine demographics

The relations Hartley speaks of are not easy to assess or control given the millions of varied individuals out there but, he suggests, institutions therefore produce 'invisible fictions' about audiences. These are constructions of such groups, their wants, needs and preferences, based upon details of the preferences of actual people but generalised to apply to the broader, anonymous many. The point is that media institutions are not ultimately interested in the audience as individuals, *per se* – as complex, social animals – but rather in objectified entities as they pertain to satisfying institutional commercial needs.

Media companies then produce 'interested' knowledge about audiences. This knowledge is described as 'interested' as it is not produced out of intellectual curiosity but because it has a more instrumental purpose. It is related to the desire to control, direct and sell audiences, just as much as those institutions might purport to respond to audience desires and needs ('we give our subscribers what they want'). Of course, the desire to attract, control and direct audiences has always been an urgent feature of a media market defined by commercial competition. However, if we take the example of television as Ien Ang does, there are clearly dangers inherent in the development of technologies that allow 'zapping', i.e. instantly turning to other channels, thus undermining the need to maintain interest and commitment to any one show, let alone channel. Websites with endless hypertext links have this quality built into them. Given the competition for attention and expendable income, no media business organisation can afford to avoid 'knowing' and planning for its audience if it wishes to at least maintain if not expand the numbers.

One way of seeing audiences, then, is as the product or effective outcome of the planning and marketing strategies of media organisations. Organisations seek to control and avoid risk via market research in order to anticipate and serve demand. As the media research company Ipsos declares on its website for the benefit of its potential clients, 'Nobody's unpredictable' (www.ipsos.com). However, in order to make this claim with such confidence, Ipsos and its media employers expend a lot of time, effort, money and ingenuity in finding out what people want, but also seek to develop available product to meet perceived needs. Thus, from your set-top box to online usage and retail purchases, what you do is tracked and contributes to data not only about general audience use but your own preferences as an individual within this aggregate, and it is against the wider aggregate that you can be evaluated and in part directed to consume ('Customers who bought *Tiny Tempah* also bought . . .') (see also Chapter 13). Whether you do or do not act predictably, of course, is another matter.

As creative, economic entities, the managers of media companies clearly have every faith in their track record and ability to innovate and maintain content and services. They work at attracting and directing audiences to their product in an almost scientific manner, although they can never rest in case they get things wrong. And, of course, they do get things wrong – often! Films flop, many, if not most, pop songs fail, audience members turn over or turn off the set if yet another reality-talent TV show appears on screen when they've had enough of them. Such unintended

Doing media studies

Locate and explore the following audience research company sites:

- Ipsos (www.ipsos.com)
- Radio Joint Audience Research (www.rajar.co.uk/)
- Nielsen (www.nielsen.com/)
- Media Mark Research Inc (www.mediamark.com/).

Write a short analytical report on one of the companies, identifying:

a. what range of services they provide and how they work;

b. which media sector they work with (naming specific media companies);

c. what kind of information about audiences they provide;

d. the uses that this information might be put to by media studies scholars, outlining any possible limitations with the approaches in evidence.

consequences in the face of media might set up some useful speculations about the assumptions that lie behind productions of the audience – that people do not always quite fit the model produced. This observation might have something to add to the next idea under consideration: that media scholars in their research also produce audiences, or at least ideas of audiences.

Media scholars produce audiences

Just as we can think of audiences as constructed when media organisations make products and target them at certain consumers, we can also think of ideas of the audience as being produced through the ways that media scholars have conceived of, and researched, them.

When people first became interested in studying media (in the early part of the twentieth century) very little attention was given to thinking through what people actually did with the various media that they consumed. This is mainly because they were focused on issues that seemed far more pressing and obvious. Mass communications media seemed to be part of dramatic changes in society, and the development of what is usually called 'mass society' (see Chapter 11). As scholars have become more interested in media audiences and their activities, there has been a tendency to over-simplify some of this earlier work. Most often, histories of media scholarship use a simple story about reactions to the development of mass media, resulting in a preoccupation with 'media effects'. This label suggests that scholars began with a simple idea of media 'messages' that produced observable effects in audiences. The story then moves to a point at which scholars considered a slightly more complex idea that there are intervening factors in the way in which media messages reach and 'affect' us, before ending with a more ambiguous and sometimes celebratory idea that audiences are active, empowered people who do things with media. While this narrative is a broadly useful basis from which to think about developments in research into media, it also tends to suggest that early media scholars worked with a very limited conception of media and their relationship with people. These approaches are often presented as positing 'hypodermic models' of communication, suggesting that media messages were thought to act like injections of a behaviour-changing drug into our bodies. These are also sometimes called 'magic bullet' or 'silver bullet' theories. There are, however, studies using experimental research which suggest that watching violence in the cinema leads to violent behaviour, for instance Jowett *et al.* (1996). Reading many of these studies today, they often seem naïve and, in attempting to focus on the direct relationship between viewing and behaviour, they miss so many of the important cultural factors involved in that relationship (see Barker and Petley, 1997). This is, in fact, a recurring criticism of attempts to make sense of media 'effects' on audiences, as our discussion of the work of David Gauntlett (below) suggests.

Equally, categorising all the work that looked at this relationship as part of a media-effects school of research is also mistaken. If we put ourselves back into the early decades of the twentieth century, we can see that the new media scholars had a major job on their hands. They wanted to research and theorise a new social phenomenon, but they did not have any existing concepts or reliable approaches with which to undertake the study. Perhaps, therefore, the work conducted at this time says more about the social and historical location of the theorists and researchers than it does about the things they wanted to study. Scholars were part of a growing social group of intellectuals who worked in the expanding universities and state organisations of the USA and European countries in particular. They valued certain forms of thinking, based upon careful study and evidence, but they worried that people outside their own educated group were vulnerable to emotional appeals, and that once manipulated they could be persuaded to believe anything and behave in ways that benefited other people. Given that the first 40 years of the twentieth century had seen the rise of a powerful Soviet state in Russia, Nazi and fascist governments in much of Europe, and powerful commercial corporations in North America that actively sought to employ mass media to realise their objectives, such fears were not groundless. Some of this context is explored in the discussion of propaganda below.

One of the primary tasks of the first generations of media scholars was to try to conceptualise the process of communication through which media and audiences are connected. Looking back, we tend to call these early attempts process, or transmission, models of communication because they use the common-sense notion that communication involves sending a message from one person to another (or to a large audience) through a medium of communication. Again, though, we tend to ignore the reason that the theorists and researchers developed such ideas. Perhaps the most widely cited example is the model devised by Shannon and Weaver (1949), and adapted by Gerbner, Gross and Melody (1973). We need to understand that Shannon and Weaver were telephone engineers trying to work out how much the quality of the then quite primitive lines needed to be improved for customers to hold effective conversations. Gerbner's particular theories of media seem less generally applicable when his own background in journalism and his interest in political persuasion are taken into account.

Perhaps the most important lesson to learn from this early work is that the way we conceive of the object of study is heavily influenced by what we want to find out. For this reason, the first phase of 'media effects' theories usually focused on research or theoretical work that aimed to explore how people's behaviour is changed by their exposure to media. It is certainly clear that there was a common theme that ran through much early media scholarship, and this reflected widespread concerns about how newly prominent media forms would impact on society (Chaffee and Hockheimer, 1985). First, these focused on the arrival of moving pictures in the cinema, then on radio (and sometimes recorded popular music), then television and advertising, then home videos, and more recently computer games and the internet. This pattern suggests that the concerns of researchers and media theorists had less to do with the audiences, and more to do with the appearance

Thinking aloud

Media effects?

What is a media effect? For a start, consider how we respond to music that gets the toes tapping or pulls at the heartstrings, or films that might make us laugh, cry or become scared. These are emotional, physiological, psychological reactions that we have described as affective responses (p. 34). Every time the hairs on your neck rise while watching a movie or hearing a piece of music, this response attests to the power of media forms and the rhetorical manipulation of their communication strategies.

However, such immediate sensations – often pleasurable – lead some to make claims about the endurance of such responses and their translation into other activities and behaviour beyond the moment of consumption. For instance, how might our long-term political affiliations be affected by how current affairs, political ideas and public figures are managed and represented in the media? What about the choices we will make in the supermarket about what to buy (as well as the choice of supermarket itself), after watching, reading and listening to a barrage of adverts for products? Indeed, given the integration of all mass media and communication forms in our everyday lives, is it not worth considering whether or not we as individuals might be more aggressive, individualised and noticeably more inattentive learners than our ancestors were before video games, or television, or horror films, or newspapers, or the printing press? All of these issues have been explored on occasion through the frame of media effects and influence – as well as claims that populations in general are more liberal, liberated, individualised and acquisitive than they once were – as a basis for both celebration and complaint by turn.

of any new medium, with some wider concerns with political change and control, social communication and behaviour, or with the very state of society.

Contextualising 'media effects' research

Perhaps the most widely quoted question directing the study of early mass media is Harold Lasswell's (1948): 'Who, says what, through what channel, to whom, with what effect?' Obviously the statement nicely combines a transmission model of media and the idea of media effects that we have discussed so far, but if we set Lasswell's question in the wider context of the university he was working in, and the problems he was grappling with, we get a different picture entirely. Far from getting his fellow scholars to focus on media effects as it seems to suggest, Lasswell's statement encouraged a vast range of studies which collectively represented a major leap in media scholarship (Lazarsfeld, 1940; Lazarsfeld and Stanton, 1941, 1944).

Lasswell was part of a wider group of researchers based at Princeton University and involved in the Radio Project, which was established in 1937 in an attempt to explore all aspects of the then relatively new medium of over-the-air radio. Led by Paul Lazarsfeld, it included, among others, influential media scholars Theodor Adorno (p. 380) and Hardy Cantril, as well as Frank Stanton, who went on to run one of the US's major radio networks, CBS. These scholars produced some diverse work, much of it hugely influential: Lazarsfeld is usually seen as the first to develop focus groups as a research method (Morrison, 1998) (and see p. 334), and Adorno's studies of music and radio were developed during this time (1941/1990, 1945, 1967). Lasswell himself contributed seminal work on propaganda, and was a key theorist of 'behaviourism' – the idea that media messages impact upon our behaviour in immediate as well as long-term ways, individually and collectively.

Doing media studies

Exploring theoretical contexts

You can do this sort of contextualising research yourself, and then speculate on the ways that this new knowledge allows you to think about the way audience studies are represented in modern textbooks. Select two or three books on audience studies and produce a list of 10 key thinkers or researchers on media audiences from those covered by the authors of those books. Do some background research and try to answer some key questions. You will find that some of these questions have been answered by the authors of each of the textbooks, but it is always worth checking from other sources yourself. The short biographies and resources offered on the internet are often all you need as long as you read two or three to check facts against each other. Key questions to ask yourself include:

■ What was the media scholar's research question?

■ Where did they work at the time?

■ Was this university well known for certain types of research?

■ Did they share ideas with other theorists which would influence their work?

You can then start to ask yourself about the degree to which this work is specific to their study, or more generalisable – i.e. applicable to wider statements about media and audience responses. Other questions worth pondering include the extent to which your theorists were concerned with ideas of mass society, used transmission models of communication, or explicitly used ideas like media effects or models of hypodermic influence. Does your research support the idea of early media work as being preoccupied with media effects, or does a broader picture emerge? Is it evident whether the social background of the theorist, or place and moment in which they worked, has an impact on their work?

Propaganda and manipulating audiences

Propaganda
is the intentional, conscious and active process of managing or manipulating information and ideas to achieve effects of a political or social nature. Methods of manipulation and management here include: censorship – restricting or stopping what can be known; *mis*information; and the generation or planting of outright 'lies'.

The concept of **propaganda** is of enormous interest to students, although it has been clouded by some misconceptions about its meaning and application, as well as its limitations in thinking about the relation of media texts to their consumers. Instructively, the word 'propaganda' itself originates in the seventeenth-century policy of the Vatican and its foreign missions that aimed at propagating the faith of the Roman Catholic church, although its modern usage is often illustrated with reference to the use of media in the wars of the twentieth century and in totalitarian social regimes.

The practice of propaganda was important in the work of scholars such as Lasswell, Lazarsfeld and also Walter Lippmann, all of who contributed to the development of the first generation of media studies. Lippmann himself worked in the US 'Ministry of Propaganda' during the first First World War (1914–18), while Lasswell made an impact with his study *Propaganda Technique in the World War* (1927). Observing the mobilisation of whole populations and the motivation of millions to fight and lay down their lives for their countries, the concept of propaganda in the age of mass communications presented an obvious site for thinking about whether or not behaviour is linked to media messages.

The *Oxford English Dictionary* defines propaganda as: 'The systematic propagation of information or ideas by an interested party, esp. in a tendentious way in order to encourage or instil a particular attitude or response.' Edward Bernays, a US Public Relations guru and contemporary of Lasswell and Lippmann, suggested his own definition of propaganda, 'the consistent, enduring effort to create or shape events to influence the relations of the public to an enterprise, idea or group' (Bernays, 2004, p. 52). For him, it described his own media campaigns throughout the twentieth century, to sell (among other things) cigarettes to women, new cars to people who already owned one and the promotion of consumerism to a (then) largely parsimonious US nation, given to believe in the virtues of saving rather than spending. To combine and clarify these definitions, therefore, we can add our own (see left).

Source: Mary Evans Picture Library

Nazi propaganda poster overtly propagandist activities are a feature of modern totalitarian states.

Historically, the intentional and conscious nature of propaganda can be illustrated by considering its association with totalitarian regimes and with societies whose management is highly concentrated around the apparatuses of the state. Such regimes still exist in places such as China and North Korea, although many studies have been made of the Soviet Union between 1917 and 1991 (Kenez, 1999) and Adolf Hitler's Third Reich which spanned 1933 to 1945 (Hoffman, 1997). Even before they came into conflict with each other, the internal organisation of the social systems of these two societies was not unlike that of many nations during wartime. Both waged a constant struggle against enemies within and without their borders: capitalists and counter-revolutionaries for the former, communists and Jews for the latter. Modes of production and communication were highly centralised and controlled in both cases, and a monopoly over film, radio and press was certainly exercised in the USSR.

Source: Mary Evans Picture Library

Propaganda poster from the Soviet Union: overtly propagandist displays have been a feature of modern totalitarian
states. This is a particularly stylised contribution.

Consequently, ideas – at least in media – were regimented and information was directed towards conformity and acquiescence to a particular worldview
(communism and fascism respectively).

During the great economic depression of the
1930s, the development and apparent success of these
opposing social-political systems in Germany and
Russia seemed to demonstrate their success and the
allied effects of the propaganda machine. The centrality of the personalities and whims of the dictators
Stalin and Hitler were transmitted in widespread and
highly visible propagandist literature and broadcasts,
magnified in the parades, rallies and 'spontaneous'
demonstrations and actions by hundreds of thousands of people in their name. For those who feared
the effects of modern 'mass' society and were concerned about the role that mass media played in such
situations, the relationships between intent and result
seemed obvious.

So, what do such instances and contexts for
the deployment of propaganda tell us about the
concept? Did it really work in producing desired
effects (or any effect at all) in those at whom it was
directed? How can we tell? In the case of these totalitarian regimes, we should be cautious of assuming anything at all about the effect of propaganda,
given the prevalence of more direct mechanisms
for producing effects in the behaviour of citizens,
including physical coercion, violent repression and
the use of fear. On the one hand, propaganda was
ubiquitous and a visible and tangible part of the

Thinking aloud

Evaluating propaganda

With hindsight, propaganda often appears to
be obvious because of its lack of sophistication; or because of the lack of sophistication
of the propaganda we notice. For instance,
American and British war films of 1939–45 are
packed with stereotypes of Germans, Japanese
and Italians, whose characteristics include sad-
ism, idiocy, cowardice and sometimes even all
three. Such two-dimensional images – as well
as all propaganda perhaps, especially viewed
from the present – may cause us some amuse-
ment and inflect the way in which we perceive
the audiences of the past. However, we should
ask whether our parents or grandparents were
naïve enough to swallow such material uncritically or even without a degree of willing complicity in this material. Likewise, we should ask the
same questions about contemporary media – the
perceptions of audiences in relation to the case
study about the Dalai Lama later in this chapter,
for example. What detailed evidence is there
that accounts for how audiences responded and
respond to propagandist messages, if at all?
How do you and your contemporaries respond
to modern media messages? Does it ever seem
like propaganda? How would you know? If you
do recognise it as such, does this suggest that
potentially we are complicit in responding to and
endorsing propaganda by tolerating it?

fabric of each of these societies – it clearly had a role but whether or not it had literal, effective value in producing results was another matter. What did matter, perhaps, was the perception that propaganda did do the things attributed to it, working through modern mass media forms to communicate quickly with masses of people. Whether or not people act as a 'mass', however, is another matter entirely, and to assume that they do involves quite a leap of faith (see Chapter 11).

We could argue that the intentional and conscious nature of propaganda makes it potentially transparent and noticeable in practice. Certainly, the historical association

Key thinker

Noam Chomsky (1928–)

An American political commentator and activist, Chomsky made his name as a linguist, theorising that human beings were imbued with an innate grammatical sense or structure in their genetic make-up. In Chomsky's theory, this enables language and thus communication to a degree that differentiates us as social and cultural beings distinct from other animals. More recently and controversially, he has become renowned for his range of popular polemical works that analyse and challenge American domestic and foreign policy. For him, US power is exercised in pursuit of capitalist profit, at the expense of the democracy and freedom that such policy and power is supposed to secure. His work is detailed and wide in scope but has been criticised for being relatively untheoretical, positing a vision of politics which presents a grand conspiracy on behalf of the powerful that serves to dupe the electorate. He reserves a great deal of ire for mass media, which are largely owned by a limited group of individuals whose interests coincide with other corporations and the powers that be, translated into the kinds of stories and coverage they present. However, whatever the limits of his work, at the centre of his polemic is a palpable commitment to human values and dignity in the face of the expedient rhetoric of politics.

The following is an extract from an interview with Noam Chomsky:

The logic is clear – propaganda is to a democracy what the bludgeon is to a totalitarian state and that's wise and good because again the common interests elude the bewildered herd, they can't figure them out. The public relations industry not only took this ideology on very explicitly but also acted on it, that's a huge industry, spending hundreds of . . . by now probably on the order of a billion dollars a year on it or something, and its commitment all along was to controlling the public mind.

[. . .]

You know the people in the PR industry aren't there for the fun of it, they're doing work, they're trying to instill the right values, in fact they have a conception of what a democracy ought to be, it ought to be a system in which the specialized class are trained to do their work for the service of the masters, the people who own the society, and the rest of the population ought to be deprived of any form of organization because organization just causes trouble.

They ought to be just sitting alone in front of the television set and having drilled into their heads daily the message which says the only value in life is to have more commodities, or to live like that rich middle-class family you're watching and to have nice values like harmony and Americanism and that's all there is in life. You may think in your own head that there's got to be something more in life than this but since you're watching the tube alone you assume I must be crazy because that's all that's going on over there, and since there's no organization permitted, that's absolutely crucial, you never have a way of finding out whether you're crazy and you just assume it because it's the natural thing to assume. That's the ideal and great efforts were made into trying to achieve that ideal and there is a certain conception of democracy behind it.

Source: www.chomsky.info/. © 1992, excerpt used with permission of Roam Agency

of propaganda with state management and total war has, perhaps, tended to limit its meaning and lead to its dismissal in some quarters. It is not a concept often applied to media operations outside times of crisis and, even then, it usually only applies to very particular spheres of production, such as the news. As mentioned, any notion of the effect of propaganda, in all of its variety, is hard to ascertain. Do such provisos mean, therefore, that propaganda has any continued relevance or use to media analysts interested in audiences?

Here we can evaluate arguments for how media propaganda works in modern pluralistic, open and 'unmanaged' societies, i.e. Western capitalist democracies. One influential study in this area has been produced by Edward Herman and Noam Chomsky, in *Manufacturing Consent* (2002). They offer up a 'propaganda model' that relates to democratic societies rather than seeing propaganda as simply an obvious feature of more repressive regimes (such as North Korea or China). They outline the way in which information and news are managed and organised by the media on behalf of the powerful (this is not a singular argument of course, as we've seen, Chapters 5, 10).

Case Study

Contemporary propaganda

→ The 'first' Gulf War began when Iraqi troops invaded Kuwait in August 1990. Despite an odious human rights record, Iraq's dictator, Saddam Hussein, had proven a useful ally in maintaining Western interests in the Middle East, although now a major supply of oil was threatened. Kuwait's record was not much better, its democratic movement suppressed by the ruling al-Sabbah family. The moral argument for any potential war of liberation thus posed considerable problems, as one ex-US army public relations office noted: '[They] had better get cracking to come up with a public relations plan that will supply the answers the public can accept' (Steward, 1990–1: 10).

In fact, it was the Kuwaitis who engaged the PR firm Hill and Knowlton to make their case, the nature of which was ignored by the US administration. Tens of millions of dollars were spent in generating news stories, videos and events, the most notorious of which was a testimony to a US congressional committee in October. 'Nayirah', a 15-year-old Kuwaiti girl, claimed that Iraqi soldiers had looted the hospital where she worked, removing babies from incubators and leaving them on the floor to die. Her account was repeatedly broadcast on US television and did much to generate support for military action.

Many journalists failed to scrutinise this story and its source (or were complicit in it): the girl was later identified as the daughter of Sheik Saud al Nasir al Sabah, ambassador to Washington and member of Kuwait's ruling family. A post-war investigation by Amnesty International failed to uncover any evidence for the atrocity story (MacArthur, 1992).

The identification of propagandist instances around such conflicts invites us to consider other encounters with suspicion. New scholars might find it profitable to examine reporting around more recent conflicts and international tensions – in Afghanistan or around the relation of the US and Iran for instance.

Case Study

Chinese 'propaganda' portrays me as 'devil', Dalai Lama says

LONDON – The Dalai Lama said Saturday he was saddened that Beijing's state 'propaganda' had left many Chinese considering him a 'devil with horns'.

On the first of five days of talks and teachings in the central English city of Nottingham, the exiled Tibetan spiritual leader said Beijing's control over information left millions thinking he was a 'demon'.

Emotional human values were lacking in modern China, he added.

'Millions of innocent Chinese will have no other way to get information except government propaganda,' he said in a talk at Nottingham Arena.

Source: www.chinapost.com.tw/china/local%20 news/tibet/2008/05/26/158092/Chinese-propaganda.htm

In this news item which appeared in the *China Post*, Tibet's spiritual leader, the Dalai Lama, is presented as reacting to the way he is reported in the Chinese media. Of course, as a political leader of Tibetan people who do not want to continue to be part of China, the way the Dalai Lama is reported in China is of vital importance to their campaign. We understand the points attributed to him, even though they make up only a few lines in a news story, because they use a series of ideas that have been widespread in discussions of media for about a century. The story contains the idea of 'propaganda', the notion of a powerful state, and the fear that this may determine how a whole people think because of the control the state exercises over the sources of information available to ordinary people. We fear that powerful people can do things to others by using the power of media.

The story contains a sense that the Chinese population is a massive audience, manipulated by the propaganda transmitted through media forms. There is, though, another audience to be considered. As we read the story, we become part of an audience of the *China Post*. You should be able to see from the URL that the *China Post* is based in Taiwan. It describes itself as 'Taiwan's leading English-language newspaper', providing 'comprehensive news to our readers without the industry puffery or political slant' (www.chinapost.com.tw/ cp/thechinapost/). We are not trying to make political points about China, Tibet or Taiwan (the situation is far too complex to deal with here), but we are very interested in the different senses of audience that are implied in the story and its reporting. Taiwan, an island off the coast of mainland China, was formerly part of the Chinese state and its independence is to some degree dependent on the support of the USA. By providing an English-language news service with a focus on Taiwanese and Chinese news, the *China Post* creates an audience at a number of levels.

Both the story and the news service which provides it give a sense of an audience being addressed. Each media text, and each media organisation that produces the texts, produces a notion of audience. Getting to grips with these ideas is a central part of our study of media forms, organisations and audiences.

Media effects and moral panics

Media effects research has developed beyond its roots in the early twentieth century, discussed above, as one branch of the field of mass communication and media studies. A continued theme of exploration is the relationship between depictions of violence and violent behaviour in media audiences. While few researchers would claim that media representations are the sole influence on individuals in their lives, some research posits that depictions of media violence constitute an important learning factor that leads to the imitation of violent acts, mainly by younger, impressionable children but also affecting other 'vulnerable' people. This position informs the use of longitudinal studies, for instance the study of a subject over a period of time to see if exposure to media violence has any long-term effects. Cecilia von Feilitzen (in Dickinson *et al.*, 1998) summarises some of the ways in which the link has been theorised. For instance, it has been suggested that TV and film viewers can become frustrated at not being able to live lifestyles similar to those often presented on screen which, as well as inspiring positive moods, sometimes make viewers frustrated and aggressive. However, there are approaches and results that counter such negative conclusions, suggesting that viewing media violence can have positive effects in providing 'catharsis'. This concept relates to a sense of letting off steam in consumers, suggesting that media violence can 'purify' and release aggression that has been built up through everyday life (Carlsson and von Feilitzen, 1998: 94). Some approaches suggest ways in which media 'effects' play a part in the general socialisation of children (aiding imagination, role play and so on). However, as a whole, such research has proven to be highly contentious in some quarters for its scientific aspirations, assumptions and procedures.

Effects research in general and studies of violence in particular attract a great deal of attention, as well as speculation, from outside the field, often in debates and coverage within media. For instance, Guy Cumberbatch has suggested that when journalists cover media issues 'well over 80 per cent of news stories (and considerably more news space) is devoted to the concerns that media violence is bad/harmful' (Cumberbatch, 1998: 267). This might be one way of accounting for the hostility towards effects research in some quarters of the field of media studies, particularly for the way in which such work is picked up and selectively interpreted within popular media debates that are themselves modern manifestations of fears about the social role of media.

The concept of moral panic is a useful one, here, for framing popular concerns about media effects, their manifestation, impact and indeed for the way in which media organisations themselves look to and make use of effects research in 'producing' versions of media audiences. Stanley Cohen first employed the term 'moral panic' most usefully and systematically in his book *Folk Devils and Moral Panics* (Cohen, 1972). This study derived in part from a consideration of the sociology of 'deviancy', of groups and their practices that seemed to be outside societal norms. It offered an examination of reactions to contemporary youth groups or subcultures, which had become noticeable in the post-war period, particularly for their spectacular appearance (Teddy Boys, Mods, Rockers, Skinheads, etc.) and their relationship with what appeared to be new media forms, such as rock and pop music and the growth of television (see p. 315).

'Moral panic', in its original use, describes a process that, for Cohen, is one in which a 'condition, episode, person, or group of persons emerges to become defined as a threat to societal values and interests' (Cohen, 1972: 28). Thus, the process model follows the way in which members or groups within societies respond to a challenge or perceived threat to their values, mores, culture and so on from 'deviant' groups or practices. The point is that threats need to be dealt with and countered in some manner, thus initiating calls for reaction, neutralisation, legislation, regulation and so on. Media have a key role to play here in advertising and defining 'moral panics' and spotting folk devils, as well as suggesting and supporting responses to them. This process can be mapped in schematic fashion as follows.

First, there is the occurrence of an event, which is deemed to be something significant or unusual enough in its impact to merit media coverage and attention that, in turn, frames the event as significant and unusual, thus generating concern. This attention in turn generates further coverage, framed by the terms of the response to the original event. At this stage the media role lies in identifying events as significant and setting agendas (what is

Key thinker

David Gauntlett (1971–)

Based upon the continued investment into effects research around the world, in tandem with the apparent inconclusiveness of this work, British theorist David Gauntlett has produced a detailed critique of this approach and its assumptions. He suggests that effects models tackle the exploration of social problems 'backwards'. By this he means that social behaviour precedes and exceeds anything in media forms and activities and in media relationships with audiences. However, researchers begin with media, thus pursuing connections and explanations for social activity from that starting point. In essence, research has tended to neglect the contexts in which media forms are produced and consumed, giving them a suspiciously privileged place. Furthermore, he suggests, media effects approaches lack sensitivity in their understanding of media texts, their variety and how they make meaning – rhetorically, generically and so on. In addition, the nature and degree of what exactly is being represented in media texts (e.g. sex, violence, antisocial behaviour and so on), which is supposed to produce effects, is never properly defined. The relative definitions of such characteristics should get alarm bells ringing!

Suggestive for our idea of the way in which media theorists have 'produced' audiences is Gauntlett's description of the tendency in effects research to assume superiority for the researcher over the individuals and groups being researched. Constantly exposed to the kinds of harmful material they seek to explore for its impact upon the wider public, researchers rarely reflect upon their own status within this communication circuit. The researcher is thus always distinguished in some way from those who are acted upon by media messages.

Gauntlett concludes that, if evidence for direct effects upon behaviour has not been found, then they are not there to be found. Otherwise, perhaps, it is that media effects research has been misdirected in its approach. Ultimately, for Gauntlett, the effects model lacks theoretical grounding, directed by assertions, social agendas and assumptions rather than reasoning, and ignores basic questions such as why would it be that individuals would imitate behaviour depicted in media? Why would this be a motivating factor in any one person's life? (Dickinson *et al.*, 1998)

Source: David Gauntlett, 'Ten things wrong with the effects model' (www.newmediastudies.com/effects1.htm)

the extent of the problem? where is it? what should be done?). Coverage then extends from the original event or occurrence to examine wider social implications and resonances. This fuels public debate, partly by media employment of 'authorised' commentators, who underline the significance and exceptional aspects of the original event. The culmination of this comment is to outline the way in which the event in focus provides evidence for theories of social or moral decay, or threat from deviant groups. The original event is thus reframed and amplified beyond its original limited context to become a concern for society at large. Finally, in response to the perceived threat, some form of social control is recommended, produced or exercised.

While media generate awareness and provide 'amplification' ('broadcast' would be a resonant synonym), contributing to the construction of moral panics, as well as providing frameworks for understanding deviancy and threat, they themselves can become 'objects' of panic. Often, such panics amount to nothing more than identifications of activity that may seem objectionable to commentators (the pleasures of young people, usually), ways in which media might be turned to illegal ends. For example, particular moral panics about media have included: concerns about predatory paedophiles on the internet lurking in chat rooms; 'Gangsta Rap' and the genre's influence on young black men or – *worse* – white, middle-class men; playing computer games leading to laziness and obesity, as well as hyperactivity and violence; the circulation of bomb-making instructions and incitements to terrorism on internet sites; and so on.

A celebrated panic over the presumed effect of the representation of media violence centred on the 1993 murder of toddler James Bulger by two other children. When the British press discovered that one of the murderers' fathers had rented *Child's Play 3* several weeks before the murder, they used the film as an explanation for the killing, the circumstances of which otherwise seemed incomprehensible. James Bulger's body was found on a railway track and a scene in *Child's Play 3* showed a murder occurring on a railway track. This is where the similarities ended but the press managed to use this to wage a war on violent films and videos. Evidently, the murderers must have seen the film and, disturbed by it, recreated this fictional event. Such was the frenzy and hyperbole created that the video was afforded supernatural powers and owners were encouraged to send their copies to newspapers for public burning (see Kerekes and Slater, 2000). There are countless other examples of public panic and allegations about media violence and its influence across media forms themselves, but they are no more than that: allegations. What they detract from (alongside the imputation of a satanic quality of evil to the murderers) is any attempt to understand what actually happened and how we might account for the development and morality of the murderers over the 10 years or so of their lives *not* spent in watching violent videos – time spent in the company of, well, people like you and me and those who run the various media, living in a society that we all share.

Likewise, when director Oliver Stone defended his film *Natural Born Killers* (1994) after it was accused of influencing two American teenagers to go on a killing spree, he observed that it was not films that influence people but instead 'perhaps a negligent or abusive upbringing, combined with defects in their psyches . . . Parents, schools and peers shape children from their earliest days, not films' (Stone, 1996: 238). This is also the finding of many researchers: it is these 'intervening variables' of upbringing and peer pressure that have more influence than a violent film 'drugging' its audience (Buckingham, 1998: 65).

Another recent example of a moral panic about media and related dangers concerns the demonisation of the internet. Indeed, we can track how many moral panics have been responses to a new medium, such as the panics surrounding the video recorder and computer games, but the internet is constantly in the headlines. Craig and Petley discovered, in their research in this area, that '1999 saw the publication of over 200 stories centred on the distribution of child pornography alone via the internet' (Craig and Petley, 1999: 192). Craig and Petley argue that 'one is as likely to find evidence of the existence of "snuff" films as to come across child pornography while surfing the internet' (1999: 198). Although such material is there, the point is that there is very little evidence to support media panic about the widespread availability of child pornography on the internet as a symptom of the millions of predators supposed to be lurking in every chat room in order to 'groom' children for abuse.

Behind such perceptions lies an abiding suspicion of the vulnerability (moral, physical, physiological, intellectual) of audience members in the face of almost preternaturally powerful media and those who know how to achieve their ends by using the various forms. The members of this audience seem themselves to be malleable figures, produced as much as objects of fear, concern and, indeed, urban myth as they are by any real empirical knowledge. Whether or not we accept such positions must surely begin with a reflection on our own membership of audiences, our responsibilities and activities.

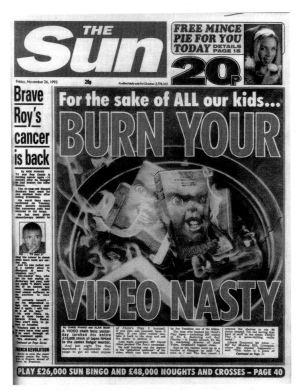

Source: © News International Syndication Ltd

Newspaper campaigns to protect readers and communities may appear to offer a public service, whipping up a moral panic and generating sales at the same time.

Case Study

An Italian moral panic over video games (or was it a case of propaganda?)

On the website Videoluca, Matteo Bittanti reports on a curious case of a moral panic at work in Italy in 2006, apparently generated by the release of the video game *Rule of Rose*. He relates how the popular current affairs magazine *Panorama* carried a cover story announcing that, in the game, 'He who buries the little girl wins' (*Vince chi seppellisce la bambina*).

In this cover story, alongside criticisms of the game by various public figures (who admit to knowing little of the game), other games are also singled out – *Grand Theft Auto*, *Bully* and *Postal 2*. The story was then picked up by popular TV shows on Canale 5 and Rete 4. After reading the magazine article, Rome's mayor, Walter Veltroni, called for a ban on the game, arguing that 'There is no way that a violent video game should be sold and distributed in our country . . . this game must not enter Italian homes . . . Our youngsters are living through difficult times, with violence present on a daily basis in all the media . . . Small children have the right to be shielded from violence.'

Bittani suggests that it is not uncommon for Italian mass media to attack video games. In the early 1990s, for instance, journalist Cesare Fiumi and psychologist Vittorino Andreoli suggested that a series of gruesome youth-related crimes that happened in Italy had been directly instigated by violent video games. On this occasion the mounting furore led directly to discussion in the Italian parliament that blamed such games directly for violent acts among young people and suggested ways of limiting access. In this development Bittani explicitly identifies a classic case of moral panic. However, Bittani suggests that, ultimately, the panic was in some manner actually related to the machinations of the game's distributor, Digital Bros. In this narrative, the intriguing thing is that the distributor's potential millions of euros of profit were threatened when the game was launched to relative indifference from the Italian media. Digital Bros enlisted promotions company Media Hook to do something about this and Bittani suggests that they lay behind the resulting controversy, which in the end benefited sales.

Source: www.videoludica.com/news. php?news=453

Doing media studies

Identifying and exploring moral panics

Is there a current example of a specific contemporary concern about media and a particular audience group that you are able to identify? If so, try to track down the origins of the story and frame it within the process model of moral panics set out above. Does this aid in identifying the validity of the stories contributing to this concern (is it in fact a panic)? Do you need more information and evidence to make up your mind and, if so, what would help? Do your investigations reveal any assumptions about media effects?

From effects to influence

Jostein Gripsrud (2002) has asked whether all media research is in some way about 'effects'. It is certainly the case, as we see in the generation of moral panics, that many public concerns about media forms are related to the results that they are perceived to produce in audiences and society in general.

In drawing this section to a close, and in anticipation of our chapter on power, it is useful here to distinguish between ideas of behavioural effect and theories and approaches to research that posit a less dramatic but more pervasive version of media 'influence' (over the ideas and beliefs held by individuals about the world and their place in it). We see this notion behind many important theories of culture, language and media, sometimes crossing over with the more direct 'effects' conceptualisation. For instance, and as in the work of de Saussure, the Russian Formalists (p. 83) considered the manner in which language shapes our understanding of reality. Another Russian, the film-maker Sergei Eisenstein (p. 404), conceived of ways of directing audience responses towards a specific political 'consciousness', through his use of 'montage' editing. The influential theorists of the Frankfurt School argued that the products of what they called the 'Culture Industry' worked at psychological and ideological levels on audiences in order to promote social conformity and the accommodation of an inequitable social system. A development of this kind of thinking, in tandem with structuralist ideas, is 'screen theory' – exemplified by the work of Laura Mulvey (p. 93). Herein, popular films are understood as contributing to the positioning of each member of the audience as a socially constituted individual who recognises their allotted role and place within society.

The assumption behind these kinds of approaches presumes a very different idea of 'effect', when compared with an apparently measurable 'before and after' notion of behavioural change in the face of media texts. In such work, media forms serve a social function, to reproduce the way the world is, its order, and in doing so, as these theorists argue, they aid in a wider maintenance of social inequalities. This approach has mattered a great deal to those on the left of the political spectrum, and to questions of individual and collective freedoms. Interestingly, this version of the media as powerful, or acting on behalf of the powerful, often presents the audience as a largely defenceless object of media forms. This is, then, another instance of media theorists producing ideas of media 'effects' that in turn 'produce' audiences. Interestingly, the model discussed here does, to some extent, echo concerns expressed by those on the right of the political spectrum. Social and political conservatives have also been concerned with the impact that various media have had upon social values. Here, media have variously been blamed for encouraging 'antisocial' behaviour in the short term and, in the long term, undermining traditional social values and modes of living, such as families organised around marriage, heterosexuality and respect for authority. For instance, because television seems to offer so much sex, violence, swearing and so on, and is ever present in the home, so society follows its lead. Whether the concern here is with the technology, the content or the lax morals of producers – or all three – is not always entirely clear. However, this is not to be cynical about those on the right and their values particularly. The same arguments are indeed trotted out by those on the left – media producers in particular are identified for being too partial and conservative in their management of messages. One argument produced against those who complain about media content, who object to portrayals of sex and violence, use of profanity and so on, is that televisions can be turned off or over. That is as may be, but perhaps the nature of media in reaching right into our homes and private spaces – messages popping up whether solicited or not – as well as infusing our public ones, is the reason behind such concerns.

We've found, then, that the audience, when looked at closely, is an intriguing concept, both obvious and elusive. Why else would it be subject to so much attention from media industry specialists themselves, if it were so immediately knowable? All of us are, mostly, a part of media audiences. We can tell this by virtue of the fact that we're forever engaged in media-related activities, such as watching television, surfing the net, reading newspapers, updating our Facebook profile and so on. However, the individualised feeling of what it is to be involved in this activity is of a different order from the conceptual category demanded by and produced by the industries themselves. Likewise, despite the empirical, scientific approaches employed, much media effects research does not seem much different, beginning with assumptions that partly construct concepts of what audiences are and what media forms do to them in advance of the results.

Ultimately, what we've done in this chapter is to deal with 'ideas' about audiences, produced in the minds of theorists, in laboratories and market research, and by political and promotional strategists, and so on. We've intentionally played up this angle and the idea of the passivity of audiences in such ideas in order to set up our next chapter, which outlines ways of making sense of the various things which audiences do with media.

Summary

Investigating what media do to audiences

In this chapter we have explored the idea that the audience is 'produced' as a result of the fact that media do things to people. In the first section we explored what exactly it meant to think of the audience and 'be' an audience member in relation to media products, social groups and so on. Audiences, we argued, are themselves modern entities or abstractions, products of media address, appeal and organisation. We saw that media companies spend a lot of money researching audiences, as these are integral to media businesses in providing subscriptions, sales and, of course, as something to be sold to advertisers who use popular media sites for their messages. We suggested that, while businesses produce 'interested knowledge' and ideas about audiences, they are not ultimately concerned with individuals as individuals.

We then considered the idea that media theorists have also produced the audience as an 'abstraction' in their relationship with media forms. We explored the foundations for particular ways of investigating and theorising audiences, which gave birth to a tradition known as 'effects research'. We suggested that there are particular ways of telling the story of this tradition's contribution to the development of media studies but that the tradition is best approached by thinking about what contexts prompted its foundational questions. Thus, we explored the concept of propaganda and ideas of media manipulation, in tandem with the assumptions that these revealed about audiences. Touching upon concerns about the 'effects

of media violence', we considered some criticisms of the effects approach and highlighted how its presumptions were picked up in popular debates about media and audiences. Here, we utilised the notion of moral panic to highlight some of the continued constructions or ways of producing ideas about audiences – in general and particular – as something that is acted upon by media texts and technologies. Finally, we drew some comparisons between approaches to media effects in terms of behaviour and broader theories about the role of media in influencing values and beliefs at a social level.

If you have followed this chapter through, engaged with the activities and thought about the issues covered, you should be able to:

■ Discuss and critique common-sense ideas of the audience. (Think again about what it means to imagine the audience and to actually be in the audience.)

■ Identify ways in which it can be said media organisations produce audiences. (Explore again the various ways in which we are appealed to, addressed and positioned by media throughout the day, as well as the wealth of market research produced by media organisations into ensuring that their audience exists! If you are unsure of this idea, explore some of the links we've pointed to in this chapter that allow you to see how media organisations speak of and produce audiences.)

■ Identify ways in which it can be said media scholars produce media audiences.

■ Discuss and critique ways in which propaganda and media effects have been addressed both in media and in media scholarship. (There is clearly more work to be done if you wish to pursue the detail of media effects research by reading further. Here, we were mainly concerned about some of the presumptions behind this approach and the way that these are taken up in media debates within media.)

■ Explore the extent to which ideas of the audience, and of media effects, are linked to 'moral panics'. (The important point here is to be aware of the terms of such debates and how best to evaluate such research and resultant claims. To this end, the following activity will allow you to explore and evaluate your own position on this line of enquiry.)

Doing media studies

Evaluating claims about media effects

It would be difficult for new scholars to conduct any meaningful research into media effects and influence, especially if we consider the long history of study in tandem with the inconclusive nature of results in this area. However, we should not avoid evaluating existing and continuing research or comment on this basis. We should be attuned, in particular, to the manner in which this kind of research is employed, by governments, pressure groups or media organisations themselves, for instance, as part of public debates about the effects of media on the 'vulnerable'. Likewise, we should be aware of the way in which these reports tend to crop up in the midst of specific moral panics about media, if not as a possible cause.

Below, for instance, are some extracts from 'Letting Children be Children – Report of an Independent Review of the Commercialisation and Sexualisation of Childhood'. This report was commissioned by the UK Department for Education and led by Reg Bailey – Chief Executive of the charity Mothers' Union – and is thus commonly referred to as the 'Bailey Report'.

(Available at: www.education.gov.uk/publications/standard/publicationDetail/Page1/CM%208078).

Bailey expressed his own approach to the 'review' in this way:

> We live in a society that is changing at what is, for many, a bewildering rate. Increased levels of wealth have created strong commercial pressures on every one of us, whether or not we have participated in that affluence. Society

also seems to have become more openly sexualised; the rapidly changing technological environment has its benefits in so many ways but has also made the seamier side of humanity inescapable.

If adults need to be emotionally and otherwise well adjusted to deal with this environment; so much more so do children. I wanted to understand the nature of these pressures on our children and young people. I wanted to understand, too, why so many parents seem to lack confidence in their ability to help their children navigate this commercial and sexualised world. Most of all I wanted to bring forward some clear and straightforward suggestions to address these issues and ensure we provide the right sort of support for parents and children alike.

This scope of the research involved:

Nearly 1000 responses from parents to an online Call for Evidence.

1025 parents of 5–16-year-olds and 520 children and young people aged 7–16 took part in a face-to-face survey.

70 parents took part in qualitative research, including interviews and focus groups.

552 children and young people took part in a survey organised by the Office for the Children's Commissioner for England and Amplify, their Children and Young People Advisory Group.

120 organisations and businesses provided written submissions and many more members of the public rang, emailed and wrote to the research team to share their views.

As part of its investigations the research team identified four themes concerning the public that were explored in the report. These are expressed as follows:

Theme 1 – the 'wallpaper' of children's lives

We are all living in an increasingly sexual and sexualised culture, although it is far from clear how we arrived at this point. Many parents feel that this culture is often inappropriate for their children. They want more power to say 'no'. Some parts of the business world and sections of the media seem to have lost their connection to parents and this is compounded in some new media where there is limited regulation. Where regulation does exist, regulators need to connect better with parents and encourage businesses to comply with the 'spirit of the regulation'. Where regulation does not exist, businesses need to behave more responsibly.

Theme 2 – clothing, products and services for children

Sexualised and gender-stereotyped clothing, products and services for children are the biggest areas of concern for parents and many non-commercial organisations contributing to the review, with interest fanned by a sometimes prurient press. The issues are rarely clear-cut, with a fine balance on a number of points – taste, preference, choice, affordability, fashion and gender preferences. Retailers are aware of the issues and sensitivities, and they are responding. They need to be explicitly and systematically family friendly, from design and buying through to display and marketing.

Theme 3 – children as consumers

We all live in a commercial world and children are under pressure from a range of sources to act as consumers. We do not want to cut children off from the commercial world completely as we believe that it brings benefits and parents tell us that they want to manage the issue themselves, supported by proportionate regulation and responsible businesses. While adults may understand that companies might look to 'push the boundaries' when advertising to them, children are especially vulnerable and need to be given special consideration. Special measures already exist in advertising and marketing regulations to protect children but some gaps exist. Regulators cannot realistically be expected to anticipate detailed developments in the new media. However, an absence of regulation does not absolve businesses from acting responsibly by themselves.

Theme 4 – making parents' voices heard

Parents have told us that they feel they cannot make their voices heard, and that they often lack the confidence to speak out on sexualisation and commercialisation issues for fear of being labelled a prude or out of touch. Business and industry sectors and their regulators need to make clear that they welcome, and take seriously, feedback on these subjects. Given the technology available, regulators and businesses should be able to find more effective ways to encourage parents to tell them what they think, quickly and easily, and to be transparent in telling parents how they are responding to that feedback. Once parents know that their views are being taken seriously, we would expect them to respond positively towards companies that listen to their concerns.

On the basis of these short extracts, the report clearly takes a broader purview than media alone, taking a nuanced approach to the contexts in which children develop. It offers a recent and much-publicised piece of work to explore in terms of its themes and approach to research. For us, it presents an object of scrutiny, born of resources that few of us can marshall. We might ask, for instance, questions such as: how are 'opinions' and concerns balanced as evidence with empirical observation and engagement? What ideas of the consumer are present? What role do media play in this report and how are the various media audiences conceived?

Your job is to formulate further questions and to investigate this report as well as ways in which it has been received in order to anchor your own response to the question: 'What do media do to people?'

Further reading

Ang, I. (1991) *Desperately Seeking the Audience*, London: Routledge.
  A classic and commonly referred to study on media audiences that still has great value today. In this ethnographic study of TV audiences, Ang is inspired by French scholar Michel Foucault and his work on power and knowledge as she looks at how producers of television approach audiences. Chapters look at both American and European TV programming and focus on issues such as rating systems and audience measurement, public-service broadcasting and oppositional TV audiences.

Barker, M. and Petley, J. (eds) (1997) *Ill Effects – the Media/Violence Debate*, London: Routledge.
  Barker and Petley are both important scholars in the study of media violence. This collection of essays is an important addition to the field, covering issues such as film censorship, media regulation, children and media violence and, importantly, the problem with effects studies. Craig and Petley's article on internet moral panic will be of worth to those with an interest in internet regulation. Drawing on research, Craig and Petley identify that the web is not the stomping ground of perverts that we are led to believe.

Critcher, C. (2003) *Moral Panics and the Media*, Buckingham: Open Univeristy Press.
  Though Stanley Cohen's *Moral Panics and Folk Devils* is usually regarded as *the* classic study to refer to when studying moral panics, Critcher's *Moral Panics and the Media* is an accessible work for those looking for an informative introduction. Critcher, co-author of an earlier moral panic study *Policing the Crisis*, readdresses Cohen's model and applies it to a wealth of case studies such as video nasties, paedophilia, AIDS and ecstasy. Although Critcher covers the majority of well-known moral panics there are some notable exceptions such as the fascination with terrorism following 9/11, and size zero. However, that should not stop any student interested in this area taking ideas from this book and applying them to any of the more recent moral panics absent from this work.

Martin, R. (2002) *Propaganda and the Ethics of Persuasion*, Orchard Park, NY: Broadview Press.
  Of the numerous books on propaganda this one has particular relevance for the new media scholar. Early chapters offer a historical study of propaganda and the use of rhetoric as a persuasive tool. Rather than primarily focusing on what we might call 'bad' propaganda, Martin also looks at commonly accepted forms of propaganda such as advertising and public relations. Examples from around the globe are offered and the chapter on propaganda, democracy and the internet brings the subject into the information age.

CHAPTER 9

Investigating audiences: what do people do with media?

Source: Getty Images

International Pillow Fight Day: Berlin. 'Flashmobs' or 'smartmobs' are examples of the contemporary 'we-think' aspect of digital media and social networking. Sometimes the power of the crowd can be set to solve serious problems, sometimes it can be directed for simple fun and silliness!

Thinking about what audiences do with media texts

In his book, *We-think* (2008), cultural commentator, analyst and UK government advisor Charles Leadbeater recounts an incident that offers a suggestive insight into the nature of media consumers. He writes of how, in 2004, the closing frames of a cinema advertisement for the game *Halo 2* featured a flickering web address – www.ilovebees.com.

Intrigued, thousands of fans visited the site which, oddly, featured news of a missing beekeeper with information about several hundred global co-ordinates, as well as a warning message of a 'system' that was in peril. As Leadbeater's account goes on, here was a site presenting confused but intriguing details and a ticking clock.

In the following few months, over 600,000 visitors to the site set out, without instructions, rules or guidance, to investigate this apparent mystery. Working independently at first and then collectively, this mass of people managed an incredible feat of co-ordination, against the clock, to engage with what ultimately turned out to be an extended game, created by the company 42 Entertainment (www.42entertainment.com/). Thus:

> The game began to come to a head on 24 August, as thousands of players turned up at the pay phones [which were at the locations of the global co-ordinates] armed with every conceivable piece of digital communication equipment . . . players of I Love Bees showed that a mass of independent people, with different information, skills and outlooks, working together in the right way, can discover, analyse, co-ordinate, create and innovate together.

(Leadbeater, 2008: 11) (For a full account online see www.wethinkthebook.net/home.aspx)

Leadbeater takes this instance as evidence for the optimistic and creative possibilities of new media, but it also serves as a useful illustration of the issues dealt with in this chapter – namely the productive activities and capabilities of media users. Here is evidence of media users doing something beyond their allotted role as simple, passive consumers of media product, behaving in ways that seem irreducible to some 'effect' of media form and message. Respondents to this website enigma worked proactively, collectively, innovatively and creatively in the service of more than individual satisfaction or pleasure.

Interestingly, too, this instance of audience behaviour may also have been a result of the particular nature of this media text and the way that it was planned and made available, an indication both of the changing relationship of producers and audiences and of the way in which the boundaries between the two are being blurred.

What we will do in this chapter

In the previous chapter, we considered the media's relationship with audiences in particular ways. We looked at conceptualisations, constructions and productions of the audience that resulted in a vision of a rather passive entity upon which the various media are thought to have influence or effect, or, indeed, which they actively seek to affect in terms of their economic activity. Having outlined some of the industrial and academic origins, insights and limits of such approaches (but not having discounted them entirely), which presume that media forms do things to audiences, we now move on to think about what audiences do with media forms.

The suggestion here is that what people do relates to questions of interpretation of the meaning of texts, as well as how they appropriate media products and use them to their own ends, in ways not only or immediately captured by any sense of the creator's intention. By the same degree, however, media products offer a finite resource that limits the range of possible uses.

The first section of this chapter deals with some of the theoretical approaches to the idea of the 'active audience'. First, we will start by looking at what we mean by this term, drawing upon what is known as the 'uses and gratifications' approach, which came directly out of the effects tradition. Then we consider Stuart Hall's 'encoding and decoding' model, itself a response to the kind of ideas presented by the identification of 'uses and gratifications', which fed into the work of David Morley. Of particular use in developing these ideas around audience activity is a tradition in feminist scholarship. Very broadly, we track a shift from suspicions about how women are affected by the negative influence of media to how they gain genuine pleasure from their media consumption, attuned to the particular resources that they bring to that consumption. We will then consider the particular categories of 'subcultures' and 'fandom', and associated theories which present us with some conceptual tools for theorising and describing the often spectacular ways in which individuals and groups appropriate, celebrate and change media products. In the final part of this section, we will consider what is happening in online versions of audience consumption and activity, how media theorists make sense of this relatively new domain and what this means for some traditional ways of viewing audiences.

The second section is most important for detailing a range of research methods for investigating audiences. These indicate ways in which you will be able to go and conduct research of your own design in order to pursue these and other ideas.

By the end of this chapter you should be able to:

- Identify key concepts and theories associated with the idea of media audience activity.

- Identify and engage with key issues and approaches to conceptualising audiences as active users and interpreters of media products and messages.

- Conduct initial research into the activity of media audiences, utilising one or more methods as appropriate.

KEY TERMS: ▶ active audiences; bricolage; cultural capital; encoding/decoding; ethics; ethnography; fandom; feminism; focus groups; gendered audiences; homology; interviews; methodology; questionnaires; subcultures; uses and gratifications; virtual communities; virtual ethnography.

Doing media studies

Finding out about what audiences do with media

For this activity you need to locate evidence of the actual audience or audiences for any one media product and what they themselves say about and do with that product. You can do this by reading the letters page of a newspaper or magazine, joining a TV programme's online discussion forum and so on. You might even try speaking to the people you spend time with at the movies or at concerts. The aim is to find instances where individuals discuss their media use and preferences in relation to these questions: what kind of things does your audience talk about? What do they reveal about their media use and response to the media product (as text, artefact, commodity)? Do these things seem significant? Does anyone reveal anything that surprises you?

Identifying audience activity

In proceeding, we should note, as we did in the previous chapter, that our use of the label 'audience' serves as a synonym for all groups of media consumers. While new media scholars will undoubtedly be struck by the fact that the field of TV studies, in talking of 'reception', has been most productive in its consideration of viewers of that medium, we need to include and attend to readers of the press and magazines, and listeners to radio and popular music, as well as computer gamers or players, online 'users' of internet facilities and so on. In encompassing these disparate groups, however, we should also be attuned to the different possibilities and means for audiences to relate to different media forms and rhetorical strategies. This distinction will have an impact upon the kinds of questions we might ask and the way that we go about seeking answers. Clearly, reading a close-print prose newspaper article is somewhat different from listening to a piece of pop music at a live concert or a radio broadcast. We should note, too, as per the reference to the productiveness of TV studies above, that some aspects of media consumption have engendered much more attention than others. Thus, while the nature of TV consumption is prodigious, media photography or even popular music studies are relatively underdeveloped in their attention to consumption.

Our motivation in this chapter has something to do with the way in which our idea of how audiences are 'produced' – by media and some traditions of academic thought – concentrates on and produces a very passive characterisation. Of course, there is an obvious 'passivity' to being an audience member, in the fact that media products are things produced 'out there' by companies which we're only interested in when we want them, or believe that we want them. For most of us, 'activity' appears to require little more than switching on the television, or browsing the internet or a rack of magazines at the newsstand. One way of seeing our role as audience members, therefore, is to see us as making a selection and then sitting back and enjoying the show!

On the other hand, isn't our relationship with media something more than this? Beginning on an anecdotal level, most of us have a sometimes curious and variable relationship with media products in all of the variety in which we encounter them. We tend to 'speak to' media texts, for instance – commenting volubly on newspaper stories and TV programmes, singing along with (or rejecting) songs on the radio, expressing exasperated disbelief in the plot turns of a movie (the killer comes back to life for one more go at the heroine after being shot, stabbed, blown up and so on). We interact with others in the audience along the same lines in our reactions to media texts – with your mum as she sits in the living room with you watching the Eurovision Song Contest or the news, with other concert-goers at a gig, with participants in online forums or games – in ways which don't seem to be uniform or predictable from the 'address' and appeal of the text.

Thinking of television in particular, a most powerful medium in the attentions of effects models, we watch in very inattentive ways in general, sometimes very 'disrespectfully' (of the creative effort, of the gravitas of some of the figures which populate our screen). Other times, however, we watch very attentively, sometimes obsessively and with a great deal of involvement, which sometimes goes beyond the moment of viewing. Some of us dedicate further activities to our media consumption, joining discussion groups, sometimes protesting or celebrating some media development or practice ('they're cancelling our favourite TV show, the news is biased'), sometimes buying further products (DVD releases, novelisations, T-shirts) which don't just seem to be about adding to the coffers of producers. In fact, in pursuing our media pleasures, some of us get involved in activities that are actually illegal and may be detrimental to the interests of producers. There is a long history of 'bootlegging' popular music concerts, for instance, in order that the fans of any one audience can indulge themselves beyond the limits set by the record company and tour promoter. Most recently, the activity of online file sharing has merited legal threats from media companies against consumers.

Anecdotally then, media consumption seems to take many forms which are not quantifiable or easily slotted into the kinds of generalities or anodyne abstractions produced by market research or the expectations of media producers. Nor is media consumption simply about a correspondence between textual meaning and cognitive understanding: we can ask, what role does our comprehension of news information or the pleasures of a computer game shoot-out have in our lives? Furthermore, in what contexts does media consumption take place and how does this impact upon how we make sense of media meanings and values for us as individuals? Such questions lead us to consider how to make sense of activity (interpreting texts, doing things with them, etc.) empirically and with some attention to the individuality and idiosyncrasies of audience members.

Audiences, then, seen from one perspective, are possibly very 'active', rather than the passive figures awaiting organisation by media institutions or direction by media messages. It is the significance and meaning of this activity of which we shall seek to make sense.

There is an important and obvious sense in which audience activity is worthy of serious attention – for the same reasons that prompted effects traditions of research. Media forms, objects and meanings are an integral part of modern life, contributing to our sense of the social but forming also a major part of our lives as individuals. One need only observe the number of TV screens in any home you visit, faces stuck in newspapers, magazines and comic books on public transport, or the individuals walking around with headphones attached to MP3 players to see this, not to mention the overwhelming place of the internet in our daily lives at work, in education and at play. What role media products and meanings play is deserving of our attention in order to discover how they are part of everyday life and what we do with them, just as much as they may seem increasingly to direct that life!

From 'effects' to uses and gratifications

As we suggested in our previous chapter, one thrust of audience research was founded upon intellectual suspicions of mass media institutions and forms in the context of mass social and political movements – fascism and communism, for instance, as well as the apparently effective use of media propaganda in both world wars. Research informed by this context, which pursued the cause and effect relationship between media messages and audience behaviour, continued into the post-war period but failed to find specific evidence of links between media content and attitude change, or increased levels of violence in individuals or society at large. By 1960, Joseph Klapper, a prominent effects researcher, concluded after a summary of research up to that date that 'mass communications does not ordinarily serve as a necessary or sufficient cause of audience effects, but rather functions through a nexus of mediating factors' (Klapper, 1960: 8). Researchers in this tradition had come to conceive of a 'limited effects' model of media influence, highlighting the importance (and neglect) of factors such as social and cultural context in the way media forms relate to the lives of individuals. By the time of Klapper's statement, and while effects research continued (as it still does), approaches to media consumption explored beyond the effects models and attendant assumptions about audiences. In the USA, innovative work in this vein was developed by Elihu Katz and, in Britain, by James Halloran, and by Jay Blumler and Denis McQuail of the Leicester Centre for Mass Communications Research. The premise for this work was set out by Katz:

> It is often argued that the mass media 'give the people what they want' and that the viewers, listeners, and readers ultimately determine the content of the media by their choices of what they will read, view, or hear. Whether or not this is a valid characterisation of the role of the

mass in relation to the media, it is only an arc of circular reasoning, unless there is independent evidence of what the people do want. More particularly, there is great need to know what people do with the media, what uses they make of what the media now give them, what satisfactions they enjoy, and, indeed, what part the media play in their personal lives.

(Katz and Foulkes, 1962: 377)

One initial aspect to emerge from such approaches was a focus on the 'uses and gratifications' that audiences brought to and gained from media producers. Instead of searching for 'effects' and changing behaviour, this approach concentrated instead, as James Lull has it, on 'how audience members positively influence their own media experiences' (Lull, 1995:73). In addition, questions about media use and how need is fulfilled were based upon an assumption that answers cannot simply be read off in any linear or direct manner from media content.

The uses and gratifications concept is usually identified as deriving from 'functionalist' theories of society. It is functionalist because it contends that audiences approach texts out of a purposeful desire to satisfy or 'gratify' necessary personal and social needs or, indeed, to 'use' media for a variety of purposeful and rational ends within a comprehensible and explicable model of social activity. Exactly how and why this happens is one of the focal points of research in this area. A key theorist and proselytiser for this approach within mass communications traditions is the aforementioned Denis McQuail, who summarises four categories for itemising the uses and gratifications that audiences pursue. These are surveillance, personal identity, personal relationships and diversion. None of these categories is exclusive, and media forms may fulfil various aspects of these for audiences at any one time.

1. 'Surveillance' refers to the use of media in order to satisfy a need for knowledge – to comprehend what is going on in the world around audience members – 'us'. On the one hand, this need for knowledge can be satisfied by the consumption of current affairs and actuality media forms – newspapers, news bulletins, documentaries and so on. This has important bearing upon the function of media as a 'fourth estate', in relation to the status of audiences as political citizens in need of insight and guidance on the maintenance of society. On the other hand, in order to be a social animal nowadays, we might need to know about media as an object of discussion – just to be able to communicate with other people during those 'water cooler' moments at work, for instance, or to be part of social media chat online. This point relates, of course, to consumption of celebrity scandal generated by paparazzi in newspapers and magazines but also to keeping up with the pop charts, soap plotlines or general gossip.

2. 'Personal identity' refers to the way in which media play a part in defining us. In some ways, this connects with the principles or needs labelled under surveillance but it can have rather more trite meanings, too. Thus, issues of taste come into play here – how our choices reflect our preferences for information, pleasure and so on but also, in turn, reinforce our sense of who we are. For instance, we may consider the kinds of people presented to us in factual and fictional media forms, judging and defining ourselves in relation to them. Indeed, many forms of media actively invite such judgements – talent and dating shows on television, and 'circles of shame' and 'clothing disaster' items in popular magazines, as well as opinionated newspaper columns and blogs. Critics play a part here, too, as do notions of media personalities as 'role models'. The notion of 'lifestyle' consumption seems relevant here as well, i.e. the way in which one might wish to be seen with the 'latest' music or at 'trendy' clubs and concerts.

3. 'Personal relationships' can be explored in terms of media uses and gratifications in a number of ways that build upon these two previous points. We may use media forms as a basis for the way to act in personal situations. For instance, pop songs may teach us about the rules and rituals of romance and emotions, teen soaps about being an

adolescent. Knowledge of and consumption of particular types of media may open doors for us in terms of personal relationships. We join communities of consumers at cinemas and pop concerts, or in online forums and games such as *Second Life* or *World of Warcraft* in which we participate and develop social relations. To some extent, too, media forms may offer us surrogate sociability and relationships. What we refer to here are some of the ways in which we interact with the media – talking to or 'with' personalities on screen, on air or in print. Of course, we most of us recognise this as a form of harmless ritual, surrogate participation in TV talent or reality shows, for instance. We do, of course, find solace in media, whether we're alone or otherwise. Songs may give us indicators of how to act with prospective partners ('I would jump in front of a train for you') but also how to cope (or otherwise) when things go wrong ('My baby done left me . . . ', 'Gonna wash that man right out of my hair').

4. The idea of 'diversion' relates to very familiar notions of escapism, fantasy, relaxation and so on that can be located around media use. Primary reasons why we may wish to listen to music may relate to pleasure or a desire to escape everyday life. Individuals seem to enjoy being scared by horror movies, 'moshing in the pit' at speed-metal gigs, killing aliens in fantasy video games and experiencing feelings of sexual arousal through pornography. Occasionally this 'diversion' may be instrumental in nature – consider the way in which children might be stuck in front of a television by their parents as a surrogate activity on a rainy day or, indeed, how any of us might attempt to empty our minds of daily stresses via net or TV channel surfing or by immersing ourselves in a favourite CD.

These are intriguing, suggestive and usable ways of thinking about media consumption, which offer a means for identifying and labelling any results we might produce when thinking of why and how audiences consume media. What is interesting about the work that developed in the uses and gratifications approach to audiences is the manner in which audience members emerge as individuals engaging with media, rather than distant and amorphous constructs of market research, theory or scientific 'objectivity'. Early work by Blumler and McQuail, for example, was predicated on an exploration of the responses of 300 individuals, who were interviewed about their TV viewing and invited to categorise for themselves the nature of their uses and gratifications. But even then, out of this size-able sample, the nuances of individuals do emerge. Here's a quote from work done in 1970–1, for instance, that itemises the responses of a 40-year-old milkman who produces eight constructions of his uses and gratifications based upon reflections about his favourite twelve shows:

1. *Covers many things – covers only one topic.*
2. *Makes me feel nostalgic – is viewed just for pleasure.*
3. *Produces feelings of frustration and helplessness – does not make me feel that way.*
4. *Entertaining; you can sit back and enjoy it with a blank mind – tells you about things that are happening.*
5. *Gives you other people's opinions and views – gives you knowledge.*
6. *Serious and heavy – light-hearted.*
7. *Challenges one's own opinions – enjoyable without having to work at it.*
8. *Like best – like least.*

Source: Blumler *et al.* (2003) reproduced at www.participations.org/volume%201/issue%201/
1_01_blumler_chapter5.htm#_ednref3

Clearly, the exploration of uses and gratifications represents something different from the abstractions of market research and promotions or the presumptions behind the idea that media produce direct and measurable effects on belief and behaviour. This approach opens up questions of the plurality of audience interpretations, recognising and affording them

Doing media studies

Your media uses and gratifications

Based upon the four categories outlined above, produce a brainstorm map of how you use media and what kinds of gratifications you derive from your consumption. How easily are you able to locate your uses and gratifications within these parameters? Does anything not fit in here? Is there any way in which you feel that media do not satisfy your 'needs'? If they don't, why not?

some space for power and self-determination. Inevitably, however, the uses and gratifications approach has also engendered some criticism, even as it continues to inform aspects of media research, particularly in response to questions about the integration of new media into the lives of individuals (e.g. Ruggiero, 2000).

Some of the salient points of this criticism are worth considering, as they underline the fact that, while this approach has an application in addressing certain aspects of media use, there are other questions worth asking and agendas that are brought to bear upon investigations of audience activity. One criticism, for instance, lies in the very functionalism and individualism that uses and gratifications research explores, which relies very much upon assumptions about and ascriptions of the audience member's personality and psychology. While such aspects are important, it is suggested that the uses and gratifications approach is limited because it lacks attention to social and cultural perspectives that might have some bearing on, and conditioning of, all of those categories explored. For example, acceptable types and sources of 'information' or 'diversion' may vary considerably within particular contexts. And what happens if one has needs unfulfilled by media? In addition, criticism of the uses and gratifications approach suggests that it takes a consumerist view of media use, where, like buying beans in a supermarket, individuals choose the media products that meet their needs, and it is thus circuitously goal-oriented and uncritical of the actual products on offer. For instance, what if I pursue diversions and define myself in my social relations through my consumption of pornography and its limited, misogynistic images of women?

We should recall, too, that the nature of media products and the apparent variety of meaning presented to us ('on offer') is not of the user's making. Thus, a major issue concerns the lack of attention within the uses and gratifications approach to content other than in very broad terms, i.e. that 'news' is sought in order to aid surveillance of the world. That media forms present information in particular ways, and often particularly repetitive and circumscribed ways – despite the apparent variety on offer – might have some bearing upon what kinds of uses are available to audiences and the degree of gratification they derive from their choices.

Ultimately, then, a uses and gratifications framework offers one approach to understanding what audiences do with media, but it has not addressed a number of important issues that we might consider to be factors in media consumption and worthy of investigation. These include: social and domestic contexts and relations; the agendas and project of media organisations and producers; and, indeed, the manner in which detailed meaning is made by and derived from specific media texts.

Theorising audiences: encoding/decoding media meanings

In narratives of media studies, scholars who pinpoint limitations in the uses and gratifications framework (e.g. Corner, 1998; Morley and Brunsdon, 1980) locate an important contribution to the development of audience studies in the work of Stuart Hall. Hall's work at the Birmingham Centre for Contemporary Cultural Studies (CCCS) in the 1970s (p. 309, 390) was influenced by the semiology of Roland Barthes and Umberto Eco as well as the political insights of Eco's fellow Italian Antonio Gramsci (p. 358). Hall's approach to audiences was a reaction to how media had been studied, observing that: 'Traditionally, mass-communication research has conceptualised the process of communication in terms of a circulation circuit or loop. This model has been criticised for its linearity – sender/ message/receiver – for its concentration on the level of message exchange and for the absence of a conception of the different moments as a complex structure of relations' (Hall, 1980: 128). While Hall did not investigate actual audiences, he sought to develop a theoretical model for thinking of the context in which media messages are made and interpreted, of the relationship between producer, text and audience. This sense of a relationship is encapsulated in his conjunction 'encoding/decoding' (the very title of his paper on this matter): messages are part of a process, encoded in texts in production and then decoded in consumption, and this process takes place within a complex social structure in which the message is not isolated. Media institutions (comprising owners and producers, with their own agendas as well as textual and professional conventions) have power to set agendas, define 'what counts' as media content and the way that it is presented and articulated. Audiences make what they can or will of the signs, systems, meanings and so on that media forms present, as well as making their readings within the social and cultural positions which underwrite how they are disposed to read and interpret these signs. Clearly, producers and audiences share these systems of interpretation, as they do social and cultural perspectives, although, as individuals with different social identities (as men, women, black, white, working class, professional), there are also a variety of other pressures on the resources that are brought to bear on interpretation. The overarching issue is, for Hall, one of power relations in society, in which media, and the messages they present, have a role to play. (See the next chapter for a more detailed discussion of the issue of social power and media.)

Hall offers a series of 'positions' of meaning for conceptualising the situation and parameters of sense-making for audiences in the face of the 'influence' of media messages, what they represent and indeed 'who' they represent. These are: dominant (or hegemonic; see p. 358), oppositional and negotiated.

The dominant set of ideas or meanings in media texts are those that present, invite or insist upon a 'preferred' reading among audiences, which, if taken on or accepted, ratifies particular ways of seeing the world. An 'oppositional' reading is one in which the preferred interpretation of a media text or message is understood but rejected by its consumer. A 'negotiated' meaning is one in which the audience take on the 'preferred' meaning but this is also tempered by 'oppositional' positions conditioned by the context of interpretation, and also by the polysemic (p. 62) nature of texts. Of course, in this relationship between production and consumption of meaning, texts are intentionally and conventionally constructed in order to anchor meaning, so all effort is made to rein in polysemia. On the other hand, one cannot guarantee how individuals will read texts, considering their position. Thus, what this model suggests is that, while interpretation is context-bound, impacting upon how we might deduce any likely result in audiences, that interpretation, like the production of meaning, is bound up in greater social structures of convention and power. In short, with all of these pressures, the message at the start of the production chain is not that which consumers take away. Thus, this tends to present a problem for models that privilege direct links between the message and the behaviour and beliefs of consumers.

Let's illustrate these ideas with a contemporary example. During the worldwide 'credit crunch' and economic crises of 2008, President George Bush decided to direct the US government to go against its free market, monetarist policies and support the financial system with an injection of around $700 billion. On 24 September 2008, Bush addressed the American nation on live TV to outline this plan. Here is some of what he said:

> Good evening. This is an extraordinary period for America's economy. Over the past few weeks, many Americans have felt anxiety about their finances and their future. I understand their worry and their frustration. We've seen triple-digit swings in the stock market. Major financial institutions have teetered on the edge of collapse, and some have failed. As uncertainty has

grown, many banks have restricted lending. Credit markets have frozen. And families and businesses have found it harder to borrow money.

We're in the midst of a serious financial crisis, and the federal government is responding with decisive action. We've boosted confidence in money market mutual funds, and acted to prevent major investors from intentionally driving down stocks for their own personal gain.

Most importantly, my administration is working with Congress to address the root cause behind much of the instability in our markets. Financial assets related to home mortgages have lost value during the housing decline. And the banks holding these assets have restricted credit. As a result, our entire economy is in danger. So I've proposed that the federal government reduce the risk posed by these troubled assets, and supply urgently needed money so banks and other financial institutions can avoid collapse and resume lending.

Source: www.whitehouse.gov/news/releases/2008/09/20080924-10.html

As good media scholars, we would wish to see these words in the context of their delivery, of course (on television, live and direct from the US Congress, Bush standing behind a lectern decorated with his emblem of office), as well as examining Bush's performance of these words. Nonetheless, this is, obviously, a formal message delivered from the most powerful man in the country to his fellow citizens, on whose behalf he wields power. It seeks to explain a current situation, to outline the nature of the crisis and, indeed, to demonstrate the action that his administration is taking. A preferred reading of this message, possibly, is one in which the threat is accepted on the terms described by the reader, who is reassured by Bush's actions, which seek to preserve the status quo on behalf of the common good. An oppositional reading might reject the overall diagnosis and solution based upon an analysis that finds fault not in some abstract root cause behind the operations of the market, but in the market and the overall system. A negotiated reading would find ground to agree with and be reassured by Bush but perhaps wonder if this action is completely reliable or necessary, perhaps looking for other solutions but generally agreeing with the aim of maintaining the status quo. How one takes up such readings is likely to depend upon one's position within American society (or even outside it). For instance, how might the following respond to such a message: a Wall Street banker, a member of the Democratic Party, a UCLA student, a bank clerk in Idaho, a single mother in Detroit, a new home-owner in Oregon, a member of the Taliban in Afghanistan?

This message, as it is presented here, might seem quite transparent as a message with an equally transparent purpose. It is also most directly about the nature of society and the role of the powerful and their relationship with a wider constituency. What then of other messages? What is the nature of preferred, negotiated and oppositional positions and readings when audiences consume fiction, films, advertisements and newspaper photographs, or radio shows and popular music and the variety of other media in which political issues are not dealt with in such obvious fashion? We have already touched upon some of the ways of reading such media messages

Key thinker

Stuart Hall (1932–)

Stuart Hall is one of a handful of theorists responsible for the prodigious growth of media and cultural studies. He took over from Richard Hoggart (p. 390) as director of the Birmingham Centre for Contemporary Cultural Studies and oversaw the development of an incredible array of influential works, the legacy of which can be felt in this book and across the field. His cultural analysis has always been 'engaged' with the nature of the society in which we find ourselves, seeking to support progressive practices across media, politics, education and so on. In the 1970s he paid attention to the nature of media panics concerning street crime in *Policing the Crisis* (Hall *et al.*, 1978) and the way in which this was tied to racist perceptions of young black men. His analysis of contemporary power and hegemonic struggle anticipated the political terrain of the 1980s and the rise of the 'New Right'. Overall, his work has proven to be optimistic in identifying ways in which analysis and popular struggle can take on the powerful and vested interests, by winning position if not always being triumphant in the end.

throughout this book (see the Chanel analysis on pages 158–165 for a detailed discussion). These have been rather hypothetical and schematic, however – conducted by the authors as media analysts. If you review our analyses, you will see, perhaps, traces of Hall's model of the relationship between text and a hypothetical or 'implied' reader. What then, we ask, of the actual, living readers who consume and make sense of media texts?

Discovering the audience: media, context and meaning

We should understand that Hall's work came out of a moment in which 'theory' occupied a privileged position for many in the academic community concerned with media messages. Any empirical work on the actual opinions, preferences and activities of audiences was viewed as likely to produce little more than 'market research' (Brunsdon and Morley, 1999). Thus, Hall is akin to those theorists discussed in the previous chapter, whose assumptions tended to 'produce' audiences and their potential responses. However, Hall offered his model as something in need of exploration, refinement and testing, well aware of the distinction between 'implied' readers and people with real lives who exist in real contexts. This realisation, for Hall, and for us now, in considering audiences in relation to our own perceptions of media meaning, offers important qualifications for how we proceed.

A student of Hall's by the name of David Morley took on the model of encoding/decoding in order to explore the way in which actual audiences from different backgrounds responded to a specific, popular BBC TV show of the late 1970s called *Nationwide*. This show appeared in the early evening and took on a 'magazine' format that combined current affairs stories with more lightweight material. It was, in effect, the epitome of 'everyday' television, neither overly 'hard' in its news and political coverage nor wholly 'ephemeral' or 'diverting' like material clearly signalled as 'entertainment' (comedy, drama and so on). This balance was of particular interest at a time when the UK was experiencing an unsettled economy and a great deal of industrial unrest and political polarisation as a result.

The programme had already been the object of a close textual reading by Morley, in conjunction with Charlotte Brunsdon (as well as others of the CCCS) (Brunsdon and Morley, 1978). Here they focused on its mode of address to its implied audience and the particularly mainstream social values and worldview it presented in its amalgam of stories and styles (Brunsdon and Morley, 1978). Morley arranged for 29 different groups of 5–10 individuals to view episodes of *Nationwide* (e.g. those covering the annual budget announcements and so on). Members of groups were selected on the basis of their socio-economic backgrounds in order to explore whether or not these would have any correlation with their interpretations in some traceable form. Groups, including bank managers and working-class apprentices, tended towards a 'dominant' reading, according with what Morley interpreted as *Nationwide*'s own values. Those who produced 'negotiated' readings included teachers, university students and trade union officials. Those who rejected *Nationwide*, producing 'oppositional' readings, included black further education students and trade union shop stewards. Overall, the results tended to confirm Hall's model of interpretation but not in a consistent fashion that supported a direct correlation between social position and receptivity to the 'dominant' reading of the values presented in the text.

In short, then, Morley's empirical audience research located actual audiences in their guise as individuals and role as members of recognisable socio-economic groups, within a tangible social and historical context. How they made meaning was clearly a complex issue, and not reducible to the banal yet vital observation that 'different people read media messages in different ways'. Perhaps the whole story did not quite emerge in this study.

Key text

The death of the author and the birth of the reader

An important development theorising the activity of the consumer of the text came out of the semiology of Roland Barthes. In an essay of 1968, the French theorist announced, rather provocatively, that the author was dead (*'La mort de l'auteur'*). He did not mean that any one particular writer was literally or suddenly dead or redundant, but presented the logical conclusion of semiotic investigation and the manner in which meaning systems, structures and signification are culturally located. He sought to challenge the notion that any writer – the Author with a capital A (or any other producer of a text) is the final arbiter of meaning, residing as an authority figure over their work and its interpretation. Barthes suggested that such a focus has, at worst, tended to lead to interpretative criticism that seeks qualification for meaning in the individual's biographical detail or their pronouncements about their 'intention', when the fixity of the very language they use escapes them. Barthes's announcement of the 'death' of the author acknowledged, on the one hand, how the producers of texts are situated in a complex web of meanings and ideas that inflect the 'originality' and 'intention' of their enterprise. On the other, it acknowledged the vital act and role of interpretation – the existence of the reader in making meaning.

This idea proved very provocative, particularly in the Anglophone world, where Barthes was too often taken very literally, rather than being seen to offer a theoretical treatise on language and the political quality of individualism in modern society, an idea evinced in the elevation of authors and other creative workers to a privileged status. Likewise, and perhaps symptomatic of the heady challenges of the 1960s, the overt radicalism of the idea upset conservative thinkers. However, Barthes's notion, when translated beyond the literary work, offered a great deal to the theorisation of the audience as 'active'.

Of importance here is a distinction between what Barthes calls the readerly and writerly text – concepts derived from his study of literary style but, like his concept of authorship, ones which are suggestive in thinking about aspects of media. For Barthes, the 'readerly' text is one in which structure and rhetorical strategies are highly conventional and the spaces available for interpretation are highly circumscribed. To some extent, this would describe a majority of the generic, formulaic and 'transparent' or straightforward nature of much media product. On the other hand, the 'writerly' text is more experimental and indeterminate, while the actual activity of 'writing' that Barthes conceptualises lies in the moment of the reader's interaction with any text, where meaning is produced, sometimes soaring off in ways that cannot be reduced to any prescriptive or descriptive formulae. Whether or not these categories lend themselves to mass, collectively produced media forms is another matter, but if 'readerly' and 'writerly' are taken to describe the process of interpretation, then this may all depend upon the nature of the actual consumer and what they do with media texts (see Barthes, 1977).

Morley's research was rather artificial in the way in which it was conducted – organising groups of similar individuals to watch pre-recorded shows in a university setting, out of their familiar context of domestic spaces, at particular times and with (or without) family members, friends and so on around them. The lesson is that such factors are clearly worthy of consideration if we really want to find out what audiences get up to as audiences, the way in which they make sense of media meanings and the way in which media 'mean' as part of their lives; or, indeed, the way in which media forms are often relatively peripheral and 'weak'.

Where the exploration of methods and questions about audiences and contexts has been particularly productive is in a range of studies influenced by feminist theory and approaches. Researchers have been particularly attuned to the domestic and social contexts of consumption, theorising pleasure, the part that gender plays in audience activity and, indeed, the role that 'gendered' texts or genres play in the lives of audiences.

The relationship of feminist theorists with female audiences and their media consumption, in particular, has been a very interesting one for what it tells us about the relationship

Key theory

Feminism

'First-wave feminism' is a term that is usually applied to the European and American suffragette movement of the early twentieth century, which gained the vote for women. 'Second-wave feminism' grew out of the changes and radical challenges of the 1960s.

The initial contribution of feminists in this period – outlined in groundbreaking work by writers such as Simone de Beauvoir (1949/1997), Germaine Greer (1971), Shulamith Firestone (1971), Kate Millett (1972) etc. – was to identify the inequality and injustice of a society that disempowered women in every possible way. In essence, men held power and the jobs and positions that made them powerful – a power that was deemed to be self-evidently the result of the natural state of affairs manifest in biological differences. Central to feminist analysis was the dictum that 'the personal is political', locating the manner in which inequalities were present in the domestic sphere and in the nature of personal relationships. As this situation was systematically identified and critiqued, it was deemed necessary to do something about it and change things – thus the notion of 'women's liberation'. Feminism was about confrontation of inequality and sexism, as well as about education, which sought to enlighten and liberate women collectively and individually through a process of 'consciousness raising'.

Inequality was something to be addressed, by exploring the experience of all women (all members of an oppressed group and by implication all potential feminists) and by asking some difficult questions about the structures, societies, culture and assumptions that held women back. By this we mean the religious and social mores that deemed that women were second-class citizens, and the medical and scientific assumptions about their physical, mental and intellectual capacities that thus made them unfit for certain kinds of work.

In their attention to media and its social role, feminists have asked questions about three categories. First, there has been an attention to women in media industries, which has explored the sexual make-up of institutions; questions of political economy (who owns the media); how, when and where media operators are trained; the working environment of organisations (regulations, contracts, hours); and the cultural practices of media workers, etc. Secondly, feminists have been concerned with the images and representations of women, asking how men and women are represented in media forms. What range of media representations is available? How does form (text, rhetoric, genre) relate to such images? Finally, and very productively in the context of this chapter, theorists have also paid attention to the gendered nature of audiences, asking: how do men and women make sense of (reading, viewing, pursuing, discussing) media texts and in what ways does gender impact upon this process?

of theorist and subject, and the way that assumptions in the field have been challenged and, occasionally, altered.

Early feminist approaches to media drew attention to the nature and impact of images of women. For instance, Betty Friedan's *The Feminine Mystique* (1963/1984) explored magazines for women, concluding that articles, pictures and editorials in total emphasised a vision of domestic, motherly, middle-class femininity, presented for readers to emulate. Molly Haskell outlined two pole positions for the way in which women were viewed and treated in the title of her book, *From Reverence to Rape* (Haskell, 1974). This study of Hollywood 'weepies', movies aimed at women, concluded that, whatever 'exceptional' and inspiring roles appeared for women, characters always ended up subsuming their vitality as independent women in a romance with a man. Thus, 'The domestic and the romantic are entwined, one redeeming the other, in the theme of self-sacrifice, which is the mainstay and oceanic force, high tide and low ebb, of the woman's film' (Haskell, 1974: 157). Analyses such as these then posited a view of media forms contributing to the 'subjugation' of women, whatever their class, race or sexuality. Media texts, as part of wider cultural production, are seen as contributing to the social construction of femininity, and the limited expectations placed upon women, who are defined through looks and body, for instance, at the expense of skills, mind or ability.

While negative images of women abound across all media forms, of particular concern for theorists such as those cited above, as well as many others (e.g. Laura Mulvey, p. 93, and see also Tuchman *et al.*, 1978; McRobbie, 1991), is the fact that media products aimed at, consumed and enjoyed by women are especially limited. Thus, such approaches to media meanings evidence a concern with media 'effect' or influence, for the way in which women are located in a culture saturated with images that present a rather limited set of roles for women and ideas about women. It naturally follows that actual women learn from these, are thus socialised, and grow into the circumscribed roles available to them. This model is one that presents women as cultural dupes, complicit in their own oppression through their consumption. As we've seen in the previous chapter, and discuss in more detail in Chapter 11, such perspectives are based upon a deep suspicion of media messages and forms as well as the nature of the audience members themselves.

There were two problems with these approaches and insights. As the Dutch scholar Joke Hermes has commented on the literature on women's magazines, the resulting pessimistic and often angry evaluations constructed and assumed what happened to consumers, 'there was no theoretical or other need to interview readers' (Hermes, 1995: 2). Likewise, and notwithstanding the fact that analyses of representations and texts have had value and continue to inform media studies, a major issue for feminists who produced critical evaluations of media forms for women in particular, evincing concern for audiences, was that many of them consumed and enjoyed them too!

TV scholar Charlotte Brunsdon has described 'the opposition between the feminist subject and housewife object of research', and how these positions of power reveal 'the historical construction of these identities' (Brunsdon, 2000: 53). Such ideas resonate with our discussion in the previous chapter of the context in which ideas are formed and of how theorists have 'produced' audiences in their thought, but of importance here is Brunsdon's exploration of the way that such distinctions have fluctuated. This is particularly due to a thrust in media studies that has explored and accentuated 'positive' aspects of media as popular culture (see p. 392), and as a resource in people's lives, in which pleasure and audience have been taken seriously.

Brunsdon, in her book *The Feminist, the Housewife, and the Soap Opera* (2000), has explored the way in which feminists evaluated their own pleasures (see also Hermes, 1995; Vance, 1984) and how they turned to explore audience activities, in order to better understand how they make meaning and the role that media play in the everyday lives of consumers. Very broadly, and in conjunction with the kinds of studies of subcultures and fans discussed below, there has been a 'turn to the audience' since the 1980s, with researchers proceeding with a more respectful and empirical approach to consumers as people. A good example to illustrate this point is Jackie Stacey's *Star Gazing* (1993). This was written within the field of film studies and during a period dominated by theoretical constructions of audiences as 'spectators', informed by ideological and psychoanalytical approaches. Stacey investigated how women understood Hollywood stars in the 1940s and 1950s, drawing on letters and questionnaires from over 300 filmgoers. Stacey's work demonstrated how cultural and national location impacted upon the ways in which audiences related to films, how they identified with stars and what meanings and purposes 'escapism' held for them.

Let's explore some insights about the relationship of female audiences and media with a brief look at genre. We have suggested elsewhere that genre is a particularly valuable way of organising meaning and audiences for producers, and also the importance of it for audiences in recognising familiar pleasures (see Chapter 2). Media theorists have also explored the way in which genres have a particularly 'gendered' quality. Aspects of pop music, film, TV, radio, newspapers and magazines, for instance, have all been studied in this way (e.g. Whiteley, 1997; Hermes, 1995; Winship, 1987). This is not simply to say that media products are just directed at women as a particular audience but that content and form, as well as aspects of delivery and distribution, accord with the nature of women's lives, social roles and wider cultural expectations or conventions and connotations of femininity. For instance, the way in which radio and TV schedules, historically, have organised programming over the day has reflected the assumption that mothers or housewives are at home. Hermes's findings on women's magazines – with their focus on family, cooking, fashion, gossip, etc. – suggest that they have utility in women's lives because they are easily picked up and put down over the course of a day's busy domestic duties. The most prodigious field for research here, if not for audience research in general, has been in TV studies and, in particular, the attention given to soap opera.

Soaps have had a historical status within academic approaches to media and in wider cultural perspectives as the acme of superficiality and ephemera. The endlessly repetitive storylines concerning romances and tangled webs of personal relationships, in the assumption of a largely passive female audience, have meant that this genre has often been seen as having little value.

Brunsdon (2000) outlines how feminists considered soap, as a typical 'women's genre', as a potential site for research because of this negativity. However, the pleasure that female viewers took from soap opera was surprising to feminists, as soap opera has an emphasis on the domestic sphere, which for them was a site of oppression and limitation. Based upon the pleasures expressed by female audiences in the face of the travails of women characters, caused by men, family, friendships and life in general, however, the genre has been 'recuperated' as offering positive and progressive pleasures in which 'feminine competence is recognised' (Brunsdon, 1997: 15).

Christine Geraghty, for instance, has suggested that 'the soap's basic premise is that women are understandable and rational, a premise that flies in the face of much TV drama' (Geraghty, 1991: 47). In this genre, women are seen as skilled in their emotional abilities,

Source: Lime Pictures

UK soaps such as *Coronation Street* and *EastEnders* have been explored by scholars as particularly 'gendered texts' for the manner in which they offer female audiences progressive pleasures based around strong female roles and portraits of domestic competence. Newer soaps such as *Hollyoaks* (and its raunchier extension *Later* above) aim at a particularly niche audience and offer comparatively traditional pleasures with a parade of buff young men and women, often in various states of undress.

Doing media studies

Everyday media use

In what ways does context and our social identity affect our media consumption and the meanings we make from our favoured texts? How can the new researcher begin to explore such questions in meaningful fashion? An exercise that you could try would be to get together a group of friends of both sexes, in order to discuss your media consumption in general – what you consume, where, how and what it means to you. You could also try focusing the discussion by getting your impromptu group to examine a media text together – reading a women's or men's magazine, or watching a 'gendered' TV programme (e.g. a soap, or a 'sports' programme, which might stereotypically work as feminised and masculinised respectively). How might you direct discussion to tease out the kinds of issues that we're interested in as scholars? What kinds of questions could you ask? What kinds of results or insights would you expect to gain? (See below for a discussion of relevant methods.)

and narratives focus on relationships being built, managed and maintained. Therefore, it can be argued that soap opera celebrates aspects of femininity and that this is recognised by female audiences in particular, whose own 'repertoires' are brought to bear in recognising, responding to and taking pleasure in such texts.

What then can the new media scholar take away from this outline of feminist-inspired research? Above all, approaches to audiences informed by feminism have been innovative in the adaptation and development of methods for exploring consumption and contexts (individual methods are outlined in detail in the second part of this chapter). For instance, we've cited Stacey's work already, which drew upon letters from respondents (see also Ang, 1985). Researchers such as Dorothy Hobson drew upon the focus group format in gathering together groups of working women in their lunch breaks, in order to get them to talk about their pleasure in soap operas. Interviews and ethnographic observation (Gray, 1992; Seiter *et al.*, 1991; Thornton, 1993), as well as 'autoethnography', have proven important in exploring domestic and social contexts for consumption. The feminist dictum that 'the personal is political' is perhaps partly responsible for the appearance of the personal pronoun in theoretical work. This is not to eschew our attempts at critical distance or objectivity. That authors regularly now insert themselves into their work as the ever present 'I' has been productive, as researchers reflect upon and acknowledge their own role and part in their work as individuals and media consumers.

Subcultures and fandom

We now turn to consider two related concepts that have proven useful for understanding particular types of media consumers. These concepts are, first, subcultures and, secondly, fandom. Both ideas have something to tell us about everyday media use among groups and individuals to whom particular media forms are more than banal or passing ephemera, and for whom the manner of media consumption has a consciously determining and active role in their identities.

Subcultures

are identifiable, if not necessarily immediately 'visible', minority groups in society who share particular values and habits that are distinctive to that group and sometimes at odds with those of the greater culture to which its members belong.

'Subcultures must exhibit a distinctive enough shape and structure to make them identifiably different from their "parent" culture . . . They must be focused around certain activities, values, certain use of material artifacts, territorial spaces, etc. which significantly differentiate them from the wider culture . . . but there must also be significant things which bind and articulate them with the "parent" culture' (Clarke and Jefferson, 1975: 10).

The concept of subculture derives from anthropology and sociology and interest in theories and instances of social deviance, i.e. how individuals and groups go against the accepted mores and habits of societies. The concept has proven highly influential in the field of cultural studies, which is where it has fed into aspects of attempts to make sense of media consumption. The term does not pertain solely to media use (if at all in some cases), but where media use is important to a subculture the category is instructive.

While subcultures have a long history, the category has proven important in identifying the ways in which young people in particular have responded to social change and aspects of mass media in modern consumer cultures since the Second World War. Indeed, contemporary subcultures are, in part, a result (albeit an unintended one) of media companies responding directly to young people as emergent consumers – identified in marketing terms through 'the teenager', and 'produced' as a group perceived to have its own needs (social, psychological, cultural) towards which mass cultural products could be directed.

Across the world, the impact of the Second World War led to social upheaval and long-term changes – economic, physical, intellectual, cultural, political, sexual and so on. In the UK, for instance, traditional urban communities were being altered by post-war rebuilding (moving people out of slums and housing damaged by bombs), new educational and workplace opportunities, the growth of the consumer society, immigration of non-indigenous peoples and so on. In this context, theorists have reflected upon the rise of a range of spectacular youth subcultures originating among the urban working class, who were most affected by these changes. Thus arose the 'Teddy Boys', 'Mods', 'Rockers', 'Skinheads', 'Suedeheads' and later 'Punks'. It has been suggested that such groups offer community, a sense of belonging in the face of change and disruption to traditional social organisation about which one can do little, especially if young. For the urban working class in the UK, for example, post-war prosperity – the acquisition of goods such as cars, washing machines, televisions and so on – has been blamed for the atrophy of the kinds of community spirit and culture necessitated by poverty and oppression. Home comfort and entertainment – particularly signalled by the coming of television (later, home computers) – enhanced the importance and isolation of domestic space and family units at the expense of collective experiences (in the street, pubs, dancehalls, cinemas and so on).

Subcultural groups came to attention in particular because of a series of disturbances and the formation of a continuing moral panic around 'youth' (Cohen, 1972). On the one hand, this moral panic concerned levels of education and threats to culture arising from the consumption of movies, popular music, magazines, comics – all usually of American origin (see also p. 290). But this panic also had something to do with the 'deviant' nature of what young people did as groups, when compared with previous generations, and

Youth subcultures are sometimes subtle and hidden from the 'mainstream'; other times they are spectacular in appearance as with these punk rockers.

Source: Alamy Images

particularly in the nature of what and how they consumed media and other consumer goods. Thus, the groups identified above – as well as more recent groups such as 'Goths', 'Emos', 'Ravers', 'B-Boys', 'Headbangers', 'Junglists' and so on – have been associated with the genres of music they consume and define as acceptable, what they wear, their haircuts and jewellery, and which clubs and locales they frequent, as well as the kinds of drinks and illegal substances they prefer (or reject, of course). That these things seem to be core to the lives of those within subcultures has been a cause for concern.

Subcultures may seem, when seen from the outside, confusing and sometimes very challenging to 'mainstream' society. In response, theorists have sought to 'read' them for how they signify semiotically and the kinds of meanings that are conveyed in the activities of participants, and how they define themselves through what they consume. *Resistance Through Rituals* (Hall and Jefferson, 1975/1991), the title of one of the first books on the topic from Birmingham's CCCS, reveals something of this approach, as well as the moment of its origin and the theories informing subcultural analysis. The term 'resistance' indicates its debt to the political thought of Antonio Gramsci and ideas of social struggle (p. 358), while 'rituals' was a reference to Roland Barthes's borrowing of anthropological insights from the work of Claude Lévi-Strauss (p. 84). Dick Hebdige, another graduate of Hall's Centre, developed the idea of a subculture as a text in his book *Subculture: The Meaning of Style* (Hebdige, 1979). Here, semiology, together with Barthesian ideas of 'bricolage' and 'homology', were utilised to examine how certain young people conducted 'semiotic guerrilla warfare' (a phrase borrowed from Umberto Eco (1975/1986).

In Hebdige's work, subcultures are interesting because they are evidence of consumers doing things beyond their allotted role of passively and compliantly digesting what is given to them. Faced with relatively circumscribed social resources, they challenge or 'resist' the way that the world is or how it is offered to them, not through any coherent political programme or action (in this sense subcultures are not 'counter-cultures') but via the kinds of rituals they follow and the style that they express. Thus, individuals and the groups to which they belong win 'space' for themselves, create community and define their values by a process of 'bricolage', which means reconfiguring the conventional meanings of the artefacts they consume and the way that they are consumed. The concept of homology refers to the 'symbolic' fit between subcultural lifestyles, disposition and attitudes, that everything that marks them out as distinctive has meaning – from the safety pin through the nose of the Punk and the shaven head of the Skinhead to the black dress of the Goth.

In this, all subcultures of interest to us to some extent represent a relationship with the nature of contemporary consumption. Often, subcultures embrace consumption and take it to extremes that – as with the New Romantics of the 1980s – can serve to unnerve the dominant culture. (New Romantics wore glamorous clothes and overtly challenged the signifiers of gender boundaries in what they wore and the way that they made themselves up.) Sometimes, subcultures reject consumer society: punk's recycled 'dustbin' wardrobe, for instance, as well as the puritanical rejection of stimulants among the 'straight edge' (see www.straightedge.com/) in the context of the rise of acquisitiveness and hedonism in the 1980s.

Of interest to us as media theorists is the role that media play in subcultures, the way in which subcultures make use of media artefacts for the meanings that they are perceived to have and how these 'speak to' and are made to have meaning for such groups. While many youth groups are associated with particular types of music, therefore – the relationship of American 'B-Boys' and rap music for instance, to the 'Ravers' of the 1980s and acid house – not all subcultures are defined by this area. Choices of film, television, magazine and, increasingly, online activity, are also of primary importance to particular subcultures. In addition, we should attend to the various responses of media themselves to subcultures, whether in generating moral panics or in terms of recognition or even of appropriation of subcultural meanings. Hebdige calls this last process 'recuperation', one in which 'Youth cultural styles may begin by issuing symbolic challenges, but they must end by establishing

Case Study

What is Emo?

'Emo' is a useful category for thinking about the role of media in contemporary sub-cultures, how they originate and what happens to such groups. 'Emo' is actually a label that has been applied to various bands that may or may not collectively constitute a musical genre. 'Emo', or emotional hardcore music, has been identified with 1990s bands such as Fugazi, Jimmy Eat World and, more recently, My Chemical Romance and Panic at the Disco (that such bands reject the label itself is worthy of note). The label then extends to fans of the bands, who are, in turn, particularly recognisable in their dress and habits.

Those who might identify themselves as 'Emo', or are labelled by others as belonging to an 'Emo' subculture, are, stereotypically, described as effete in appearance and manner – men and women dress in similar ways, blurring 'obvious' gender boundaries – with long, lank hair, black dress, buckles, jewellery and canvas-style shoes. In this sense, the 'Emo' look shares something with 'goth' subculture, which originated in the 1980s as an offshoot of punk, as well as aspects of stylings associated with followers of the independent and alternative music scene of that decade (Hodkinson, 2002).

Readers who style themselves as 'Emo' will find much that is remiss with this brief account (we've got the terms all wrong, no doubt), but a number of developments around it are typical of subcultures. First, there is the debate between bands and followers over the 'authentic' nature of what Emo is – musically and culturally; accusations over bands 'selling out' and the appearance of Emo fashions in high-street stores suggest a moment of recuperation.

Secondly, Emo has attracted the attentions of non-music-based and non-sympathetic media organs, forming the basis for a minor moral panic. This centres upon the apparently maudlin message and look of bands such as MCR and its followers, and a link (whether actual or imagined) with teen suicides and online forums and sites dedicated to the topic of suicide. More recently, as the subculture has expanded and travelled beyond its Anglo-American roots, its members have engendered attention in Mexico, as *Time* magazine has reported. In this report, one gets a sense of the recognisable aspects of a subculture that has attained 'stereotype' status, and its relationship with other groups and the perceived 'norms' of dominant culture. Ioan Grillo identifies those who belong to the Emo subculture as 'the kids who wear exaggerated haircuts and immerse themselves in moody music. In short: the kids jocks have been beating up for decades.' Here then one has a sense of the 'victim' and 'outsider' status of Emo. Grillo traces the way in which this subculture has met with some hostility in Mexico among existing subcultural imports 'As well as running riot in Queretaro, a mob also attacked emos in the heart of Mexico City.' Interviewees claim that they are regularly threatened and assaulted: 'The attackers, catalogued as "anti-emos", include some from other urban tribes such as punks, metallers and cholos but many are just ordinary working-class teenagers and young men. They deride the emos for being posers who are overly sentimental and accuse them of robbing from other music genres.' Such things seem relatively inconsequential but the seriousness with which they are treated and the consequences that they engender illustrate the real bonds and meanings that subcultural identities and territorial investments members bring to their groups.

Source: www.time.com/time/arts/article/
0,8599,1725839,00.html - 2008.

new sets of conventions; by creating new commodities, new industries or rejuvenating old ones' (Hebdige, 1979: 96). Thus, the signs of subcultures – dress, musical preferences, activities (dance, language and so on) – become converted into mass-produced objects. This process and these frames for comprehending subcultures may also aid us in exploring the related category of the 'fan' and 'fandom'.

'Fan' is derived from the word fanatic, a term that guides the dominant ways that such individuals have been viewed. Joli Jenson suggests that these relate to a view of fans collectively as a 'hysterical crowd' or alone as an 'obsessed individual' (Jensen, 1992: 9). The collective image is reinforced by the sight and sound of crowds at football matches or screaming mobs at pop concerts – from the days of Frank Sinatra to the Beatles, and more recent manifestations. The individual fanatic is exemplified by figures such as John Lennon's murderer, Mark Chapman, John Hinckley, who attempted to assassinate US president Ronald Reagan, and repeated instances of celebrity stalkers and, indeed, celebrity fanatics, such as Chris Crocker with his YouTube dedications to Britney Spears. When Jensen first made her observations, 'fandom' as a 'practice' was relatively unexplored. While negative associations endure, studies of fandom, informed by the more 'respectful' attitude of theorists towards media consumers, have proliferated as part of the wider exploration of the way in which audience members are active in their interpretation of media texts, and the way that these contribute to the construction of their identity and social participation (Cook and Bernink, 1999).

As with the label 'subculture', 'fan' does not refer simply to a relationship with mass media. It seems that one can be a fan of anything, although it would be unusual to apply the term to an academic who had spent her life reading, collecting and analysing the works of T.S. Eliot, when compared with, say, an aficionado of SpongeBob SquarePants cartoons. We might argue over the relative merits of these cultural texts but the distinction between them and the relative cultural respectability of each in our society, and the regard for the affiliation one shows to each, indicates something of the limits of fan as a label. The term is also often used quite casually to describe anyone who might show some affection or a regular devotion to something – watching *X Factor* every week, or buying *Lucky Luke* comic books. However, the longer 'fanatic' suggests a greater attachment, and our comparison might also suggest, perhaps, an attachment to something that is perceived to be not quite worthy of such attention. After all, one can probably gain a reputable, well-paid teaching post sharing an appreciation of Eliot and his works with students but it might be a little harder to achieve this based upon a knowledge and affection for the denizens of Bikini Bottom.

We would suggest, then, that what marks out the fan (at least in the way we wish to employ the term) is a commitment and attachment that is distinct from the regular consumer. In this, their consumption compares to the habits of those in subcultural groups. A useful way of thinking about fandom further, perhaps, is as one way of consuming media within a whole set of possible and dynamic relations. Thus, one way of defining fandom is through relations of 'taste'. Fans resist 'dominant cultural hierarchies' (Jenkins, 1992: 17–18),

Doing media studies

Subcultures and media

Do you belong to an identifiable subculture? If not, are you able to identify a contemporary group that might fit the bill?

Based upon any subcultural group you are able to locate, itemise its distinguishing features and activities. What kinds of media consumption, if any, characterise this group? How might the concept of homology aid in explaining these features?

Is this group already 'known' to the media itself or is it 'hidden'? If so, where does it feature and how is it represented? Is this representation positive or negative in any way?

If you do not belong to this group, how would you go about 'getting close' to it in order to explore how it works and what it means for participants? Even if you do belong, what kinds of approach do you think might work in getting closer in order to explore this group and its media consumption?

considering texts from their chosen interest to be of 'good taste', treating them 'as if they merited the same degree of attention and appreciation as canonical texts' (i.e. those things officially sanctioned in society as respectable, such as Eliot's poetry or Shakespeare's plays). Aficionados, in turn, mark out the objects of fandom as superior to the rest of the fare on offer across different media forms. Interestingly, and while stereotypes of fans of science fiction or fantasy as 'geeks' abound, there is little that is common or consistent across the 'objects' of fandom. Compare, for instance, the work of a rock band such as the Grateful Dead (who have their own distinctive followers – 'Deadheads') and devotees of the film *The Big Lebowski* (dir. Cohen and Cohen, 1998) (who hold conventions centred on Jeff Bridges's character, Dude) with collectors of Euro-cult cinema (see below). With no obvious or consistent connections, what defines the objects of fandom are the practices and devotion of fans that accrue around them (Hills, 2002).

It is worth dwelling upon the concept of taste for a moment in order to fully grasp the role it plays in the establishment of social hierarchies within fandom and in fandom's relationship with the wider culture (see: Hills, 2002). Here, theorists of fandom have found the work of French sociologist Pierre Bourdieu useful. In his studies of French society, Bourdieu originated a concept of 'cultural capital': 'a possession of cultural and symbolic power working to produce and reinforce social distinctions' (Hartley *et al.*, 2002: 45). Bourdieu sought to describe the ways in which taste could be explained schematically, rather than accepted as subjective and innate in individuals with taste. For Bourdieu, taste was naturalised in relation to economic capital, supporting social inequalities: the powerful, and their cultural preferences (in art, their manners, design of house, clothing, etc.), seem effortlessly, naturally, superior and deserving of the rank.

Within fandom, for fans at least, their taste and commitment to the objects of their devotion is what marks them out from other consumers and, indeed, within the fan community. John Tulloch (Tulloch and Jenkins, 1995) has described fans as a 'powerless elite': they wield little power in society but mark themselves out as an 'elite' through their knowledge and validation of the media they consume. They are powerless, too, in relation to the actual management and production of their favoured products. They are unable to influence the content of their favourite media texts (when the quality or integrity of a TV

A *Star Trek* convention for fans. Fans are as often highly visible sector of the active audience.

Source: Getty Images

programme is perceived to be in decline, for instance) nor, in most cases, are they able to halt the cancellation of the production of output (comics, recordings, TV shows) when it is no longer economically viable (see the discussion of fans and producers below).

In his book *Textual Poachers* (1992), Henry Jenkins studied fans of the science fiction TV programme ('space opera') *Star Trek* and the manner in which this show has meaning for them, in particular for the way in which they appropriate it, making it part of their lives and adding new meanings to it. The term 'textual poachers' derives from the work of French theorist Michel de Certeau, who wrote of how, in cultural terms in everyday life, the disempowered were like trespassers on the grounds of the powerful, wherein they would 'poach' dominant meanings and values and make them their own (a concept not unlike those behind the theories of subculture). The way that fans do this can be quite personal, in their relationship with their favoured texts, but is also manifested through the production of their own texts, such as stories, art and songs. Fan activity also extends to organising fan clubs, conventions, producing fanzines (fan magazines), amateur fan films, T-shirts and other media artefacts. These are distributed to fellow fans via specialised networks and, increasingly, over the internet. In this creation of community, belonging and shared meanings, fandom again compares with youth subcultures, particularly in the way that, as 'poachers', fans appropriate meaning and make it their own and integral to their identities.

Fan fiction 'written and read by fans themselves centring on the object of their fandom' (Jenkins, 1992: 45) is sometimes known as 'slash' fiction, a term that derives originally from fan stories that fantasised about the sexual pairing of Captain Kirk and Mr Spock from the series (in shorthand – Kirk/Spock – thus emphasising the 'slash' in that conjunction). Slash fiction is incredibly popular within fandom of different descriptions and can be easily located on the internet. Often, such work, as well as other fan productions, infringes the intellectual property rights (p. 225–229) of the creators or causes problems when fantasies are generated around figures that, while fictional, are under the age of consent (e.g. slash fiction about Harry Potter characters for instance). Jenkins notes then that fans can come into conflict with the producers of media texts because they are using the ideas of others, therefore 'The relationship between fan and producer, then, is not always a happy or comfortable one and is often charged with mutual suspicion, if not open conflict' (Jenkins, 1992: 32). An example of the ways in which fans have conflicted with producers was when the animated sitcom *Family Guy* was cancelled by the US Fox network. After initial discontent was expressed about this decision in online message boards, online petitions were created to show that there would be support for a new season of the show. Coupled with the high DVD sales of the show and the fan support, Fox decided to commission a fourth season, much to the delight of fans. In this case, it would appear that the internet can serve as an equaliser of sorts, although repeated examples of a failure to influence producers on behalf of fans tends to confirm the rule.

By and large, therefore, fan production in extending the textual meanings of shows like *Star Trek*, or in circulating concert bootlegs of rock bands, out-takes and so on, can be seen to fulfil a desire for more product and meaning. Interestingly, and despite the relative niche aspects of fan cultures, such groups are increasingly pandered to by producers. The generation and regurgitation of DVD box sets, reissues, repackaging and so on of back-catalogue items, as well as the 'limited' edition for new releases across media forms, is an obvious means of exploiting and recuperating fan activity.

We've noted in passing that fandom has benefited from digitisation and the invention of the internet. This provides a rich resource for researchers interested in this aspect of audience activity. Jenkins (1992; Tulloch and Jenkins, 1995) notes how fans were early adopters of new media forms to aid their activities, providing an 'ethnographic' study of a newsgroup centred on the early 1990s US TV series *Twin Peaks*. Clearly influenced by Jenkins's study, Matt Hills briefly studies an online *X Files* newsgroup to provide an 'ethnography of the cult audience' participating in online discussion (Hills, 2002: 174). Clerc (1996) discusses the growing online participation of female fans in newsgroups amidst

Case Study

Euro-cult cinema fandom

Euro-cult cinema is a category determined by and used commonly within the international fan community (see www._lovelock-andload._net and www._fabpress._com). It refers to low-budget horror and thriller films that emerged from Western Europe from the late 1950s onwards. These films, which were once regarded as banal Hollywood imitations or 'trash', like many fan objects, have become highly revered by their followers and transformed into something with more cultural value. The *giallo* can be seen as one of the more popular sub-areas of Euro-cult cinema. The *giallo* film was based on pulp crime novels that were popular in Italy from the mid-twentieth century; this led to the production of film adaptations of several *giallo* stories. Although some of the films were released internationally, audiences outside Italy did not get to experience the *giallo* until the home video boom of the early 1980s, when low-budget films were released by enterprising home video labels to meet demand. In the early 1990s, British and American horror fans learnt about the *giallo* through fanzine publications, such as Britain's *Giallo Pages* and America's *European Trash Cinema*, which created interest and paved the way for the generation of a Euro-cult cinema fan culture centred partly around the *giallo* film. Around this time, a British video label called Redemption was formed and released a number of *gialli* in their original language and original cinematic aspect ratio. This allowed a new generation of film fans to experience the *giallo* for the first time. The advent of DVD led to more *gialli* being released, particularly in America and Italy. Recent labels, such as the British company Shameless, continue to release titles on DVD.

What is particularly interesting about Euro-cult cinema fandom are the forms of fan production that take place within the community. New media have allowed fans to not only have a greater level of interaction with the community but also to move from amateur fan production to professional production. An example of this would be the British fan publishing house FAB Press. Originally, FAB Press published the fanzine *Flesh and Blood* and then moved towards producing limited runs of lavish books, several devoted to well-known *giallo* director Dario Argento. Another example would be the website lovelockand-load.com. Not only does the website sell fan-produced T-shirts, which feature designs taken from Euro-cult film posters, but it also has a message board where fans from all across the world discuss their fan interests. Some of the participants build fan-made DVDs using video taken from commercial DVD releases and add English-language audio or subtitles. These fan DVDs are not sold commercially and are only traded with fellow fans. They make available films which might not be released in English-speaking territories. A CD containing mixes of Euro-cult soundtracks has also been produced.

By looking at this example, we can see how fan production has changed: digital technologies are being used to produce texts of a professional standard. We can also see how fans 'poach' from texts in order to create their own artefacts.

Further reading

Gallant, C. (2000) *Art of Darkness: the Cinema of Dario Argento*, Guildford: FAB.

Hutchings, P. (2003) *The Argento Effect*, in Jancovich, M. (ed.) *Defining Cult Movies: the Cultural Politics of Oppositional Taste*, Manchester: Manchester University Press.

Koven, M.J. (2006) *La Dolce Morte: Vernacular Cinema and the Italian Giallo Film*, Oxford: Scarecrow.

New media, new media studies

Fan, Fiction and Twitter

Inger-Lise Bore and Jonathan Hickman

New media create new opportunities for fans to create and share their own interpretations of media texts. For example, a group of fans of the US television show *The West Wing* use Twitter to 'tweet' as characters from the drama. In doing so, they have created a new fan activity for us to study.

Jane Feuer (2007) has described *The West Wing* (*TWW*) as an American mainstream quality TV drama series. It was created by Aaron Sorkin and originally shown on NBC between 1999 and 2006, and it focuses primarily on the lives of the US democratic president, Josiah Bartlet, his family and senior members of his staff.

When we first began studying this activity we approached *TWW* 'twitterverse' (as participants call it) as a work of fan fiction, with each participant acting as a collaborating author. Their joint output has the potential to expand the timeline of the original *TWW* story. This is particularly significant because the show itself has finished. There will be no new episodes to provide viewers with further narrative development or background information, so this Twitter activity offers one way to fill in gaps in the original text and satisfy fans' cravings for new episodes (Costello and Moore 2007).

Our research considered how this *TWW* twitterverse worked as a text, exploring how Twitter mediated the content creating a complex hypertext story which may be experienced differently by different readers at different times, according to who they follow on Twitter.

In this sense, our object of study differs from conventional 'fanfic' research.

When we moved our attention from the text to its producers – many of whom we were fortunate enough to interview – we continued to reassess the way in which we understood this practice. Fanfic writing is believed to be dominated by female fans (Cumberland 2002: 176).

However, the majority of our research participants identified themselves as male. Moreover, only one of our interviewees, @donnatella_moss, had written any other form of fanfic. Other characters who we interviewed either understood what fanfic was but rejected that label for this practice, or claimed to be unaware that such fan practices existed.

The output of this *TWW* twitterverse can appear to its audience as a unified story, but in fact it is formed and shaped by independent participants who have a variety of motivations for their participation. One of the interviewees told us that in real life he works in politics in Washington. He originally conceived of the activity as a way to discuss politics openly online without compromising his position. Several other interviewees saw the activity primarily as an exercise in creative writing, and are motivated by their own writing aspirations. Some participants had seen other *TWW* Twitter accounts and created a character with the hope of engaging with the established twitterverse, while others began as a solo activity and were subsequently adopted by the other users and drawn into the twitterverse.

To differentiate these practices from conventional fanfic we now tend to refer to *TWW* twitterverse as an improvised simulation. The participants are simulating how these characters might come across if they existed in the 'real' world, rather than in a TV show, and if they were using Twitter. Our observation suggested that the accounts can easily be read as 'real' Twitter accounts as they conform to the normal style of tweets – employing normal Twitter practices such as the RT, hashtagging and @ replies.

Our observation and interview data demonstrated that 'staying in character' was a key guiding principle for all participants. Providing what is deemed an 'authentic' performance allowed all of these participants to perform *TWW* fandom by displaying their knowledge and understanding of their chosen character, as well as their awareness of politics and current affairs. It also enables them to demonstrate their creative skills as they adapt that character for Twitter.

For more project links see: https://bitly.com/wwtwitter

Follow the story here: http://twitter.com/#!/joshualyman/colleagues

References

Costello, V. and Moore, B. (2007) 'Cultural outlaws : an examination of audience activity and online television fandom', *Television and New Media* 8(2): 124–43

Cumberland, S. (2002). 'The five wives of Ibn Fadlan: women's collaborative fiction on Antonio Banderas web sites', in *Reload: Rethinking Women+ Cyberculture*, ed. M. Flanagan and A. Booth, 175–94. Cambridge, MA: MIT Press

Feuer, J. (2007). 'HBO and the concept of quality TV', in *Quality TV: Contemporary American Television and Beyond*, ed. J. McCabe and K. Akass, 145–57. London: I.B. Tauris

Doing media studies

Investigating fandom

Identify a 'fan' website: this could be devoted to a pop band, film, TV show, game, sports team, person, etc. What is the 'fan object' and what kinds of things are said and done around it? What kinds of values are in evidence in this activity? Is there any sense of a hierarchy of fandom here? What relationship does your example of fans have with media producers?

male dominance and Baym (1999) also looks at gendered audiences by considering the merging of audience studies and computer communication. She uses an ethnographic study of an online soap opera fan community to understand how women construct their individual identity and participate in a community. All of these developments, and the kinds of activities exemplified by fans, are important to understanding wider 'audience' or 'user' activity online and, indeed, how this is changing our conceptualisation of media consumers and their relationship with producers.

Online audience activity: creating communities, meaning and identity

In this section, we will explore ways of making sense of online activities in relation to the creation of virtual communities and social networks. The importance of this concept can be illustrated through the example of Facebook. Current statistics from Facebook itself claim that it has over 800 million active members and is the one of the most visited sites in the world (www.facebook.com/press/info.php?statistics). With claims such as these, it is hard to ignore the issues presented to attentive media audience researchers by sites such as Facebook, alongside others like Myspace and Bebo. High user numbers suggest that here is a phenomenon worthy of our attention, but what is particularly interesting about sites such as these is the way in which audiences present themselves and interact with one another. In this case, the audience is truly and visibly active. Not only are people communicating with each other in a variety of different ways but they are also 'producing' meanings through their interactions and contributions. In addition to having profiles on social networking websites, people may also have blogs (web logs) that they carefully maintain as a repository for their thoughts, opinions and so on. Some online users might upload video, or even create videocasts or podcasts. Photos are uploaded to sites such as Flickr and are shared and commented upon by other users – some may be familiar to those who post such material, others may be strangers.

We can speculate that the nature of audience behaviour is changing or that these online sites and the opportunities afforded users present new ways of being media consumers, even as they integrate familiar and more long-standing modes of media consumption. It is important, therefore, that we are aware of the ways in which people are using new media and what ideas this presents for thinking about 'audiences' and potential research projects.

What is a virtual community?

The term 'virtual community' was coined by the theorist Howard Rheingold, who defined it as: 'A group of people who may or may not meet one another face to face, and who exchange words and ideas through the mediation of computer bulletin boards and networks. In cyberspace . . . we do everything people do when people get together, but we do it with words on computer screens, leaving our bodies behind' (Rheingold, 1993). Mário Guimarães suggests that a variety of activities can take place between people with mutual interests in online communities, and users obtain different gratifications when they participate in them (Guimarães, 2005: 141–56). Nessim Watson adds that this type of environment 'depends not only upon communication and shared interests but also upon communion' (Watson, 1997: 104). Nancy Baym suggests that, although many attributes of face-to-face communication are not available in cyberspace, this has not disrupted our communication skills. She indicates that this is because new forms of expression (e.g. emoticons), which can also be used creatively, have evolved on the internet and in online communities (Baym, 1995: 151–3). So, online communities, like subcultural groups and fandom, may generate their own conventions, languages and values that make them distinctive.

In order to understand the nature of virtual community, it is worth outlining the role that the internet has had in this development, as well as its difference from the web. The internet is a global network of computers, while the web is a user-friendly interface that runs on the internet. The World Wide Web (the web) was invented by Tim Berners-Lee between 1990 and 1991 (see www.w3.org/People/Berners-Lee/). He sought to find a way in which people could use the internet with the goal of creating a space where people could communicate by sharing information. It is this ethos of sharing that has allowed the internet to grow to such a spectacular degree, as it allows audiences actively to produce material and meaning, and to interact with each other and established professional media producers to a degree unimaginable in the recent past. Collaboration was vital in order for the web to grow. Without anyone producing websites, it would not be as densely populated as it is right now, nor would it have encouraged the establishment of virtual communities. We've mentioned already social networking sites such as Facebook and Bebo, while some further examples of where virtual communities can be found include:

- Bulletin board systems (also known as discussion forums): forums are usually part of a website, offering a place for the online user or 'surfer' to discuss subjects related to the content of that site. The forum system usually requires membership in order for the user to post a topic or view the forums.

- Newsgroups: similar in many respects to discussion forums, newsgroups were one of the earliest forms of virtual communities on the internet. Newsgroups are still very much in existence and can be accessed via client software: Microsoft's Outlook Express, for example. They are sometimes used to distribute films, music, games and software illegally.

- Blogs: though not generally accepted as virtual communities, blogs offer users the ability to communicate with the individual author (or authors) and engage in discussion based around specific issues.

- Chat rooms: 'real-time' environments, where users can talk among a large group of people.

- Massively multiplayer online role-playing games (MMORPGs): popular games such as *World of Warcraft* (www.worldofwarcraft.com) and even the online virtual world *Second Life* (http://secondlife.com/) can be classified as MMORPGs. As suggested by the name, these sites have a very large membership, who interact in a virtual world.

In Rheingold's optimistic view of the internet, online communities open up a new site for the public sphere, where free interaction can take place and people from different global locations are able to engage in discussion and exchange. Rheingold has also shown an awareness of how the relative anonymity afforded by online activity can have both positive and negative effects. Those who might feel unable to voice their opinions in society may find the anonymity to be useful in allowing them to contribute to discussion. Conversely, those who are perfectly reasonable and non-confrontational in real life can become unnecessarily aggressive online, using the cloak of anonymity to act in this way (see, for example www.penny-arcade.com/docs/internetdickwad.jpg).

James Slevin suggests that, while 'all media requires skills' (Slevin, 2000: 65), internet use demands the need for particular capabilities, resources and attentiveness (2000: 66). This suggests that being online is not just about having the skills to work a computer but that it is also important to learn and employ the languages and tactics that been have adopted online, like emoticons and abbreviations in virtual communities. Such usage may mark out online users in communities as insiders or outsiders (Jordan, 1999: 70). This sense of the different status levels online is useful for exploring some of the categorisations of internet user activity.

Ananda Mitra carried out a study on the soc.culture.indian community group, in which he examined its postings. He discovered that, although many members of the community actively participated by responding to messages, the majority of users were reading but not making a response. These people are identified as 'lurkers' (Mitra, 1997: 62). Michele Willson agrees that only a small number of people actually participate, as 'many operate from a voyeuristic or viewer position' (Willson, 1997: 153). Nessim Watson indicates, in his work on Phish.net, that these lurkers reflect the lack of commitment that can occur in the online world in comparison with societies in 'real' life (Watson, 1997: 105). Willson believes that this is because 'Within a virtual community individuals are able to choose their degree of interaction' (Willson, 1997: 152). Steve Jones agrees that this type of participant is negative to communities, as this sort of activity online surely creates an isolated form of being; if you are lurking, you are not interacting and are therefore no more social than a wallflower (Jones, 1997: 13).

In order for online communities to be successful as communities in terms of sociability, they draw on codes of conduct and ethics which may be derived from 'real life' interaction. They have their own set of rules in order to function correctly. This is where the term 'netiquette' comes from. Netiquette refers to online etiquette, generally accepted rules and ways of communicating in virtual spaces. A simple example of netiquette would be not writing in block capitals, as this is regarded as shouting. Further examples of netiquette include: not using someone else's name and pretending to be them; not using abusive or threatening language; not posting negative remarks regarding people's sex, race or gender; not 'spamming' message boards or chat rooms with useless or repeated messages (see www.internet-guide.co.uk/netiquette-guide.html).

Even though virtual communities have such rules, they can be liberating, empowering and democratic for the inhabitants, when compared with the real or 'corporeal' world. If optimistic academics such as Rheingold are to be believed, virtual communities present a utopian ideal that offers a solution to many issues in the 'corporeal' or bodily world. However, virtual communities are not exempt from prejudice and are not without their own problems. Steve Jones (1995) sounds a note of caution, seeing cyberspace as a cultural construction that is not a value-free environment. Its use reflects the structure of values and beliefs that circulate or hold together 'real' society, and is capable of reinforcing existing power relations and inequalities in the same way as any other institutional form. After all, if you have someone who is prejudiced in real life, they are still likely, if not more so, to be prejudiced in an online environment.

We should also be aware that virtual communities are often actively moderated so as to prevent spamming and the posting of unwanted topics or comments. The moderator therefore takes the role of 'gatekeeper', deciding what is and is not acceptable. This decision making is subject to the moderator's own personal values and beliefs. An example of this can found at the Mobius Home Video Forum (www.mhvf.net). Mobius had a reputation for being heavily moderated. When the films of US documentarist Michael Moore were being discussed, a number of posts were deleted as they did not accord with the moderator's political stance.

We should also be aware that not everyone is able to have internet access. This is where the digital divide can become an issue. The digital divide can be understood as 'Different access and use of the internet according to gender, income, race and location' (Couldry, 2004: 190). So, for example, some parts of the world may not have internet access, and people in some countries may not be able to afford internet access. This means that some people are excluded from being able to be part of such communities. Even though virtual communities might present us with a utopian ideal, they still recreate society and bring with them unwanted baggage.

As we established earlier, a characteristic of the web is the sharing and contributing of knowledge. The general consensus of online discussion forums, for instance, is to provide support and help to others and to further one's knowledge in the particular subject area catered for. Posters are asked to 'stay on topic' in forums, for example; in a computer support forum devoted to processors, if someone posted a comment about a TV soap opera they would be warned for being off topic and possibly banned for not following forum rules. Wellman and Guila (1999) see online communities as electronic support groups, offering help and support to people who require specific information. They suggest that 'helping others can increase self-esteem, respect from others, and status attainment' (Wellman and Guila, 1999: 176).

The issue of 'status' is of particular interest here, as some posters and active members in virtual communities are not primarily there to help others but to enhance their reputation among online peers. This is when we might see hierarchies appearing in virtual communities, where at the top is the moderator or forum owner and below are those who have the higher number of contributions to the forum. But, just because a user has a large number of contributions, it does not mean that they are an authority on a particular issue – they just might not have anything better to do. Bourdieu's notion of cultural capital is useful here, as those who contribute to forums, such as fans, might want to demonstrate their power and knowledge through answering and responding to questions (Bourdieu and Passeron, 1990). Because of this competitive environment, newcomers to online environments might perceive them to be uncomfortable places, as they may find it difficult to fit in.

Source: Copyright 2009, Linden Research Inc. All Rights Reserved

Virtual communities such as *Second Life*® offer users immersion in a world that is both similar to and different from our own – where one can explore fantasy scenarios of escape or reproduce everyday life.

Identity and deception

One way in which we come to terms with and address a community is to present ourselves in a particular way. Sociologist Erving Goffman's (1959) studies of 'real-life' interaction suggested that we role-play and present public personas, which we deem to be appropriate for certain types of social intercourse. Do we behave the same way online? There are many extreme examples of people using the anonymity of the internet to create a fictional 'narrative' of themselves and presenting that to other users. Even if we do not consciously do this, some studies suggest that we actively construct identities for

Case Study

eBay

Individuals and collectives generate and manage some online communities from their own independent action. Other communities are allied to commercial operations – in relation to media and other activities and products. There are interesting dynamics to be explored and understood in such sites, therefore, as users/audiences enter into dialogue with each other under the gaze and management of companies, who provide their pleasures and support their activity. In this regard, a curious and unusual site for attention is that of eBay.

eBay Inc. is an internet company that manages the online marketplace ebay.com. The brand was founded, in 1995, by Pierre Omidiyar, who wanted to provide an online platform that would allow for the selling of products and services by a community of individuals and small businesses. eBay is promoted as an online space where people can connect through what they call 'social commerce', which is defined as 'a powerful combination of commerce, communication and community that enhances traditional buying and selling' (eBay, 2012). This is achieved within an auction environment, where members sell and bid for items; 'buy it now' prices can also be set, which allow users to purchase goods immediately.

eBay is the type of online platform that requires specific skills and capabilities (Slevin, 2000: 66).

Users need knowledge of the conventions and tactics required to be a successful seller. These are related to the formal conventions set up by the site's owners but also the 'cultural' conventions that have been established by users themselves. The virtual community of eBay has established its own conventions about acceptable behaviour and, particularly, about the establishment of trustworthy, peer-reviewed identities. As the site is dedicated to financial transactions, trust and reputable identities for both buyers and sellers are essential. Newman and Clarke have discovered that online auctions account for a great amount of online fraud (2003: 93). The opportunities they describe include bid shilling, where the seller or the seller's friend takes on a false identity and attempts to bid on their own item to make the bidding price increase. Another is bid shielding, where a buyer and partner make a really high bid to scare away other bidders then, at the last moment, the bid is withdrawn and the associate wins at a low price. Then there is non-delivery, where the seller receives the payment and does not ship the item or delivers a cheaper product. Finally, they discuss non-payment, where bidders do not make a payment (Newman and Clarke, 2003: 96).

Interestingly, while the pursuit of financial reward is possibly the primary pleasure of eBay, many secondary pleasures also occur from discussion board participation, which sometimes relate to the nature of buying and selling, other times to completely unrelated topics, such as favoured TV shows, politics, food addictions and so on. Herein, one can observe the characteristics of virtual communities identified by Rheingold, such as instances of users finding pleasure and satisfaction in the formation of friendships and the giving and receiving of support (Rheingold, 1991: 57–80).

ourselves when online which may be extensions of or alternatives to those we inhabit in regular 'physical' interactions.

Sherry Turkle's (1995) study *Life on the Screen* looks at the construction of online identities in virtual environments. She found that cyberspace provides people with the opportunity to express themselves more freely and allows them to discover an 'authentic', more fulfilling sense of self-identity, with many users, more often than not, inhabiting multiple identities online. For example, when online, some people might present themselves as being of a different gender, race, physical ability, sexuality or even appearance, and hence act through different languages and discourses to construct different 'online' experiences, through different interactions in various communities or online one-to-one relationships.

Charles Cheung suggests that the internet 'provides a range of ways in which net users can carefully select, polish and embellish aspects of their selves to present to their friends, families and unacquainted Web surfers, without risking the embarrassment or harassment that may be experienced in face-to-face interaction' (Cheung, 2004: 50). So, the internet can provide a hiding place – a disguise, enabling us to invent a persona and interact under different rules from those by which we are defined 'in person'. This issue has been at the forefront of the 'moral panic over online paedophile activity' (Waterson, 2000) and also the current online privacy and fraud debate, where we are told to be aware that the people with whom we interact online may not be who they say they are.

Though people create identities, it doesn't always mean that they are reputable sources of information. This is discussed by Judith Donath (1998) in her valuable work on identity and deception in online communities. She suggests that 'deception to the information-seeking reader is potentially high' – users can create any identity they wish, claiming to be experts or changing their gender – and that the only way to enhance one's reputation in an online community is by posting interesting topics or providing support to fellow users (Donath, 1998: 31). She also highlights other forms of identity deception, such as 'trolling', where rogue posters attempt to disrupt the community by giving 'bad advice', and 'flaming', which is when users are insulted (Donath, 1998: 44). Donath reminds us that people online may not always be reliable, something that is important when studying virtual communities.

New virtual spaces, new audiences

In recent years, new media forms have allowed the development of a much more interactive aspect to online communication (and indeed across other media). The term 'Web 2.0' is sometimes enlisted to identify this change, marking out the fact that we seem to have moved on from an earlier, more 'primitive' stage of electronic activity. While the term is relatively meaningless in itself, the shift it refers to is marked by the advent of blogs, wikis, social networking sites and other new forms of online communities, such as YouTube and Vimeo. With these sites, the emphasis is placed on collaboration and networking rather than simply visiting to consume set content in a manner analogous to the one-way nature of old media. The popularity of sites such as Facebook, Myspace and YouTube demonstrates that audiences are no longer just using the internet primarily as a source of information but are actively involved in production, and in changing the way in which media are both created and consumed. One only has to look at the way in which the first incarnation of Napster, the infamous file-sharing software, changed the ways that music was distributed and consumed to see that the boundaries between producers and audiences are being blurred.

Another instance of this blurring can be found in citizen journalism. Bowman and Willis (2003) define citizen journalism as the act of citizens 'playing an active role in the process of collecting, reporting, analysing and disseminating information'. On many recent occasions, such as the Chinese earthquake of 2008, early news of the tragedy was broken on the social

Doing media studies

Investigating virtual communities

Identify a virtual community and have a look at some of the discussions present. You may have to join the forum in order to look at the discussion. Consider the following questions:

■ How do members of this community construct and present their identities?

■ What is the relationship between the members of this community?

■ What strategies are used to reinforce and maintain the relationship?

■ Are there any values or activities that seem to be unique to this particular community?

networking site Twitter, and further details were published on blogs and distributed on networking sites. An early example of citizen journalism was demonstrated in the 7 July 2005 London bombings, where members of the public, some of whom were actually trapped in the London Underground, were taking pictures and video of the event as it unfolded. Some of the images were broadcast by major news channels and used in newspapers. Citizen journalists are also able to raise issues that are ignored or not accurately reported by mass media, and cover them, without any regulatory presence, on their blogs. The two-way nature of the blog allows for readers to engage in discussion and also add to the news story, sharing details and their own accounts. Here we can see the collection, distribution and consumption of news changing, and mass media having to change in order to accommodate this new form of news reporting.

Researching media audiences

Methodologies

Now that we have explored some ideas about audiences and their activities, how are we to find out meaningful things about them ourselves, about what they do with media products, why they do the things they do, what meanings media forms have for them and the role that media play in their lives? This section is dedicated to outlining briefly some of the methods which researchers have deployed in pursuing these questions. The term 'method' is simply a way of labelling the organised technique and systematic process by which we go about these investigations. We have encountered a number of other methods so far in this book that have been concerned with analysing the text: rhetoric, genre, semiology, narratology and content analysis.

As we suggested in the last chapter, in discussing being part of an audience, the concept seems rather obvious and close at hand as we are, all of us, at some time or another, members of an audience, readership or online community. This might suggest that researching media consumption is an entirely obvious procedure. Of course, media companies ask questions of audiences and survey their behaviour all the time, in pursuit of what we've called 'instrumental' knowledge that can be used for the purpose of enhancing what they do in order to keep the same customers satisfied. However, the kinds of questions and issues we seek to explore with audiences are particular and often peculiar to media studies. While people think about and speak with each other about their media consumption all the time, some questions we might wish to ask might seem very odd indeed. It would be very unusual to be confronted by someone asking you to talk about the way in which your reading of your daily newspaper allows you to function as a citizen in relation to ideas of the public sphere, or if you asked a group of five-year-old children about representations in Disney films and how they understood gender depictions in *High School Musical*. The kinds of subjects that we are interested in are not necessarily obviously manifest in what people say or do, nor can they always be accessed so directly.

It is not, therefore, that media audiences are difficult to identify, or especially difficult to 'get at', although some can be for legal and moral reasons (try getting into a school to ask five-year-olds about Disney films, for instance). These legal and moral issues may present concerns for us as researchers just as much as for the audience we investigate and may dictate whether or not they are likely to be interested in being investigated. Think of the difficulties involved in researching the reality of online paedophiles, or Chinese web-users looking for sites relating to democratic material or current affairs reporting on Chinese government repression in Tibet. Such extreme examples draw attention to the nature of how and why we embark upon research, as well as the ethical dimensions of how we proceed – issues dealt with below.

The methods explored in this section constitute a range of available tools; each one allows the researcher to do different things. How we employ one or more of these methods relates to the kinds of questions we ask of media forms, and their consumption and use. Whether or not the kinds of research we do yields results will relate to the 'fit' between question and method. It will also relate to the nature of the relationship as researchers that we have with our 'subjects', i.e. those very audience members who consume and use media. The particularities of the issues that concern us as media researchers, our concepts and explanatory jargon, may seem weighty, sophisticated and formidable. However, this array should not lead us to assume a position of superiority in the relationship we take up with the subject of research, as if our questions and observations are tools that will elicit a 'truth' about those subjects and what they do with media forms that only we can arrive at. As we have said before, all of us already know what media mean and, indeed, what we do and why we do it. In our guise as media researchers, we may simply have different perspectives on why these things matter, what matters and in which contexts. Likewise, despite the apparent innocuousness of much media – products are more often than not fun, frivolous, ephemeral – these mean a lot to audiences, and the way that they mean within the audiences' lives means that we must consider them with care, attention and respect.

Such considerations will condition how we go about any research, its tone and, indeed, what we make of the data we produce. And it is data that research into audiences produces. While we might 'know' what media mean and why we consume various products as audience members, trying to articulate these meanings, placing them in meaningful explanatory contexts, and understanding and articulating them, is a job of reflection and interpretation. Researching audiences can be very time-consuming and laborious, but also rewarding. Sometimes, what one 'discovers' or elaborates on as a result of research and interpretation can be quite spectacular or even banal: both might be significant.

The methods discussed here will only become meaningful if you employ them but, in order to put them to work, you need some understanding of what they are as well as what kinds of questions about audiences they will allow you to address and answer. Using these methods effectively will depend upon the kinds of research questions you ask and how well informed you are about how others have employed them. Each time you read research work from the field of media studies – whether concerning audiences or not – do reflect upon what the writer has to say about the method they have employed.

Questionnaires and interviews

Questionnaires or surveys are a common audience research method and the format informs the organisation of interviews. Potentially, surveys allow the researcher to reach a much larger 'sample' or number of people (or respondents) than any of the other audience research methods presented here. This is based upon designing a set of questions and circulating them to respondents for them to answer and return in their own time. However, what one makes up for in quantity tends to be lost in quality, as questionnaires are quite blunt tools. Thus, this method is best used to present a list of unequivocal questions that, usually, can be answered quickly and concisely by respondents. Multiple choice options or rating systems (e.g. 'On a scale of 1 to 10, where 1 is poor and 10 is excellent, give a rating for JLS's latest video') are often employed in questionnaires, which might be presented by the researcher to subjects, posted or uploaded online. For example:

Q. Which regional newspaper(s) do you read?

	Always	Often	Occasionally	Never
Birmingham Evening Mail	105	200	303	10
Express and Star	15	25	33	20
Birmingham Post	10	21	13	50

Bertrand and Hughes (2004) identify four appropriate uses of questionnaires in media audience research: demographic surveys (age, ethnicity, gender and so on – details that most of us supply to census takers); ratings surveys (who watched what); attitude and opinion surveys; and surveys of behaviour (who does what, goes where and so on).

In order to draw meaningful conclusions from responses to questionnaire content, a large sample needs to have been drawn that is statistically significant in relation to an object of research. 'Significance' will of course be dependent upon circumstances. For example, consider local cinema-goers – say at a 10-screen, out-of-town multiplex with an average of 2000 visitors per night. Even if we wanted to make sense of, say, the reasons for visiting for any one night's sample of visitors, we would probably need responses from 10 per cent (200) of this figure to begin to draw conclusions or to claim that any insights were significant, rather than idiosyncrasies.

If used effectively, questionnaires can be a useful research method. Questions need to be carefully worded so as to avoid confusion for both interviewer and respondent. 'Closed' questions tend to be more useful, as they limit possible responses and are more manageable for analysis. A closed question invites a yes or no answer or a simple identification (e.g. what newspaper(s) do you read every week?). Open-ended questions can be successful, although they invite reflection and elaboration (e.g. what do you like about 'x' newspaper?). Data resulting from such questions would be variable and hard to collate. If you use this method, the questionnaire should be kept as short as possible, so that you are able to garner as many responses as possible in good time. A useful way of proceeding is to 'pilot' a version of your questionnaire in order to evaluate its usability with respondents and to allow fine-tuning of your questions.

Ultimately, questionnaires deliver data that, if you've produced the 'quantities' associated with this method, offer statistical insights that you will then be able to generalise from. To what extent you are able to go beyond the kinds of things done in market research, however, will, of course, depend upon the kinds of questions you have posed.

One further thing that questionnaires can do is to introduce researchers to individuals who are willing to spend time in more detailed interviews, participate in focus groups or allow researchers to observe them in the process of consuming their preferred media and the context in which they do so.

Interviews take advantage of the fact that people can tell you things about themselves. They are an invaluable method for exploring the feelings and reactions that audience members or fans have for their preferred pleasures, for obtaining oral histories and as a way of interrogating media workers about their roles. Interviews can be, at one extreme, unstructured and free-ranging in response to the circumstances of the interaction of interviewer and interviewee, or at the other, based on a fixed sequence of largely 'closed' questions. Fully structured interviews are often used for market research, interviewing and other survey work. The respondent is asked a set of pre-planned questions and their answers are coded into tightly defined categories, in similar fashion to questionnaires. Semi-structured interviews are generally the most useful form of interviewing. For the purpose of a semi-structured interview, you are generally trying to get yes/no type answers, but you are likely to provide the opportunity for your respondent to expand on their answer. For example, you might ask the following initial question in an interview concerning audiences for radio news:

Q. Was there any topic not covered in the news bulletin that you think should have been included?

A. (Respondent answers with a yes or no.) If the respondent answered yes you would ask them what it was that they thought should have been included.

Obviously the opposite of structured interviews, unstructured interviews allow for an open discussion that can be guided towards appropriate areas. Rather than having a series of prepared questions, the researcher may have identified a number of themes or issues they wish to cover in the session beforehand.

When identifying who to talk to, it is important to establish whether your subject is an *actor* or an *informant*. Actors are involved in the activity you are investigating; informants are not directly involved, but have information that may be of use to you. When interviewing for factual information, you should bear in mind that it may well be influenced by the values, attitudes and beliefs of the person you are interviewing.

Interviews can take place in a variety of locations. Ideally they should take place in person, but on occasions you may need to interview your subject by telephone or even virtually, using email, instant messaging software or chat rooms. Interviews should be relaxed, fairly informal encounters. It is advisable to record interviews, as it is not possible

Case Study

Using questionnaires

Lyn Thomas, in her book *Fans, Feminism and 'Quality' Media* (2002), used questionnaires in order to access fans of the UK radio show *The Archers* and TV detective show *Morse*. This method was used to identify individuals who would be willing to speak in depth about their pleasures and the kinds of issues dealt with in these texts that she was interested in exploring – debates around gender, feminism, nationality, tradition, etc. None of these subjects is likely to be the kind of thing one can access in any nuanced manner through questionnaires.

Thomas distributed questionnaires about *Morse* at a screening of an episode at the National Film Theatre and at other events

dedicated to her texts. This meant that she was able to identify 'dedicated' consumers, willing to go out of their way, beyond their typical consumption, and, potentially, more likely to offer responses. Thus, she writes of one instance at an Arts Festival 'performance' of *The Archers* radio show that, for an audience of 900 people 'I gave out 300 forms, and 158 people returned completed forms at the end . . . the high response rate (just over 50 per cent) is also indicative of the strength of fan cultures around the programme and of its popularity. In the weeks following I sent out questionnaires to my sample of 158. Some 110 were returned . . . indicative of regular listeners' commitment to the programme, but it is also perhaps linked to the class profile of the sample' (Thomas, 2002: 63). The fact that these media consumers were largely middle-class, middle-aged and white perhaps disposed them towards responding dutifully, as did their attachment to the texts under scrutiny and the potentially enjoyable pay-off of indulging the knowledge and attachment to the shows that they had as dedicated fans.

to transcribe interviews on the fly. Recorded interviews can be played back repeatedly, revealing different issues or points that you may have missed during the moment. Make sure you ask permission to use a recorder, and stress confidentiality if your respondent is concerned. Note taking can be a distraction and prevent you from concentrating on what the person is saying. However, an occasional bit of note taking tells the respondent you are interested in what they are saying. When asking questions, put the other person at their ease (even if you are the nervous one). Let them know how you want the interview to proceed: Why are you seeing them? What type of questions will you be asking? How much time will the interview take up (is this OK with them)? Start with straightforward, non-threatening, fairly factual questions, but stay away from questions that will produce simple yes or no answers – you want to get them talking. Try to get them to talk about concrete examples where they can comment about something specific. Keep your questions short and deliver them in easily understandable language. Try to ensure that your questions have a logical order. If you want to ask them anything controversial, save this for nearer the end of the interview, when it won't matter so much if they dry up or refuse to answer any more of your questions.

Listening is a difficult skill for most interviewers. It is easy to miss what someone is saying by thinking about the next question you are going to ask. Concentrate on what they are saying and don't worry if there is a pause before you can come up with the next question. Let the person know that you are listening to what they are saying, preferably by using non-verbal communication such as the occasional head nod. Don't summarise what they have just said or finish their sentences for them. These interventions can be very irritating for your respondent.

You may be asking people to describe and to reflect on activities that they take for granted and engage in habitually as part of their daily routine. Give them a little time to think about the question you have just asked them. Don't interrupt during this thinking time and don't interrupt when they are speaking. When they have finished what they are saying you can explore the issue further. Use 'how', 'in what way', 'why' questions or an expectant silence to explore issues in more detail.

There is considerable debate about whether an interviewer should empathise, agree or disagree during an interview. Some people may wish to know your opinions – others may not. Some may give you a more useful reply if they know you have a good knowledge of the subject – others may explain an issue more thoroughly if they think you are slightly naïve (but not clueless!). It's probably best not to disagree too strongly or challenge someone directly, unless they are being gratuitously offensive. However, in such cases it's probably a good idea to bring the interview to a swift conclusion.

Not all interviews are a success but, by good preparation, suitable questions and a relaxed and respectful approach, you can improve your chances of getting good material. Always remember that your interviewee has volunteered their time to assist you.

Focus groups

Focus groups are interviews in a group setting where the researcher is able to question several people in relation to a research topic. This method allows the generation of conversation between group members around the topic, often in response to a specific 'stimulus' set before them, such as a media text. Thus, if research concerned media moral panics, specific extracts from the tabloid press might be used as a point of discussion, or a music video might be played in a discussion of representation in such forms.

In studying audiences, it would be necessary to gather relevant respondents. Thus, if you were looking at teenage female responses to a fashion blog, you would need to ensure that your focus group consists of teenage females. Alternatively, if you were attempting to discover the meanings an audience associates with a specific radio station or show, you would need to make sure that your focus group includes a cross-section of that audience, such as different ages, races and genders, otherwise it would not have much value.

Focus groups should have between six and eight participants – any more and it can be difficult to moderate, any fewer and it might be difficult to generate conversation. The role of the moderator in a focus group is crucial. If a focus group goes well, the moderator will have very little to do. A good moderator will have little involvement with the conversation, only being on hand to get the conversation started and also to keep the conversation focused on the topic. On occasion, there might be a dominant member of the group or some members may not be speaking. It is the job of the moderator to monitor the group dynamic and to try to get everyone to speak. If the moderator has too great an involvement with the group, it can impact upon the quality of the overall results. Focus groups are usually recorded, either using an audio or video recorder, as it is very difficult to make full notes during the session. Video recordings can be particularly useful, as you are able to study body language and group interactions.

Ethnography

Ethnography is a method of fieldwork research derived from anthropology. This method is one where the researcher attempts to enter into the 'culture' or way of life of a particular group and provide an account of its meanings and activities from inside, based on what they mean to members of that culture. However, in ethnographic accounts there is always a further concern: what interpretation does the ethnographer *make* of group activities and meanings? This concern is particularly important because it defines ethnography as an *interpretative* activity.

Ethnographic insights are gained by observing how people interact with each other, but also by interviewing people about their own and their fellow group members' cultural practices. As a result, ethnographic writing within anthropology usually contains elements such as lengthy verbatim quotes, biographies and case studies. Raw ethnographic data are predominantly qualitative. Without interpretation, this material tells us little beyond what can be gleaned from the descriptions of the researcher and the self-descriptions of those interviewed. Thus, ethnographers must always be aware of their own subjectivity: the way that they stand in relation to those that they study. Ethnographers might be of a different class and cultural affiliation from the people that they write about, so the interpretations they make of social and cultural practices will necessarily be grounded in their own life experience. Ethnography forces us to confront our roles as researchers of other people's lives and behaviour. This applies as equally to ethnographies of media consumers or participants as it does to traditional anthropological ethnography.

The anthropologist Clifford Geertz, who has written interestingly and readably about this area, has warned potential ethnographers that they must be aware of the constructedness of the accounts that they produce: 'What we call our data are really our own constructions of other people's constructions of what they and their counterparts are up to' (Geertz, quoted in Moores, 1993: 62). So, we should be aware that, when we talk to someone about their TV viewing, for instance, they are constructing a particular account of their viewing practices, from which we further construct our own interpretation. A handy set of questions to bear in mind when considering ethnographic accounts is: who is writing, about whom, from what relative position, and in what material circumstances? This provides a neat way of assessing the nature of your own ethnographic accounts and those of others. Are you, or they, claiming to be a neutral observer or an interested party?

While ethnography has been used for researching fan cultures, online communities and subcultures, an area that has been most productive in its use of ethnographic methods has been that of TV viewing. Implicit in the range of academic studies has been the idea that TV viewing is a part of everyday life and not an isolated, antisocial activity – as it has often been viewed in the past. For ethnographers of the TV audience, viewing is interwoven with other cultural and social practices, and so cannot be studied outside of its 'natural' context, which is the domestic setting in most cases. As Roger Silverstone has commented:

> *Television is everyday life. To study one is at the same time to study the other. There are TV sets in almost every household in the Western world . . . their texts and their images, their stories and their stars provide much of the conversational currency of our lives. TV has been much studied. Yet it is precisely this integration into the daily lives of those who watch it which has somehow slipped through the net of academic enquiry.*

(quoted in Morley, 1992: 197)

James Lull (1990) has suggested that the TV audience ethnographer can find out all that they want to know about viewing practices in an observation period of between three and seven days. It has to be said that most TV audience ethnographers tend to spend far

Case Study

Ethnography in practice? The Oregon Soap Opera Study

Four media researchers wanted to investigate why and how people watched soap operas (Seiter *et al.*, 1991). They got hold of their informants by advertising in the local paper, offering potential interviewees $5 per hour to take part in the study. They had numerous calls, but whittled these down to 26 informants – all of whom had promised to get hold of between two and nine other interviewees to take part in the study as well. Altogether, they got 64 participants for the study. The interviews took place in the homes of those informants who had responded to the newspaper advertisement. The researchers thought that these were sufficiently 'natural' settings for their study, although they accepted that such practices would not meet the standards of traditional ethnography. They argue that none of the research into TV audiences meets these standards, because the periods of contact are necessarily brief when compared with the kinds of fieldwork anthropologists do.

During the account of their study, the research team regularly use quotes from viewers to support their assertions. For instance, on the subject of women viewing distractedly, the following woman (RG) is quoted: 'I'll clean, but I'll have the TV on so I can hear it . . . if you can hear what's going on . . . like, you know, if there is a good fight or something going on, I always run in here and watch what's going on' (Seiter *et. al.*, 1991: 231). The study found that women who structured household tasks tended to build soap-watching into the day and not watch distractedly, whilst those women who thought of housework as 'endless' would usually do something else as they watched. Interestingly, they also found that soap viewers tended to fill in gaps caused by missing episodes or distracted viewing, by getting the information from discussions with friends. Those of us who are regular soap viewers would recognise the collective nature of soap, and how it tends to encourage these sorts of discussions. The Oregon team also found that soap viewers are well aware of the constructed nature of soap, and often comment on the writing or acting in their favourite examples of the genre. This evidence counters disparaging views of audiences such as soap viewers being unable to tell fiction from reality. They clearly can, but prefer to suspend disbelief to enhance their enjoyment of the shows. Interestingly, the Oregon study found a huge gap between some textual accounts of the 'passive' female soap viewer and the views expressed by their informants. On the whole, women viewers tended not to identify with the 'feminine' female characters but, instead, the villains of the piece or the stronger women characters in general.

shorter periods than this with those that they are observing. Ien Ang (1985), in her study of *Dallas* viewers, did not come into physical contact with her informants *at all*. She compiled her account from letters sent to her by fans of the show. Thus, TV audience ethnographers often only have the most fleeting contact with those that they study, which suggests perhaps that ethnography is sometimes used as a catch-all term to describe any audience study with an interest in the interpretation of qualitative data.

Virtual ethnography, or cyberspace ethnography, extends the anthropological method to online activities and communities. The popularity of the internet and its ease of use have attracted much attention not only from the general public but also from academics. David Bell believes that the 'very existence of the Internet and its easy accessibility make it a very attractive "site" for fieldwork' (2001: 195). With the existence of message boards, blogs, chat rooms and social networking profiles, it is obvious to see why this is so. Christine Hine believes that virtual ethnography 'can be used to develop an enriched sense of the meanings of the technology and the cultures which enable it and are enabled by it' (2000: 8).

There is no routine way to carry out a virtual ethnography, just suggestions which can help the ethnographer achieve highly beneficial results. While the ethnographer should have a high level of involvement in the online community they are researching, too much involvement can lead to a mistrust of the ethnographer, which would subsequently affect the behaviour of those participating. This point is also mentioned by Bell: 'we have to remember that participation in any social setting transforms it – even if we do declare our intentions, our presence impacts on the behaviour of those around us' (Bell, 2001: 199).

An example of the research methods used in a virtual ethnographic study is found in Bakardjieva and Smith (2001), which shows how people integrate the internet into their everyday lives. They take a number of people from different backgrounds to see how they use the internet. A number of these users participate in online communities due to problems in their lives or the need to communicate with family abroad. They discuss 'Merlin', a 58-year-old unemployed mechanical engineer. He used the internet in order to 'gain access to a professional community of people that he needed but was denied in the real world' – the people belonging to this community were mechanical engineers (Bakardjieva and Smith, 2001: 73). This gives one reason for people joining online communities: we join them in order to be part of a group, in which we can share a discussion on a niche subject with other like-minded people. But there are also many other examples of the virtual ethnographic approach used in different contexts.

Ethics and audience research

Ethics refers to the moral principles that define and guide acceptable standards of behaviour. These affect us socially and in our specific role as researchers, whether we choose to acknowledge them or not. Ethical considerations guide our integrity as researchers in formulating research as well as its reception. For instance, we seek to establish from the outset of any project that our work is valid, justified and that we did what we said we were going to do, rather than simply making it up, in accordance with the academic expectations and standards of honesty and reliability. More specifically, ethical principles impact upon our relationship with our subjects of research – from media producers to the audiences in focus in this chapter. Thus, when employing the methods outlined here and seeking to investigate what real people do with media forms, ethical considerations should always be at the forefront of any researcher's mind.

The wider research community – from the classroom, to a course, to a department within a college or university, to the wider field or discipline, to academia 'in general' – is responsible for setting and overseeing standards. In turn, the individual researcher is responsible to this wide community. If ethical issues are not considered or are ignored, the researcher could, at best, be open to criticism from peers and, in some severe cases, professional censure and even prosecution. One body responsible for giving guidance to the field of media studies in the UK is the Economic and Social Research Council (ESRC), which gives extensive guidance on the subject, as well as setting out the expectation that researchers address related issues in applying for funds. Here are some of the ESRC's precepts:

- *Research should be designed, reviewed and undertaken to ensure integrity and quality.*
- *Research staff and subjects must be informed fully about the purpose, methods and intended possible uses of the research, what their participation in the research entails and what risks, if any, are involved.*
- *The confidentiality of information supplied by research subjects and the anonymity of respondents must be respected.*
- *Research participants must participate in a voluntary way, free from any coercion.*
- *Harm to research participants must be avoided.*
- *The independence of research must be clear, and any conflicts of interest or partiality must be explicit.*

(*Source:* www.esrcsocietytoday.ac.uk/ESRCInfoCentre/about/CI/CP/Social_Sciences/issue60/
research_ethics.aspx)

Clearly, the concern is with the researcher as much as any respondent, and occasionally researchers can be deeply affected by their experiences. This is worth dwelling on for a moment. Given the familiarity and 'everydayness' of media presence and use, this may be one of those moments where new researchers seem sceptical about the nature of 'risk' and ethical considerations involved in researching television, or magazines or gaming, for instance, when compared with, say, investigations of social poverty, injustice and so on in social sciences. Media studies presents its own series of ethical issues for consideration and, in relation to audiences especially, we've already noted the importance of media texts and meanings in individual lives, as well as the need to treat respondents with respect. In audience studies, we often seek access to homes, personal lives, individual preferences, memories, pleasures, thoughts and so on. In pursuing what 'we' are interested in, 'they' might be bemused, confused and sometimes uninterested in responding to the things we ask about, or not forthcoming in any manner! Furthermore, and in any involvement with 'real' people, however banal the research, attachments may form, information comes out (not always related to the subject under investigation) and researcher and subject may find themselves at odds with each other in terms of values, personality, class and so on.

An example from some recent research illustrates these points. In a project funded by the ESRC, Bev Skeggs, Nancy Thumim and Helen Wood researched the viewing practices and interpretations of reality TV programmes of 40 women in the London area. They began with textual analysis of programmes, followed by interviews in which they sought to locate participants 'sociologically' in terms of their social, cultural and economic contexts, and lifestyles. They followed this with viewing sessions, watching TV programmes with the women and recording their responses while they viewed, ending with follow-up focus groups. Both instances here reveal something about the expectations of the respondents. The first quote below reveals something about the expectations of one group of respondents who assumed that the researchers would occupy a similar ground to themselves:

Our middle-class participants also often assumed that the researchers would share with them the cultural attitude of derision towards 'reality' television, and indeed television per se, as a bad object . . . That is not to say that these women did not watch and express pleasure in 'reality' television, but when asked to discuss particular programmes they did so by displaying their skill in holding the form at a distance, as the following exchange with Ann (who in the initial phone contact claimed not to watch 'reality' television) illustrates:

Ann: *Oh yes, oh my goodness, yes I love* Supernanny, *I even bought the book.*
Bev: *Really, I'll write this one down, book [laughs].*
Ann: *Oh goodness, I am watching 'reality' TV.*
Bev: *So you would purposefully watch* Supernanny?

(Skeggs *et al.*, 2008: 9–10)

In another group, questions of identity emerged in terms of nation, race, class and gender and led to a moment of awkwardness in an interview:

An extreme example was the interview with Saj. Saj is a Pakistani woman who did not have enough English for the interview (we only discovered this on arrival at her home). But Saj is a fan of Supernanny *(broadcast on Channel 4) and was keen to take part in the project and so the interview continued. The interview was uncomfortable for both parties because it became clear that Saj viewed the interviewer as a representative of the state, offering her bank statements as if to prove her legitimacy. She also desperately wanted to answer the questions 'correctly' in order to say the 'right' things about her daily life in Britain, and was determined to display a positive attitude to 'reality' television. It was as if Saj thought the interview was a citizenship test and that we wanted to hear that she thought Britain and British television was 'good'.*

(Source: Skeggs *et al.*, 2008: 11 © 2008, Sage Publications)

This last example, too, illustrates the regular need to anonymise the identities of respondents – on this occasion the worry evinced by the Asian woman may have related to a genuine problem about her legal status as a citizen. Often, researchers alter names and identities in order to protect the privacy of respondents.

It is not uncommon for such instances of confusion and unease to occur and it behoves the researcher to be prepared for and attuned to such instances. As far as possible, we always need to plan for and take into account ethical considerations, and take care of ourselves, too! Our own moral, political and social orientations can impact upon research and, indeed, what we make of the data we generate as a result.

Summary

In this chapter, we have explored some of the ways in which we might make sense of the activities and contexts in which audiences make meaning and respond to media. We began with a discussion of some anecdotal ways of thinking about media consumption and of the kinds of relationship we have with media texts. We suggested that sometimes we're very engaged, other times quite distant from those things we consume and their meanings. On the one hand, this presents problems for those models of research that privilege the media message and the receiver at the expense of contexts of consumption. Above all, however, we suggested that we need to explore how people actually consume media and media meanings for the simple fact that they play such an integral role in our lives.

We explored a range of approaches to discovering what audiences actually do with media. The first, which came out of the dissatisfactions of 'effects' research and constructions of audiences, explores the 'uses' and 'gratifications' that media consumers derive from consumption. This approach has its uses, but we pointed to some of its limits in understanding social contexts rather than individual choice and, indeed, the relationship of specific textual features with the interpretative acts of audiences. Using the theoretical model developed by Stuart Hall – of encoding/decoding – we explored ways of thinking about the contexts of consumption and the kinds of pressures that might impact upon the way that we understand media meanings. Hall's model formed the basis for work by David Morley, which we can see as an impetus for a whole range of work that has sought to explore what real people actually do with media. We argued that this impulse has been most productive in the thrust of feminist work, which has been instrumental in exploring the contextual nature of media consumption.

We explored some parallel ideas here in the frameworks of subcultural studies and theories, and those of fans and fan communities. As in feminist research, work done in these areas traces a shift to a respectful approach to audiences, one in which popular pleasures have been taken seriously. What we learnt about audiences has value for the kinds of activities that are now taking place online. We explored, therefore, ideas of virtual community and the way in which individuals are active online in creating cultures and identities. As we saw, the nature of digital media raises questions about the distinctions between the audience and producer now that we all of us, potentially, have access to produce and distribute meaning.

In the final section of this chapter, we explored a number of issues and methods relating to researching audiences. Our outline of methods was brief but here the utility of each (in tandem with suggested reading and our main bibliography) should begin to suggest ways of doing media studies in this area. The final words were on the nature of ethics, for the integrity of how we proceed and the way that we relate to audiences should be a guide for all that we do as scholars.

You should now evaluate what you know and are able to do as a result of this chapter. If you have followed the chapter through, engaged with the activities and thought about the issues covered, you should be able to do the following:

■ Identify key concepts and theories associated with the idea of media audience activity. (Of course, these are only brief summaries of some broad thrusts in media studies. You will need to follow these up with further reading to get to grips with detail, as well as with the differences between studies of audiences for different media forms.)

■ Identify and engage with key issues and approaches to conceptualising audiences as active users and interpreters of media products and messages.

■ Conduct initial research into the activity of media audiences, utilising one or more methods as appropriate. (We are, all of us, part of media audiences at various times, as are most of our acquaintances. Likewise, the proliferation of online activity means that, potentially, wider audiences and users are available to us as objects of research. The meaningfulness of your own research and the utility of the methods you employ will come from having a go, exploring and testing your own ideas in relation to those questions and topics that are important to you. In tandem with those other ideas and modes of analysis – of texts and media businesses – you should also now be able to link up ideas and ways of making sense of media-related activities, as part of a complex web of relationships.)

Doing media studies

Investigating audiences

Choose one (or more) of the following questions about audiences and outline a brief plan of research, identifying which method or methods you would employ. Outline any ethical issues that might arise in conducting this research, as well as any logistical issues (excluding those of language and cost):

■ What are the pleasures of 'committing crimes' when playing contemporary computer games for young middle-class men?

■ What ideas about body, femininity and relationships do teenage girls derive from reading problem pages in adolescent magazines?

■ 'Who' make up the audience for Barcelona's Sónar (www.sonar.es/portal/eng/home.cfm) and what does this tell us about the role of music festivals in a multicultural Europe?

■ On what terms can 'warez' file-sharing groups be considered to be a subculture?

■ What kinds of ideas and values of community form around internet pornography sites?

■ What role do tabloid newspaper reports of immigration and asylum seekers play in the views of women readers?

■ How do people watch football on digital TV?

Further reading

As we have suggested, there is a wealth of material from TV studies on audiences, as well as a growing literature on fandom. Most of the titles mentioned and summarised are worth exploring in detail, particularly in terms of how scholars have employed methods for understanding audience activity. Here are some further suggestions:

Barker, M. and Brooks, K. (1998) *Knowing Audiences: Judge Dredd, its Friends, Fans and Foes*, Luton: Luton University Press.
This book explores the way in which audiences relate to action films such as the Hollywood blockbuster *Judge Dredd* starring Sylvester Stallone. The research is placed in the wider context of audience studies as a whole in order to grapple with various traditions and assumptions and as such is a useful guide to the field. This research evaluates 'effects' claims but also the significance of ideas of audience activity. The research explores the relations between people's prior orientations to the film, and their eventual responses to and judgements of it.

Morley, O. (1988) *Family Television: Cultural Power and Domestic Leisure*, London: Routledge.
This study developed Morley's initial explorations as detailed in this chapter. Morley interviewed 18 families in order to answer question such as how are TV materials interpreted and used by different families? He concentrates on nuclear families in the East End of London and his findings reveal how television fits into the home as the site of leisure for the husband and a sphere of work for women, even when they work outside the home. The kinds of answers he finds to his questions reveal the gendered nature of consumption and the ways in which his respondents related to 'gendered' texts.

Thornton, S. (1995) *Club Cultures: Music, Media and Subcultural Capital*, Cambridge: Polity Press.
Thornton takes an ethnographic approach to the participants of what was then the emergent 'rave' culture, exploring the ways in which it had meaning for its members. At the heart of this are some interesting insights into the role of popular music in the culture and discourses of authenticity, underground and mainstream. Thornton's role as a participant observer is also explored.

Electronic resources

Read about research ethics in art, design and media at www.biad.uce.ac.uk/research/rti/ethics/

PART FOUR

MEDIA AND SOCIAL CONTEXTS

Across the previous three parts of this book, we have explored ways of making sense of the meanings of media texts, the processes of production and also the ways in which the audiences of media texts have been theorised. In this part, we take a sideways step to consider the broad social contexts in which all of these things take place.

The different themes that we explore in the next chapters are based on four broad perspectives that media theorists have taken in making sense of the social role of media.

The first chapter (Chapter 10) concerns issues of power and ideology, bringing together some of the themes that have already been touched upon in previous chapters. Questions of the way in which representations work, of issues of the control of media organisations and the effects of media texts and technologies on audiences all feed into this discussion. Power is a central concept in making sense of social organisation and the way in which media forms play a part in power relations has been a dominant site of analysis.

The second chapter (Chapter 11) is based upon responses to the nature of mass communication forms, and the way they have defined the nature of 'mass society' and its development. These responses, both positive and negative, give us a sense of some of the fears and hopes of media theorists about the social role of media and their relationship with ordinary people.

The third chapter (Chapter 12) develops these ideas to consider how media forms have played a central part in defining the modern. What we mean by the modern and modernity is explored here, in order to make sense of what theorists are saying about the 'ending' of such concepts and what it means now to be 'after' or 'postmodern'. These difficult concepts are all related to the inexorable growth and spread of media, the integral part they play in contemporary life and society, and the way that the media have played a role in challenging the very foundations of meaning.

The final chapter in this part (Chapter 13) considers the role of media in defining and maintaining a consumer society. The key medium or practice here is, of course, advertising.

As readers will note, many of the ideas cross over these chapters and, to reiterate, these are organised along lines of theme and perspective in order to allow some insight into the social role of media. As a whole, this part will draw upon the knowledge developed in previous parts, and more developed activities will depend upon new scholars beginning to synthesise the different skills that they have acquired.

Chapters in this part:

Chapter 10: Media power
Locates questions of media meaning and ownership in relation to the dynamics and potential inequalities of social power

Chapter 11: Conceptualising mass society
Explores the centrality of mass communications to positive and negative ideas of contemporary society as comprising 'masses' and ideas of culture

Chapter 12: Modernism, postmodernism and after
Develops ideas from the previous chapter to consider the centrality of media to ideas of the modern and their contribution to concerns that we have entered a new media-saturated era

Chapter 13: The consumer society and advertising
Examines the role of media forms in the development and maintenance of contemporary consumption

CHAPTER 10

Media power

Thinking about media power

Source: Getty Images

Rupert Murdoch, founder, chairman and CEO of News International.

'It's the Sun wot won it!'

'Murdoch's power must be curbed!'

'Silvo Berlusconi: the most powerful man in Italy?'

'Twitter revolution across the Middle East'

'Danish cartoons mocking Mohammed prompt riots: five dead'

'Michael Moore's Sicko "unfair influence in election year"'

'Preacher: Rock and Roll will bring the white man down to the level of the Negro'

The headlines presented above are drawn from a variety of contexts and refer to a range of media forms but they all illustrate assumptions about power in relation to media. Over the past 100 years, media forms, organisations and owners have been blamed repeatedly for lowering cultural and social standards, for undermining individuality and for spreading passivity, as well as panic and lies. Often, specific media texts, owners and features are pinpointed by media outlets themselves for the impact and supposedly determining effect that they have had. In the UK, for instance, the *Sun* newspaper claimed that it had won the 1992 General Election on behalf of John Major's Conservative Party, ridiculing Neil Kinnock, the leader of the opposition on election day. While the paper often complains about the British government surrendering its power of self-determination to the European Union, it rarely focuses upon the power of its owner, Rupert Murdoch. Australian by birth and a naturalised American, Murdoch is the owner of the greatest share of media in the UK. It is claimed that his newspapers and TV companies tend to reflect those social values and politics which support his business agenda. If it is indeed the *Sun* that wins elections, therefore, it is possible that it wins them for him, and for the kind of political ideas that have supported the rise of his business empire. At the time of writing, this business is under scrutiny as a result of accusations of 'phone-hacking' by reporters at the UK newspaper *News of the World*. For the first time in a generation, UK politicians on all sides have been vocal in questioning the role of Murdoch media in British life and there is a real threat to the rules of media ownership which have underwritten his reach in the UK, if not internationally.

Such instances highlight one of the most important reasons for a consolidated study of media and power. In contemporary society, television, radio, press, and now the web are the main conduits for news and the kind of information necessary for us to operate as active citizens, as social and cultural beings. In spite of the challenges of new digital platforms and access points, this places a great deal of responsibility in the hands of a relatively small number of people and institutions. By the same token, the fact that we can make this claim about the importance of media, of the centrality of mass communication to society and our lives, suggests the way that the presence of various forms, if not their 'influence' upon us, has grown inexorably in recent decades.

What we will do in this chapter

Our opening example is a useful starting point in trying to understand arguments about the social role of media. Our first job is to recognise why the idea of power is important and to get to grips with what power means, and where it lies in society and in relation to media. With these insights, we can then explore a productive and provocative idea for explaining the role of media in relation to power in the form of ideology. This has been a key way that media and cultural theorists have thought through the relationship of power and media. There are a number of theories of ideology, and we examine three key ones from the past 150 years — offering an argument for why they matter — before looking at more recent notions about ideas and power. The chapter is rounded off by a reflection on what power is and who exercises it.

By the end of this chapter you should be able to:

- Identify and engage with core ideas and key terms around the relationship of power and media.

- Identify sources of power in contemporary society and evaluate the role of media for each one.

- Research into aspects of media power in society and draw conclusions in relation to key issues and debates.

KEY TERMS: ▶ agency; civil society; class; control; determinism; discourse; dominant and subordinate groups; government and state; hegemony; hierarchies; idealism; ideology; interpellation; liberalism; Marxism; materialism; media power; popular power; power; resistance; RSAs and ISAs; self-determination; structuralism.

Doing media studies

Getting started

In order to aid you in working through the ideas in this chapter, it is useful to consider how you might answer the following questions:

- What does the idea of power mean to you?

- Where does power lie in society: who has power and who does not?

- In what ways do you think that the issue of power is related to media in terms of textual meanings, businesses, audiences and their position as consumers?

We've been flagging up a range of ideas, debates and approaches relevant to questions of power in the previous three parts of this book. How might these support your answers to the questions posed above?

Conceptualising power

Power
is the ability to determine the actions of others, as well as our ability to determine our own actions.

Individuals or groups who hold and exercise power are termed dominant individuals or groups. Those over whom power is exercised are termed subordinate individuals or groups.

From their inception, many people have worried about the **power** of mass media over individuals and society in general. Questions are often raised about the direct influence of advertising, music or television (see Chapter 8). On other occasions, people have been concerned about the power that individuals gain over media messages when they own and control large media organisations. Likewise, others have asked what role media play in maintaining the status quo in society or, indeed, in effecting change. What we need to ask is what is meant by power and how we can make sense of these different perspectives on media power. We can begin with a usable definition in order to direct our investigation:

Our definition suggests there are two related aspects to power. The power of control – the ability to determine the actions of *others* – is generally viewed in a negative light because it implies that its exercise might limit the liberty of those others. The power of *self*-determination is tied to the idea of liberty from the exercise of power, or from obligations to those in power. Theories of liberalism, liberation and libertarianism derive their names from the Latin root word *liber*, meaning free, and are concerned with the extent to which individuals are unfettered by the power of other individuals, states, governments and so on.

Equally, one social group can control the actions of others, and the oppressed group, so called, can seek a collective self-determinism. However, the power of self-determination can easily become translated into the control of others. Thus, what one person or group sees as liberation, others might see as oppression. The ability to exercise power over others brings benefits for individuals and dominant groups, in the form of greater economic wealth, for instance, as well as the egotistic pleasure of being able to 'have your own way'. Of course, there are also claims that power can be used in more altruistic ways, for the greater good, whereby groups and individuals seek to balance the degree to which their liberty is controlled. In proceeding, we can think of two main ways in which power is exercised: through force and through ideas.

1. *Physical force.* Individuals and groups often use violence to get others to do what they want, and often the threat of violence is enough to make people obey the directions of others. If a dominant group seeks to keep control without physical force – which needs effort and resources – that group needs to divide any potential opposition in order to weaken them and secure the widespread acceptance of the group's power. In order to maintain power, individuals and groups have traditionally gained support for their dominance by 'buying off' some groups of potential challengers with a share of their power and wealth.

2. *The force of ideas.* The most successful form of support will be a situation in which any subordinate group accepts their own subjugation, believing it to be natural. Historically, societies acquiesced to the rule of monarchs on the basis that such rulers were thought to be divinely appointed, and their power was believed to be an immutable aspect of the structure of the universe. To rebel against such a situation was to rebel against nature and God.

The dynamic between the use of physical force and the force of ideas recurs throughout this chapter. We would suggest that the more overtly oppressive and obvious the exercise of power, the more likely it is to be resisted; the less oppressive and obvious, the more likely it is that people will try to accommodate themselves within it. The social processes and practices that we study under the title of politics are those of securing an acceptance of the power of one group over another – Democrats versus Republicans in the USA, for instance, or Christian Democrats versus Social Democrats in Germany. Of course, people who have power exercised over them often do not just accept it. Some will openly defy it, others try to subvert it or ridicule it, and others will try to accommodate themselves and what they want within the confines of this control.

We should add that power is not simply a matter of overt party politics but it is a thing of everyday life, of personal relationships, of the workplace, and occurs in the home, in education and, of course, in the operations of media organisations, the meanings of media products and our relationship with them as consumers and readers. In moving towards questions of media power, however, let us consider who exactly the powerful are in society and how power is organised.

Locating power

Academics have traditionally thought about the distribution of power as a hierarchy. That is, a small number of powerful people at the top of the social heap, and a large number of subordinate people below, in gradations towards the bottom. In proceeding, however, we should address the question of who the powerful are in this hierarchy. Who are the 'subordinates', the 'oppressed'? To answer this, scholars have looked at ideas of social class, at other social groups, at the role of the government in state power, at the power of resistance and at those with alternative views to the state's. Outside of the concern with the state and social organisation, there are also distinctions in gender, race and sexuality to account for.

Class

is a way of categorising social groups according to hierarchies of wealth, occupation, taste and *culture*.

Let's look at what this hierarchy of power means through the way in which **class** has been conceptualised. A class is a group of something, so social classification is the process of identifying different people as belonging to different groups with different amounts of social power, usually measured in terms of economic status. Political philosophers have all struggled with questions about the nature and purpose of inequalities of power between different classes and the consequences of such differences in power, which are disproportionate to numbers.

Those lower down the hierarchy always outnumber the rich and powerful, a situation which has often led to discontent, despite the exercise of physical force and the operation of ideas in the maintenance of this imbalance. There are many historical examples of attempts by ordinary people to throw off oppression, believing that things would be better without the lords who controlled them and took the wealth they created. In Europe, these struggles became the foundation for theories such as democracy and socialism, which argued that it was possible to have a form of society where everyone had a stake in it, even if the degree of investment and equality proposed in such theories varied.

Economic and sociological theories of class were formulated during the nineteenth century, at a time when old forms of social order gave way to newer modes such as democracy. At the top of the ladder were the '*upper* class', whose position and wealth were inherited – the aristocrats, monarchs and so on that had hitherto ruled. The label '*middle* class' refers to those entrepreneurs, capitalists and professionals (the bourgeoisie in Marxist thought), defined by the generation of their own wealth, ownership of property and their 'cultured' nature. You will notice that the hierarchical nature of these terms means that the final one – *working* class – is actually interchangeable with *lower* class. Thus, *working* class (or *proletariat* in Marxist terms) traditionally refers to that majority defined by their labour power – men, women and children who were required for the manufacturing process (Joyce, 1995; Cannadine, 2000).

With the advent of modern consumer societies, the decline of industry in the West in particular, and the rise of a service economy, the meaning of class seems to have changed and, to some degree, has slid down the public and academic agenda. However, contemporary analyses of power have not quite left the concept of class behind. Contemporary attempts to reconstitute theories of class have concentrated on the idea of a 30/30/40 society (Hutton and Peel, 2003). In Britain, for instance, 40 per cent have secure, well-paid jobs, homes of their own and are reaping the benefits of the country's wealth. The next 30 per cent are less secure, working in short-term, often part-time employment and rely on some form of social benefit to make ends meet. The final 30 per cent are often termed the 'under-class', who slip in and out of the social register and who may be disenfranchised and highly disadvantaged as a result.

As author Will Hutton has commented on his thesis:

Such an arrangement was sanctioned by an amoral conservative political, business and financial class that deployed the power of the monarchical British state and the accompanying icons of gentlemanly prestige to privilege markets and denigrate a shared conception of the public realm. But the annoying conclusion the book drew (for both the old left and the new right) was not to despair of capitalism, but rather, recognising its fecundity and power, to propose its reform around so-called 'stakeholder' principles. This involved incorporating values of inclusion, commitment and fairness in the bedrock of capitalism, which would be further entrenched by constitutional reform to give Britain a less monarchical democracy and a better chance of expressing the public interest.

www.guardian.co.uk/politics/2005/jan/09/politicalcolumnists.comment

Nowadays, class politics in modern Western societies seems less about workers and owners than it was during the great industrial period, and more about levels of ownership and display, as well as about cultural differences. The last category has certainly come to the fore as debates about class appear to have waned. Thus, other important theories of power have become increasingly relevant. Feminists and anti-colonialists, for instance, pointed to the fact that power was not just distributed between different classes, but also between women and men, and between people of different ethnic origin. In turn, movements behind these ideas influenced others, notably gays and lesbians, to start demanding equality of treatment and wider acceptance in society.

We should now say a word in relation to society's more formal and official structures of power. For instance, it is easy when thinking about people with power in society to think about the people in the government – they feature so often in media reports. Clearly, the government of a country has a degree of power that it uses to make laws – many of which affect the nature of media, ownership and operation. However, the power of a particular government is dependent on the state, and on other powerful groups in society. The state is the collection of agencies that have power within all areas of a country. There are primary agencies concerned with the operations and regulation of any state, such as the legal system, the civil service, the police and the army. Most modern states have secondary agencies that provide services for the society covered by the state, like education, social security and health provision. All of these have particular legal positions within society. These agencies exist before a specific government comes into power and, in theory at least, the government is subject to the rule of law as much as we are as citizens. In addition, the government needs the state agencies to enact and enforce the laws and policies that it has passed. An individual government can and does, however, change these agencies and their nature. Most modern Western states are 'representative democracies', where we vote for a representative in an elected body and, directly or indirectly, a leader of the government. We could contrast this with the idea of 'popular democracy', where people would directly control those factors that affect their life, either by controlling the actions of the state, or by replacing it by a smaller-scale structure. Because most Western societies have had relatively stable representative democracies, it is often hard to understand that elected governments gain their power from the support of the dominant social classes and their interests. Historically, the move to representative democracy in Europe, for instance, came not from the idealism of democracy, but from the growing desire among men of the capitalist class for political power to match their economic power. The first rules that governed who could vote were aimed at enfranchising men of property, rather than seeking votes for all adults. We can see that governments that do not work to the benefit of the dominant social class are often short-lived. In recent years, governments that have wanted to change society in Spain, Chile, Nicaragua, Grenada, Nigeria, Haiti and Venezuela have all been threatened by or actually removed by army *coups d'état*, undermined by anti-government agitation, often from foreign powers. Likewise, multinational global businesses, often with assets greater than some countries, have been pinpointed on many occasions for the manner in which they undermine the integrity of modern nation states (Monbiot *et al.*, 2003). To turn to a media example we could consider the potential influence of the aforementioned Rupert Murdoch over media in various countries, in support of the interests of News Corporation and its stakeholders. As one article in *The Economist* might suggest, any suggestion of influence is also tempered by the waxing and waning of business fortunes:

> *Mr Murdoch inherited a newspaper business and boldly turned it into a multi-media empire. Arriving in Britain in the 1960s, he invented the modern tabloid newspaper – a stew of sexual titillation, moral outrage and political aggression. In America he broke the stranglehold of the three major broadcast TV networks. His Fox News Channel has enraged liberals – and piled up profits.*
>
> *The coups continue, but the judgment looks increasingly faulty. Mr Murdoch grabbed Myspace in a typically bold deal, then watched helplessly as it was bulldozed by Facebook. In 2007 he brilliantly exploited weaknesses in the Bancroft family to seize Dow Jones and the Wall Street Journal, but apparently failed to notice that the newspaper business was collapsing. Dow Jones's value was later written down by half.*

> (Anon, *Last of the moguls Rupert Murdoch is the last member of a dying breed. Time for him to step back The Economist; 21 July 2011.* © The Economist Newspaper Limited, London (2011).

At the time of writing, exposés of phone-hacking by NI newspaper journalists in the UK were prompting calls to limit Murdoch's media interests and the reach of his power.

Media and power

Most people who want to be media workers see such work as an opportunity for self-determination and individual fulfilment. They are drawn to media careers as offering an opportunity for self-expression, self-realisation and, maybe, personal reward in terms of wealth and celebrity. There is also potential in media work for the acquisition of social power – through such wealth and celebrity and, indeed, in the very act of reaching audiences with ideas and messages. For us, therefore, questions are raised concerning how media forms and organisations confer power upon individuals and groups, and their capacity to exercise power and to exert control at a social level. There is, though, no clear consensus among scholars on where power lies in relation to media forms, organisations and individuals. So, there is no simple set of facts to be learnt here, but rather a range of important questions to be investigated, and a number of theories to be tested and debated. To help you do this, it is useful to relate particular theories or approaches to three ways of viewing media and power. These are, first, notions of powerful media, secondly, the idea that media make people powerful and, thirdly, the idea that media act as agents of the powerful.

Powerful media

The source of the 'power' of media is often portrayed as intrinsic to the processes of communication – something in the technology or particularity of media texts and technologies. Such power is seen as operating at an emotional, psychological and physiological level, affecting behaviour in some manner. Its influence is thought to be strongest on vulnerable individuals, and their reactions are viewed as having important implications for the rest of society.

Good examples of this approach would include fears that viewing television *per se* is bad for you, or that seeing examples of TV violence will lead to real violence, or that pop lyrics can unduly influence young people. This position is often linked to arguments that the content of the media should be controlled (see Chapter 6). We can identify incidents that outline some of the ways in which media power has been conceptualised in this manner (see case study below).

Media make people powerful

Here, the source of power is usually identified as deriving from the ability of those who control media organisations. Again, the assumption is that media are powerful, but here the concern is about those who exercise control over that power. It is feared that media workers, or the media owners who appoint and direct media workers and organisational policy, are awarded undue political and social influence as a result of their position. Concerns about editorial bias in newspaper or TV news reporting would fall into this category, and often arise in discussion of 'public sphere' and political economy approaches to media studies (see Chapter 5).

Media as agents of power

This model begins with an acceptance that media technologies are powerful inasmuch as they reach lots of people, and the technologies and means by which they convey messages are important because they have become habitual, perhaps indispensable, aspects in our

Case Study

The Columbine High School massacre

 On 20 April 1999 two teenage students, Eric Harris and Dylan Klebold, went on a killing rampage at Columbine High School in Colorado, USA. They murdered 12 fellow students before both committed suicide. In the search for explanations that followed, a variety of factors were seized upon that are pertinent to the debates and assumptions about powerful media.

The two were outsiders who belonged to a marginal group in the school who wore a trench coat uniform, echoing the image of the protagonists of the then hit film *The Matrix* (dir. Wachowski, 1999). They also enjoyed destructive video games. Such things drew attention, but a feature of their lives that was pinpointed as the causal factor in their actions (albeit without *any* evidence) was the fact that the killers were keen fans of Marilyn Manson.

→ Manson is an American 'Shock Rocker' whose images and music flirt with ideas such as social rebellion, Satanism and sexual perversion and who has (intentionally) drawn the ire of fundamentalist religious groups in the USA. Manson's music, it was claimed, with its doom-laden ambience and nihilistic message directly *influenced* the youths to kill.

Bowling for Columbine, an award-winning documentary film about the shootings, was directed by Michael Moore in 2002. In it, the director interviews Manson about the apparent influence of his music on such fans. In this quote, Manson suggests that this media moral panic over the meaning and influence of his songs ignored broader social pressures and deflected debate and attention away from arguments over widespread gun ownership in the USA, the Gulf War and, indeed, sexual scandal in high office. As Manson says in the film:

The two by-products of that whole tragedy were violence in entertainment and gun control. And how perfect that was: the two things that we were going to talk about with the upcoming election. And also, then we forgot about Monica Lewinsky and we forgot about, uh, the President was shooting bombs overseas, yet I'm a bad guy because I, well I sing some rock-and-roll songs, and who's a bigger influence, the President or Marilyn Manson? I'd like to think me, but I'm going to go with the President.

lives. This model also builds upon the idea that the power of individuals is important but that media power is far more pernicious than the dictates of any one individual or small group of shareholders, for instance. What matters in this model is a wider notion of social power – the context of ideas and relations, in which the operations of media must be understood. Here, media forms, technologies, operatives and organisations are bound up already in the exercise of the power of dominant groups in society. Power, here, does not originate with media, but media act as 'agents' as part of a wider social process, in which the powerful groups of society make their interests the dominant ones in society, to which all other groups acquiesce, even when those interests may be detrimental to them. Explanations for this process lie in theories of ideology and its operations, to which we now turn, and we explore them in more detail.

Ideology

Ideology
is ideas presented or hidden as 'truths'.

Look up the word **'ideology'** in a range of media studies books and you will notice that it has been a central and complex concept in thinking about media, power and society. As a starting point, we will use the definition in the left column.

Clearly, from this definition, ideology has something to do with ideas, but it is initially hard to see how ideas can be 'hidden', or how they can be presented as 'truths'. However, we often make a distinction between opinions and truth, and anyone can hold an opinion on anything without necessarily producing evidence in support of it: it does not have to be objectively right. Truth, on the other hand, is that which is incontrovertible and demonstrable – or so we assume. While truth is seen as objective, opinions are often seen as subjective – informing ideas, perspectives and interpretations of the world and, indeed, of truth itself. Our definition does, however, suggest that what we take for truth can be problematic and contentious upon closer inspection.

This is the essence of the concept of ideology: it is a set of shared ideas that seem, to those who hold them, to be natural and unquestionable; they seem to spring up unbidden as fundamental components of the reality of the world. We all use the term 'common sense' to describe what we take for granted. If we think about the literal meaning of the

Case Study

Silvio Berlusconi in power

Figures like Silvio Berlusconi are a useful focal point for considering the manner in which media ownership is thought to make people powerful, as well as debates around this issue, its consequences and some of its ambiguities.

Berlusconi began his career in Italian property and moved into media ownership in 1980, when he launched Canale 5, Italy's first national commercial TV network. He went on to acquire media holdings in other European countries, moving into publishing books, magazines and newspapers. His political career commenced when he founded the Forza Italia political movement, and in the general election of March 1994 he gained a majority of votes to become prime minister.

Fears were expressed in Italy and, indeed, across the EU, that Berlusconi's success was in no small part due to the support afforded him by his own media outlets and the lack of a significant sphere of debate, let alone opposition, across the remaining Italian media. These fears extended to questions over how Berlusconi would be held to account during his tenure as PM and how he would exercise his power. Interestingly, during this period he was head of a company called Fininvest whose major competitor – the national state broadcaster RAI – was deregulated and dismantled by his coalition administration.

While his media assets are a visible factor in his pursuit and management of his power, Berlusconi's case presents ambiguities for the way in which we think about media power. In the run-up to his initial election, Berlusconi ran a massive campaign of advertising for his party across the three TV networks he owned. Evidently, therefore, his media ownership made him powerful. Nonetheless, his power and position have waxed and waned – he was ousted by Romano Prodi in 1996, for instance, but subsequently returned to power.

During the European Elections of 2004, many Italian mobile phone users received text messages signed by Berlusconi urging them to vote. However, despite the controversy and fears that the messages were, by implication, an advert for him and his party, Berlusconi did not do as well as expected in the election. Nonetheless, fears about the state of politics in Italy continue, in terms of the way that Berlusconi's control limits the sphere of debate, even if it does not seem to be the case that this media owner simply gets his way all the time. Media criticism of Berlusconi is most vociferous from outside of Italy (notably in *The Economist* which described him as the man who screwed a whole country), and is such that the organisation Reporters without Borders suggested that the president 'is on the verge of being added to our list of Predators of Press Freedom', which would be a first for a European leader (http://en.rsf.org/).

Source: Corbis

Silvio Berlusconi – media mogul, head of the Forza Italia movement and Italian premier. Berlusconi's roles and position raise interesting questions about how media make individuals powerful and the nature of that power.

phrase, we can see that it relates to aspects of our shared or common understanding. But what if apparently shared views actually reflected only the interests of a privileged section of society, that they justified the power of the people in power, for instance – not just the political groups in government, but those who control the economy, or who operate the legal system? In most societies there seems to be a wide acceptance that some people have a right to greater wealth or power than others, even while there are many who have no power and little wealth and even suffer greatly as a result. To accept this state of affairs as in some way natural or inevitable is to sink under the weight of ideology.

An example here of how ideology works would be that of European people under the Catholic faith, who once believed that the sun revolved around the earth and that our world was at the centre of the universe. Everyone thought the same. Since they were young they had known this to be so; anyone who suggested otherwise had to be mad or a heretic and could even be punished for transgressing the law in thinking differently. Functionally, this belief was part of an edifice that affirmed the God-given authority of the head of the Church – the Pope – as well as the divine right of monarchs.

Perhaps such cosmological subjects were not the kinds of things on the minds of ordinary people every day but it is important to recognise how the everyday is affected by ideology, in terms of the way in which we behave, those to whose authority we accede and the ideas by which we live. A brief example from the world of television offers some insight into the role of media here in the contemporary world. Ideology suggests that the ideas, and thus interests, of the powerful few dominate those of the many, and in this way we can see how television acts as an agent for this idea, manifesting it in its texts and practices. For instance, the growth in recent years of TV 'talent'-cum-reality shows (*X Factor*, *American Idol*, *Making the Band* and so on) expresses the value and worth of the individual over the many. Such shows are predicated upon the elevation of the few over the mass, defined by rather inef- fable qualities – the *X Factor* relatively circumscribed ideas of talent and personal qualities ('sex appeal', a 'pop' voice). At the end of the process of selection lies wealth and celebrity, a permanent elevation of the one from the many. This validation is confirmed each year by the thousands who sign up for the competitive stages of such shows and those of us who tune in. Sure, many will say that this is just entertainment, a bit of fun, and where's the harm? Likewise, such shows are not exceptional – television with its hierarchy of stars (actors, pre- senters, reporters and so on) has been like this for a long time. What is important here is that such a state of affairs is normalised; it is just the 'way things are'. Once we begin to consider such issues in this manner, we are again in the realm of the operation of ideology.

We'll go on to consider media examples in more detail but many of the examples of text- ual meanings and features which have been already been discussed throughout this book draw upon concepts of ideology. Stereotypical representations (see Chapter 3), Roland Barthes's concept of 'Myth' (p. 58), as well as the ways in which genres and narratives pro- vide 'closure' to portraits of the world in factual and fictional forms, are worth reviewing in relation to this discussion. However, in order to get at the roots of the study of ideol- ogy – the key strands of thought – as well as getting to grips with its operation in relation to dominant and subordinate groups in society, we must now turn to explore the influence of Marxist thought.

Unpacking ideology: the contribution of Marxism

Ideology is literally 'the study of ideas', which is how it began as a philosophical subject across Europe at the time of the French Revolution. Its development into a label for a par- ticular way of thinking and, more recently, a pejorative term for blinkered political thought, came by way of thinkers in political science and sociology, in particular Karl Marx.

Our starting point in understanding Marx's importance lies in his criticism of 'political economists' from the eighteenth and nineteenth centuries, who were trying to make sense of the coming of industrialisation and the development of modern economies and capitalism. Writers like Adam Smith in *The Wealth of Nations* (Smith, 1776/1977) and David Ricardo in *Principles of Political Economy and Taxation* (Ricardo, 1817/2006) proposed a set of theories that made sense of the emerging economic system of exploitation of resources (human, material) and profit maximisation. They argued that, for this system to work properly and meet its potential, there should be a general liberalisation of the kinds of restrictions that characterised contemporary society, which were largely undemocratic and ordered around the dominance of an autocratic elite for the fulfilment of their own privileges. These thinkers argued that freeing up the economic, legal and political spheres – giving unfettered liberty to the operation of the market – would lead each individual to pursue his own interests, generating value (or capital – wealth) that would in turn benefit all.

Marx developed a critique of these ideas based upon the empirical evidence around him, such as the growth of slums, long working hours and poor pay for the majority, child labour, colonial plunder that in effect enslaved whole continents for the benefit of industrialised nations and the incredible wealth of a minority. He suggested that, rather than freeing everyone into a new period of increased wealth, fairness and freedom, capitalism simply gave power and wealth to a new elite which exercised its own power in oppressing those required to maintain its status. This elite group, whom he called the bourgeoisie, comprised those factory owners and investors who were driving and benefiting from industrialisation at the expense of the old landowning elites – the aristocracy.

If this was all that Marx had offered, he would not have proven so influential. What made his writing so important was the connection of these arguments to thinking about *ideas* and their value in power relations, in an attempt to make sense of the profound political and social changes in Europe at that time. He had originally studied with the German philosopher G.W.F. Hegel (1770–1831), who argued that it is the dominant ideas at large in any one era that determine the 'material' nature of society – its physical, empirical organisation and maintenance. The basis of Hegel's theory was that ideas have an existence all their own. He proposed that one set of ideas is dominant in society at any one time; these ideas he termed the 'thesis'. While such a set of ideas is dominant, opponents of this way of thinking formulate alternatives that cohere into what he termed the 'antithesis' (the *anti*-thesis). In time, the two ideas would clash and merge to form a new agreed set of ideas, the 'synthesis'. In turn, this synthesis would form the new dominant way of thinking, continuing the idealist process or what he called the dialectic.

Hegel added that each cycle of ideas (or zeitgeist – meaning a prevailing 'spirit of the age') changed the way people thought and thus led them to bring about a major change in the organisation of society. During the period of the eighteenth and nineteenth centuries, this would have made sense of the transition in Europe, from a traditional feudal order (governed by monarchs and aristocrats who were deemed to be appointed by God and supported by religious writings and teachings) to a modern, capitalist order (dominated by the self-made bourgeoisie and supported by ideas of reason, enlightenment and constitutional democracy).

Key thinker

Karl Marx (1818–83)

Marx was born in Trier, Germany, and studied at Bonn and Berlin universities at a time when democracy was only just emerging among European nations, despite fierce opposition from their rulers. His radical ideas and philosophy developed early, seemingly at odds with his comfortable middle-class background, and most of his life was spent in political exile as a result of his overtly revolutionary aims and practices. In 1844 he met Friedrich Engels, who became his political collaborator, and together they wrote *The Communist Manifesto* (Marx and Engels, 1848/1969). His later years were spent in England researching his magnum opus, *Capital* (Marx, 1867/1967), and in organising the International Working Men's Association. His thoughts, for good and bad, influenced generations of radicals, political activists, freedom fighters and tyrants.

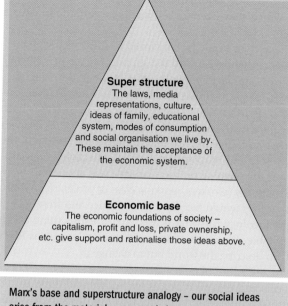

Super structure
The laws, media representations, culture, ideas of family, educational system, modes of consumption and social organisation we live by. These maintain the acceptance of the economic system.

Economic base
The economic foundations of society – capitalism, profit and loss, private ownership, etc. give support and rationalise those ideas above.

Marx's base and superstructure analogy – our social ideas arise from the material or economic base which in our era is that of capitalism.

Marx's innovation was to invert Hegel's idealism to argue that the way a society was organised – its material basis – would determine ideas and the way that people thought about the world. He suggested that it was the organisation of society that changed first and that any new way of running things would lead to a new set of ideas that explained things. These ideas came from those who stood to benefit from the new social order, because such ideas justified their advantage. Marx used the analogy of a building to explain how his theories worked. He saw the economic organisation of society as the equivalent of a building's foundations, and all the other ideas and institutions in society as like the visible building. You may find this referred to as the 'base and superstructure' analogy in other books.

So, Marx argued that the ideas served to justify a particular organisation of society, and rather than being openly advertised as such, and available for scrutiny and evaluation, they were obscured. They were presented, not as one possible and historically situated way of thinking, but as self-evident truths. The ideas, outlook, practices and philosophy of the bourgeoise, which originated in and justified their status and position, acquired the 'quality of truth' or 'common sense' and so perpetuated their growing power and status as somehow 'natural' and 'obvious'. This quote from *The Commmunist Manifesto*, which speaks directly to the dominant group, gives a sense of this analysis:

> But don't wrangle with us so long as you apply, to our intended abolition of bourgeois property, the standard of your bourgeois notions of freedom, culture, law, etc. Your very ideas are but the outgrowth of the conditions of your bourgeois production and bourgeois property, just as your jurisprudence is but the will of your class made into a law for all, a will whose essential character and direction are determined by the economical conditions of existence of your class.
>
> The selfish misconception that induces you to transform into eternal laws of nature and of reason the social forms stringing from your present mode of production and form of property – historical relations that rise and disappear in the progress of production – this misconception you share with every ruling class that has preceded you.

Source: Marx/Engels Selected Works, Volume one, pp. 98–137 Publisher: Progress Publishers, Moscow, USSR, 1969 Translated: Samuel Moore in co-operation with Frederick Engels, 1888.

Transcription/Markup: Zodiac and Brian Basgen Copyleft: Marx/Engels Internet Archive (marxists.org) 1987, 2000. Permission is granted to copy and/or distribute this document under the terms of the GNU Free Documentation License.

The ideology of the powerful, Marx argued, would be unquestionably accepted by both the powerful themselves and those they exercise power over, simply because it acquired the status of 'truth'. Operating out of self-interest, for instance, can be excused and justified as just 'human nature' (plenty of examples exist of selflessness that might equally be cited as evidence of our natures to contest this truism). This idea of acceptance is very important because, in any discussions of the link between media language and power, people often infer that there is some sort of conscious manipulation of language by the powerful, as if ideology were merely a form of propaganda. There are, of course, many instances of just this sort of calculated manipulation at work, through censorship, through media proprietors interfering in their publications and through state control. However, the concept of ideology provides us with a more sophisticated notion: that there is a dynamic mechanism at work within power structures, by which they become self-justifying and 'natural' to a point where they are unquestionable.

It is easy to see why the powerful themselves would be convinced by ideas justifying their greater power and wealth. This is just what happened with the support for the new liberal/capitalist ideas among the new speculators and factory-owning elite of the mid to late nineteenth century. It is harder to see, though, how individuals who lose out in a hierarchical society would support and believe in such ideas. Marx argued that the majority in society – those who labour for a wage (employed by those with capital, who accrue more capital through the labour of others) – have an objective collective interest that is antithetical to that of the minority. This is where political, economic and utopian concepts of collectivity – socialist and communist – come from. For Marx, the ongoing political struggle was about encouraging the collective consciousness of the majority (workers, working class or proletariat – those who own only their labour power), that they would recognise the injustice and irrationality of their position (in turn exposing the ideology for what it was) and do something about it. Whether social revolution was inevitable as a result of such recognition or not, as Marx famously said, the point is not merely to describe the world but to change it!

Although he was an active journalist and editor of radical newspapers, Marx himself died before the coming of mass media forms and organisations as we understand them today. In addition, he wrote little about culture and its relation to ideology but this sphere is one that has proven to be of central concern to many theorists, who have taken up his mode of analysis and produced a prodigious amount of work occupied with the ideological role of media as agents of power. Elsewhere, we discuss the contribution of Roland Barthes's notion of myth (p. 58) and the thinkers of the Frankfurt School (p. 380). Here, we explore the ideas of two thinkers who have influenced thinking in media studies around the operations of ideology. In the next section, we deal with the contribution of the structuralist thinker Louis Althusser, and with Antonio Gramsci's theory of hegemony. These offer differing appraisals of the strength and role of ideology, how it might aid our thinking about the social role of media, acquiescence and the possibilities for resisting power.

Antonio Gramsci and hegemony

The Italian Antonio Gramsci developed his approach to ideology in the 1930s. Gramsci was struck by the robustness of capitalism in the face of its obvious iniquities. Of particular interest was the way that the kinds of large-scale worker's revolution apparently anticipated in Marx's analyses of the economy had failed to materialise. At that time, Russia – a country that had undergone a revolution in 1917 in the name of Marxism – had come under the dictatorship of Stalin, who authorised the physical and cultural oppression of his own people, a people who were supposed to be the beneficiaries of freedom from capitalism. For radical thinkers like Gramsci, such an alternative to capitalism appeared to be no such thing, one form of oppression surrendered to another. The era in which he was working was also that of the emergence of the repressive regimes of Mussolini's fascists in Italy and Hitler's Nazi party in Germany.

Gramsci's contribution was to consider the complexities of ideology as developed by Marx and how it worked to actively maintain acceptance of the rule of the powerful in such contexts, when the mass of people suffered disproportionately.

Central to Gramsci's thought was the concept of *hegemony*. This is a Greek word that means leadership. Gramsci's use refers to the way in which economic and cultural 'leadership' is demonstrated by a dominant group, how consent for it is sought and won, and where in society this takes place. Gramsci distinguished between the mechanisms of political and civil society. The former can be thought of as the domain of the state and its agencies that maintain the power of the elite through coercion – the exercise of power through

Thinking aloud

Is Marx relevant?

Despite dismissals of Marxist ideas as having died with the fall of the Soviet bloc and as irretrievably tied to totalitarian oppression, journalist Francis Wheen, in his biography of the great philosopher, offers arguments for a continued attention to Marx's work. Faced with the prospect of writing about a 'discredited, outmoded, irrelevant figure' he reveals that:

> The more I studied Marx, the more astoundingly topical he seemed to be. Today's pundits and politicians who fancy themselves as modern thinkers like to mention the buzz-word 'globalisation' at every opportunity – without realising that Marx was already on the case in 1848. The globe-straddling dominance of McDonald's and MTV would not have surprised him in the least. The shift in financial power from the Atlantic to the Pacific – thanks to the Asian Tiger economies and the silicon boom towns of West-coast America – was predicted by Marx more than a century before Bill Gates was born.

(Wheen, 1999: 2–5)

This quote from *The Communist Manifesto* gives a sense of the prescience that Wheen writes about:

> Modern industry has established the world market, for which the discovery of America paved the way. This market has given an immense development to commerce, to navigation, to communication by land. This development has, in turn, reacted on the extension of industry; and in proportion as industry, commerce, navigation, railways extended, in the same proportion the bourgeoisie developed . . . We see, therefore, how the modern bourgeoisie is itself the product of a long course of development, of a series of revolutions in the modes of production and of exchange.
>
> [. . .]
>
> The bourgeoisie cannot exist without constantly revolutionising the instruments of production, and thereby the relations of production, and with them the whole relations of society . . . All fixed, fast frozen relations, with their train of ancient and venerable prejudices and opinions, are swept away, all new-formed ones become antiquated before they can ossify. All that is solid melts into air, all that is holy is profaned . . . The need of a constantly expanding market for its products chases the bourgeoisie over the entire surface of the globe. It must nestle everywhere, settle everywhere, establish connections everywhere.
>
> The bourgeoisie has, through its exploitation of the world market, given a cosmopolitan character to production and consumption in every country. To the great chagrin of reactionaries, it has drawn from under the feet of industry the national ground on which it stood. All old-established national industries have been destroyed or are daily being destroyed. They are dislodged by new industries, whose introduction becomes a life and death question for all civilised nations, by industries that no longer work up indigenous raw material, but raw material drawn from the remotest zones; industries whose products are consumed, not only at home, but in every quarter of the globe. In place of the old wants, satisfied by the production of the country, we find new wants, requiring for their satisfaction the products of distant lands and climes.

Source: Marx/Engels *Selected Works*, volume one, pp. 98–137. Publisher: Progress Publishers, Moscow, USSR, 1969. Translated: Samuel Moore in co-operation with Frederick Engels, 1888.

Transcription/Markup: Zodiac and Brian Basgen Copyleft: Marx/Engels Internet Archive (marxists.org) 1987, 2000. Permission is granted to copy and/or distribute this document under the terms of the GNU Free Documentation License.

The continued relevance of Marx's ideas have been reinforced by geographer David Harvey in a range of publications. These in turn come out of a lifetime of engaging with *Capital*, Marx's magnum opus. In *A Companion to Marx's Capital* (2010), Harvey suggests that a crucial task in appraising Marx's work is 'to open up a space of dialogue and discussion in such a way as to bring the Marxian vision of the world back onto center stage, both intellectually and politically. Marx's works have far too much to tell us regarding the perils of our time to consign them to the dustbin of history.' (Harvey, 2010: 242).

(Harvey's lectures can be heard at: http://davidharvey.org/).

Doing media studies

Exploring ideologies through their 'shelf-life'

Several objections have been raised against the notion of ideology and the work of Marx: for instance, how did he 'spot' ideology if we are all subject to it? If it is so effective and 'naturalised', how can we be aware of its operations? Why are 'theorists' so privileged? On the one hand, Marx had his own explanations for this process in that the systematic examination of any society's claims about itself and its values – which is the work of the thinker – measured against the nature of that society's practices, exposed its contradictions and thus its dominant ideology. Additionally, the time in which he wrote was one of great change and struggle over ideas and politics – what had once seemed secure and immutable had seemingly been swept aside. To reiterate the quote above: 'all that is solid melts into air'. Thus, ideology is not 'static' and is subject to change – how

we live and what we believe is different from the society of Marx's day. On the other hand, there is much that we do share – particularly the core validation of hard work, wealth generation, individualism and so on.

A useful way of understanding the dynamic of ideology and the 'shelf-life' of some presented ideas is to examine *old* media products for what they say about the world and the social values that they represent. For this activity, seek out any film, TV programme, musical record, magazine or advert that is older than you are. Examine your text for what it says about the world: what assumptions does it present (about men and women, family, society, relationships, etc.)? Do these assumptions and values seem different in any way from those of contemporary society? What continuities are revealed? What distinctions? What conclusions can you draw from your observations?

physical control of the military, police, law, etc. The civil sphere is a more diffuse realm, incorporating organised religion, education, the media and popular culture, as well as the private spheres of the family and the home. And it is in the civil sphere that the complexity of social life is ordered and reproduced and where social ideas are circulated.

Civil society is the site where intellectual, moral and cultural leadership is established. The worldview of the ruling class circulates from its intellectuals (in theories, philosophies, works of art), through to the level of the popular culture of the wider society and everyday 'common sense' about the way of the world. In this way, leadership is not a position that has been physically or even noticeably seized on behalf of one privileged section of society but seems something obvious and even spontaneously agreed to. Under the hegemony of the powerful, the oppressed accept and actively consent to their oppression because they believe it to be natural. The things that people learn in school, the values of the home and the assumptions behind the presentation of news or in the narratives of TV drama all circulate the worldview of the powerful, in a way that is unquestioned.

However, argued Gramsci, the oppressed would counter the power exercised by the elite. The powerful would never hold absolute power. Wherever there was power being exercised, there was also resistance to that power and negotiations about the limits and

Key thinker

Antonio Gramsci (1881–1937)

Gramsci was a radical Italian journalist and political activist, who was imprisoned under Mussolini's fascist regime in the 1920s and 1930s. He spent his time in prison clandestinely developing his political theories, although he died before Italy was restored to democracy at the end of the war. His most influential contribution was to develop the Marxist idea of ideology via his concept of hegemony, in order to explain how dominant ideologies reinforced the status quo, and how they could be resisted and undermined. His writings did not become widely known in the English-speaking world until the 1970s, when they proved influential in the field of cultural studies in its British guise, particularly in relation to concepts of 'resistance' to the power by the oppressed and disadvantaged.

parameters of hegemony. Gramsci's notion of leadership accounted in part for the way in which those in power acceded to some struggles for power, giving way over some things – welfare support or increased wages, for instance – but ultimately maintaining power and the overall status quo of inequality. This, then, can be termed a 'war of position', in which some ground is gained and some conceded in turn. Thus, any student of power needs to examine the struggle over it: not simply the attempts to exercise it by the powerful but the means by which it is recognised and resisted, where it is resisted and how it is resisted.

This idea of resistance to power became popular with academics concerned with the ideological operation of media – an increasingly vital part of civil society in the later part of the twentieth century. Gramsci's ideas directed attention to the way that hegemony operated in media practices and textual representations, but also to the way in which 'resistance' emerged. In this way, media texts, for instance, could be viewed as more than vessels for ideas, becoming sites of struggle over meaning, where not only producers and consumers but also academics had a part to play. In this way, Gramsci's work offers a sense of the role of human beings as agents in their own destiny. This stands in contrast to another thread of thought that became influential at the time that his ideas were being widely disseminated and discussed – structuralism.

Louis Althusser and structuralism

A range of theoretical work labelled 'structuralist' came to prominence in Europe in the 1960s and 1970s, influencing thought around the world in a range of academic disciplines and creating some controversy over its core ideas and conclusions. The field is usually associated with the ideas of radical French intellectuals. These include the anthropologist Claude Lévi-Strauss, the semiologist Roland Barthes (whom we met in Chapter 1), analysts of narrative (see Chapter 2), psychologist Jacques Lacan and the Marxist philosopher Louis Althusser.

As the name suggests, structuralism is interested in structures and its method derives from the analysis of systems of signs suggested by the linguistics of Ferdinand de Saussure (see Chapter 1). It investigates and connects the underpinning structure in language – the basis of sense making in semiology – with examinations of the underpinning structures in society – as Marx did – and, by extension, the structures of the media and of cultural forms and practices.

Like Gramsci's, Althusser's work is useful in thinking about how ideology works, particularly when extended to the mechanics of media. In his thought, as in Marx's, the economic basis of society is vital and ultimately determining of the way things are, but he conceived of a more fluid and sometimes independent role for ideas and the way they continued to structure inequalities of power, wealth and opportunity. On the one hand, he pointed to obvious, physical forms of social control and the social agencies which maintained them – the military, police, courts and penal system. Labelling these repressive state apparatuses (RSAs), he suggested that they alone were not enough to maintain the social relations of an inequitable system of production. The acquiescence of the majority to their position is achieved by other less obvious means – through the carrying of ideological messages through education and organised religion, within the family and its nurturing structures, and, of course, through media. These areas he termed ideological state apparatuses (ISAs). The concept of an ISA is a useful one, as it focuses attention upon the state and its role in perpetrating the power of the powerful. In democratic societies, governments are changeable, distinguished by their policies from other groups that seek power through elections. A country's government is normally in charge of the organisations of the state, which are usually unchanging, although political policy determines the funding and application of the energies of each (more or less resources for education, transport, etc.). In most countries, the police, the military, the penal system, civil service, education and some media areas are under some degree of control by the government.

The concept of an ISA indicates that state agencies influence in an ideological way. The legal system sets out what kind of behaviour is acceptable and the degree to which material

Doing media studies

Power and resistance

When looking at the power of media, we should not neglect another aspect of power: resistance to it. Even the exercise of ideological power is met with resistance. It is unlikely that members of a subordinate group are going to knowingly do something that disempowers or disadvantages them. So maybe we are 'fooled' into consuming ideologically charged texts, or possibly some or all of us consume texts that allow us to evade or resist control of our ideas.

Are all media forms, at base, selling the same ideas about the world? Is there any evidence from your own media consumption of texts and practices where ideas about the world or, indeed, the way in which the media present the world to us are challenged? If your own consumption does not suggest such material, are you able to find any evidence of 'alternative' networks of media production and distribution where challenging ideas are circulated? (For pointers see Chapters 3 and 7.)

Source: Corbis

Louis Althusser

Source: Rex Features

Michel Foucault

Source: Corbis

Karl Marx

Source: Alamy Images

Antonio Gramsci

Approaches to power in media studies, as in disciplines such as sociology, history, literary studies, politics and so on, has been influenced by European thinkers interested in the social role of ideology.

goods or lives are, or are not, valued. For instance, in the USA, if you call a police officer because your house is being burgled, your property will be protected and the intruder prosecuted (in fact, you may be within your rights to shoot any intruder – injuring or killing them); if you are seriously ill or maybe undernourished and have no job or health insurance, there is no one you can call to help or blame. Property is protected while human life and dignity are not.

The concept of the ISA includes schools, colleges and universities, all of which establish values of competition and individuality based upon qualifications that provide the basis for gaining relative wealth and power. Mass media are seen as providing views of the world which reflect the benefits of those already powerful, whether in the form of game shows that encourage individual acquisition of wealth or movies supporting the value of individual heroism and celebrity, features in newspapers or lifestyle programming, and so on.

This, then, is a view of the media as agents of power, and sounds very much like Gramsci's in its distinction between civil and political society. However, where Althusser diverges is in a much more mechanistic and determining view of ideology. Thus, it is possible to see Althusser's concept as one that also explores how media work as powerful forms in his allied concept of interpellation. This term derives from the French for questioning (either by the police or within parliament between politicians) or 'hailing', i.e. the way in which someone might call to you in the street: 'Hey!', 'Oi you!', etc. What matters is the way in which we respond to being addressed.

Key thinker

Louis Althusser (1918-90)

Althusser attempted to expand further upon Marx's philosophy of ideology, reappraising his original tracts in *For Marx* (Althusser, 1965/2005) and *Reading 'Capital'* (Althusser and Balibar, 1965/1997). Despite Gramsci's work, which was little known, by the time of Althusser's work on Marx, the Soviet Union and European communist parties had reduced Marxism to more of a dogmatic political creed than a basis of philosophical investigation. This dogmatism produced a crudely 'deterministic' version of ideology, meaning that all social ideas within capitalist societies were castigated as in some way tainted by the interests of the dominant class. This unsophisticated approach did little to account for the fact that society does change and the way in which capitalism had prospered instead of generating discontent among the exploited. The post-war economic boom of European countries like France had produced apparent satisfaction among working-class people, rather than discontent and consciousness of their own comparatively unequal status when compared with the middle classes. Althusser's contribution, therefore, was to account for the manner in which ideology worked to maintain order and how it worked, sometimes independently of the material conditions of society. As his work implicitly encompassed media and culture, it influenced debates in media studies in the 1970s and, while his influence has waned considerably, traces of his ideas abound. They lie behind a whole range of influential media theories and analyses with which it is still worth engaging. They need to be understood in order to make sense of some of the contentions about power that have informed our field and the ways in which arguments about the social role of media have been formed.

Imagine that you are the one who is the subject of a questioning or hailing – you are 'positioned' to recognise that you are being spoken to and that a particular response is needed. We have seen this at work throughout our analyses of media texts in this book, in the way that we are addressed directly or implicitly in our various identities by media rhetoric – in magazines for instance (e.g. *She, You, Men Only, Trout Angler*). In this thought, ISAs act in a manner which positions us within a system of values and ideas, in which we recognise our place and how we should respond and act in the world. The fact that this does not take place consciously – we are not involved in an endless series of questions and answers, we just do – illustrates the way in which ideology acts to produce our very subjectivity or sense of ourselves. This is a profoundly troubling idea, of course, because it suggests that our very consciousness and sense of our individuality and self-determination might itself be ideological in nature. We ourselves, inasmuch as we are conscious, are the products of power: indeed our consciousness is 'ideological'.

These ideas are highly abstract and rather disturbing because they change and challenge the concept of ideology presented by Marx and Gramsci, and our position in relation to it, radically. Ideology in this model does simply act in the interests of a minority group, making their 'truth' acceptable and subject to investigation or questioning so that we can discover how things really are. Ideology, here, acts in a deeply psychological fashion. This seems to exclude any possibility of human agency in pursuit of freedom from oppression and exploitation. In fact, one cannot imagine any place outside ideology in which to achieve enlightenment about the nature of society and the imbalances of power. One is positioned by and within ideology, born into and trapped in a highly deterministic iron cage from which there is no escape! And media forms play an important role in this structure of power. However, this mechanistic view of things seems to be counter-intuitive for explaining how and why things are challenged and, indeed, have changed because of the actions of individuals and groups.

In each case we have examined so far, however, ideas and theories directed at wider political purposes have been reined in to the service of media analysis. This underlines one view of our field as given to serious questions about the social role of media, even when the object of our endeavour might seem superficially frivolous: is Mickey Mouse important in the social play of power and ideology, for instance? As we've argued elsewhere, of course he is (p. 10) – to suggest otherwise might in fact be deemed to be, well, ideological. There is nothing more diverting in our search for power than insisting that power is to be found only in certain places. Our attention is to media as sites of power and of ideology, rather than seeing power as something which is located in parliaments and determined by the status of political representatives, or held by those who control media companies, for instance. This idea of the diffuseness of power is explored further in the concept of discourse and the ideas of another French theorist, Michel Foucault.

New media, new media studies

New power and resistance?

The so-called 'Arab Spring' of 2010 saw popular uprisings in Egypt, Tunisia, Syria, Libya and other countries of the Middle East and North Africa. This insider comment by Egyptian blogger and media researcher Noha Atef gives a sense of how new media tools were used as a tool to challenge the power of dictatorships:

In the same month, two peoples of the Middle East took to streets, trying to overthrow dictators who had been ruling them for more than 25 years. Cairo and Tunis share the same problems of poverty, unemployment and continuous price hikes. And both of them were counted among the ten worst countries to be a blogger, and also they were listed as enemies of the internet.

In the Middle East, common people are not allowed to communicate freely, because of political oppression, social conservatism or both. Now, a new type of media has enabled them to voice their opinions with the option of staying anonymous, allowing them to be heard. The story started with a citizen journalism covering the few protests taking place initially and developed with social networks aiding mobilization of offline actions on the streets.

The first wave of popular protests in the Arab world was in Cairo late 2004, as some intellectuals gathered and started to chant 'Enough!' calling President Hosni Mubarak to step down. This was the first time a chant against the president was heard; people were orally circulating the story. In 2005, the scene was repeated, this time some people managed to take pictures, and others wrote down the chants, sharing them with friends. This encouraged more people to participate, and the protests were getting bigger offline and online. Egyptians number over 58 millions and internet penetration is 21.2% with hardware and access relatively cheap (20 cent/hour).

Social media take-up and protest was driven by young, middle class and educated people producing social media content, the rest is consuming it, until 3G mobile phones found their way to the country and aided wider democratic participation. In Egypt, you rarely meet someone does not own a mobile phone, despite poverty (55% of what?), so many Egyptians have more than one set and usually prefer the phones with an embedded camera. With such penetration, we have a tool in the hand of almost everyone that allows the documentation of Egyptian life, from the election forgery to the belly dancing! This online activity and sociability helped to provoke discussion of critical causes such as torture.

See how many mobiles are recording

A turning point in recent developments was 6th April 2008. This date marks the first general strike in the history of Egypt, an event started by a group on Facebook asking people to stay at home. Though its success is still debatable, it was disturbing enough to the regime to get more brutal with citizens, arresting the two admins of the Facebook group and torturing one of them. Yet, Facebook was not blocked, Egypt is the type of internet enemy who tend not to block a websites, but to block its editors; it means to arrest them illegally! ➜

Though, you clearly find smart use of social network during the ongoing protests, Twitter as an example; had the hashtag #Jan25 trending worldwide, as protestors are sending instant updates, activists are tweeting the numbers of arrests and injuries and lawyers who volunteered to offer legal support, have their own lists to connect them throughout the country.

Over the days of protest, Hosni Mubarak regime used internet and mobile cut to punish protestors, and stop the word spread, between 28th January to 2nd of February both internet and mobile services were blocked, though so many discussions on Egypt appeared in social networks, on Twitter, the tweets on protestors were abundant enough to trend the country name world wide, in English, French, Spanish and Italian! After all heads of mainstream media were turned to the massive protests, social media was used by citizens worldwide to show solidarity with Egyptians, every night new tweets, blog posts, vlogs and mash-up videos uploaded to show support to Egypt uprising.

Now, as a social media student, the question I wish to get it answered is how the protestors in Tahrir square in Cairo were communicating over the time of their strike; how hundreds of thousands (2 millions in Aljazeer English estimation) were making their decisions and spread it among each others without having a mobile service or being online? I believe they have been using sorts of social non-digital media, something I will get it cleared from my friends who are in the protest now, but the violence and killings by plain clothes give them no opportunity to tell their media experience in the uprising.

You can read more from Atef at: http://advocacy.globalvoiceonline.org/author/noha-atef/ and at www.tortureinegypt.net/

Discourse, power and media

Gramsci's ideas about hegemony, the struggle for position and the possibilities for challenging dominance and oppression became influential in the 1970s, as studies of power in society started to take account of inequalities between groups beyond the all-encompassing categories of social class. Thus, the lineaments and operations of gender, ethnicity and sexual orientation became subject to scrutiny for their role within power relations. Often involved in the political struggles that they studied, theorists increasingly focused attention on the domain of culture, of the representations and language that was used in the reproduction of power and in the struggle over it. In modern society, media forms and operations are therefore central to such concerns. For instance, and as we've seen in discussions of representation, one idea is that repeated and limited representations of some social groups (women, migrants, gay men) – in TV, for instance, and across the press – has a relationship with their social status and power (see Chapter 3). Since the 1960s, too, there has been a great deal of success as a result of this attention in countering the language and cultural practices of inequality and 'hate', in terms of sexism, racism and other prejudiced language and perspectives. This attention to the operation of language and social practice has resulted in the emergence of an idea and method that has become increasingly prominent in the work of scholars of power: **discourse**.

Michel Foucault and discourse

This section outlines the key notions of discourse. Starting by defining discourse, we then explain why there is such diversity in the use of the idea. Initially, we can suggest that discourses are the kinds of language we use to talk about something, and the assumptions that lie behind what we think, say and do. This definition places the emphasis on the use of language and on the ideas that we utilise when we speak or act. The most influential theorist in this area has been Michel Foucault.

Discourse
Foucault's own definition of discourse is of 'practices that systematically form the objects of which they speak' (Foucault and Sheridan, 1972: 49).

Key thinker

Michel Foucault (1926–84)

Foucault was a French scholar, originally mentored by Althusser, who produced most of his work in the 1960s and 1970s, amidst the rise of structuralism. He had a diverse academic background in philosophy, history and psychology. Foucault increasingly distanced himself from his peers' emphasis on reinterpreting Marxism, and the limits of structuralist analysis (as evidenced by Althusser), by offering detailed analyses of ideas and practices that run throughout history, providing interpretations that seemed contrary to convention. At first glance his studies of madness, criminal justice and sexuality seem radically diverse. However, his main interest was in the way that ideas change through time, and how language and power were centrally involved in these changes and in bringing about ways of knowing the world or what he termed 'regimes of truth'. Foucault has been associated with a set of ideas that are usually termed post-structuralist (after structuralism). Post-structuralists extend and deal with some of the perceived limitations of structuralist thought and theory. The central way they do this is to concentrate not on structures, but on practices. Not how our society is structured, but what we do in it. Not how our language is structured, but how we use it. Not how our subconscious is structured, but how we use ideas (see also p. 456).

Foucault meant by his definition that discourses are ideas embedded in what we do, say and think and that these create the terms upon which we know the world. Of course, this sounds a bit like ideology. It might have been a lot simpler if he had used the term 'ideology' that everyone else used, but he wanted to shift the emphasis in theoretical thinking, from approaches such as Althusser's absolutely determining structures, to ideas of practice – everyday actions and the physical world that we make and in which we live, as well as what we say – as the basis of meaning, and struggle as the basis of power.

Thus, it is important to understand how discourse is a different concept from ideology, and in that difference lies some of the controversy that has surrounded the concept and the work of Foucault. First is Foucault's attempt to get away from a model of power derived from ideas of hierarchies – with the sovereign (e.g. king or queen) or dominant group at the top of the heap. He sought to get beyond an idea that power is simply held by any one person or group absolutely and then exercised over others. Power is more diffuse in its reach and operations, he argued. Neither is power necessarily about prohibiting and forbidding practices; it also authorises and produces practices and knowledge.

Where controversy lies is in the way in which Foucault breaks with the lineage of theorists from Marx onwards and the way that they had made sense of ideology. The Marxist critique of ideology sought to illuminate the nature of the world as it truly is, to expose the way in which 'ideas' were presented as truths, operating to obscure reality as it really was in a manner antithetical to the interests of the majority and the creation of a better, more equal, world. However, rather than speaking of truth or seeking to illuminate the truth of the world, Foucault speaks of 'regimes of truth' that are produced by practices and languages – discourse. In his work, this idea is illuminated by discourses of medicine, sexology, science, psychology – things that, in themselves, we believe to be in some way 'objective' in their pursuit of knowledge. However, Foucault argues that each of these fields is guided by a set of its own practices, procedures, concepts and agendas, and thus any insights are, in turn, determined by the ways in which one speaks and proceeds according to the discursive parameters of medicine, science and so on. The very terms and concepts available to us in order to describe a concept determine it and how it is known.

For Foucault, ideas do not conspire to deceive us by layering over or glossing reality but are, instead, the very stuff of reality and of 'truth' itself! In this way, 'regimes' of truth operate in relation to power, in order to authorise the pursuit of knowledge, to determine what we can do or how we act in relation to others. For instance, our faith and ability to lock up criminals in prisons, to define individuals as 'insane' and lock them up in asylums, or perhaps to support the dropping of bombs on villages in countries that are sympathetic to 'terrorism' and thus antagonistic to 'our' liberty might all be identified as results of regimes of truth which make such things possible. A further illustration of the seemingly contrary nature of his ideas lies in his analysis of the Victorian attitude to sex. Conventional ideas of the people of that period have it that they were extremely prudish about sex and sexuality, seeking to conceal and 'repress' discussion of such matters. On the contrary, argued Foucault. It was during the Victorian period that there was an explosion in ways of speaking about and defining sex – in science, medicine, the law, psychology, demographics and so on. This growth in these ways of talking in turn defined ways of knowing and understanding sex and sexuality – what was normal, deviant, the different categories of sexuality, legal prohibitions and networks of punishment and treatment (for the deviant) but also support and reinforcement for normality – through marriage practices and so on (Foucault and Hurley, 1990).

One of the more optimistic things Foucault had to say was that where there is power, there is always 'resistance'. And yet his ideas lead us into a very sticky situation politically and morally. After all, to what absolute touchstone can we then appeal to for guidance and agreement or even action? Perhaps there are only micro-levels of truth and agreement we can reach and act upon. The ramifications of these ideas are pursued further in the section on postmodernism in Chapter 12.

What then do these ideas have to offer our study of media? Although he gave very little attention to the media, this approach has been developed recently by a number of theorists, building upon the way in which Foucault's ideas have influenced studies of culture. The concept of 'practice' has been particularly useful for thinking about how professionals operate in media organisations, for instance (Wall, 2006), as well as the parameters by which we judge representations and representational technologies. The development and use of photography, for instance, as part of a desire to 'know' and define the world, has been explored in the work of John Tagg and others (Tagg, 1988; Rose, 2006). More regularly, discourse focuses mainly upon what people say and write, and thus the field of journalism has been particularly ripe for study, defining the terms of debate upon which 'news' – that which matters – is defined, trusted and understood (Richardson, 2006). The British linguist Norman Fairclough has been particularly influential here. It is worth taking one of his case studies in order to bring out elements he derives from Foucault for his media studies (see p. 366).

How, then, do all of these ideas and approaches to power add up? Can we use them and indeed should we use them? After all, to explore the idea that power imbalances exist in society, we would suggest, presupposes in some way that there might be something wrong with this state of affairs, making it incumbent upon us to do something about this, however slight. On the other hand, some would contest that we live in a society that, while unequal, is a relatively stable and functional one: it doesn't need changing. In this vision, the role of the media is functional and acceptable in maintaining the world as it is.

While we have progressed in chronological form through a series of ideas, they all offer nuanced ways of thinking about, in particular, media as agents of power. While Foucault's notion of discourse may seemingly undermine previous attempts to theorise power in relation to ideology, the concepts are not wholly antithetical, nor are the provocation of discourse, 'realms of truth' and so on accepted uncritically by theorists. One cannot ignore the fact that, even in the realm of what is said, who speaks and what counts suggest that hierarchies of discourse, in relation to the positions of the powerful and the subordinate in society, do matter. Nowhere is thinking about these issues more important than in the variety of media we encounter and consume in our daily lives.

Case Study

Crimewatch

Crimewatch is a long-running reality TV programme, which features reports and reconstructions on serious crime, wanted criminals and so on, making appeals directly to the viewing public for aid. Fairclough focuses on the way that *Crimewatch* and similar TV police 'appeals' and 'reality' programmes construct the relationship between the public and the police, and ideas about crime and its pursuit.

In Foucauldian terms, although *Crimewatch* features a wide range of criminal cases, all the items 'talk' about, and so 'form', the broad field of law and order, and this relationship, as an 'object' of knowledge. The analysis he provides is particularly interesting in the way that it highlights how different ways of talking – the voices and speech of the police; the ordinary voices of the public (the victims of crime); and the voices of the TV staff – are integrated to construct a particular version of the relationship of the public with the police. These discourses operate to naturalise and legitimise ways of seeing and dealing with crime, of who can act, who is trusted and what one can expect from the processes of law and order.

Fairclough examines the formulaic nature of the programme's titles, the use of re-enactments and other features, and suggests that there is a 'fudging' of the difference between the police and the presenters (police officers present and presenters do police work by appealing for witnesses). He argues that 'the ambivalent mix of reconstruction and re-enactment, and the mixing together of dramatised narrative and public appeal, resituate police work in the familiar and homely world of television entertainment . . . which powerfully domesticates and so legitimises police work' (Fairclough, 1995: 168).

The context in which the programme has become a success is vital to understanding the value of this show and others like it. It is one in which public perceptions of crime as a threat and problem have exceeded actuality. Indeed, it is one in which public faith in politicians, governments and institutions of the state (judiciary, penal system, etc.) have lost credibility and authority. Fairclough provocatively suggests that the programme is, therefore, an 'intervention to shore up the crumbling public legitimacy of the state' (Fairclough, 1995: 151).

Across the world, radio and television, particularly news programming, regularly attract the ire of political groups for being biased in favour of ideas that they disagree with. Complaints are often posed as arguments about the selection and interpretation of facts, the weighting of a particular viewpoint and whether media workers are closet liberals or reactionaries. In the UK, for instance, when faced with such arguments, BBC operatives in particular often fall back in glib fashion upon a position which suggests that to offend opposing viewpoints equally means that the organisation is doing something right. (Google 'BBC and bias', or 'liberal media bias', for instance, and you'll discover a hotbed of accusations and debate on this issue.) However, to think about media as agents of power would pose questions about the manner in which news programming (and political analysis particularly) is 'cordoned off' from broader social issues and ways of seeing news, rather than being about the simple viewpoint of a political party. It would pay attention to the way in which agendas for news items are selected – what counts as news, for example? We can accept that fluctuations in stock markets and the fortunes of businesses and investment banks have an impact upon us all but a great deal of current affairs programming seems overly concerned with the profit levels of companies and returns to shareholders, say, rather than the quality of life of the majority of people who do not hold shares, own penthouses and so on. Likewise, this would focus on the way that the debates about issues are conducted in programmes themselves – what are the accepted terms of debate and how is debate conducted, for instance? All of this serves to present a particular set of values describing the 'proper' way to investigate and report the world, and how to debate issues in a 'professional' manner that might, in fact, exclude other viewpoints and agendas that are not just reducible to the existing features of news (see, for example, our discussion of Sky News and Palestine on p. 460). In fact, a sense of media as agents of power might argue that the objectivity and 'political' focus of news and current affairs programmes serve only to underwrite a performance of the process of 'democracy' that is actually no such thing!

Summary

Investigating media power

In this chapter we have investigated the relationship of media and power. We defined power, as well as thinking about the nature of where power lies in society, of who the powerful are and, by extension, who those others who lack power are – subordinates, oppressed and so on. Our discussion developed three ways of thinking about media: that media forms (technology, rhetoric) are powerful, that media make people powerful and that media are agents of power.

In order to develop an increasingly sophisticated sense of power, we considered the lineage and concept of ideology. We explored how Marx made sense of the operation of ideas in society and how the ideas of the dominant groups, or class, become 'accepted' or taken to be truths. In this way ideas, which have social origins and are laden with vested interests, are naturalised, appearing to be 'common sense'. These ideas were developed in the theories of Antonio Gramsci and Louis Althusser, who further sought to understand where and how ideology operates. The ideas of both thinkers are important in comprehending the broader political and economic world and why and how these were imported into media studies. The differing degrees of optimism or pessimism about human agency are for us to evaluate and consider in relation to media operations. In the face of social change and the way that individuals have challenged representations, issues of access and so on, we would suggest that the exercise of power is not wholly determining or effective.

Our final section considered the idea of discourse and, in particular, the work of Michel Foucault. Foucault's approach may seem, like Althusser's, to be pessimistic but is one that extends our concern with power to issues of practice and the way in which truths are constructed; and, indeed, how the nature of language sets the parameters for what we know and how we know it.

This seems a very complex set of ideas, and new scholars need to explore them in more detail and become accustomed to their use, as they offer us a useful way of researching and understanding the social role of media. Your task is to build upon these foundations and proceed with a sense that power is a vital concept in the media scholar's armoury.

You should now evaluate what you know and are able to do as a result of this chapter. If you have followed the chapter through, engaged with the activities and thought about the issues covered, you should be able to do the following:

- Identify and engage with core ideas and key terms around the relationship of power and media. (Think about the different models we've presented and where you encounter arguments about media power.)

- Identify sources of power in contemporary society and evaluate the role of media for each. (Develop your understanding here by seeking out information on where power lies in society, as well as issues around media ownership, access and so on.)

- Research aspects of media power in society and draw conclusions in relation to key issues and debates. (Doing the activity below will allow you to test your understanding and exploration of these ideas.)

In addition, of course, we should note that this chapter offers only a brief summary of some complex ideas that really do need further exploration at source, and our further reading suggestions and reference materials offer pointers for those who wish to pursue this area of investigation.

Doing media studies

Finding evidence of media power

If you have followed this book through sequentially, you should have now developed a range of analytical resources and engaged with various theories and ideas about media and society. In doing the activities in this part, it would be a progressive move to draw upon what you have done so far to develop more sophisticated approaches to your own research and thinking.

We began this part by listing some newspaper headlines that illustrate ways of thinking about media power. We have also provided illustrations for each of three models of media power – media forms are powerful, media make people powerful and the media as agents of power. You should now find three of your own examples. These can be drawn from any sources – media, academia or even from conversations you might hear about you every day. Never neglect the 'common-sense' ways in which audiences feel about media. In each of your examples, think about how the source relates to the power model – what evidence or assumptions are present? Is an argument about media presented? Are you convinced?

Develop a dossier on media power. Outline what kinds of concerns (if any) you, or social groups, might have about this power. What are we able to do about such concerns? In light of some of the evidence of how individuals and social movements are using new media, what arguments are there for thinking about democratic possibilities and potential for resistance to power? Is there evidence of 'new media' used as a tool for the powerful, for repressive purposes?

Further reading

Eagleton, T. (2007) *Ideology: An Introduction*, London and New York: Verso.
   Eagleton is a literary theorist and his work is informed by Marxist approaches to analysis. This book explores some of the key thinkers and works on the subject of ideology and, despite claims that the concept has waned as an object of understanding in recent years, he brings this up to date. Eagleton is a witty and erudite writer who brings very complex ideas to life with ease, always aware of the historical and contemporary context, which is used to provide illumination.

Matheson, D. (2005) *Media Discourses: Analysing Media Texts*, Maidenhead: Open University Press.
   This book offers a detailed insight into the use of discourse as concept and method in the analysis of a range of media texts, in order to explore who 'talks', what is represented and how power relations are challenged or reinforced. Matheson explores different media genres, such as news, advertising and weblogs.

Miller, D. and Philo, G. (eds) (2000) *Market Killing: What the Free Market Does and What Social Scientists Can Do About It*, Harlow: Longman.
   The various authors in this book argue that the expansion of the free market in the last part of the twentieth century produced a rise in inequality and violence, and allowed a criminal economy and the degradation of social and cultural life. Its main objective is to question the position of academia on these developments, suggesting that many academics in the social sciences, media and cultural studies have avoided critical issues and instead become occupied in obscure theoretical debates. By default, they are complicit with the current order of things, rather than in pursuit of a critical stance. This book

touches upon many of the themes raised in this chapter and is a useful, if controversial and challenging, place to consider how theorists relate to their power as well as their responsibilities.

Wayne, M. (2003) *Marxism and Media Studies: Key Concepts and Contemporary Trends*, London: Pluto Press.

This work takes a Marxist perspective on the study of the media, drawing upon Marx *et al.* in order to understand the economic, ideology and power relations of current practices and meanings in film, television, internet and print. Wayne's book is well illustrated with analyses of Disney, TV shows such as *Big Brother* and so on, which serve to underwrite an argument for this approach and its value.

CHAPTER 11

Conceptualising mass society

Asking questions about 'mass society' and media

'The BBC has unintentionally been responsible for the biggest scare known in Britain since the advent of broadcasting. Half the country over the weekend has been flooded with rumours of a great upheaval in London.' *Evening Standard*, 18 January, 1926.

'many timid folk were genuinely startled by the news' *The Times*, 18 January, 1926.

'Humour and satire are dangerous implements when they are applied to mankind in the mass. The BBC will be wise if, in future, it takes no risk with its public's average standard of intelligence.' *Irish Times*, 18 January, 1926.

Broadcasting the Barricades was transmitted by the BBC on the evening of 16 January 1926. Written by one Father Ronald Knox, it was presented in an innovative way that married drama and the style of current affairs reporting that radio and television have made so familiar to us. The show began as if it were an academic lecture before an interruption announced that a riot was under way in Trafalgar Square. A series of increasingly dramatic incidents were reported, underlined with sound effects as if from the scene of events themselves: a minister had been hanged by the rioters, the Savoy Hotel and Big Ben blown up. Such was the apparent realism of the broadcast (despite its intentionally parodic nature) that the BBC later broadcast a statement, printed in the next edition of *The Times*:

'Some listeners, who apparently only heard part of Father Knox's talk at 7.40 this evening did not realise the humorous innuendoes underlying the imaginary news items and have felt uneasy as to the fate of London, Big Ben and other places mentioned in the talk. The preliminary announcement stated that the talk was a skit on broadcasting and the whole talk was, of course, a burlesque. We hope that any listeners who did not realise it will accept our sincere apologies for any uneasiness caused. London is safe. Big Ben is still chiming, and all is well.'

A variety of factors combined to add to the reception of the drama and circulation of discussion about it. Snow delayed delivery of newspapers on subsequent days (none of which reported revolution in London) while there were genuine fears of civil unrest prompted by class divisions: revolutions in Russia and Germany were recent events while a general strike by UK unions took place shortly after in 1927. Likewise, broadcasting was still a relatively new thing and, indeed, the audience was relatively small.

Nonetheless, this incident and the way that it, and others like the US *War of the Worlds* broadcast (outlined below), have been perceived over subsequent years at first seem indicative of the power of 'mass' media and ideas about the malleable and uniform nature of modern populations – 'the masses'.

A way of considering this event and reactions to it is to scrutinise the very terms employed for their meanings and the underlying assumptions of this story in the wider social context of the event. Who are the 'masses' and public referred to in responses to this story – and others like it? What do such terms mean? Where do they come from? What uses have they had and continue to have? Accounts of the BBC broadcast and reactions to it can be found at:

Raymond Snoddy, 'Show that sparked a riot', http://news.bbc.co.uk/newswatch/ukfs/hi/newsid_4080000/newsid_4081000/4081060.stm

Paul Slade, 'Holy terror: the first great radio hoax', www.planet-slade.com/ronald-knox1.html

What we will do in this chapter

In this chapter, then, we will aim to contextualise and investigate ideas of mass society and the masses in relation to ideas about media. Building upon the previous chapter on power and ideology, we will consider the way in which intellectuals have formulated ways of viewing modern society, and how their hopes, fears and agendas have constructed versions of 'massness' that have determined ways in which modern society and the role of media in it have been understood. The assumptions behind these ideas, as we shall see, are related to changing concepts of class distinction, education and culture, as well as the relationships between these categories.

We begin by offering a historical context for this chapter before unpacking the word 'mass' and two perspectives on mass society. In rough chronological order (but without implying a simple narrative) we examine a British tradition of thinking about media and society, as exemplified by the scholar F.R. Leavis. We then consider American reactions to mass society – a discussion that is useful to read in conjunction with that on audiences (see Chapter 8). Then we offer detailed insight into a group of German thinkers known as the Frankfurt School and their concept of the industrialisation of culture.

The next section investigates the work of more recent developments in British thinking about mass society and media that we label 'culturalism'. This can be considered to be something of a reaction to these earlier ways of thinking, developing through the work of a series of thinkers and schools completely at home within contemporary media culture. We finish, then, with a consideration of some of the ongoing debates about the limits of the direction of thinking about mass society and culture.

By the end of this chapter you should be able to:

- Outline origins and contexts for debates about 'mass society', culture and media.
- Outline, evaluate and contrast key terms used in debates about mass society in relation to the key theorists in this area and the contributions they made to the debates.
- Engage with ideas of mass society and definitions of culture in support of your own media research and theorisation.

KEY TERMS: ▶ authentic culture; commodity fetishism; critical theory; culturalism; culture; culture industry; Frankfurt School; Left-Leavism; mass communication; mass society; pluralism; popular culture; positivism.

Doing media studies

Getting started

One of the problems that new scholars have in understanding the roots of media theory (and the value of this understanding) lies in comprehending the terms of debate and assumptions behind them. Sometimes, the contexts for how people thought and why they thought in the way they did bemuses new scholars. Nowadays, for instance, media technologies and products are so much a part of almost everyone's lives, in all walks of life, that it is difficult to comprehend how negatively many different people in society viewed them in the past.

As the discussion of postmodernism in the next chapter suggests, the boundaries between what was once thought to be worthwhile and the worthless is an ambiguous one in an age when comic books sell at auction houses for thousands of dollars alongside first editions of the novels of Charles Dickens, and where academics study TV shows such as *The Sopranos* or the aesthetics of first-person shooter computer games. Nonetheless, there is a residue of the distaste that was once expressed about these kinds of popular pleasures, too, in the perception of media studies itself that we discussed in the introduction.

A starting point for this chapter, then, is to think about some key terms in ways that are meaningful and important to you. What does 'culture' mean to you? What does it mean to speak of cultural worth? Where can culture be found – are there particular places or people associated with it? Are you in any way 'cultured'? Answers to these questions are at the heart of the ideas discussed here and you should consider why they were so important to the people involved.

Contexts: mass society, mass media and social change

The development of truly 'mass' media in Western societies in the early decades of the twentieth century was the culmination of a number of changes that had unfolded across the previous 150 years, and which transformed first Europe, then North America, and ultimately the rest of the world (Weightman, 2007). The key characteristics of this period were apparent in a rapid population growth and urbanisation, the development of innovative and increasingly efficient technologies, and a shift in the way wealth was created, from agriculture and hand-crafted goods to the factory system.

The social strata changed as the new mercantile middle classes and the new urban working class wrested power away from an elite group to establish forms of democracy and a modern capitalist economy. Social struggles – often violent and vehemently resisted by the powerful – enabled the growth and spread of democracy, and social, economic and working conditions began to improve. These struggles and changes gave a new importance to the large groups of urban populations who were increasingly thought of by social commentators as 'masses' (Hobsbawm, 1996a, 1996b). The term 'mass' is an incredibly loaded one and, as we'll see, arguments and debates about this group and about mass society are indivisible from issues of power, class and democracy.

Comparatively speaking, these developments, spread over the late nineteenth, twentieth and early twenty-first centuries, marked years of incredible change, both in society itself and in the ways in which society is understood (think about how the web has impacted on how we live in the past 20 years, for instance). It is for this reason that this chapter examines in detail some of the key theorists who made sense of these changes in thinking about society, media and culture. We must also note, though, that these theorists were not just analysts of social power, they were part of the society in which it operated. Not only did these theorists seek to understand and explain how the classes and cultures of a society related to each other, they themselves had a class position. We then need to understand this key idea of class in greater detail, and then to grasp how these classes and their relationships were characterised. To do this we need to develop the definition of class introduced in the previous chapter, and then see how it was related to the idea of mass society.

In the early twentieth century, cataclysmic events such as the First World War of 1914–18 and the Russian Revolution of 1917 indicated the extent to which life in the modern world was characterised by rapid change, undermining the safety of tradition and continuity. This situation was paralleled by the growth of new forms of communication, like mass-circulation newspapers, radio and cinema, that seemed to herald even bigger changes to come. However, technological, political, cultural and demographic changes created great anxiety about the nature of society among many social theorists and cultural commentators. These fears were distilled into one idea: the mass society.

Theories of mass society

Mass communication theorist Denis McQuail (McQuail, 2005) suggests that there are a number of meanings to the concept of 'mass' used in phrases like 'mass communication', 'the mass audience' and 'mass culture'. He concludes that the dominant concept of 'mass' connotes, in the main, a negative view of large, aggregated, undifferentiated social constructs that lack order.

As we've suggested, 'mass society' was an idea that developed over the nineteenth century, and came to dominate debates about society, culture and media in the early twentieth

The growth of populations, cities and anonymised modes of living in industrialised countries in the last two hundred years, coupled with new forms of communication, produced new ways of describing and thinking about society and people – as masses.

Source: Rex Features

century. At their heart, the theorists of mass society shared a belief that industrialisation, capitalism and democracy itself had changed society from a set of relationships between individuals in small communities to one where any sense of individuality had been lost in the alienating atmosphere of the modern city and the factory system. The new forms of communication – particularly cinema and broadcasting – were seen as part of this process of 'massification'. Most of the commentators, theorists and analysts of these changes – at least up until about 1968 – felt that these were detrimental to civilised society. Do note, however, that this last date does not indicate an absolute cut-off point. Such ideas continue in a variety of forms (for an explanation of the chosen date see below).

Thinking aloud

The power of the masses

Most of the ideas we deal with in the first part of this chapter are based upon a suspicion of mass society and those largely nameless millions who compose that group – whether characterised as mob, urban working class, 'nation' or any other unit. However, we should recognise some of the positive views of mass society that celebrated the power of people to take their collective destinies into their own hands. The revolutions and agitations across Europe in the nineteenth century, which extended the vote and social benefits to the majority, were the result of collective action, as were legal reforms over work, holiday allowance, pensions, sick pay and so on. Such things were fought for, not doled out by benign employers and rulers.

Certainly, Marx and his followers supported a positive view of the power of the collective. For them, working-class agitation and collective self-consciousness would result in the establishment of a better society for all – so they believed. On the other hand, albeit with a more cynical view, perhaps, were those such as Mussolini and Hitler, who believed in the collective power of the nation or race, which could be harnessed and directed by 'strong men' such as themselves.

At the time of writing, ideas of 'crowd-sourcing' and the largely benign perspective on the popular rebellions of the 'Arab Spring' (p. 362) are perhaps indicative of a positive view of 'masses' and their potential power when weighted against modern dictators.

Beyond the pessimism and negativity about the character of 'mass' society were a whole range of different positions and nuanced arguments. To understand the range, it is instructive to look at some different versions of mass society theory.

In this part of the chapter, we will examine two of the earlier traditions of thought that tried to come to terms with the shifts in society we have just examined. They share an idea of mass society, but work this through in very different ways. The first, associated with the British academic Frank R. Leavis, is rooted in the arts and the study of literature, while the second was established in the USA and is associated with the development of the social sciences.

The culture and society tradition

The arguments about mass society produced by Leavis echoed a lineage of thought across Europe that developed in reaction to the coming of industrial society. He drew heavily on the arguments of the Victorian cultural commentator, poet and educationalist Matthew Arnold, one of the most influential British thinkers of the nineteenth century. In *Culture and Anarchy* (Arnold, 1882/1932), Arnold expressed his revulsion and fear in the face of the social development of industrial Britain and its apparent vulgarity. He criticised all social groups of the new mass society for their materialism and failure to protect and benefit from the great cultural achievements of the past. For Arnold, the measure of value in a society did not lie in the wealth it generated but in the culture it produced – literary works by authors such as Shakespeare, Donne and Milton, as well as in fine art and music. The power of such culture for Arnold lay in its apparently transcendental qualities and potential to bring classes together, to offset political antagonism and the degradation of modern life, evidenced in urban slums and popular pleasures to be found in pubs and music halls.

Leavis disliked what he saw as the superficiality and inauthenticity of modern 'mass' life, and the popular culture that developed in his own time. For him, the stuff consumed by most people was film, radio shows, popular music, newspapers, pictorial magazines and book clubs that trivialised the classic material they sold (i.e. cheap versions of classic literature). All of this was the fruit of modern media production and distribution, much of which he disliked also because of its American origins – in content and method of

Key thinker

Frank R. Leavis (1895–1978)

Leavis entered Cambridge University after the 1914–18 war in which he fought, his methods and ideas impacting deeply upon the study of English and culture within British universities and the way in which these subjects were thought about more widely. He challenged the then dominant view that to be 'cultured' meant to have studied the 'classics' – i.e. Latin and Greek language, literature and art. This was the kind of material that was privileged in the English public school system and at universities. For him, it was English literature (novels, plays, poetry) which was the repository of a 'Great Tradition' of an active culture of 'feeling' and human sensibility. His critical writing and work for the magazine *Scrutiny* (1932–53) led to the establishment of the subject of English Literature in universities and schools. Working with his wife, Q.D. Leavis, and others, he simultaneously offered a critique of popular culture and championed the study of modern English literature as a way of returning to an understanding of the human condition and a preservation of humane feeling in an alienating modern society. His 'method' and the serious attention to the detail of 'the text' are, in part, at the base of many approaches to media studies.

Thinking aloud

What's wrong with America?

We'll see a recurring motif in our discussions in this chapter. This is an explicit, often implicit, distrust of all things American – media (films, music, comic books, etc.), ideas, as well as people and politics. On the one hand, this might be dismissed as a historical perspective manifested in attitudes of the long-dead thinkers considered in this chapter. Why do you think they had such a negative view of the USA? Do you think that such perceptions are a thing of the past? What evidence is there of any negative perspectives of the USA and its culture in contemporary thought? How are these presented and what do you feel about such perspectives?

production and promotion. In the face of such widespread and popular pleasures, Leavis's central concern was with the meaning and nature of culture.

'Culture' is one of those words in the English language with many meanings and we will offer some of the changing uses throughout this section at different locations. Here we define culture initially in the terms used by theorists like Arnold and Leavis.

Over his lifetime of writing, Leavis's views became increasingly despairing, faced with the spread of what he saw as a pernicious, debased, 'mass' culture. The essence of his position can be summed up as follows. In *pre*-industrial society (which reached its apotheosis some time around the English Elizabethan period), people participated in a shared 'organic' culture (see the later definition) that was destroyed by the advent of 'mass' society. Under modern industrialisation, individuals were, as Marx suggested, 'alienated' from their full potential and humanity, reduced as they were to cogs in a machine, with little investment in the quality of what they produced or in the 'art' of everyday life.

Culture (version one)

For Arnold, Culture (with a capital C) was 'The best that has been thought and said' and in this sense it is used by Leavis (and the Frankfurt School) as a label for identifying a set of attainments in fields such as fine art, classical music, literature and dance. These attainments are usually labelled as the province of 'high culture' and the products of the great names of history (Shakespeare, Michelangelo, Voltaire, etc.). However, these ideas are often also allied to concepts of an 'authentic' 'folk culture' – i.e. something produced by ordinary people themselves within the context of their own organic traditions. This last sense is distinct from the idea of a 'popular culture' made from the products generated by mass media.

Despite its origins in European industrialisation, for Leavis 'mass' society was in large part an American phenomenon, based upon ideas of individual, lowest-common-denomination cultural ideals served by commercial interests. In thinking of how a better society might be forged from the modern, and human values retrieved and preserved, he rejected the utopian and egalitarian ideals of Marxism, based as they were in political action. Instead, and based upon the idea that it was a vision of Culture that mattered, he proposed the establishment of an elite of active 'cultured' individuals who could maintain – through art and its appreciation – the kind of authentic human condition and feeling which pre-industrial people felt in their unalienated social relationships. Through education among those outside the elite, he argued, defences could be built against some of the worst excesses of 'popular' culture. Leavis advocated the promotion of 'discrimination' in taste, which, he believed, would lead to a resistance to, and rejection of, the shoddiness of mass-produced culture and its negative effects. For him, the 'effect' of mass culture was not behavioural, but a general debasement of the quality of life and what we now call 'dumbing down', although the very term would appal Leavis as itself vulgar evidence of that process.

Leavis offered a cultural programme, which did not have an explicit political dimension, although his politics have often been interpreted as quite reactionary and anti-democratic. His work was put into practice through his influence upon education, however. For instance, his book with Denys Thompson, *Culture and Environment* (Thompson and Leavis, 1933), was intended for the benefit of schoolteachers as part of the cultural mission to educate children in standards of taste that would 'protect' them from mass media. In this way, they offer examples of the processes of degradation and suggest questions to ask of students that are designed to inculcate 'proper' values. Below are some examples. (Note: Gresham's Law posits that the precious metals used in the manufacture and circulation of coinage will gradually be reduced by the introduction of baser metals. Thompson and Leavis extend it as a metaphor for the debasement of the cultural realm.)

- 'In the light of the "Gresham Law", what kind of influence do you expect the cinema to have on general taste and mentality?' (Thompson and Leavis, 1933: 114)
- 'Broadcasting, like the films, is in practice mainly a means of passive diversion, and it tends to make active recreation, especially active use of the mind, more difficult. How far in your observation is this so, and how far need it be so?' (ibid: 115)
- 'What are likely to be the views on politics, equality of educational opportunity, capital punishment . . . of a regular reader of, respectively, the *Daily Mail* (or the *Daily Express*), the *New Statesman*, the *Week-End Review*, the *New Leader*?' (ibid: 139)

How do *you* respond to such questions? Are they at all answerable and on what terms? What are the assumptions behind them? Whatever your answers, this kind of approach had enormous influence over cultural theory in Britain, as well as over generations of teachers of English literature, their teaching practice and students at all levels of education, for decades. The attitudes expressed here continue to have influence in debates about the relationship of popular culture and young people in particular, and are often echoed when one hears complaints about the decline of ideas, manners and education, usually in arguments against media studies courses and research.

The American context

The intellectual background to theories of mass society and communication as developed in America is rooted in two important areas. The first relates to the development of the

New media, new media studies

Dumbing down?

A contemporary site around which concerns about 'dumbing down' are focused is the web. In particular, it is the interactive, collective production base of the culture of Web 2.0 which is manifest in Wikipedia, YouTube and the social media that generate comment of a nature familiar to anyone who has read Leavis and other critics of 'mass society'. Andrew Keen is one such critic. In his book *The Cult of the Amateur: How Today's Internet Is Killing Our Culture* (2007) he launches a diatribe against the culture of the web and the 'collective intelligence' of Google search results, crowd-sourcing and suchlike:

As I write, there is a brutal war going on in Lebanon between Israel and Hezbollah. But the Reddit user wouldn't know this because there is nothing about Israel, Lebanon, or Hezbollah on the site's top twenty 'hot' stories. Instead, subscribers can read about a flat-chested English actress, the walking habits of elephants, a spoof of the latest Mac commercial, and underground tunnels in Japan. Reddit is a mirror of our most banal interests. It makes a mockery of traditional news media and turns current events into a childish game of Trivial Pursuit.

What is your response to such comments? What evidence is there to support or contest Keen's points? In what way is it useful to speak of 'online culture'?

human or social sciences and the second to a 'moral panic' (p. 290) about certain versions of modern society and culture among intellectuals.

First, then, we can point to what we now call the social sciences – and notably sociology and psychology – which were taken up and developed in the early part of the twentieth century. In particular, North American scholars were highly influenced by ideas of 'positivism'. In this context, 'positivism' refers to a belief that scientific method and results are in some way 'objective', untainted by the culture and social position of the researcher, and where others are left to make moral judgements about the nature of the object of their study and any results (Hacking, 1981). The scientific credentials of work on the media and its cultural impact were often widely accepted because scientific 'proof' was provided from a 'disinterested' researcher. Such approaches were also based upon the idea that, by studying the behaviour of people, researchers could begin to understand how they thought and, in the case of media consumption, how they were influenced directly by its content and appeals (see also Chapter 8).

An equally prominent aspect of the media and cultural theory of pre-war America was a moral panic about the feeling that this young society had changed dramatically, from an individualistic yet communal and pluralist society into a society characterised by the opposite of these values – a mass society. This shift was perceived as a threat to the very heart of American social, cultural and political life. This perspective on mass society represented a different sense from those found in continental Europe, which were not wholly negative (see 'Thinking aloud', p. 402). For instance, European political movements based on fascist or socialist principles saw mass action as the basis for political change for the better, while Americans, particularly in intellectual circles, looked to more liberal and individualistic versions of politics. In Europe, 'mass' media was enormously appealing to those seeking to affect those masses they claimed to speak for, and, as we discuss in the next chapter, there was a greater receptivity to the idea that mass forms such as film and recorded music could challenge the status quo and habitual thought, as well as being used as blunt tools of propaganda.

Thus, American cultural theorists like Dwight Macdonald (1957a,b) counter-posed the idea of a pluralist society – heterogeneous and based upon individual rights – with that of a mass society. A good example of this opposition in practice, of how American political ideas enjoined with a moral panic and notions about the influence of mass media, can be found in the procedures of the House Un-American Activities Committee (or HUAC), which was most active between the mid-1930s and 1950s. The investigations of this committee concerned the infiltration of American life, culture and ideas by foreign political propaganda. Its work began in the pre-war period by focusing on communist activities, before switching to the activities of Nazism during the war (when the Soviet Union became an American ally). As the conflict ended, the attention turned once more to communism and the threat from the Soviet Union during what is now known as the 'Cold War'.

As the Cold War escalated, many Americans were fearful about the possibilities of enemy infiltration and ideas being spread by 'fifth columnists', or Americans sympathetic to communist ideals. The paranoia of 1950s Cold War America is evinced in the low-budget genre B-movies of the day, such as *Invasion of the Body Snatchers* (dir. Siegal, 1956), in which alien invaders take over the bodies and minds of Americans. They offer a new utopia of equivalence and peace but at the cost of emotion, individualism and free choice. Whether the film is representing fear of communism or offering a critique of the bland reality of American individualism and the conformity of that society is subject to debate.

During the period 1947–54, particularly through the energies of Senator Joseph McCarthy, the HUAC paid attention to attacking left-wing ideas in Hollywood. This was, in its own terms, not just an attack on the idea of communist infiltration and propaganda, but also on the essentially un-American nature of Hollywood, because it was then the epitome of technologies and practices producing a 'mass' society. Although McCarthy's witch hunt of all progressive and radical ideas is relatively well known and well documented (see George Clooney's film *Good Night, and Good Luck* (2005), for instance, and Gladchuk (2006) and Bentley (2002)), it was not simply an aberration of a paranoid American right. It reflected a widespread fear of authoritarian ideas, which was common to all shades of the political spectrum, and lies at the very heart of the way American academics dealt with the modern communication media, and the long-term attention given to 'effects' theories and concerns over the behaviour of those susceptible to media messages (see Chapter 8).

So far in this chapter we have examined two ways of conceptualising mass society, which developed through two very different approaches. For Leavis and his associates, mass society was a worrying development, most obviously linked to American society,

Case Study

Mass manipulation in the USA?

→ On 30 October 1938, one of the most notorious events in media history (and perhaps in media studies history) occurred, when Orson Welles and his Mercury Theatre players performed an updated and dramatised radio version of H.G. Wells's science fiction story *War of the Worlds*. It was introduced as a dramatic work by Welles himself and thereafter, in very effective and innovative fashion, as if a 'live' broadcast from an actual alien invasion itself. Here is an extract from a news report about the drama and its impact that appeared in the *New York Times* on 31 October 1938.

Radio Listeners in Panic, Taking War Drama as Fact:

Many Flee Homes to Escape 'Gas Raid From Mars' – Phone Calls Swamp Police at Broadcast of Wells's Fantasy

A wave of mass hysteria seized thousands of radio listeners between 8:15 and 9:30 o'clock last night when a broadcast of a dramatization of H. G. Wells's fantasy, 'The War of the Worlds', led thousands to believe that an interplanetary conflict had started with invading Martians spreading wide death and destruction in New Jersey and New York.

The broadcast, which disrupted households, interrupted religious services, created traffic jams and clogged communications systems, was made by Orson Welles, who as the radio character, 'The Shadow', used to give 'the creeps' to countless child listeners. This time at least a score of adults required medical treatment for shock and hysteria.

In Newark, in a single block at Heddon Terrace and Hawthorne Avenue, more than twenty families rushed out of their houses with wet handkerchiefs and towels over their faces to flee from what they believed was to be a gas raid. Some began moving household furniture.

Source: © 1938 *The New York Times* All Rights Reserved

This event also led to an early and influential study of media effects and the psychology of panic by Hadley Cantril (Cantril *et al.*, 1940; see also Hand, 2005). The incident (if such reports are to believed) echoed and outstripped in scale the British case presented at the start of this chapter.

Responses to such cases serve to illustrate ideas about the power of media forms to reach and to convince people as to the truth of media messages – whether as dramatic scenario, advertising claims about a product or propagandist direction.

Fan sites that examine this incident and others like it around the world, as well as programme extracts, can be found online at www.war-ofthe-worlds.co.uk/ and www.mercurytheatre.info/ (see also our discussion of *Ghostwatch*, p. 150, and *The Blair Witch Project*, p. 95).

that needed to be resisted through education and attention to traditional forms of culture. For the social scientists of the American tradition, mass society was a phenomenon that needed to be measured and calculated so that appropriate social policy antidotes could be identified and applied. We must now study a third approach to mass society theory that was developed in Europe. The theorists of this tradition are most often called the Frankfurt School, though, as we will see, for most of their work they were based in the USA in a wide range of universities.

The Frankfurt School

The people, theories and methods associated with the Frankfurt School provide some of the most important influences on the emergence and development of a field of media studies. A familiarity with this school of thinkers and their ideas is crucial to any comprehension of the dimensions of theories about mass society and the role of modern communications in it. The name itself describes a range of thinkers who were associated with the establishment, in 1923, of the Institute for Social Research at the German University of Frankfurt. The most notable of these figures, for our purposes, are Theodor Adorno and the School's director, Max Horkheimer. Other names of importance are Walter Benjamin, Erich Fromm, Leo Lowenthal and Herbert Marcuse. At the periphery of the original group we could include Siegfried Kracauer, while a contemporary theorist associated with the School is Jürgen Habermas.

The training and scholarly background of this group incorporated philosophy, sociology, psychoanalysis, musicology and literary theory. The broad importance and nature of the ideas they developed can be illustrated by contextualising the Frankfurt School within a complex and turbulent time. All of them had some kind of radical theoretical agenda that came under the broad auspices of Marxist theory and attempts to develop Marx's ideas for the twentieth century. Many of the personalities were also of Jewish origin and these two details explain the decision of the School in 1933 to decamp to the USA, where it remained until 1953. Of course, 1933 was the year in which Adolf Hitler came to power in Germany – his ideas and followers espoused an extreme hatred of Judaism, Marxism and intellectualism.

As a group, the School is associated with the concept of critical theory. Their theory is critical first in that it seeks to evaluate the terms and claims of society in the same way that Marx did. For instance, if a culture claims to be run on democratic principles, do such claims stand up to scrutiny? Secondly, it is a self-conscious theory in which the thinkers seek to recognise their own position and interests as they affect their 'objectivity' or insight. Thinkers, as we've suggested at the outset of this chapter, are not divorced from the world or their own interests in it that might, conceivably, have an impact on the conclusions they reach about it. Ultimately, these thinkers sought to deal with the philosophical limits and problems of Marxism, particularly the kind of dogmatic or vulgar interpretation of his ideas evinced by Stalin and the Soviet Union at that time. For the theorists associated with the School, theory was active: theorisation of society was a process that could not be allowed to ossify in its attempt to contribute to social revolution. In particular, theirs was an attempt to revitalise those aspects of Marxism concerned with the realm of ideas and ideology as opposed to the economy. This explains their concern with the realm of culture, its promise and their fears about how it had been colonised by capitalism in search of profit and as a tool of ideological manipulation, as opposed to enlightenment and personal fulfilment. Their work is also related to the study of the political economy of the media (see Chapter 5).

In relation to our earlier discussion of ideology, theorists of the Frankfurt School compare with another contemporary Marxist – Antonio Gramsci – in attempting to account for the perseverance of capitalism but also the appearance of its most extreme manifestation

Doing media studies

Investigating ideas about mass society

Read the following quotes on the masses and mass society – the emphases are our own:

■ 'A vast residuum of the working class, which, raw and half-developed, has long lain half-hidden amidst its poverty and squalor, and is now issuing from its hiding place . . . marching where it likes, breaking what it likes' (Arnold, 1882/1932: 105).

■ 'Many too many are born . . . Just look at these superfluous people! They steal for themselves the works of inventors and the treasures of the wise: they call their theft culture . . . Just look at these superfluous people! They are always ill, they vomit their bile and call it a newspaper' (Nietzsche, 1883–5/1967: 76–8).

■ 'The great agent of change and, from our point of view, destruction, has of course been the machine-applied power. The machine has brought us many advantages, but it has destroyed the old ways of life, the old forms, and by reasons of the continual rapid change it involves, prevented the growth of new. Moreover, the advantage it brings us in mass-production has turned out to involve standardization and levelling-down outside the realm of mere material goods. Those who in school are offered (perhaps) the beginnings of education in taste are exposed, out of school, to the competing exploitation of the cheapest emotional responses; films, newspapers, publicity in all its forms, commercially-catered fiction – all offer satisfaction at the lowest level, and inculcate the choosing of the most immediate pleasures, got with the least effort' (Thompson and Leavis, 1933: 3).

■ 'People go to the movies instead of moving! Hollywood characters are supposed to have all the adventures for everybody in America, while everybody in America sits in a dark room and watches them have them! Yes, until there's a war. That's when adventure becomes available to the masses' (Williams, 1945/1987: 47).

■ 'There is no doubt that in our headlong rush to educate everybody, we are *lowering our standards* . . . destroying our ancient edifices, to make ready the ground upon which the barbarian nomads of the future will encamp in their mechanized caravans' (Eliot, 1949: 108).

■ 'Almost everybody is worried about the extension of the frontiers of the vulgar, the corrupt, and the trivial. In competition and contrast with high culture, the trepidation everybody felt about its "mass" counterpart was warranted in such political growths as Hitler's demagogy, the Communist's "people's democracies" and the "Americanisation" of Europe' (Macdonald, 1957a: 75).

Write a short answer to each of the following questions:

1. What ideas about social change, mass society and the masses are expressed here?

2. What kind of relationship exists between the authors (intellectuals) and those that they write about or speak for?

3. What ideas about media forms are expressed here? On the evidence presented here, what are the similarities and differences between these thinkers?

in the form of the fascism of Hitler and Mussolini which emerged in Europe in the first decades of the twentieth century. One of the notable features of Hitler's fascism was his appeal to 'the masses', that individuals must sublimate their own interests in favour of the *Volk* or nation. To these ends he marshalled the tools of mass communication – radio, newspapers, publishing, popular music, posters and films. This process would strike us as obviously propagandist, and typical of a highly centralised and controlled society such as Nazi Germany. However, what prompted the most famous insights of the theorists associated with the Frankfurt School was what they found during their enforced period of exile in the USA, and how they turned critical theory to examine the claims of the 'land of the free'. This is encapsulated in Adorno and Horkheimer's concept of the culture industry.

Defining the culture industry

The USA was and is clearly a country that defines itself as democratic, a country within which there is an unfettered support of capitalist principles in pursuit of the 'American dream' of success. To the Frankfurt School thinkers this pluralist, largely unregulated system was the opposite of that of the totalitarian and centralised state of Nazi Germany. It was one where individuals considered themselves to be free, exercising choice in every sphere of their lives in pursuit of 'life, liberty and the pursuit of happiness'. One area in which this seemed apparent was in the realm of entertainment and culture, which was also varied and marked by a high degree of choice. There were films, radio shows (and many stations to choose from among them), a variety of newspapers, magazines and a vibrant source of music in jazz and other popular musical forms.

However, for Adorno and Horkheimer, upon closer critical inspection, this pluralism and liberty was a deception that was particularly structured into this field of entertainment on the basis of a desire for profit and thus an alignment with capitalist business methods and values, all aimed at generating and maintaining profit. Media, therefore, were viewed as sites that involved the rationalisation (organisation, streamlining according to repeated principles) and industrialisation of culture to the point at which it became an agent of the very system of exploitation. In this way, the 'culture' provided by the media industries becomes the epitome of the values of the dominant social group and partial social interests.

For these theorists, the transformation of 'culture' into the banal, mass-produced product of the factory was rooted in the very fact of Hollywood's production-line studio system, generic radio shows, advertising, magazine publishing houses, as well as the existence of 'Tin Pan Alley' where songwriters wrote tunes to order!

Authentic culture

Culture industry

Those organisations involved in the economic rationalisation, organisation and exploitation of entertainment, cultural or aesthetic work to generate profit and to maintain the operation of a market system.

The term '**culture industry**' is itself intentionally oxymoronic and designed to provoke. For Adorno and Horkheimer, a proper or 'authentic' culture was evinced by either pre-capitalist forms, such as the tales and songs that ordinary people had created and maintained themselves (folk culture, oral traditions), or the work of great artists in literature (novels, poetry, drama), art (sculpture, painting, etc.) or music – collectively high culture. As a musicologist and composer himself, Adorno had more than a passing interest and knowledge of the music of figures such as Mozart or Beethoven. To him, the works of such figures bore the stamp of the unique artistic personality.

Formally (meaning the use of paint in a painting, the organisation of movements and motifs in a symphony, for example), proper cultural works were constructed in terms of their own internal logic and not according to some predetermined formulae – as one finds in a horror film or a magazine romance story. Thus, one of the merits of 'art' work for Adorno is, literally, its difference from the uniformity of the status quo and the world in which we exist. In proper cultural work, privileged by the artist's vision, we comprehend a world (in our sensory apprehension of a painting or musical concerto) with which banal reality compares unfavourably. While 'proper' culture may be beautiful and joyous, its status disrupts our complacency with the world and the system; in its integrity of feeling, its perfection and its uniqueness, the falseness of the world under the exploitative system of capitalist industry is thus revealed, as is the shoddy nature of social relations, feelings and economic existence. For Adorno, proper culture represents what it means to be truly and authentically free!

Faced with these ideas, you may object that even the worst Hollywood films take us beyond 'banal reality' to places of the imagination, to emotional stories of love and so on; likewise, with other media products, such as pop songs and human-interest stories in magazines, which affirm the human spirit. In this critique, however, Adorno and Horkheimer argue that these pleasures are 'false' and deceptive in their operations and objectives. We can understand this better by unpacking the features of the products of the culture industry in more detail and examining the way in which they differ from the vision of 'authentic' culture set out above.

Features of the culture industry

Reflecting on his original ideas on the culture industry some years after their publication, Adorno revealed that he and Horkheimer had considered using the term 'mass culture'. This was rejected, however, on the basis that it might be mistaken for a popular art that stemmed *from* the people – or masses – themselves, reflecting their interests, rather than one created *for* them in the interests of the system, i.e. capital. The concept of culture as industry for Adorno, then, is an abomination. It produces art (or entertainment) where every detail has been predetermined in formulaic fashion for consumption by a mass audience. In appealing to as many people as possible (thus maximising profit), the products of the culture industry exhibit a number of key features and produce theoretical (if not proven) long-term effects in its audience.

First, the products of the culture industry are characterised by 'standardisation' and 'pseudo-individualisation'. The first idea concerns the way in which all products adhere to simple formulae (hero kills bad guy and gets girl in films, popular songs follow the verse/chorus structure and 'I love you' formulae, horoscopes promise vague successes, etc.). The latter idea suggests that, despite the sameness of media products, they appear to be different, through the substitution of new actors and actresses and locations in film, or the delivery of songs in new arrangements by a variety of singers. These things appear to be different but they are not, as the essential formulae remain the same. We should also note that the plots and ideas of songs – romantic idealism and individual triumph – reiterate aspects of the ideology of bourgeois capitalism: it could be you! Despite the variety on offer across these products (a hundred songs in the hit parade, several new releases at the cinema), Adorno suggests that, at base, everything is the same. Superficially, there appears to be something for everyone, simply so none may escape the system.

Different but the same – the products of the culture industry are characterised by 'standardisation' and 'pseudo-individualisation' in the thinking of theorists of the Frankfurt School.

Source: Alamy Images

Secondly, the undifferentiated character of the products of the cultural industry (its massness) reproduces the audience in its own image – dull, unimaginative, repetitive. The culture industry positions and demands that the audience respond in a collective way, that they laugh and cry at the same things. In this it orders the audience and induces a form of ideological distraction from the reality of the world. These products create and satisfy a need that is deemed to be false (tears and laughter can be turned on by combinations of rhetorical effects and stock situations), and certainly not spontaneous. Products are 'pre-digested', so that every outcome and pleasure is anticipated, inducing a form of regularity and obedience in the very act of consumption.

Thirdly, the products of the culture industry induce in their consumers a feeling of 'catharsis'. Despite the fact that films, songs, etc. are constructed rather like work itself (repetitive and ordered, ultimately laborious), they offer the opportunity for a good laugh or cry that gets rid of the tensions and frustrations of work. What this means, however, is a spurious and 'commodified' form of leisure (if leisure is about escape from work) that does not lead to enlightenment or freedom – as in culture proper. On the contrary, this experience merely makes one fit for another day's work after the weekend's release – in dancing, watching movies and so on! Throughout the week we can be distracted from our own problems, the dullness of work and our collective oppression by worrying about the z-list celebrities whose lives we follow in the papers or in fictional form in soap operas.

A further feature of the culture industry lies in the particular nature of the commodification, or packaging and selling of culture. This is the idea of commodity fetishism, based upon an elaboration of an idea developed by Marx.

Marx sought to consider how relations and conditions of life were different under industrial capitalism with its system of mass production, compared with the way things once were (the principle of buying and selling and gaining wealth was not a modern invention, after all). He discussed how physical objects or mass-produced products took on particular identities in the marketplace, where competition over price takes place. If we take the example of a coat, for Marx it can be thought of as having a 'use-value', i.e. we buy coats because they keep us warm or dry as needed. However, many different manufacturers who pay workers a set wage to produce them manufacture masses of coats. A price is put on such products, which are to be sold in the market where many other products compete for our attention and money. Here, products acquire 'exchange value', not necessarily related any more to utility or to what went into their making. For instance, all coats are presumably designed to give warmth or to keep the wearer dry, but some cost a little and others a lot, sometimes without any difference in style or material and with little discernible use-value at all, as they are made from materials that are less than robust! Furthermore, there is no consistent logic for explaining price differences. Some coats might be 'hand-made', but the hands may be those of children paid a pittance in Third World sweatshops; conversely, some mass-produced, factory-made goods are sold at very high prices simply because of the name of the designer or producer's label.

For Marx, the process by which such commodities are produced (and by whom), how much was paid to the maker and the way in which goods acquire such market value disappears from view. What matters is that they have acquired a worth that does not necessarily convey this process and therefore appear before us as if by magic. Marx's use of 'fetish' here is derived from some religions, in which objects are invested with supernatural properties and worshipped. For Marx, modern societies treat products – commodities – as if they were such fetishes – magical things wherein the explanation for their existence disappears in favour of the 'worship' of their monetary value and social worth. (My haute-couture blouson might fall apart at the first drop of rain, but wearing it marks me out as wealthy and as having good taste.)

So how, then, is this idea transposed to the world of culture and entertainment? For Adorno and Horkheimer, the products of the culture industry are sold to us on the basis of their cost price and, indeed, the value that they generate, both of which are divorced from any interest in an evaluation of their cultural meaning and qualities. By way of example, we can pinpoint how films are marketed in terms of how much they cost to make and how much they have taken at the box office. During the time of writing, the final Harry Potter film, *Harry Potter and the Deathly Hallows (Part 2)*, was released and critical evaluations were superseded by daily reports of how box-office records had been shattered. Similarly, in the realm of popular music, success and some form of quality are measured in terms of sales – number one on the hit parade, for instance, is deemed to be the ultimate achievement. Anyone tuning in to any contemporary chart show on television or radio will find that acts are often defined in terms of units shifted in particular territories or attenders and receipts at gigs, material that is offered up as equal in excitement to the 'rebellious' attitude of the act, their 'sexiness' or the tenderness of a lyric. Of course, and as Adorno and Horkheimer lamented, even in the world of 'high' culture, too, works of art are graded according to price (or 'pricelessness', even) – each new sale of a Picasso or Bacon is widely reported to have generated a new record price! At the time of writing, and against the backdrop of global economic depression, excited media reports related how a Francesco Guardi painting of Venice's Rialto Bridge sold in London for almost £27 million ($42.8 million, €29.8 million).

Assessing the culture industry

Undoubtedly, the vision of the culture industry is a pessimistic one that, like many ideological critiques (as seen in the previous chapter), suggests that the objects of our media pleasures and sources of information about the world are deceptive. Certainly, many theorists reject such conclusions and dismiss the elitism of Adorno and Horkheimer's position.

Thinking aloud

From culture industry to cultural industries

In the analysis of Adorno and Horkheimer, the term culture industry is an oxymoron enlisted with disdain. For them, the idea of industrial production is antithetical to the integrity of 'culture' proper. Whether or not this critical term registers or not, in recent years the term 'cultural industries' has emerged in public and academic discourse. This term has a wholly different descriptive and non-evaluative emphasis, tied usually to a focus on the value of nurturing 'creativity' as a driver in contemporary post-industrial economies. These terms occur repeatedly in the policy statements of both national and supra-national governments. The Council of Europe, for instance, has co-ordinated a wealth of information on such trends from Albania to Finland (see www.culturalpolicies.net). At a global level, UNESCO has pronounced on the virtue of the cultural industries and what is meant by this term:

The cultural industries, which include publishing, music, cinema, crafts and design, continue to grow steadily apace and have a determinant role to play in the future of culture.

Their international dimension gives them a determining role for the future in terms of freedom of expression, cultural diversity and economic development. Although the globalisation of exchange and new technologies opens up exciting new prospects, it also creates new types of inequality.

The world map of these industries reveals a yawning gap between North and South. This can only be counteracted by strengthening local capacities and facilitating access to global markets at national level by way of new partnerships, know-how, control of piracy and increased international solidarity of every kind (http://portal.unesco.org/culture).

This vision is clearly of a different order from that of the Frankfurt School thinkers. It marks a shift, too, from an era in which this sector of activity was a minor arm of the economy, to one in which the role of cultural production is central. As discussed in Chapter 7, however, the global nature of media organisations in particular and the role that their products are seen to play in the process of cultural imperialism may yet lead us back to a reconsideration of Adorno and Horkheimer (for a discussion of the contemporary 'cultural industries' see Hesmondhalgh, 2002).

However, we would suggest that there is much about this work that is both convincing and productive, and certainly understandable in the context in which it was produced. We should not forget that, in comparison with more conservative critics of mass culture and the masses, Adorno *et al.* were genuinely, politically and humanely concerned with the condition of the majority – why else would elitists bother with Marxism, which aims to transform society to the benefit of that majority?

To dismiss Adorno, for instance, as an elitist misses a number of points. First, one critique of the theory summarised here, and of his other writing, would protest its difficulty and apparent impenetrability. His writing is difficult partly because of his synthesis of so many other difficult ideas, but also because it intends to be quite singular. His is a form of writing that differentiates itself from the everyday, run-of-the-mill, popular journalism of the culture industry, which for him turns difficult ideas into nuggets of wisdom or fact that merit a response from the reader of 'well, fancy that!', but are then discarded because they are predicated on the principles of consumption – i.e. what's next? His writing is, itself, a rather artistic thing that compares favourably with the cultural forms he endorsed.

Secondly, it is worth noting that he was highly critical of the manner in which high art was itself fully incorporated by the system and commodified for the bourgeoisie. Anyone

Doing media studies

Exploring the culture industry

It would be useful to build upon our summary of Adorno and Horkheimer's ideas by reading what they said in more detail (a link below leads you to online publications). To get you thinking about their ideas and their style, here are some extracts from *Dialectic of Enlightenment*:

> all mass culture is identical, and the lines of its artificial framework begin to show through. The people at the top are no longer so interested in concealing monopoly: as its violence becomes more open, so its power grows. Movies and radio need no longer pretend to be art. The truth that they are just business is made into an ideology in order to justify the rubbish they deliberately produce. They call themselves industries; and when their directors' incomes are published, any doubt about the social utility of the finished products is removed.

> [. . .]

> The ruthless unity in the culture industry is evidence of what will happen in politics. Marked differentiations such as those of A and B films, or of stories in magazines in different price ranges, depend not so much on subject matter as on classifying, organising, and labelling consumers. Something is provided for all so that none may escape; the distinctions are emphasised and extended. The public is catered for with a hierarchical range of mass-produced products of varying quality, thus advancing the rule of complete quantification. Everybody must behave (as if spontaneously) in accordance with his previously determined and indexed level, and choose the category of mass product turned out for his type.

> Consumers appear as statistics on research organisation charts, and are divided by income groups into red, green, and blue areas; the technique is that used for any type of propaganda.

> [. . .]

> There is nothing left for the consumer to classify. Producers have done it for him. Art for the masses has destroyed the dream.

(Adorno and Horkheimer, 1997) See also: 'The Culture Industry: Enlightenment as Mass Deception' at http://marxists.org/reference/subject/philosophy/works/ge/adorno.htm

Based upon your own media consumption, evaluate the ideas of standardisation and pseudo-individualisation. Are they convincing in understanding the role of media in our lives? Are there elements unaccounted for? How convincing is the notion of a culture industry when applied to contemporary media forms and institutions?

doubting this should consider the nature of the contemporary art world, with its marketable scandal, high prices and celebrity artists such as Damien Hirst, Jeff Koons, Chris Ofili, Tracey Emin (lately enlisted to contribute an 'edgy' work to the official home of the UK's prime minister), etc. Likewise, the analyses of mainstream film, popular music and other forms seem increasingly relevant, as films are developed by teams of scriptwriters, in consultation with focus groups and organised around product placement, while different cuts are tested before preview audiences. The same process is worked through in public in TV talent shows, which manage to whittle down thousands to one 'individual' (or group of 'individuals') who nonetheless fit the same mould of all previous winners.

Finally, in the technical detail of their analyses of the culture industry, Adorno and Horkheimer are convincing. Media products are indeed alike, uniform, standardised, produced in corporate fashion with the purpose of making a profit. By any estimation, films, songs, TV programmes and so on are, indeed, incredibly formulaic and repetitive. This is demonstrable and indisputably so. However, whether or not one can simply deduce from this the nature of the experience of audiences and how those 'masses' of people who consume such products – 'us', 'we', 'they' – think is another matter. In this manner, the thinking of Adorno, Horkheimer and many others of the Frankfurt School displayed a lack of knowledge of who the 'masses' of mass society were, as well as assumptions that they shared with some of those others encountered so far in this chapter.

Who are 'the masses'?

Just as theorists of the media have moved from ideas of 'the culture industry' to that of the 'cultural industries' (see the 'Thinking aloud' box 'From culture industry to cultural industries', above), they have also distinguished between the idea of mass culture (produced for the masses and which produces 'massness' in them) and a more flexible idea of 'popular culture'. The latter idea accounts for what people do with mass-produced products and acknowledges, also, that they are produced in a context in which producers and consumers share aspects of culture. Tracing and understanding these shifting senses of culture, and using them to make sense of your own research, is an important part of becoming a student of the media. To help us think through these changes, it is productive to identify a series of individuals and their ideas that we place under the broad label of 'Left-Leavism' and 'culturalism'. These terms are used to describe the approach of a group of academics working from the 1950s, who were active in socialist politics but gave an important emphasis to questions about modern culture in their academic work. The most influential individuals here were Richard Hoggart, Raymond Williams, Edward P. Thompson and Stuart Hall. A historian concerned with the traditions of the neglected 'masses' in history, Thompson (1924–93) came from an upper-middle-class background, while the Jamaican-born Hall (1932–) came to Britain after the war and has probably been the individual most responsible for nurturing the theories and theorists of what has come to be known as cultural studies. Hoggart and Williams were part of a small section of working-class children whose secondary and university education in the 1930s was gained with the aid of financial scholarships when opportunities for such individuals were quite limited. It was here that these individuals came into contact with Leavis's work.

Unsurprisingly for a generation of aspirant, but committed, socialists (thus the left of Left-Leavism) like Hoggart, Williams, Thompson and Hall, Leavis's ideas and social critique offered a sense of striving for something better in the face of an apparently degraded and degrading culture of capitalism. But Leavis's failure to understand what actually happened in working-class culture was seen as a major limitation by these academics. They drew upon observations from their own experience, empirical research and Marxist theory both to understand Leavis's failures and to outline their own grasp of culture and the originality of their insights. These writers were pivotal in shifting the ground of the elitist cultural tradition in Britain, and in offering an alternative to the theoretical abstraction characteristic of continental theory produced by Althusser *et al.* (p. 359).

There are two parts to this alternative. The first is in the detail of cultural analyses of ordinary people's lives. The second is that ordinary people were active in the making of their own culture, even if it was set amidst the forces of history, mass culture and society. The most influential figure in the shift from mass to popular approaches is Raymond Williams, whose ideas we shall examine first.

Raymond Williams: culture is ordinary

Williams's published writing is extensive in its quantity and coverage, but it is worth using two key ideas he presented as a way of understanding his significant contribution to our conception of the changing idea of mass culture. He argued that no one who ever thinks of people as masses includes themselves in the category, as he observed 'the masses are other people'. Furthermore, he suggested that 'culture is ordinary'. By these phrases and the arguments that he used to support them, he pushed theorists to rethink the way they understood the relationships between modern mass media, social class, power and ideas of culture.

Taking each in turn, we can bring out the essence of Williams's argument, and its striking difference from the pessimistic ideas of mass society presented by the British tradition, exemplified by Arnold and Leavis, the American tradition in modern social sciences, and the European-rooted Frankfurt School theories.

First, let us consider what lies behind the proposition that 'the masses are other people'. Exploring the concept of the masses in Williams's breakthrough book *Culture and Society* (1958/1961), he sought to point out that the earlier mass society theories had been proposed from a position where the theorists saw themselves as examining other people. As most theorists had come from upper-class or upper middle-class backgrounds, their arguments were always about a group of people whom they thought of as separate from themselves. With a sense of the positive aspects of his own working-class background, Williams felt many of the assumptions made about ordinary people's lives were incorrect, and that, in their ignorance, theorists created a sense of other people as a lump or mass that did not share what they saw as the valuable aspects of elite lifestyles. This separation, and the particular processes and assumptions associated with the life of elites, also qualified the way in which they perceived and valued culture. As he wrote:

> We now regularly use both the idea of the 'masses', and the consequent ideas of 'mass-civilization', 'mass-democracy', 'mass-communications' and others. Here, I think, lies a central and very difficult issue which more than any other needs revisions . . . Yet, masses was a new word for mob, and the traditional characteristics of the mob were retained in its significance: gullibility, fickleness, herd-prejudice, lowness of taste and habit. The masses, on this evidence, formed the perpetual threat to culture . . . [but] who are the masses? In practice, in our society and in this context, they can hardly be other than the working people . . . I do not think of my relatives, friends, neighbours, colleagues, acquaintances, as masses; we none of us can or do. The masses are always the other, whom we don't know and can't know . . . To other people, we also are masses. Masses are other people.

> (Williams, 1958/1990: 287–9)

The pithy conclusion he drew was that there are, in fact, no masses: 'there are only ways of seeing people as masses'. Once one grasps this fact, then, it is possible to understand the origins and function of such concepts.

Key thinker

Raymond Williams (1921–88)

Williams represented a new type of British intellectual that came to prominence in the 1960s. He was born into a working-class family in the Welsh/English borders, attended a grammar school with the support of a scholarship (i.e. support for fees, books and so on), when most working-class people had little senior school education, before studying English literature at Cambridge University under Leavis. He started work in adult education, and wrote a number of widely read books on culture and class, as well as fictionalised portraits of his origins. He made a major impact in academia and, indeed, in popular thought with *Culture and Society*, which became a bestseller in the UK in 1958. Williams went on to become one of the defining cultural voices in post-war Britain, taking up a professorial post at Cambridge, and becoming progressively more radical as he grew older.

Culture (version two): a whole way of life

This anthropological sense of the term is distinct from the notion of culture as a body of special artefacts. It allows for the practical and collective aspects of making meaning in ordinary life. This definition encompasses texts and the way that they are consumed and interpreted within the contexts of a culture. Thus, this definition also allows for popular culture to be not only that produced by the majority of people themselves in the ways in which they live but also the way in which those products which are produced for them ('mass' culture) are taken into their lives as meaningful.

The next observation to consider is that 'culture is ordinary', and what Williams meant by this. This is, in fact, the title of an article written early in his career, in which he demonstrated the originality of his approach to understanding modern **culture** at a number of different levels. First, the article was mainly about him and his life. While earlier theorists had hidden themselves in their writing, Williams uses the personal pronoun 'I' all the time, and the article draws on his own early life in a working-class community and his experiences of life as a student at Cambridge, in a largely upper-class community.

Secondly, he uses storytelling devices drawn from literature to structure his argument within a narrative about a series of journeys, both physical and symbolic. He starts the article by telling the story of a return visit to the small town in which he grew up, and then uses this to tell of the physical and social journey he made when he 'went up' to university. Rather than providing a series of propositions about culture, he uses the description of his own life experiences, and his literary devices, to interrogate the meaning and importance of the word culture. He suggests that:

We use the word culture in these two senses: to mean a whole way of life – the common meanings; to mean the arts and learning – the special processes of discovery and creative effort. Some writers reserve the word for one or other of these senses; I insist on both, and on the significance of their conjunction.

(Williams, 1958/1990: 76)

In this reflection on the concept of culture, we can see both the idea inherited from Leavis and Arnold of culture as certain forms of special achievement, and of an anthropological sense of the way we live our lives. Culture here is not created by a specially talented or exceptional group of individual artists, authors and so on, at a remove from life, nor, in relation, is it just something that can be appreciated by an equally privileged minority as a special preserve of human values, implying that this elite, by extension, was specially human. The concept of culture as a 'whole way of life' takes into account, insists, in fact, that meaning, significance and creativity are more widespread and democratic than those limited selections that make it into art galleries and libraries, for instance. It is about how people live and the way in which they make their lives and why they do what they do.

By focusing on the idea that culture came from and was about ordinary lives, Williams influenced a generation of scholars of culture and society. To understand this influence and its reach, traced in aspects of many approaches and perspectives in this book, as well as the utility of Williams's ideas, we should refer to a further concept: that of a 'common culture'.

In the work of Arnold, Leavis and, later, in the influential commentary of the poet T.S. Eliot, contemporary with Williams, the elitist concept of culture was to school 'the masses' in those things valued by the elite. This was predicated upon a belief that this extension would 'cultivate' the majority to invest in those things and practices which embodied the values of the elite, rejected all those nasty things like mass-produced culture (films, pop songs, etc.), as well as political action that disturbed the 'natural' order of things with horrible ideas such as equality and the redistribution of wealth. This meant that society would have a 'culture in common', in the sense of everyone sharing in what Leavis called 'The Great Tradition'. However, this also implied that whatever the majority valued and did was tantamount to being worthless and easily rejected.

Williams's idea of a 'common culture' is somewhat different. Built upon the idea of 'a whole way of life', it offered instead a sense of culture, not as a limited preserve of 'the best' of art and so on, but as a site of shared values that included recognition and validation of the lives and meanings of ordinary people. Thus, he envisaged 'a society where values are at once commonly created and criticised, and where the divisions and exclusions of class may be replaced by the reality of common and equal membership' (Williams, 1967: 308).

Once one places this idea in context, it becomes less abstract and particularly relevant to arguments about media. The context of Williams's commentaries was the post-war boom in the UK (echoed across Europe, America and Japan) and the growth of a consumer society. One feature of this development was a massive growth in mass communication – the coming of television, in particular, but also the birth of rock and roll, and a growing commodification of leisure and of private life that continues to this day. For Williams, it was important that these developments allowed access for all social views and cultural perspectives, and that they did not just reiterate values of acquisitiveness and selfish individualism. In this way his ideas resonate with concepts such as the ideological critique of capitalist economies, of arguments about the public sphere, representation, multiculturalism and, of course, with debates about the nature of democracy in modern society.

Richard Hoggart: *The Uses of Literacy* to the Centre for Contemporary Cultural Studies (CCCS)

The emphasis in Williams's work on studying the ordinary, everyday nature of culture as integral to people's lives, exploring how meanings are central to culture, and tying culture explicitly to a democratic zeal, can be seen to underlie the next set of ideas we need to understand. Richard Hoggart (1918–) is the thinker whose name is often linked to Williams. Although his reputation as a theorist is less assured, his impact upon thinking about media, culture and society was considerable and became established with the publication of a book called *The Uses of Literacy* (Hoggart, 1958). The book was a bestseller, particularly important to the post-war generation of working-class men and women who were taking advantage of the now free educational, social and vocational opportunities afforded by the establishment of the post-war welfare state in the UK.

Hoggart's approach was comparable to Williams's in the manner in which he sought to challenge some of the fantasies that intellectuals had about working people, which allowed them to project on to them their ideas about 'masses'. He counters the dehumanised and anonymised way in which that label works, through insights and colour from within the world of those masses. In this way the book reads like a novel or autobiography, as he paints an enormously detailed portrait drawn from his own Leeds childhood.

Instead of judging them on values imported from outside their world and projected on to them, Hoggart sought to understand how ordinary people made use of the resources available to them within it.

Thus, to critics of mass culture from Adorno to Leavis, popular songs, for instance, as evidence of the shoddiness of mass-produced products, may have appeared to be imaginatively poor and conventional, too. However, Hoggart does not see in this a corollary in the human qualities of members of the audience themselves and says of pop songs that 'their aim is to present to the hearer as directly as possible a known patter of emotions; they are not so much creations in their own right as structures of conventional signs for the emotional fields they open' (Hoggart, 1958: 161) Such songs are resources, appropriated on the terms of the people themselves, who ignore much about them and yet 'make much else better than it really is, to continue putting their own kind of vision into what may not really deserve it' (Hoggart, 1958: 325). Hoggart admitted that the kinds of things modern people found pleasure in might lack the finesse of the popular culture of the past – the kinds of things that thinkers like Leavis and Adorno suggested had died out. However, Hoggart wondered why such ideas romanticised the people of the past, while failing to see that there was virtue in the way that contemporary communities made the best of things and tried to live decent and respectable lives with what they were given: 'is it not also worthy of remark that working-class audiences today, after nearly one hundred years of hard and often ugly urban life, should hold as strongly as they do to themes which, though very simply apprehended, are by no means unadmirable?' (Hoggart, 1958: 162). Nonetheless, Hoggart himself, as Williams was also wont to do on occasion, repeats some of the pessimism of other theorists. Of particular concern for him was the context we've described above – the growth of consumer culture. The explosion in mass media and goods after the Second World War he described as offering a 'candy-floss world' (think about the imagery

Thinking aloud

Periodising ideas of 'mass society' or why 1918–68?

At the beginning of this chapter, we framed our discussion of mass society and the development of related theories in the years 1918–68. It is worth asking why these dates are used, and whether this kind of periodisation has value. Despite the fact that some of the ideas that have influenced our discussion in this and the previous chapter come from an earlier period, by 1918 many of the key technologies and institutions that formed modern mass media were in place. That year also marked the end of the cataclysmic world war and, as such, seems a useful historical 'marker'. We could also argue that the subsequent decades witnessed a high point of theoretical and ideological appeals (for good and bad) to the concept of people as 'masses', defined by nation and class.

1968 is not a point where this kind of thinking ended but it is again another useful marker. This was a year of worldwide protests against the totalitarian systems of the Eastern Bloc but also of student uprisings in opposition to the feeling that Western democracies and capitalism were also totalitarian and served to deny freedom. For our purposes, what is intriguing is that out of this ferment came the theories and practices that challenged and systematically dismantled both traditional ways of thinking and foundational concepts that had supported the kind of elitism that produced the intellectual prejudice about masses and their culture (or lack of it). While not beginning in 1968, this year gave an impetus to new voices and ways of thinking about race, ethnicity, sexuality and gender that countered the dominance of the WASP (White, Anglo-Saxon, Protestant) hegemony. For good and bad, the development of the field of cultural analysis underpinning media studies and its cognate fields reflects this fragmentation and challenge.

Thinking aloud

'Mass' and 'popular' culture

As demonstrated by Adorno's thoughts about the kind of label he considered using for the object of his studies, such choices matter. As the word 'mass' is loaded with significance, so is the word 'popular' when enlisted in describing cultural forms and consumption (see discussion of Williams and Hoggart). Does 'popular' describe the perceptions of the audience (it is enjoyed by them), and/or its wide reach? Could 'high' culture be popular in the same way or is the term used as a synonym for the products of the culture industry and particular attitudes to them? Does the use of 'popular' always allow for acknowledgement of audience choices and needs? To what degree do such terms allow for shared values between producers and consumers? Such uses are important and have been subject to debate, particularly as they pertain to ideas about the choices and selections made by consumers themselves and the degree to which cultural commodities relate to their 'real' needs and any part they might play in determining their qualities and meanings. Such labels are always imbued with value judgements and you should look out for instances of their use in your own media consumption and interactions.

of the idea and texture of the stuff itself!) of magazines, movies and later television. For him, this stuff, particularly in advertising and the kinds of superficial lifestyle promotion that abounded, had the potential to undermine the creativity and cohesion of working-class life that he sought to recognise and celebrate.

In their time, Hoggart and Williams both became minor celebrities, certainly lauded as 'popular' thinkers, whose comments on contemporary society were solicited and listened to. Hoggart, in particular, served on a number of government committees concerned with culture and media. The important thing, here, was not simply that the ideas of these two thinkers were sought out but that they themselves advised that ordinary people should be listened to, taken account of and taken seriously. In effect, that ways of thinking of people as masses ought to be dissolved.

Hoggart's attempts to investigate popular culture and the meanings it had for people, rather than simply reading it off from the superior vantage point of the theorist, was a great innovation in a world where culture had become a particularly important object of scrutiny. Based upon taking contemporary popular culture seriously, Hoggart's other great initiative was to establish the first dedicated academic site for its study, in the form of the Centre for Contemporary Cultural Studies (CCCS) based at the University of Birmingham.

The 'Centre' was established by Richard Hoggart in 1964, and then led by Stuart Hall from 1967 until 1979 (it was closed down by the university in 2002 amidst some controversy). During this time, scholars working at the Centre produced an enormous number of studies that impacted radically on how academics thought about culture. The CCCS took students from a vast array of disciplines, actively sought recruits from outside the mainstream of white, middle-class, male academics and threw them into collaborative projects, discussions and research into the nature of culture, politics, identity, theory, intellectuals, class, gender, ethnicity, history, sociology, sexuality, psychology, the media and anything else that merited attention. What is remarkable is how graduates of the Centre, once established in teaching posts in other universities, came to dominance with a new notion of modern society, its analysis and articulation in cultural, public and social policy.

Learning from Williams and Hoggart, but with a greater affection for the cultural products of the post-war world (the music, the films, the television and so on), they replaced an idea of mass culture with one of popular culture and a more nuanced sense of the role that people themselves played in creating the meanings of the material they consumed, enjoyed and often had some hand in producing. This is not to say that such thinkers wholly abandoned any sense of the negative aspects of the products of media for instance.

An awareness of the function and operations of ideology and power in society and in media tempered any overly celebratory position. Nonetheless, their work has covered a wide range of topics, and related to many different political ideas, investigating different perspectives on culture and engaging with ideas from continental European theory, from Antonio Gramsci to the Structuralists – as discussed in the previous chapter. By this we mean that they picked up Williams's analysis of the way that terms like popular and culture have meanings rooted in different class positions. Indeed, as class has seemingly waned as a category of public debate and theoretical analysis, theorists such as Richard Dyer, Paul Gilroy, David Morely, Charlotte Brunsdon, Anne Gray, Stuart Hall and many others have been attuned to gender, ethnicity and sexuality as equally vital to making, and making sense of, culture.

Summary

Conceptualising mass society

In this chapter we have developed our thinking about the social role of media through an investigation of and engagement with concepts of mass society. Thus we began with a consideration of the idea of mass society and how this related to historical contexts of social change and the rise of mass communications and mass media. This context then set up our exploration of some negative responses to these changes.

We first considered the British theorist F. R. Leavis and his lineage, notably his debt to Matthew Arnold. Leavis's negative perception of modern culture was evinced in the products of mass media and their degrading effect on modern life. His response generated an educational project that sought to generate an appreciation of his definition of culture (his 'Great Tradition' of the works of literature) through education, in order to 'innoculate' the masses against mass culture. We then explored some of the context for American responses to the development of mass society, the investment in social science, and the widespread fears of the way that the anonymous nature of 'massness' was antithetical to American values and sense of a pluralist society.

Then we considered the central concepts of the Frankfurt School, in the form of the ideas of Adorno and Horkheimer. Their central concern was with the commodification of culture, which resulted in what they termed the culture industry. The mass-produced output of film studios, radio, record labels and so on they dismissed as inferior to 'authentic' culture and its

character. The products of the culture industry, they suggested, were marked by standardisation, pseudo-individualisation and the development of commodity fetishism. The main effect of all of this was ideological in nature, for the manner in which consuming these products offered inauthentic pleasures to ordinary people, who were, in turn, turned into obedient 'masses' by the culture industry.

Finally, we explored a post-war line of thought in the form of Left-Leavism and culturalism. We moved from a concept of 'mass culture', as seen and objectified by unsympathetic intellectuals, to an idea of 'popular culture'. Thus, we explored the work, context and concepts of Raymond Williams, who argued that culture is ordinary and, in tandem with the insights of Richard Hoggart, sought to counter the presumptions of thinking of people as masses. From both, we saw the birth of a whole lineage of thought that explored culture as a lived thing of collective meaning and struggle, rather than as simply something preserved at a remove from ordinary life – in museums or galleries – or produced by the organs of mass media.

You should now evaluate what you know and are able to do as a result of this chapter. If you have followed the chapter through, engaged with the activities and thought about the issues covered, you should be able to do the following:

■ Outline origins and contexts for debates about 'mass society', culture and media. (Of course, given the brevity of the historical details we've given, you need to further your investigations and reading to get a fuller picture.)

■ Outline, evaluate and contrast key terms used in debates about mass society in relation to the key theorists in this area and the contributions they made to the debates. We've given you some core ideas here which come up explicitly or implicitly in the work of others. Be aware that there are different reactions and evaluations to these ideas and theorists in our field.

■ Engage with ideas of mass society and definitions of culture in support of your own media research and theorisation. What we present here is not just a historical argument. As we've suggested, these ideas do continue in different ways and your job is now to consider how these ideas work and their utility to your own media studies.

We can conclude from this chapter that while media have played a central role in society and its development, they have had profound effects upon the way in which theorists have made sense of both society and people themselves. We should perhaps ask questions about the validity and limits of such work, given that the voices and practices of 'the masses' have rarely figured in it – just as the culturalists did and continue to do. Also, we should not be lulled into a sense that what we have presented tells a 'progressive' story, that we have moved from limited ways of thinking by intellectuals to a more enlightened state. Your job should be to search out more contemporary ways of speaking of 'masses': what euphemisms are enlisted to talk of ordinary people in general terms, especially with regards to the media? What uses do these ideas have and how do they echo what we have encountered here?

Doing media studies

Researching cultures and contexts

If you have followed this book through in order, you should by now have developed a range of analytical resources and engaged with various theories and ideas about media and society. In doing the activities in this part, it would be a progressive move to draw upon what you have done so far to develop more sophisticated approaches to your own research and thinking.

In order to explore the ideas introduced in this chapter and their utility, it is necessary to consider our contemporary culture, media contexts and the core concepts we've dealt with. Are there still ways of seeing people as masses? Do we still use such terms or are there other labels for this idea? Are you one of 'the masses'? What are these terms and how are they manifested? What do you think are the assumptions of the people who use such terms?

It is, too, useful to review the answers to the questions posed at the beginning of this chapter. What does 'culture' mean to you? What does it mean to speak of cultural worth? Where can culture be found – are there particular places or people associated with it? Are you in any way 'cultured'?

Further reading

All of the theorists cited in this chapter need reading in depth, but new scholars will find Hoggart and Williams most accessible, although some attempt to make sense of the context in which their key works were published is necessary. Useful works that give a more extended gloss on theories of culture, media and mass society can be found in the following.

Barlow, D. and Mills, B. (2009) *Reading Media Theory*, Harlow: Longman.
   This unique and extremely useful part-textbook, part-reader, gives you access to some of the seminal primary texts relating to the material in this chapter (and others). Each reading is supported by detailed annotations, introductions and reflections from the editors, which will help you find your way into and around the material as well as critically assess it. Students will find extracts of work by theorists such as F.R. Leavis, Adrono and Horkheimer, Stuart Hall, Jürgen Habermas, Raymond WIlliams, Roland Barthes and Jean Baudrillard.

Carey, J. (1992) *The Intellectuals and the Masses: Pride and Prejudice Among the Literary Intelligentsia, 1880–1939*, London and Boston: Faber & Faber.

Carey is a literary scholar and concentrates on the ideas of writers of fiction and journalism in this book. It gives real detail, context and a sense of the currency of the kinds of negative ideas set out in our chapter here, across Europe. What is interesting, in particular, is the conclusions he reaches, which suggests that some of the theoretical strands in recent thought are explicitly elitist, despite the apparently democratic stance of some theorists.

Dworkin, D. (1997) *Cultural Marxism in Postwar Britain: History, the New Left, and the Origins of Cultural Studies*, Durham, NC and London: Duke University Press.

Dworkin's narrative is wide-ranging and comprehensive. He deals with the complexity, origin and development of the kinds of ideas dealt with in our chapter here in extraordinary depth. This work is challenging but useful for making sense of how Anglophone scholars of culture engaged with European theory and the political foundations behind their ideas. This gives a very thorough insight into the development and importance of the CCCS.

Jenks, C. (2002) *Culture*, London: Routledge.

Another useful overview of the concept of culture that locates it in relation to the lineage of social studies, expanding in particular on the relationship of this idea with ideology. Jenks also gives a sense of how ideas developed beyond the CCCS – from subcultures onward, and how 'culture' figures in a wide range of contemporary fields and disciplines.

CHAPTER 12

Modernism, postmodernism and after

WTF?

What kind of world are we living in and how can we tell? For at least half a century, Western countries have seen an incredible expansion of an all-pervasive consumer society and have supported welfare systems that promise equality and some form of comfort for all. Consumption itself has been aided by the coming of television and its installation in virtually every home, offering a 'window on the world' in the form of documentaries, drama, news and entertainment but also a shop window into a dizzying array of consumer durables and lifestyles. For many people, it is these items – from T-shirts to trainers, to new technologies and four-wheel-drive cars — that are now the things that are important to their social identities, rather than old-fashioned things like nation, class, religion, ethnicity or gender. How true is this for you?

Soviet communism, since 1917 the ideological opponent of the Western system, collapsed in on itself in the early 1990s, heralding what one observer prematurely termed the 'end of history' and of one form of political struggle itself (Fukuyama, 1992). 'Politics', once defined through parties and the allegiances of those 'masses' and minorities we identified in the previous chapter, seems to have given way to a consumable parade of personalities, smiles and sound bites, where PR and spin are more important than substantial policies. From MP3 players to mobile phones and the internet, communication has personalised and sped up, expanded its coverage, collapsed barriers of time and space, and also, perhaps, altered its very nature as a mode of relating people to each other. Consider, for instance, the image of a crowded club, where everyone present is tweeting other people on their smartphones, some of whom are feet away across the club, others of whom are elsewhere entirely!

People name their children after celebrities, text speak or even famous brand names (Nike, Subaru, Stallone, Armani, etc. are all first names found in maternity wards nowadays), and anyone can be famous for any reason or no reason at all, as media concentrate on an endless regurgitation of 'reality'. We seem more concerned about the lives of TV contestants, soap stars and/or the actors who play them than we are about our own kith and kin. Films and TV programmes refer endlessly to other films and TV programmes, and endlessly recycle ideas to a point when all we can do is casually tick off the cited reference without any sense of judgement of intent.

And on and on we could go, as media and media realities suffuse our everyday existence. Modern media, we would argue, construct our sense of past, present and future to such an extent that this is the one undeniably original facet of contemporary life: no one in history has lived like this before, so overwhelmed with information and images, sounds and ideas, to the point where we don't notice that this is now the world for us! But what does it mean to say this and how can we explore these claims about modern life and media?

car to plane), such technologies countered the distance between people in space and time, making mass communication possible and relatively instantaneous. In turn, the development of mass communications and media impacted upon theories and ways of making sense of this era of change.

Modernists, modernism and media

Modernism

Modernism describes a tendency among artists in various fields in Europe and America, working from the early part of the twentieth century onwards (they are thus 'modernists'). While such a catch-all grouping cannot do justice to important distinctions between media and individuals, what characterises all of their works is experimentation with content, form and materials (whether paint, musical notes, words or images).

Avant-garde

is a French military term for those soldiers who advanced ahead of the main force – the vanguard in English. It came to be applied to the pioneering individuals and groups in the arts whose work aimed to 'forge ahead' and to be new, consciously attacking tradition and the values and assumptions of the establishment or 'bourgeoisie'.

A characteristic of the modern age, then, is that science, philosophy and social theory interrogated traditional ways of viewing the world and how it should best be understood. Karl Marx's analysis, for instance, exposed the ideological fetters that maintained inequality and prevented individuals reaching their full potential; Sigmund Freud's ideas about the psyche ventured deep into the human unconscious, to explain our deepest fears and motivations. Many theorists celebrated the age of mechanisation and rationality for the way in which mankind's ingenuity broke down barriers of time and space through travel and communication, finding new ways to exploit the planet and natural resources. It must also be said, however, that there were many who were distinctly suspicious of the modern and what 'progress' meant – as we noted in our previous chapter. Certainly, the people of those countries and continents upon which Western prosperity and identity were founded often had a less than progressive sense of the process of Enlightenment (see Said 1978/2003).

One area in which new ideas and the challenge of what it is to be 'modern' in the face of such developments was encountered and explored – positively and negatively – was among creative workers and in their works. In fine art, literature, drama, music and, of course, across media forms, creative workers sought to evaluate the terms of modes of representation and find new ways of working and representing the world. Many sought to become the acme of the 'modern' and to make themselves and their works 'modernist', at the forefront of change. Thus, an **'avant-garde'** of individuals in an enormous variety of fields and places created a huge impact and no little controversy by rejecting habitual forms, tampering with the very foundations of art and culture in order to challenge the expectations and perceptions of the reading, listening and viewing public with the 'shock of the new' (Hughes, 1991).

In literature, authors such as James Joyce, in novels such as *Ulysses* (1922/2000) and *Finnegans Wake* (1939/2000), and Berthold Brecht in his *Epic Theatre* (1964/1994) experimented with language and narrative structure in ways that eschewed involving the 'reader' or audience in a simple good story for the purpose of frivolous entertainment. The art of Pablo Picasso and Georges Braque, as Cubists (1907–), fragmented the nature of representational art. In music, Igor Stravinsky (1913–) disrupted the pleasing harmonies of classical forms with discord and dissonance (see Ross, 2008).

So challenging to traditional expectations and convention, both artistic and moral, and often deliberately shocking was this work that reactions could be extreme. Joyce's work was banned in his native Ireland and proscribed by the Pope. When the Cubists exhibited their paintings in America as part of the 'Armory Show' (in 1913), there were protests, outrage and disbelief that this was art (a recreation of the exhibit at the University of Virginia can be found at http://xroads.virginia.edu/~MUSEUM/Armory/armoryshow.html). Likewise, when Igor Stravinsky's *Rite of Spring* was first performed in Paris in 1913, fist-fights broke out between those in the audience who were affronted by this experiment and those who welcomed it. We should note that the outraged among the audiences for these works were the respectable bourgeoisie, the well-off in society, whose worldview, morality and politics were the ones being challenged. This extract from the manifesto of those artists behind the 'Dada' movement – which rejected outright the values of bourgeois art and logic – conveys a sense of the challenging intent behind their approach:

TO THE PUBLIC

Before going down among you to pull out your decaying teeth, your running ears, your tongues full of sores,
    Before breaking your putrid bones,
    Before opening your cholera-infested belly and taking out for use as fertilizer your too fatted liver, your ignoble spleen and your diabetic kidneys,
    Before tearing out your ugly sexual organ, incontinent and slimy,
    Before extinguishing your appetite for beauty, ecstasy, sugar, philosophy, mathematical and poetic metaphysical pepper and cucumbers,
    Before disinfecting you with vitriol, cleansing you and shellacking you with passion,
    Before all that,
    We shall take a big antiseptic bath,
    And we warn you
    We are murderers.

Source: Extract from *Manifesto* signed by Ribemont-Dessaignes and read by seven people at the demonstration at the Grand Palais des Champs Elysées, Paris, 5 February 1920. Reproduced at Dada Online (www.peak.org/~dadaist/English/Graphics/index.html)

Arguably, the practices of modernism as they developed in the traditional arts – those of painting, literature, drama, classical music – are inextricable from the coming of modern mass media. The invention of photography in the nineteenth century, for instance, shattered the faith in the traditions of painterly realism (p. 135). After all, what artist's skills could compete with the instant capturing of light reflected off a face, or a scene, preserved in its entirety on paper, as an apparently exact likeness, within seconds? This development actually freed painters to reconsider their craft and aims anew, directly informing the development of movements such as Impressionism (1860–), in which artists played with light, colour and the very materials of painting. This practice of reflecting on the process of representation led directly to experiments with materials and form in Cubism (1907–), which in its analysis of movement and perspective responded directly to the coming of film. Marcel Duchamp's famous painting, *Nude Descending a Staircase* (1912), for instance, expressed movement through a series of superimposed figures in one frame, as if capturing a sequence from a reel of celluloid in one space. Likewise, other Cubist works presented collages that emulated the juxtapositions of stories and images on newspaper front pages.

Mass media, then, impacted upon the world of art and the way that its creators aspired to be 'modern'. In addition, there were many artists, as well as individuals within media organisations, who aspired to explore the modernist potential of forms like film, radio, print journalism and photography. Given the commercial and conventional nature of mass media, this seems at once counter-intuitive and logical, depending upon how one views the variety of modernist principles. This impulse seems on one hand to be counter-intuitive, as modernist art in all its guises was largely a minority pursuit. While modernists might have sought to challenge perception and morality, this was largely the perception and morality of those groups who were educated in and who could afford the time and leisure to consume and engage with art – i.e. the bourgeoisie. Likewise, and as authors such as John Carey (1992) have argued, aspects of modernism were about making art 'difficult' and deliberately hard to comprehend, in order to preserve this sphere from those 'masses' who were in the ascendant and apparently taking over society. The growth of literacy, education and the traditional cultural works widely available – records and radio broadcasts of classical music, the establishment of museums and art galleries, and so on – all went hand in hand with political democratisation. In addition, some of those thinkers we encountered in our

Modernist art experimented with form and representation, exploring issues of perception and reality. Sometimes this was to illuminate and radically change perception, sometimes to alienate ordinary people from the world of art.

previous chapter would have been highly suspicious of any impulse to create 'art' or achieve modernist ends through mass media forms simply because of what they saw as the shoddy nature of each medium.

However, counter to antagonism towards mass media, there was a logical exploration by some modernists of various forms – after all, media technologies represented the essence of the new! This was allied to a tendency to celebrate the age of mass society and the ascension of ordinary people – the masses themselves. Thus, throughout the twentieth century, we discover movements that theorised and utilised media in order to educate and liberate the majority from oppression and its habitual way of seeing things, in support of potentially progressive political ideas. In fact, we could trace a march of modernist approaches throughout some of the most fascinating and innovative media work and, indeed, in media theory itself.

One of the most challenging and exciting things about studying media lies in a recognition of the way in which the direction of a great deal of theoretical work has been informed by the creativity, writings and analytical insights of many of the great practitioners in photography, cinema and music. The field has borrowed, too, from modernist work and ideas in other forms, such as fine art, theatre and literature, for example, the German dramatist Berthold Brecht. It is difficult to reduce the enormously varied work and styles of media influenced by modernist approaches, but there are some recurring and interrelated features and motifs. Let us now explore these in more detail in order to understand some of the interactions between media practice and modernism. These will become important to understanding some of the claims about media in a postmodern age.

First, we can identify in modernist media a concern with form and structure. This refers to the exploration of the 'essence' or crucial properties of any medium as an obvious aspect of the work itself. For example, while photography is perceived to be a relatively straightforward means of capturing reality, its effects are formed by variations in light and tone, as well as perspective. Such things were experimented with in the work of artists such as Man Ray, and in his images blurring, incandescent and unusual textures abound. In music, it is tone, timbre, scale and duration of sound (and non-sounds), for instance, that give form. Examples of 'modernist' sensibilities have been crucial to the development of jazz and the work of artists such as Miles Davies and John Coltrane, and can also be heard in dub reggae experiments of Lee Perry and King Tubby. In the work of such artists, one often hears explorations of the nature of sounds and their ordering, playing with repetitions and sound qualities to extremes. In the field of rock music, the atonal qualities and use of feedback in the work of bands such as the Velvet Underground mark them out as modernist. The music critic Alex Ross has suggested that such artists took blues, rock and roll and formulaic 'Tin Pan Alley' forms and made them something else more adventurous and unsettling (Ross, 2008). Furthermore, he notes how modernist composers, from Stravinsky to Steve Reich, in turn, have learnt from popular forms, suggesting the dialogue that has taken place over media.

Key thinker

Walter Benjamin (1892–1940)

A member of the Frankfurt School, Walter Benjamin's ideas about culture and mass media are much more optimistic than some of his fellow thinkers from that group, particularly about the political potential of mass media such as cinema and photography. This optimism sat alongside his enthusiasm for modern art movements like Surrealism, which for him explored the nature of freedom in the modern world (Benjamin, 1929/1997). While other thinkers were suspicious of contemporary propaganda, as well as the negative and ideological nature of the 'Culture Industry', as Adorno and Horkheimer put it, Benjamin crystallised his thoughts in a famous and much quoted essay, *The Work of Art in the Age of Mechanical Reproduction* (1936/2008). His ideas in this essay began by exploring the way in which traditional culture was being changed in the modern age. His fellow theorists tended to value traditional art as somehow 'authentic', unique and untainted by commerce when compared with the superficialities of mass media, although for Benjamin, paintings, sculptures and so on were overlaid with a very restrictive sense of ritual. He called this the 'aura' of a work, which connoted the reverence that one was supposed to experience in the presence of great art. However, all of these ideas for Benjamin came not from any value in the artwork itself but all of those values surrounding it: the way it was treated and revered, its ownership and often restricted exhibition, were all symbolic testimonies to the worth of its owners and the values they evinced in maintaining the almost religious treatment of art.

In mass forms such as photography and cinema, suggested Benjamin, there was no 'true' original, freeing art and representation from its reliance on ritual and smashing the 'aura' of art. In addition, such things were not restricted to private ownership by a minority and could be brought before the many. Thus, he observed that:

> These two processes lead to a tremendous shattering of tradition which is the obverse of the contemporary crisis and renewal of mankind. Both processes are intimately connected with the contemporary mass movements. Their most powerful agent is the film. Its social significance, particularly in its most positive form, is inconceivable without its destructive, cathartic aspect, that is, the liquidation of the traditional value of the cultural heritage. This phenomenon is most palpable in the great historical films. It extends to ever new positions. In 1927 Abel Gance [a French film-maker] exclaimed enthusiastically:

> 'Shakespeare, Rembrandt, Beethoven will make films . . . all legends, all mythologies and all myths, all founders of religion, and the very religions . . . await their exposed resurrection, and the heroes crowd each other at the gate.'

> *Source*: www.marxists.org/reference/subject/philosophy/works/ge/benjamin.htm)

So, for Benjamin, and indeed for many others like film-maker Abel Gance, these new forms offered a chance for a new art, for new ways of seeing, in tandem with progressive ideas about the world.

A second aspect of modernist media practice derives from the first and this concerns the problematising or foregrounding of the very act of representation. Thus, one finds repeated instances of an exploration of the 'making' of film, for example. In the films of the French director Jean-Luc Godard, film-making often appears as a subject itself and, in his more avant-garde work, he shows little concern for the conventions of 'classical realism'

Thinking aloud

Avant-garde pop

It has been argued that the most famous or most heard piece of avant-garde music (even if most have never listened to it more than once) is the Beatles 'song' 'Revolution Number 9' from their self-titled album of 1968 (otherwise known as 'The White Album'). Influenced by innovative modern composers such as Stockhausen, this is a sound montage of 'found' clips that include a BBC test broadcast (a voice repeats the words 'number nine' endlessly) as well as the recording of an unborn baby's heartbeat. If the avant-garde was about subversion and challenge to conventional attitudes, few moments can have been so full of potential impact as this one, sandwiched between the pop tunes of the most famous band in history (MacDonald, 1994/2005).

(see Chapter 14) (Morrey, 2005; Temple and Williams, 2001). Thus, one sees in his more radical work microphone booms drifting into shot or actors breaking from the role they are playing to address the director or audience directly. Sometimes, narrative structure is reordered, as Godard famously suggested: 'A story should have a beginning, a middle, and an end . . . but not necessarily in that order.'

Further features of modernist media, and ones that tend to mark them out from conventional and overtly industrial objectives and orientation, are an avowedly anti-commercial approach and an alienation of audience expectations. Indeed, there is a rejection of the 'mass' audience produced by media organisations directed by a search for profit – modernists seek to get audiences to follow them and their lead, rather than pandering to habitual tastes. Thus, we can find instances in all media forms of artists providing subject matter that shocks – some photojournalism would fit in here.

Likewise, there are modes that distance the audience from becoming involved in the story or gaining pleasure instead of an understanding of the greater social picture conveyed in a work or the aesthetic qualities of the work itself. This tendency is often directed by a theoretical or avowedly political approach to the production of work, which in turn appears as a use of manifestos and/or analytical essays. As explanations of works and intent, such manifestos and analyses accompany and qualify the finished product, directing how others go about making media texts and, to some extent, providing a basis for understanding them at the moment of consumption. A contemporary example of modernist-styled practice in popular music was centred upon a punk-feminist movement commonly known as Riot Grrrl (Rosenberg and Garofalo, 1998; Schilt, 2003). Bands associated with this movement included Bikini Kill, Heavens to Betsy, Huggy Bear and Sleater-Kinney. Intent upon challenging the male-dominated world of rock, various groups that have aligned themselves with this label have produced statements of intent that direct why and how their music was made. An extract from one recent example that gives a long list of motivations and directions for making music and related practices is as follows:

BECAUSE us girls crave records and books and fanzines that speak to US that WE feel included in and can understand in our own ways.

BECAUSE we wanna make it easier for girls to see/hear each other's work so that we can share strategies and criticise-applaud each other.

BECAUSE we must take over the means of production in order to create our own moanings.

BECAUSE viewing our work as being connected to our girlfriends-politics-real lives is essential if we are gonna figure out how we are doing impacts, reflects, perpetuates, or DISRUPTS the status quo.

BECAUSE we recognise fantasies of Instant Macho Gun Revolution as impractical lies meant to keep us simply dreaming instead of becoming our dreams AND THUS seek to create revolution in our own lives every single day by envisioning and creating alternatives to the bullshit christian capitalist way of doing things.

BECAUSE we are interested in creating non-hierarchical ways of being AND making music, friends, and scenes based on communication + understanding, instead of competition + good/ bad categorisations.

BECAUSE we hate capitalism in all its forms and see our main goal as sharing information and staying alive, instead of making profits of being cool according to traditional standards.

Source: www.feastofhateandfear.com/archives/hanna.html

There is a wealth of material from media history and a wider cultural practice for scholars to explore in relation to the ideas of the modern and modernism. However, what we need to take away from this outline is the idea of the importance of media in defining the modern and in the interaction with modernist principles, the idea that media forms might play a role in exploring how we see the world and, indeed, supporting and aiding progressive ideas. This ambition stands in explicit opposition to models that see media as simple tools for propagandist manipulation, or as inevitably ideological apparatuses that keep the masses in their place in order to service only the aims of capital in generating profit.

Case Study

Cinema, the modern and modernism

→ Modernist principles have been behind some of the most memorable films and film movements since the Lumière brothers first showed their life studies in 1895. These movements include German Expressionist Cinema (1920s), which was influenced by painting, poetry and literature (Roberts, 2008). Expressionist films were so called as they 'externalised' the inner emotions of characters (usually angst, insanity, depression and paranoia), expressed in exaggerated set design, lighting and acting style. Films such as *The Golem* (dir. Wegener, 1920) and *The Cabinet of Dr Caligari* (dir. Wiene, 1920) explored the irrational, Freudian aspects of life, and still look striking.

We can also point to the Soviet montage cinema (or 'materialist' cinema, reflecting the Marxism of its creators) of the same period. Lenin, the leader of the Russian Revolution, had announced that cinema was the most revolutionary and important medium, due to its ability to appeal to the masses – in Russia, then still a largely illiterate and 'backward' peasantry. Figures such as Vselevod Pudovkin, Sergei Eisenstein and Dziga Vertov responded to the initial optimism of the Bolshevik revolution of 1917 by formulating a Marxist theory of film and its revolutionary potential. Their modernism was predicated on making films that shattered the illusions and ideologies of mainstream entertainment, already dominated by Hollywood. As Vertov announced in his manifesto for documentary films:

WE declare the old films, the romantic, the theatricaled etc., to be leprous.
  – Don't come near!
  – Don't look!
  – Mortally dangerous!
  – Contagious.

WE affirm the future of cinema art by rejecting its present.
  The death of 'cinematography' is necessary so that the art of cinema may live.
WE call for the acceleration of its death.

(Vertov, 1922/1944: 69)

Eisenstein and others based their practice on the process of editing (or 'montage'), for them the 'essence' of the cinematic form. Informed by Marxist dialectics, they did not seek to

→

present a seamless reality as in mainstream narrative film but to 'analyse' reality through the ability of film to edit scenes and perspective together, to make ideas and images *clash* and lead viewers to a new vision of reality: a 'correct' political reality based on class warfare. Eisenstein's films, such as *Strike* (1925), *Battleship Potemkin* (1926) and *October* (1928), placed the workers at their centre, in place of the bourgeois individualist hero, and had an incredible impact upon how people viewed the possibilities of the medium.

We've mentioned the work of Godard and there is a whole field of contemporary art cinema that takes on modernist principles, working at the margins of most national cinemas (you might explore the art cinema of your own country here by way of comparison). Most recently, the principles and echoes of a modernist attack on the 'mainstream' has been successfully pursued by the Danish Dogme 95 group that includes Lars von Trier and Thomas Vinterberg. Their motivation is set out in their statements which express disappointment with the manner in which previous cinema movements have run out of steam (e.g. Godard and his fellow 'new wave' directors), as well as rejecting the bloatedly commercial blockbuster 'event' movies that emerged in the 1980s and 1990s.

> Today a technological storm is raging, the result of which will be the ultimate democratisation of the cinema. For the first time, anyone can make movies. But the more accessible the media becomes, the more important the avant-garde, It is no accident that the phrase 'avant-garde' has military connotations. Discipline is the answer . . . we must put our films into uniform, because the individual film will be decadent by definition!

(www.dogme95.dk/)

The Dogme 95 group produced a manifesto or 'Vow of Chastity' for making film by which directors in the group swore to abide, in order to create truthful films, stripped back to an essential cinema devoid of 'tricks'. Rules, or dogma, include insisting that all filming was done on location, avoiding the importation of props or the use of sets; sound and music must be diegetic; the camera must be hand-held, in order to follow action; only colour film is allowed; superficial action is forbidden (i.e. murders, weapons, etc. must not be used); temporal and geographical alienation are forbidden – the film takes place here and now; genre films are not acceptable and the director is not to be credited, thus reinforcing the 'collective' nature of film-making.

Source: www.dogme95.dk/; the 'remodernist manifesto' is at http://jesse-richards.blogspot.com/; Stevenson, 2004.

There are also manifestos for film in the digital age. The 'pluginmanifesto' (written by Ana Kronschnabl (2004) and reproduced at www.geertwachtelaer.com/pluginmanifesto.htm) for instance, aims to create a framework that film-makers can use to produce films for the internet, reproducing the attention to the needs and creative opportunities of this new medium.

Here's an extract published under 'copyleft' conditions (a more liberal version of copyright) which has been amended and adapted over the period of its circulation:

> Limitations can be creative – if you do not have a wind machine, use a fan. If you do not have the bandwidth, do not expect the cinema.

> Filmmaking on the Internet is at a truly exciting time. Currently, very little exists that has been designed for viewing on the Net. Much has been carried across from other mediums e.g. TV and film. This is not good. It means that the work being shown cannot be appreciated in the form it was originally intended. It also does web films a disservice because audiences complain about the lack of 'quality': their expectations are for the traditional film, seen in its familiar context.

> In the same way that film found its own form in relation to the theatre, and TV in relation to film, the web filmmaker needs to search for the appropriate form for

films on the Internet. It is incumbent upon the independent filmmaker to be at the forefront of these new technologies less they be subsumed by the media conglomerates. Independent filmmakers, geeks and artists have an ideal opportunity to experiment and push these technologies creatively.

Use Codecs and compression creatively.

Use the tools that are appropriate for the job. Filmmaking for the Internet is not filmmaking for the cinema. We should be taking the tools invented for the medium such as Flash, .html, compression algorithms etc. and pushing them to see what they can do in creative terms; our creative terms. That is the job of the filmmaker and artist. The camera and celluloid defined films for the cinema; computers and the Internet will define media for the new millennium.

Filmmakers and Geeks should be friends.

Filmmakers, in order to be good at their craft, have always had to have a certain level of technical knowledge. Many of the short films appearing on the Internet have been made by those familiar with the technology, rather than traditional filmmakers. This is good. However, how much better would those films be if people who had spent their lives learning the craft got together with people who could make the technology work for them? Co-operative and artistic endeavours, the clash of assumptions, and traditional ways of doing things can produce surprising and challenging new work.

Never forget the medium and the viewing context.

Above all, don't believe the hype! Convergence is certainly happening but the potential of these mediums is just being glimpsed. What is made for the Internet now can enlighten the forms of the future. The challenge is to create these forms now. This is not a televisual system that sits in the corner of our living rooms, but the Internet: a huge system of information storage and retrieval for individual users, with no centralised control. Seize the day and make your work available to millions of people. Be part of shaping the world's next, great art form.

Copyleft DSL (http://dsl.org/copyleft/dsl.txt); plugincinema www.plugincinema.com; www.pluginmanifesto.com

Doing media studies

Writing a media manifesto

Imagine that you are a media producer, aiming to say something about the world and explore the possibilities of your medium, as well as advertising your own originality (we will take it for granted that you wish to make money although whether profit is the motive is another matter). How would you put your ideas into practice? Try putting your ideas into manifesto form for the benefit of other media workers and your potential audiences. Concentrate on the values that you wish to follow and that you want to see in your own work. Don't worry about your experience or skills; it is your opinion and ambition that matter in marking you out as distinct from everything and everyone else.

What became of progressive ambitions and the reason they were stalled can be found in the contention that the 'modern' has ended and that we are now, all of us, 'after' that period: *post*modernists.

Postmodernism and postmodernity

'Postmodernism' is a term that is, ironically, as old as modernism itself (Anderson, 1998), but which became established as a prominent idea in academia in the 1980s. The term and associated ideas quickly escaped to inform media debates and wider public discourse, to the point where it became and is still perhaps a 'buzzword'. However, so many different people in so many different contexts use the term postmodernism to refer to so many things that it is hard to pinpoint exactly what it means. This has led many people to dismiss the phrase and the theory behind it as meaningless academic gobbledegook (Sokal, 2008). An example of the confusion here is indicated in the term itself (see below), its ubiquity and application to media, history, politics, identity, nations, positive or negative responses to the idea and condition, confusion over whether it is the same as, an extension of, or different from modernism, and whether or not it has currency at all!

Theoretically, postmodernism has been prodigious in critiquing the ideas of modernity, and ideas and movements such as Marxism and structuralism. Indeed, many of the key theorists have come out of those earlier movements, which makes mapping the ideas and key thinkers difficult and sometimes confusing, especially as postmodernism is sometimes conflated with or intersects with academic ideas such as post-structuralism and deconstruction. It is, therefore, important to gain a basic understanding of some core ideas in order to apprehend the contemporary field in any depth.

The first and most prominent theorists of this concept were the Frenchmen Jean Baudrillard and Jean-François Lyotard, and the American Fredric Jameson, although the insights and ideas of Michel Foucault on discourse, Jacques Derrida on language and Thomas Kuhn on science are also often enlisted in tracking the roots of postmodern ideas (even if these theorists have eschewed the label). The spread of the core ideas about postmodernism, the response to them and the wider context that they sought to describe were dramatic. Philosophers such as Richard Rorty, sociologists like Zygmunt Baumann and Slovaj Zizeck, and geographers such as David Harvey, as well as writers on popular culture like Norman Denzin, Dick Hebdige, Iain Chambers, E. Ann Kaplan, Angela McRobbie and Lisa Appignanesi, picked up the idea and made very productive use of it in the specific study of media and popular practice. There are also many critics of the idea of the postmodern and much of the theory associated with it, including Jürgen Habermas and the literary theorist Terry Eagleton (1996, 2004).

The central idea that theorists of the postmodern advance is that we have entered a new phase in society or historical period, which is distinct from the modern: thus, post, or after, modernity. This phase in society is one that is characterised by a change in various aspects. First, there has been a shift in the way in which the world is organised economically; a new phase of capitalism has come about which Jameson (1991) calls 'late' capitalism. Modern capital is not so much founded upon the production of things but on ideas and information, and on money (or its promise) from international financial services. It is supported, of course, through the dominance of media. Secondly, the suggestion is that the way we understand the world we live in has changed, in that what once constituted our collective belief in the modern era has been revealed to have no secure foundation (Lyotard, 1979/1984). The postmodern challenges the assumptions underwriting the modern, as it undermined the previous age of religion and faith. Thirdly, all of this is reflected in the style or formal properties of the artefacts produced by our cultural industries and, indeed, the extent to which they are now an indispensable part of our lives; perhaps are our lives in many cases (Baudrillard, 1983).

These organisational, philosophical and stylistic changes are then termed postmodernism – a word that itself causes a myriad of confusions in the very way in which it is presented. You'll find many versions of the term: postmodernity, Postmodernism, post-modernism, Post Modernism, Post-Modernism and even 'pomo'. Perhaps the most

Case Study

Demolishing modernism

➡ Architect Charles Jencks began to talk about postmodernism in his book *The Language of Post-modern Architecture* (Jencks, 1990), wherein he gave a specific date and time for the beginning of this new period: 3.32 p.m. on 15 July 1972. This requires some explanation in relation to architecture as this date and the incident it relates to offer an interesting illustration of wider forces at work that characterise the postmodern era.

We can look to the Swiss designer Le Corbusier and his work as the exemplar of architectural modernism, for his experiments with materials, space and design. It was Le Corbusier who described homes rather dispassionately as 'machines for living', whose utopianism sought to create living spaces designed along rational principles and whose ideas influenced generations of designers and planners. One of these was Minoru Yamasaki, who designed the Pruitt-Igoe housing project in St Louis, USA. The project opened in 1956, designed to house low-income families relocated from shanty-town dwellings in America's Deep South. However, the homes and site were not 'used' in the rational manner planned for it and its inhabitants by the architect. The precept of 'machines for living' had not factored in that people are rather unmachinelike. Pruitt-Igoe became rundown and notorious in a matter of years, to the point where it was decided to demolish the whole site. It was dynamited at 3.32 p.m. on 15 July 1972, and with it went some of the optimism behind the American welfare system and wider ideals of progress.

Coincidentally, Yamasaki also designed the New York World Trade Center with its famous 'twin towers'. On 11 September 2001 this physical and symbolic centre of American might and capitalism was demolished in a terrorist attack, along with the loss of 3000 lives. The terrorist group al-Qaida was blamed for the attack – a group that bases itself around a fundamentalist version of the Islamic religion. Its tenets thoroughly reject all aspects of 'the modern' – scientific, technical, political, social and philosophical. Just as our technological, media-saturated world is postmodern in stepping past what came before, so too are Osama bin Laden and his acolytes, in their attempt to step back to a pure version of the world untainted by modernity.

noticeable thing about this term is its obvious contradiction: post (after) modern. How can we be after the 'now', the up to date? Well, one way is to think about the concepts that we introduced in the first part of this chapter that are associated with the modern and modernity, such as progress, optimism for the future and the betterment of humankind, rationality and so on. The argument of postmodern thinkers is that the certainty and faith in these ideas that characterised the sense of the modern has collapsed. The postmodernist thrust is that the equation between modernity and rational progress is illusory. The rise of technology, for instance, while it has brought us much that is vital to widespread comfort and leisure, facilitated the mass slaughter of two world wars and the development of the H-bomb. Technological progress, in tandem with rational order and organisation, led directly to the industrial slaughter of millions in the Nazi death camps. Our motor cars, aeroplanes and refrigerators, which give us so much pleasure, are blamed for contributing to the pollution that is (according to a majority of scientists) warming up our planet at a rate that will soon be irreversible (if it is not already). The results of this collapse are thus contained in the contradictions of the oxymoronic term 'after' the modern.

Another demise has been announced in the end of the modern and modernism in cultural work. Although artists under this label were defined by opposing traditional certainties and 'classical' style in cultural work, one narrative suggests that modernist style, precepts and works were ultimately 'recuperated'. Those who were the object of the challenge of modernism – the educated, culturally learned bourgeoisie – became most receptive to it. On the one hand, the 'difficult' nature of modernist works, from Picasso's paintings to T.S. Eliot's poetry, spoke in accents readily understood by those already familiar with the traditions being undermined. Such work was, or has been, recuperated, and its radical promise spiked, through its envelopment in respectability and commerce. Modernist works are taught on school syllabuses, inhabit museums and galleries and, of course, change hands for incredible sums among the wealthy (and prints thereof adorn living room walls, T-shirts, tea towels, etc.). Equally debilitating is the fact that mass media forms have effectively plundered the sounds, images and ideas of the modern and made any challenge they presented ultimately toothless. This is not the same as our suggestion that media forms themselves took on modernist ideas – such initiatives have also been plundered – but rather, from advertising to mainstream pop, to Hollywood film, the styles and ideas of modernism have been appropriated by a culture industry hungry for new ideas that will sell more products, more effectively, to increasingly jaded audiences. Here the modern desire for the new is reduced to a simple consumption, to use something up until it is exhausted.

By way of example, to illustrate this recuperation, the challenges of the cinematic forms have become part of the pallet of all movie-makers, who have stepped over the original purpose and intent behind jump cuts, montage, expressionism, narrative disruption and so on simply to reinforce the stylistic thrills of the movies. The work of Quentin Tarantino, Tim Burton or David Fincher, for instance, may all be lumped in here as taking stylistic elements from art films in order to produce a 'cool' look to their work. This recuperation of opposition turned into consumption is most evident in the manner in which the signs of modernism crop up endlessly in promotional materials. Thus, 'Picasso' is now a signature on a car and the artist's name is lent, via his daughter Paloma, to a perfume; the discordant tunes of the Velvet Underground accompany car tyre adverts; while surrealist films are turned into adverts for beer and so on. The uniqueness of modernist styles and imperatives, which once stood outside and in opposition to conventional, conservative and commercial ways of seeing, hearing and speaking about the world, are now fully incorporated and so disarmed. Postmodern theorists see this development as integral to understanding aspects of contemporary style in media and a whole range of forms, from art to architecture, in which ideas are robbed of their intent and social purpose and made 'flat', 'empty' and 'depthless'.

Themes of postmodernism

The developments in modernist culture we've described compound a wider 'crisis' of meaning described as characteristic of the postmodern age. In order to fully understand such arguments and the relationship with media further, it is perhaps useful to outline a series of ideas that are prominent in the myriad books and articles of and about postmodern theory. We can see these as the themes of postmodernism, ways of describing what is played out in social life, in politics, in academic thought, in economics, in our cultural artefacts and so on. We've attempted to choose titles for these themes that give some sense of the bold and sweeping style of ideas about postmodernism, supported by a summary of the argument being made. The ideas are 'the death of history'; 'the death of meaning'; 'the collapse of cultural boundaries'; 'the death of the subject; and 'spectacle'.

'The death of history'

As we have suggested, writers on the postmodern often talk about things dying, collapsing or imploding, and you cannot get more sweeping than the apparently absurd proposition that 'history is dead' or that we are at the 'end of history'. However, for theorists, history has 'died' in various ways. First, the certainties in a future different from and better than the present have been lost. Theories of science and technology once seemed to suggest a solution to all our social problems. These technical and scientific solutions are one of the major factors in our sense of the modern. However, science and technology have also created more problems than they have solved: acid rain, the greenhouse effect and global warming, holes in the ozone layer, the depletion of non-renewable natural resources, polluted air, rivers and land, a speed-obsessed society caught in traffic jams, which threatens to destroy itself with nuclear, biological and chemical weapons.

It is argued that we no longer accept the 'grand narratives' of modernity that defined the West and the idea of progress towards a better future. Thus, faith in the certainties of communism or capitalism, conservatism, liberalism or socialism to solve our political and social issues seems like wishful thinking, and people are increasingly alienated from the political processes of representational democracy.

We should add, too, that our faith in actual history as a form of study seems less secure than it once did, undermining our sense that we can know the past. History is, after all, just another form of storytelling, when seen from a particular perspective, with its own generic conventions and assumptions. How then are we to judge between a novel that recreates a fiction of past events and academic histories? Is it just that one has footnotes and the other doesn't (White, 1987)?

Postmodern ideas suggest that our sense of the past has become 'flat'. If we do not believe in a future, we do not need a past to measure our progress and distance from it. The past, therefore, becomes simply a set of images, of styles to be used and reused, with little sense of their historical origin. What was History – a structured, coherent past that gave meaning to the present and future – now becomes a series of stylistic 'cycles', a treasure chest of images without meaning. Since the 1980s, for instance, a variety of products have been sold in adverts across media forms that conjured up images of the past, via the way in which that period had been imagined in a series of films and TV series, such as *Happy Days, That 70s Show* and so on, often set to the popular music of the relevant era. Images, sounds and impressions of different historical periods are mixed and matched without any sense of coherence or fidelity to even a pretence of accuracy or authenticity. The NBC TV show *American Dreams* (dir. Attias and D'Elia, 2002) is a good example here. It is set in Detroit in the mid-1960s, and concerns various family and teen relationships. A central plot device involves the regular recording and broadcast of the influential US pop show *American Bandstand*, which ran in the period and which was produced in the city. In *American Dreams*, stock footage of the show from the period, which characters watch on their televisions, is interspersed with 'in the studio' recreations which feature contemporary artists performing as artists from the 1960s. Thus, Kelly Rowland appears as Martha Reeves of Martha and the Vandellas, performing 'Dancing in the Streets', and Wyclef Jean appears as Curtis Mayfield. Alongside this, and efforts to signal the authenticity of recreations, the show plotlines often mix up chronologies of the period, political and cultural, making a logical nonsense of some storylines – if viewers are bothered enough to work them out. In turn, such motifs and explorations of the historical are repeated in series such as *Mad Men* (2007–) in the US and *The Hour (2011–)* in the UK.

'The death of meaning'

Contemporary society is saturated with images to a degree that makes it qualitatively different from previous eras. Adverts, televisions at home and in public places, video on phones, workplace computers linked to the internet, T-shirts, etc. bombard us all day every day with images. Theorists like Jean Baudrillard have argued that this saturation has changed our sense of what such images represent for us and consequently call into question the nature of reality. For him, the mass media have created a new sense of consciousness for us through this saturation, creating an endless present that juxtaposes one image against

Thinking aloud

Nostalgia isn't what it used to be

Frederick Jameson has bemoaned the 'nostalgia for the present' that characterises contemporary life and the inhibiting effect that this has. The endless regurgitation of signs and culture means we are trapped in a loop of remembrance. For instance, a glance at the TV schedules for recent years reveals that they are often full of nostalgia or list shows (*I Remember 1999*, *The Top 100 Kids Shows of All Time*), or constructed around repeats (*Classic Gold*, *VH1*, etc.). The music industry has been largely supported of late by reselling the work of older artists in new formats, likewise with the regurgitation of movie 'classics', directors' cuts and so on via DVD. On the web, some of the most successful websites have been Classmates.com in the USA, SchoolFriends in Australasia and Friends Reunited in the UK, South Africa, Singapore, Hong Kong and Malaysia. At these sites, participants recall their school days, college years and former jobs, amidst adverts for nostalgia shows and music compilations (p. 471). For Jameson, wallowing in the past is a highly dubious activity that prevents any attempt to deal with our contemporary condition and face the future.

another, to the point that they no longer have meaning in relation to real events or things, but have meaning only within the context of the mass media, and our experience of it. Images thus only seem to refer to each other.

For theorists such as Umberto Eco (1975/1986) and Baudrillard (1986/1988) we are lost in the 'hyperreality' of the mass media age – images and media forms are more real to us than empirical reality. For these thinkers, therefore, there has been an 'implosion of the real', where words and images lose their meaning and their ability to talk about or reliably reference an actual external reality. Across media forms we see claims to realism and authenticity (see Chapter 4), but our ability to judge when faced with such bombardment and simulations overwhelms us. We see pictures of celebrities such as Pippa Middleton, Paris Hilton or Penelope Cruz, for instance, as well as gaining insights into aspects of their most intimate secrets from paparazzi shots, from 'friends' and so on quoted in gossip columns. We recognise such figures and the information about them in relation to the hundreds of others we see across media forms, rather than in relation to a sense that there are 'real' people out there represented by such images. But then such individuals are often more present to us than our own acquaintances. Publicists often generate stories in the tabloid press about 'rows', 'outrages', 'scandals' and the 'truth' of such lives in order to generate coverage that coincides with movie releases, other promotions or an emergence from rehab. For us, they exist only because of the media, and so have no meaning outside it. The argument is that this is what matters to us now, as it is the media that inform us and form the dominant mode of our leisure activities.

Such apparently trite examples have even greater political ramifications. Based upon such observations, Baudrillard provocatively announced that the (first) Gulf War did not happen (Baudrillard, 1995). What we saw instead, he says, were images taken from cameras mounted on the noses of planes and missiles in which resulting civilian casualties were euphemistically labelled 'collateral damage', and those tens of thousands killed on the 'enemy' side balanced around 70 on the 'allied' side. Baudrillard asks: to what degree could this be termed a conventional war when compared with historical versions of what war has meant, let alone the way in which we have judged war via media forms? This conflict looked and sounded more like a video game – in those shots of combat – and Hollywood movies – as American and British forces worried themselves over press

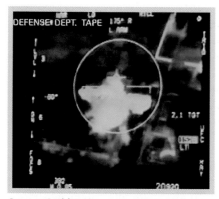

Source: Corbis

The 'death of meaning': to Jean Baudrillard, media representations of contemporary conflicts look and sound like video games, deflecting concern for human casualties in terms such as 'collateral damage'.

conference presentations which were timed for US TV prime-time live broadcast. Even the name for the military operation ('Desert Storm') was copyrighted at an early point.

A further part of this 'death of meaning' is presented to us in the way that images are put side by side in newspapers and on television. This is both intentional in sequencing and also in the clash and collage of how images and sounds come to us. Stories of famine on television are interrupted by adverts for slimming aids or sanitary towels with wings, while the news is presented as a drama with special effects and high-tech graphics – lest our interest wanes and amidst such stimulation we become 'bored', the greatest affliction in contemporary life.

'The collapse of cultural boundaries'

In both postmodernist style and postmodern social organisation there has been a collapse of sorts between the boundaries of different cultures and values. In culture, for instance, differences between respectable 'high art' and popular forms, trash, kitsch and other ephemera are no more. Typical media consumers, such as postmodern academics, now watch soap opera on television and go to the opera, which itself might be about pop culture and celebrities (e.g. *Jerry Springer the Opera*, *Anna Nicole*). Classical violinists (Vanessa Mae, Nigel Kennedy, Bond), opera singers (the Three Tenors), actors in soap operas and footballers can all be pop stars, and pop stars can become writers, movie stars and opera singers (Il Divo), and so on. Hierarchies of cultural value have disappeared, and every media text is viewed as having the same worth as traditional cultural artefacts. *The Sopranos* and *The Wire* are accorded the same respect and serious treatment as Shakespeare's *oeuvre*, for instance. Other boundaries – between fact and fiction, between 'real' life and media, for example – are also subject to collapse, as we've seen.

In the postmodern world, the boundaries of nation states and of ethnicity have become much more permeable than they once were, signalling other forms of cultural change. In Britain, post-war migration of peoples from former colonies has changed the landscape, feel and sound of the nation: chicken tikka masala is now the most popular national dish. Across Europe, for most white, middle-class youths, Black American rap about the brutal and brutalised life in the inner city 'ghetto' is the music of choice. Such cultural interactions are fed back again into hybrid media forms, as reggae and rock and rap mix in music, for instance.

'The death of the subject'

This idea suggests that it is our very sense of ourselves that is disintegrating. If the texts we consume have no meaning, the cultures and traditions we inherit and inhabit are permeable, we cannot place ourselves in relation to a reality and so we lose ourselves. This is often described as leading to a form of schizophrenia, in which our sense of a coherent self is 'decentred' from the secure anchors and reference points it once had.

Under modernity, people often had a very clear sense of their own identity, rooted in the community in which they lived (defined by social class, nation, ethnicity), and their gender role in society. Now things are less certain, and we seem to be different people at different times, depending upon the context. To refer back to our idea of the collapse of cultural boundaries, for example, this has been particularly resonant for those generations of individuals who come from migrant backgrounds. Is a third-generation Algerian Muslim woman living in Paris French, French-Algerian, a Muslim or all of these things depending upon the moment, her own self-view or the way in which she is labelled and addressed by others? To modern men, who are now at home with concepts such as paternity leave and feminism, the notion of masculinity seems very different and equivocal when compared with its dominant forms only one or two generations ago. Unalloyed machismo sits alongside 'metrosexuality' and 'ironic' ladism (see below for a discussion of irony). Thus, it is suggested that people have become 'playful' about their identities and the way that they define themselves, presenting contradictory ideas or challenging existing notions of how someone should be. Nowhere is this more apparent, perhaps, than in the identities and roles we inhabit online and in virtual communities (p. 328).

'Spectacle'

The strong sense of pessimism that is apparent in the themes of postmodernism that we have already identified is reinforced in this final theme. The death of meaning, the subject, the proliferation of depthless media signs and the collapse of 'grand narratives' effectively means that the individual can do nothing to change things. In fact, the notion that change is possible makes no sense in this context, and the foundations for truth, morality, reason and so on seem to have dissolved. We are left with the question: what do we do with our lives? In relation to the grand ambitions of modernity, they have no meaning and no purpose. One solution, therefore, is simply to lie back and enjoy the spectacle of it all. Just enjoy the aesthetic experience of pattern and sensory stimulation of the media age. This is our reality and the contemporary condition.

You will have to work with the ideas in this chapter before they become clearer and relevant to your world and media consumption, and a good way to do this is to try to integrate the summaries provided in this chapter with the writings of the theorists themselves (see the 'Doing media studies' box at the end of this chapter). We have provided a starting point for exploring the themes in more detail but to be an effective and informed scholar you should visit the original work of any of the theorists discussed above. Likewise, some of these ideas are played out in media texts that are characterised by a number of features labelled as particularly postmodern.

Postmodern media texts

We should be able to examine contemporary media texts and identify certain textual or stylistic qualities that relate to the themes of postmodernism that we have outlined. Some texts are produced by individuals and groups who seem to be intentionally exploring these ideas and are highly conscious of contemporary issues. Other texts will have such qualities because they are unconsciously reflecting their creation in postmodernity, or even a simple

Doing media studies

Exploring definitions

We have purposely avoided offering a definition of postmodernism here, as it might be misleading to do so given the range of ideas about what it is, when and where it is, indeed 'if' it is at all. In order to get a taste and expand upon the summary of key ideas we've provided, your task is to collect 10 definitions of postmodernism from as many varied sources as possible. Be attuned to the variations and different uses of the word as you do so, and search in works from disciplines outside media studies. Compare and contrast the features of these definitions to see what they agree or disagree on. What features and names do they emphasise?

economic desperation that recycles other texts or imitates those that are consciously post-modern without being 'in' on the joke, as it were. While any repeated attempt to distinguish between the two poles beyond the level of subjective evaluation is perhaps a cul-de-sac, a good example of 'intent' here concerns the Irish rock band U2 and the recording of its album *Achtung Baby* (in 1991). Lead singer Bono turned up to the studio with a song called 'The Real Thing'. Producer Brian Eno (himself a practitioner whose work now seems to be a forerunner of the post) took him to task for this, lamenting that the singer was unaware of the fact that contemporary philosophers were debating the naïvety and unreliability of concepts of reality. Bono's response was to rework the song as a suggestive postmodern tract, celebrating the object of his affections as: 'Even better than the real thing.' The band then went on to reinvent and spoof themselves throughout the 1990s, veering between irony in songs and performance, and constructions of rock and roll authenticity.

In thinking about how texts look, sound and feel, we should reiterate a point made earlier. A character of postmodern textual rhetoric, organisation and signification lies in the plundering not only of the palette of approaches that we label 'modernist' but, beyond that, of a whole history of signs and signification. In many postmodern texts, therefore, there is no coherent 'look', sound or tone, which is often due to this mix-and-match approach. The aim of this 'collage' is simply to amalgamate stylistic surfaces that look 'cool', rather than employing such styles with any greater or coherent purpose.

Let's consider an example here by way of illustration. The photographer David Lachapelle (www.davidlachapelle.com/home.html) produces work for fashion house adverts but also works as a 'fine artist', selling one-off prints of his photographs for millions of dollars (thus potentially reversing Benjamin's celebration of the loss of 'aura'). His photographs are often constructed as giant tableaux in the studio, with frame, scope, settings and colour texture evoking the great art of the Renaissance period. Figures and scenarios in these images look as if they have stepped both from the paintings of the past and from contemporary advertising or pornography at the same time. The point of all of this is not entirely apparent, beyond the creation of a momentary spectacle.

From this example we can pick up a further point about postmodern texts, which is that their 'tone' is uncertain, making it unclear for readers how they are to be interpreted. The collage and clash of styles undermines any sense of coherence or intent. The effect of this is sometimes explained as indicating a postmodern reliance upon 'irony'. Rhetorically, irony refers to the way in which intended meaning in a statement is the opposite of that actually used. An example, now well out of date no doubt (unless we are using it to be doubly ironic), would be the use of 'bad' meaning good. More recently, one could pinpoint another colloquialism, which is the use of 'shit' to refer to, variously 'everything', 'drugs' and, most ironically, things that are highly valued, as in 'that's the shit!' (e.g. as in Ludacris's 'That's my shit', from the album *Release Therapy*).

Source: Rex Features

David Lachapelle, *American Jesus, Thy Kingdom Come.* Mixing religious iconography derived from the Western fine art tradition, this image presents the pop singer Michael Jackson as a biblical martyr (it was shot long before the singer's death). Is it a serious contribution to works praising God or a tongue-in-cheek pastiche?

'Irony' may be in the eye of the beholder, when faced with the spectacle of modern media that give few cues about how to read a text. How are we meant to react to films such as the *Saw* sequence or Eli Roth's *Hostel* (2005)? The latter film seems at first to be a teen movie about US backpackers chasing girls and fun, before descending into a horror tale in which the protagonists are lured to a Slovakian town in order to be graphically tortured to death. By any estimation, the scenes depicted are harrowing and extremely explicit (a woman has a blowtorch taken to her face, for instance). Is this entertainment? Is it commentary (we watch rich Europeans torturing young people for kicks, which is what we are doing in turn by watching the movie)? Is it the same old prejudice against a constructed 'other' (the brutal Slovak)? Is it just another example of spectacular excess? Is there any point in asking such epistemologically based, 'modernist' questions wherein one might expect to locate motive and meaning?

Films such as *Hostel*, as well as phenomena like first-person shooter video games, 'death metal' music and 'Gangsta' rap, also exemplify a related aspect of the characterisation of postmodern media. This suggests that such works assume 'amoral' positions, in which who is good or bad and what position we are meant to take on the world represented is indistinct. In fact, the amorality includes the consumer, too, as we are not invited to take a critical distance but simply wallow in the pleasures of shooting and torturing people, and so on. In such examples and conclusions, we see an example of postmodernism as a moment in which 'anything goes'.

Case Study

The Simpsons

The animated TV show *The Simpsons* is the quintessential postmodern text. Its gestation, its character and the responses it generates encapsulate the nature of postmodern society. Matt Groening, the creator of the show, was heavily influenced by the alternative, underground culture that developed in the 1960s and 1970s, and first came to prominence as a comic book writer/artist with his satirical strip *Life in Hell*. This misanthropic look at the world usually centred on the situation of a rabbit by the name of Binky or a gay couple called Akbar and Jeff. The strip came to the attention of some of the producers on a 1980s TV live-action comedy sketch show, *The Tracey Ullman Show*, and Groening was asked to develop some animations of his work for it. Instead, he came up with *The Simpsons* as a series of skits that proved so popular they won a spin-off deal.

The Simpsons features the eponymous family that comprises dad Homer (whose name evokes the great Greek author of *The Iliad* and *The Odyssey*), mother Marge, and their children Bart (an anagram of Brat), Lisa and Maggie. These are all named after Groening's own parents and siblings. Stories take place in an American town called Springfield, the exact location of which is uncertain (it is Midwest but also by the sea!).

In the course of their adventures, the family have confronted their own foibles at home, work, school and in society at large. They have travelled in time and space and met God and the Devil, as well as an incredible array of historical and living celebrities who have provided voices for the show – including former British prime minister Tony Blair, who 'appeared' during his time in office.

Many episodes consciously play with the conventions of animation and the sitcom genre, endlessly quoting and pastiching both popular and high culture. In its time, the show – one of the longest-running and consistently popular TV series ever – has drawn the ire and approval of US presidents by turn. Consumed at any level (straight comedy for adults or kids, or philosophical treatise on ordinary life), one of the most remarkable things about *The Simpsons*, for all of its fantasy plots and 2-D status, is that its characters and their lives are consistently more convincing and human than many of its live-action competitors!

Here are the plot summaries to two episodes that, even in this form, encapsulate the spirit of the show and its postmodern nature (summaries for every show can be found at the official website www.thesimpsons.com/).

'Homer to the Max'

Original airdate: 7 February 1999

When he finds out that a character on the TV show *Police Cops* is named Homer Simpson, the real Homer decides to change his name to Max Power. The new name earns him new, high-profile friends like Trent Steel, a young businessman. Steel invites 'Max' and his wife Marge to a garden party, where they meet such luminaries as Bill Clinton. While Clinton tries to seduce Marge, Homer learns that the gathering is part of an effort to save the Springfield redwoods, and joins the protest. After chaining themselves to the giant trees, 'Max' and his buddies are attacked by police. As he runs from the cops, 'Max' accidentally pulls down the tree he's attached to, which in turn knocks down the entire forest. Humiliated, he retreats from his new friends and returns to being Homer Simpson.

'Mom and Pop Art'

Original airdate: 11 April 1999

Homer becomes a conceptual artist, creating striking 'outsider art' that catches the eye of Astrid Weller, a beautiful Springfield art dealer. Astrid arranges for Homer to have his own show, but when the Springfield elite gather for the opening many are disappointed by his work. Homer decides that he must create something truly groundbreaking, so he floods the entire town, turning Springfield into an American Venice. His piece is a hit and everyone, including artist Jasper Johns (who 'guest stars'), voices their approval.

These two episodes play with a number of key postmodern textual features and themes. The titles, for instance, feature a running gag as the family all run to sit on a sofa in front of the television before the show starts. In 'Mom and Pop Art', the couch is dropped from the bomb bay of a warplane and the family ride it down to earth, directly quoting the final scene of the Stanley Kubrick film *Dr Strangelove* (1964). On one level, the 'gag' relies here upon spotting the reference; it might also be funny due to the absurdity of the image.

Homer is forever treating television as if it were reality, so integral to his life is it ('friend, mother, secret lover' he calls it in one episode, frequently hugging his set). In fact, *The Simpsons*, like a Chinese box, is often about this TV family watching television. The TV show they watch, *Police Cops* (the title is an absurd tautology, 'They're cops, they're police, they're Police Cops!' goes the trailer and titles), pastiches the 1980s show *Miami Vice* most obviously, with its well-dressed heroes. As his TV namesake does, Homer adopts a suave silk scarf, and his friends and acquaintances begin to associate him with his TV namesake. However, when the show's ratings dip, the producers abruptly turn the TV Homer into a lazy oaf and, as such, the Springfield Homer's reputation plummets. Thus, he changes his name to 'Max Power', a name that once again impresses everyone arbitrarily, despite Homer's long-standing status as an unreliable oaf.

Across both episodes, 'real' people guest star as themselves (Woody Harrellson and Jasper Johns) and others are spoofed – Bill Clinton's reputation as a womaniser, for instance. Most interesting is the engagement with the world of conceptual art. Here, Homer's accident with a self-assembly barbecue (a disaster as usual) is mistaken for art by a dealer and the Springfield cognoscenti. 'Outsider art' is a term applied to rough-and-ready works created by individuals who are unacquainted with the art world as such (and thus outside its discourses). Homer exhibits at Springfield's gallery, The Louvre: American Style, but his work is already passé at the moment he becomes famous. Dejected, his daughter tells him about Christo, an artist famous for buildings in cloth and creating huge installations that change landscapes, whom Homer emulates. Most telling in this episode is the repeated appearance of Jasper Johns, who, as a trailblazer of American abstract art, is famous for painting replicas of the American flag. Now an icon, his work and that of contemporary artists, such as Jackson Pollack, challenged the very nature of art and paved the way for the postmodernists!

A straightforward and pleasant task is to take some time to watch episodes from the 23 seasons of this show and think about its value as a cultural work and the ways in which it speaks about the postmodern.

Ultimately, any attempt to 'judge' or take a position on postmodern texts in any meaningful manner is undermined by those themes we've explored already. As we have seen, under postmodernism, any attempt to locate texts in relation to the 'real' is highly problematic. Thus, there is no purchase in trying to understand Roth's *Hostel* in relation to a violent world, or any 'real' aspect of Europe and Slovakia. Instead, it should be seen, so the argument goes, as referring only to other media and forms of representation – be they the teen films already mentioned, urban myths about Europe or moral panics about snuff movies (see Chapter 4). Postmodern texts mean inasmuch as they continually refer to each other. We call this quality 'intertextuality' and 'quotation'.

The referencing of media texts by other media texts is both obvious and apparently intentional (see the reference to *Dr Strangelove* in our analysis of *The Simpsons* above) but also unintentional. Intentionality can be detected in a variety of ways, particularly as postmodern media often literally amalgamate 'bits' of different media to make new texts. The use of sampling in music, for instance, is a good example, as new records can be made out of loops of work produced by other singers and musicians. 'Mashups' of sounds and video, whether done live or recorded into new products (e.g. at YouTube), also exemplify this practice.

Intertextuality is largely unintentional because our world is so saturated with meaning and media that endless polysemy and citation is unavoidable. For instance, can anyone in a movie thriller take a shower without evoking the shower scene in Alfred Hitchcock's *Psycho* (1960) (or Gus Van Sant's shot-by-shot remake of the film in 1998)? Umberto Eco gives a sense of the context in which intertextuality overtakes us by giving the example of a lover who cannot simply say, 'I love you madly' but says instead, as if in quotation marks (thus undermining integrity), 'As Barbara Cartland would put it, "I love you madly"' (Boyne and Rattansi, 1990). Whether or not anyone would actually say such a thing, we bear the weight of such endless references. To this end, then, media texts are akin to a mirror placed in front of a mirror, in which we see an endless chain of images or signs. Intentionally or otherwise, media forms constantly recycle and quote themselves, becoming 'self-referential'. Thus we can view soap powder adverts presented as soap operas; newspaper articles on soap operas and pop music stars; soap stars becoming pop stars; video as a promotion for music and stars using techniques drawn from film, television and advertising; pop stars and music as the basis of TV programmes.

We could go on and on in trying to produce an exhaustive list of postmodern 'devices' but any useful observations are likely to derive from repeated examination of texts in action. As in any textual analysis, we need to be aware of the fact that these ideas and features abound and may not all be present in texts, if at all. Of course, some textual practices look and feel very conventional and unremarkable in terms of the issues we have

Doing media studies

Postmodernism texts

Produce a textual analysis of a media text and address the following questions:

- What kinds of formal features does your text have? Can these be considered postmodern in any way (e.g. intertextuality, recycling, quotation)?

- Do any of the ideas or themes of postmodernism seem relevant to how you understand your text (e.g. a cynical attitude to social values, underlining of the fragmentation of social values)?

For this activity you might like to consider some of the specific texts we have mentioned in this chapter and across the book – *The Simpsons*, reality TV shows or *The Blair Witch Project*, for instance, or rap music. If you feel confident enough to explore further, look for either a website (including social networks, blogs, etc.), a recent film (genre pieces are often useful for an initial analysis – contemporary horror such as *Hostel* (dir. Roth, 2005), teen movies like *American Pie* (dir. Weitz, 1999), comic book adaptations such as *Iron Man* (dir. Favreau, 2008), *Dark Knight* (dir. Knight, 2008), or *Green Lantern* (dir. Martin Campbell, 2011), a TV programme (*L'île de la Tentation, MTV Europe, Al-Jazeera News*), a newspaper (try looking at the travel or fashion sections in newspapers, or examine some celebrity magazines) or piece of popular music (try 'world music' or releases related to TV talent shows). You might also consider extending your analysis to a more 'anthropological' study by examining how friends use smartphones (as artefacts in their lives and via a textual analysis of the particular phone and how it is set up individually).

described; this does not mean that we won't interpret them as postmodernist, however. Of course, we need to be attuned to the way in which different forms work: reading a newspaper and listening to music seem to be much less obvious sites for understanding postmodernism than watching a reality TV show, for instance. The way to proceed, as always, is to approach media texts as a theorist asking questions about postmodernism and engaging with the ideas which we've dealt with here, and which we see in outline in the case study on *The Simpsons*.

Critiquing postmodernism?

At this point we should advise you that, to be a theorist, you should not feel that you must 'accept' that postmodernism is 'correct': the concept is much too varied and contradictory for this (in fact, much more so than we have been able to convey). Likewise, one should feel the same about any of the approaches that we have introduced over the course of the book: theories, methods and interpretations stand upon their merits and the validity and strength of the arguments put forward.

Here, our aim has been merely to see what theorists of postmodernism are talking about. Many academics are sceptical about or critical of much of what advocates of postmodern ideas argue, and you may agree with them but you will also agree that, before you can critique something, you need to understand it. Rather than accepting the idea of postmodernism as 'fact', what we have to consider is whether the concept has any validity and what position we should take on it, or indeed, whether or not a position is possible or desirable.

On the one hand, as we have seen, theorists like Lyotard and others have proposed that, in the postmodern age, the all-encompassing 'grand narratives' (or 'meta'-narratives) of modernity – of human liberation, progress and a belief in science and its explanatory powers – are redundant because they have faltered with the collapse of communism, disasters like Chernobyl, the credit crunch and so on. Likewise, so many 'micro-narratives' have emerged, perspectives, experiences and explanations that do not fit cosily into 'Western' rationalism, a view of the advance of democracy in tandem with the superiority of capitalism and so on. These 'views from the margins' may be the insights of those peoples dominated by the great empires of the West that cruelly colonised Africa, the East and so on, and continue to do so via globalisation. Or, insights may come from closer to home, from the women's movement, which has exposed a history of oppression and of the way that 'feminine' values (the personal, emotions, caring, etc.) have been systematically excluded and devalued in Western traditions.

Such wholesale debunking of the guiding ideas of Western thought and progressive political ideas that characterise postmodernism have not been welcomed in some quarters, and have prompted an intense series of exchanges between theorists. Jürgen Habermas, for instance, has suggested that the narrative of modernity is simply unfinished and not worth discarding prematurely (Habermas, 1988). That critical voices have emerged is simply part of this development and it is premature to speak of 'endings' (to what extent is the announcement of 'ending' by postmodernists a narrative too?). Likewise, theorists such as Paul Gilroy have argued that, for the non-white peoples of the world, and for women in every society, a narrative of liberation has certainly not 'ended', as liberty is still being fought for (1993a, b). Frederick Jameson has been highly critical of the way in which postmodernism heralds a new phase in capitalist economies, where even the cultural and personal sphere has been commodified to the detriment of human freedom and thus needs critiquing and resisting. Every aspect of our lives, he suggested, is suffused with signals about the value of money and money making – from the art and décor in our homes to those media forms we consume. Nowadays this seems even more pertinent, as every time we surf the internet, whatever we are looking for, be it goods or information or friendship, we are not only confronted with endless reams of advertising (overt and covert – see the next chapter), but our movements and searches are tracked by software in order to organise the order of sites in search engines and to map our tastes, so that we and our tastes are knowable. In fact, our consumption is itself a form of labour, as everything we do in the digital age is related to the information we seek and generate (see Beller, 2006).

Terry Eagleton, one of the wittiest and most humane voices in the field of social and cultural theory, has also proven a sterling opponent of aspects of the postmodern. In a recent book, suggestively titled *After Theory* (Eagleton, 2004), he observes that there has been some form of crisis in his field in the past few decades. From the late 1960s, he argues, movements such as feminism have challenged traditionally blinkered academic thought. New generations have put the study of popular culture on the agenda and pleasure has been taken seriously as a category, not least of all because of its obviousness and for the fact that it features so largely in people's lives as an end in itself. This is, he says, to be welcomed and is in some way indicative of the postmodern turn. However, like Jameson, he points out that pleasure is a highly commodified aspect of modern society. If we look at the history of capitalism, bourgeois ideology developed a highly disapproving attitude to pleasure, as it detracted from the ability of labourers to work and to generate profit. While pleasure is no bad thing, nowadays, he argues, capital exploits pleasure shamelessly and promotes it (or particular versions of pleasure) to us in commodified form as essential to our existence: 'In that way we will not only

Intellectuals

are people who earn their living by the use of mental labour.

Thinking aloud

What is an intellectual and what do they do?

Some of the debates about postmodern thought concern the degree to which thinkers seem to be complicit with some of the pessimistic conclusions they come to – about politics, meaning and social action, for instance. Such debates centre upon the function of ideas in society and the role of the intellectual therein.

Intellectuals include academics in universities, along with other educators, and also embrace technocrats who manage organisations, scientists and technologists who design the machines of the modern age, social and political leaders, and, of course, people who work in media, managing ideas and forms of communication. Modern 'mass' societies require people who can solve problems, organise production and state services, and communicate ideas. For this reason, over the twentieth century the role of intellectuals grew in scale and importance, and their power to influence and control ideas grew as well. The social group of intellectuals, then, is central to understanding modernity, postmodernity and postmodernism.

People who earn their living through research and thinking can be thought to inhabit a particularly privileged position when it comes to evaluating society – they have the time, space and authority, literally, to stop and think! Thus, as Noam Chomsky has argued, thinkers have certain obligations. Writing at the height of the Cold War and appalled at the manner in which some scientists, economists and other thinkers were actively supporting American action in Vietnam, he declared that:

> With respect to the responsibility of intellectuals ... [they] are in a position to expose the lies of governments, to analyse actions according to their causes and motives and often hidden intentions. In the Western world, at least, they have the power that comes from political liberty, from access to information and freedom of expression. For a privileged minority, Western democracy provides the leisure, the facilities, and the training to seek the truth lying hidden behind the veil of distortion and misrepresentation, ideology and class interest, through which the events of current history are presented to us.

(Chomsky, 1967)

Much of postmodern thought, while provocative, may also be indicative of an abnegation of the responsibility of the intellectual. To announce the end of history while people still struggle for life, or to celebrate the consumer society as dominant when so many do without, might seem a little premature.

Ultimately intellectuals are but another social group the identity and integrity of which is as recuperated and commodified as any other. 'Highbrow' journals such as *Prospect* or *Foreign Affairs* have produced lists of 'top' public intellectuals. This hit parade approach was recently added to by the *Observer* which sought to evaluate the role and place of the intellectual in British life, doing so with a list of 300 contenders:

> But if the list is anything to go by, then the dominant professions from which contemporary British public intellectuals are drawn are journalists (20%), writers (19%), historians (14%) and critics (13%).

> A big surprise is the relatively poor showing of thinkers whom one would expect to be making a significant impact on public discourse – philosophers (4%), scientists (4%), economists (3%) and politicians (2%). But the main conclusion to be drawn from this survey is that the trope that intellectuals begin at Calais is simply wrong. The British aversion to the I-word seems to be at odds with the facts. This country has an impressive array of lively, creative and argumentative minds. And if you doubt that, just watch them take this thesis to pieces.

'Why don't we love our intellectuals?'

John Naughton,

Observer, Sunday 8 May 2011

consume more goods; we will also identify our own fulfilment with the survival of the system' (Eagleton, 2004: 6).

Eagleton is also welcoming of the recognition of the 'differences' within societies – gendered, sexual, ethnic, etc. However, he argues that theorists of postmodernism have made too great a play on 'difference' and the collapse of social movements, undermining any sense of a common humanity that might bring people together, rather than leave them atomised and powerless before the unthinking and unmerciful global system of capital. Old moralities and values have disappeared and all that is left is the celebration of money and profit – thus our frenzied obsession with celebrity, fame and acquisitiveness that is written all over the media. The point for this theorist, then, is to contest a great deal of postmodern theory for the way in which it, wittingly or otherwise, disarms any sense that the world could be different. (Why change it and on what basis, if every value is relative, and modern ideas such as progressive politics are repressive in some way because they conceive of people as 'mass' groups with common interests and humanity?) Beginning from what seems a pessimistic perspective, Eagleton is actually one of life's great optimists for insisting that the world can take other, better forms because we can imagine it so!

As Eagleton has said, since the 1960s new space has been afforded to the voices of groups hitherto excluded from intellectual life, as women, people of colour and so on have gained space in universities. And the work of these new theorists has gone hand in hand with social movements that have made fundamental changes in the ordering of the world and within our communities. Who could conceive of the scale of achievement for women in the past four decades, as they have attained a greater presence in the workplace and in the running of the country, without feminism? Who could conceive of the way in which the West relates to the developing world without post-colonial theorists and writers on race and ethnicity, whose impassioned insights challenged the racism of societies like the UK as it dealt with the migrant communities of the post-war world? Who could conceive of laws on equality and discrimination without the physical actions of the many who voiced their opposition to sexism and homophobia, and those who formulated laws and legislation countering traditional and 'common-sense' ways of thinking that mean that TV screens, radio and film – by and large – can no longer deal out the most obvious and degrading of stereotypes as they once did.

Most people, when they first come across ideas of postmodernism, see them as extremely disabling or totally pessimistic and relativistic, to the point of pointlessness.

Thinking aloud

Still modern?

The use of the term 'modern', occasionally 'modernisation', has continued currency, although it is worth examining for its euphemistic deployment. Politicians use the word a lot, describing the reform or rationalisation of public services, for instance (increasing efficiency, cutting jobs, updating equipment, etc.) and in tandem with cries for social change. You can examine this the next time you see a speech from David Cameron, Barack Obama, Nicholas Sarkozy or Angela Merkel. More regularly for us, the word and the sense of the modern is often allied to the presentation and development of new media technologies, such as mobile phones with video, internet access, i-Pads, flat-screen televisions, etc. When you come across adverts for such goods, it is useful to examine them for the way in which they deploy ideas of the new and the modern, and what kinds of ideas are connoted.

Next they start to see postmodernism everywhere, and come to believe that not only is there something in the idea but that it is the only useful way to understand contemporary culture. Like the latest convert, they are the most committed. It is only after you have used the idea a little that you begin to see the limitations and contradictions of different positions. Alongside the dazzling theories and characterisations of a change in society, philosophy and so on, we should also note the continuities in particular ways of thinking and doing things. Many people are still 'modern'; not everyone has eschewed values or morality. Some ideas of progress continue unabated. In this sense, postmodernism offers a set of ideas and arguments about the world which sit alongside others – for us to evaluate and engage with.

Summary

Exploring modernity, postmodernity and media

In this chapter we have attempted to investigate a range of ideas that explore the relationship of the media to the nature of society and the way that theorists have made sense of it. We began with a consideration of modernity and modernism in media. We saw how the modern was a way of describing the kind of society and attendant ideas that developed with mass societies. Modernism is a way of thinking about the kinds of cultural practices that attended this new era, how these concepts were impelled by the development of media and the way that media forms themselves were the site of modernist practices.

This understanding of the values and practices of the modern was then used to explore the idea that modernity has come to an end. The name for the era that has come after the modern is thus 'postmodern'. We explored the character of this new era, in which the organisation of society, our orientation and the nature and status of the culture and media we consume are all thought to have altered.

We investigated key themes of the postmodern: the death of history, meaning and subject, as well as the collapse of cultural boundaries and the coming of a society in which the spectacle is paramount, in order to evaluate claims that the modern has ended. We then used these themes to consider how media texts also evince postmodern qualities. Some of the features of postmodern texts included irony and quotation, alongside an amoral position on the worlds they represent. Our examples provided some ways of thinking about these qualities but you will need to continue exploring media texts (and evaluating our interpretations).

Our final section presented some critical positions on postmodernism and evaluated the role of thinkers in the midst of what seems to be a rather pessimistic set of ideas about society and our destiny. This section should give you a sense of the way in which theories about media and society are not a set of 'facts' but arguments to be evaluated and tested.

If you have followed this chapter through, engaged with the activities and thought about the issues covered, you should be able to:

- Outline and evaluate the key ideas used in debates about the modern and postmodern. (We have summarised some main points but keener distinctions, detail and examples can be pursued through secondary reading and engagement.)

- Apply the themes of postmodernism listed in the chapter to particular media texts in order to identify their postmodern qualities. (Such analyses will go hand in hand with your confidence in the themes of postmodernism but, like our ongoing engagement with media texts and practices, examples and insights abound in our everyday consumption. Being attuned to evaluating what is going on in media and society will only enhance your advancing scholarship.)

- Evaluate the usefulness and limitations of postmodern theory. As our exploration of media and society continues, in tandem with our various concepts and methods, your evaluation will depend upon your own position as a social being. Your own motivation is important here in weighing up these key ideas for yourself, inasmuch as they prove meaningful and useful to you and your research.

Doing media studies

Exploring the postmodern 1

If you completed the 'Doing media studies: Exploring definitions' activity introduced on finding definitions of postmodernism, this will mean that you have now identified a range of further sources that will aid you in mapping the range of ideas in this area. We have not provided a list of further reading here as it is imperative, if you wish to fully understand and engage with postmodern ideas in your media studies, that you read widely. Thus, you should locate and read examples of the original writings of key thinkers like Baudrillard, Jameson, Lyotard or Eco (there are plenty of titles in our references section at the end of this book).

Questions you should ask concern how the summaries we provide here of the 'themes' of postmodernism are dealt with specifically in their work. Some of the discussions in previous chapters will also give you grounding in some of the assumptions behind their work and the ideas to which they react.

Finally, and depending upon any area of media in which you are interested, you now need to search for analyses specific to your medium. This will aid you in advancing your own studies.

Exploring the postmodern 2

A useful way of exploring your grasp of postmodernism in relation to media – specific texts and broader aspects of the medium – is to consider the role of 'new' media in our lives and culture. Brainstorm a set of ideas exploring postmodern themes and features in relation to social media and aspects of web activity (mashup facilities for instance or file-sharing, social media sites such as Facebook or Chat Roulette). What broad observations and themes come out of your observation?

CHAPTER 13

Andrew McStay

The consumer society and advertising

Configuring consumer society

The histories of consumption and advertising are intimately and innately tied together. Instrumental to the character and development of the West, the rise of mass consumerism and advertising extended the reach of the West across the globe. The effects are cultural, technological, economic, political and ecological.

While the globe undergoes an economic reshuffle with non-Western powers such as China, India and Brazil being in the ascendant, over the last twenty years advertising itself has also undergone seismic change as the practice has oriented itself in a twenty-first century defined by networks and digital devices. In addition to technological changes in media, the ways in which people engage with advertising and media over the last twenty years have developed.

As other chapters in this book describe, these tend to be framed in terms of 'participatory culture', 'convergence', 'co-production' and other terms having to do with people taking a more active hand in their mediated experiences. Other key digital developments in advertising relate to the intensification of data mining and the targeting of advertising.

What we will do in this chapter

The aim of this chapter is to explore key ideas relating to consumption and advertising from new media studies perspectives. This involves grasping the general contours of consumption and processes of branding. Centrally, it also requires that we understand in some detail how advertising works and how it is changing in light of digital developments in media. As already alluded to, these changes are both technological and sociological.

We will begin by sketching a historical context of the rise of consumerism in the West and begin to consider the proposition that we live in a 'consumer society'. This chapter proceeds to both assess developments in advertising and offer an outline of precisely what advertising is. This is less than obvious and I have attended many academic conferences where speakers have misunderstood the basic notion of what constitutes the advertising business. We will thus explore aspects of the organisation of the advertising industry and the ways in which this is changing in light of digital developments. In addition to detailing what constitutes advertising, we will also examine modes of critiquing advertising. As detailed in other chapters, we turn to textual analysis and semiotic-inspired accounts that help us understand layers of meaning within advertising texts. However, and more uniquely, we will be paying particular attention to critiques of advertising relating to privacy. The words privacy and advertising may not be associated in your mind just yet, but all will become clear as we progress. In addition to considering the formation of advertising, consumer society and changing dynamics of media we will conclude by considering Adbusters, the Canada-based publication dedicated to overturning a vision of the West predicated on consumption.

By the end of this chapter you should be able to:

- Understand processes of consumption and branding.
- Explore and engage with issues and debates in and around theories of consumerism.
- Critically examine the concepts of advertising and consumption and their social role and interaction with media industries.
- Identify key features of a changing advertising industry.
- Understand questions about privacy in relation to online behavioural advertising.
- Recognise voices that challenge the status quo of consumerism as a way of life.

KEY TERMS: ▶ advertising; consumption; marketing; public relations (PR); privacy.

Historical context of consumerism and advertising

Some historical background is useful to understand how we have arrived at a Western society so intensely predicated on consumption. Mass production and the development of mass consumption are closely tied to the technical and scientific advances of the nineteenth century. Cheap manufactured goods, made available through the technological achievements of the Industrial Revolution (particularly the second part), altered virtually everyone's style of life and standard of living. The first part of the Industrial Revolution started in the later half of the eighteenth century and involved the development of the steam engine; the second around one hundred years later in the nineteenth century revolved around the development of electricity, the internal combustion engine, refined science-based chemicals and pharmaceuticals, efficient steel casting, the diffusion of the telegraph and telephone. Cumulatively, these technological developments radically altered the organisation of production, distribution and consumption of goods. In negating scarcity, more merchandise in more varieties was available than at any other time in human history. Except for the most destitute (and there were many), nearly any ordinary person – in Europe first, and then across America – could afford to own implements, tools and appliances which had only been available to the wealthiest classes in earlier centuries.

In addition to the changes wrought by better transportation and technical innovation, the Industrial Revolution had massive effects on politics, economics, culture, education and society, some of which we have tracked in previous chapters of this book. In giving rise to an exponential increase in non-essential goods and consumption, we also witness the rise of the professional advertising industry.

Prior to rapid industrialisation, in the days of largely agrarian production, thrift, saving and the avoidance of debt were virtues. The Industrial Revolution brought with it a drive to consume and challenged these previously necessary virtues. Increased industrial output meant that if too few people spent their money consuming the rapidly widening array of goods available, store shelves would never empty and the emerging modern economy would seize up. Arguably, along with rising literacy, everyday folk were educated in the arts of taste and how to be obedient consumers. These developments were tracked at the time in classic studies of consumption by sociologists such as Thorstein Veblen (1899/1975) who identified competition for status among social groups as a key driver of consumption, noting the rise of a 'leisure class' who were conspicuous in their mode of consumption.

To maintain and encourage the processes of consumption, the mass advertising industry emerged as a means of notifying consumers about products, developing sophisticated techniques for inducing desires and needs among ordinary people for things that hitherto they did not realise they needed. Whereas consumers once sought reliable goods, manufacturers and their advertising agencies sought reliable consumers.

In addition to the relationship between consumption and advertising, we should note early on that advertising was and continues to be a key driver for commercial media, facilitating the growth of press, radio, television, movies, and now digital media. Thanks to developments in printing presses and developments in reproducing photographs, early forms of advertising were largely carried in newspapers. The origins of newspapers in the West, for instance, can be found in what were called 'mercuries' or 'news sheets'. In countries such as the Netherlands and the UK, where modern commerce and the Industrial Revolution originated, these were pamphlets that began to appear in the largest towns and cities and were used by the merchant middle classes in the seventeenth century.

Doing media studies

Exploring advertising values

Using textual analysis techniques established in earlier chapters, identify and examine an advert for a beauty product.

What is the nature of the rhetorical technique and claims of your chosen text and how does it compare with those of the past, as alluded to above? What ideas about the modern beauty industry are represented in these adverts? What messages are used to communicate these? What myths are propagated? (See also our analysis of the Chanel advertisement on pp. 158–165 by way of comparison.)

Until the 1960s the front page of *The Times* was given over to classified advertisements of all descriptions. These items of commerce were as important as up-to-date information on international current affairs for the business leaders who took this newspaper.

Source: nisyndication.com

They contained lists of prices, stocks, materials being imported from other countries, other financial information, and the details of markets and fairs occurring, as well as adverts for horses and so on. Alongside these details, perhaps the most significant adverts were for miracle cures and medicines. It is noteworthy that these types of miracle cure products, so prevalent at the beginning of the modern advertising industry, compare with many modern products. For example, adverts for moisturisers, anti-hair-loss lotions and other products quite arguably represent modern-day quackery and snake oil salespersonship (for more on historical context see Dyer, 1982/1993).

Cultures of consumption

Consumption is an activity that now involves virtually every single person on the planet. As we suggested in our brief outline of the context for the rise of the consumer society, this activity is a historically specific one. Whether it is those in the wealthy First World, who consume the vast majority of resources and products, or those in the Third World, who produce many of the resources and products necessary to make First World lifestyles possible, consumption

To consume

to eat or drink; to obsess; to use up; to destroy or be destroyed; to waste; to waste away.

has ramifications for all of the planet's inhabitants. The *Collins English Dictionary* (1993) defines the verb '**to consume**' as presented in our side bar.

The finite aspects of this action, implied in aspects of this definition, suggest some of the consequences of our collective consumption of the world's resources. For the moment, and for our purposes, however, consumption as an activity means using up and purchasing. Consumption is also about decisions to purchase or consume, and how and why we make those decisions (Miller, 1997).

Born into a culture of consumption and having acquired habits that make this activity seem entirely natural, we rarely take stock of chains of production, consumption and influences behind decision-making processes. Many economists continue to argue that consumers are rational and purchase products on the basis of functional decision making to further their own interests (Miller, 1995). On the other hand, the very act of modern consumption is seen in some quarters as highly irrational and potentially damaging to both individuals and society as a whole.

On the one hand, then, consumption can be seen as a positive part of wider society, as necessary to being modern (or postmodern) and a benefit to the economy. Without consumption, our economies would collapse. Moreover, consumer spending on what may be described as luxuries or goods that are surplus to essential human needs (basic food, clothing, shelter) is taken to be a sign of an overall healthy economy. In addition, and even bearing in mind contemporary concerns over obesity and the like connected to over-consumption, those living in advanced economies live longer than any other society that lives now or has ever lived, which is partly due to the availability of consumer goods that make life much easier than in the past. On the other hand, and alongside worries about the exhaustion of the resources that make commodities available, negative perspectives on consumption bemoan the uncritical promotion of materialistic values. This critical viewpoint suggests that consumerism involves equating personal happiness with the purchasing of material possessions, furthering the actual act of consumption for its own sake. Behind this is a suspicion of the superficiality of attendant values in affluent societies whose economies are driven largely by consumerism and in which collective and individual identity is in part sought through consumption of goods and services. We can further understand the implications of these positions by examining some of the ways in which theorists have made sense of the nature and meaning of contemporary consumption and its social role.

Theorising the consumer society

Sociologist Zygmunt Bauman argues that shopping isn't just about choosing between products or brands; it is the modus operandi, or way of operating, for those living in 'developed' societies. Bauman observes that 'the avid, never ending search for new and improved recipes for life is also a variety of shopping' (2000: 74). Life is not so much about articulated or unarticulated 'needs'; it is about desire. Desire in this case is about the compulsion to consume in all aspects of life and not just those related to manufacturing, marketing and advertising. It has to do with the orientation of people living within consumer societies. Consumers, then, are looking for instant gratification, and tend to be impatient and lose interest quickly if not stimulated. Desire here is a deferral to the next possible object of satisfaction, though this is never enough to satisfy longing and desire. Put simply: we are never satisfied! Desire is a flame that must be fostered and fuelled, and the dissipation of this represents a marketer's nightmare.

The French theorist Jean Baudrillard, who is also discussed in our section on postmodernism, carried out seminal work examining consumption in modern societies. Although his most influential texts were written in the 1960s and 1970s, he remains a powerful guide to the meaning and practices of contemporary consumer cultures. In his account of consumption he suggests that:

> *you never consume the object in itself (in its use-value); you are always manipulating objects (in the broadest sense) as signs which distinguish you either by affiliating you to your own group taken as an ideal reference or by marking you off from your group by reference to a group of higher status*
> (1968: 62)

So, to unpack what this means, the idea is that we consume what objects stand for rather than the objects themselves and their product function. Whereas use-value refers to the functionality of a product (e.g. a refrigerator stores food), sign-value refers to consumption used as a marker that positions us in some way. So, for example, a fridge labelled SMEG may instead link to the wider cultural aspirations of purchasers. It means consumers are using brands to maintain difference, to be part of a wider fashion or as a means of making a personal statement – 'I'm wealthy', 'I'm cool', or even 'I don't care about brands' when they position themselves as avoiding them.

Perhaps, therefore, it is the brands that we consume rather than the goods themselves? Whereas brands were originally benchmarks of quality that consumers could trust, their identities are now much more sophisticated in terms of the way they are positioned by marketers and advertisers in the minds of consumers. Contemporary manufacturers spend a lot of money creating these identities in the minds of consumers, particularly in sectors where there is little differentiation between products (e.g. perfumes, refrigerators and the mid-range car market). To some extent, consuming is about defining within a matrix of brand relationships which groups you do and do not belong to. Mac users, for instance, are often very vocal about their distinction from PC users.

We might say that identity is created through difference and it is thus interesting to examine the impulse that drives us to delineate ourselves this way. Sociologist Peter Corrigan has suggested that a key strategy of the early advertising industry was to take advantage of a vision of the social world wherein people define themselves in relation to others in their peer group and, importantly, where people feel under scrutiny from peers (Corrigan, 1997; also see Ewen, 1976). Arguably, manufacturers created a social world where their products became a solution to problems that arose because a marketised version of the world was accepted by people.

We can think about how this process of differentiation has been extended to the process of branding and the ways in which meanings and lifestyle aspirations are attached to products. As Ritzer (1997) observes, from a certain perspective, we consume signs (messages, images and associated ideas) rather than commodities. Thus, when shopping, do you consume objects themselves or the identities you perceive as attached to them? Is a brand a guarantor of quality or could it, in a sense, be worth more than the product itself, especially when some goods at a physical level are largely indistinguishable? The important point here is that consumers need to be literate as consumers and to be able to 'read' the system of consumption in order to know what to consume. Because members of a particular society know the codes, we know the meaning of what it means to consume one commodity rather than another. Of course, one can buck trends and break the rules, but one has to know what the rules are to begin with. Signification is a game and like all games, we may develop proficiency and expertise.

This idea of consumption as a mode of communication is developed in the ideas of French sociologist Pierre Bourdieu. In discussion of consumption in relation to taste and the art world, he suggests that: 'Consumption is, in this case, a stage in the process of communication, that is, an act of deciphering, decoding, which presupposes practical or explicit mastery of a cipher or code' (1984: 2). In terms of 'taste' in the world of art, for instance, he suggests how the 'cultured' have mastery of the codes that allow them to consume works of art, which to others are indecipherable but that are still seen to have value.

Thus, 'taste' here is what distinguishes the 'bourgeoise' from other social groups as 'naturally' refined (see the discussion of fandom, p. 315, for a further comparison here).

The same principle is equally applicable to wider consumer society and the choices one makes therein. Commodities such as clothing, cars, perfumes, computers, baked beans, coffee, magazine subscriptions, mobile phones, sunglasses, choice of social network site, what you like or share, etc., are perhaps no longer defined by their use but rather by what they signify. In the performative arena of consumer society, surface appearance is all-important. Of course, one must also be able to pull off the illusion of authenticity. One's status should be effortless after all. What products signify is not defined exclusively by what commodities do and the functions they perform, but by their relationship to the entire system of commodities and signs. While not mathematical, we may discern a scheme of interrelationships. The world of consumer objects thus represents a language with which we express and articulate a desired self to the world. It is necessarily linguistic because it is shared, social and communal (few people have a sense of taste than no one else shares). This idea of a system of signification compares well to the way in which semiologists have characterised language (see Chapter 1). Indeed, it is instructive that Roland Barthes (1992) extended his analysis to the world of fashion and advertising as a meaning system.

Baudrillard (1968; 1970/1999) argues that mass media, and advertising in particular, have greatly enhanced and generalised what he calls a process of 'simulation'. In this context, simulation refers to the games that brands and their consumers wittingly and unwittingly play with each other. Instead of being presented with 'reality' in the perception of consumer goods, at least in terms of product function ('my 4×4 car is necessary for overcoming difficult roads and terrain as I live in the country'), people are treated to simulations involving the constant recombination of signs, or elements of consumerist code that must be read for the values and distinctions it represents (e.g. power, prestige, ability to look down on people and capacity to properly care for family). Indeed, in consumer society, simulations eventually nudge out the real.

Baudrillard argues that the simulative function of consumer society accounts in part for the seeming insatiability and continual dissatisfaction of consumers, and our desire to keep acquiring more 'stuff'. People define themselves through acquisition and seek difference, i.e. they establish their social and personal identity through differentiation, rather than in the nature of a particular object in consumption. Dissatisfaction and insatiability stem from Baudrillard's premise that the need for difference is never fulfilled, particularly as new products and trends come to the market. There is no rational closure ('Socially I've made my point in wearing the most expensive hat available, I do not need to buy anything more') as the spectacle of consumerism is irrational, although possessing its own perverse logic.

In consumer society, advertising agencies represent expertise in reading trends, fashions, signs and other codes. They are able to use these systems of signification for clients to help position their products in the minds, desires and affections of consumers. Baudrillard also argues that simulated relationships emerge from this system and that these also characterise modern society. For example, advertisers imitate personal, intimate modes of communication to produce a sense of intimacy with and around consumable objects and services. A recent campaign for T-Mobile highlights this well (both shown on YouTube). In 'Life's for sharing' set in London's Liverpool Street Station and 'Welcome back' set in London's Heathrow Airport Terminal 5, we witness the commodification of participation as a mass dance appears to break out spontaneously. Akin to Baudrillardian notions of simulated intimacy, this is an update for a socially mediated age. In these adverts, widely watched on television, and viewed and shared online, interactive theatre was brought into the realms of the everyday. Articulating a conception of sociality as a means of branding, T-Mobile leveraged values of connectivity, joy, spontaneity, frivolity and community by means of a planned accident. Rather than attempting to be the most popular, it becomes the facilitator. While this is not surprising for a company whose business is 'communications', it is an

Source: The Advertising Archives

important point to mark. Where traditionally brands have fought to be number one (being cheaper, faster or having greater coverage), T-Mobile's advertising strategy taps into communicational discourses that connect the real and the virtual. Perhaps unconsciously ironic, the advert is also a criticism of advertising itself and represents a public reclaiming of the streets from commerce and private interests (as per the language of flashmobs, the appropriation of social space, and modes of resistance against soulless and joyless private buildings). What T-Mobile sought and achieved is to leverage sociality as a form of fuel or energy with which to drive its advertising campaign. Simulated intimacy is thus produced between people doing the advertising and potential customers, as well as between potential customers and the products being advertised.

For Baudrillard (1970/1999), contemporary consumption is many things: a sign of affluence, a function of enjoyment and modern leisure, and something related to individualism, offering liberation, fulfilling needs and thus aiding in the development of a sense of the self. More than this, consumption as a mode of signification (a system or code of signs) is ingrained in our way of life for us in economically advanced societies. In this sense, then, consumption and our role within it has something to do with power.

Be they clothing, toys or gadgets, we see that our acquisition of objects is not so much about individual pleasure (although this is an important aspect of consumption), but rather the confirmation of our acquiescence to a certain type of logic. To consume is to belong, to confirm one's place in the wider social system, i.e. it is a mode of conformity.

Here, consumption might seem something that is 'forced' upon us. However, Baudrillard also observes that there is no 'in' or 'out' of consumption and consumer society. To quote:

let's face it, firming the thighs of a size 8 supermodel is no challenge.

There's not much point in testing a new firming lotion on size-eight supermodel thighs, is there? That's why Dove's Firming range was tested on ordinary women with real lives to live – and real, curvy thighs to firm. After using Dove's nourishing and effective combination of moisturisers and seaweed extracts, we asked if they'd go in front of the camera. What better way to show the unretouched, unairbrushed results?

new Dove Firming Range

Source: The Advertising Archives

The UK campaign for Dove promoted the use of 'real women' in explicit contrast to other 'idealised' media and advertising images. It is interesting to note, however, that the parent company Unilever owns many 'competing' brands and produces many of those idealised images.

The consumer experiences his distinctive behaviour as freedom, as aspiration, as choice. His experience is not one of being forced to be different, of obeying a code. To differentiate oneself is always, by the same token, to bring into play the total order of differences, which is, from the first, the product of the total society and inevitably exceeds the scope of the individual. In the very act of scoring his points in the order of differences, each individual maintains that order, and therefore condemns himself only ever to occupy a relational position within it.

(1968: 62)

This appears more complicated than it is: Baudrillard is arguing that, in his account of consumer society, we consider ourselves free because we are free to choose between brands. If I choose Diesel jeans, I define myself against 'suit wearing' and 'Dad-like' Levi's wearers. In terms of maintaining order, he is arguing that, by playing the game of identity, signification and difference through consumption, we maintain this version of consumer society and our position within it as defining ourselves through brands. We can thus continue to investigate the relationship of identity and consumption further through a discussion of theories of branding and how this process operates.

Case Study

Simulating intimacy

The idea of a simulated intimacy and the contradictions it involves can be usefully illustrated with reference to a marketing campaign centring on the soap and moisturiser brand Dove. In 2007 they developed a strategy centring on a motif of speaking to, hearing and using 'real women' in adverts. It was built upon dissatisfaction among consumers of beauty products about adverts presenting idealised representations of women and products as aids to reaching desirable, but often unachievable, goals for consumers. The message of the campaign was manifest in the range of women and bodily shapes used, and an overall sense that Dove is 'on your side'. Such relationships are not uncommon in adverts, of course, but this one is reinforced by an international campaign about images of women in adverts attached to Dove and the launch of a Self-Esteem Fund, which supports the aim: to make a real change in the way women and young girls perceive and embrace beauty. We want to help free ourselves and the next generation from beauty stereotypes.

Too many girls develop low self-esteem from hang-ups about looks. Consequently, many fail to reach their full potential later in life. The Dove Self-Esteem Fund is an agent of change

to educate and inspire girls on a wider definition of beauty (www.campaignforrealbeauty. co.uk/).

In the sphere of cultural politics, this is a worthy cause to champion. However, one has to wonder about the sincerity and integrity of this whole enterprise, particularly when one realises that the parent company Unilever also owns the Lynx brand (Axe outside the UK) for men, originally launched in France in 1983. This is not a brand known for its positive work in female representation (Spurgeon, 2007). As this comment from the Lynx UK website reveals, its view of women is the antithesis of that found at Dove:

Summer 2007 saw the re-formulation of all fragrances. The new and improved range gave guys even more opportunities to pull. Kelly Brook and her team of Lynx Mynxes hit our screens in the Miami based Bom Chicka Wah Wah Rally, a nationwide search for the UK's ultimate 'Players', teams of three mates who have had success with the ladies but want to take their skills to the next level and improve their game.

(www.unilever.co.uk/ourbrands/personalcare/ lynx.asp)

The obvious point to make here, of course, is that this duality smacks of hypocrisy, but that simply reveals the functionality of the intimacy created. And, of course, this intimacy between consumer and brand is equally important to both products! The Lynx brand articulates a different sense of intimacy, in conspiring with the desire of Lynx-men to 'pull' women.

Branding, identity and consumption

So, for a process that has to do with signs and surfaces, branding cuts deep into our drives, motivations, fears, wants and desires. But how does it work and what exactly is 'branding' anyway? As mentioned, branding differentiates one product from its competitors in the market, but it is also much more than this. The term 'brand' itself originated many centuries ago in the Old English word *brandr*, meaning 'to burn'. Later, this was how farmers and owners of livestock marked their animals to identify them and branding became a method of differentiating 'stocks' in village marketplaces. As a feature of contemporary society, branding can be thought of as working at a variety of levels. Marketing theorist and commentator Kotler (2003) describes how branding operates within the business of marketing in relation to consumers conferring attributes, functionality, emotional benefits and identifying 'brand essences' of products. As we have mentioned, a brand is a benchmark of quality that may, in turn, reflect the trustworthiness of the brand as a guarantor of quality, but it is also something more.

Utilising the example of Nokia, Kotler explains the idea of 'brand essence', which relates to the deeper and more abstract goals consumers are looking to satisfy in acquiring branded goods. For example, on asking someone why he or she might want to buy a Nokia mobile phone, they may respond that the phone looks well built: this is an attribute. On being asked why it is important that the phone be well built, the consumer may respond that it means the phone will be reliable, which is a functional benefit. When asked why reliability is important, the consumer may respond describing how they want to be available for family or colleagues at all times, which is an emotional benefit. Our consumer will thus be able to help them if they are in trouble and thus the brand essence may be that the brand makes its consumer feel like a 'Good Samaritan'.

This sequence of related qualities revealed through questioning is known as 'laddering up', as it helps marketers gain a deeper understanding of consumer motivation. Through psychographic research (examining values, attitudes and opinions), marketers and advertisers thus break down audiences in terms of what motivates them to purchase products and services. Through innovations in the 1960s and 1970s in psychographic research, a new form of branding occurred. This went beyond simple market distinctions (marking your brand out from competitors), to one based on a way of being.

Thinking aloud

Consumption and postmodernity

In conjunction with the way in which consumption is part of identity formation in contemporary society, we can identify a further feature of postmodernity in addition to those discussed in the previous chapter. In recent decades, the countries that were once the drivers of industrial society – Western Europe and the USA – have seen a decline in manufacturing and all the other production-based aspects of modernity. Commonly characterised as 'post-industrial', such countries have seen the development of new 'soft' industries, such as computing and software, investment in the service industries, tourism and the creative sector (including the advertising industry).

In contrast to functional differences, we have motivational and identity-based differences. So, who do you want to be today? An Apple user who 'thinks different' from the PC herd? A buff-bodied All-American Abercrombie and Fitch type? A post-punk ironic Diesel kid? A techno-savvy Starbucks-sipping laptop-luvvie Google thinker, or one of countless other off-the-peg identities ready to be adopted and purchased?

Brands are much more than product identifiers; they permeate and influence our identity and make-up. While there are of course other influences, consumerism plays a role in how we present and conceive of ourselves. Philosophically, this is quite a radical notion but everyday experience shows it to be true. Brands are a means of articulating who we might like to be. In relation to our discussion in the previous chapter on the 'death of the subject' and the changing and flexible nature of identity under postmodernity, our relationship with brands seems to play a particularly important role here.

Desire is expensive to produce and nurture and it is for this reason that a considerable amount of manufacturers' budgets are spent on promotional aspects of marketing. When we ask, 'What is the role of the advertising industry in contemporary consumer society?', we may argue that advertisers and marketers are the storytellers, the dream makers and, most centrally, the mythmakers. In semiotic terms, they naturalise the relationship between signifiers and signifieds for given strategic goals (see Chapter 1 on semiology and Chapter 10 on ideology). Agencies thus work with their clients to create brands that have strong signifying power, and which manage to evoke desire within consumers to consume their signs/brands by consuming their products.

The organisation and practice of advertising in the digital age

Although the cultural ramifications of advertising practice are important, we should also understand the way that the industry is organised and how it works. To understand how consumerism relates to advertising, we first have to clearly understand what advertising is and its relationship with other activities, such as **marketing** and **public relations (PR)**. To focus only on effects is to develop a distorted account of promotional activities. We can begin with some definitions, in order to make this distinction.

Marketing
refers to the process of identifying consumer needs, market opportunities and producing products and services (including pricing, distribution and promotion) in order to generate a profit. In some cases, marketing departments will handle advertising 'in-house'. In others, they will outsource to an advertising agency. Marketing is also concerned with anticipating customers' future needs and wants, often through market research.

Public relations (PR)
refers to the management of communication between organisations and the public. PR processes seek to gain positive exposure for organisations in media and other outlets in ways that do not require payment of a direct nature (i.e. media space is not bought).

Advertising
can be thought of as a form of communication designed to generate awareness of products, services and organisations. Its purpose is to persuade people to purchase, subscribe to or consume a particular brand, product, service or organisation. Advertising is created for recognisable organisations, for example companies such as Diesel or Coca-Cola, or not-for-profit organisations such as Friends of the Earth or governments. It is typically defined in terms of communication through paid-for media space.

Traditionally, the process of **advertising** is made up of advertisers (the people who have products and services to offer), their agencies (the people that design advertisers' advertising), and media (the organisations that sell advertising space to advertisers). Sometimes the organisation that buys media space from media companies is part of the agency, and sometimes it is separate. It depends on the size of the agency and whether it is a full-service agency. There are many types of agencies with some handling all possible communications for a client and others specialising in specific areas (for example, web and interactive, social media, health care, and those who specialise in creative work but do not buy media for their clients). Advertising agencies are increasingly owned by large conglomerates. Many of the ones you may recognise (e.g. Saatchi and Saatchi) have been swallowed up by large holding companies, such as the French-based Publicis (www.publicis.com/). It is instructive to have a look at Advertising Age's 'Datacenter' (http://adage.com/datacenter/) for a global overview of which conglomerations are buying up agencies and how respective agencies are performing, particularly as their ranking changes yearly. For information on agencies operating in the UK (the big ones tend to be truly global) have a look at either the print version of *Campaign* or view it online (www.campaignlive.co.uk/home/).

As you can see, there are crossovers between these promotional disciplines and a full-service agency may handle public relations issues for a given client. This blurring increases in light of social and other digital media where one need not buy space (in the way we might buy space in newspapers or airtime on television). Whereas advertising was once safely defined by the purchasing of media space thorough which to communicate a message, this is no longer true. For example, in the early 1990s (just before the web became available) Bovee and Arens defined advertising as 'the nonpersonal communication of information usually paid for and usually persuasive in nature about products, services or ideas by identified sponsors through the various media' (1992: 7). Traditionally then, advertising utilises paid-for media to reach large swathes of people. This involves space in newspapers, magazines, television, cinema, radio or outdoors (such as billboards), to reach people constructed as 'audiences'. As the media environment has changed, this media-based definition is no longer absolute.

While there are crossovers between advertising, marketing and PR, they are still separate enough to warrant their own roles. People who work in advertising tend to work in one of four areas – creative, planning, management or media – although there are many more aspects (such as research and administration). Creative is where people originate, write and design advertising. Although this is the most well-known aspect, in reality it accounts for a relatively small portion of overall roles in the advertising process. Creative teams are divided into copywriter (writing) and art director (visuals), although in day-to-day life these roles blur and merge. It is their job to breathe life into a client's advertising needs, and create advertising that resonates with its audiences and persuades or informs in some way. Their role is to give form to the advertising strategy and obtain prospective targets' eyeballs, ears and minds. Given the amount of advertising that competes for attention in our cluttered media environments, this presents quite a challenge.

Planning is otherwise known as representing the voice of the consumer. Their job is to gain insights into prospective target audiences via qualitative and quantitative research. They have to be able to turn rich and complex data on audiences into something tangible, and develop insights into how advertising should communicate with specific parts of the population. They do not craft the final creative message, but they strongly influence what should be said in the advertising by means of developing strategy (what needs to be done and how it is to be achieved).

Account managers or executives are people who liaise with the client and agency. In a sense, they are the face of the agency and it is important they maintain smooth relationships so as to be able to sell an agency's work to a client, and also to make sure that clients stay with their agency and do not go looking for a new one.

Media aspects are broken down into two elements. There are those who plan media usage and where advertising is to be placed, and those who actually buy media space. Media planners will have a solid understanding of the properties of each medium and how it is consumed. For example, weekend newspapers tend to be consumed in a much more leisurely fashion than weekday newspapers. They are also kept for longer, which means repeat viewings of adverts. Ultimately, a media planner's role is to ensure maximum positive exposure of adverts through media. Media buyers, on the other hand, are responsible for the purchasing of media space and airtime, and seek to get the best possible prices for their clients. For more on the specifics of roles within agencies, have a look at the Institute of Practitioners in Advertising website (www.ipa.co.uk/) and the Advertising Association (www.adassoc.org.uk/).

As demonstrated, it is difficult to argue with the notion that advertising is, among other things, a process of generating 'false' needs. Advertising rightly receives much flak for contributing to over-consumption, materialistic values and a range of other negative qualities and practices. While many of these arguments are valid and correct, it is worth being clear about what we are critiquing. Indeed, too many criticisms of advertising fail to understand that advertising is simply a tool. They attack the technique rather than the aims to which it is put. In addition to being utilised by commercial corporations, advertising is also employed by many organisations, including governments and not-for-profit groups such as charities. Advertising is an instrument of communication – it can be used both for good and for ill. As such, critiques of consumer society should perhaps be directed at the way it is used, not at the tool itself. For example, it is hard to argue with claims that advertising serves positive purposes in promoting Unicef, Médecins Sans Frontières, Amnesty International, Greenpeace and other similar organisations.

As with other areas of media and related industries, digital developments are continuing to drive change. As mentioned, these changes are both technological and sociological (relating to how people use media). As people increasingly spend more time with digital

Thinking aloud

Advertisers and semiology

People who work in advertising tend to have an interest in the people who consume their adverts, in what makes them tick and what motivates them. Especially in the creative areas of advertising, they also tend to be highly interested in culture, cultural production, the artefacts that emerge from this, and what they mean to people. Agency employees are thus adept at playing with cultural codes so as to present a client's product or service to their audience in the most effective light. Creatives in advertising are dependent, therefore, on the politics and conventions of (digital) culture, fine art, graphic design, media, photography, pop music, subcultural activities, typography, web design/aesthetics, a variety of literary tropes and many other areas of cultural production. As such, they are experts in understanding and harnessing the power of intertextuality, combining and recombining signs to produce campaigns and messages that position brands in a desirable light. This is not to suggest that agency folk spend their time discussing the finer points of semiotic theory, although many will have studied semiotics at university, but they do spend a great deal of time reflecting on how a brand should be positioned and what vehicles might best achieve this.

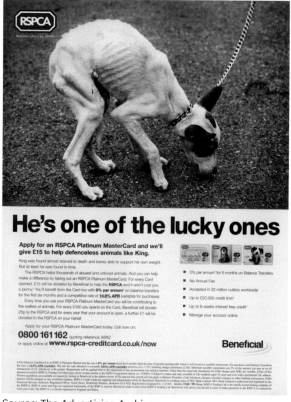

Source: The Advertising Archives

Advertising serves not for-profit, social causes as well as commercial ones.

media, and become more discerning and media-literate, this allows advertisers to widen channels of communication and increase the potential of reaching us. Ofcom (which sets the standards and regulations for UK media) defines media literacy as 'the ability to access, understand and create communications in a variety of contexts' (2006: 2). This literacy provides advertisers with opportunities to flex creative muscle in terms of the platforms they use to reach their targets and the nature of the creative message (which may be more sophisticated than straightforward sales appeals to 'buy me!'). Thus advertising platforms are developing considerably from the traditional **'above-the-line'** media formats.

Of particular interest to this chapter is the rise of online and digital advertising. In 2010 online was worth 25 per cent of all money spent on advertising, with television at 26 per cent. After these press followed at 18 per cent; direct mail 1 per cent; press classifieds 6 per cent; outdoor 5 per cent; directories 4 per cent; radio 3 per cent and cinema 1 per cent. The total amount of money spent in the UK alone came to £16.562 billion (IAB, 2011). Although on hearing the term online advertising you might think of banners and pop-ups, these in reality are a very minor part of the online advertising business. Thankfully, pop-ups are mostly a platform of the past. For example, in 2010 search advertising dominated the online media market, with 57 per cent of all clients' money spent on online advertising being spent on paid-for search advertising. This is typified by the page that results from a Google search, which brings up preferred search links on the right-hand side in tandem with paid-for listings.

Indeed, as of 2007, the amount of money spent advertising on Google in the UK alone is now worth more than all of the money spent by clients on the UK's main commercial channel, ITV1 (Sabbagh, 2007). Google is perhaps the best example of a success story to emerge from the dot.com boom period. As well as changing the way that humanity organises and accesses knowledge, it has revolutionised the advertising business. Interestingly, the inventors of Google originally had very little interest in advertising and were instead deeply suspicious of blending advertising with search results (Battelle, 2005). While other portals were cluttered with banner advertisements, Google was keen not to slow the service down with extra load time. Although Google is now ubiquitous and wealthy, up until 2001 it was struggling to find a business model that would generate any revenue.

In addition to the not-so-exciting sponsored Google link, we can illustrate some of the other things that are happening to advertising. Whereas up until relatively recently a media planner's job was relatively simple as they only had a small number of media platforms to choose from, digital media alone now includes display advertising, locative media, geo-tagging, augmented reality, viral formats, metaverses, social media campaigns, classifieds, search and the humble sponsored link. Also, their job is not only to choose channels, but also to think about how content may interact across different platforms in a 'transmediated' or 'convergent' fashion. A key change is in the way that advertising is now less often pushed at us, but rather that we may seek, share and even create content. For example, consider the 2007 American Superbowl. Television slots during the Superbowl are the most expensive advertising spaces in the world – ever. However, in line with notions of convergence, co-production and prosumerist discourses discussed in other chapters, in 2007 consumers themselves produced one of the advertisements. The American public relations agency Ketchum (note the blurring distinctions between advertising and PR!) recognised that the snack brand Doritos' 18–24 target audience was a highly tech-savvy market who spend a great deal of time online and reasoned that, to build stronger brand relations with their customers, why not let them design the adverts themselves and let them 'Crash the Superbowl' (IPRA, 2007). The number of viewings via YouTube and similar televisual content players ensured that Doritos had massive exposure before the game itself, as well as mass exposure during the game (Google 'YouTube > Crash the Superbowl' for a selection of entries for the competition).

Such developments seem to resonate with other ways in which the boundaries between producers and consumers of media are breaking down. In UK advertising, perhaps the

'Above-the-line' media

encompasses high-profile traditional mass media such as television, news-papers and radio. The term originates from when advertis-ing agencies were paid commission for sourcing media outlets for a client's advertising. 'Below-the-line' is when a standard charge replaces commis-sion. Typically, it refers to sales promotion such as direct mail and email. 'Through-the-line' involves all media types. The idea here is that all communications sing together so to deliver a more comprehensive campaign.

Viral advertising

(and viral marketing) is a phenomenon of online activity that exploits existing networks in order to spread advertising messages, brand awareness and so on. It is commonly framed in terms of the self-replicating infectiousness of a biological virus and the way in which it spreads through a body. Viral advertising may be composed of 'pass along' messages, coupons, static animation, photography, Flash Player imagery, 'advergames', and, of course, videos.

most famous example is that of Cadbury's 'Gorilla' (as well as 'Eyebrows') that was remixed, given different soundtracks (progressing from Phil Collins to 50 Cent to the EastEnders theme tune!). The point to recognise is the radical alteration of a media environment low on technical and social interaction, to one where we may interact more closely with brands, their adverts and on occasion their agencies. A critical question we should ask about this new relationship of advertiser and consumer is: are consumers in control or is this a simulation of control in which consumers 'labour' to do the work of agencies themselves? This refers not only to the technical task of making, remixing or mashing up adverts, but also redistribution across social networks and microblogging platforms. Through the use of word-of-mouth-styled **'viral' advertising**, and advertising that relies on users and consumers to forward advertising to peers, agencies have managed to access media-savvy audiences, reduce their costs on media by asking consumers to spread their messages for them, and gain credibility by getting friends to share their content. Such audience activity, modes of consuming and distribution of advertising is tantamount to what Lazzarato (1996) designates 'immaterial labor'. This concept refers to a situation where cultural and informational output of people is harnessed or exploited by others for purposes of capital generation. In this situation, it is unclear whose creative labour has produced the advertising, who it belongs to, and who is responsible for distributing the advertising – the agency, the user, or somewhere in between.

Viral messages are typically characterised by humour, originality and also timeliness, due to ease of production and dissemination across newer forms of media. There are exceptions to humour-based adverts, for example Dove's 'Photoshop', but on the whole they tend towards absurdity, jokes and on occasion wit. They are also often risqué, going beyond conventions permissible in traditional above-the-line media. For instance, one advert for the lingerie company Agent Provocateur features pop star Kylie Minogue, dressed in her underwear, riding a bucking bronco. This advert was deemed too risqué for its intended outlet in cinemas but went 'viral' instead, resulting in 360 million viewings via video-sharing sites such as YouTube. Another advert for Diesel models itself on an 1980s porn film. Likewise with the UK launch of the condom manufacturer Trojan, who were able to say things about their brand online that they could not do through traditional platforms. Trojan's adverts were picked up and circulated by viewers to the tune of 35 million views. The textual qualities of such adverts also lend an anarchic value, as seen with other brands such as MTV, Xbox, Ford and so on. To explore these issues, see the viral advertising company 7th Chamber (www.the7thchamber.com/) for an example of how viral adverts are promoted, seeded, disseminated and analysed. As mentioned on their services offered page, they gather 'analytics on the wheres, whens and whos watching, LOL-ing and WTF-ing your social media content' (7th Chamber, 2011). Also see Kontraband (www.kontraband.com/), one of the 7th Chamber's networks, for many examples of viral adverts.

Doing media studies

Branding the self online

Examine your own Facebook, Myspace (if these exist once you're reading this) or other social media page (analyse someone else's if you do not use one). How have you styled yourself? What pop/subcultures do you align yourself with, if any? How have you organised your pages in terms of layout and type font? What do you link to? Are your 'favourites' strategically chosen? What forms of prose/lexicon do you use? Semiotically speaking, how have you framed your profile pictures? What cultural language or discourses does it draw upon? Ultimately, what does 'Brand You' consist of and how have you constructed it? To what extend does it differ from what you consider to be the 'real' you?

Lastly, what advertising or promotion does your site feature and do these adverts reflect your lifestage and interests? Does the advertising reflect your behaviour and interests online?

The fact that they are forwarded between peers means that consumers can be thought to be using advertising texts as a mechanism in creating their online identities and using edgy advertising as a means of 'branding the self'. It is another example of the ways in which we manufacture and manage idealised versions of ourselves through social media. These practices are born out of a consumer culture interested in self-promotion, self-branding and the production of ourselves as market-friendly objects.

Beyond conscious acts of mashing up, remixing and reposting commercial content, what is interesting for those of us involved in studying consumption is how media owners and data-tracking companies monitor our online behaviour. Account planners within advertising agencies traditionally analyse populations in terms of demographics (age, gender, marital status and socio-economic grades), geo-demographics (location), psychographics (values and attitudes), lifestyle (interests and buyer behaviour) or mediagraphics (types of media consumed). There is now an enormous growth in monitoring consumers and their activities in real time as they use media. This provides all concerned with much more detailed information than hitherto available.

Data mining
refers to the automated analysis of databases and information using tools that look for trends or anomalies without knowledge of the meaning of the data.

Data mining

It probably does not come as a surprise to discover that many companies track your consumption patterns and movements online. What is remarkable is the centrality of data to the digital economy and the extent to which information is mined as we traverse the web. This is known as '**data mining**'.

The aim of data gathering is to refine product offers and advertising to deliver a more personalised and individual experience. As opposed to traditional big-brand advertising, which works on a broadcasting model with the knowledge that there will be a large degree

Advertising in the digital age works on an increasingly and subtly individualised basis, as Amazon's recommendation facility demonstrates.

Source: © 2010 Amazon.com, Inc or its affiliates. All Rights Reserved

of wastage, personalised advertising aims to go further than the narrowcasting model and engage users on a more or less individual basis. This is a key change in how the media work. That is to say, the intensification of data mining has resulted in increased online personalisation and tailored media consumption, as opposed to mass ritual experiences. Driving these developments, 'data mining' involves the extraction of meaning from large bodies of information so as to facilitate refined targeting.

This is what drives online behavioural advertising, i.e. tracking users' browsing activity over a period of time for the purposes of serving advertising tailored to what organisations working on behalf of advertisers assume are users' interests (McStay, 2011a, b). Behaviourally targeted advertising that utilises longitudinal profiling techniques has been in operation since around the late 1990s. The most common form of behavioural advertising is third-party web-based behavioural advertising that involves an additional party in the form of advertising networks (other types of behavioural advertising involve collecting data through ISPs or simply tracking behaviour across one website or domain).

Advertising networks are companies that connect web publishers and media owners with relevant advertisers, or agencies working on their behalf. Advertising networks' success stems from the number of web publishers they have signed up to their services. They collect and use information when an internet user visits one of a number of websites participating in that particular network. The modus operandi of behavioural advertising is to display advertisements according to who is looking at a particular web page, rather than according to the content of the page itself. This is an important point as to know who is looking at a web page requires a fair amount of information about their online travels.

Online behavioural advertising uses previous online user activity (having to do with pages visited, content viewed, searches, clicks and purchases) so as to generate a segment or cluster that is employed to match a user with a relevant advertisement. For example, having bought a new external hard drive I might then log onto Facebook and find adverts for either hard drives, or (more usefully) related products such as USB pen drives. My interests revolve around mountain biking, so most adverts I receive tend to relate to this. The point, though, is that I may visit sites unrelated to mountain biking, for example the *Guardian* website, where I receive adverts for bike-related products. On mountain bike forums I then receive adverts related to products I have bought elsewhere (desk lamps, for example). Advertising, then, may have nothing to do with a page's content and everything to do with the person looking at the screen based on their prior behaviour. These methods of tracking users across the web so as to display more relevant advertising have created polar perspectives of surveillance and efficiency. On the one hand it raises questions about access to our data trails and rights to privacy; on the other it makes advertising more relevant and pays for many services we use for 'free' (we may well consider ourselves as giving payment in other ways). As services that mine by location such as Foursquare become more popular, and people increasingly 'check in' with services such as Facebook, advertising becomes even more refined, tailored and personalised.

Such techniques are part of a wider phenomenon of 'dataveillance'. This involves the surveillance of electronic data. Technically speaking, it is 'the systematic use of personal data systems in the investigation or monitoring of the actions or communications of one or more persons' (Clarke, 1999: 2). Tracking techniques include, but are not limited to, marketers' 'loyalty' schemes; internet tracing including cookies, adware and spyware;

Thinking aloud

Under surveillance?

Online technologies and their tracking of your daily consumption habits have privacy implications. What you do online, when you do it, and with whom, as well as what you say, look at and so forth may be examined. Do you think such techniques are invasive, or simply part of everyday life nowadays? Is the concept of privacy being redefined in light of new media developments?

chip-based identification such as radio frequency identification (RFID) and biometrics. We can, of course, also add behavioural advertising to this list that involves the use of cookies.

While there are many arguments to suggest that online tracking technologies compromise our individual privacy, others suggest that many of these dataveillance and tracking tools help streamline daily life. Companies that use dataveillance in order to develop a direct relationship with users, based upon their personal activity, are thus engendering relevance and offering a personalised service. However, many dataveillance theorists argue that it is not isolated acts of monitoring that are problematic, it is when information is collected, 'aggregated' and combined with other datasets. Ball *et al.* (2006), in their comprehensive report on the condition of surveillance and surveillance studies, note that it is fruitless to think of the scenario as sinister or totalitarian. They rightly see it as the outcome of 'bureaucratic' processes that have to do with the intensification of systems of control so as to achieve a desired outcome. In our case, this has to do with control over markets.

According to Danna and Gandy (2002), it is the unintended consequences of data gathering that give rise to problems. For example, certain groups may receive special treatment based on ability to pay, while others fall by the hard shoulder of consumer culture. Other areas that require us to be critically aware are the ways in which information processing and clustering (grouping) may reinforce and perpetuate traditional identity stereotypes (for example, disability, gender, race, class, nationality and sexuality). As people interested in cultural studies, this raises questions about the cultural logic that underpins the mining of data and the inferences it draws from relationships (e.g. as you are a given demographic and are interested in X, you may be interested in Y). What we might designate 'the politics of code and algorithms' are a concern due to the generalisations made about consumers through their click-stream data. Though plainly computer code may not hold views, it may contain biases (Turow, 2003; Terranova, 2004). Outside of critical and cultural literature, algorithmic errors have long been recognised as problematic in the marketing research literature due to problems associated with choice of appropriate metrics, selection of variables, cross-validation and external validation (Punj and Stewart, 1983). Stereotyping is inevitable where the nuances of complexity have not been ironed out and the heuristics involved in profiling are fallible.

Rejecting consumption as a modus operandi: adbusting and 'culture jamming'

While consumption for those of us in capitalist societies appears a way of life and inevitable, there are many who reject this and posit alternative visions for how we might live. Adbusting, as promoted by the crusading magazine, *Adbusters*, is the flip side of corporate-driven consumer culture. It is an environmental philosophy with a twist: if external reality may be polluted, might our 'internal realities' be polluted by informational toxins? Their answer is a most definite yes. Adbusting, also known as 'subvertising', is about 'jamming' culture and the circulation of commercial messages and consumerist values they promote (Lasn, 1999). 'Culture jamming' is thus the disturbance of the cultural logic of branding. It takes advertising and spoofs it to highlight social concerns and, above all, to reject consumerism and the ways in which it nurtures desire without end. 'Culture jamming' intends to throw a spanner into circuits of culture and what its practitioners believe to be the predominance of advertising and corporate culture in defining who we are, what we purchase, and the identities that are created and sold to us by advertisers. It rallies against consumption as a cultural status quo, and among other things decries the superficial relationship between identity and consumerism. On this basis, it seeks a more authentic way of being.

Founded by Kalle Lasn and Bill Schmalz, Adbusters was originally a magazine with its main office based in Vancouver, British Columbia, Canada. It describes itself as a 'global network of artists, activists, writers, pranksters, students, educators and entrepreneurs who want to advance the new social activist movement of the information age' (Adbusters, 2008). Adbusters has affiliation with sister organisations such as L'Association Résistance à l'Aggression Publicitaire in France, Adbusters Norge in Norway, Adbusters Sverige in Sweden and Culture Jammers in Japan. Adbusters has also launched numerous international social marketing campaigns, including 'Buy Nothing Day' and 'TV Turnoff Week'. These events seem self-explanatory but the very idea of adhering to an injunction to buy nothing at all for a day, or to keep our televisions off (do computers count?) entirely for seven days, indicates the pervasiveness and reach of our consumer and media culture.

Adbusters does not consider itself as belonging to the political left or right, but describes itself as being 'straight ahead'. Adbusters argues that, environmentally speaking, in both mental and physical terms, the growth of the consumer society has been catastrophic. Although most well known for its anti-consumerist stance and spoofing, or jamming, of advertisements, it is a magazine of some sophistication (see http://adbusters.org/spoofads for examples of spoof ads – many will be familiar). It is worth noting that the Adbusters Media Foundation also operates an 'advertising agency' for not-for-profit companies. Adbusters is thus not anti-advertising per se; it is against the way in which it believes advertising has been utilised by corporate companies and government, and the influence that advertisers have over wider mass media.

The future of advertising and marketing

Crystal-ball gazing is a dangerous activity, particularly when forecasts are published in books that take some time to reach their audience and are expected to have a shelf life of at least a few years. However, there are discernible arcs and trends that can be teased out from the history of advertising and media. The results of these have already been alluded to in this chapter. Key words include: participation, location and data. If we cast our minds beyond the immediate history of media we see a distinct trend from broadcasting models of media to more tailored forms. There is no reason why this should decrease in intensity although one should be mindful of bandwagons and 'the next big thing'. Mobile media have been lauded for a number of years as the next big thing for advertisers. This stems from straightforward reasons: people tend to always have their phones with them, they may provide location-sensitive data, and so many people possess them. Few people keep any other medium so close to them.

The downside for advertisers involves issues of privacy and the fact that people are not as keen as advertisers might like in disclosing where they are and what they are doing. Whereas social networking provide benefits of connectivity, the benefits of location-based services such as Foursquare are less obvious. Locative technologies are interesting, though, particularly when we think in terms of interacting with places where we happen to be. In addition to being a receptacle for targeted advertising of shops and amenities, locative and contextual information helps us users negotiate new spaces. There is much interesting opportunity for advertisers to engage with potential customers.

As mentioned in other chapters, increased levels of participation are a key trend in contemporary media use. This is no less the case with marketing. While big-brand advertising campaigns that utilise television and ritualistic media will not abate, we increasingly turn to our peers for assistance in product decisions. It is important then for those wishing to market their products that they engage in sophisticated public relations activity through social networking so as to be cast in the best light. Important, too, for brands' reputations is that they respond quickly to product or service failures. While social media may quickly make people aware of brands and new products, they can ruin brands within a short space of time. New media tend to be much more communal than traditional media forms and, as we know, people in communities gossip. Many in the business community see markets as being about conversations and relationships (keep in mind the discussion of simulated intimacy earlier). What this means is that, rather than manufacturers pushing their wares at us, businesses now have to negotiate with us and 'talk' with us. Although these Web 2.0 discourses are hyperbole, the discussion itself represents noteworthy media and cultural development. Whereas in the early days of heavy consumerism manufacturers sought and arguably fashioned mass consumption through mass media, today's highly competitive environment means that companies have to react to and engage with us on a much more individual level. More recently, as businesses become measured by reviews, feedback, tweets and comments, a power shift has occurred as consumer choice is widened. However, while this is true, the cultural logic of participation in consumerism reinforces consumerism both as a modus operandi and a way of life.

A key challenge then for marketers is how to steer this conversation and present brands in the best possible light. Thus, while the bastions of marketing, advertising and public relations still hold, there is much crossover between these disciplines. It is noteworthy too that many companies that once proudly described themselves as advertising agencies no longer have the word 'advertising' on their homepages. So as not to be pigeonholed they refer to themselves using words such as creativity, ideas, disruption and communication. It appears that advertising is becoming passé.

New media, new media studies

Online search advertising

As media students and scholars we do well to recognise the relationship between the changing media environment and the role of advertising therein. One thing has not changed though: advertising continues to fund the majority of media channels, although the ways in which it does this have changed. As the relationship between media and advertising develops, so should modes of analysis and critique. Whereas historically, much attention to advertising utilised semiotic-inspired critique of advertising, we now require additional tools. Whereas in the past much analysis of advertising revolved around the text, how it is constructed, what it might mean when considered within a wider cultural matrix, we now turn to other factors. There is a simple reason for this: much online advertising is, textually speaking, not very sophisticated. More remarkable are the mechanisms that target and place advertising. Take, for example, advertising on Google's services (e.g. email and search engine). Most striking is the lack of visual representation (it is often just a link or a sentence). Second is how relevant some of the advertising is. It is utterly unbranded and based on algorithmic analysis that only aims to engender applicability to the consumer. Relevance and usefulness to consumers is generated by minimal mediation. The key virtue of search advertising for advertisers is that it targets consumers when they are most interested and searching for information about products and services. For consumers, the upside is that we do not receive irrelevant information about products and services we are not interested in. In addition to semiotic modes of analysis that assess complex advertising texts, we should better understand: the technologies that underpin behavioural advertising; how data is bought/sold/shared between data gatherers; the political and legal environment that facilitates privacy incursion; theories on privacy and the economics of new media.

Summary

Investigating the consumer society and advertising

In this chapter, we have examined some of the relationships between media, consumption and advertising. We have seen that 'consumer societies' started to gather real momentum during the industrial period, when goods became easier to produce and reproduce. This led to the necessity of a consuming public that acquires goods not only for needs, but also wants – although the debate between what is a want or a need is a can of worms in itself. Advertising was one of the means of communicating to newly forged consumers, telling them what was available but also what could be done with consumables. Advertising has both developed enormously and barely changed. As mentioned, many of the strategies today, particularly in the beauty and cosmetics market, are highly similar to advertising well over one hundred years old. The promise of youth does not seem to age. When flicking through magazines or wandering through a department store, this is worthy of some reflection.

As advertising developed, it became more focused around the process of branding. This has to do with differentiation of products. Although branding originally referred to the 'hallmark' of the product, it came to mean something more than this and began to take on aspirational factors. To some extent, products and their brands have divorced, arguably with the brand taking on primary significance. Again, there are very few of us who are not affected by brands although there are many that claim not to be. As Bauman describes, brands form ingredients for the recipe of life in 'advanced' societies. Saatchi and Saatchi, an advertising agency, refer to brands as 'lovemarks'. They are seductive icons that bypass rational assessment that none of us escape, despite protestation to the contrary.

However, in the popular imagination advertising can mean all sorts of things, and it's worth being precise so we know exactly what we are investigating and critiquing. Advertising is frequently confused with the packaging of goods and other areas of commercial communication having more to do with marketing. For critique to have any meaning, we should at least be clear about what we are discussing. Advertising is usually thought of as something that is characterised by the utilisation of paid-for media. However, digital media have upset this tidy definition. As mentioned in the discussion of viral advertising, many people repost advertising content on social media sites, so giving creators free media space. Blurring boundaries even more, some are keen to get further involved and on occasion even make or remix adverts themselves. More generally, much advertising has become interactive.

Other key developments in online advertising involve dataveillance and the tracking of consumers' surfing patterns. While some might argue that data gathering is unimportant, it certainly means something to data miners. The economics of data mining drive digital developments forward. Should this be unclear, it is worth asking: how exactly does Google make money? It does this through the precise targeting of advertising. Likewise, as we do not pay to use Facebook, it has to make money somehow. This is done through the buying and selling of consumer data. As suggested in the chapter, use of Ghostery to determine which data miners are gathering information at any time is highly illuminating. Although large-scale broadcast branded advertising is not going to disappear any time soon, it is fair to say that the future of advertising is about getting closer to consumers and their consumption patterns.

While it remains useful and interesting to assess traditional advertising forms as a social index or barometer of culture (in regard to stereotypes of femininity or masculinity, for example), it is currently pointless to examine behavioural advertising from a textual perspective, as has been predominant within analyses of traditional advertising by scholars in media and cultural studies. A much wider appreciation of systems of production is required. Approaches involving political economy (also see Chapter 5) are useful so as to understand institutional aspects of new media ownership, behavioural advertising systems, and the political and legal systems they operate within. We should also examine closely our interaction with behavioural advertising systems.

As we surf digital content and our data selves are bought and sold by data harvesters, we might also enquire about the nature of the stereotyping. Again, these clustering techniques are not without a cultural political dimension, particularly in regard to forms of the heuristics, biases of profiling and the ways in which we are labelled.

Questions are thus raised about privacy. Do we really want people and organisations listening in on our conversations or following us around the web? Whereas traditional media such as press, television and other forms may be used in relative anonymity, newer media tend to be bound to digital networks involving monitoring and surveillance. Also, unlike television and traditional media, the internet is an open structure and by logging on we open ourselves and potentially our data to the entire internet. As boundaries between private and public are utterly blurred, it is the inability to process this idea that leads to improper care of personal data. As we surf the web we behave as if cocooned, isolated and private. In reality, what we do is highly public as we leave data trails across the web to be gathered and analysed.

Loosely put, privacy concerns revolve around the challenging of the distinction between public and private life. A right to privacy follows from the premise that privacy acts as a form of clothing, barrier or mediator. Privacy then is something we wear in digital environments and something we should care for. Some may of course choose to remove it for incentives, while those unwilling or unable to pay for services may be coerced into being naked. From this we can further clarify the division between traditional advertising and behavioural. Although they are part of the same continuum, and behavioural techniques are an extension of traditional market and audience research, behavioural strategies seek to render us transparent so as to more fully map our likes, favourites, wishes, dislikes and even moods.

Then there are those who actively challenge such developments. Adbusters acts as a rallying point for those who eschew consumerism and corporate advertising techniques. Although some of their views are extreme, they highlight well some of the effects that consumerism has on the environment, both physical and mental. As such, they call upon interested individuals to do more than criticise from the outside, but to get involved and participate in the jamming of capitalist culture and consumer society.

If you have followed this chapter through, engaged with the activities and thought about the Issues covered, you should be able to:

■ Identify, research and outline the key features of the advertising industry, and practices and concepts of consumption and branding. (As with our approach throughout this book, it is useful to continue to analyse those adverts and their different modes of delivery as they come to you in your own consumption. Likewise, locate and explore the nature of some of the companies we have mentioned throughout this chapter in order to see what they do and how they do it.)

■ Explore and engage with issues and debates around theories of consumerism and the consumer society.

■ Begin to recognise the impact of social media on advertising practices.

■ Understand that contemporary practices of advertising raise ethical questions about privacy and the distinction between what constitutes private and public.

By developing your reading and research, and by making connections between chapters, you should be well placed to explore and evaluate the role of advertising and media in contemporary consumer society.

Doing media studies

Evaluating the consumer society

Research and articulate the relationship between advertising and consumption further. Some suggestions:

■ Research Adbusters and do some adbusting or culture jamming of your own. Choose a brand or company and spoof it. The best spoofs tend to have an underlying political message, but be delivered with wit.

■ Essay: in 1500 words provide an answer to the following question: 'What are the pros and cons of consumer society today?' Discuss in reference to self-interest, materialism and economic benefits.

■ Consider the extent to which discourses of Web 2.0 have affected the advertising industry, paying particular attention to Lazzarato's notion of immaterial labour.

Further reading

Adbusters (magazine) (www.adbusters.org)

As described in the chapter itself, *Adbusters* is indispensable reading for critics of advertising and cultural environments where brands play an inordinately large role in lifestyle choices. It is misleading, however, to think of *Adbusters* as simply a rant against the advertising and media industries, as instead it often contains moving articles on the fallout of a culture predicated on idealised versions of beauty and other pressures present in consumer societies.

Ultimately, it is about how humans relate to their physical and mental environments. It also contains insightful analysis into alternative models of economics that consider human happiness more important than fiscal progress.

Adland (http://commercial-archive.com/)

Adland – entirely unrelated to Tungate's book – describes itself as the 'beyond-a-blog, commercial-laden delirium of heaven and hell for advertising addicts'. It is a great resource of interesting advertisements spanning all media forms from around the globe. If you are interested in creativity and advertising, you could do worse than have a look at this free resource.

Klein, N. (2000) *No Logo*, London: Flamingo.

Although having seemingly been around for ever, this is a highly relevant and topical book; its ubiquity and popularity belie its depth and scope. Essentially, it is about corporate irresponsibility and the relationship between brands and lifestyle choices. Whereas products purchased at one time had to do with utility, we now use products and brands as a means of defining ourselves. Klein also highlights questionable treatment of workers in terms of employment conditions, wages and workers' rights.

McStay, A. (2009) *Digital Advertising*. Basingstoke: Palgrave Macmillan.

This book lays out the wider terrain of digital advertising and associated cultural processes. It traces the growth of digital advertising, starting with its use as fringe advertising media, to become a dominant global advertising media form. Examining advantages, disadvantages and ethical dilemmas of using digital media, this book requires you to consider your own ideas about the field. Chapters combine industry and critical perspectives, alongside example material and interviews with the editor of *Adbusters*, media owners and senior figures from the wider international advertising industry.

McStay, A. (2011) *The Mood of Information: A Critique of Online Behavioural Advertising*. London: Continuum.

This book will be particularly useful if you are interested in the privacy and behavioural advertising material in this chapter. You may find some of the material a little advanced, but it represents the most thorough examination and critique of behavioural advertising and dataveillance you will find.

Tungate, M. (2007) *Adland: A Global History of Advertising*, London: Kogan Page.

Books on advertising come in all sorts of guises but this one offers its readers a detailed account of the history of professional advertising. It is extremely well researched and brings to life the trajectory of the advertising businesses and the people instrumental in forming it. It is not an academic book (you might find it in WH Smith!), but it forms excellent reading for anyone wanting to know more about the history, rise and development of the advertising industry.

PART FIVE

HISTORIO-GRAPHY

There is just one chapter in this part of the book, which concerns questions of media and history, and the methods by which we might produce histories. As in the previous sections, this chapter builds upon themes, approaches, skills and assumptions built up across the rest of the book and draws upon the various approaches introduced throughout.

In this part, we do not offer a history of media but, instead, think about what such a thing might look like and how we might go about 'doing' media history. Thus, this chapter explores the particular nature of media history, the fact that media represent history in their various forms and, indeed, the fact that media are part of our wider sense of history.

Chapter in this section:

Chapter 14: Media histories
Explores the role of media in making history and how to make sense of the history of media forms and institutions

CHAPTER 14

Media histories

Source: Corbis

Exploring media and history

Pebble Mill was the first purpose built broadcasting centre for television and radio production in the UK. It opened in Birmingham in 1971, and was finally demolished in 2005. It signalled a commitment by the BBC for production outside London. At its height over 1500 staff worked at Pebble Mill, and the building was responsible for around 10 percent of BBC output. Radio and Television production in Birmingham has now moved to the Mailbox in the centre of Birmingham, and to the Drama Village in the Selly Oak area of the city.

There is an interesting project aimed at exploring the history of this production base that takes advantage of a range of new media forms. The project can be accessed at two sites: Pebblemill. org, which collects interviews and sources as well as a Facebook site (http://www.facebook.com/ pebblemillstudios?sk=info).

The latter has over 800 members, many who worked at Pebble Mill - in all areas of production, administration etc - and who have uploaded artefacts and contributed to this collective memory project.

While there are some existing histories of work produced at Pebble Mill, this project is of a different order for the way in which it explores memories of production in a democratic manner and including anyone and everyone involved. In so doing this online collective produces the raw materials from which wider histories of broadcasting practice might be constructed. Group participation in recording history in such online sites — making institutional, professional, collective and personal histories — is strikingly different from other media and history work which is managed by professionals with some sense of what the outcomes might look like.

Such sites offer ways of thinking about how the history of media production is a part of everyday life — just as media products have become a means of defining our lives and collective histories. At the very same time we must wonder what it must have been like before the internet enabled the sort of participation on which such Facebook groups and others are built that allow these new ways of producing history collectively and make it available. Just think: no email, no online social networking, no MSN, no Wikipedia, no file sharing, no i-Tunes, no Skype and so on. Imagine! So, the further lesson here is that like all media the internet too has a history. Each medium came into existence for a combination of reasons, and understanding them is the purpose of media history. By starting with a phenomenon like Facebook, we can quickly start to generate some fundamental questions that lie behind our social experience: How is it that the internet came about? Who created it and to what end? In what ways has it been used and how can we explain and understand the ways in which it is being used now? How does the internet as a whole interact with other media? How has it impacted upon those media? Even more interesting perhaps is the wider question of how has the internet impacted upon society and culture as a whole?

What we will do in this chapter

In this chapter we will explore the meanings of history and what this field has to say about studying media. You will have noticed that even though in the earlier chapters of this book we have focused on production, texts and then audiences we often discussed each with historical examples. These little snippets of media history explain an idea or give you a broad understanding of the issues we are working with. In this chapter we will reflect a little more on this process of making media histories. We will also consider what media have to say about history too, about what media forms and institutions as well as what we do with media can contribute to our understanding of the past.

To this end we will explore some of the themes and key ways of approaching historical questions, ways of doing media history, as well as approaches to evaluating the historical materials and methods available to us as media scholars.

We will not be attempting the much harder task of writing the complete history of the various media. There are many such histories available to you in any library, and it is important that you read and study as many of these histories as you can on whatever topics you select for your own research. At the same time it is important that you start to develop a critical engagement with these histories. Writing media histories involves far more than simply reproducing the historical accounts published in these books in the library. Although they have been written by media scholars who have spent significant amounts of their time on their studies, an important part of your development as a media student needs to involve developing an awareness of the usefulness and limitation of existing studies, and the skill to conduct your own. Accordingly, this chapter will introduce you to the skills of the media historian, so that you can produce your own histories of media, interpret the histories written by others, and explore the ways in which media produce history.

By the end of this chapter you should be able to:

- Define what is meant by history and historiography.

- Discuss the distinctive features of media histories, and explain the uses and limitations of media as history.

- Generate questions for studying media history.

- Produce a timeline to represent the chronology of media development.

- Research relevant secondary and primary sources and evaluate their reliability as historical evidence.

- Make research plans for histories based upon aesthetic, political-economic, technological and socio-cultural approaches.

KEY TERMS: 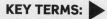 aesthetic; archives; chronology; contemporary; historiography; history; media as history; oral histories; the past; political-economic, technological and sociocultural histories; primary and secondary sources; timelines.

Thinking about media history

Before we can actually do media history, we need to give some thought to how we should approach the task. This necessitates some thoughtful reflection. There are so many histories around us – and media forms in particular are full of many histories from popular to serious in tone – that it is very easy to believe that we understand clearly and instinctively what history is, and how we could do it. As we have seen so many times in this book, though, scholarly study demands a different sort of approach from that widely carried out outside universities. Although we may actively access histories – perhaps as part of our online fan activities or through TV history programmes – once we start reflecting on exactly what history is, and how we should and could study media history, we begin to see there is more to being a media historian than we would first think. It certainly involves far more than getting at some facts about the past from the internet. To introduce you to the sort of reflection that has taken place among scholars we first want to ask: what is history, and then, what is media history?

What is history?

The past
is simply the time before the present. That is, everything and every aspect of existence and events – large, small, noticed or unnoticed – before the immediate 'now'. As you get to the end of this sentence your reading of it is already a thing of the past.

We each have a strong sense of history. **The past** precedes the present, things were different before, and what we have today is the result of what once happened. It seems quite strange, therefore, to ask the question: what is history? However, in proceeding we need to get to grips with some fundamental distinctions in order to conceptualise the process of researching and producing histories, what **history** is made out of, and what is at stake in 'doing' it. Any historical project needs to recognise the distinction between three things: the past, history and **historiography**.

Defining the past, history and historiography

The word 'contemporary' is often confusing in the context of the past and the present because it can refer to either place in time. In essence something that is contemporary exists at the same time as something else. However, that can mean it is in existence now (contemporary to us) or that it existed at the same time as someone or something we are talking about (they were contemporaries). We use the term quite often, so you will have to be careful that you realise whether we are talking about contemporary with the present, or contemporary with past events we are examining.

These definitions and distinctions are likely to 'make strange' the issue of what exactly history is. By talking about history as stories, and historiography as the act of writing history, we are making explicit the selective nature of how we understand the past, and how it is made for us.

History
refers to a narrative or a story about what happened in the past. We also use the term for the chronological record of events that we understand to form the past. Finally, people also talk about history as the university or school discipline that seeks to record or understand the past.

Thinking about the past

One of the tasks of the historian is to think 'into' the mindset of the past, exploring and assessing it within its own terms of reference, as well as our own. The mistake we sometimes make in thinking of the past is in imagining that living in a complex technological age makes us, as individuals and a society, superior or more complex than those billions who have lived and died before us. This results in what historian Edward Thompson calls 'the enormous condescension of posterity' (Thompson, 1963: 13).

A good example of the attitudes Thompson has in mind is the story of the 'invention of film' and how it was unveiled. A common version is that when the Lumière brothers unveiled their moving images in 1895, a short piece showing a train arriving

Historiography

is literally the act of writing the past. It is, then, what historians do. That is, the guiding principles, theoretical foundations and methods of historical research, and the re-presentation of the past. We specifically use the term to refer to the writing of history based on analysis, evaluation and the selection of authentic, original source materials and the use of these in a narrative. Finally, historiography can be used to mean a selection of historical literature, usually relevant to a specific topic or subject. So, it can refer to the articles and books about the coming of sound in cinema in the USA, the development of sound broadcasting in Europe, or the nature of the press during the First World War.

at a station, it so panicked the audience of factory workers that they stampeded from the hall showing the film. When this is told with authority it takes on the assertion of a historical fact. However, a number of problems present themselves with this account, and by looking at some of the facts of the past a variety of details can be assembled that question this version of events, suggesting that the account is probably apocryphal, possibly part of the promotion for Lumière films, and reflecting poorly on the original audiences for these films.

We can speculate that such apocryphal tales are a projecting backwards of fears and debates about the 'effects' of media forms on audiences on to the history of their pleasure in cinema. A cautionary take on such a tale suggests that it is far too easy to reproduce unthinking perspectives on media audiences of the past as somehow primitive and further back along a kind of developmental curve that leaves us in a privileged position. We might indeed be more socially and materially privileged than some of our forebears but we should not imagine that our perception, acuity or pleasure is in any way necessarily superior. The story here relies upon the counterpoint of a 'developmental' sense of history – that of historical development as rupture or fracture. The story relies upon a sense of cinema as 'invention', a new device complete with new practice (representing movement in real time), impacting upon the world as something revolutionary.

'Cinema' (or 'kinema' as it came to be known at that early time – from the Greek for motion) was in place already by the time of its supposed 'invention'. By this we do not mean at the technological level as a particularly original amalgamation of lenses, celluloid strips, process and development but as a series of professional practices centred upon public entertainment. Photography, itself the basis for cinema (16 frames a second on those first cameras and projectors), was being used by figures such as Eadweard Muybridge (1830–1904), Etienne Marey (1830–1906) and T.A. Edison (1847–1931) in devices such as the Kinetoscope in order to 'show' motion. Theories of the 'persistence of vision' were already well known and exploited in 'flickerbook' animations – a quick succession

Key thinker

E. H. Carr (1892–1982)

E. H. Carr's *What Is History?* (1961) is one of the most influential of all works dealing with the philosophy behind the historian's project. Some of the central arguments are provocative for anyone with a faith in the idea that history merely records the facts of the past. He argues that such 'objective' or 'empiricist' history is not possible. Carr suggested that the problem with such views is that the historian, as man or woman, cannot divorce themselves from the age in which they live, from the outlook and interests that characterise social perception and with that the perception of the past and what it means. He thus distinguished between 'facts of the past' (things that happened) and 'historical facts' (the things that happened that historians select for their stories of the past). So, he argued that when we read histories we need to recognise that what constituted facts were decisions made by historians, that 'facts speak only when the historian calls on them: it is he who decides to which facts to give the floor, and in what order of context' (Carr, 1961: 11). This is not to suggest that Carr thought history a redundant enterprise but instead that we should, in approaching any account, 'examine the historian' for who they are and where (or when) they come from as much as what they have to say to us! He saw historiography as 'an unending dialogue between the past and present' (Carr, 1961: 30).

of sequential photographs are shown rapidly – anticipating the process of cinema projection itself. Likewise, lens projection was used in puppet shows and fairground attractions around the world in order to tell stories, often achieving a range of highly expressive capabilities. The main objection to this foundational story, of course, is that it is hard to believe that anyone would mistake a silent, black-and-white representation of movement for unfettered reality. We should at least ask if the audience at the Lumière factory could imagine that a new railway line had been laid outside their factory in the minutes that they sat in darkness.

Such ideas of the past – of development and rupture – are often manifest in hyperbolic history writing and some student work. Whenever we use phrases along the lines of 'Steve Jobs took personal technology to the next level' or 'CGI technology made Hollywood blockbusters of the 1990s even more real for audiences' or 'The new propaganda techniques fooled audiences during the war', we slip into simplistic and condescending assumptions about the past. The lesson is that things are always more complex and, like much of the approach to media as scholars, we need to 'make strange' the common-sense ideas we sometimes bring to making sense of the world.

What is media history?

What is it that is distinctive about media history, then, as opposed to plain old unadorned history? Is media history, in fact, distinctive? Is there a particular way of doing history with, about or around media that is different from whatever mainstream, normal or 'pure' history might be? Whatever issues arise from these questions, the most obvious thing to observe is that media history is a way of thinking about the past with media at the centre of attention. In other words, media history is a way of looking at the past on the terms of the nature, use and dimensions of media informed by the various perspectives outlined in this book.

Source: Corbis

Produced by pioneering French film-makers Auguste and Louis Lumière, *L' Arrivée d'un train à La Ciotat/Arrival of a Train at La Ciotat* was filmed at La Ciotat, Bouches-du-Rhône, France, on 28 December 1895 and first screened to a paying audience on 6 January 1896. Did audiences, as some stories suggest, run screaming from this image? If such tales are myths what do they suggest about our view of the past and the history of media?

Key Theory

Totalising History

The French philosopher and historian Michel Foucault saw tendencies in historiography as aimed at producing 'totalising' histories where singular events and pluralities are reconciled to become part of a linear story with an underlying explanatory concept ('man', class, economics, progress, etc.) which leads inevitably to the constitution of the present and an understanding of the present as inevitable (Foucault and Sheridan, 1972: 9–10). In this way, his ideas have been identified as part of a postmodern moment, although he distanced himself from such labels.

Foucault's approach to history was what he termed 'genealogical' for the way in which it explored divergent, plural ways of life, knowledge and interactions of power (a major Foucauldian concern) which undermined attempts at linearity or a 'grand narrative' about the sweep of history. Like E.P. Thompson he tended to examine those events and people who were marginalised by traditional histories, and although he studies the histories of madness, sexuality and criminality rather than media his ideas have been influential (and controversial) in new histories of media. His arguments are a good guide to students of media history who wish to dig up the complexity of the past from the certainty of many of the stories we are currently presented with.

Within media studies and its sub-branches of journalism studies, advertising studies, film studies, popular music studies and TV studies we can find further sub-branches dedicated to historical research of that medium. The interests of the scholars in these areas encompass media texts, political economy and cultural study, as well as related issues around the development of technologies and their employment and use around media industries. It is in this scope of attention that the specific 'media-ness' of media history can be found. Media historians are well served by a whole subfield of specialised books and journals such as *Media History, Historical Journal of Film, Television and Radio, Journal for MultiMedia History* and *Early Popular Visual Culture*. Scholars who produce work for such journals, making contributions to this field, are often interested in contemporary media too. Historical research is often employed to better understand the nature of contemporary media practices, institutions and cultures. Explanations for the habitual ways in which we think and organise ourselves and are organised, institutionally, culturally, socially and politically, can sometimes be found in the study of the past.

However, media historian and theorist James Curran (2002) has suggested that the writing of media history is beset by a number of problems. First, there is the sense that most media histories focus on a single medium in isolation. He argues that this tends to result in very inward-looking accounts of, say, the development of television or film, with little sense of the wider historical role of such media.

Secondly, he suggests there is the related sense that media history is 'mediacentric'. By that he means that the histories tend to emphasise the same analytical tools and references that are found in the subfield of studies of any medium. Just as film studies tends to emphasise textual approaches to how films make meaning, for instance, film history has tended to tell us about the developing content of films; just as press studies tends to emphasise the role of news organisations, so press history has focused upon the development of those institutions. Even when media history extends its purview, it tends to relate wholly upon the plane of the media industries themselves and is, again, inward-looking and gives us little insight into the relationship of media and wider social contexts.

Curran's third point expresses a worry that these tendencies contribute to a weakening of interest in 'mainstream' media history. Thus, in the field of media studies 'non-historians' such as Marshall McLuhan have produced the most influential accounts. For Curran, such accounts privilege the development of technology, for instance, at the expense of a wider address to the nuances of context.

Taking these insights on then, we should be mindful that any study of the history of media is also, indivisibly, a study of how media make history and contribute to a sense

Doing media studies

Asking questions about the past

You can develop your grasp of how a historical analysis could inform our understanding of the present by generating questions about the past for yourself. For instance, present-day discussion about the development of transnational news services can lead us to ask questions about why broadcasting developed on a national scale in the first place, and why it is so often associated with forms of localness. Likewise, we can ask interesting questions about the way that popular music culture and the music industries have been organised around promoting and selling 'recordings'. We could explore the way in which recordings developed in different formats from 10-inch 78rpm shellac discs, to 12-inch 33rpm and 7-inch 45rpm vinyl discs, to 12-inch singles, and later DAT tapes and CDs, and how, with the advent of digitisation and MP3s, streaming, file sharing and so on, the assumptions, culture and economy of popular music have begun to alter.

Now try this for yourself. Using the short list of contemporary practices listed below, generate one or two questions about the histories that might explain them:

- the use of digital photography in news and entertainment papers and magazines;
- ideas of viral marketing used by PR professionals;
- interactivity in sports broadcasting;
- the role of trailers in the promotion of new film releases;
- the coverage of party politics in social media.

Now generate a list of five contemporary issues of your own, and then develop one or two questions for each issue.

of wider social, economic, cultural, political history. In an attempt to grapple with these issues Anabelle Sreberny-Mohammadi (1995) has inverted the way we usually explore the relationship between media and society as a whole to explore the ways in which different historical 'epochs' are characterised by the different communication technologies available at that time. Thus she explores the way in which 'orality', or speech, defined the ancient world and cultures such as those of the Greeks. 'Print' defined the English Middle Ages through to the age of industrialisation. Lately, we live in a period defined by electronic media, explored in her work via the example of US television. Her argument is that all of these forms are important in themselves, affecting how many people can be addressed and what methods of addressing them can be used as well as modes of interaction. This approach is one that evaluates the social and political impact these technologies have had, and explores their relationships with power and the ways in which access to channels of communication have been controlled and limited.

Media as history

One of the major challenges for the media historian is that media are involved in writing histories themselves, and often these are histories of any one medium itself. In this sense we could consider media themselves as a form of history. It is something of a cliché for instance to suggest that it is journalists who write the 'first draft' of history. However, correspondents from the far reaches of the world, and at home (wherever we live), are recording, evaluating, filtering and interpreting the world for us. Newspapers and TV, while

Woodstock

Source: Corbis

largely concerned with the unfolding 'now', anchor and locate their insights with reference to the immediate and sometimes the distant past.

There are three interrelated issues that we should reflect on here. First, because media record events and capture aspects of the moment, media texts are an aspect of the materiality of history. As media historians we can study media history, in part at least, through media texts from the past that are available to us. Embedded in the daily production of

Source: Corbis

Terrorist attacks on 9/11

Moon landings

Source: NASA

media and their recording or preservation is a history of media as a whole. Or at least these recordings provide us with some very valuable material to study; thus, media texts are historical texts. We will return to the question of how we should deal with these texts as media historians below, but we should pause a minute to note that history and ideas of the past – our past – are represented in and recorded through media texts, and revealed in media practices and institutions.

Secondly, media write histories both of the world and themselves. You only have to think about the abundance of TV histories, the way radio historicises music as 'golden oldies' in nostalgia shows and channels, and of 'where are they now?' features in magazines, to sense how great this activity is. Indeed, the internet sometimes feels like one gigantic, ongoing record of, and commentary about, the past. Films such as *Atonement* (dir. Wright, 2007), *A Knight's Tale* (dir. Helgeland, 2001), westerns, souvenir issues of newspapers, 'on this day in history' features on the internet, back-catalogue music sales, television reruns and revivals (as well as repeat channels, history and biography channels) and so on, all add to our sense of our past, its meaning and texture and our sense of significant moments, what counts and who counts in such stories. Media undoubtedly tell us about the very concept of history itself – of the wider politics, society, culture and context of its production and reception or use.

Doing media studies

Getting to grips with media as history

Media have been present to record events in ways and to a degree not available to our pre-modern ancestors. As suggested above, our sense of history is perhaps conditioned by filters and 'media moments' which affect the way in which we ourselves recall and memorialise them.

A key, albeit relatively insignificant, moment in English history, for instance, for a lot of people in England, is the winning of the football World Cup in 1966. For many the moment is crystallised in the words of BBC commentator Ken Wolstenholme: 'There are people on the pitch, they think it's all over. It is now.' In the UK, the phrase has become synonymous with this moment but also a moment of sporting glory, the 1960s in general and ideas about the value of the nation. Within the broader UK – across Wales, Scotland or Northern Ireland, the event may have less significance, indeed it may be understood in very different ways. For Germans (West Germany were the opponents that day as the country was still divided and had two teams), it has a different place in cultural memory, as it has for other football fans in other countries.

Identify and list *five* international events (try to find events outside your own country) that have been experienced internationally via media and shared beyond the boundaries of any one nation's perspective. Outline the event: what it was, where and when it occurred as well as identifying what kinds of media represented the event.

Examples: the Iranian revolution of 1979; first man in space; Indian Ocean tsunami; release of Nelson Mandela; opening of the Berlin Wall.

Finally, media set the agenda for our sense of history and what it is. Here the sense that history is being written is less clear, and it is in the assumptions that are made in the programming and editorial content of different media that we can start to sense something of their power to set the agenda for our ways of thinking. Taking each of these issues in turn we can get a sense of how we should engage with media and with history. As we have suggested, certain areas of media output give significant space or time to history as part of the editorial content. However, that should not lead us to believe that ideas of history are not implicitly at play on other occasions. For instance, even though the historical is rare in news reports – after all they tend to deal with 'current affairs' – it is certainly possible to argue that the way that news reporting is organised can lead to 'amnesia' about the past which eschews complex explanations of contemporary events. This tendency is revealed most forcefully when it is challenged by a dissenting voice, as detailed in our case study.

Case Study

Historical amnesia: George Galloway gives Sky News a history lesson

Here is an extract from a transcript of an interesting exchange between UK MP George Galloway and Sky newsreader Anna Botting. This took place in 2006 and is unusual for the way in which Galloway takes issue with how a story concerning the Middle East has been represented. His interjections seek to make points about historical events pertinent to current affairs, issues that the newsreader seemingly seeks to avoid. While this is a contentious item, and Galloway himself is not a historian, and would not be considered a reliable source by everyone, it illustrates how media workers, in 'recording' history, rarely have time to stop and consider the lessons and complexity of the past in making sense of the present.

Newsreader: . . . very good evening, good morning rather to you, Mr Galloway. How can you justify your support for Hezbollah and its leader Sheikh Hassen Nasrullah?

Galloway: What a preposterous way to introduce an item! What a preposterous first question! Twenty-four years ago, on the day my daughter was born, and I have just celebrated her 24th birthday, I had to dash at the maternity to see giving birth, from a mass demonstration in London against the Israeli invasion and occupation of Lebanon. Israel has been invading and occupying Lebanon all 24 years of my daughter's life. The Hezbollah are a part of the Lebanese Resistance who are trying to drive, having successfully driven most Israelis from their land in 2000 . . . It's Israel that is invading Lebanon! It's Israel that is attacking Lebanon, not Lebanon that's attacking Israel! You've just been carrying a report 'Ten Israeli Soldiers on the border getting ready to invade Lebanon', and you ask us to mourn that operation as if there were some kind of war crime! Israel is invading Lebanon and has killed 30 times . . .

Newsreader: (Interrupting)

Galloway (does not stop): . . . more Lebanese civilians than have died in Israel. So, it's you who should be justifying the evident bias, which is written on every line of your face and is in every nuance of your voice and is loaded in every question that you ask.

Newsreader: Right, the . . . you put your finger on the button, didn't you when you said that the Hezbollah was set up back in the 1980s in order to remove every Israeli soldier from Lebanese soil as you said had achieved that in 2000. This is a set-back.

→ Galloway: No, they didn't! This is a key point you are concealing from your viewers! Israel was forced out of MOST of South Lebanon in 2000! It still occupies a part of Lebanon since 2000.

Newsreader: (Interrupting) . . . subject to this latest UN draft resolutions [. . .]

Galloway: No, oh, please! Have a slightly longer memory than four weeks. I'm talking about the thousands of prisoners taken during the Israeli occupation, illegal occupation of South Lebanon. These are the prisoners that have to be released in exchange of the Israeli soldiers that were captured in the beginning of this wave of the crisis.

Source: The full transcript can be read at www. counterpunch.org/galloway08152006.html and the exchange viewed on YouTube

Galloway certainly held a controversial position within Britain, and knowing that he was adept at media interviews, Botting used a common journalistic rhetorical device to push Galloway to explain and justify his position. His response is to attack the general assumptions of the reporting of news, to claim that journalists are not paying attention to the history of the conflict on which they are reporting, and to make the contention that it is the

news service which needs to justify its position. One does not need to accept Galloway's position, or his version of history, to realise that the exchange shows that there are a number of ways to look at the issue, and that alternative positions on the contemporary state and history of these events have to be justified, while the editorial line of the news service is presented as fact.

As some commentators have suggested, one of the problems with modern media, and television in particular is that they suffer from a kind of historical amnesia.

A useful paper on the idea of historical amnesia can be found in an essay by Frederic Jameson on the 9/11 attacks (see Jameson, 2002). For discussion of this idea online see: Nick Stratton 'Historical Amnesia in the International Media about Haiti/Aristide myth' at Ezildanto.

(www.ezilidanto.com/zili/2011/03/the-historical-amnesia-in-the-international-media-about-haiti/); Stephen Roblin, "Historical Amnesia": Reporting The Conflict In Somalia' at 'Countercurrents' (www. countercurrents.org/roblin300509.htm). On the UK riots of summer 2011 see Rich Rubenstein's blogpost 'The British Riots and Historical Amnesia' (www.reasonstokill.com/2011/08/the-british-riots-and-historical-amnesia/).

Doing historiography

So far we have set out the sorts of issues we need to be aware of when we undertake media history. For the rest of this chapter we will set out some of the key ways in which you can conduct a media history of your own. There are three main areas of skill, which develop from the most basic mapping of history, through more development and engagement with the sources out of which histories are written, and finishing with a discussion of how we can write different forms of media history.

Producing chronologies: a sense of time

Chronology
is the arrangement of events in the order that they happened.

One of the simplest ways in which we can understand the history of media is through the order and relative distance from each other that things happened in the past. Whenever you start a particular historical analysis it is worthwhile trying to get the basic **chronology** right in your mind. Once you have a sense of the order, and timescale, in which things happened, then the more developed activities of interpretation become far easier.

A key way to grasp the historical sweep of different media is to be able to picture them all in your mind in a way that reveals their relative developments. Timelines are a useful way to achieve this. As we will see, there is a tendency with basic chronologies of media to build them on technological developments, and while an awareness of the development of the technology on which our mass media are based is very helpful, it can also lead us to the mistaken conclusion that technology is the major determinant of media development. For a basic **timeline** it is useful to represent three phases through which each medium goes: emergence (where the technology for communication is in place, but the institutions have not been widely established); maturity (when the medium is organised around recognisable institutions and professional practices); and adapted (where another medium takes over some of the medium's cultural functions). To illustrate: radio emerged as a technologically possible communication medium during the first quarter of the twentieth century, reaching maturity from 1925 onwards, and then adapting some time after 1950 as television took radio's place as the primary domestic medium. Television itself was technically possible well before the Second World War, reached maturity in the 1950s, and over the past 20 years has had to adapt first to the coming of video and then DVDs, and more recently streamed internet content.

Timelines work just as well with more specific studies. For instance we could examine the much shorter history of the computer game medium, which has become part of the wider new and web media forms that have characterised the late twentieth and early twenty-first centuries.

It is important that we are aware of the fact that, however useful a particular timeline (or the chronology on which it is based) is, it remains a selective representation of the history of that medium. Chronologies of dates and events themselves do not announce their

Timeline
is the representation of a chronology on a line of evenly spaced dates.

Doing media studies

Producing timelines

Undertake some research into the dates that these sorts of developments happened in each of the following media. Represent the periods with different forms of line, as we have done with radio and television:

- ■ ___ represents the emergent period;
- ■ _ _ _ the mature period; and
- ■ .... the adapted period.

Medium	1850	1875	1900	1925	1950	1975	2000
Press							
Photography							
Recorded music							
Radio			___ __ _ _ _				
Television				___ __			
New and web media							

Looking back at your representations, are you able to put some of these relative developments into words? How would you describe the development of media as a whole? What do you notice about this development over a century and a half?

significance or give explanations as to why selected events are pertinent to our understanding. Indeed, facts, figures and names in themselves offer little insight into the nuances, structure and meaning of everyday life and activity in the past – whether centred upon media or any other aspect of the world. Whatever we do with facts, figures and names, they constitute tools involving evaluation and selection as well as accuracy, awareness and thought about their relevance when used. For instance, in constructing a timeline for the development of radio, Martin Shingler and Cindy Wieringa mapped 76 events over 150 years covering over 12 pages of their book on the medium (Shingler and Wieringa, 1998). Such a detailed analysis reveals important key dates in the development of this medium, and is an excellent way to grasp something of the rich development of radio. However, like all chronologies it is also selective in which dates the authors see as significant. First, it gives most prominence to technological developments, particularly as the medium emerged. Secondly, once radio's mature period is being chronicled, the examples are almost always taken from the UK or the USA. Finally, most of the events selected in the mature and adapted phases of radio history relate to speech-based radio, rather than the dominant forms of music radio. In fact even using a generous interpretation, only 6 of the 76 events listed relate to music broadcasting. This emphasis reflects the overall balance of the book, and so it acts as a good introduction to what follows. However, we cannot see it as any form of objective history of radio, even though the listing of dates and facts seems to suggest otherwise. It merely accounted for what the authors thought was significant in the development of radio.

A critical sense of chronology is therefore an essential skill of the media historian. Not only do you need to develop a strong sense of what happened when, you also need to be aware that the events which we arrange on our timelines represent a particular emphasis, and therefore tell a particular version of history. You need to apply this same critical awareness when you construct your own timelines, and when you work through the chronologies produced by other media historians.

Case Study

Computer games

→ In this representation we have taken just three key aspects of computer games – the consoles, first-person shooter games and real-time strategy games – and plotted their development against each other.

Again, simply by laying out the different events against each other, patterns begin to develop. What explanations could you speculate for any of these developments and their patterns? If we add some further facts to enhance our list, how does that change our sense of the development of the games industry? For instance, by 31 March 2005, the PlayStation and PSone had shipped a combined total of 102.49 million units, becoming the first video game console to reach the 100 million mark. One of the most popular real-time strategy games, StarCraft, has sold 9.5 million copies worldwide. The storyline of the game follows a war between three races: the Terrans, the Zerg and the Protos. Half-Life's game-play influenced many first-person shooters for following years. It has since been regarded as one of the greatest games of all time with over 8 million copies sold. Half-Life is one of the best-selling PC first-person shooters to date.

→

Videogames consoles (Key consoles and year of release)	First-person shooters (Key games)	Real-time strategy games (RTS) (Key games)
Atari 2600 (1977)		
Nintendo Entertainment System (NES) (1986)		
Nintendo Entertainment System (SNES) (1992)	Wolfenstein 3D (1992)	Dune II: The Building of a Dynasty (1992)
	Doom (1993)	War Craft: Orcs & Humans (1994)
Sony PlayStation (1995)		Command & Conquer (1995)
		War Craft II: Tides of Darkness (1995)
	Duke Nukem 3D (1996)	Command & Conquer: Red Alert (1996)
	Quake (1996)	
	GoldenEye (1997)	Total Annihilation (1997)
Half-Life (1998)		Star Craft (1998)
Sega Dreamcast (1999)		Age of Empires II: The Age of Kings (1999)
Sony PlayStation 2 (2000)		
Microsoft Xbox (2002)		War Craft III: Reign of Chaos (2002)
	Halo (2003)	
	Doom 3 (2004)	Warhammer 40,000: Dawn of War (2004)
	Half-Life 2 (2004)	
Microsoft Xbox 360 (2005)		
Nintendo Wii (2006)		
Sony PlayStation 3 (2007)	Crysis (2007)	

Chronology courtesy of Brett Taylor

Qualitative data is not apparent in the timeline, and the mere appearance of a console or game does not in itself reveal its historical significance. In fact when the timeline was developed, its author was selective about which consoles, types of game and actual games he selected. His awareness of the scale of hardware and software sales determined his choice of item, and led to the distinctiveness of the timeline.

Doing media studies

Analysing other scholars' chronologies

Select a published history of a medium, or aspect of a medium, you are particularly interested in and abstract a timeline from the written account. Analyse the pattern of events and reflect on how the pattern you can see on the timeline relates to the narrative the author gave in their written account. Are there any differences between the two? If so, how can you account for these differences? Finally, is it possible to see why the author chose the events they did just by looking at the timeline? Do they emphasise technological, textual, institutional or cultural histories? Is there a sense of phases of an emergent, mature and adapted medium? Are the events part of a totalising history, where the selected events are there because they serve to show only the factors that lead directly to the current state of the medium?

Sources and archives

By now you should have a very strong sense that doing media historiography involves far more than copying facts and interpretations out of existing published or online accounts. Although all media historians rely on existing histories, they use them as only one of their sources of information about the past. As with any kind of academic research we can make a distinction between types of sources, where they can be found and what we are able to do with them. We can thus distinguish between primary and secondary sources.

Distinguishing between primary and secondary sources

Primary sources are those that we study directly or 'first hand'. In historical work they are original materials from the time period under scrutiny and have not been filtered through the lens of academic interpretation. They are 'raw', if you will. Primary sources might therefore include: media products (artefacts, commodities, texts) themselves; web pages, diaries, journals or blogs; interviews (promotional, legal proceedings, personal, via telephone, letter, email); letters; original documents (such as patents for inventions, the Royal Charter for the BBC, contracts); photographs; minutes and proceedings of meetings; statistical work (market surveys, public opinion polls, audience measurements, sales figures, census data).

Secondary sources are accounts written or produced after the fact, with the benefit of hindsight or critical distance. They are, as the name suggests, interpretations and evaluations of primary sources. Secondary sources do not usually constitute historical evidence although they do contain in them references, quotes and so on that derive from primary sources and, if adequately referenced, give the account its credibility (if we were studying academic writing and publishing per se of course such sources might indeed become 'primary'). Thus, secondary sources include: biographies; institutional histories; student dissertations; indexes; journal articles; and monographs. These sources also include all of those media sources that tell us about the history of media such as sleeve notes to CDs; biography channel TV documentaries; summaries and essays on the news of the week in newspapers.

Secondary sources provide commentary, discussion, evaluation and interpretation of evidence. These sources are the most systematically organised of any materials we seek in producing history. You will certainly find that any university library has histories of a whole range of media sectors, with specialist studies on a whole range of times and societies. Increasingly, summary versions of these histories can be found in online encyclopedias, and increasingly whole journal articles and books are available online. These are the kinds of scholarly work you should consult to find out about the background to your

Doing media studies

Surveying secondary sources

You will find that practice now in identifying secondary sources quickly will pay dividends when you have to do this for assignments and dissertations later in your studies. You should familiarise yourself with the libraries you use and how they organise their collections. Histories of different media are likely to be collected separately, and you may well find useful books organised under very different headings. You should think of the research job here as akin to a children's treasure hunt, where you move from clue to clue, but where the prize is the picture of the library's holdings and cataloguing system, rather than a single book.

Start with one book on the history of a medium you are interested in, and using the bibliography and citations in that book identify a further five books. You should find that at least one of those is available in your library. Locate this one, and choose five more references to search for. Just before you move on to another stack in the library look along the shelf to see what other books on your chosen topic are available at the same class mark. After just half an hour you will have identified a whole range of books and places where you can access secondary accounts of your chosen topic. With the titles that your library did not have to hand, speak to the library staff about how you could borrow these other books. Libraries will have a variety of lending agreements with other libraries which would allow you to borrow the book from elsewhere if it was essential to your studies.

media research (accounts of the founding of a newspaper or computer game production company for instance); what scholars have already said about a subject; and how they have approached it. In historical work, this is the historiography – the writing about the past, that which makes history out of the past. Thus, secondary sources are usually consulted to survey the historiography of a subject – to gain clues as to how to do or approach a topic, to address or generate questions about the adequacy of existing coverage, insights and conclusions.

Primary sources are the material out of which history is constructed. This is the material that records aspects of the past but is at best partial in that, however much of it is available to us, it and our use of it inevitably presents us with a fraction of the past. More often than not, however, historical sources, especially around media, are unevenly available, and in some forms can prove to be scarce. Where media texts have a market value, they are often more readily available, and as the channels for distributing media texts have extended major media organisations have bought up the back catalogues of other media companies, digitised them and made them available commercially. This makes some TV programmes, films, musical recordings, radio programmes and published journalism and photography available to us as primary sources. In addition, this material tends to be released with extended sleeve notes, or additional audio-visual material which can tell us a lot about the time and place that the texts were originally released.

Other material is harder to find. Again, though, institutional documents, statistical information and earlier policy documents have been digitised and can be accessed online. Some larger organisations have made consistent efforts to collect together these records of the past, and some have even organised them to make searching easier. These archives of historical material are invaluable to the media historian.

Doing media studies

Identifying commercially available media texts

Select a series of different media and time periods and research how widely available texts within this field are. You could approach this text in a number of different ways. Secondary sources may name some programmes or publications and you could then search for these on online retailers who have major holdings of that sort of material, or with the original publisher. Alternatively, start with a text you know, identify if that is available commercially, and once you locate a first text search for others using details of the publisher or broadcaster, the producer or creative workers, simply by the date. You could do something as simple as a search for 1970s TV dramas broadcast on commercial and public-service TV stations; perhaps music recorded by women in the 1920s; or news stories in popular newspapers about trade union industrial action in the 1950s and 1980s. Then again it could be early websites from the 1990s. Your own selections would be as interesting as the research.

- How successful were each of your searches?
- Why do you think the materials you found were available?
- How many sources that you wanted to find were available?
- Why do you think some were available, and others not?

Archives: collections of primary sources

Primary sources in media can be found in many places but historians often locate their activities around identifiable archives and 'do' history through archival work. An archive is any collection of materials. It does not really matter whether or not the materials were collected 'officially', or with the intention of coherence or preservation or as a repository for scholars or other interested parties. It helps the historian find what they are looking for, of course, if an archive is catalogued or ordered – which is itself an interpretation of sorts.

Media archives present scholars with the same issues they face in addressing the contemporary world of mass production and consumption. So many things were produced in the past that were deemed to be ephemeral and without lasting significance that few thought it worth preserving much of it (today's newspapers line tomorrow's litter trays). Likewise, the nature of media forms and how they were regarded was such that it was neither expedient nor possible to preserve some materials pertaining to organisation or output. Cinema in particular has suffered from the nature of its early material forms, which has affected its memory. As Matthew Sweet has written of British cinema:

> When cinema was young, it had no memory, no history. It told no stories of its pioneers: kept no records of its endeavours. The medium celebrated nothing but its flickering present. Past successes, when they were no longer saleable on the lowest circles of the exhibition system, became a burden and hazard to their owners. Forgotten titles were left to moulder in back rooms and storage cupboards, where they sometimes took their revenge by bursting into flames. More often, their volatility was cured by the furnace, or by scrap merchants who juiced old reels of celluloid for the silver and camphor they contained. When the trailblazing producer Cecil Hepworth went bankrupt in 1924, his entire back catalogue of negatives was bought by a dealer who melted them down into resin for water proofing the canvas of aircraft wings. Two thousand films, which had showcased Britain's first generation of stars, were liquefied.

(Sweet, 2005: 3)

Thus, the process of preservation (and therefore access to the past) can be difficult and problematic. Media industries have not necessarily found it useful or practical to preserve a record of their past. TV and radio, for instance, were both invented before the advent of audio and video tape. Disc records made of shellac (pre-vinyl material) were available and indeed recorded examples of the earliest radio transmissions do exist. But these were both costly to reproduce and, at the time, their use was hard to justify.

Furthermore, what possible reason would there be to maintain such a record? For a long time, everything was done 'live' and without thought for posterity. Interestingly, nowadays many media organisations are very careful about maintaining their archives. Recordings, images, texts are all eminently reusable and resaleable in our digital, media-saturated age. Furthermore, depending on where you live and dependent upon regulation, it may be necessary for media companies to keep a full record of their output for legal reasons. Sometimes, thanks to copyright laws, national archiving services have preserved complete print runs of newspapers, magazines and comic books alongside more regular 'literary' works.

The job facing the historian is both one of constructing adequate and convincing accounts of the past out of available materials and also, often, compensating for the lack of materials. On occasion, therefore, their job is one of 'retrieval', piecing together insights and compensating for absences in the records.

In some cases media archives can seem overwhelming in size, again presenting the researcher with problems of selection and emphasis, not to mention time and money available to conduct meaningful research. Here is the British Library's claim about one section of its holdings:

> *The pop music section of the British Library Sound Archive holds one of the most wide-ranging collections of popular music in the world. We do not believe in any simple definition of what constitutes 'pop' music and our collection reflects the diversity of styles that have been popular over the years, from early 20th-century music hall to the latest rock and dance music. We try to collect and preserve copies of every recording commercially issued in the UK. We also acquire pop videos, radio and television programmes and make our own recordings at festivals, conferences and seminars. All of these, together with our extensive reference library and online services combine to provide the premier public research facility for pop music in the UK.*

www.bl.uk/collections/sound-archive/pop.html

Thinking aloud

The politics of the archive

The availability and accessibility of artefacts reflects the nature of each medium, the institutional organisation behind it and the way in which it has been culturally valued. Newspapers and magazines have often been privileged, archived by national (and local) libraries. Many products of popular mass culture have been afforded little regard and often treated as ephemeral, dismissed as the trite products of a commercial, consumer culture and even unpreserved by those who produced them. The products of popular music for instance can be particularly difficult to locate and access. Historically, films have been equally difficult to access, in spite of the work of the national archive. While many works have merited commercial release on new platforms, first as video and now DVD, much remains unavailable.

In conjunction with these issues of the preservation of media artefacts, the politics of the archive are also inflected by social imbalances of class, race and gender. One

→

project designed to address the gender imbalance of the TV archive for instance is the AHRC-funded (Arts and Humanities Research Council), 'A History of Television for Women in Britain, 1947–1989', which is running in 2010–13. The project investigates British television's provision of programming of all genres addressed directly to an audience of women from its relaunch after the war to the end of the terrestrial period in 1989, a historical period which saw significant social change in relation to women's lives, the reorganisation of gender relations, the home and consumption. Researchers are looking at production context, programme texts themselves where they still exist (or reconstructed from paper traces where they don't) but are also consulting the audience for this television through interviews with women of different generations and regions across Britain. One of the main aims is to have an impact on archiving policies which have neglected programmes for women: this is a project with a clear feminist agenda.

At the time of writing, readers are welcome to participate in the project by joining a dedicated Facebook group (www.facebook.com/pages/Womens-Television/120561311355829)

The project team will use this group page to share news and publicise project events to members. Researchers particularly hope that members will use the page to chat about their memories of 'television for women'! The project team is Rachel Moseley, Helen Wheatley and Mary Irwin (University of Warwick) and Helen Wood and Hazel Collie (De Montfort University).

Finally, and despite obvious yet uneven difficulties in accessing media past, there are a variety of means at our disposal for constructing a sense of what lost and unavailable radio and TV programmes were like and how they were received. Contemporary reports, reviews and memoirs are all useful, as are less formal sources. Thus, media output has figured in important and indispensible ways in the scope of popular memory, marking out a collective history and the individual sense of social development. With the advent of the internet and digital distribution, outside of the formal, organisational record and archive, sometimes at the margins of legality, the 'fan-archivist' and online community have made memories and artefacts available.

Case Study

A job of historical retrieval

TV historian Jason Jacobs has sought to investigate the early days of British TV drama. His focus was on its incarnation between 1936 and 1939, when it was shut down due to the war (it was thought that signals might guide enemy bombers to central London) and its revival in 1946 up to the advent of ITV in 1955. In this 'aesthetic' history (see below), Jacobs's problem was that virtually no recorded examples of early British TV drama exist. This absence left unchallenged, oft-repeated assertions that programmes were little more than 'photographed stage plays' fitting in with the early view of TV as 'radio with pictures'. Jacobs used BBC written archives (production notes, scripts, viewer feedback, critical reviews, etc.) in order to 'reconstruct' how TV looked. His conclusions suggest that despite limitations in the medium, producers offered a range of innovative dramas and techniques. TV producers were, from the outset, 'self-conscious' about their medium and what constituted its possibilities and how to treat material and communicate with audiences. As a contribution to the field, innovating in technique and assumptions about how to deal with a major 'absence' of archival material, Jacobs challenges existing accounts, suggesting further ways in which historians might open up the exploration of a period considered 'lost' (Jacobs, 2000).

What seems initially to be a marvellous cornucopia of material for the media historian of the record industry can quickly invoke despair when faced with the challenge of deciding what to select for study. However, there are two key ways in which one can deal with both scarcity and over-abundance: by being focused and asking for help. If you have a clear sense of what you are looking for and why, you will spend far less time on fruitless searches because you will avoid meandering or the feeling of being overwhelmed. Archives are also usually staffed by knowledgeable and dedicated staff who can help you locate material if you have a clear sense of purpose and you spend some time building a relationship. Often the staff are delighted to find someone who shares their interests, and if you can communicate your enthusiasm and your professional approach they will be pleased to suggest examples and help you locate them.

It is certainly beneficial to be aware of local, national and online archives early on in your studies, and to have visited or accessed them to gain some sense of their holdings. Later, when you are researching for an assignment or a dissertation you will be able to judge swiftly where you can find the material you want, you will be familiar with how it is stored and catalogued, and you may have established a relationship with staff who can help. The web is a great way to identify these archives, and university and major city libraries will often have lists of specialist archives they hold, and ones that they know about elsewhere.

Searching online, and by making enquiries at your university or major public library, you can identify a range of archives that you can access with documents on an area of media history you are interested in. In the UK there are prestigious archives for film, newspapers, photography and BBC broadcasting. Most countries have their own equivalents. Local libraries often have local history archives, and they may well have materials that relate to a major media figure with some local connection. These less well-known archives may well hold material that has not yet been analysed, and could be the foundation for original work in your studies.

Oral histories

Media history does not have to derive from 'official' documents, media texts or artefacts. It can be derived from what people say in the form of oral history. Oral history is built from the verbal testimonies of individuals. These individuals may be media producers of any ilk, contemporary figures (politicians, businessmen) or consumers or audiences. Testimonies may be records of first-hand experiences from the time of production or consumption (think of individuals interviewed at the sites of award ceremonies, interviews with audiences about programmes for instance), or the moment of memory when an interviewer or historian asks for information or a recollection.

It is remarkable what sorts of information and interpretation one can gain from oral histories. Staff within your academic department may well have been involved in media production at a key moment of media history, and their testimony will throw light on events you are trying to record and interpret. Your parents or grandparents will have experienced very different periods of media consumption over the years, and their accounts can bring colour to the dry facts of timelines you may have constructed and offer strong qualitative detail on events.

New media, new media studies

Online memory making

In 2000, couple Steve and Julie Pankhurst launched the website Friends Reunited (www.friendsreunited.com). Inspired by the US-based Classmates.com, the Pankhursts provide a place for people to find out about what their old school-mates were up to and to re-establish contact with each other. The site organised exchanges between subscription-paying members based around listed schools and universities. By the end of its first year Friends Reunited could claim several thousand members, within another year over 2 million – an incredible take-up rate. At one point, the site claimed 18 million users, although not all were fully regis-tered subscribers. Like most web-based ventures the success of the site can be measured in financial terms and its waxing and waning fortunes are indicative of the uncertainties of modern media. The site was acquired by the UK independent TV company ITV plc in 2005 for £120 million. In March 2009, ITV announced that it would sell Friends Reunited as part of wider restructuring, selling the site for £25 million to brightsolid Limited, a firm owned by DC Thomson, a publishing firm most famous for comics such as the *Beano*.

Friends Reunited is in many ways a paradox: its operation and speed of success were only possible because of that most modern of media, the internet, yet the site is effectively retrospective – based on memory and nostalgia. The site is organised around forums dedicated to sharing memories of school, teachers and growing up, as well as wider aspects of social life. The comments in its public forum gener-ated some controversy and several libel cases, and it was cited in the break-up of numerous marriages as old flames reignited relationships. There have been spin-off CDs, books and TV programmes as well as imitators and spoof sites (Convicts Reunited anyone?). Subscribers to the site range from 'silver surfer' users in their later years, to individuals just out of school who are not only using the site as a contact base but seek to memorialise their recent experiences.

Friends Reunited can tell us a lot about the relationship between history and media. Although we may not always realise it, the site enables us to explore our own personal histories, and if we participate in it, to make that history. On the site our school lives are produced by what is recorded there, and we select what is there, for our own ends, both well meant and malicious. Ultimately, in its social media organisation and various forums, it has offered intensified, perhaps even new, ways of developing collective memory. The challenge for new scholars is to get to grips with the continuities of such media but also the way in which they challenge our thinking about media forms and social activities such as memory making.

Evaluating sources

Primary sources are vital fragments of the past. They offer us glimpses of what happened and, if we are sensitive to what we find, they can allow us to build a grounded interpreta-tion of the events of a particular time, and of their significance. We must be constantly aware of the reliability of the source and of its status as evidence. As we have seen, material survives from the past in uneven ways, and may have been preserved and made avail-able for a variety of reasons, many of which will make these sources selective and partial.

Doing media studies

Recording oral histories

Perform a simple oral history by asking someone with personal experience of production or consumption of media in the past. Perhaps they will remember a key point at which significant things happened or when things seemed to change. They will be able to tell you how they understood these changes. Get them to track back to an age before cable television, the internet, downloads, colour newspapers or MP3 players.

Think about the evidence they provide you with: how reliable do you think it could be? How much do you think the evidence will be limited by their memory of, or sense of nostalgia for, the events; or by the need to justify what they did at that time? What kind of evidence is it? How could you utilise it, or material like it, in research around media history?

Equally, we have to be aware of the selection we made when we searched. If we have fixed ideas of what we want to 'prove' it will not be surprising that we find evidence of just that as we research primary sources. The danger is probably greatest when we hold on to rather sweeping senses of history. Focused, small-scale studies which are carried out with an open mind, analysed systematically, and interpreted with the intention of understanding how things would have been understood at the time often make the best scholarly work. This is especially true when there are so many major media histories available as secondary sources.

Sources only become meaningful, however, when they are placed within a developed piece of historiography. As we have seen, accounts of the past are always 'stories', 'constructions' or 'arguments', but they are the most convincing when supported, as far as possible, by those indispensable anchors of factual evidence marshalled in support of interpretation and argument. It is to this aspect of doing media history that we now turn.

Writing media history

You have probably seen it written, or heard it said, that the triumphant side in any struggle – the winners of wars – always writes its history. This is an instructive aphorism because it tells us something about the relationship of power, perception and narratives in history. Whenever we research or write history we take some kind of position. This is not to say that scholars are wilfully prejudiced. They are themselves determined by the conditions that produced them. Our gender, class, nationality, education and politics may tend to colour what we are interested in, what we find out, how we write, and why we write history. This is not necessarily a conscious, or even a 'bad' thing: there are plenty of examples of overt 'projects' aimed at reclaiming people or events forgotten or marginalised in existing histories. Nevertheless, when reading history it is worth remembering to make a note of who the historian is.

That is not to say that a historian's background will determine the form of their history, but by asking these sorts of questions we are able to pinpoint that it has, largely, been white middle-class men who have written histories. This is mainly because those in positions of power (in politics, wider social institutions or media) have, hitherto, been white, middle-class Western men. That is certainly true of the main authors of this book. We have

Key thinker

Interrogating the media historian Asa Briggs

Asa Briggs (1921–) established his reputation within the mainstream of traditional history, specialising in the study of the Victorian era. His status as a founding historian of broadcasting history came with the publication of five volumes of *History of Broadcasting in the United Kingdom* starting in 1961. Not surprisingly, given the date, this work was mainly a history of the BBC: commercial TV was not established in the UK until 1955. In many respects Briggs can be labelled as an institutional historian, interested in policy making rather than personalities, decision-making processes and the contexts for the narrative that emerge out of the fragmentary perspectives on their subject. His major work on a media organisation reflects the approach he brought to the kinds of institutional, structural social studies he published previously.

Interestingly, Briggs's study was also commissioned and paid for by the BBC, a relationship that, perhaps, tempered any critical perspective that could be brought to bear upon the development, ethos and place of such an institution in national life. Ultimately awarded a title (a Lordship) and arguing for the PSB status of the BBC may place Briggs in a less than objective position for some commentators. Likewise his later position on the Board of Southern TV (a commercial company bidding for a broadcasting franchise) may have something to do with the critical position he adopted in surveying the history of ITV in *The Franchise Affair* (Briggs and Spicer, 1986).

His histories are seen from the 'inside', within the bosom of the establishment, viewing the history of the BBC largely from the perspective of its personnel, in relation to regulation. He tends to neglect the BBC's output and the wider reception by those millions who have constituted the BBC's audience as well as its funders as licence payers.

Of course, historians cannot cover every available angle and Briggs's encyclopedic work is itself a starting point for researchers seeking to locate their own project when examining the BBC. This institution is itself something of a dream for researchers as it has, like many public and paternalistic institutions, obsessively recorded almost every aspect of its activities since its establishment.

our own perspectives that we rely upon, consciously or not. We also have our own default settings in our approach to our field and however hard we try to present a nuanced and varied set of accounts, methods and versions of media studies we will never achieve total objectivity. The point here is to draw particular attention to the importance of interrogating the approaches of existing histories, and exploring the spaces available to the truly innovative scholar of media history, as well as the difficulties presented by 'recovering' of media history.

Our brief interrogation of Asa Briggs suggests that there are a number of different ways of writing media history. Each has its own value in opening up our understanding, but each also has its own limitations, and tendencies to fall into traps that might inflect the account. At the extremes these trap-tripping tendencies can be so pronounced that they actually invalidate the historical analysis itself. Because the past can never be captured in all the complexity that it existed we must always select what we believe is the most significant from all that could be available to us. For that reason the way that we write our histories is of paramount importance. Let us consider a range of possible approaches to media history that also schematically outline the ways in which we could go about researching, focusing and writing our histories. These four approaches we label:

1. aesthetic,

2. political-economic,

3. technological,

4. socio-cultural.

Aesthetics: histories of rhetoric, form, text

Traditionally, aesthetics refers to matters of beauty and taste. It also refers to issues and principles underlying the composition and presentation of creative texts – what they look like and why they look like they do, as well as what they seek to achieve in their relationship with audiences. Acknowledging our debt to the textual studies of literature, we could also call an approach that took account of these things a 'poetics' of media forms. The approach to aesthetics as textual practice, as communication, would track developments in expression, convention, tradition as well as innovations and experiments, their take-up by other media practitioners and across any medium (or media) or their possible rejection.

The aesthetic approach to history, then, encompasses aspects of those modes of textual analysis and understanding outlined in previous chapters in terms of the rhetoric, genre, narrative and semiological meanings of media products, but now focused on understanding the ways in which these have changed. We can draw on the skills of textual analysis we outlined in the first part but now use them to bear upon any historical text, or groups of texts, as a way into understanding them within their historical context or within a line of historical development and change. Historically, we can evaluate the achievements in various media forms, tracking developments, changes and experiments in form. We have already done something in this field when we looked at defunct genres in Chapter 2. A consideration of movies in this way might take account of how early films, restricted to black-and-white, soundless images, developed and extended a particular narrative style later incorporating sound and colour in order to attain 'realism'. Another approach might be to consider how newsgroups and social networks are organised and how 'emoticons' developed and have been used as part of the communicative discourse of online cultural practice.

Classic study

A.L. Rees, *A History of Experimental Film and Video* (1999)

Rees's analysis of a neglected part of film history shows how to investigate material and textual practices that are marginalised by the emphasis on mainstream texts. He recognises that film cognoscenti have developed a canon of avant-garde films to parallel the canon of Hollywood films which dominate traditional film histories. He explores how these alternative films of the experimental canon relate to wider art and political movements, and how they were disrupted by film-making in Britain rooted in media theory from the 1960s onwards. Although he draws heavily on a series of films as the basis of his historiography he widens the discussion to draw on a range of other historical sources, and his understanding of the social milieu in which the film-makers worked is well developed. Although a fairly short study it makes a marvellous secondary source for anyone wanting to study a single part of this history in more detail.

One aspect of this aesthetic approach to history is inevitably related to the formation of judgements about the most valued media products and ideas about what constitutes its best features and most worthy product, perhaps also marking out the worst. However, if we think of media texts in this manner, does this mean that we are appraising the most popular works, those media products and individuals (actors, writers, directors, for instance) who have proven the biggest hit with audiences, measured by units shifted, tickets sold, 'bums on seats'? Popularity measured in this manner does not always guarantee endurance or respectability, otherwise the *Police Academy* series of films might be considered to be the acme of the cinematic art. As Dave Harker (1992) has demonstrated, this approach would certainly affect our sense of the history of popular music and culture. As he commented, while the 1960s might often be commemorated through the work and achievements of the Beatles and particularly the LP *Sergeant Pepper's Lonely Hearts Club Band*, the biggest-selling LP of the period in the UK was in fact the soundtrack of the Hollywood musical *The Sound of Music* while singers such as Jim Reeves, Ken Dodd and Engelbert Humperdinck were equally dominant in the singles chart.

One argument in support of the validation of the best of media, whatever the criteria, is that this is exactly what producers, intermediaries and consumers are given to do. Media construct arguments around value based upon sales and audience numbers: the pop charts, newspaper sales figures, box office receipts, website hits, etc. But then there are awards schemes, often unrelated, superficially at least, to sales: Grammy and Emmy awards, Oscars, Baftas, etc. There are also 'greatest hits', 'best (and worst) of' selections used to sell magazines, TV programmes, DVDs and so on. Pop magazines such as *Q*, *Mojo*, *Uncut*, *NME*, tend to produce lists of the top 100 albums of all time on a regular basis while TV companies recycle their own product as 'The greatest TV ads of all time'. Our casual consumption of media, as well as our more committed allegiances as 'fans', subscribers and so on, is often constructed about value judgements: which websites are most entertaining or user-friendly, or which pop artists are the best. Critics (and media theorists) do this too but their selections tell us that any pursuit of an 'absolute' sense of good or bad can be a dead end.

If we examine the kinds of material that consumers and critics have valued in the past, as well as what they have neglected, and if we take 'endurance' (continued popularity and interest) as a benchmark then these categories appear to be remarkably unstable and changeable. Nonetheless, the production of what are called 'canons' – collections determined by taste and judgement – is important in critical and consumer thinking. While academics may have eschewed obvious and overt judgements about the material that they research this does mean that explicit aesthetic value judgements are missing in their work and approaches to history and research in general. Books such as this one often use repeated and familiar examples of films, newspapers and so on to illustrate their arguments and insights. Indeed, even if we shy away from making any aesthetic judgement about media texts we can track histories of popularity and critical acclaim as a way of historicising how and why media texts have taken the forms they have.

A history of journalism and the press for instance may be able to distinguish between the economics and audiences of broadsheets and tabloids but we could argue that this is to miss an obvious point of how they look and appeal to audiences. How they speak to readers and present stories is an integral part of their make-up and meaning. An investigation of a range of media forms, from film to advertising to popular music and speech radio, would soon reveal the sometimes static, sometimes dynamic, nature of rhetoric and genres, of how there is not a 'progression' to better or more refined aesthetic expression but certainly ways in which rhetorical devices have been wedded to popular appeal. Examples here might include the narrative realism of Hollywood and the limits of what is acceptable in portraying profanity, sex or violence, the enduring 12-bar, 3-minute format for pop, with its relatively limited subject area of heterosexual romance, the page design of social networks such as Facebook and Myspace, progressive levels of attainment

Doing media studies

Preparing an aesthetic history

Taking into account the factors discussed above, design a small research project that could explore historically located media texts. Remember, the more focused the study the better, and the more it examines a neglected area of study the more distinctive it will be. Avoid issues that would make your study 'totalising' in approach (i.e. assuming that absolute issues can be solved absolutely), and be thoughtful about how you select the sources you will draw upon. Identify a range of media texts, either contemporary with each other or to trace developments over history. Identify the sorts of issues that are likely to be debated around these texts and then identify the best textual analysis tools to tackle your analysis.

as organising principles in computer games. An investigation of aesthetics could, feasibly, marshal a sample of texts across a time period in order to investigate media rhetoric and its development.

Political-economic histories of the media

To think of the politics and economics of the media and related histories is to explore media as a business within a capitalist system. The economic aspect is at once one of the most important and determining aspects of media, but one that is sometimes under-explored. Such an approach would attend to a range of statistical data including costs – materials, contracts, charges, profit, loss, business reports, and disposable income of consumers. Wider contexts of economic growth and recession and so on would impact upon an understanding of the economic history of media. It would also examine the structures of ownership and control in media organisations and their economic and regulated relationships with their audiences.

This approach tends to qualify or problematise some high-minded ideas around 'aesthetic' questions and the nature of creativity in the media, especially when we consider that award-winning journalistic exposés of injustice in the press, tear-jerking popular music, 'rebellious' or 'transgressive' advertising and the movie-maker's 'art' are more often than not predicated upon the profit-maximising aims of media businesses.

One of the unavoidable facts of the nature of media, historically at least, is that they have proven to be prohibitively expensive to produce. Start-up costs for films, television, newspapers, radio and so on served to limit the kinds of people who have established media industries as well as determining the kinds of things that can be done with their products. In essence, if costs are high, then the pursuit of profit to some extent determines form and function as well as the accessibility of output – what a consumer can expect to pay for media output. Economics then plays a determining part in media production at a practical and aesthetic level as well as conditioning consumer relations. The conditions and conventions of media forms are not just products of abstract communication strategies, but then, before we strike too cynical and determining a note, media have proven to be singular kinds of businesses in that they are located around creativity and ineffable qualities such as audience appeal which cannot be thoroughly planned for or anticipated. As the venerable scriptwriter William Goldman, rather hyperbolically, announces in his book *Adventures in the Screen Trade* (Goldman, 1983), in the world of Hollywood commercial film 'nobody knows anything'. That, or they can't be sure about what exactly constitutes a successful film. For all of the recourse to focus groups, audience surveys, niche marketing and so on, the waxing and waning of the appeal of artists, programmes, films

Classic study

Russell and David Sanjek, *Pennies from Heaven* (1996)

The title of the Sanjeks' book is taken from that of a popular song of the mid-1930s, and combined with its subtitle *American Popular Music Business in the Twentieth Century* indicates the way it combines a detailed analysis of songwriting and recording of the past 100 years with an account of the business practices and economic society in which the songs were produced and sold. The book is over 700 pages long and based upon a decade-by-decade chronology. Nevertheless it manages to bring the detail of financial analysis alive by contextualising it using the people who produced and exploited the songs and the technology which reproduced them. A widely respected history, it is a model of how to conduct a long and detailed account that makes the single moment comprehensible, and the full history meaningful.

and magazines, demonstrates that there is no sure thing in this sector. Thus, as we explore elsewhere, historically media businesses are those in which a great deal of risk has been involved. Economic approaches would thus account for investment in particular media forms (experiments with form, supporting technological developments, etc.). Economic history also accounts for the relationship of media with wider monetary frameworks – taxation, trade tariffs on exports and imports, inflation, subsidies – all of which affect the production and distribution of media texts and meanings and indeed the activities of audiences and consumers.

Technological history

This is an approach that privileges attention to the technological developments that have facilitated the status of modern media as an area of 'mass' communication. The nature of mass media is indivisible from its technological status, from the steam printers that supported the press of the Victorian era, the celluloid, chemistry and electricity of cinema, wireless telegraphy in radio and of course the binary systems of more recent digitisation and

Doing media studies

Preparing a political-economic history

Again, reflecting on what has been said above, design a small research project that could explore how media organisations and the consumers of media products can be understood in terms of their political and economic relationships. The economics part of such studies often deters students and yet is often the most straightforward to conduct once you have got to grips with the analysis of media businesses we introduced in Chapter 5. Again this is an excellent approach for studying neglected areas of alternative production in music, broadcasting, film or the free press. Focused and detailed studies are always the most successful. It is not necessary to find out lots of economic statistics about companies or consumers because by applying underlying principles it is possible to analyse individual companies in their historical location. Having said that, it is remarkable how much information is often available about the economic structure of consumption and production at different times. By combining secondary and primary sources, quite sophisticated studies can be developed.

computer networking. Economic determinants have a role to play here in thinking about technologies and their development, and take-up by producers and users. Technologies associated with media have, traditionally, been prohibitively expensive to develop. What kinds of technology get developed, how and why and the outcome of their use is a matter for some consideration. Likewise, the aesthetic qualities and possibilities of media have been determined and enhanced by the available technology (sound, colour, reproduction – think about all of these aspects in whichever medium you next consume).

As James Curran bemoans (2002), one of the problems that often occurs in histories of technologies is that resulting narratives privilege the technology as somehow determining its application, use and success. This historiographical trap is usually called '**technological determinism**'. A related concept is a thesis of inevitability that relies upon a form of idealism as if 'inventions' are floating in the ether, awaiting discovery and thus application. With the benefit of hindsight, of course, when technologies become 'naturalised' or 'acculturated', their uses and benefits appear to be self-evident, inevitable even. There is, however, nothing inevitable or obvious about technology, its discovery or development, and ultimate form, appearance and application.

While technology is important, integral to our sense of the media – from the print and paper of the press to the bytes of digitised information in MP3s – it is embedded within a range of economic, cultural and social contexts that determine it as much as it appears to determine them. Raymond Williams (1992) has argued that the technological determination model presupposes that innovations are researched and produced within some kind of scientific bubble by 'great men'. The great men of media technology would thus be the genius inventors such as Thomas Edison, Guglielmo Marconi, John Logie Baird or Steve Jobs of Apple. These individuals and their genius lie at the heart of explanations of the appearance and use of media technologies which in turn support some of the stories we tell ourselves about society and history and the importance of the individual. This label of 'great men' is also useful in its focus on particular individuals (men), revealing how history often privileges stories of men at the expense of women and the role that they play in media and wider society.

Technological determinism

the theory that the technology developed by any one society in any era determines societal and cultural make-up (thus, the Stone Age, Computer Age, etc.).

Social and cultural histories of the media

In a sense, all media history is social and cultural in nature. The aesthetic shape, economic use and technological dimensions are incomprehensible without recourse to the societies

Doing media studies

Preparing a technological history

Because of the limits of technological determinism, this is the most difficult area in which to write histories. It is notable that this is also one of the most common types of histories of media. This is perhaps because the sources for factual information are the clearest in this area. Patents and the introduction of technological processes are usually quite well recorded, and for those interested in such issues there is some fascinating technical detail to master. However, the challenge of engaging with technology in a way that is not totalising is intriguing, and successful studies are likely to add considerably to our understanding of media. Probably, the main thing to do here is avoid obvious assumptions, and make sure that we think of the technologies as enabling. Marshall McLuhan (who ironically is often seen as a technological determinist analyst of the media past) has given a useful guide for our analysis when he suggested that the social significance of a technology usually works out as being very different from the motivations behind its invention (McLuhan and McLuhan, 1988).

Classic study

Michael Chanan, *Repeated Takes* (1995)

Chanan's study is subtitled *A Short History of Recording and Its Effects on Music*. The full title would suggest an idea that technological developments somehow determine social and cultural change, while in fact Chanan deftly relates technology to the complex social and economic world from which it comes. He is strong on the facts and detail of technological development of record formats, recording machines and domestic playback equipment, but he relates these to the detail of the organisation and practice of the music industry and other media. He shows how a lot of factual information can be communicated in an interesting manner, and how a narrative can explore the implications of changes in their historical moment, and in the longer history of sound recording.

and cultures in which media are produced and are consumed. By 'social history' we refer to the way in which media, their form and function are determined by contexts. Media have not in any simple way determined the form of our society, and media are not simply technological inventions, but products of the social arrangement of our society. Media have developed along lines that reflect the investment in some forms of communication over others. In totalitarian societies media were seen as potential agencies of control, and a state-controlled media developed to meet this social agenda. In relatively rigid hierarchical societies, media took on a paternalistic form, attempting to guide and set an agenda for the broader society. Such societies tend to have significant regulation and ownership controls. In more liberal, capitalist societies media are seen as another sphere for profit-maximising economic activity. The final social ingredient is the belief that media could serve democracy, acting as a public sphere in which debate and the free flow of information and ideas take place, or even a space where everyone can participate in communication. Of course, in truth, most societies that have developed over the past century have contained elements of all these ingredients and aspirations, and their media reflect an unfolding shift between these different imperatives. A major thrust of social media histories is to try to account for the links between ideas, social structure and mass media policy and practice.

This emphasis on the order of our societies also includes the study of the role of media in culture as 'a whole way of life'. These histories have tended to focus on the development of audiences, or the institutionalised cultures of professional media practice. These are perhaps the most demanding of histories to write because we cannot simply identify and discuss historical events from a contemporary cultural position, but must try to unpack the

Classic study

Susan Douglas, *Listening In* (1999)

Douglas's study is part subtitled as 'Radio and the American Imagination' and it offers a startlingly different analysis of the development of radio in the USA from the one usually built on technologically determined listening and institutional politics and high finance. She explores the changing form of radio, and a range of ways in which Americans imaged themselves from early use of wireless technology by male hobbyists to envisage a new geography of their world, through radio's institutional birth, the often welcome intrusion of African-American jazz into a white-American domestic world, the popularity of radio comedy that played with racial stereotypes, the role of information in world wars and the forms of music and speech which connected with new generations once television had become America's main domestic medium. The way Douglas has researched her take on the medium as a social and cultural form, and the way she writes that story in an accessible manner is a model for future histories.

Doing media studies

Preparing a socio-cultural history

Although the area of social history has been dominant within the wider field of media history, there are significant opportunities to design and carry out original studies. While most studies have been broad and sweeping, perhaps following developments in a single medium across decades, there are plenty of opportunities to focus on single moments in media history. Comparisons between the social context of different media at the same point in time are not very common. Studies which examine the competing pulls of totalitarianism, paternalism, commercialism and democracy at a single place and time would reveal much more than many of the more sweeping histories which tend to a totalising idea. Finally there are real opportunities to study the culture of media workers, the small institutions in which they worked, and the way in which professional values and workplace culture operated.

Generate proposals for some social histories which could be conducted within one of these undeveloped areas. Think about the factors we have identified as relevant in the conduct of such a history, and be aware of the limitations that earlier histories have faced.

sorts of cultural and ideological views that drove people to argue for different media, and to judge the media products which were produced. The field of cultural studies has been particularly productive in exploring how people's identities related to their consumption of media products which became part of their popular culture. These have been especially strong in relation to popular music and to the idea of youth culture, but latterly television and occasionally radio and other popular media have been the basis for cultural histories. By contrast, while the top-level staff of major media organisations have been the subject of quite detailed media histories, with the exception of some romanticised studies of the mavericks of the alternative and independent media, the everyday culture of professional media workers has been somewhat neglected in media history.

Media have been such a central part of the past century that almost any history of this period must engage with the history of media. The social networks of culture, the policies and political agendas of decision makers, and a more general sense of national milieux that contribute to group outlook and expectations, traditions, taboos and habits all make up the key field of social media histories. To approach social questions around media histories is to be concerned with the wider role of media in society and indeed how media are integrated and determined by particular contexts, assumptions, demands and conventions.

While Curran's critique of media history that we introduced earlier would suggest otherwise, it is clear from the classic studies of each approach that when done well it is often difficult to keep the approaches or perspectives listed above from 'leaking' into each other. While each insight is valuable, without the context of other approaches, histories can tend towards sterility. Whichever approach you choose to take in your own studies, ensure that you develop your textual, political-economic, technological or social history with some reference to the other ideas. The balance between a clear chronology, an awareness of the reliability of primary sources, reference to the secondary work of others and a focus on a clean line of argument is often very hard to sustain. You should worry less about producing the perfect history and concentrate on finding out things that really matter, treating them in a systematic and reflective manner. You have a number of very good histories to use as models. They can guide you, but in the end historiography is about writing accessible accounts of what actually happened.

Summary

Investigating and producing media history

In this chapter we have explored what we mean by history, and discussed what features of media history make it distinctive. We have also discussed some of the limitations of media history as it has been practised. With a critical awareness of this work you will be able to produce thoughtful historiographies of your own. The ideas and approaches that we have sketched out here offer only a starting point for thinking about this enterprise and one that needs to be considered in conjunction with the insights and approaches set out in the rest of the book. In the same way, it is hard to conceive of any of those other approaches – to regulation, text, audiences and so on, that does not in some way, implicitly or explicitly, deal with aspects of the historical in what they have to say about the media.

What we need, as scholars and thinkers, are names, concepts, frameworks and ideas for locating the ways in which we navigate our way around our subject in an attentive manner. We cannot do everything; and we cannot actually capture the past other than in a partial sense, and sometimes our job as scholars is to acknowledge such limitations. In doing so, however, we can at least sketch out how we might offer further avenues for work and consideration – had we time enough!

If you have followed through the discussion and activities you should now be able to challenge yourself to produce your own histories. These might be set as an assignment, or you may choose to give a historical dimension to a dissertation. Whatever their form it is useful to have a checklist of approaches based upon the schema we laid out in this chapter.

At the beginning we set out the things you should aspire to do by the end. If you have followed through the chapter and our exercises, drawing upon skills already developed, the things you should be able to do include the following:

■ Define what is meant by history and historiography.

■ Discuss the distinctive features of media histories, and explain the uses and limitations of media as history.

■ Generate questions for studying media history.

■ Produce a timeline to represent the chronology of media development.

■ Research relevant primary and secondary sources and evaluate their reliability as historical evidence.

■ Make research plans for histories based upon aesthetic, political-economic, technological and socio-cultural approaches.

It is certainly important that you can with some clarity explain what we mean by history and something of the considerations and skills of historiography. It is certainly helpful if you can write these out as simple definitions and a skill toolkit.

The skill toolkit includes the ability to generate research questions, often derived from contemporary issues, or from absences in current histories. It is certainly worth skimming through the chapter and making a list of the absences we have highlighted, as they will give you an extensive range of possible historiographies that you could apply to a range of media. Equally important is the ability to abstract chronologies in your area of study from secondary sources, or from initial research, and represent them on a timeline. This provides an overview for all your subsequent work.

At a more advanced level you will need to identify, analyse and interpret primary sources, often using archives. As you select and incorporate them into a written account you need to make judgements about their reliability as evidence for any claims you are going to make. It is one of the qualities of a good media historian that they are sensitive to what can be claimed, and what cannot. The greatest challenge, though, is writing up the history. Here you need to choose an appropriate approach – emphasising aesthetic, political-economic, technological, or socio-cultural factors – but contextualising it with an awareness of the other ways of focusing your history. It is especially rewarding to see how other scholars have met this challenge, and learn from their successes.

Doing your media studies

As you are reading this end part of the book, it is likely that you have worked your way through the contents of the individual chapters and would like to see how all of this can be summarised and concluded. Alternatively, you have jumped to this part of the book in the hope that the conclusion contains a quick summary, so you can decide if the rest is worth reading. The aim of this conclusion, however, is not to outline the end of a journey, but to prompt the start of a new one, whichever category of reader you fit into. It is a way of taking stock – and that is, in part, what we will do here – but this conclusion is mainly about what to do next. It is about doing your own media studies.

In the Introduction, we made the point that we have not set out to produce a comprehensive account of the entire range of media for you to learn. There are lots of examples in the chapters that should give you a good sense of the diversity of media and the way that they function in modern society. We have tried to choose examples which make you think about the diversity of media in modern society in a way that treats each example as distinctive. Most often, the example was a way of applying an idea or a concept, or a way of getting you to do something.

Everything in this book is there as a way of demonstrating that students learn best by doing, and that your study – media studies – is an active process. The entirety and range of media are too pervasive, too complex, and have too long a history for anyone to produce an analysis comprehensive enough to satisfy everyone. Additionally, like all college and university subjects, different people have different views on all of that complexity. The book has been organised and written to help you become a media scholar. That is, to help you become someone who can actively understand some part of the all-pervasive variety and complexity of media for yourself.

The Introduction also laid out the proposition that you should build your active scholarship on the studies of media that already existed. Again, though, we have not attempted to produce a summary of all the existing studies of the variety of media forms, organisations and modes of consumption. That is a massive task in itself, and there are already some very good books that aim to do just that. As with the real-world examples that we selected, we have chosen existing studies when they show why and how to take a particular approach, or they have been a key contributor to the way that other scholars in the field of media studies think and analyse phenomena and practices. Being a scholar will involve both studying media and studying studies of media.

If you have worked through the book, it should have become clear that being a scholar involves taking on a different perspective from the one we normally apply when we engage with media as a casual consumer. We need to be less interested in our own passions and opinions (although these have value), and more interested in being focused and systematic in our analysis and reflections. We should want to understand the world as it actually is, rather than argue that it is the way we would like it to be. This is a very ambitious goal, and such an understanding is well beyond the achievement of a single individual. That is why becoming a media scholar is also about joining a community of other people who are doing media studies. This community includes your lecturers, all the other students making such a commitment at your university or college, and all the academics and students undertaking media studies across the world – whether they sit under the label of the field or outside of it. When they have practised enough, some of these scholars will have their work published so other members of this community can read, judge and respond to it, as well as learn from and use it.

What you will need to do

As authors of this book, we argued right from the start that taking the particular perspective of a scholar means doing a number of things. It certainly involves building on the studies of media that already exist. By reading and thinking about these studies you can learn a lot:

- **Questions:** you can start by understanding the sorts of questions that are asked about media and their place in society. You can also judge which ones have been answered, and which ones remain in need of investigation. What is worth noting from such studies too is the productive way in which questions are phrased in order to promote investigation and reflection.

- **Technical terms:** you can learn about and use the technical language in which we discuss the issues around media. Understandably, given that we want to be focused and systematic, this language is more precise than the terms used in general conversation about media; sometimes we use the same words with more precise meanings, and we also use terms and ideas that you will not find in general usage.

- **Analytical tools:** you can also learn and use 'the tools of the trade', the analytical concepts and approaches that allow us to comprehend the dynamics of media texts, organisations or moments of consumption to understand what is going on. We aspire to be 'clean-fingered mechanics', making sense of the functions and operation of all aspects of media.

- **Theoretical ideas:** you should not just take the published writing of a scholar as truth; you need to engage with their arguments and the ideas they deploy to set these against the studies you carry out and your own thoughts. In doing so, you need to evaluate the usefulness and limitations of the way they have abstracted the complexity of the world into a set of ideas we can use to think through the issues.

  Like in a mechanic's apprenticeship, by building on the studies of others we learn how to do the job. At its best, to use another metaphor, we can 'stand on the shoulders of giants'. Many of the people who have studied media have been some of the greatest minds and scholars of the last century and by building our own work on theirs we can raise ourselves up, and see further than we could have without paying attention to their work. However, that should not mean we take what they say for granted. Their approaches, like those you will develop, will have uses and limitations. They point the way for further studies, and your job is to carry out at least some of those studies at the same time as you learn to be a scholar yourself. There are a series of other things you should have started to learn to do, therefore:

- **Raise your own questions:** these will be questions which remain unanswered in the work of other scholars. They may remain unanswered because they ignored them to focus on something else, or because their background biased them away from looking at that aspect of the world. Then again, it could be because the world has changed, and new questions must be posed. There are certainly an enormous number of questions about media that remain unanswered, and there are lots of opportunities for you to contribute part of the answer.

- **Engage with debates that matter to you:** because we contribute only part of the work of the academic community, we can choose areas that others have neglected, or which matter to us in particular. These tend not to be the grand ideas that the first media scholars tried to grapple with. We understand now that they were perhaps too grand, and that we need a tighter focus. And, in the face of the all-pervasiveness and complexity of media, there are so many issues that need investigating. Such issues of debate are usually impossible to answer conclusively, but we can usually contribute some empirical facts or insightful observations, so that we can push the debate on some distance.

- **Conduct your own analysis:** with a good set of tools, and a clear understanding of what the appropriate tool is at the appropriate time, we can undertake analyses of media texts, processes of production and regulation, or forms of media consumption. Such analyses should be linked to a clear question, and a wider issue of debate about something that really matters. Just taking a TV programme apart, for instance, is not intellectually productive unless it enlightens us in some way, or makes us see things in a manner that we did not see them before.

- **Develop your own theories:** the most advanced thing you can do is to offer generalised conclusions about the aspect of the world you have studied. This is to offer a theory of your own. It sounds a quite grand thing to do, and it certainly involves a lot of intellectual training and a focused and systematic mind. However, it is not such a far-fetched suggestion that by the end of your own studies you will be developing such theories. These are merely the conclusions, speculations and generalisations that you are asked to produce as part of your assignments and dissertations. Such a task is certainly the most demanding thing you will do as part of your study, but that is why it is given the most credit when your work is assessed as part of the courses you take in your own university or college.

What you will need to cover

This book is organised around five parts which reflect useful ways to think about the key questions in media studies, and the scholarship that has already engaged with those questions. As you start your own media studies, it is valuable to have in your head a broad sense of what characterises each of these five areas.

1 Media texts and meanings

'Text' is one of the key pieces of technical terminology in media studies. Of course, the word is in general usage, but in our field we use it to refer to the output of media in terms of their meanings. It is always important to remember that you will already know what a media text means. Media studies scholars have tried to explain not just what something means, but why it means what it means. That ambition should be at the centre of any studies you do in this area. Although scholars have offered a range of approaches, they each aim to deal with this fascinating question. Although some published works are quite philosophical, it is actually possible to take each of the ideas and turn them into analytical tools. It is important to remember that each of these tools has a purpose – they each unlock some aspect of how the text made meaning – and you must start with the purpose and not the tool if your analysis is going to have any value. As important, too, is the fact that you will need to use these tools of analysis in combination – where we unlock and connect several ways in which the text makes meaning – because it is only as you produce a rounded analysis that insight emerges. We established some basic approaches to textual analysis using ideas of rhetoric, semiology and discourse, and then examined wider structures of meaning in genre and narrative, before moving on to ask important questions about representation, and about the relationship of media and the idea of realism.

2 Producing media

Because we experience media primarily through texts, we cannot immediately imagine how they came into existence. If you are on a course where you undertake media production of your own, you will have learnt something about the technology and production processes which lie behind programmes and publications. Each of these processes is part of a massive industrial structure, which stretches from the film producers of Hollywood and Bollywood, through nationally based broadcasters and transnational satellite stations, to publishers, music companies and internet firms. All such companies are supported by a range of journalists, photographers, promotions workers and creative staff. To understand this diversity, we need some basic principles that we can derive for political-economic studies. These will include an understanding of the economic organisation of production, the hierarchies in different types of firm, and something of the ownership and control of media businesses. We must also be aware that firms cannot do as they please, and to some extent all media companies are subject to some forms of regulation of company ownership, production process or access to texts. Such ownership comes out of government policy, which in turn reflects a sense of the public good and a notion of the influence of media in society.

3 Media audiences

Studies in this area have probably had the most attention outside universities, and the higher profile seems to be linked to fears, or even moral panics, about the role of media in society. It is often taken for granted that audiences are common-sense categories of media consumers, and media must obviously influence the individuals and groups who make up these audiences. However, a more critical view would see that audiences are produced by media organisations in the production of their texts, and the means they use to first address them and then organise them as affluent consumers. At the same time, academics have constructed an idea of audiences as subject to the control of media power. This idea was often linked to the concern with media as a source of manipulation and propaganda. However, as media studies has developed, we have begun to realise that questions about what media do to people are often simplistic, and that we have had increasingly to ask questions about what people do with media. These latter studies have tended to focus on the culture of social groups, and the way that media operate within our lives and our senses of ourselves.

4 Media and social contexts

The shift in audience studies away from questions of effects to questions of culture is paralleled in a set of wider questions about media and our society. These are some of the most fundamental, and philosophical, issues with which we have to grapple in media studies, and they are often connected to some of the most abstract of media theories. Nevertheless, they also deal with some quite straightforward issues of debate that are generally discussed outside the academy. First, there are those issues related to the idea that media forms constitute a powerful force within society, either directly, or in providing powerful people with a means of influence. Secondly, media are seen to be a key part in a major shift in society that was well established by the start of the twentieth century, in which people started to talk about a mass society. Thirdly, by the end of the twentieth century, theorists were asking if society had again changed, this time into a postmodern age in which the certainties and confidence in the future had ebbed away, to be replaced by a more ironic detachment in which media had disconnected our senses of meaning from direct experience of the world. Each of these debates about power, mass society, the modern and the postmodern is intimately related to the nature of contemporary consumer society and the promotional activities of commercial media.

5 History

Finally we attempted to provide you with some skills of historical analysis through which you could understand texts, production and social audiences in their historical context. This remains quite a demanding activity because of the simultaneous role played by media in recording and narrating history. Nonetheless, with a systematic approach, a sense of chronology, and attention to aesthetic, technological, political-economic and social approaches to history, we can begin to appreciate both the continuities and disruptions of a whole variety of media forms.

What to do next

This book is intended as a stimulus for action, and so it is only right that we end with some straightforward things you could do to consolidate your studies, practise your new skills, and prepare yourself for the assignments and dissertations that will follow as your studies continue in your college or university.

Keep in touch with issues of debate around the media

Get into the habit each week of reading and analysing the coverage of media issues in the press, in broadcasting and on the internet. Many major newspapers have a weekly media supplement with several pages of news and features on media, and a section of jobs which, over the weeks, will allow you to build up a picture of the issues that matter to media professionals, and a sense of the range of companies and employment opportunities available. The *Guardian*'s Monday media supplement is the best known in the UK and, like the other titles in most major nations, it is available online as well as in print. There are a range of media-oriented features on radio, and occasional TV documentaries on media topics or media history. These programmes are increasingly available throughout the world on the internet. The web has been host to a vast amount of comment and news about media across the world. It really is worth setting up an RSS feed aggregator that brings together the content from all websites and notifies you when new posts are added.

Read a journal article regularly

Academic journals are the place that active scholars place their most up-to-date research. By reading regularly, you will get a sense of what issues are of interest to other media scholars. The journals usually publish two or three times a year, so if you regularly keep an eye on four or five journals, you will have a fruitful supply of articles. As the journals are published for other practising academics in specialised areas, some of the articles can be a challenge to read, but it is a bit like learning a new language: the more you practise, the easier it is to understand. Your university library will carry a wide range of paper publications, and increasingly current and back issues are available online through your library's website.

Apply what you have learnt regularly

Take 5–10 minutes out of every day to step back from your own media consumption and to apply some of the questions and analytical skills you have learnt. When you watch television do a quick semiological analysis. When you listen to your iPod, imagine all the companies involved in creating and distributing the music or podcasts to you. Ask yourself how they made money, and how you came to be listening to that bit of audio. As you pass advertising hoardings, just stop to ask yourself who the advert is aimed at, and how it uses media rhetoric to sell the product it advertises. When you pick up a newspaper on the train, see if you can find out which company produced it and how long it has been in existence. See how many examples of postmodernism you see in a day. Just doing these things regularly, and in an informed, systematic way, will turn you into a true scholar who can think through the issues and apply the theory quickly and accurately. There is true pleasure to be found in seeing the world in a new way.

Communicate about your media

It would be flattering to suggest that new scholars, born into new media landscapes, are best placed to engage with and understand these practices. This is not necessarily the case as many aspects of media studies have, to some degree, involved standing back from the everyday assumptions of media production and consumption in order to formulate meaningful questions. However, since the advent of digitisation, mobile technology and the internet, a whole host of practices have emerged that seem to challenge as much as continue traditional modes of communication. Formulating questions about a world of communication into which you have been born and raised is a useful place to start your studies. In addition, contemporary modes of communication from blogs to social media networks and sites such as Vimeo and YouTube, as well as the ease with which podcasts can be made and disseminated, mean that it is possible to communicate ideas to a wider community (of scholars, the plain interested and sometimes plain hostile) in a myriad of original ways. Blogging about your reading and ideas, in short bursts and often, is one way to address and perhaps build a community of interest beyond the classroom or scholarly community. This is perhaps the biggest opportunity for new scholars to consider what is new about media and how new modes of communicating research can work.

Ultimately, then, media studies is something you will do in relation to the degree that media interest you. This is where the great joy of the subject lies. For new scholars, grounded in what seems to be a rapidly changing environment, drawing upon and testing established concepts, you are well placed to ask the questions that will truly make media studies your subject.

Glossary

'Above-the-line' media: high-profile traditional media such as television or newspapers. The term originates from when advertising agencies were paid commission for sourcing media outlets for a client's advertising.

Advertising: a form of communication designed to generate awareness of products, services and organisations. Its purpose is to persuade potential 'customers' to purchase or to consume a particular brand, product or service.

Affect: the intellectual, emotional, psychological or physical responses to the rhetorical address of media texts.

Artefact: the physical form of media products.

Audience: an anonymous and variable collective of individuals addressed (as a group and individuals) by the organs of 'mass' media communication.

Avant-garde: a French military term for those soldiers who advanced ahead of the main force – the 'vanguard' in English. It came to be applied to these pioneering individuals groups in the arts whose work aimed to 'forge ahead' and to be new, consciously attacking tradition and the values and assumptions of the establishment or 'bourgeoisie'.

Cartel: a formal agreement among firms in an oligopolistic industry. Cartel members may agree (collude) on such matters as prices, total industry output, market shares, allocation of customers, allocation of territories, bid-rigging, establishment of common sales agencies, and the division of profits or combination of these. (See OECD, 2002 in Chapter 7.)

Chronology: arrangement of events in the order that they happened.

Class: a way of categorising social groups according to hierarchies of wealth, occupation, taste and culture.

CNN effect: a name for the process by which media influence government political policy at home and abroad.

Cognition: how we as individuals acquire knowledge as well as apply it; the process through which we comprehend events and ideas in order to understand the world.

Commodity: the economic or exchange value of media products.

Concentration: the degree to which control of a particular sector of media (or any other economic sector) is in the hands of the most dominant firms.

Consume: to eat or drink; to obsess; to use up; to destroy or be destroyed; to waste; to waste away.

Content analysis: a quantitative method of analysing the denotative content of media output based upon defined samples and recognisable categories.

Convergence: a term for the merging of different technologies and industries to create new forms of cultural product and new modes for their production and delivery. The term also refers to the flow of content across multiple media platforms, the co-operation between multiple media industries, and the migratory behaviour of media audiences, who will go almost anywhere in search of the kinds of entertainment experiences they want.

Copyright: the ownership rights that subsist within a creative work for its author to be recognised as its creator, to decide how the work will be used, and to derive income from that use.

Culture, version one: for Matthew Arnold 'The best that has been thought and said' and in this sense it is used by F.R. Leavis (and the Frankfurt School) as a label for identifying a set of attainments in fields such as fine art, classical music, literature and dance.

These attainments are usually labelled as the province of 'High Culture' and the products of the great names of history (Shakespeare, Michelangelo, Voltaire *et al.*). However, these ideas are often also allied to concepts of an 'authentic' 'folk culture' – i.e. something produced by ordinary people themselves within the context of their own organic traditions. This last sense is distinct from the idea of a 'popular culture' made from the products generated by mass media.

Culture, version two: a whole way of life. This more anthropological sense of the term is distinct from the notion of culture as a body of special artefacts. It allows for the practical and collective aspects of making meaning in ordinary life. This definition encompasses texts and the way that they are consumed and interpreted within the contexts of a culture. Thus, this definition also allows for popular culture to be not only that produced by the majority of people themselves in the ways in which they live but also the way in which those products which are produced for them ('mass' culture) are taken into their lives as meaningful.

Culture industry: those organisations involved in the economic rationalisation, organisation and exploitation of entertainment, cultural or aesthetic work to generate profit and to maintain the operation of a market system.

Data mining: the automated analysis of databases and information using tools that look for trends or anomalies without knowledge of the meaning of the data.

Diachronic: (in semiology) attention to language in terms of organisation and principles over time.

Diegesis: the internal story world portrayed in a media text.

Discourse: in Michel Foucault's work this refers to practices (language and actions) that systematically form the objects of which they speak.

Economies of scale: all of the ways that a corporation can save money through size – being big and acting big.

Empirical: based on experience or observation, and verifiable by observation or experiment, without recourse to a scientific or philosophical theory or system.

Ethnography: literally 'writing culture'. A study that involves observing and writing a description and analysis of some form of lived cultural practice and orientation.

Fabula: a pattern that film spectators create through assumptions and inferences: we do not see the fabula on the screen or hear it on the soundtrack.

Free market: a condition where business is governed by laws of supply and demand, rather than by government interference, regulations or subsidies.

Gender: the cultural nature of the differences between the natural biological sexes of male and female.

Genres: recognisable groupings, subsets or types of media forms comprising the paradigmatic elements (stories, rhetoric, signification) that are drawn upon in the creation of individual syntagmatic texts.

Globalisation: 'the intensification of world-wide social relations, which link distinct localities in such a way that local happenings are shaped by events occurring many miles away and vice versa.' (See Giddens, 1990 in Chapter 7.)

History: a narrative or a story about what happened in the past.

Historiography: literally the act of writing the past.

Ideology: ideas presented or hidden as 'truths'.

Intellectuals: people who earn their living by the use of mental labour.

Langue: a whole system of signification and its elements – the distinctions and oppositions which allow meaning to emerge, determined by the rules and principles of combination shared by the communities who recognise and use this system of signification.

Marketing: the process of identifying consumer needs and thus producing products and services (including pricing, distribution and promotion – i.e. advertising) in order to meet those needs and to generate a profit.

Media studies: analysis of mass media; study of media as an academic discipline.

Modernism: describes a tendency among artists in various fields in Europe and America, working from the early part of the twentieth century onwards (they are thus 'modernists'). While such a catch-all grouping cannot do justice to important distinctions between media and individuals, what characterises all of their works is experimentation with form and materials (whether paint, musical notes, words or images).

Monopoly: a condition in which one company or seller has control over the entire market.

Narrative: the organisation of textual elements into a pattern in terms of space, time and perspective. It is the narrative that encourages us to read specific parts of the text as 'events' which are ordered through time (temporal succession) and which we conceive as the cause of other events (causation).

Oligopoly: market condition in which sellers – i.e. businesses – are few. The result is that the actions of any one of them will affect the market price as well as their competitors.

Paradigm: a term that refers to what we could call the 'vertical' relations between any words in a sentence or sign in a system – an element which could be substituted for another similar sign.

Parole: any particular 'utterance' derived from the system of signification or langue.

Past (the): the time before the present.

Policy: government plans of action which set goals to be achieved by directing or influencing decisions that are made by media companies or consumers.

Political economy: 'the study of the social relations, particularly the power relations, that mutually constitute the production, distribution, and consumption of resources.' (See Mosco, 1996 in Chapter 5.)

Power: the ability to determine the actions of others, as well as our ability to determine our own actions. Individuals or groups who hold and exercise power are termed the dominant individual or group. Those over whom power is exercised are termed subordinate individuals or groups.

Propaganda: the intentional, conscious and active process of managing or manipulating information and ideas to achieve effects of a political or social nature. Methods of manipulation and management include: censorship – restricting or stopping what can be known; misinformation; and the generation or planting of outright 'lies'.

Public relations (PR): the management of communication between organisations and publics. 'PR' processes seek to gain positive exposure for organisations in media and other outlets in ways that do not require payment of a direct nature.

Public-service broadcasting (PSB): a system whereby broadcast media receive some or all of their funding from the public, usually through state subsidies or specific taxes, such as compulsory licence fees on radio or television receivers, collected by the broadcaster.

Realism: a rhetorical and signifying strategy (in media texts) for representing the worlds those texts refer to. In this way it is best to think of 'realisms'.

Regulation: legal or self-imposed controls or restrictions on media organisations, involving their ownership, or production processes and their output, as a means to achieve a policy goal.

Representation: to represent something is to describe or depict it, to call it up in the mind by description or portrayal or imagination. To represent also means to symbolise, stand for, to be a specimen of, or to substitute for.

Rhetoric: the construction and manipulation of language by the creator of a text for affective purposes.

Semiology: literally 'the study of signs'; the study of meaning and the different systems that make meaning possible.

Stereotyping: stereotyping is a process involving the expression of an exaggerated belief about a group that serves to qualify or justify the conduct towards that group of those who hold and express that belief.

Subculture: identifiable, if not necessarily immediately 'visible', minority groups in society who share particular values and habits that are distinctive to that group and sometimes at odds with those of the greater culture to which its members belong.

Synchronic: (in semiology) the study of language and the processes of meaning-making in use at a particular time.

Synergy: a number of processes working together within a system for greater benefit than they could achieve alone.

Syntagm: signs in language are organised in linear fashion to make more complex structures such as sentences which demonstrate the possibilities of paradigmatic selection.

Syuzhet: the arrangement and presentation of the story events according to specific principles.

Text: the site of the meaning value of media products.

Timeline: the representation of a chronology on a line of evenly spaced dates.

Vertical integration: the organisation of production whereby one business entity controls or owns all stages of the production and distribution of goods or services. This allows the business to collect profits from all aspects related to the media content.

Viral advertising (and viral marketing): a phenomenon of online activity that exploits existing networks in order to spread advertising messages, brand awareness and so on, analogous to the self-replicating infectiousness of a biological virus. Viral advertising may be composed of 'pass along' messages, coupons, static animation, photography, Flash imagery or 'advergames'.

References

Introduction

McLuhan, M. (1964) *Understanding Media: The Extensions of Man*. New York: Signet.

Mintel International Group Limited (2006) 'Children's comics and magazines', www.mintel.com at http://oxygen.mintel.com/sinatra/reports/display/id=173790

World Association of Newpapers (2006) *World Press Trends – 2006 Edition*, www.wan-press.org/

Chapter 1: How do media make meaning?

Barilli, R. (1989) *Rhetoric* (Theory and History of Literature), Minneapolis: University of Minnesota Press.

Barthes, R. and Lavers, A. (1972) *Mythologies*, London: Jonathan Cape.

Bordwell, D. and Thompson, K. (1988) *Film Art: An Introduction*, New York: Random House USA Inc.

de Saussure, F. (1983/1986) *Course in General Linguistics*, edited by Charles Bally and Albert Sechehaye with Albert Riedlinger, translated and annotated by Roya Harris, Open Court, Chicago and La Salle, IL: Open Court.

de Saussure, F. (1993) *Saussure's Third Course of Lectures on General Linguistics (1910–1911)*, London: Pergamon Press.

Eco, U. (1992/2004) *The Name of the Rose*, London: Vintage.

Frith, S. (1988) *Music for Pleasure: Essays in the Sociology of Pop*, Cambridge: Polity Press in association with Basil Blackwell, Oxford.

Herrick, J. (2008) *The History and Theory of Rhetoric*, Boston: Allyn & Bacon.

Yewdall, D.L. (2007) *The Practical Art of Motion Picture Sound*, Oxford: Focal Press.

Chapter 2: Organising meaning in media texts: genre and narrative

Allen, R. and Gomery, D. (1993) *Film History: Theory and Practice*, Columbus: McGraw-Hill.

Arisotle (1996) *Poetics: translated with an introduction and notes by Malcolm Heath*, London: Penguin.

Biskind, P. (1999) *Easy Riders, Raging Bulls: How the Sex 'n' Drugs 'n' Rock 'n' Roll Generation Saved Hollywood*, London: Bloomsbury.

Booker, C. (2005) *The Seven Basic Plots: Why We Tell Stories*, London: Continuum.

Bordwell, D. (1985) *The Classical Hollywood Cinema: Film Style and Mode of Production to 1960*, London: Routledge.

Bowen, K. (2003) 'Top Ten Dying Game Genres', 23 March. Retrieved 17 September 2008, from http://archive.gamespy.com/top10/march03/genres/index.shtml

Brunsdon, C. (1997) *Screen Tastes: Soap Opera to Satellites*, London: Routledge.

Caughie, J. (ed.) (1981) *Theories of Authorship: A Reader*, London: Routledge & Kegan Paul in association with the British Film Institute.

Eco, U. (1966) 'The narrative structure in Fleming' in his *The Bond Affair*, reprinted in B. Waites, T. Bennett and G. Martin (eds) *Popular Culture: Past and Present*, London: Croom Helm.

Fiske, J. and Hartley, J. (1989) *Reading Television*, London and New York: Routledge.

Freeman, M.P. (1993) *Rewriting the Self: History, Memory, Narrative*, London: Routledge.

French, P. (2005) *Westerns: Aspects of a Movie Genre and Westerns Revisited*, Manchester: Carcanet.

Hollows, J. and Jancovich, M. (eds) (1995) *Approaches to Popular Film*, Manchester: Manchester University Press.

McVeigh, S. (2007) *The American Western*, Edinburgh: Edinburgh University Press.

Mulvey, L. (1975) 'Visual pleasure and narrative cinema' in *Film Theory and Criticism: Introductory Readings*, L. Braudy and M. Cohen (eds), Oxford: Oxford University Press.

Ofcom (2006) 'Ofcom review of public service television broadcasting: the role of television in society: audience opinions and perceptions'. Retrieved 17 September 2008, from www.ofcom.org.uk/consult/condocs/psb/psb/sup_vol_1/audience/summary/

Propp, V.Y. (1928) *Morphology of the Folktale*, Austin, TX: University of Texas Press.

Shone, T. (2005) *Blockbuster: How the Jaws and Jedi Generation Turned Hollywood into a Boom-town*, London: Scribner.

Todorov, T. (1977) *The Poetics of Prose*, Oxford: Blackwell.

Wells, P. (2000) *The Horror Genre: From Beelzebub to Blair Witch*, London: Wallflower.

Wright, W. (1975) *Six Guns and Society: A Structural Study of the Western*, Berkeley, CA: University of California Press.

Chapter 3: Media representations

Burton, G. and Dimbleby, R. (1988) *More than Words: Introduction to Communication*, London: Hodder Arnold.

Davis, N., Cole, E. and Rothblum, E. (eds) (1993) *Faces of Women and Aging*, London: Routledge.

de Lauretis, T. (1991) 'Queer theory: lesbian and gay sexualities', *Differences: A Journal of Feminist Cultural Studies* 3(2): iii–xviii.

Dyer, R. (1993) *The Matter of Images: Essays on Representations*, London and New York: Routledge.

Dyer, R. (1997) *White*, London and New York: Routledge.

Dyer, R. (2002) *The Culture of Queers*, London: Routledge.

Ellis, J. (1992) *Visible Fictions: Cinema, Television, Video*, London: Routledge.

Fuss, D. (ed.) (1991) *Inside/Out: Lesbian Theories, Gay Theories*, London: Routledge.

Gledhill, C. (1991) *Stardom: Industry of Desire*, London: Routledge.

Haggerty, G. and Zimmerman, B. (eds) (1999) *Encyclopedia of Lesbian and Gay Histories and Cultures*, London: Routledge.

Horroicks, D. and Kolinsky, E. (ed.) (1996) *Turkish Culture in German Society Today* (Culture and Society in Germany), Providence, RI: Berghahn Books.

Johnson, K.H. and Cleese, J. (2006) *Superman: True Brit*, New York: DC Comics.

Kangasvuo, J. and Karkulehto, S. (2006) 'Preface: Querying queer', in *SQS, Journal of Queer Studies in Finland*, 1(1).

Lippmann, W. (1922) *Public Opinion*, bnpublishing.com. New York: Macmillan.

Mercer, K. (1994) *Welcome to the Jungle: New Positions in Black Cultural Studies*, London: Routledge.

Millar, M. (2004) *Superman: Red Son*, New York: DC Comics.

Perkins, T. (1997) 'Rethinking stereotypes' in Y. Jewkes and T. O'Sullivan (eds), *The Media Studies Reader*, London: Hodder Arnold.

Thompson, A. (ed.) (2007) *The Media and the Rwandan Genocide*, London: Pluto Press/Fountain Publishers.

Wells, L. (ed.) (2004) *Photography: A Critical Introduction*, London: Routledge.

Chapter 4: Reality media

Barker, H. and Taylor, Y. (2007) *Faking It: The Quest for Authenticity in Popular Music*, London: Faber & Faber.

Barthes, R. (1968) 'L'Effect de reel', *Communications*, 11:84–9.

Burnett, R. (1991) 'Realism, naturalism and their alternatives' in R. Burnett *Explorations in Film Theory: Selected Essays from Ciné-tracts*, Bloomington: Indiana University Press.

Carroll, N. (1991) *Mystifying Movies: Fads and Fallacies in Contemporary Film Theory*, New York: Columbia University Press.

Carroll, N. (1996) *Theorizing the Moving Image* (Cambridge Studies in Film), Cambridge: Cambridge University Press.

Ellis, J. (2000) *Seeing Things: Television in the Age of Uncertainty*, London: I.B. Tauris.

Finlayson, A. 'Language' in Ashe, F., Finlayson, A., Lloyd, M., MacKenzie, I., Martin, J. and O'Neil, S. (1999) *Contemporary Social and Political Theory: An Introduction*, Buckingham and Philadelphia: Open University Press.

Heider, K.G. (2006) *Ethnographic Film*, Austin: University of Texas Press, 23.

Hockey, D. (2001) *Secret Knowledge: Rediscovering the Lost Techniques of the Old Masters*, London: Thames & Hudson.

Jacobson, R. (1971) 'On realism in art' in L. Matejka and K. Pomorska (eds) *Readings in Russian Poetics: Formalist and Structuralist Views*, Cambridge, MA: MIT Press.

Long, P. (2008) *Only in the Common People: The Aesthetics of Class in Post-war Britain*, Newcastle upon Tyne: Cambridge Scholars Publishing.

Loshitzky, Y. (1998) *Spielberg's Holocaust: Critical Perspectives on 'Schindler's List'*, Bloomington: Indiana University Press.

Luhmann, N. (2000) *The Reality of the Mass Media*, translated by K. Cross, Cambridge: Polity Press.

New Collins Dictionary (1987) Managing ed. W.T. McLeod, London and Glasgow: Collins.

Perry, I. (2004) *Prophets of the Hood: Politics and Poetics in Hip Hop*, Durham, NC: Duke University Press.

Rheingold, H. (1991) *Virtual Reality*, New York: Summit.

Rheingold, H. (1994) *The Virtual Community: Homesteading on the Electronic Frontier*, Reading, MA: Addison-Wesley.

Sanders, E. (2002) *The Family*, London: Thundermouth.

Tagg, J. (1988) *The Burden of Representation: Essays on Photographies and Histories*, Basingstoke: Macmillan.

Williams, R. (1977) 'A lecture on realism', *Screen*, 18(1), 61–75.

Winston, B. (1995) *Claiming the Real: Documentary Film Revisited*, London: British Film Institute.

Winston, B. (1996) *Technologies of Seeing: Photography, Cinematography and Television*, London: British Film Institute.

Winston, B. (2001) *Lies, Damned Lies and Documentaries*, London: British Film Institute.

Chapter 5: The business of media

Anderson, C. (2006) *The Long Tail: Why the Future of Business Is Selling Less of More*, New York: Hyperion.

Bagdikian, B. (2002) *The Media Monopoly*, Boston: Beacon Press.

Balnaves, M., Donald, D. and Donald, S.H. (2008) *The Global Media Atlas*, London: British Film Institute.

Bantz, C. (1985) 'News organizations: conflict as a crafted cultural norm' in D. Berkowitz (ed.) *Social Meanings of News: A Text-reader*, California: Sage Publications, 123–37.

Biskind, P. (1999) *Easy Riders, Raging Bulls: How the Sex-Drugs-and-Rock 'n' Roll Generation Saved Hollywood*, London: Simon & Schuster.

Born, Georgina (2004) *Uncertain Vision: Birt, Dyke and the Reinvention of the BBC*. London: Secker & Warburg.

Burns, Tom (1977) *The BBC: Public Institution and Private World*. London: Macmillan.

Chang, Y. (2007) 'The role of the nation-state: evolution of STAR TV in China and India', *Global Media Journal* 6(10).

Corbin, K. (2008) 'AOL Buying Social Networking Site', internetnews.com. Retrieved 30 March 2008 from www.internetnews.com/webcontent/article.php/3733861/AOL+Buying+Social+Networking+Site.htm

Demers, D.P. (2002) *Global Media: Menace or Messiah?*, Cresskill, NJ: Hampton Press.

du Gay, P. (1997) *Doing Cultural Studies: The Story of the Sony Walkman*, London and Thousand Oaks, CA: Sage Publications in association with the Open University.

Espinosa, P. (1982) 'The audience in the text: ethnographic observations of a Hollywood story conference', *Media, Culture and Society* 4(1): 77–86.

Ettema, J. and Whitney, D. (1982) *Individuals in Mass Media Organizations: Creativity and Constraint*, London and Thousand Oaks, CA: Sage Publications.

Fishman, M. (1980) *Manufacturing the News*, Austin: University of Texas Press.

Florida, R. (2004) *Cities and the Creative Class*, London: Routledge.

Florida, R. (2008) *Who's Your City? How the Creative Economy Is Making Where You Live the Most Important*, New York: Basic Books Inc.

Gill, R. (2009) 'Creative biographies in new media: innovation in web work', in Andy C. Pratt and Paul Jeffcutt (eds) *Creativity, Innovation and the Cultural Economy*. Routledge: London, 161–78.

Goldhaber, M.H. (1997) 'The attention economy and the net', *First Monday*, 2(4).

Golding, P. and Elliot, P. (1980) *Making the News*, London: Longman.

Golding, P. and Murdock, G. (2000) 'Culture, communications and political economy' in J. Curran and M. Gurevitch (eds) *Mass Media and Society*, London: Arnold, 11–30.

Habermas, J. (1962) *The Structural Transformation of the Public Sphere: Inquiry into a Category of Bourgeois Society*, Cambridge: Polity Press.

Hesmondhalgh, D. (2002) *The Cultural Industries: An Introduction*, London: Sage Publications.

Hotelling, H. (1929) 'Stability in competition', *Economic Journal*, 39(153): 41–57.

Kettler, D. and Loader, C. (2002) *Karl Mannheim's Sociology as Political Education*, New Brunswick, NJ: Transaction Publishers.

Mosco, V. (1996) *The Political Economy of Communication: Rethinking and Renewal*, London and Thousand Oaks, CA: Sage Publications.

Murdock, G. (1994) 'Money talks: broadcasting, finance and public culture', in S. Hood (ed.) *Behind the Screens: The Structure of British Television*, London: Lawrence & Wishart.

Murdock, G. (2004) 'Building the digital commons: public broadcasting in the age of the internet', *The 2004 Spry Memorial Lecture*, Vancouver and Montreal.

Negus, K. and Pickering, M. (2004) *Creativity, Communication and Cultural Value*, London and Thousand Oaks, CA: Sage Publications.

Scott, J. (1999) *Gender and the Politics of History* (Gender and Culture Series), New York: Columbia University Press.

Shoemaker, P. J. (1991) *Communication Concepts 3: Gatekeeping*, Newbury Park, CA: Sage.

Shone, T. (2005) *Blockbuster: How the Jaws and Jedi Generation Turned Hollywood into a Boom-town*, London: Scribner.

Smythe, D.W. (1981) *Dependency Road: Communications, Capitalism, Consciousness, and Canada*, Norwood, NJ: Ablex Pub. Corp.

Tunstall, J. (1971) *Journalists at Work: Specialist Correspondents: Their News Organizations, News Sources, and Competitor-colleagues*, Beverly Hills, CA and London: Sage Publications and Constable.

Weber, I. (2003) 'Localizing the global: successful strategies for selling television programmes to China', *Gazette: The International Journal For Communication Studies* 65(3): 273–90.

White, D.M. (1950) 'The gatekeeper: a case study in the selection of news', *Journalism Quarterly* (27): 383–90.

Williams, R. (1981) *Culture* [s.l.], London: Fontana Paperbacks.

Willis, P. (1976) 'The man in the iron cage: notes on method', *Cultural Studies* (9).

Chapter 6: Media regulation and policy

Barnard, S. (1989) *On the Radio: Music Radio in Britain*, Milton Keynes and Philadelphia: Open University Press.

Barnouw, E. (1966) *A Tower in Babel: A History of Broadcasting in the United States, to 1933*, New York: Oxford University Press.

Bennett, T. (1991) 'Putting policies into cultural studies' in L. Grossberg, C. Nelson and P. Treichler (eds) *Cultural Studies*, London: Routledge, 788.

Briggs, A. (1961) *The History of Broadcasting in the United Kingdom*, London and New York: Oxford University Press.

Briggs, A. and Burke, P. (2001) *A Social History of the Media: From Gutenburg to the Internet*, Cambridge: Polity Press.

Curran, J. and Seaton, J. (1981/1997) *Power Without Responsibility: The Press and Broadcasting in Britain*, London and New York: Routledge.

Engelman, R. (1996) *Public Radio and Television in America: A Political History*, Thousand Oaks, CA: Sage Publications.

Frith, S. (1988) 'The pleasures of the hearth – the making of BBC light entertainment' in *Music for Pleasure: Essays in the Sociology of Pop*, Cambridge: Polity Press.

Hare, G. (2003) 'Popular music on French radio and television' in S. Cannon and H. Dauncey (eds) *Popular Music in France from Chanson to Techno: Culture, Identity, and Society*, London: Ashgate, 57–76.

Hendy, D. (2000) 'Pop music in the public services: BBC Radio One and new music in the 1990s', *Media, Culture and Society* 22(6).

Hilmes, M. (2003) 'British quality, American chaos: historical dualisms and what they leave out', *Radio Journal* 1(1): 13–28.

Kretschmer, M. and Kawol, F. (2004) 'The history and philosophy of copyright' in S. Frith and L. Marshall (eds), *Music and Copyright*, Edinburgh: Edinburgh University Press.

Lessig, L. (2004) *Free Culture: How Big Media Uses Technology and the Law to Lock Down Culture and Control Creativity*, New York: Penguin Press.

Lewis, P.M. and Booth, J. (1989) *The Invisible Medium: Public, Commercial and Community Radio*, Basingstoke: Macmillan Education.

Litman, J. (2001) *Digital Copyright: Protecting Intellectual Property on the Internet*, Amherst, MA: Prometheus Books.

Livingstone, S. and Bober, M. (2006) 'Regulating the internet at home: contrasting the perspectives of children and parents' in D. Willett and R. Buckingham (eds), *Digital Generations: Children, Young People, and the New Media*, London: Routledge, 352.

McChesney, R.W. (2004) *The Problem of the Media: US Communication Politics in the Twenty-first Century*, New York: Monthly Review Press.

Mitchell, J.W. (2005) *Listener Supported: The Culture and History of Public Radio*, Westport, CT: Praeger.

Neill, K. and Shanahan, M.W. (2005) *The Great New Zealand Radio Experiment*, London: Thomson.

Rothenbuhler, E. and McCourt, T. (2002) 'Radio redefines itself, 1947–1962' in M. Hilmes and J. Loviglio *Radio Reader: Essays in the Cultural History of Radio*, New York: Routledge.

Scannell, P. and Cardiff, D. (1991) *A Social History of British Broadcasting*, Oxford, UK and Cambridge, MA: Blackwell.

Sweet, M. (2005) *Shepperton Babylon: The Lost Worlds of British Cinema*, London: Faber & Faber.

Wall, T. (2000) 'Policy, pop and the public: the discourse of regulation in British commercial radio', *Journal of Radio Studies*.

Wall, T. (2006) 'Calling the tune: resolving the tension between profit and regulation in British commercial music radio', *Southern Review* 39(2).

Wall, T. (2007) 'Finding an alternative: music programming in US college radio', *Radio Journal* 5(1): 35–54.

Williams, K. (1997) *Get Me a Murder a Day: A History of Mass Communication in Britain*, London: Hodder Arnold.

Chapter 7: Media production in a global age

Al Jazeera (2011) Egypt' s protests in social media. *Al Jazeera* [internet] 25 January. Available at: http://blogs.aljazeera.net/middle-east/2011/01/25/egypts-protests-social-media [Accessed 22 February 2011].

Alterman, J.B. (1998) *New Media, New Politics? From Satellite Television to the Internet in the Arab World*. Washington: The Washington Institute for Near East Policy.

Alterman, J.B. (2004) 'The information revolution and the Middle East', in Nora Bensahel and Daniel L. Byman (eds), *The Future Security Environment in the Middle East*. Santa Monica, CA: RAND. Available at: www.csis.org/media/csis/pubs/the_information_revolution_and_the_me.pdf [Accessed 22 February 2011].

Altheide, D. (2006) 'Terrorism and the politics of fear', *Cultural Studies = Critical Methodologies* 6(4): 415–39.

Altheide, D. (2007) 'The mass media and terrorism', *Discourse and Communication*, 1(3).

Appadurai, A. (1996) *Modernity at Large: Cultural Dimensions of Globalization* (Public Worlds, Vol. 1), Minneapolis: University of Minnesota Press.

Artz, L. and Kamalipour, Y. (2003) *The Globalization of Corporate Media Hegemony*, New York: New York University Press.

Ayish, M. (2002) 'Political communication on Arab world television: evolving patterns', *Political Communication* 19(2): 137–54.

Bakir, V. (2001) 'An identity for Europe? The role of the media' in M.J. Wintle (ed.) *Culture and Identity in Europe: Perceptions of Divergence and Unity in Past and Present* (Perspectives on Europe), Aldershot: Avebury, 177–200.

Bakir, V. (2010) *Sousveillance, Media and Strategic Political Communication: Iraq, USA, UK*. New York: Continuum.

Bakir, V. and McStay, A. (2008) 'When the script runs out . . . what happens to the polarized war body? Deconstructing Western 24/7 news coverage of Operation Iraqi Freedom 2003', in K. McStay and A. Randell, *The War Body on Screen*, New York: Continuum, 165–181.

Balnaves, M., Donald, D. and Donald, S.H. (2008) *The Global Media Atlas*, London: British Film Institute.

Barber, B.R. (1996) *Jihad vs McWorld*, New York: Ballantine Books.

Bar-Ilan, J. and Gutman, T. (2005) 'How do search engines respond to some non-English queries?', *Journal of Information Science* 31(1).

Baudrillard, J. (1995) *The Gulf War Did Not Take Place*, Bloomington: Indiana University Press.

Beaton, J. and Wajcman, J. (2004) *The Impact of the Mobile Telephone in Australia: Social Science Research Opportunities*, Canberra: Academy of Social Sciences.

Boyd, D.A. (1977) *Egyptian Radio: Tool of Political and National Development*, Lexington: Association for Education in Journalism.

Boyd-Barrett, O. (1998) 'Media imperialism reformulated' in D. K. Thussu (ed.) *Electronic Empires: Global Media and Local Resistance*, London: Arnold, 157–76.

Boyd-Barrett, O., Seymour-Ure, C. and Tunstall, J. (1977) *Studies on the Press*, London: HMSO.

Bytelevel Research (2010) Byte Level Research Announces Best Global Web Sites of 2010 [internet] 4 March. Available at: www.bytelevel.com/news/reportcard2010.html [Accessed 22 February 2011].

Carlson, M. (2007) 'Order versus access: news search engines and the challenge to traditional journalistic roles', *Media, Culture and Society* 29(6): 1014–30.

Cherribi, S. (2006) 'From Baghdad to Paris', *Harvard International Journal of Press/Politics*, 11(2): 121–38.

Colwell, T. and Price, D. (2004) 'Rights of passage: British television in the global market', Television Research Partnership. Retrieved 4 April 2008 from www.pact.co.uk/uploads/file_bank/1698.pdf

Couts, A. (2011) Egypt's 'Facebook generation' pressures Mubarak to step down. *Digital Trends* [internet] 11 February. Available at: www.digitaltrends.com/social-media/egypts-facebook-generation-pressures-mubarak-to-step-down/ [Accessed 22 February 2011].

Demers, D.P. (2002) *Global Media: Menace or Messiah?*, Cresskill, NJ: Hampton Press.

Donald, S. and Evans, H. (1999) *Picturing Power in the People's Republic of China: Posters of the Cultural Revolution*, Boulder, CO: Rowman & Littlefield.

The Economist (2011) 'Egypt rises up', 5 February 2011.

European Privacy and Human Rights (EPHR) (2011) *European Privacy and Human Rights* [internet] 26 January. Available at: https://www.privacy-international.org/ephr [Accessed 22 February 2011].

Facebook press room (2008) Statistics. www.facebook.com/press/info.php?statistics

Financial News (2008) 'Thomson/Reuters: Transatlantic authorities clear Thompson-Reuters merger', 20 February. Retrieved 24 March from www.efinancialnews.com/archive/tag/Thomson/1/content/2349848694/restricted

Galtung, J. and Ruge, M.H. (1965) 'The structure of foreign news: the presentation of the Congo, Cuba and Cyprus crises in four Norwegian newspapers', *Journal of Peace Research* 2(1): 64–90.

Gerbner, G., Mowlana, H. and Nordenstreng, K. (eds) (1993) *The Global Media Debate: Its Rise, Fall and Renewal*, Norwood, NJ: Ablex.

Giddens, A. (1990) *The Consequences of Modernity*, Oxford: Polity Press in association with Basil Blackwell.

Gillan, A. (2009) Third postmortem to be carried out on Ian Tomlinson. *Guardian.co.uk* [internet]. 21 April. Available at: www.guardian.co.uk/uk/2009/apr/21/tomlinson-g20-assault [Accessed 22 February 2011].

Google Annual Report (2009) Available at http://investor.google.com/pdf/2009_google_annual_report.pdf

Green, D.C. (2003) 'Search engine marketing: why it benefits us all', *Business Information Review*, 20(4): 195–202.

Hawkins, V. (2002) 'The other side of the CNN factor: the media and conflict', *Journalism Studies* 3(2): 225–40.

Herman, E.S. and Chomsky, N. (2002) *Manufacturing Consent: The Political Economy of the Mass Media*, New York: Pantheon Books.

Herman, E.S. and McChesney, W.R. (2001) *The Global Media: The New Missionaries of Corporate Capitalism*, London: Continuum.

Horten G. (2002) *Radio Goes to War: The Cultural Politics of Propaganda during World War II*. Berkeley, Los Angeles, London: University of California Press.

Hoskins, A. (2001) 'Mediating time: the temporal mix of television', *Time and Society* 10(2–3): 213–33.

Human Events.com (2006) Muhammad cartoon gallery, 2 February. Retrieved 26 March 2008 from www.humanevents.com/article.php?id=12146&offer=&hidebodyad=true

Internet World Stats (2010a) *Internet usage statistics.* [internet] www.internetworldstats.com/stats.htm [Accessed 22 February 2011].

Internet World Stats (2010b) *Internet world users by language.* [internet] www.internetworldstats.com/stats7.htm [Accessed 22 February 2011].

Jenkins, H. (2006) *Convergence Culture: Where Old and New Media Collide*, New York: New York University Press.

Jones, J. (2007) 'Branding trust: the ideology of making truth claims through interactive media', in V. Barlow, and D. Bakir (eds), *Communication in the Age of Suspicion: Trust and the Media*, Basingstoke: Palgrave-Macmillan, 304–23.

Kleinwatcher, W. (1993) 'Three waves of the debate', *The Global Media Debate: Its Rise, Fall and Renewal* in G. Mowlana, H. Gerbner and K. Nordenstreng (eds), Norwood, NJ: Ablex Publishing Corporation, 13–20.

Krazit, T. (2010) Slight dip in Google's January search market share. *Cnet* [internet] 11 February. Available at: http://news.cnet.com/8301-30684_3-10452235-265.html [Accessed 22 February 2011].

LaTulippe, S. (2011) The Internet and Muhammad Bouazizi. *Strike the Root* [blog] 19 January. Available at: http://strike-the-root.com/internet-and-muhammad-bouazizi [Accessed 22 February 2011].

Lerner, D. (1958) *The Passing of Traditional Society. Modernizing the Middle East*, Glencoe, IL: The Free Press.

Lerner, D. and Schramm, W. (1967) *Communication and Change in the Developing World*, Honolulu: East-West Center Press.

Lewis, P. (2011) Ian Tomlinson death: IPCC rules Met officer 'reckless' in conduct.Guardian.co.uk [internet] 9 May. Available at: http://www.guardian.co.uk/uk/2011/may/09/ian-tomlinson-death [Accessed 17 May 2011].

Loory, S. (2005) 'CNN today: a young giant stumbles' in *Critical Studies in Media Communication* 22(4): 340–3.

Lull, J. (1995) *Media, Communication, Culture: A global Approach*, Cambridge: Polity Press in association with Blackwell Publishers.

Lynch, M. (2006) *Voices of the New Arab Public: Iraq, al-Jazeera, and Middle East Politics Today*, New York: Columbia University Press.

MacBride, S. (1980) *Many Voices, One World*, New York: UNESCO.

MacBride, S. and Roach, C. (1993) 'The New International Information Order' in G. Gerbner, H. Mowlana and K. Nordenstreng, *The Global Media*

Debate: Its Rise, Fall and Renewal, Norwood, NJ: Ablex, 3–11.

McCarthy, C. (2010) Who will be Facebook's next 500 million? *CNet*. [internet] 21 July. Available at: http://news.cnet.com/8301-13577_3-20011158-36.html [Accessed 22 February 2011].

McChesney, R.W. (2004) 'The political economy of international communications' in P.N. Nain and Z. Thomas, *Who Owns the Media? Global Trends and Local Resistances*, London: Zed Books, 3–22.

Machin, D. and van Leeuwen, T. (2007) *Global Media Discourse: A Critical Introduction*, London: Routledge.

McKenna, J., Boyd-Barrett, O., Sreberny-Mohammed, A. and Winseck, D. (1997) *Media in Global Context: A Reader* (Foundations in Media), London: Hodder Arnold.

McLuhan, M. and Fiore, Q. (1967) *The Medium is the Message*, Harmondsworth: Penguin Books.

McLuhan, M. and Powers, B.R. (1989) *The Global Village: Transformations in World Life and Media in the 21st Century*, New York and Oxford: Oxford University Press.

McQuail, D. and Siune K. (1986) *New Media Politics: Comparative Perspectives in Western Europe*, London: Sage Publications.

McStay, A. and Bakir, V. (2006) 'Privacy, online advertising and marketing techniques: the paradoxical disappearance of the user', *Ethical Space: the International Journal of Communication Ethics* 3(1): 24–31.

Miles, H. (2005) *Al-Jazeera: The Inside Story of the Arab News Channel That Is Challenging the West*, New York: Grove Press.

Miles, H. (2006) 'Al Jazeera', *Foreign Policy*, July–August: 20–4.

Mohammed Image Archive (n.d.) Mohammed Image Archive: depictions of Mohammed throughout history. Retrieved 26 March 2008 from www.zombietime.com/mohammed_image_archive/

Morley, D. and Robins, K. (1995) *Spaces of Identity: Global Media, Electronic Landscapes and Cultural Boundaries*, London and New York: Routledge.

Morozov, E. (2011) 'Taming cyberspace', *Index on Censorship*, 40(1), 50–55.

Moss, L. (2007) 'Tempest brews over Al Jazeera English', *Multichannel News*, 7 May: 57, 60.

MPAA (2010) *Theatrical market statistics* (www.mpaa.org/2010-US-Theatrical-Market-Statistics-Report.pdf)

Nordenstreng, K. and Varis, T. (1974) *Television Traffic – a One Way Street?*, Reports and Papers on Mass Communication No. 70, Paris, UNESCO: UnipubInc. 62.

Nye, J.S. (2004) *Soft Power: The Means to Success in World Politics*, New York: Perseus Books Group.

OECD (2002) *Glossary of statistical terms*. Retrieved 30 March 2008 from http://stats.oecd.org/glossary/detail.asp?ID=3157

Ó Siochrú, S. and Girard, B. (2002) *Global Media Governance: A Beginner's Guide*, Oxford: Rowman & Littlefield

Pieterse, J.N. (1995) 'Globalisation as hybridisation', *Global Modernities*, London: Sage, 45–68.

Quinn, S. and Walters, T. (2004) 'Al-Jazeera: a broadcaster creating ripples in a stagnant pool' in R. Berenger (ed.) *Global Media Go to War: Role of News and Entertainment Media during the 2003 Iraq War*, Spokane, WA: Marquette Books: 57–73.

Rahim, S.A. (1984) 'International communication agencies: an overview' in G. Siefert and M. Gerbner (eds), *World Communications: a Handbook*, New York and London: Longman, 391–9.

Rantanen, T. (2004) *The Media and Globalization*, London: Sage.

Robinson, P. (2002) *The CNN Effect: The Myth of News, Foreign Policy and Intervention*, London and New York: Routledge.

Rohumaa, L. and Bradshaw, P. (2011) *The Online Journalism Handbook*, Harlow: Longman.

Rusbridger, A. (2009) 'I've seen the future and it's mutual', *British Journalism* 20: 19–26.

Sadiki, L. (2010) Opinion: Tunisia: The battle of Sidi Bouzid. *Al Jazeera* [interent] 27 December. Available at: http://english.aljazeera.net/indepth/opinion/2010/12/20101227142811755739.html http://news.cnet.com/8301-13577_3-20011158-36.html [Accessed 22 February 2011].

Sakr, N. (2002) *Satellite Realms: Transnational Television, Globalization and the Middle East*, London: I.B. Tauris.

Schafer, M.L. (2011) Egypt, China Attempt to Plug Information About Egyptian Protests. *Lippmann Would Roll* [internet] 30 January. Available at: http://lippmannwouldroll.com/2011/01/30/egypt-china-attempt-to-plug-information-about-egyptian-protests/ [Accessed 22 February 2011].

Schiller, H.I. (1976) *Communication and Cultural Domination*, White Plains, NY: International Arts and Sciences Press.

Schiller, H.I. (1979) 'Transnational media and national development' in K. Schiller and H.I. Nordenstreng (eds), *National Sovereignty and International Communication*, Norwood, NJ: Ablex Publishing Company, 21–32.

Seib, P. (2004) 'Hegemonic No More: Western Media, the Rise of Al-Jazeera, and the Influence of Diverse Voices', Montreal: International Studies Association.

Semati, M. (2004) *New Frontiers: International Communication Theory* (Communication, Media and Politics), Lanham, MD: Rowman & Littlefield Publishers.

Skuse, A. (2002) 'Radio, politics and trust in Afghanistan: a social history of broadcasting', *Gazette: The International Journal for Communication Studies* 64(3): 267–79.

Steven, P. (2004) *No Nonsense Guide to Global Media.* London: Verso.

Tatham, S. (2005) 'Al-Jazeera: can it make it here?' *British Journalism Review* 16(1): 47–52.

Thurman, N. (2007) 'The globalisation of journalism online: a transatlantic study of news websites and their international readers', *Journalism Quarterly* 8(3): 285–307.

Tomlinson, J. (1999) *Globalization and Culture*, Cambridge: Polity Press.

UNESCO Constitution (2002) Available at: http://portal.unesco.orp/en/ev.php-URL_ID=15244&URL_DO=DO_TOPIC&URL_SECTION=201.html

van Ginneken, J. (1998) *Understanding Global News: A Critical Introduction*, London, Thousand Oaks, CA: Sage Publications.

Virilio, P. (2002) *Desert Screen: War at the Speed of Light* (Athlone Contemporary European Thinkers), London; New York: Continuum International Publishing Group – Mansell.

Volkmer, I. (1999) *News in the Global Sphere: A Study of CNN and Its Impact on Global Communication*, Luton: University of Luton Press.

Warburton, Nigel (2010) MUHAMMED AND THE FUNDAMENTALISTS, 21 May at http://blog.indexoncensorship.org/2010/05/21 pakistan-muhammed-censorshi/

Weinraub, B. (1993) 'Directors battle over GATT's final cut and print', *New York Times*, 12 December). © 1993 The New York Times All Rights Reserved.

White, R.A. (1993) 'The new order and the third world' in G. Mowlana, H. Gerbner and K. Nordenstreng (eds), *The Global Media Debate: Its Rise, Fall and Renewal*, Norwood, NJ: Ablex.

Wojcieszak, M. (2007) 'Al-Jazeera: A challenge to the traditional framing research', *International Communication Gazette* 69(2): 115–28.

Wood, J. (1992) *A History of International Broadcasting*, London: Peter Peregrinus.

Chapter 8: Producing audiences: what do media do to people?

Adorno, T.W. (1941/1990) 'On popular music' in *On Record: Rock, Pop and the Written Word*, S. Frith and A. Goodwin (eds), London: Routledge.

Adorno T.W. (1945) 'A social critique of radio music', *Kenyon Review*, VII(2).

Adorno, T.W. (1967) *Introduction to the Sociology of Music*, New York: Continuum.

Ang, I. (1985) *Watching Dallas: Soap Opera and the Melodramatic Imagination*, London, New York: Methuen.

Ang, I. (1990) *Desperately Seeking the Audience*, London: Routledge.

Ang, I. (1996) *Living Room Wars: Rethinking Media Audiences for a Postmodern World*, London and New York: Routledge.

Barker, M. and Petley, J. (1997) *Ill Effects: the Media/Violence Debate*, London: Routledge.

Bernays, E. (2004) *Propaganda*, New York: Ig Publishing.

Buckingham, D. (1998) *Teaching Popular Culture: Beyond Radical Pedagogy*, London and Bristol, PA: UCL Press.

Carlsson, U. and von Feilitzen, C. (eds) (1998) *Children and Media Violence*, the UNESCO International Clearinghouse on Children and Violence on the Screen, Fothenburg: NORDICOM.

Chaffee, S.H. and Hockheimer, J. (1985) 'The beginnings of political communication research in the United States: origins of the "limited effects" model', in *The Media Revolution in America and Western Europe*, E.M. Rogers and F. Balle (eds), Norwood, NJ: Ablex, 267–96.

Cohen, S. (1972) *Folk Devils and Moral Panics: The Creation of the Mods and Rockers*, London: MacGibbon & Kee.

Craig, T. and Petley, J. (1999) 'Invasion of the internet abusers: marketing fears about the information superhighway' in *Ill Effects: The Media Violence Debate*, M. Barker and J. Petley (eds), London: Routledge, 240.

Cumberbatch, G. (1998) 'Media effects: the continuing controversy', in *The Media: An Introduction*, A. Briggs and P. Cobley (eds), Harlow: Longman, 520.

Dickinson, R., Linne, O. and Harindranath, R. (eds) (1998) *Approaches to Audiences: A Reader* (Foundations in Media), London: Hodder Arnold.

Gerbner, G., Gross, L. and Melody, W.H. (eds) (1973) *Communications Technology and Social Policy: Understanding the New 'Cultural Revolution'*, Chichester: John Wiley & Sons.

Gill, R. (2008) 'Empowerment/sexism: figuring female sexual agency in contemporary advertising', *Feminism and Psychology* 18(1): 35–60.

Gripsrud, J. (2002) *Understanding Media Culture*, London: Hodder Arnold.

Hartley, J. (1987) 'Invisible fictions: television audiences, paedocracy, pleasure', *Textual Practice* 1(2): 121–38.

Herman, E.S. and Chomsky, N. (2002) *Manufacturing Consent: The Political Economy of the Mass Media*, New York: Pantheon Books.

Hoffman, H. (1997) *The Triumph of Propaganda: Film and National Socialism, 1933–1945*, Providence, RI: Berghahn Books.

Jowett, G., Jarvie, I. and Fuller, K. (1996) *Children and the Movies: Media Influence and the Payne Fund Controversy* (Cambridge Studies in the History of Mass Communication), Cambridge: Cambridge University Press.

Kenez, P. (1999) *A History of the Soviet Union from the Beginning to the End*, New York: Cambridge University Press.

Kerekes, D. and Slater, D. (2000) *See No Evil: Banned Films and Video Controversy, Critical Vision*, Manchester: Headpress.

Lasswell, H. (1948) 'The structure and function of communication in society' in L. Bryson (ed.), *The Communication of Ideas*. New York: Harper and Row, 37–51.

Lasswell, H. (1972) *Propaganda Technique in the World War* (1927; reprinted with a new introduction, for the Garland Edition by Harold D. Lasswell 1972), London: Garland Publishing.

Lazarsfeld, P.F. (1940) *Radio and the Printed Page: An Introduction to the Study of Radio and its Role in the Communication of Ideas*, New York: Duell, Sloan and Pearce.

Lazarsfeld, P.F. and Stanton, F.N. (1941) *Radio Research, 1941*, New York: Duell, Sloan and Pearce.

Lazarsfeld, P.F. and Stanton, F.N. (1944) *Radio Research 1942–1943*, New York: Duell, Sloan and Pearce.

MacArthur, J.R. Jr (1992) *Second Front: Censorship and Propaganda in the Gulf War*, Berkeley, CA: University of California Press.

McQuail, D. (1969) *Towards a Sociology of Mass Communications*, London: Collier-Macmillan.

McQuail, D. (1997) *Audience Analysis*, London: Sage Publications.

Morrison, D.E. (1998) *The Search for a Method: Focus Groups and the Development of Mass Communication Research*, Luton: University of Luton Press.

Shannon, C.E. and Weaver, W. (1949) *The Mathematical Theory of Communication*, Urbana, IL: University of Illinois Press.

Steward, H.D. (1990–1) 'A public relations plan for the US military in the Middle East', *Public Relations Quarterly* (Winter 1990/1): 10.

Stone, O. (1996) 'Don't sue the messenger', in K. French, *Screen Violence*, London: Bloomsbury, 237–9.

Chapter 9: Investigating audiences: what do people do with media?

Ang, I. (1985) *Watching Dallas: Soap Opera and the Melodramatic Imagination*, London and New York: Methuen.

Bakardjieva, M. and Smith, R. (2001) 'The internet in everyday life', *New Media and Society* 3(1): 67–83.

Barthes, R. (1977) 'The Death of the Author' in *Image, Music, Text* (trans Stephen Heath), New York: Hill & Wang, 142–8.

Baym, N. (1995) 'The emergence of community in computer-mediated communication' in *Cybersociety: Computer-mediated Communication and Community*, S.G. Jones (ed.), Thousand Oaks, CA: Sage, 256.

Baym, N. (1999) *Tune In, Log On: Soaps, Fandom, and Online Community*, London, Thousand Oaks, CA: Sage Publications.

Bell, D. (2001) *Introduction to Cyberculture*, London: Routledge.

Bertrand, I. and Hughes, P. (2004) *Media Research Methods: Audiences, Institutions, Texts*, London: Palgrave Macmillan.

Blumler, J.G., McQuail, D. and Brown, J.R. (2003) 'The conduct of exploratory research into the social origins of broadcasting audiences', *Particip@tions* 1(1).

Bourdieu, P. and Passeron, J-C. (1990) *Reproduction in Education, Society and Culture*, London: Sage.

Bowman, S. and Wills, C. (2003) 'We Media: How audiences are shaping the future of news and information', J.D. Lasica, The Media Center at the American Press Institute.

Brunsdon, C. (1997) *Screen Tastes: Soap Opera to Satellite Dishes*, London: Routledge.

Brunsdon, C. (2000) *The Feminist, the Housewife and the Soap Opera*, Oxford: Clarendon Press.

Brunsdon, C. and Morley, D. (1978) *Everyday Television – Nationwide*, London: British Film Institute, Educational Advisory Service.

Brunsdon, C. and Morley, D. (1999) *The Nationwide Television Studies*, London: Routledge.

Cheung, C. (2004) 'At home on the web: personal webspace and identity' in D. Gauntlett (ed.) *Web Studies 2.0*, London: Edward Arnold, 53–8.

Clarke, J. and Jefferson, T. (1975) *Politics of Popular Culture: Culture and Sub-culture*, Birmingham: Birmingham University Centre for Contemporary Cultural Centre.

Clerc, S.J. (1996) 'DDEB, GATB, MPPB, and Ratboy: The X Files Media Fandom, Online and Off' in *Deny All Knowledge: Reading the X-Files*, D. Lavery,

A. Hague and M. Cartwright (eds), New York, Syracuse University Press, 233.

Cohen, S. (1972) *Folk Devils and Moral Panics: the Creation of the Mods and Rockers*, London: MacGibbon & Kee.

Cook, P. and Bernink, M. (1999) *The Cinema Book*, London: British Film Institute.

Corner, J. (1998) *Studying Media: Problems of Theory and Method*, Edinburgh: Edinburgh University Press.

Couldry, N. (2004) 'The digital divide' in D. Gauntlett (ed.) *Web Studies 2.0*, London: Edward Arnold, 185–94.

de Beauvoir, S. (1949/1997) *The Second Sex*, London: Vintage.

Donath, J. (1998) 'Identity and deception in the virtual community', *Communities in Cyberspace*, M.A. Smith and P. Kollock (eds), London, Routledge, 328.

eBay (2012) http://pages.ebay.ph/aboutebay/thecompany/companyoverview.html

Eco, U. (1975/1986) *Travels in Hyperreality: Essays*, Oxford: Harcourt.

Firestone, S. (1971) *The Dialectic of Sex: Case for Feminist Revolution*, London: Jonathan Cape.

Friedan, B. (1963/1984) *The Feminine Mystique*, New York: Dell Publishing Co.

Geraghty, C. (1991) *Women and Soap Opera: A Study of Prime Time Soaps*, Cambridge: Polity Press.

Goffman, E. (1959) *The Presentation of Self in Everyday Life*, Woodstock, NY: Overlook Press.

Gray, A. (1992) *Video Playtime: The Gendering of a Leisure Technology*, London: Routledge.

Greer, G. (1971) *The Female Eunuch*, London: Paladin.

Guimarães, M.J.L. (2005) 'Doing anthropology in cyberspace', in *Virtual Methods: Issues in Social Research on the Internet*, C. Hine (ed.), Oxford: Berg Publishers, 256.

Hall, S. (1980) *Culture, Media, Language: Working Papers in Cultural Studies, 1972–79*, London/Birmingham: Hutchinson/Centre for Contemporary Cultural Studies, University of Birmingham.

Hall, S. and Jefferson, T. (1975/1991) *Resistance Through Rituals: Youth Subcultures in Post-war Britain*, London: HarperCollins Academic.

Hall, S., Critcher, C., Jefferson, T., Clarke, J. and Roberts, B. (1978) *Policing the Crisis: Mugging, the State and Law and Order*, London: Macmillan Press.

Hartley, J., Montgomery, M., Rennie, E. and Brennan, M. (2002) *Communication, Cultural and Media Studies: The Key Concepts*, London: Routledge, 47.

Haskell, M. (1974) *From Reverence to Rape*, London: Penguin.

Hebdige, D. (1979) *Subculture: The Meaning of Style*, London and New York: Methuen.

Hermes, J. (1995) *Reading Women's Magazines: An Analysis of Everyday Media Use*, Cambridge: Polity Press.

Hills, M. (2002) *Fan Cultures*, London: Routledge.

Hine, C. (2000) *Virtual Ethnography*, London: Sage Publications.

Hodkinson, P. (2002) *Goth: Identity, Style and Subculture*, Oxford: Berg Publishers.

Jenkins, H. (1992) *Textual Poachers: Television Fans and Participatory Culture*, New York and London: Routledge.

Jensen, J. (1992) 'Fandom as pathology: the consequences of characterization', in *The Adoring Audience: Fan Culture and Popular Media*, L.A. Lewis (ed.), London: Routledge.

Jones, S.G. (ed.) (1995) *Cybersociety*, London: Sage.

Jones, S.G. (1997) *Virtual Culture: Identity and Communication in Cybersociety*, London: Sage.

Jordan, T. (1999) *Cyberpower: The Culture and Politics of Cyberspace and the Internet*, London: Routledge.

Katz, E. and Foulkes, D. (1962) 'On the use of the mass media as "escape": clarification of a concept', *Public Opinion Quarterly* 26(3).

Klapper, J.T. (1960) *The Effects of Mass Communication*, New York: Free Press.

Leadbeater, C. (2008) *We-think*, London: Profile Books.

Lull, J. (1990) *Inside Family Viewing: Ethnographic Research on Television's Audiences*, London: Routledge.

Lull, J. (1995) *Media, Communication, Culture: A Global Approach*, Cambridge: Polity Press in association with Blackwell Publishers.

McRobbie, A. (1991) *Feminism and Youth Culture: From 'Jackie' to 'Just Seventeen'*. Basingstoke: Macmillan Education.

Millett, K. (1972) *Sexual Politics*, London: Abacus.

Mitra, A. (1997) 'Virtual commonality: looking for India on the Internet', in *Virtual Culture: Identity and Communication in Cybersociety*, S. Jones (ed.), London: Sage Publications, 272.

Moores, S. (1993) *Interpreting Audiences: The Ethnography of Media Consumption*, London: Sage Publications.

Morley, D. and Brunsdon, C. (1980) *The Nationwide Television Studies*, London and New York: Routledge.

Morley, D. (1992) *Television, Audiences and Cultural Studies*, London: Routledge.

Newman, G. and Clarke, R. (2003) *Superhighway Robbery: Crime Prevention and E-commerce Crime*, Cullompton: Willan Publishinig.

Rheingold, H. (1991) *Virtual Reality*, New York: Summit.

Rheingold, H. (1993) *The Virtual Community HB: Surfing the Internet*, Reading, MA: Perseus Books.

Ruggiero, T. E. (2000) 'Uses and gratifications theory in the 21st century', *Mass Communication and Society* 3(1): 3–37.

Seiter, E., Borchers, H., Kreutzner, G. and Warth, E-M, (eds) (1991) *Remote Control: Television Audiences and Cultural Power*, London: Routledge.

Skeggs, B., Thumim, N. and Wood, H. (2008) 'Oh goodness, I am watching reality TV', *European Journal of Cultural Studies* 11(1): 5–24.

Slevin, J. (2000) *The Internet and Society*, Cambridge: Polity Press.

Stacey, J. (1993) *Star Gazing: Hollywood Cinema and Female Spectatorship*, London: Routledge.

Thomas, L. (2002) *Fans, Feminism and Quality Media*, London: Routledge.

Thornton, S. (1993) *Record hops to raves: authenticity and subcultural capital in music and media cultures.* Unpublished thesis, University of Strathclyde.

Tuchman, G., Kaplan Daniels, A. and Benet, J., (1978) *Hearth and Homes: Images of Women in the Mass Media*, Oxford: Oxford University Press.

Tulloch, J. and Jenkins, H. (1995) *Science Fiction Audiences: Watching Doctor Who and Star Trek*, London: Routledge.

Turkle, S. (1995) *Life on the Screen: Identity in the Age of the Internet*, London: Simon & Schuster.

Vance, C.S. (ed.) (1984) *Pleasure and Danger: Exploring Female Sexuality*, Boston and London: Routledge & Kegan Paul.

Waterson, J. (2000) 'The abuse of power', *Socialist Review*, No. 244 at http://pubs.socialist reviewindex.org.uk/sr244/waterson.htm

Watson, N. (1997) 'Why we argue about virtual community: a case study of the Phish.Net fan community', *Virtual Culture: Identity and Communication in Cybersociety*, London: Sage Publications, 272.

Wellman, B. and Guila, M. (1999) 'The network basis of social support: a network is more than the sum of its ties' in *Networks in the Global Village*, B. Wellman (ed.), Boulder, CO: Westview Press, 408.

Whiteley, S. (1997) *Sexing the Groove: Popular Music and Gender*, London: Routledge.

Willson, M. (1997) 'Community in the abstract: a political and ethical dilemma?' in *Virtual Politics: Identity and Community in Cyberspace*, D. Holmes (ed.), London: Sage, 256.

Winship, J. (1987) *Inside Women's Magazines*, London, New York: Rivers Oram/Pandora List.

Chapter 10: Media power

Althusser, L. (1965/2005) *For Marx*, London: Verso Books.

Althusser, L. and Balibar, E. (1965/1997) *Reading 'Capital'*, London: Verso Books.

Cannadine, D. (2000) *Class in Britain*, Harmondsworth: Penguin Books.

Fairclough, N. (1995) *Media Discourse*, London and New York: Edward Arnold.

Foucault, M. and Hurley, R. (1990) *The History of Sexuality: The Will to Knowledge v.1*, Harmondsworth: Penguin Books.

Foucault, M. and Sheridan, A. (1972) *The Archaeology of Knowledge*, London: Tavistock Publications.

Harvey, D. (2010) *A Companion to Marx's Capital*. London: Verso.

Hutton, W. and Peel, M. (2003) *The Lowest Rung: Voices of Australian Poverty*, Cambridge: Cambridge University Press.

Joyce, P. (ed.) (1995) *Class* (Oxford Reader), Oxford: Oxford Paperbacks.

Marx, K. (1867/1967) *Capital: A Critique of Political Economy – Volume 1: Capitalist Production*, London: Lawrence & Wishart.

Marx, K. and Engels, F. (1848/1969) *Selected Works, Volume one* (tr. S. Moore in co-operation with F. Engels, 1888), Moscow: Progress Publishers. Available at: www.marxists.org/archive/marx/works/1848/communist-manifesto/

Monbiot, G., Balanya, B., Doherty, A., Hoedeman, O., Ma'anit, A. and Wesselius, E. (2003) *Europe Inc.: Regional and Global Restructuring and the Rise of Corporate Power*, London: Pluto Press.

Ricardo, D. (1817/2006) *Principles of Political Economy and Taxation*, New York: Cosimo Inc.

Richardson, J.E. (2006) *Analysing Newspapers: An Approach from Critical Discourse Analysis*, London: Palgrave Macmillan.

Rose, G. (2006) *Visual Methodologies: An Introduction to the Interpretation of Visual Methods*, London: Sage Publications.

Smith, A. (1776/1977) *The Wealth of Nations*, Chicago: University of Chicago Press.

Tagg, J. (1988) *The Burden of Representation: Essays on Photographies and Histories*, London: Palgrave Macmillan.

Wall, T. (2006) 'Calling the tune: resolving the tension between profit and regulation in British commercial music radio', *Southern Review* 39(2).

Wheen, F. (1999) *Karl Marx*, London: Fourth Estate.

Chapter 11: Conceptualising mass society

Adorno, T.W. and Horkheimer, M. (1997) *Dialectic of Enlightenment*, London: Verso Books.

Arnold, M. (1882/1932) *Culture and Anarchy: Landmarks in the History of Education*, Cambridge: Cambridge University Press.

Bentley, E. (ed.) (2002) *Thirty Years of Treason: Excerpts from Hearings Before the House Committee on Un-American Activities, 1938–1968*, New York: Thunder's Mouth Press.

Cantril, H. (1940) with H, Gaudet and H. Herzog, *The Invasion from Mars: A Study in the Psychology of Panic*, Princeton, NJ: Princeton University Press.

Eliot, T.S. (1949) *Notes Towards the Definition of Culture*, Oxford: Harcourt.

Gladchuk, J. (2006) *Hollywood and Anticommunism: HUAC and the Evolution of the Red Menace, 1935–1950*, London: Routledge.

Hacking, I. (ed.) (1981) *Scientific Revolutions* (Oxford Readings in Philosophy), Oxford and New York: Oxford University Press.

Hand, R. (2005) *Terror on the Air! Horror Radio in America, 1931–1952*, Jefferson, NC: McFarland & Co. Inc.

Hesmondhalgh, D. (2002) *The Cultural Industries: An Introduction*, London: Sage Publications.

Hobsbawm, E. (1996a) *The Age of Capital: 1848–1875*, London: Vintage.

Hobsbawm, E. (1996b) *The Age of Revolution: 1789–1848*, London: Vintage.

Hoggart, R. (1958) *The Uses of Literacy*, Harmondsworth, Middlesex: Penguin Books.

Keen, A. (2007) *The Cult of the Amateur: How Today's Internet Is Killing Our Culture and Assaulting Our Economy*. London and Boston: Nicholas Brealey.

Macdonald, D. (1957a) 'A corrupt brightness', *Encounter*, VIII(6).

Macdonald, D. (1957b) *The Responsibility of Peoples, and Other Essays in Political Criticism*, London: Victor Gollancz Ltd.

McQuail, D. (2005) *McQuail's Mass Communication Theory*, London: Sage Publications.

Nietzsche, F. (1883–5/1967) *Thus Spoke Zarathustra: A Book for Everyone and No One*, Harmondsworth: Penguin Books.

Thompson, D. and Leavis, F.R. (1933) *Culture and Environment: The Training of Critical Awareness*, London: Chatto & Windus.

Weightman, G. (2007) *The Industrial Revolutionaries: The Creation of the Modern World, 1776–1914*, London: Atlantic.

Williams, R. (1958/1961) *Culture and Society 1780–1950*, Harmondsworth: Penguin in association with Chatto & Windus.

Williams, R. (1958/1990) *Culture Is Ordinary*, London and Stoke-on-Trent: Workers' Educational Association, Raymond Williams Memorial Fund.

Williams, R. (1967) 'Culture and revolution: a response' in T. Eagleton and B. Wicker (eds), *From Culture to Revolution: the Slant Symposium 1967*, London and Sydney: Sheed and Ward, 296–308.

Williams, T. (1945/1987) *The Glass Menagerie Screenplay*, New York: Signet.

Chapter 12: Modernism, postmodernism and after

Anderson, P. (1998) *The Origins of Postmodernity*, London: Verso Books.

Baudrillard, J. (1983) *Simulations*, New York City: Semiotext(e) Inc.

Baudrillard, J. (1995) *The Gulf War Did Not Take Place*, Bloomington: Indiana University Press.

Baudrillard, J. and Turner, C. (1986, transl. 1988) *America*, London: Verso.

Beller, J. (2006) *The Cinematic Mode of Production*, Hanover, NH: Dartmouth College Press, University Press of New England.

Benjamin, W. (1929/1997) *One-way Street and Other Writings*, London: Verso Books.

Benjamin, W. (1936/2008) *The Work of Art in the Age of Mechanical Reproduction*, London: Penguin Books.

Boyne, R. and Rattansi, A. (1990) *Postmodernism and Society*, London: Palgrave Macmillan.

Brecht, B. (1964/1994) 'The modern theatre is the epic theatre: notes to the opera Aufstieg und Fall der Stadt Mahagonny', in *Brecht on Theatre: The Development of an Aesthetic*, New York: Hill & Wang, 352.

Carey, J. (1992) *The Intellectuals and the Masses: Pride and Prejudice Among the Literary Intelligentsia, 1800–1939*, London and Boston: Faber & Faber.

Chomsky, N. (1967) 'A special supplement: the responsibility of intellectuals', *New York Review of Books* 8(3).

Eagleton, T. (1996) *The Illusions of Postmodernism*, Oxford: WileyBlackwell.

Eagleton, T. (2004) *After Theory*, London: Penguin Books.

Eco, U. (1975/1986) *Travels in Hyperreality: Essays*, Oxford: Harcourt.

Fukuyama, F. (1992) *The End of History and the Last Man*, Harmondsworth: Penguin.

Gilroy, P. (1993a) *Small Acts: Thoughts on the Politics of Black Cultures*, London: Serpent's Tail.

Gilroy, P. (1993b) *The Black Atlantic: Modernity and Double Consciousness*, London: Verso.

Habermas, J. (1988) *The Philosophical Discourse of Modernity*, Cambridge: Polity Press.

Hughes, R. (1991) *The Shock of the New: Art and the Century of Change*, London: Thames & Hudson Ltd.

Jameson, F. (1991) *Postmodernism, or, the Cultural Logic of Late Capitalism*, Durham, NC: Duke University Press.

Jencks, C. (1990) *Language of Post-modern Architecture*, New York: Rizzoli International Publications.

Joyce, J. (1922/2000) *Ulysses*, London: Penguin.

Joyce, J. (1939/2000) *Finnegans Wake*, London: Penguin.

Kronschnabl, A. and Rawlings, T. (2004) *Plug In and Turn On: A Filmmaker's Guide to the Internet*. London: Marion Boyars.

Lyotard, J.-F. (1979/1984) *The Postmodern Condition: A Report on Knowledge*, Minneapolis: University of Minnesota Press.

MacDonald, Ian (1994/2005) *Revolution in the Head: The Beatles' Records and the Sixties*. London: Pimlico.

Morrey, D. (2005) *Jean-Luc Godard*, Manchester: Manchester University Press.

Porter, R. (1990) *The Enlightenment*, London: Palgrave Macmillan.

Roberts, I. (2008) *German Expressionist Cinema: The World of Light and Shadow*, London: Wallflower Press.

Rosenberg, J. and Garofalo, G. (1998) 'Riot Grrrl: revolutions from within', *Signs* 23(3): 809–41.

Ross, A. (2008) *The Rest Is Noise: Listening to the Twentieth Century*, London: Fourth Estate.

Said, Edward (1978/2003) *Orientalism* (25th Anniversary Edition). Harmondsworth: Penguin.

Schilt, K. (2003) ' "A little too ironic": the appropriation and packaging of Riot Grrrl politics by mainstream female musicians', *Popular Music and Society* 26(1): 5–16.

Sokal, A. (2008) *Beyond the Hoax: Science, Philosophy and Culture*, Oxford: Oxford University Press.

Stevenson, J. (2004) *Dogme Uncut: Lars von Trier, Thomas Vinterberg, and the Gang That Took on Hollywood*, Santa Monica, CA: Santa Monica Press.

Temple, M. and Williams, J.S. (eds) (2001) *The Cinema Alone: Essays on the Work of Jean-Luc Godard 1985–2000*, Amsterdam: Amsterdam University Press.

Vertov, D. (1922/1944) 'We. A Version of a Manifesto' in I. Christie and R. Taylor (eds), *The Film Factory: Russian and Soviet Cinema in Documents*, 1896–1939, London: Routledge, 69–7.

White, H. (1987) *Content of the Form: Narrative Discourse and Historical Representation*, London and Baltimore: Johns Hopkins University Press.

Chapter 13: The consumer society and advertising

7th Chamber (2011) *Our Services*. [online]. Available from: www.the7thchamber.com/services/ [Accessed 20/06/11].

Adbusters (2008) *About Adbusters*. [online]. Available from: www.adbusters.org/network/about_us.php [Accessed 17/01/08].

Ball, K., Lyon, D., Wood, D.M., Norris, C. and Raab, C. (2006) A Report on the Surveillance Society. [online]. *The Surveillance Studies Network*. Available from: www.ico.gov.uk/upload/documents/library/data_protection/practical_application/surveillance_society_full_report_2006.pdf [Accessed 06/12/10]

Barthes, R. (1992) *The Fashion System*, Berkeley, CA: University of California Press.

Battelle, J. (2005) *The Search: How Google and Its Rivals Rewrote the Rules of Business and Transformed Our Culture*, London: Nicholas Brealey.

Baudrillard, J. (1968) *The System of Objects*, London: Verso Books.

Baudrillard, J. (1970/1999) *The Consumer Society: Myths and Structures*, London: Sage.

Bauman, Z. (2000) *Liquid Modernity*, Oxford: Polity Press.

Bourdieu, P. (1984) *Distinction: A Social Critique of the Judgement of Taste*, Cambridge, MA: Harvard University Press.

Bovee, C.L. and Arens, W.F. (1992) *Contemporary Advertising*, Boston: Richard D. Irwin, Inc.

Clarke, R (1999) *Introduction to Dataveillance and Information Privacy, and Definition of Terms*. [online]. Available from: www.anu.edu.au/people/Roger.Clarke/DV/Intro.html [Accessed 12/2/04]

Corrigan, P. (1997) *The Sociology of Consumption*, London: Sage.

Danna, A. and Gandy, O. (2002) 'All that glitters is not gold: digging beneath the surface of data mining', *Journal of Business Ethics* 40(4): 373–86.

Dyer, G. (1982/1993) *Advertising as Communication*. London: Routledge.

Ewen, S. (1976) *Captains of Consciousness. Advertising and the Social Roots of Consumer Culture*, New York: McGraw-Hill.

IAB (2011) *Full Year 2010: Internet Advertising worth over £4 billion*. [online]. www.iabuk.net/media/images/iabresearch_adspend_adspendfct-sht2010_7818.pdf [Accessed 28/06/11].

IPRA (2007) *Consumer PR – Doritos Crashes the Superbowl*. [online]. Available from: www.ipra.org/detail.asp?articleid=266 [Accessed 22/01/08].

Kotler, P. (2003) *Marketing Management*, Upper Saddle River, NJ: Prentice-Hall.

Lasn, K. (1999) *Culture Jamming: The Uncooling of America*. New York: Eagle Brook.

Lazzarato, M. (1996) 'Immaterial labour', in *Radical Thought in Italy*, eds. P. Virno and M. Hardt, 132–46. Minneapolis: University of Minnesota Press.

McStay, A. (2007) 'Regulating the suicide bomber: a critical examination of online viral advertising and simulations of self-broadcasting', *Ethical Space: the International Journal of Communication Ethics* 4(1–2): 40–8.

McStay, A. (2009) *Digital Advertising*. Basingstoke: Palgrave Macmillan.

McStay, A. (2011a) *The Mood of Information: A Critique of Online Behavioural Advertising*. New York: Continuum.

McStay, A. (2011b) 'Profiling phorm: an autopoietic approach to the audience-as-commodity', *Surveillance and Society*. 8(3), 310–22.

McStay, A. and Bakir, V. (2006) 'Privacy, online advertising and marketing techniques: the paradoxical disappearance of the user', *Ethical Space: the International Journal of Communication Ethics* 3(1): 24–31.

Miller, D. (ed.) (1995) *Acknowledging Consumption*. London: Routledge.

Miller, D (1997) 'Consumption and its consequences', in Mackay, H. (ed.), *Consumption and Everyday Life*. London: Sage, 14–50.

Ofcom (2006) *Media Literacy Audit: Report on Media Literacy Amongst Children* [online]. Available from: stakeholders.ofcom.org.uk/binaries/research/media-literacy/children.pdf. [Accessed 28/06/11].

Punj, G. and Stewart, D.W. (1983) 'Cluster analysis in marketing research: review and suggestions for application', *Journal of Marketing Research* 20(2): 134–48.

Ritzer, G. (1997) *Postmodern Social Theory*, New York: McGraw-Hill.

Sabbagh, D (2007) Google shows ITV a vision of the future. [online]. *The Times Online*. Available from: http://business.timesonline.co.uk/tol/business/industry_sectors/media/article2767087.ece [Accessed 30/10/07].

Spurgeon, C. (2007) *Advertising and New Media*. London: Routledge.

Terranova, T. (2004) *Network Culture: Politics for the Information Age*. London: Pluto Press.

Turow, J. (2003) 'Americans and Online Privacy: The System is Broken'. [online]. *Annenberg Public Policy Center*, University of Pennsylvania. Available from: www.asc.upenn.edu/usr/jturow/Internet-privacy-report/36-page-turow-version-9.pdf, date [Accessed 22/01/11].

Veblen, T. (1899/1975) *The Theory of the Leisure Class*, New York: Augustus M. Kelley.

Chapter 14: Media histories

Briggs, A. (1961) *The History of Broadcasting in the United Kingdom*. London, New York: Oxford University Press.

Briggs, A.T. and Spicer, J. (1986) *The Franchise Affair*, London: Century.

Carr, E.H. (1961) *What Is History?*, London: Macmillan.

Chanan, M. (1995) *Repeated Takes: A Short History of Recording and its Effects on Music*, London and New York: Verso Books.

Curran, J. (2002) 'Media and the making of British society, c.1700–2000', *Media History* 2(1): 135–54.

Douglas, S.J. (1999) *Listening in: Radio and the American Imagination, from Amos 'n' Andy and Edward R. Murrow to Wolfman Jack and Howard Stern*, New York: Times Books.

Foucault, M. and Sheridan A. (1972) *The Archaeology of Knowledge*, London: Tavistock Publications.

Goldman, W. (1983/1986) *Adventures in the Screen Trade: A Personal View of Hollywood and Screenwriting*, London: Abacus.

Harker, D. (1992) 'Still crazy after all these years: what was popular music in the 1960s' in *Cultural Revolution? The Challenge of the Arts in the 1960s*, B.J. Moore-Gilbert and J. Seed (eds), London: Routledge.

Jacobs, J. (2000) *The Intimate Screen: Early British Television Drama*, Oxford: Oxford University Press.

Jameson, F. (2002) 'The dialectics of disaster', *South Atlantic Quarterly* 101(2), Spring: 297–304.

McLuhan, M. and McLuhan, E. (1988) *Laws of Media: The New Science*, Toronto and Buffalo, NY: University of Toronto Press.

Rees, A.L. (1999) *A History of Experimental Film and Video*, London: BFI Publishing.

Sanjek, R. and Sanjek, D. (1996) *American Popular Music Business in the 20th Century*, New York: De Capo.

Shingler, M. and Wieringa, C. (1998) *On Air: Methods and Meanings of Radio*, New York: Arnold.

Sreberny-Mohamrnadi, A. (1995) 'Forms of media as ways of knowing' in John D. H. Downing, Ali Mohammadi and Annabelle Sreberny-Mohammadi (eds) *Questioning the Media: A Critical Introduction*. London and Thousand Oaks, CA: Sage, 23–38.

Sweet, M. (2005) *Shepperton Babylon: The Lost Worlds of British Cinema*, London: Faber and Faber.

Thompson, E.P. (1963) *The Making of the English Working Class*, London: Gollancz.

Williams, R. (1992) *Television: Technology and Cultural Form*, Hanover, CT: Wesleyan University Press.

Index

Terms in **bold** indicate glossary entries.

Aamir 13
Abercrombie, N. 77
aberrant reading 62
'above-the-line' media 437, **488**
Achtung Baby (U2) 414
adbusting 424, 441–2, 445
Adorno, T. 285, 380, 382–7, 393, 402
advertising 7–8, 120, 160, 171, 173, 175, 176, 419, **488**
  agencies 426, 430, 434–6, 442–4
  behavioural 440–1, 444–5
  consumer society and 424–45
  digital age 434–41
  future of 442–3
  not-for-profit campaigns 434, 436, 442
  online 435, 437, 438, 440, 443–4
  personalised 439–40
  PR and marketing 434
  privacy and 424, 440–1, 442
  simulated intimacy 430–1, 432, 443
  viral 438, 444, **490**
aesthetic approach 469, 474–6, 478, 481
affect 36, 40, 47, 160, **488**
affective response 34, 46, 47
agency 103, 140, 361, 367
Agent Provocateur viral ad 438
Akademiks 63
Al Jazeera 239, 260–2, 263–4, 267
al-Qaeda 243, 408
alibi 159, 164
Aliens 79, 88, 89
Allen, L. 50, 197
alliteration 38
allusion 38, 62
Alterman, J.B. 259, 261, 262
Althusser, L. 356, 359–62, 364, 367, 388
amazon.com 78, 178, 198, 439
American Dreams (NBC TV) 410
analepsis 88
analysing media texts 32, 66–7
  reality media 158–65
  rhetoric 33–48, 64–5

semiology 49–64, **490**
  see also meaning
Anderson, C. 198–9, 200, 201
Ang, I. 280, 315, 337
AOL 181–2, 242, 243
Appadurai, A. 266
Arab Spring (2010) 362–3, 374
Arab Spring (2011) 266
Archers, The 333
archetypes 106–8
architectural modernism 408
archives 467–70
Arctic Monkeys 36, 197
Aristotle 35, 81, 87, 134
Arnold, M. 375–6, 381, 388–90, 393
artefact 30, 174, 192, 276–8, 468, **488**
Artz, L. 254, 266
Associated Press 238, 239, 257
asylum seekers 102, 105, 108
audience 180, 184, 193, 384, 435, **488**
  active 301, 303–4, 324–30
  affective response 34, 46, 47
  artefact form and 276–7, 278
  as collective 279–80
  as commodity 174, 185–6
  commodity form of product 276–7
  consumption activity 437–8
  definitions 276–85, **488**
  genre and 73–4, 77–9, 82
  implied 48, 310
  investigating 300–339
  manipulation of 286–90
  mass 176, 383, 403
  media, context and meaning 310–30
  media effects 290–4
  media uses/gratifications 304–10
  online activity 324–30
  producing 274–96
  realism and 136–7
  researching 280–1, 330–9
  as response 278, 279
  as social group 279–80
  as spectator 313

textual meaning and 277, 279
  theorising 307–10
  see also effects research
auteur 80, 81, 91, 311
autoethnography 315
avant-garde 140, 399, 402–3, 405, **488**
award schemes 475
Azad, A.K. 253–4
Azeez, W. 119

Bagdikian, B. 184
Bakardjieva, M. 337
Bakir, V. 182, 243, 258, 260
Ball, K. 441
Balnaves, M. 181, 251, 253, 257
  global media 238, 241, 245, 248
  Hollywood's dominance 245, 247, 256
Bar-Ilan, J. 242
Barber, B.R. 265
Barilli, R. 35
Barker, H. 154
Barker, M. 283
Barthes, R. 58–9, 63, 84, 139, 160, 307, 311, 317, 359, 430
  on myth 353, 356
  on *Paris Match* 158–9
Battelle, J. 437
Baudrillard, J. 249, 407, 411–12, 428–32
Bauman, Z. 407, 428, 444
Baym, N. 324, 325
BBC 78, 248, 260–1, 310, 370
  business issues 174, 176, 180, 187–9
  development 450, 459, 469–70, 473
  radio 223, 333
  reality programmes 143, 145–6, 150–1
  regulation 220–2, 223–4
  representations 109, 114–17, 119
  World Service 237, 262, 265
Beaton, J. 259
Bebo 8, 182, 324, 325

behavioural effects 284–5
Bell, D. 337
Benjamin, W. 380, 402
Bennett, T. 208
Bentley, E. 379
Berlin (Pillow Fight Day) 300
Berlusconi, S. 344, 352
Bernays, E. 13, 286
Berne Convention (1886) 225
Bernink, M. 319
Bertelsmann AG 27, 189, 237
bias 117, 366
Big Brother 77, 125, 146, 151, 266
Big Lebowski, The 320
Biskind, P. 78, 175
Bittanti, M. 294
Black Britain website 119
Blair Witch Project 95–6, 418
blogs/blogging 4, 149, 197, 200, 240,
    324–5, 329, 330, 438
Blumler, J. 304, 306
body image 274–5
Bollywood 13, 139, 258
Bono 414
Booker, C. 85
bootlegging concerts 303–4, 321
Bordwell, D. 41, 85, 87, 89, 140
Bore, I-L. 323–4
Botting, A. 460–1
Bouazizi, M. 262, 263
Bourdieu, P. 320, 327, 429
Boyd, D.A. 264, 265
Boyd-Barrett, O. 239, 258
Boyne, R. 417
Bradshaw, P. 240
brand name/recognition 160–1
branding 60, 172, 176, 193, 430,
    442–4
    identity 429, 433, 438–9
Brecht, B. 399, 401
bricolage 317
Briggs, A. 211, 221, 473
British Library 468
broadcasting 4, 200
    development (UK/USA) 214–15,
        248–50
    regulation (history) 208–9, 250
broadcasting model 439–40, 442
broadsheets 36, 171, 172, 475
Broomfield, N. 144–5
Brunsdon, C. 81, 307, 310, 313, 393
Brzezinski, M. 185
Bulger, James 292–3
'bullet-time' technologies 88
bulletin board systems 325
Burke, P. 211
Burton, G. 108
Bush, G.W. 308–9
businesses, media 168
    audience as commodity 175–6
    audiences produced by 279–83
    commodity relations 174–5
    conceptualising 170
    corporate influence 180
    cost structure/risk management
        177–9
    culture of production 192–7

in digital age 197–202
    distribution 180, 184
    economies of scale 179–80, 489
    free market 173–4
    Hotelling effect 176
    investigating 171–2
    long tail 198–9
    organisational studies 185–92
    revenue 174–5
    size and concentration 179–83
Butler, J. 111

cable television 249–50
Cadbury's 'Gorilla' advertisement 438
CALEA 246–7
Cameron, J. 88, 89
Campion, C. 107
Canal+ 27, 168
Cannadine, D. 347
canons 80, 475
Cantor, J. 274
Cantril, H. 285, 379
capital 404, 407, 419, 421
capitalism 173–4, 254, 256, 289, 349,
        354, 390, 407–8, 410, 441, 445
    ideology 380, 382–4, 387, 419
    Riot Grrrl and 403, 404
captioning 35, 62
Cardiff, D. 221–2
Carlsson, U. 291
Carr, E.H. 454
Carroll, N. 138
cartel 238, 239, 247, 251, **488**
cartoons 243, 244, 319, 344
catharsis 291, 384, 402
Caughie, J. 81
CBS 182, 255, 256
celebrities 124–7, 146–7, 319, 411
censorship 207, 208–9, 211
    internet 234–5, 243, 245, 267
Chabrol, C. 12
Chaffee, S.H. 284
Chanan, M. 479
Chanel advert 159–65, 310
Channel 4 100, 114, 115
chat rooms 292, 325
Cherribi, S. 260
Cheung, C. 329
children 8, 83, 280–1, 297–8
China 2, 173, 234–5, 329, 331, 424
    propaganda 286, 290
Chomsky, N. 255, 288, 289, 420
chronology 461–5, 480, **488**
cinema 216, 467
    classical 85–7, 140–1, 402–3
    modern and modernism 402,
        404–6, 409
    see also film
citizen journalism 149, 197, 259,
        329–30
citizenship 184, 208, 246
civil society 356, 358, 359
Clarke, J. 315
Clarke, R. 328, 440
class 347–9, 361, 363, 373, **488**
    representation 102, 105, 115, 120
    see also working class

classic realist film 85–7, 140–1, 402–3
Cleese, J. 107
Clerc, S. 321–2
cliché 38, 108
closure 79–80, 89–91, 97
CNN 150, 242, 261, 266
CNN effect 249–50, 267, **488**
codes 60–1, 429
cognition 33, **488**
Cohen, C.J. 112
Cohen, S. 291, 316
Columbine High School massacre
        350–1
Colwell, T. 258
comics 4–5, 7, 30
commercial broadcasting 248–50
commodity 30, 63, 175–6, 276,
        384, **488**
    fetishism 384, 393, 430
communication flows 259, 260–2
Communications Act (2003) 211, 214
commutation test 56–7, 123, 125, 161
competition 173–4, 179
computers (children's ownership) 8
concentration 179–80, **488**
conglomerates 180–1, 247, 255–9
connotation 58, 104–5, 106, 122, 125
    Chanel advert 162, 163
    Paris Match image 158
consume 31, 428, **488**
consumer society
    branding 430, 433–4
    digital age 434–41
    historical context 426–7
    theorising 428–32
consumption 8, 9, 31, 210, 303, 386
    as audience activity 437–8
    branding and identity 429, 433–4
    conformity and 431
    cultures of 427–8
    defining 428
    future of 442–3
    global activity 424
    history of 426
    postmodernity and 433
    rejecting 441–2
    signification 429–30, 431
content analysis 122–3, 127, **488**
control, media power and 346–50,
        353, 355, 358–60, 362
controls 207–9, 218, 223, 230
conventions 75, 77, 85, 89, 95
    Chanel advert 160–2
    codes and 72–4, 76, 80, 82, 87–8
convergence 247, 248, 424, 437, **488**
Cook, P. 319
cookies 440–1
'copyleft' 405–6
copyright 225–9, 247–8, 253–4, **488**
Corbin, K. 182
corporate influence/culture 180, 441
Corrigan, P. 429
cost structure 177–9, 183, 201
Costello, V. 323
Couldry, N. 327
Couts, A. 264
Cowboys and Aliens 70, 73, 75, 86

Craig, T. 293
Creative Commons Licensing 229
creative workers 186–7, 190, 192–7
creativity 81, 225, 385
Crimewatch 366
critical distance 11, 32
critical political economy 173
critical theory 380, 382
'crowd-sourcing' 374, 377
CSI 75, 90–1
Cubism 399, 400
cultural capital 320, 327
cultural imperialism 235, 256, 258, 264, 385
cultural policy 212–14
cultural production 186, 385
cultural values 80–2
culturalism 371, 387, 393
culture
    authentic 376, 382–3, 393, 442
    collapse of boundaries 409, 412, 422
    definitions 376, 388–90, 393
    high/low 80, 376, 382–7, 392
    mass society and 375–7
    of production 192–7
    see also mass culture
culture, version one 376, **488–9**
culture, version two 389–90, **489**
culture industry 295, 382–7, 393, 402, **489**
'culture jamming' 441–2, 445
Cumberbatch, G. 291
Cumberland, S. 323
Curran, J. 211, 222, 456, 478, 480

Dada movement 399–400
daguerrotype 135, 138
Daily Mail 100
Daily Mirror 34, 35, 37, 130
Dalai Lama 287, 290
Danna, A. 441
data mining 424, 439–41, 444–5, **489**
de Certeau, M. 321
de Lauretis, T. 113
De Saussure, F. 49, 58, 61, 63, 73, 154
    on language 295, 359
    semiological terms 51–4, 55, 56
de-territorialisation 266
death of history 409–10, 422
death of meaning 410–12, 413, 422
death metal music 415
death of scarcity 199–201
death of the subject 412–13, 422, 433–4
deception 328–9, 385–6
decoding 49, 61, 301, 307–10, 339, 429
Demers, D.P. 181, 235, 251, 255, 256
democracy 35, 183–4, 256, 262, 266, 390
    media and 146–9, 207, 220, 479
    political power and 348–9
demographics 338, 439
denotation 58, 104, 125, 154, 158
    Chanel advert 162, 164
deregulation 181, 218, 254, 257

radio 223, 224
television 147
Derrida, J. 154, 407
Descent, The 79
Deutsche Telekom 168–9
deviance/deviant groups 291, 292
diachronic approach 51, 56, 74, **489**
Dickinson, R. 291, 292
Die Hard 4 255–6
diegesis 86, 90, 134, **489**
Diesel adverts 432, 438
digital divide 238, 327
digital rights management 228, 247
digitisation 16, 64, 137, 182, 228, 247, 259, 321
    advertising and 434–41
    media business and 197–202
Dimbleby, R. 108
discourse 363–7, **489**
Disney 10, 27, 237, 247, 255, 330–1
distribution 177–8, 180, 184
diversion 306
documentary forms 41, 133–4, 141–6, 404
Dogme 95 group 405
Donald, S. 265
Donath, J. 329
Doritos Superbowl advertising 437
Douglas, S. 479
Dove ad campaign 431, 432, 438
Dr Strangelove 416, 417
Du Gay, P. 192, 193
Duchamp, M. 400
dumbing down 222, 376, 377
Dyche, E. 94
Dyer, R. 113, 127, 393, 427

Eagleton, T. 407, 419, 421
Eastwood, C. 75, 125
eBay 328
Eco, U. 49, 61–3, 85, 307, 317, 411, 417
economic intervention 209
economies of scale 179–80, 199, 254, **489**
Edison, T.A. 4, 454, 478
editorial rhetoric 42, 44–7, 47
Egypt 262, 263–4, 362–3
effects research 274–5, 295, 379
    evaluating claims 297–8
    theories/models 283, 284–5
    uses and gratifications 304–10, 339
Eisenstein, S. 12, 295, 404, 405
Eliot, T.S. 319, 381, 390, 409
Elle 50
Elliot, P. 189, 190
ellipses 38
Ellis, J. 124, 149
EMAP 148, 171
Eminem 120, 125
Emo subculture 317, 318
empirical 133, 150, **489**
encoding 49, 61, 301, 307–10, 339
Endemol 77, 146
Engelman, R. 222
Engels, F. 354, 355, 357

Eno, B. 414
entertainment, global 245, 247–8
Espinosa, P. 192–3
ESRC 338
establishing shot 47
ethics 149–53, 217, 326, 337–40
ethnography 141, 193, 321, 335, **489**
    soap operas 324, 336
    virtual 337
Ettema, J.S. 189
euphemism 38
Euro-cult cinema 322
Europe 378
    EU regulation 212, 246, 252, 258
    film industry 252–3, 254, 322
    public-service broadcasting 251
Evans, H. 265
exchange value 384
expectations, genre and 79–82
Express and Star 182–3
Expressionist films 404
extra-diegetic elements 86

fabula 87–8, 89, 92, 324, **489**
Facebook 182, 237, 262–3, 267, 296, 325, 329, 438, 440, 444, 451, 469, 471
Fairclough, N. 365, 366
Family Guy fans 321
fans/fandom 77, 333, 430
    subcultures and 319–24, 340
fantasy and aristocracy 137
Farrelly Brothers 86, 93
fascism, mass society and 381
female characters 86, 93
femininity 111–12, 312, 315
feminism 311–15, 333, 339–40, 419, 421
    and heterosexual narratives 91
50-Cent 107, 108, 120, 438
file-sharing 185, 197, 247–8, 304, 329
film 12–13, 41, 78, 112, 124–5
    classical realist 85–7, 140–1, 402–3
    disruption-enigma-resolution 85–7
    filmmaking and 81, 245–7, 405–6
    narratology 84–7
    origins 4, 454–5
    see also Bollywood; Hollywood; horror films; Western films
Film 4 115
Fincher, D. 86, 88, 409
Finlayson, A. 154
Fiore, Q. 265
first-person shooter games 415, 463–4
Fishman, M. 191
Fiske, J. 79
flags 58, 60, 158–9
Flaherty, R. 141–2
flashbacks/flashforwards 88, 92
Flickr 324
Florida, R. 195
focus groups 285, 297, 315, 334–5, 476
foley operators 40, 193
folk culture 83–4, 376, 382

folk music 137, 155
Ford, J. 81
Formalists/Formalism 83, 85, 87
Foucault, M. 113, 360, 363–7,
    407, 456
Foulkes, D. 305
Foursquare 440, 442
fourth estate 149, 305, 398
Fox TV 197, 255, 321, 349
France 81, 106, 118, 158, 209,
    217, 238
Frankfurt School 295, 356, 376,
    380–3, 385, 387–8, 393, 402
free market 173–4, 179, 184,
    309, **489**
    global media 250–5, 257, 258, 267
freedom 149–56
    of expression 207, 209, 217,
        259–62
    of speech 207, 257, 262
freelance writer 195–6
freesheets 179
Freud, S. 13, 399
Friedan, B. 312
Friends 274, 275
Friends Reunited 411, 471
Frith, S. 41, 222
Fromm, E. 380
Fukuyama, F. 396
functionalist approach 305, 307

Galloway, G. 460–1
Galtung, J. 258
Gance, A. 402
Gandy, O. 441
gangsta rap 36, 73, 102, 107,
    292, 415
Garofalo, G. 403
gatekeeping 190–2
Gauntlett, D. 283, 292
gaze, masculine 93, 278
Geertz, C. 193, 335
Geldof, B. 149
gender 111–13, 123, 127, 274,
    324, **489**
    audience activity and 311–15
    power and 348, 363
generic programming 76–7, 78–9,
    95–6
Genette, G. 83
genre 70–82, 160, **489**
    Chanel advert 160–2
    codes/conventions 76, 80, 82,
        160–2
    consumer dimension 78–9, 82
    cultural values 80, 82
    defining 72–3
    dynamic and hybrid 75–7
    dynamism and exhaustion 73–82
    expectations and 73–4, 78–82
    gendered 313–14
    hybrid 75–7, 95–6, 412
    ideological closure 79–80
    innovation and repetition 77–8
    meaning-making 79–80
    narrative 82, 95–6
    organising audiences 77–9, 82

paradigm/syntagm 73, 74
    repeat purchasing 177
geo-demographics 439
Geraghty, C. 314
Gerbner, G. 252, 257, 258, 284
German Expressionist Cinema 404
Ghostwatch 150–1
giallo film 72, 322
Gibson, M. 121, 141
Giddens, A. 245
Gill, R. 196, 278
Gillian, A. 241
Gilligan, A. 37
Gilroy, P. 393, 419
Girard, B. 241–3, 248, 250–2, 254, 257
Gladchuk, J. 379
Glasgow Media Group 136
Gledhill, C. 124
global media production 234–66
    blogging and 240
    critics of conglomerates 255–9
    cultural/social effects 265–6
    definitions 237–64
    entertainment 245, 247–8
    free markets and regulation 250–5
    heterogenerisation 266
    hybridisation 266
    impact of 263, 264–6
    indigenisation 266
    information as basis 238–41
    new environments 241–3
    political effects 264–5
    regulation 243–5, 250–5
    roots 238–41
    as spur to deveeloopment 264
    television and 248–50
global village 6, 265–6
globalisation 245, 419, 424, **489**
    evaluating and resisting 255–64
Glover, J. 150, 151
Godard, J-L. 12, 81, 88, 402–3, 405
Goffman, E. 328
Goldhaber, M. 200
Golding, P. 173, 189, 190
Goldman, W. 476
Good Night, and Good Luck 379
Google 64–5, 182, 200, 234–5, 377
    advertising on 437, 443, 444
    News 237, 241–2
government 344, 346–9, 353,
    359, 366
    see also policy; regulation
Gramsci, A. 307, 317, 356, 358–61,
    363, 367, 380, 393
'grand narratives' 410, 413, 419
Gray, A. 315, 393
Green, D.C. 243
Gresham's Law 377
Grierson, J. 12, 137, 141, 142
Grillo, I. 318
Gripsrud, J. 295
Groening, M. 415
Gross, L. 284
Groundhog Day 89
Guardian 130, 210, 241
Guila, M. 327
Guimarães, M. 325

Gulf War 249, 289, 411–12
Gupta, R. 13
Gutman, T. 242

Habermas, J. 183–4, 380, 407, 419
Haggerty, G.E. 113
Hall, S. 307–10, 317, 339, 387, 392–3
Halloran, J. 304
Halo 2 300–1
Hand, R. 379
Hare, G. 209
Hargreaves, D. 274
Harker, D. 475
Harrison, K. 274
Harry Potter 5, 137, 321, 385
Hartley, J. 79, 281–2, 320
Harvey, D. 357, 407
Haskell, M. 312
Hawkins, V. 249
Hawks, H. 81
Hebdige, D. 317, 319, 407
Heeb magazine 121
Hegel, G.W.F. 354–5
hegemony 308, 356, 358–9, 363
Hendy, D. 224
Hepworth, C. 467
Herman, E.S. 255, 289
Hermes, J. 313–14
Herrick, J. 35
Hesmondhalgh, D. 190, 385
heterogenerisation 266
heteronormativity 113
heterosexuality 112, 114
Hickman, J. 323–4
hierarchies 347, 353, 356, 364, 365
Hills, M. 320, 321
Hilmes, M. 222
Hine, C. 337
historical realism 134–9
historiography 450–81, **489**
    approaches/doing 453, 461–5
    archives 467–70
    chronologies 461–5, 480, **488**
    defined 453–4, **489**
    primary/secondary sources
        465–72
history 450, 453, **489**
    death of 409–10, 422
    media as 457–61
    sense of 460
    writing 472–80
Hitchcock, A. 81, 88, 417
Hitler, A. 286, 287, 380, 381
Hobsbawm, E. 373
Hobson, D. 315
Hockheimer, J.L. 284
Hockney, D. 135
Hodkinson, P. 318
Hoffman, H. 286
Hoggart, R. 309, 387, 390–3
Hollywood 93, 313, 378–9, 383,
    404, 475
    blockbusters 78, 91, 103, 175, 455
    global dominance 245, 247, 255–6
Holocaust 152
homology 317, 319
homosexuality 113–16, 257, 421

horizontal integration 180
Horkheimer, M. 380, 382–7, 393, 402
Horrocks, D. 109–10
horror films 79, 88, 95–6, 104
    snuff movies 152–3, 293, 417
Horten, G. 265
Hostel (Roth) 415, 417, 418
Hotelling effect 176, 180, 201
Hour, The 410
house style 39–40, 191
humour 108–9, 114, 116, 121
Humphrys, J. 9, 10, 37
Hurley, R. 365
Hutchings, P. 85
Hutton, W. 348
hybrid genres 76–7, 143, 266
hyper-reality 132, 411
hypodermic models 283, 285

I Am Legend 140
I Love Bees 301
I, Robot 73
i-Tunes 198, 199, 451
iconic signs 102, 125, 158
    relationship 51, 59–60, 104,
        161, 163
idealism 349, 355
identity 193, 305, 412–13
    branding and 429, 433–4
    virtual communities 328–9,
        339, 413
ideological state apparatus 359–61
ideology 93, 111, 173, 351–62, **489**
image, stars as 125, 126
imperialism
    cultural 235, 256, 258, 264, 385
    media 256, 258, 264
Impressionism 400
in media res 86, 163
independent companies 180
indexical relationship 51, 60, 154,
    162–3
India 8, 13, 253–4, 424
indigenisation 266
individualist ethos 124–7, 378, 390
Industrial Revolution 134, 426
Indymedia 259, 263
influence of media workers 185, 192
innovation 174, 176–7, 194
intellectual property rights 192, 247
    music industry 218, 219, 225–9
    WTO and 251, 252, 253–4, 255
intellectuals 80, 378, 419–21, **489**
interactivity 197, 328–9, 442–3
internet 4, 137, 237, 263, 325,
        362–3
    censorship 234–5, 243, 245, 267
    children's use of 8, 280–1
    data tracking 439–41
    death of scarcity 199–201
    distribution and 184, 197–8
    ethnography and 337
    global news and 240–1
    interactivity 328–9
    ISPs 215–16, 243, 246–7, 440
    moral panics 292, 293
    open source software 259

    regulation 212, 218, 243
    user-generated content 149
interpellation 360–1
intertextuality 417–18, 436
interviews 193, 331, 332–3, 334
Iraq 37, 130, 249, 260–2, 289
irony 413, 414–15
Italy (moral panic) 294
ITV 78, 469, 471

Jackson, V. 143–4
Jacobs, J. 469–70
Jakobson, R. 83, 134, 138
Jameson, F. 407, 411, 419, 461
Japan 176, 212
jargon 14, 16
Jaws 85, 88
Jefferson, T. 315, 317
Jencks, C. 408
Jenkins, H. 248, 319–20, 321
Jensen, J. 319
JLS 56, 57, 64
John, Elton 103, 106
Johnson, K.H. 107
Jones, J. 259
Jones, S. 326
Jordan, T. 326
journalism 36–8, 191, 240–1, 403
journalists 188–90, 211, 216
    citizen 149, 197, 259, 329–30
journals 19, 22–4
Joyce, J. 399
Joyce, P. 347
juxtaposition 44–5, 46
Jyllands-Posten 243, 244, 267

Kamalipour, Y. 254
Kangasvuo, J. 113
Karkulehto, S. 113
Katz, E. 304–5
Kawol, F.
Keen, A. 377
Kenez, P. 286
Kerekes, D. 293
Kermode, M. 79
Kinetoscope 454
Klapper, J. 304
Kleinwatcher, W. 251, 257
Kolinsky, E. 109–10
Kotler, P. 433
Kracauer, S. 140, 380
Krazit, T. 241
Kretschmer, M. 225
Kuhn, T. 407

Lacan, J. 359
Lachapelle, D. 414
laddering up 433
language 49, 52–4, 59–61, 73, 363
    specialist 12, 14, 16, 138
langue 54, **489**
Lanier, J. 137
Lanzmann, C. 152
Lasn, K. 441, 442
Lasswell, H. 285, 286
lateral integration 180
LaTulippe, S. 263

Lavers, A. 59
Lazarsfeld, P. 285, 286
Lazzarato, M. 438
Le Corbusier 408
Leadbeater, C. 300
Leavis, F.R. 375–7, 379, 381, 388–90
    Left-Leavism 387, 393
Leone, S. 75
Lerner, D. 264
Lessig, L. 229
Lévi-Strauss, C. 84, 158, 317, 359
Lewis, P.M. 223, 241
LGBT studies 113
liberalism 346, 349, 354, 356, 366
limited effects model 304–5
Lippmann, W. 107–8, 286
Listening In 479
locative technologies 442
'logic' narrative 88
long tail 198–9
Lopez, J. 132–3, 154
Loshitzky, Y. 152
Low, R. 216
Lowenthal, L. 380
Lucas, G. 73, 85, 86, 141
Luckhurst, T. 10
Luhmann, N. 133
Lull, J. 266, 305, 336
Lumière Brothers 4, 450, 453–4, 455
Lynch, M. 259, 262
Lyotard, J-F. 407, 419

MacArthur, J.R. 289
MacBride, S. 252, 257
McCabe, E. 130
McCann, Madeleine 103, 106
McCarthy, C. 237
McCarthy, J. 378
McChesney, R. 218, 255
McCourt, T. 223
Macdonald, D. 378, 381
MacDonald, I. 403
MacDonald, T. 105
McKenna, J. 255
Machin, D. 238–9, 245, 248–50, 255–8
McLuhan, M. 5–6, 34–5, 265–6,
        456, 478
McQuail, D. 252, 276, 279, 304–6, 373
McRobbie, A. 313, 407
McStay, A. 243, 260, 440
'McWorld versus Jihad' 265
Mad Men 410
magazines 7, 50, 114, 148–9,
        279, 361
    see also women's magazines
'magic bullet' theories 283
Man Ray 401
Manning, L. 150, 151
Manson, Marilyn 350–1
'Manson family' 152
Marcuse, H. 380
market research 310, 332, 441
marketing 428, 432–5, 438,
        441–4, **489**
Markson, E. 112
Maroc Telecom 168, 169
Marshall, N. 79

Martin, C. 125
Marx/Marxism 399, 407
    dialectics 398, 404
    mass society 374, 376, 380,
        384, 386
    political economy 172, 380
    power 347, 353–8, 360–1,
        364, 367
'mashups' 75, 417, 439
mass audience 176, 383, 403
mass communication 4–6, 184, 286,
        304, 373, 381, 388–90, 393
mass culture 80, 376–7, 386,
        390–3, 468
mass media 54, 80, 102, 108, 133, 186
    modernist art and 400–1
    social change and 373–87
mass society
    American context 376, 377–80
    contexts 373–87
    culture and 375–7
    definitions 387–93
    ideas about 381, 391
    masses as other people 388
    origins 373–4, 376
    theories of 373–82
    Williams on 388–90
materialism 354–5, 359–60, 361
Matrix, The 88, 350
meaning 34, 53, 55
    anchoring 35, 62, 163
    context 30–1, 310–30
    creating 324–30
    death of 410–12, 413, 422
    encoding/decoding 61,
        307–10, 339
    in media texts 70–97
    negotiated 308, 309
    oppositional 308–9
    preferred 62, 308
    rhetoric and 34–6
    semiology 49–64, 73
    as social conventions 52, 64
    systems/signifying 56–7, 160
    textual 30–3
media
    context 6–14
    definitions 3–6
    as history 457–61
    imperialism 256, 258, 264
    literacy 437, 438
    mass *see* mass media
    output and consumption 276–9
    political economy of 172–85
    power and *see* power
    producers and rhetoric 60–2
    state-controlled 479
media effects 283
    influence and 275, 284, 293, 295–7
    limited effects model 304–5
    moral panics and 290–4
    on social values 295
    see also effects research
media history 450–2
    approaches 453–61
    definitions 453, 455–7
    historiography 461–5

socio-cultural histories 478–80
sources and archives 465–72
writing 472–80
media studies 489
    areas covered 484–6
    context of 6–14
    criticisms of 9–11
    defined 1–6
    first steps 1–3, 20–1
    journals 19, 22–5
    rationale for 7–9
    requirements 482–4
    skills development 486–7
    studying others' studies 11–12
media texts *see* analysing media texts;
        text, media; textual analysis
mediagraphics 439
mediation process 102
Melody, W.H. 284
Mercer, K. 120
mergers 179, 181–2, 255
meta-narratives 33, 419
metaphor 9, 14, 38, 53
'metatextual realism' 96
method acting 135
metonym 38, 109
Metz, C. 83
Mexico (Emo subculture) 318
micro-narratives 419
Microsoft 280–1
Miles, H. 253–4, 26
Millar, M. 107
Miller, D. 428
Millett, K. 312
mimesis 134
mise en scène 41, 45, 55, 125, 139, 140
misrepresentation 119
Mitchell, J.W. 222
Mitra, A. 326
MMORPGs 325
Mobius Home Video Forum 327
'mock'-umentary 145
modern 398–9
modernism 396–7, 413, 421, **489**
    characteristics of 399
    demise of 408–9
    media and 399–406
modernist media 401–5
Mohammed cartoons 243–4, 267, 344
Monarchy: The Royal Family at Work
        144, 145–6
Monbiot, G. 349
monopolies 179, **489**
montage 44, 89, 139, 295, 404
Moore, B. 323
Moore, M. 327
    Bowling for Columbine 132, 351
    Fahrenheit 9/11 132, 144
    Sicko! 132, 141, 144, 344
moral panics 316–18, 329
    media violence 290–1, 292–3, 417
Morgan, P. 130
Morley, D. 266, 307, 310–11, 336,
        340, 393
morphemes 83
Morrey, D. 403
Morse 333

Morse code 61
Morrison, D.E. 285
Mosco, V. 173
Moss, L. 261
motivated cut 46–7
moving image (rhetoric) 42, 44–8
MPAA 247, 254
MTV 39, 82, 177, 182, 256
Mubarak, President H. 263–4, 362–3
multi-accentuality 60, 61, 63
multiculturalism 390
Mulvey, L. 24, 93, 295, 313
Mundell, E.J. 274
Murdoch, R. 189, 197, 255, 344, 349
Murdock, G. 173, 184
music 36, 41–2, 48, 63, 212, 401
    copyright 228, 229, 230
    phonologism 154–5
    subcultures 316, 317–18
        see also pop music
My Big Fat Gypsy Wedding 100
MySpace 182, 197, 324, 329, 438, 475
mythology 64, 158, 159, 163–4

Napster 248, 329
Narnia 137
narratemes 83
narration
    point of view and 89–91
    unreliable 91, 92
narrative 90–4, 472, **489**
    Chanel advert 160
    classical form 85–7
    disruption, enigma, resolution 85–7
    emergence of micro 419
    film 84–7
    genre and 82, 95–6
    'logic' 88
    modernism and 403
    photographs and 92, 94
    plot and story 85, 87–9
    postmodernism and 413, 419
    space (sense of) 89
    as structure 83–5, 95–6
    time (representation) 88–9
narrowcasting model 440, 442
Nationwide study 310–11
Natural Born Killers 293
Naughton, J. 420
NBC 168, 247, 248, 323
negotiated reading 308, 309
Neill, K. 223
Netflix 78
netiquette 326
New Zealand radio 223
Newman, G. 328
Newman, K. 151
news 92, 190–2, 366–7
    agencies 238–9
    citizen journalism 149, 197, 259,
        329–30
    commodification of 239–41
    dominance by conglomerates
        257–8
    Indymedia 259, 263
    international flow of 257
    internet and 240–1

rolling 249
television 105, 239
Western domination 257–9
News Corporation 173, 237, 247, 255, 349
News International 27
News of the World 106, 189, 344
newsgroups 325, 474
newspapers 34, 130, 182, 197, 293, 344
circulation/revenue 7–8
combination of signs 55
freesheets 179
online 8, 240–1
origins 4, 426
verbal rhetoric 36–8
see also broadsheets; tabloids
newsreaders 105, 118, 126–7
NHK (in Japan) 176
niche audiences 77, 176, 200
niche markets 178–9, 180
Nickelodeon 256
Nietzsche, F. 154, 381
Nintendo 19, 27, 464
Nochlin, L. 134
Nokia 433
non-verbal devices 40
Nordenstreng, K. 257
North Korea 286
nostalgia 411, 472
not-for-profit advertising 434, 436, 442
NPR (National Public Radio) 222, 223
NRK (in Norway) 280
Nugent, B. 274
NUJ Code of Conduct 216, 217
NWICO 257–8, 259
Nye, J.S. 265

objectivity 12, 33, 63, 378, 380
OECD 239
Ofcom 78, 100, 208–9, 211, 214, 437–8
oligopolies 179, 180, **490**
online
advertising 435, 437–8, 440, 443–4
audience activity 324–30
journals/information 24–5
memory making 471
see also internet
Only Way is Essex, The 77, 147
open source software 259
oppositional reading 308–9
oppression 346–7, 354, 356–8, 361–3, 367, 419
oral histories 332, 470–1, 472
Oregon soap opera study 336
ORF (in Austria) 280
'organic' culture 376
organisational studies
divisions and executive control 185–6
gatekeeping 190–2
production processes 190–1
staff (role and function) 186–90
organisations *see* businesses, media

O Siochrú 241–2, 248, 254
on regulation 243, 250, 251–2
UK and UNESCO 251–2, 257
output, media 30–2, 209, 276–9
owners/ownership (media) 209, 350

paedophiles 292, 293, 329
Pakistan (internet censorship) 243
Palestine 367
Pankhurst, S. and J. 471
paparazzi 411
paradigm 55, 73, 74, 147, **490**
Paramount Pictures 247, 256
Paris Match 158–9
parole 55, **490**
participatory culture 424
Passeron, J-C. 327
passivity (of audiences) 296
past (the) 453–5, **490**
patronage 186
PBS (in USA) 176
Pearl Harbor 140
Peel, M. 348
Peirce, C.S. 49, 51, 63, 102
Penn, A. 75
Pennies from Heaven 477
Perkins, T. 109, 110, 127
Perry, I. 154
personal relationships 305–6
personalities 124–7, 174
pessimism 413, 420, 421
Petley, J. 283, 293
phone-hacking 189, 235
phonologism 154–5
photo journalism 403
photography 4, 92, 94, 414
devices used 42–7
modernism and 401, 402
realism and 135, 138, 140, 141
Picasso, P. 399, 409
Pickering, A.S. 274
Pieterse, J.N. 266
Pitt, B. 102, 125, 126
Plato 11, 134, 154
Playboy 281
Playstation development 463–4
pleasure, commodified 419
plots 85, 87–9
pluralism 378, 382, 393
podcasts 54, 197, 324
point of view, narration and 89–91
policy 204–6, **490**
analysis 210–17, 219
consultation 211
defining 208–10, 230–1, **490**
documents 213, 230, 231
identifying 210–12
issues 218–30
objectives 213, 216
see also **regulation**
political-economic histories 476–7, 480, 481
political and civil society 356, 358
political economy 350, **490**
of global media 252, 256, 264, 267
of media 172–85, 201, 380
politics of archive 468–9

politics of representation 116–22, 127
polysemia 60, 61, 161, 417
Chanel advert 163
media producers and 62
negotiated reading and 308
stardom 126
pop music 4, 31, 104, 125, 154, 175–6, 382, 390
British Library archives 468
hybrid forms 412
judging value 475
narrative 74, 79, 93
postmodern 412, 415
punk-feminist 403–4
regulating 218, 219, 225–9
rhetoric 39, 41
social networking sites and 197
storyline 82
see also gangsta rap; music
popular culture 375–7, 387, 389–93
see also mass culture
pornography, child 293
Porter, R. 398
Portugal 217
positivism 378
post-industrial societies 433
postmodernism/postmodernity 81–2, 121
consumption and 433
critiquing 418–22
cultural boundaries 412, 422
death of history 409–10, 422
death of meaning 410–12, 413, 422
death of the subject 412–13, 422
as disabling 421–2
emphasising difference 421
ideas of 407
irony and 414–15
media texts 413–18
pessimism 413, 420, 421
political ideas 419
Simpsons 415–17
spectacle 413, 415
themes of 409–13
poststructuralism 364, 407
power 431, 472, **490**
conceptualising 346–9
defined 346, **490**
discourse and media 363–7
force of ideas 346
gender and 348
ideology and 351–62
imbalances 365
locating 347–9
Marx on 347, 353–8, 360–1, 364, 367
of mass society 374
of media 344–67
of media workers/owners 350
official structures 348–9
ourselves as products of 361
relations 173, 186
resistance and 359, 360, 362–3, 365
social 90, 351
social class and 347–9

Powers, B.R. 266
pragmatism 51
Prague School 83
preferred reading 62, 308
presentational rhetoric 39–42, 163
press 4, 7–8, 211, 257
    circulations 7–8
    freedom 257
    history of policy 211
    origins 4
    see also magazines; newspapers
Price, D. 258
primary sources 465–6, 467–70,
    471–2
Priutt-Igoe housing project 408
privacy 424, 440–1, 442, 445
production 178
    culture of 192–7
    processes 190–2
professionals/professional culture
    169, 171–2, 185, 186–7, 189,
    191, 192–7
prolepsis 88
propaganda 117–18, 250, 262,
    265, 294, 304, 355, 378,
    402, 455, **490**
    audience manipulation 286–90
    contemporary 289–90
    entertainment as 256
    fact and 256
Propp, V. 83–5
pseudo-individualisation 16, 383,
    386, 393
Psycho 417
psychographic research 433, 439
public-service broadcasting
    176, 187–8, 218, 250,
    467, **490**
    Europe 251
    online 223
    regulation 219–24
    researching 224
public good 173, 224
public relations 122, 434–5, 437, 442,
    443, **490**
public sphere 183–4, 249, 342, 350,
    390, 479
Pudovkin, V. 404
Pulp Fiction 88
Punj, G. 441
punk-feminist movement 403–4
punk rock 155

Queer as Folk 114, 115
queer theory 113
questionnaires 331–2, 333
Quinn, S. 260
'quotation' 417

race/ethnicity 74, 118–23,
    158–9, 412
racism 80, 108, 119–20, 363, 421
radio 4, 77, 120, 153–4, 265, 333, 379
    commercial stations 175, 177, 223
    development timeline 462, 463
    local 175, 176, 217
    policy (UK/USA) 214–15

regulation 217, 220–4, 250
    rhetoric 39, 42, 47
Radio Project 285
Raging Bull 135
Rahim, S.A. 251
rap music 126, 154–5, 418
    gangsta 36, 73, 102, 107–8,
    292, 415
ratings surveys 332
Rattansi, A. 417
RDF 145–6
readerly text 311
real-time strategy games 463–4
realism 103, 132–9, 474–5, **490**
    classical 85–7, 140–1
    sound 153–5
reality media
    conceptualising realism 132–9
    representation 103–6
    Take a Break magazine 148–9
    TV 76–8, 100, 132–3, 146–7,
    150–1
Rear Window 88
recording industry 179, 247–8
Redstone, S. 256
Rees, A.L. 474
referent, sign and 102, 162
regulation 180, **490**
    analysis 210–18
    Creative Commons 229
    defining 208–10, 230–1, **490**
    external/internal 211, 215–16, 222
    free markets and 250–5
    issues 218–30
    pop music 218, 219, 225–9
    public policy 204, 207–10
    regulatory bodies 206–7, 209–14,
    223–4
Reich, S. 401
Reid, M. 144
Reith, J. 220
repeat purchasing 175, 176–7
Repeated Takes 479
representation 88–9, 160, 363, **490**
    burden of 120–1, 127, 161
    conceptualising/defining 102–16
    of gender 111–12, 311–12
    individuals 103–6, 124–7
    politics of 116–22, 127
    stereotypes 106–11
repressive state apparatuses 359
researching media audiences 330–7
resistance 359–60, 362–3, 365
responsibility 149–56, 183–4
Reuters 235, 238, 239, 257
revenue (for businesses) 174–5
Rheingold, H. 137, 325, 326, 328
rhetoric 16, 33–48, 50, 54, 60–1,
    64–5, 160, 474–6, **490**
rhetorical analysis 33–48
rhetorical devices 36–8, 40, 42–8, 62,
    89, 153–4, 160–1, 475
rhyme 38
RIAA 248
Ricardo, D. 354
Richardson, A. 183, 196, 365
Riot Grrrl 403

risk management 177–9
Ritzer, G. 429
Roach, C. 252, 257
Roberts, I. 404
rock music 155, 401, 414
Rohmer, E. 81
role models 305
'Romans in Films' 59
Roselmack, H. 118
Ross, A. 399, 401
Roth, E. 415, 417, 418
Rotha, P. 12
Rousseau, J-J. 154
royalties 186, 227, 229
Rusbridger, A. 240, 241
Russian Formalists 83, 87, 295

Sakr, N. 260, 262
Sanjek, R. and D. 477
Saving Private Ryan 91, 92
Scannell, P. 221–2
Schiller, H. 258, 264
Schindler's List 152
scholars 11–12, 283–5
science fiction 79, 86, 91, 104
Scorsese, M. 135
Screen 23–4, 83
screen theory 295
Se7en 86, 88
search engines 65–6, 237, 241–3, 437
Seaton, J. 211, 222
secondary sources 465–6, 472
Seiter, E. 315, 336
self-determinism 344, 346, 361
self-regulation 211, 215–16
Semati, M. 254, 266
semiology 73, 102, 104, 311,
    317, **490**
    advertising and 434, 436
    Chanel advert 159–65
    foundations of 49–54
    Paris Match image 158–9
    tools/techniques 54–62
    uses/limits 63–4
September 11th 243, 246, 408, 458,
    461
7th Chamber 438
sexism 80, 108, 312, 363, 421
sexuality 111–16, 348, 363, 365
Shanahan, M. 223
shares/shareholders 168–9, 180
Shklovsky, V. 87
Shoah 152
Shone, T. 78, 175
Shropshire Star 182–3
Shyamalan, M. 88
sign-object relations 51, 58–60
sign value 42, 44, 429
significance test 56–8
signification 53–4, 58, 60–1, 103–4,
    162, 429–31
Signorielli, N. 123, 274
signs 54–7, 601, 64, 159–60, 162–3
'silver bullet' theories 283
Simpsons, The 415–17, 418
Singapore (MDA) 217
Singer, B. 90, 92

situation comedies 74, 80, 81
Siune, K. 252
Sixth Sense, The 88
Skeggs, B. 338–9
Skillset 2
Skuse, A. 265
Sky 197, 367, 460–1
Skype 200, 451
slash fiction 321
Slevin, J. 326, 328
slow motion 88
Smith, A. 172, 354
Smythe, D. 175
snuff movies 152–3, 293, 417
soap operas 114, 313–15, 324, 336
social change 373–87
social extension 136–7, 138
social groups 107–11, 426
social networking sites 182, 196–7,
    237, 324–5, 329, 362, 438,
    442–4, 474
social power 90, 351
socio-cultural histories 478–81
socio-economic groups 310–11
    see also **class**
Sony 28–9, 179, 197, 237, 247, 464
soul music 154
sound 39–42, 86, 153–5
sound effects 40, 193
sources 465–72
Soviet Union 286–7, 378, 380
Spears, B. 274, 275, 319
spectacle 59, 413, 415
Spielberg, S. 85, 88, 91, 92, 152
spoken word 39, 153–4
Sreberny-Mohammadi, A. 457
Stacey, J. 313, 315
standardisation 383, 386, 387, 393
Stanislavsky, K. 135
Stanton, F. 285
Star Gazing 313
Star Trek fans 320, 321
STAR TV 173, 197
stars/stardom 124–7, 174
Statute of Anne 225
stereotypes 80, 318, 353, 444, **490**
    gender/sexuality 111–16
    nature and function 108–11
    negative 107–8, 110, 114,120–1
still images (narrative) 93
Stone, O. 293
Stonewall research 114, 116
story/storytelling 82–3, 85
Stravinsky, I. 399, 401
structuralism 35, 83, 359–62,
    364, 393
Style Guide 394–0
subcultures 291, 315–24, 340, **490**
Subhash, K. 13
subject, death of 412–13, 422, 433–4
subjectivity 12, 33
Sugar Rush 115
Sun 36, 197, 293, 344
Superman archetype 107
supply and demand 174, 199–201
Surrealism 402
surveillance 246–7, 305, 440–1, 444–5

surveys 332
Sutton, D. 150, 151
Sweet, M. 216, 467
symbolic relationship 51, 60, 104, 158
synchronic approach 51, 56, 74, **490**
synecdoche 38, 163
synergy 5, 177–8, 180, 201, 254, **490**
syntagm 55, 73, 74, 162, **490**
syuzhet 87–8, 89, **490**

T-Mobile campaign 430–1
tabloids 36, 37, 171, 475
Tagg, J. 141, 365
Take a Break magazine 148–9
Tarantino, Q. 88, 409
taste 176, 211, 320, 376, 429–30
Tatham, S. 260, 261
Taylor, C. 112
Taylor, Y. 154
technological determinism 478, 479
technological history 453, 462–3,
    477–81
telephone (changing role) 4
television 55, 75, 118, 124–5, 333,
    442
    24/7 coverage 249, 255, 260
    audiences 303–4, 335–7
    children's viewing 8, 83
    genres 74, 77–8, 80
    globalisation and 248–50, 258
    news 105, 239
    reality TV 76–8, 100, 132–3,
        146–7, 150
    sitcoms 74, 80, 81
    talent shows 57, 77, 192, 353, 387
Terranova, T. 441
terrorism 13, 245, 255–6
    9/11 attacks 243, 246–7, 261,
        408, 458, 461
text 32, 52, 474–6, **490**
    audience defined 276, 277, 279
    postmodern 413–18
    see also analysing media texts
textual analysis
    Chanel advert 159–65
    Paris Match image 158–9
    semiology in 53–4
    see also analysing media texts;
    narrative
textual meaning 30–3, 197
    see also rhetorical analysis
theorists/theorising 11–13
There's Something About Mary 86, 93
Thom, S. 197
Thomas, L. 333
Thompson, A. 118
Thompson, D. 376–7, 381
Thompson, E.P. 387, 453, 456
Thompson, K. 41
Thomson-Reuters 239
Thumin, N. 338
Thurman, N. 241
Tiggemann, M. 274
Time Warner 181–2, 237, 247
timelines 462–5, 470, **490**
Times, The 36, 197, 427
Tin Pan Alley 382, 401

Todorov, T. 83, 86
Tomlinson, I. 241
tone 39–40, 414
Top Gear 109, 116
Total Recall 73, 91
totalitarianism 286–7, 382, 479–80
Tracey, M. 189
transmission model 284, 285
travellers (in UK media) 100, 103
TRIPS 253–4
Trojan viral advert 438
Truffaut, F. 12, 81
trust 150, 151, 200
truth 141–6, 149–56, 351, 364–5, 367
Tulloch, J. 320, 321
Tunisia 262–3
Tunstall, J. 189
Turkle, S. 329
Turow, J. 441
Twentieth Century Fox 247, 255
Twitter 4, 197, 240, 262, 323–4, 344
typification 106–8

UNESCO 251–2, 257–8, 259, 385
    on Al Jazeera 261, 267
Unilever 432
Union flag 58
United Nations 243, 251, 252, 264
United Press Association 238, 239
United States
    CALEA 246–7
    Copyright Office 226
    deregulation 218
    DRM 228
    FCC 215, 246
    foreign policy via news media
        264–5
    FTC 181
    negative views of 376
    radio policy 220, 222–3, 250
    Telecommunications Act 214–15,
        254–5
    Un-American Activities Committee
        378
Universal Music Group 168, 179
Universal Studies 247
unregulated media 207, 217–19,
    229–30
use-value 384, 429
uses and gratifications approach 301,
    304–10, 325, 339
Uses of Literacy, The 390–3
Usual Suspects, The 90, 92

value of products, judging 474–6
value systems 221–2, 255–8
van Ginneken, J. 238, 239, 252
van Leeuwen, T. 238–9, 248–50,
    252, 257
    on conglomerates 255, 256
    film/TV exports 245, 258
Varis, T. 257
Vaughan, T. 86
Veblen, T. 426
Velvet Underground 401, 409
verbal rhetoric 36–8, 104
verbal signs 55–6

Verhoeven, P. 73, 91
verisimilitude 40, 130, 134, 139, 140
vertical integration 180, 247–8, **490**
Vertov, D. 404
Viacom 247, 255, 256
videogames 4, 76, 132, 134, 137, 415
    development of 463–4
    media violence and 293–4
    MMORPGs 325
Vimeo 329
violence, media 290–4, 417
viral advertising 438, 444, **490**
virtual communities 324–30,, 340, 413
virtual ethnography 337
virtual reality 132, 134, 137
visual signs 55–6
Visnews 239
Vivendi 168–9, 237
Voice-Over-Internet-Protocol 246, 247
voice overs 86, 90
Volk, S. 150–1
Volkmer, I. 249, 251, 264, 266
Volosinov, V. 60–1
von Feilitzen, C. 291

Wachowski, A. and L. 88, 350
Wajcman, J. 259
Wall, T. 212, 222, 223, 224, 365
Walters, T. 260
War of the Worlds (1938) 379

Ward, L. 8
Warburton, N. 243
Warner Brothers 247
Warner Music Group 179
Watson, N. 325, 326
'we-think' 300–1
Weaver, W. 284
'Web 2.0' 329, 377, 443
websites 91–2, 149
    see also internet
Weinraub, B. 253, 254
Welles, O. 379
Wells, L. 96, 103
West Wing, The 323–4
What Happens in Vega 86
Wheen, F. 357
White, R.A. 259
Wieringa, C. 463
Wikipedia 263, 329, 377, 451
Williams, R. 141, 143, 211, 216, 381,
    387, 391–2, 478
    cultural production 186–7, 190
    culture is ordinary 388–90, 393
Willis, P. 193
Willson, M. 326
Winston, B. 134, 136
Wired 197
Wojcieszak, M. 261, 262

Wolstenholme, K. 459
women 123, 312–13
    representation/role 91, 93, 112
women's magazines 50, 72–3,
    148–9, 313
women's movement *see* feminism
Wonderbra advert 276, 277, 278
Wood, H. 338, 469
workers, media 192–7
working-class 105, 120, 136, 316,
    347, 374, 381, 387–9, 391–2
World Bank 251, 252
World Wide Web Consortium (W3C)
    243
Wright, W. 84–5
writerly text 311
WTO 251, 252, 253–5, 259, 267

Xbox 161, 464
Xinhua news agency 234

Yahoo 241, 242
Yamasaki, M. 408
Yewdall, D.L. 40
youth subcultures 291, 316–17, 318
YouTube 197, 199–200, 237, 242,
    319, 329, 377, 430, 437, 438

zeitgeist 354
Zimmerman, B. 113